Psychology: The Core

Charles G. Morris   Albert A. Maisto

PEARSON

Prentice
Hall

Upper Saddle River, New Jersey 07458

Library of Congress Cataloging-in-Publication Data

Morris, Charles G.
   Psychology the core / Charles G. Morris, Albert A. Maisto—1st ed.
     p. cm.
   Includes bibliographical references and index.
   ISBN 0-13-603344-X
   1. Psychology—Textbooks   I. Maisto, Albert A. (Albert Anthony).   II. Title.
   BF121.M5987 2008
   150—dc22   200803372

Editorial Director: Leah Jewell
Executive Editor: Jessica Mosher
Project Manager, Editorial: Judy Casillo
Editorial Assistant: Jessica Kupetz
Director, Media and Assessment: Shannon Gattens
Manager, Media and Assessment: Brian Hyland
Director of Marketing: Brandy Dawson
Senior Marketing Manager: Jeanette Koskinas
Marketing Assistant: Laura Kennedy
Associate Managing Editor: Maureen Richardson
Project Manager, Production/Liaison: Harriet Tellem
Senior Operations Supervisor: Sherry Lewis
Associate Director of Design Development Services:
  John Christiana

Art Director: Kenny Beck
Interior Design: Anne DeMarinis
Cover Design: Anne DeMarinis
Cover Illustration/Photo: *Water Lily on Translucent White
  Background*. A studio image of a White Water Lily, or White
  Lotus, on a white background. Chad Kleitsch / Science
  Faction / Getty Images, Inc.
Director Image Resource Center: Melinda Patelli
Manager, Rights and Permissions: Zina Arabia
Image Permission Coordinator: Debbie Latronica
Composition/Full-Service Project Management: Black Dot
  Group/Sandra Reinhard and Marilyn Rothenberger
Printer/Binder: RR Donnelley

Pearson Education Ltd.
Pearson Education Australia PTY, Ltd.
Pearson Education Singapore, Pte. Ltd.
Pearson Education North Asia Ltd.
Pearson Education, Canada, Ltd.

Pearson Educación de Mexico, S.A. de C.V.
Pearson Education-Japan
Pearson Education Malaysia, Pte. Ltd.
Pearson Education, Upper Saddle River NJ

10 9 8 7
ISBN-10: 0-13-603344-X
ISBN-13: 978-0-13-603344-8

Brief Contents

Online Content: **www.psychologythecore.com**

Contents

3 Sensation and Perception   59

4 States of Consciousness   91

5   Learning   119

6   Memory   147

13 Therapies 343

14 Social Psychology 369

Online Content: www.psychologythecore.com

Appendix | Measurement and Statistical Methods A-1

Preface

These are exciting times. The Internet is revolutionizing the way in which we access information as well as the sheer amount of information that is available to us. At the same time, there is concern about the cost of textbooks; students are looking for low-cost, environmentally-friendly course materials that help them save time and get a better grade. Not surprisingly, the relationship between printed media and electronic media is at the center of discussion. This book is our response to this discussion.

The printed textbook, *Psychology: The Core*, covers the core content of psychology—the essentials that every introductory psychology student should know. The book is briefer than a standard introductory text—allowing for a lower cost to students and using less printed paper. It includes study aids students have told us they find useful—concept maps, note-taking features, and a laminated study card highlighting the most challenging topics in introductory psychology. The Web site www.psychologythecore.com provides more in-depth treatment of topics, up-to-date statistics, cutting edge research, simulations, video clips, and real-world applications of psychology. A monthly author blog provides an opportunity for us to post interesting links, new research findings, and responses to questions from our readers. Annual updates to the site ensure that readers will have access to all the latest findings, and our printed text should require revision less often. **Welcome to *Psychology: The Core*.**

Unifying Themes

The goal of *Psychology: The Core* is to present a scientific, accurate, and thorough overview of the essential concepts of psychology and to help readers see its exciting applications to real life. We also believe it is important to recognize recurring themes that run throughout contemporary psychology. In Chapter 1, we introduce a set of five **Enduring Issues** that cut across and unite all subfields of psychology (see page 13).

Each chapter opens with a section highlighting the enduring issues to be encountered in that chapter. Several times in each chapter, we call attention to the way in which the topic under consideration reflects one of these issues. In this way, we show the surprising unity and coherence of the diverse and exciting science of psychology.

Person–Situation:
To what extent is behavior caused by processes that occur inside the person and to what extent is behavior caused or triggered by factors outside the person?

Nature–Nurture:
Is the person we become a product of innate, inborn tendencies or a reflection of experience and upbringing?

Stability–Change:
Are the characteristics we develop in childhood more or less permanent and fixed or do we change over the course of our lives?

Diversity–Universality:
Each person is like every other person and, in other respects, each of us is like no other person. Anywhere humans exist, there will be both similarity and diversity.

Mind–Body:
How are mind and body connected?

ENDURING ISSUES in the Biological Basis of Behavior

As with the first chapter, all five Enduring Issues will be encountered. The core of this chapter—the notion that biological processes affect thoughts, emotions, and behavior—directly addresses the age-old debate about the relationship betwe... It also sheds light on th... environme... tent to wh... the nervou... Moreover, biological...

ENDURING ISSUES PERSON/SITUATION

Contextual Cues and State-Dependent Memor

Whenever people try to memorize something, they are also unintentionally picking up information about the context in which the learning is taking place. That information becomes useful when the person later tries to retrieve the corresponding... nt when the person tries t... uccessful. The effects of... room whe... prove you... sometime... call crucia...

ENDURING ISSUES NATURE/NURTURE

Exceptional Memories

"S" and other people with exceptional memories are not born with a special gift for remembering things. Rather, they have carefully developed memory techniques using certain principles. For example, Luria discovered that when "S" studi... m. When reading a long a... specifica... cite the... each one... meaning... memory. time, your...

ENDURING ISSUES STABILITY/CHANGE

Neural Plasticity

The brain is the one organ in the body that is unique to each individual. From the beginning, your brain has been encoding experience and developing the patterns of emotion and thought that make you who you are. At the same time, your... and adjusting t... of maintain... the brain... **neural plas...** experience...

ENDURING ISSUES DIVERSITY/UNIVERSALITY

Sex Differences in Mate Selection

Evolutionary psychologists cite mate selection as another example. In choosing a partner, males and females tend to pursue different strategies. Why? Evolutionary psychologists answer this way: Human females usually have only one child... ild than men do—going through p... adaptive f... long-term... prospecti...

ENDURING ISSUES MIND/BODY

Sensory Experience

Each sensory experience—the color of a flower or the sound of a fire engine—is an illusion created in the brain by patterns of neural signals. The brain, isolated inside the skull, is bombarded by "impulses," or "firings," of coded neural signals arriving on millions of nerve fibers. The impulses on the optic nerve reliably produce an experience we call *vision*, just as impulses moving along an auditory nerve produce the experience of *hearing*, or audition. The one-to-one relationship between stimulation of a specific nerve and the resulting sensory experience is known as the *doctrine of specific nerve energies*. Even if the impulses on the optic nerve are caused by something other than light, the result is still a visual experience. Gentle pressure on an eye, for instance, results in signals from the optic nerve. And from these signals, the brain creates a visual experience—"seeing stars" when we're hit in the eye is so familiar that even cartoons depict it.

The online materials at www.psychologythecore.com include a rich array of resources to complement the textbook, including more in-depth treatment of topics, up-to-date statistics, cutting edge research, simulations, video clips, and critical thinking exercises along with real-world applications of psychology. The online content is updated regularly, providing readers with access to the latest research and examples.

Chapter 4: States Of Consciousness

- ☑ **Concept Map**
- ☐ **Preview**
- ☐ **Thinking Critically**
- ☐ **Applying Psychology**
- ☐ **Recent Studies**
- ☐ **World Around You**
- ☐ **Study Tools**

Thinking Critically:
Critical thinking exercises include thought-provoking topics such as corporal punishment, media violence, eyewitness testimony, road rage, and ethnic conflict.

Applying Psychology
and **World Around You:**
These demonstrate the ways in which psychology sheds light on issues of widespread interest including the benefits of studying psychology, memory improvement, problem solving, losing weight, resolving conflicts, coping with stress, recognizing depression, finding help, and understanding the roots of ethnic conflict.

Recent Studies:
Every chapter describes recent, progressive research in the field of psychology to inform and challenge our current understanding of phenomena such as the effect of playing violent video games, the evolution of language, and virtual therapy.

Author Blog:
This Web log provides an opportunity for the authors to post interesting links or new research findings and to respond to questions from students. The blog is updated monthly to draw attention to new research that is especially interesting or that extends our understanding of psychology in new directions or to provide examples of current topics that illustrate key points in the text.

For Students: Saving Time and Getting a Better Grade

Go to **www.psychologythecore.com** to help you make stronger connections between the world around you and what you are learning in your introductory psychology course. The site is updated regularly and is an important part of what you are learning—information from this site will help you prepare for your test, so be sure to check it out.

The first time you log in, you will need the access code packaged with your textbook. If you do not have a code, go to **www.mypearsonstore.com** and enter the ISBN of your text to purchase access.

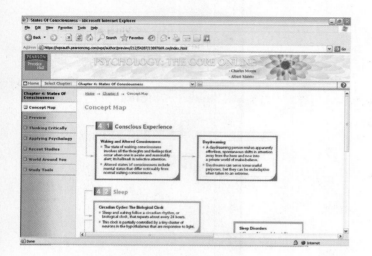
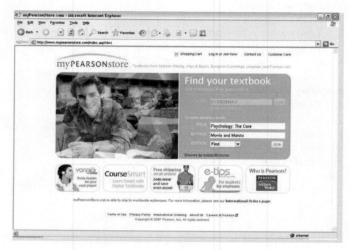

Students have provided us with feedback on the study tools they find most useful. In response, we have included the following features in *Psychology: The Core:*

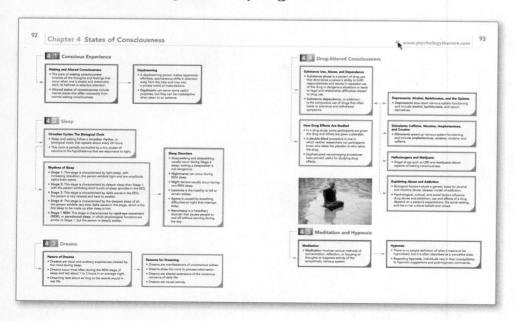

Concept Maps: These are a useful way of understanding how all the content in the chapter fits together. The maps start each chapter and highlight the key objectives in a highly visual manner.

Concept Maps Online: These provide a way to navigate the content online. Just click on the section of the concept map you want to review.

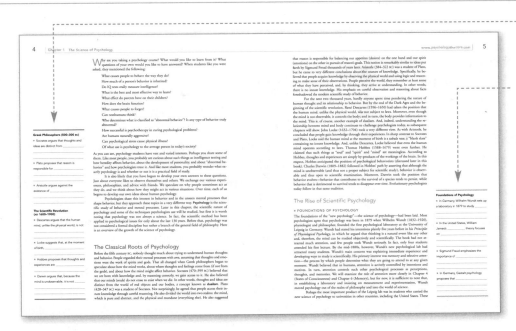

Note-taking: Throughout the chapter, parts of the maps are placed in the margins of relevant sections; these parts are designed as note-taking features to help highlight and note the most important concepts in each section. The book is perforated and three-hole punched, so relevant chapters are portable and can be brought to class for easy note-taking.

Online Note-taking Answers: These notes are filled in with responses to any questions asked in the note-taking feature.

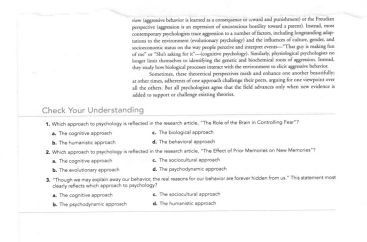

Practice Quizzes: With room to fill in responses, quizzes are included at the end of every major section to help you determine whether key content has been understood—**before** your next class test. Answers are found at the back of the book.

Online Quiz: Additional quizzes are available online at www.psychologythecore.com to help you prepare for your next test.

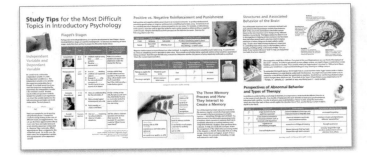

Study Sheet: The study sheet included with your book provides study tips for the most difficult-to-understand concepts in introductory psychology on one side and a history of psychology timeline on the other side.

To find more study tools online at www.mypearsonstore.com, just enter the ISBN 0-13-603344-X and check out the "Everything That Goes With It" section under the book cover.

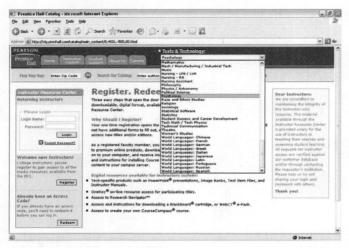

http://prenhall.com/irc

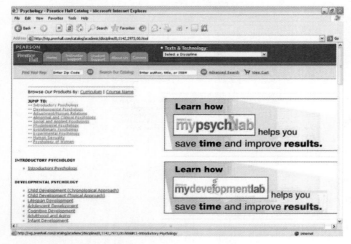

http://prenhall.com/replocator/

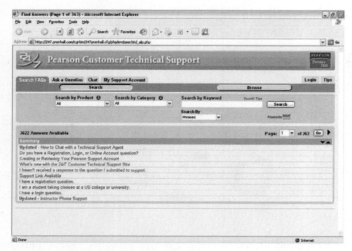

http://247.pearsoned.com

Instructor Supplements

For access to all instructor supplements for Morris/
Maisto *Psychology: The Core* including the test bank
(with questions for both the printed text content and
the online content), PowerPoint slides, videos, and
more, simply go to http://prenhall.com/irc and follow the directions to register (or log in if you already
have a Pearson user name and password).

Once you have registered and your status as an
instructor is verified, you will receive a log-in name
and password via e-mail. Use your log-in name and
password to access the catalog. Click on the "online
catalog" link, then "psychology," followed by
"introductory psychology," and finally, the
Morris/Maisto *Psychology: The Core* text. Under the description of each supplement is a link that will allow
you to download and save the supplement to your
desktop.

Printed versions (hard copies) of the supplements
can be requested through your Pearson Education sales
representative. If you do not know your sales representative, go to http://prenhall.com/replocator/ and
follow the directions to locate your sales representative.

To receive technical support for any of your Pearson products, you and your students can contact
http://247.pearsoned.com.

Acknowledgments

Although a first edition, much of the content for this text builds on material from our text *Understanding Psychology,* 8th edition. Thanks to all who reviewed previous editions:

Jack Harnett, *Virginia Commonwealth University*
Joseph Lao, *Borough of Manhattan Community College*
Jennifer Peluso, *Mercer University*
Cheryl Bluestone, *Queensborough Community College*
Dixon A. Bramblett, *Lindenwood University*
Terry Pettijohn, *Ohio State University*
Joe Grisham, *Indian River Community College*
Joy Easton, *De Vry University*
Tom Frangicetto, *Northampton Community College*
Jason Kaufman, Ph.D., *Inver Hills Community College*
Gregory Manley, *University of Texas, San Antonio*
Karen Tinsley, *Guilford College*
Jim Dalton, *Sanford-Brown College*
Carolyn Tremblay, *Orlando Culinary Academy*
Daniel Dickman, *Ivy Tech*
Christian Fossa-Anderson, *De Vry University, South Florida*
Fred Whitford, *Montana State University*
Stephen M. Colarelli, *Central Michigan University*
Michael Durnam, *Montana State University - Bozeman*
Kelly Charlton, *University of North Carolina, Pembroke*
John Lindsay, *Georgia College and State University*
Blaine Weller, *Baker College*
Dr. B. Hannon, *University of Texas, San Antonio*
Leslie Reeder, *Wallace Community College*
Jason Kaufman, Ph.D., *Inver Hills Community College*
Dr. Gary J. Springer, *Texas State University, San Marcos*
Dr. Sharon Sawatzky, *Butler County Community College*
Dr. Dan Muhwezi, *Butler County Community College*
Layton Seth Curl, Ph.D., *Metropolitan State College of Denver*
David Copeland, *University of Southern Mississippi*
Gregory G. Manley, Ph.D., *University of Texas, San Antonio*

Special thanks to reviewers of our new book who helped us determine the key content to include in our text and the up-to-date research to include online:

David E. Copeland, *University of Nevada, Las Vegas*
Jennifer Dashiell, *North Carolina A&T State University*
Wendy Domjan, *The University of Texas, Austin*
Edward Fernandes, *East Carolina University*
Don Knox, *Midwestern State University*
Marilyn Milligan, Ph.D., *Santa Rosa Junior College*
Jane Ogden, *East Texas Baptist University*
Chitra Ranganathan, *Framingham State College*
George M. Slavich, Ph.D., *University of California, San Francisco*

About the Authors

Charles G. Morris Charles G. Morris received his B.A. from Yale University and his M.A. and Ph.D. in psychology from the University of Illinois. He joined the University of Michigan in 1965 as Assistant Professor of Psychology and was promoted to Associate Professor in 1971 and Professor in 1987. He served as Associate Dean in the College of Literature, Science and the Arts and as Associate Chair of the Department of Psychology. Upon his retirement in 2002, he was appointed Emeritus Professor. He is a Fellow of the American Psychological Association and the American Psychological Society.

He is the author of more than two dozen books, more than a dozen articles, and more than thirty papers and presentations. His books include *Psychology: An Introduction*, *Understanding Psychology*, *Basic Psychology*, *Psychology: Concepts and Applications*, and *Contemporary Psychology and Effective Behavior*.

His early research centered on leadership, group interaction, and group problem solving. More recently, his publications and presentations have focused on various aspects of undergraduate education, on contemporary views of leadership, and on the "Big 5" personality traits.

Albert A. Maisto The Carnegie Foundation's U.S. Professor of the Year for 1997–1998, Albert A. Maisto is the Bonnie E. Cone Distinguished Professor of Teaching at The University of North Carolina at Charlotte, where he is also Associate Dean of the Honors College. Maisto earned both a Ph.D. and an M.A. in Psychology from The University of Alabama, with an emphasis in Mental Retardation and Applied Cognitive Development. While at UNC–Charlotte, Professor Maisto has held several positions including Coordinator of the Undergraduate Psychology Program, Faculty President, and Assistant to the Vice Chancellor for Academic Affairs. Earlier in his career he served as a visiting Professor to The University of Nottingham in England, and he spent two years on the faculty of The University of Connecticut. Throughout his career Dr. Maisto has distinguished himself as an exemplary instructor of general psychology winning the prestigious Bank of America Award for Teaching Excellence.

Maisto's portfolio includes dozens of published articles in refereed journals, professional papers, and a successful series of Introductory Psychology textbooks published by Pearson Education.

Chapter 1
The Science of Psychology

http://www.psychologythecore.com

The world is changing all the time. Researchers in the field of psychology are constantly coming up with fascinating new findings, and our students tell us often about the importance of understanding how the content in their introductory psychology text relates to the world around them. So, to make stronger connections between the world around you and what you will be learning in this introductory psychology course, check out **http://www.psychologythecore.com**. This Web site is updated regularly and will be an important tool for your learning. The information at this site can help prepare you for your next test, so be sure to access it. To log in, you will need the access code packaged with your textbook. If you do not have a code, go to **http://www.mypearsonstore.com** and enter the ISBN of your textbook (0-13-603344-X). From this page, you may purchase access.

Students also tell us that **concept maps** are a useful way of understanding how all the content in the chapter fits together. Consequently, each chapter will start with a concept map for students to use as a way to navigate the content online.

Throughout each chapter, portions of the maps appear in the margins of relevant sections as **note-taking features** to help you remember the most important concepts in each section. *Online—you will find these notes with responses to the questions asked filled in.*

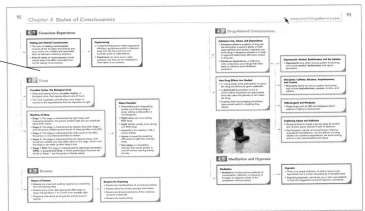

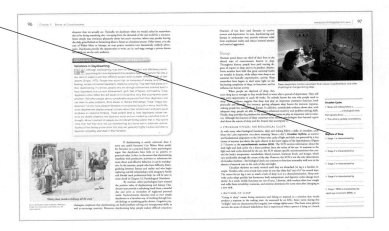

Chapter 1 The Science of Psychology

Psychology is the scientific study of behavior and mental processes.

1 1 The Classical Roots of Psychology

Greek Philosophers (500–300 BC)

- Socrates argues that thoughts and ideas are distinct from the world of real objects and our bodies—a concept known as **dualism**.
- Plato proposes that reason is responsible for balancing our appetites (desires) on the one hand and our spirit (emotions) on the other in pursuit of reason's goals.
- Aristotle argues against the existence of innate knowledge and emphasizes observation and reasoning, foreshadowing the modern scientific study of behavior.

The Scientific Revolution (AD 1600–1900)

- Descartes argues that the human mind, unlike the physical world, is not subject to laws.
- Locke suggests that, at the moment of birth, the mind contains no innate knowledge. Unlike Descartes, he proposes that even the human mind operates according to laws.
- Hobbes proposes that thoughts and experiences are simply by-products of the workings of the brain.
- Darwin argues that observable behavior, not the unobservable mind, can be studied scientifically. Behavior that contributes to the survival of a species tends to persist, while behavior that is detrimental to survival tends to disappear over time.

1 2 The Rise of Scientific Psychology

Foundations of Psychology

- In Germany, Wilhelm Wundt sets up a laboratory in 1879 to study mental processes scientifically. His student, Edward Titchener, is the founder of **structuralism**.
- In the United States, William James's **functionalist theory** focuses on how learning and perceptual abilities are used.
- Sigmund Freud emphasizes the importance of unconscious processes and early experience.
- In Germany, **Gestalt psychology** proposes that the whole of our perceptual experience is more than just the sum of its parts.

Women in Psychology

- Despite the prevalence of men among the founders, women have contributed significantly to psychology from its beginnings.
- Today, women receive the majority of undergraduate and graduate degrees in psychology.

1 3 Contemporary Approaches to Psychology

- The **biological approach** is concerned with the relationship between biological processes and consciousness and behavior.
- John B. Watson, who redefines psychology as the study of observable, measurable behavior and nothing more, establishes the **behavioral** approach, a view later popularized by B. F. Skinner as **behaviorism**.
- Psychologists who adopt the **cognitive approach** believe that mental processes can and should be studied scientifically.
- The **humanistic approach** emphasizes the importance of human strengths and virtues; **positive psychology** continues in this tradition.
- Sigmund Freud originates the **psychodynamic approach**, which emphasizes the centrality of unconscious desires, fears, and memories as determinants of behavior.
- Psychologists who take the **evolutionary/sociobiological approach** build on Darwin's foundation by exploring the ways in which human behavior patterns and mental processes have been beneficial to our emergence and survival as a distinct species.
- The **sociocultural approach** emphasizes the importance of culture, gender, race, and ethnicity as factors that affect virtually all aspects of human behavior.

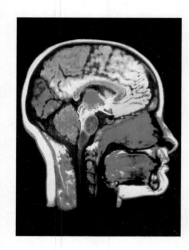

1 4 Enduring Issues in Psychology

- Person–Situation: To what extent is behavior caused by *internal* thoughts and feelings, as opposed to *external* events?
- Nature–Nurture: Is behavior the result of hereditary or environmental forces?
- Stability–Change: Is the behavior of an individual stable throughout the life span or does the behavior change over time?
- Diversity–Universality: To what extent are all people alike?
- Mind–Body: What is the relationship between one's experiences and one's biological processes?

1 5 Psychology as Science

- Psychologists rely on the **scientific method** to *describe, explain, predict,* and eventually achieve some measure of *control* over what they study.
- As data are collected, psychologists propose **theories** to explain the data; in turn, these theories generate **hypotheses** (predictions) that can be tested through further research.

1 6 Research Methods in Psychology

Descriptive Methods

- **Naturalistic observation**—Systematic study of behavior in natural rather than laboratory settings; main drawback is **observer bias**.
- **Case studies**—Detailed descriptions of one person or a few individuals that yield in-depth portraits.
- **Surveys**—Interviews or questionnaires used to collect information.

Correlational Research

- This research technique is based on the naturally occurring relationship (correlation) between two or more variables.
- **Correlational research** can be used to describe a relationship but not to establish cause and effect.

Experimental Research

- The **experimental method** can be used to study cause-and-effect relationships.
- The experimental method involves the manipulation of an **independent variable** by the experimenter to determine whether it affects the **dependent variable** of interest.
- Results from participants in the **experimental group** are compared to those in the **control group** to determine whether the independent variable had the predicted effect.

Multimethod Research

- Psychologists often use more than one method to study a single problem.
- If the results from many studies that used different methods are in agreement, the researcher can have added confidence that the theory is correct.

Importance of Sampling

- Researchers typically study only a small **sample**, or subset of the population, then use the results of that limited study to generalize cautiously about larger populations.
- To improve the generalizability of their results, researchers use **random samples** and **representative samples**.

1 7 Ethics and Psychology

Ethical Principles That Guide Research in Psychology

- Participants must be informed, in advance, about the nature of the research, including potential risks and limitations on confidentiality.
- Researchers who use nonhuman animals in research must ensure appropriate consideration of the subject's comfort, health, and humane treatment.

Why are you taking a psychology course? What would you like to learn from it? What questions of your own would you like to have answered? When students like you were asked, they mentioned the following:

What causes people to behave the way they do?

How much of a person's behavior is inherited?

Do IQ tests really measure intelligence?

What is the best and most effective way to learn?

What effect do parents have on their children?

How does the brain function?

What causes people to forget?

Can nonhumans think?

Who determines what is classified as "abnormal behavior"? Is any type of behavior truly abnormal?

How successful is psychotherapy in curing psychological problems?

Are humans naturally aggressive?

Can psychological stress cause physical illness?

Of what use is psychology to the average person in today's society?

As you can see, psychology students have vast and varied interests. Perhaps you share some of them. Like most people, you probably are curious about such things as intelligence testing and how heredity affects behavior, about the development of personality, and about "abnormal behavior" and how psychologists treat it. And like most students, you probably wonder what exactly psychology is and whether or not it is a practical field of study.

It is also likely that you have begun to develop your own answers to these questions. Just about everyone likes to observe themselves and others. We exchange our various experiences, philosophies, and advice with friends. We speculate on why people sometimes act as they do, and we think about how they might act in various situations. Over time, each of us begins to develop our own ideas about human psychology.

Psychologists share this interest in behavior and in the unseen mental processes that shape behavior, but they approach these topics in a very different way. **Psychology** is the scientific study of behavior and mental processes. Later in this chapter, the scientific nature of psychology and some of the techniques psychologists use will be studied, but first it is worth noting that psychology was not always a science. In fact, the scientific method has been applied to psychological issues for only about the last 130 years. Before that, psychology was not considered a formal discipline but rather a branch of the general field of philosophy. Here is an overview of the growth of the science of psychology.

The Classical Roots of Psychology

Before the fifth century BC, nobody thought much about trying to understand human thoughts and behavior. People regarded their mental processes with awe, assuming that thoughts and emotions were the work of spirits and gods. That all changed when Greek philosophers began to speculate about how the mind works, about where thoughts and feelings come from (if not from the gods), and about how the mind might affect behavior. Socrates (470–399 BC) believed that we are born with knowledge and, by reasoning correctly, we gain access to it. He also believed that our minds (souls) do not cease to exist when we die. In other words, thoughts and ideas are distinct from the world of real objects and our bodies, a concept known as **dualism**. Plato (428–347 BC) was a student of Socrates. Not surprisingly, he agreed that people access their innate knowledge through careful reasoning. He also divided the world into two realms: the mind, which is pure and abstract, and the physical and mundane (everything else). He also suggested

---

Greek Philosophers (500–300 BC)

■ Socrates argues that thoughts and ideas are distinct from _____

_____

_____

■ Plato proposes that reason is responsible for _____

_____

_____

■ Aristotle argues against the existence of _____

_____

_____

The Scientific Revolution (AD 1600–1900)

■ Descartes argues that the human mind, unlike the physical world, is not

_____

_____

■ Locke suggests that, at the moment of birth, _____

_____

■ Hobbes proposes that thoughts and experiences are _____

_____

■ Darwin argues that, because the mind is unobservable, it is not _____

_____

_____

that reason is responsible for balancing our appetites (desires) on the one hand and our spirit (emotions) on the other in pursuit of reason's goals. This notion is remarkably similar to ideas put forth by Sigmund Freud thousands of years later. Aristotle (384–322 BC) was a student of Plato, but he came to very different conclusions about the sources of knowledge. Specifically, he believed that people acquire knowledge by observing the physical world and using logic and reasoning to make sense of their observations. People perceive the world, they remember at least some of what they have perceived, and, by thinking, they arrive at understanding. In other words, there is no innate knowledge. His emphasis on careful observation and reasoning about facts foreshadowed the modern scientific study of behavior.

For the next two thousand years, hardly anyone spent time pondering the nature of human thought and its relationship to behavior. But by the end of the Dark Ages and the beginning of the scientific revolution, René Descartes (1596–1650) had taken the position that the human mind, unlike the physical world, was not subject to laws. Moreover, even though the mind is not observable, it controls the body; and in turn, the body provides information to the mind. This is, of course, another example of dualism. And, indeed, understanding the relationship between mind and body continues to challenge psychologists today, as subsequent chapters will show. John Locke (1632–1704) took a very different view. As with Aristotle, he concluded that people gain knowledge through their experiences. In sharp contrast to Socrates and Plato, Locke said the human mind at the moment of birth is a *tabula rasa*, a "blank slate" containing no innate knowledge. And, unlike Descartes, Locke believed that even the human mind operates according to laws. Thomas Hobbes (1588–1679) went even further. He claimed that such things as "soul" and "spirit" and "mind" are meaningless. According to Hobbes, thoughts and experiences are simply by-products of the workings of the brain. In this respect, Hobbes anticipated the position of psychological behaviorists (discussed later in this book). Charles Darwin (1809–1882) followed in Hobbes' path by asserting that although the mind is unobservable (and thus not a proper subject for scientific study), behavior is observable and thus open to scientific examination. Moreover, Darwin took the position that behavior evolves—behavior that contributes to the survival of a species tends to persist, while behavior that is detrimental to survival tends to disappear over time. Evolutionary psychologists today follow in that same tradition.

The Rise of Scientific Psychology

■ FOUNDATIONS OF PSYCHOLOGY

The foundations of the "new psychology"—the science of psychology—had been laid. Most psychologists agree that psychology was born in 1879 when Wilhelm Wundt (1832–1920), physiologist and philosopher, founded the first psychological laboratory at the University of Leipzig in Germany. Wundt had stated his intentions plainly five years before in his *Principles of Physiological Psychology*, in which he argued that thinking is a natural event like any other and, therefore, the mind can be studied objectively and scientifically. The book had not attracted much attention, and few people took Wundt seriously. In fact, only four students attended his first lecture. By the mid-1880s, however, Wundt's new psychological lab had attracted many students. Wundt's main concern was explaining immediate experience and developing ways to study it scientifically. His primary interest was memory and selective attention—the process by which people determine what they are going to attend to at any given moment. Wundt believed that in humans, attention is actively controlled by intentions and motives. In turn, attention controls such other psychological processes as perceptions, thoughts, and memories. We will examine the role of attention more closely in Chapter 4 (States of Consciousness) and Chapter 6 (Memory), but for now, it is sufficient to note that, in establishing a laboratory and insisting on measurement and experimentation, Wundt moved psychology out of the realm of philosophy and into the world of science.

Perhaps the most important product of the Leipzig lab was its students who carried the new science of psychology to universities in other countries, including the United States. These

Foundations of Psychology

■ In Germany, Wilhelm Wundt sets up a laboratory in 1879 to study _____ _____

■ In the United States, William James's _____ theory focuses on _____ _____

■ Sigmund Freud emphasizes the importance of _____ _____

■ In Germany, Gestalt psychology proposes that _____ _____

Wilhelm Wundt

William James

included G. Stanley Hall (who established the first American psychology laboratory at Johns Hopkins University in 1883), J. M. Cattell (a professor at the University of Pennsylvania in 1888, who was the first American to be called a "professor of psychology"), and British-born Edward Bradford Titchener. Titchener (1867–1927) became the leader of American psychology soon after he was appointed professor of psychology at Cornell University (a post he held until his death).

Titchener's ideas differed sharply in many respects from those of his mentor. Titchener was impressed by recent advances in chemistry and physics, which had been achieved through analysis of complex compounds (molecules) in terms of their basic elements (atoms). Similarly, Titchener reasoned, psychologists should analyze complex experiences in terms of their simplest components. For example, when people look at a banana they immediately think, "Here is a fruit, something to peel and eat." But this perception is based on associations with past experience. Titchener wanted to discover the most fundamental elements, or "atoms," of thought. Titchener broke down consciousness into three basic elements: physical sensations (what people see), feelings (such as liking or disliking bananas), and images (memories of other bananas). Even the most complex thoughts and feelings, he argued, can be reduced to these simple elements. Titchener saw psychology's role as identifying these elements and showing how they can be combined and integrated—an approach known as **structuralism**. Although the structuralist school of psychology was relatively short-lived and has had little long-term effect, the study of perception and sensation continues to be very much a part of contemporary psychology (explored later in Chapter 3: Sensation and Perception).

One of the first academics to challenge structuralism was an American, William James (1842–1910). In his youth, he studied chemistry, physiology, anatomy, biology, and medicine. Then, in 1872, he accepted an offer to teach physiology at Harvard. There, James read philosophy in his spare time and began to see a link between it and physiology. For him, the two seemed to converge in psychology. In 1875, James began a class in psychology at Harvard (commenting later that the first lecture he ever heard on the subject was his own). He set aside part of his laboratory for psychological experiments. He also began work on a textbook, *The Principles of Psychology*, which was published in 1890.

In preparing his lectures and his textbook, James studied structuralist writings thoroughly and decided that something in Titchener's approach was wrong. He concluded that the atoms of experience—pure sensations without associations—simply did not exist. People's minds are constantly weaving associations, revising experience, starting, stopping, and jumping back and forth in time. Perceptions and associations, sensations and emotions, cannot be separated; consciousness flows in a continuous stream. For James, when people look at a banana, they see a banana, not a long yellow object.

Still focusing on everyday experience, James turned to the study of habit. People, he reasoned, do not have to think about how to get up in the morning, get dressed, open a door, or walk down the street. James suggested that when people repeat something several times, their nervous systems are changed so that each time they open a door, it is easier to open than the last time. This was the link he needed. The biologist in him firmly believed that all activity—from the beating of the heart to the perception of objects—is functional. If we could not recognize a banana, we would have to figure out what it was each time we saw one. In other words, mental associations allow us to benefit from previous experience.

With this insight, James arrived at a *functionalist* theory of mental life and behavior. **Functionalism** is a school of psychology concerned not just with learning or sensation or perception, but rather with how an organism uses its learning or perceptual abilities to function in its environment. This theory raised questions about learning, the complexities of mental life, the impact of experience on the brain, and humankind's place in the natural world—questions that still seem current today. Although impatient with experiments, James shared Wundt and Titchener's belief that the goal of psychology was to analyze experience. Wundt, however, was not impressed. After reading James's textbook, he commented, "It is literature, it is beautiful, but it is not psychology" (Hunt, 1994, p. 139).

Meanwhile, in Germany, a group of psychologists headed by Max Wertheimer, Wolfgang Köhler, and Kurt Koffka was attacking structuralism from another angle. As did James, they thought that the attempt to break down perception and thought into discrete elements was misguided. When people look at a tree, they see just that, a tree, not a series of branches. Look at Figure 1–1. A white triangle can be seen in the center of the pattern although the object consists only of three circles from which "pie slices" have been cut and three 60-degree angles. And when one views a series of still pictures flashed at a constant rate, motion is perceived (for example, movies or "moving" neon signs) even though the eyes see only a series of still pictures.

Phenomena such as these were the force behind a new school of thought that became known as **Gestalt psychology**. Roughly translated from the German, *gestalt* means "whole" or "form." When applied to perception, it refers to the human tendency to see patterns, to distinguish an object from its background, and to complete pictures from a few cues. In other words, the whole of our perceptual experience is more than just the sum of the parts. As will be seen in Chapter 3, Gestalt psychology paved the way for the modern study of perception.

Though none of these early "schools" of psychology exist today as they did early in the twentieth century, together they laid the groundwork for contemporary psychology.

■ WOMEN IN PSYCHOLOGY

After reading the brief history of modern psychology, you may have concluded that the founders of the new discipline were all men. But did psychology really have only fathers and no mothers? In the early twentieth century, psychology was predominantly a male profession with a distinctly American accent (Strickland, 2000). However, women have contributed significantly to psychology from its beginnings. In 1906, James McKeen Cattell published *American Men of Science*, which, despite its title, included 22 female psychologists. Cattell rated three of these women as among the thousand most distinguished scientists in the country. The list included Mary Whiton Calkins (1863–1930) for her analysis of how people learn verbal material and her contributions to self-psychology; Christine Ladd-Franklin (1847–1930) for her work in color vision; and Margaret Floy Washburn (1871–1939) for her pioneering research examining the role of imagery in thought processes. Moreover, Mary Whiton Calkins and Margaret Floy Washburn were elected to the presidency of the American Psychological Association.

In recent decades, the presence of women in psychology has grown by leaps and bounds. Women now receive roughly three fourths of the baccalaureate degrees awarded in psychology. The vast majority of all psychology graduate students are women, and most doctorate degrees in psychology are earned by women. As the number of female psychologists has grown, so have their concerns about traditional psychological theories, research, and clinical practices. As we will

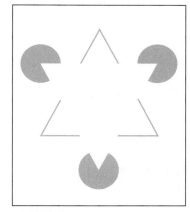

FIGURE 1–1
An illusory triangle.
When sensory information is incomplete, people tend to create a complete perception by supplying the missing details. In this figure, we fill in the lines that let us perceive a white triangle in the center of the pattern.

Women in Psychology

■ Despite the prevalence of men among the founders, women have

_____

_____

■ Today, women receive the majority of _____

_____

see, it was assumed during much of the twentieth century that what was true of males was true of everybody. To the extent that women differ from men, females often were found "lacking." Moreover, reports of gender differences historically have tended to focus on the extremes, exaggerating small differences and ignoring much greater similarities (Hyde, 2005; Spelke, 2005). Finally, the very questions that psychologists ask and the topics that they study reflect what they consider to be important; male and female psychologists differ to some extent in that regard.

Check Your Understanding

1. It was not until the late _____that psychology came into its own as a separate discipline.

2. Women have made significant contributions to the science of psychology since its beginnings.

    a. True   **b.** False

3. As a contestant on a television show, you are delighted that you took a psychology course when you read the clue, "Founder of the first psychological laboratory," and you know that the correct answer is, "Who was _____?"

    a. B. F. Skinner   **c.** William James

    b. John B. Watson   **d.** Wilhelm Wundt

Contemporary Approaches to Psychology

Contemporary psychologists apply many different approaches in their attempts to gain insight into behavior and mental processes. As will be seen, each approach sheds somewhat different light on psychological processes.

■ THE BIOLOGICAL APPROACH

From the time of the early Greek philosophers, the relationship between biological processes on the one hand and consciousness and behavior on the other has been a subject of great interest. Physiological psychologists are especially interested in determining the extent to which behavior, thoughts, and emotions are affected by physical conditions in the body. In its strongest form, the **biological approach** presumes that biological processes are the sole determinant of thoughts and behavior.

Some physiological psychologists are interested in the workings of the brain and nervous system. How does the brain enable people to perceive the world through their senses? How does it allow us to think, speak, sleep, move our bodies, and feel emotions such as anger, sadness, and joy? Others are interested in the body's biochemistry and the ways in which hormones, psychoactive medications, and "social drugs" affect people. How are the hormones of puberty related to mood swings? How do drugs such as marijuana and cocaine work? Still other physiological psychologists are interested in the impact of heredity on normal and abnormal behavior. To what degree is individual intelligence hereditary? Do illnesses such as alcoholism and depression have a genetic component? What about differences in the ways in which men and women think, act, and feel? Although we will encounter questions about the relationship between mind and body throughout the book, in Chapters 2 through 4 we will look especially closely at what we can learn from the biological approach to psychology.

■ THE BEHAVIORAL APPROACH

As seen earlier, Thomas Hobbes believed that such things as "soul" and "spirit" and "mind" are meaningless. John B. Watson (1878–1958) could not have agreed more strongly. In *Psychology as the Behaviorist Views It* (1913), Watson asserted that the whole idea of consciousness, of mental life, is superstition. One cannot define consciousness any more than one can define a soul, he argued. One cannot locate it or measure it, and, therefore, it cannot be the object of

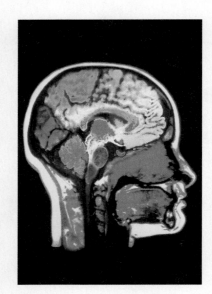

Recent advances in neuroimaging techniques enable physiological psychologists to investigate how specific regions of the brain are involved in complex behaviors and mental processes.

scientific study. For Watson, psychology was the study of observable, measurable behavior—nothing more. This **behavioral approach** to psychology was extremely influential throughout much of the twentieth century.

Watson's approach to psychology, known as **behaviorism**, was based on the work of the Russian physiologist Ivan Pavlov (1849–1936), who received a Nobel Prize for his research on digestion. Some years before Watson's article appeared, Pavlov had noticed that the dogs in his laboratory began to drool as soon as they heard their feeder coming—even before they could see their dinner. The Russian physiologist had always thought that salivation was a natural response to the presence of food, so he found the dogs' anticipatory response odd. He decided to see whether he could teach them to drool at the sound of a ringing bell, even when no food was in the room. He explained his successful results as follows: All behavior is a response to some stimulus or agent in the environment. Thus, to control behavior one must control the environment (Pavlov, 1927). In ordinary life, food makes dogs salivate. All Pavlov did was to train his animals to expect food when they heard a certain sound.

In a famous experiment with an 11-month-old child, Watson showed that people can also be conditioned. Little Albert was a secure, happy baby who had no reason to fear soft, furry white rats. But each time Albert reached out to pet the rat Watson offered him, Watson made a loud noise that frightened Albert. Very soon, Albert was afraid of white rats (Watson & Rayner, 1920). Thus, conditioning changed the child's behavior radically.

Watson saw no reason to refer to consciousness or mental life to explain this change. Little Albert simply responded to the environment—in this case, the association between the loud noises and white, furry objects. Watson felt the same was true for everyone—that all behavior could be explained with the stimulus-response formula. Psychology, he felt, must be purged of "mentalism."

Watson found a kindred spirit in B. F. Skinner (1904–1990), who became the leading spokesman for behaviorism in the mid-twentieth century. Skinner, as did Watson, believed that psychology should involve only the study of observable and measurable behavior. He too was primarily interested in changing behavior through conditioning—and discovering natural laws of behavior in the process. But Skinner's approach was subtly different from that of his predecessor: Skinner rewarded his subjects for behaving the way he wanted them to behave. For example, he would put an animal (rats and pigeons were Skinner's favorite subjects) in a special cage and allow it to explore. Eventually, the animal would reach up and press a lever or peck at a disk on the wall of the cage, at which point a food pellet would drop into the cage. Gradually, the animal learned that the pressing of the bar or the pecking at the disk always brought food. Skinner thus made the animal an active agent in its own conditioning.

In Chapter 5, we will explore in depth what we can learn about psychology from the behavioral approach.

■ THE COGNITIVE APPROACH

In the late 1960s, the grip of behaviorism on the field began to loosen. On the one hand, research on perception, personality, child development, interpersonal relations, and other topics that behaviorists had ignored raised questions they could not readily explain. On the other hand, research in other fields (especially anthropology, linguistics, neurobiology, and computer science) was beginning to shed new light on the workings of the mind. Psychologists came to view behaviorism not as an all-encompassing theory or paradigm, but as only one piece of the puzzle. They began to look into the "black box" of the human mind and put more emphasis on humans (and other animals) as sentient—conscious, perceptive, and alert—beings; that is, as active learners, rather than as passive recipients of life's lessons.

In contrast to behaviorists, psychologists who adopt the **cognitive approach** believe that mental processes can and should be studied scientifically. Although people cannot observe memories or thoughts directly, they can observe behavior and make inferences about the kinds of cognitive processes that underlie that behavior. For example, we can read a lengthy story to others and observe the things they remember from that story, the ways in which their recollections change over time, and the sort of errors in recall (comprehension) they are prone to make. On the basis of systematic research of this kind, we then can gain insight into the

Contemporary Approaches to Psychology

■ The biological approach is concerned with _____

■ John B. Watson redefines psychology as _____

■ Psychologists who adopt the cognitive approach believe that _____

■ The humanistic approach emphasizes the importance of _____

■ Sigmund Freud originates the psychodynamic perspective, which emphasizes _____

■ Psychologists who take the evolutionary/sociobiological approach build on _____

■ The sociocultural approach emphasizes the importance of _____

cognitive processes underlying human memory (explored later in Chapter 6: Memory). Moreover, with the advent of new brain-imaging techniques (described in Chapter 2), cognitive psychologists have begun to address questions about the neurological mechanisms that underlie the cognitive processes of learning, memory, intelligence, and emotion, giving rise to the rapidly expanding field of cognitive neuroscience.

As a result of this shift in focus, even the definition of psychology has changed. Psychology is still the study of human behavior, but psychologists' concept of "behavior" has expanded to include thinking, feeling, learning, remembering, making decisions and judgments, and so on. If the behaviorist model of learning resembled an old-fashioned telephone switchboard—in which a call or a stimulus comes in, is relayed along various circuits in the brain, and an answer or a response goes out—the cognitive model resembles a high-powered, modern computer. Cognitive psychologists are interested in the ways in which people acquire information, process or transform that information using their cognitive "hardware" and "software," and use the results to make sense out of the world, to solve problems, and so on.

In just a short time, cognitive psychology has made an enormous impact on almost every area of psychology and, along with biological psychology, has become one of the most prominent approaches in contemporary scientific psychology.

■ THE HUMANISTIC APPROACH

The **humanistic approach** emphasizes the importance of human potential, self-esteem, self-expression, and self-actualization (the notion of becoming all that one is capable of becoming). Free will and individual choice play an important role in this approach to psychology that also tends to focus on mental health, well-being, self-understanding, and self-improvement, rather than on mental illness. Abraham Maslow (1908–1970) made important contributions to the study of motivation and emotions (see Chapter 8). Carl Rogers (1902–1987) significantly affected the study of personality and the practice of psychotherapy (Chapters 10 and 13). But the humanistic approach as a whole has never been totally accepted by mainstream psychology, in large part because questions of meaning, values, and ethics are not easily subjected to scientific analysis.

In recent years, psychologists studying **positive psychology** have begun to reinvestigate some of the questions that humanistic psychologists first raised a half century ago. According to this view, psychology should devote more attention to "the good life": the study of subjective feelings of happiness and well-being; the development of such individual traits as intimacy, integrity, leadership, altruism, and wisdom; and the kind of families, work settings, and communities that encourage individuals to flourish (Gable & Haidt, 2005; Seligman & Csikszentmihalyi, 2000; Seligman, Steen, & Park, 2005). Positive psychologists argue that psychologists have learned a great deal about the origins, diagnosis, and treatment of mental illness but relatively little about the origins and nurturance of mental wellness. For example, psychologists understand a lot about how individuals survive and endure under conditions of extreme adversity, but far less about ordinary human strengths and virtues. They know more about intelligence than about wisdom, more about conformity than originality, more about stress than about tranquility, and more about prejudice and intergroup hostility than about tolerance and intergroup harmony.

■ THE PSYCHODYNAMIC APPROACH

Of all the pioneers of psychology, Sigmund Freud is by far the best known—and the most controversial. A medical doctor, unlike the other scientists just discussed, Freud was fascinated by the central nervous system. He spent many years conducting research in the physiology laboratory of the University of Vienna and only reluctantly became a practicing physician. After a trip to Paris, where he studied with a neurologist who was using hypnosis to treat nervous disorders, Freud established a private practice in Vienna in 1886. His work with patients convinced him that many nervous ailments were psychological, rather than physiological in origin.

Freud's clinical observations led him to develop a comprehensive theory of mental life that differed radically from the views of his predecessors. For example, Freud held that human beings are not as rational as they imagine and that "free will" is largely an illusion. Rather, we are motivated by a dynamic cauldron of primitive sexual and aggressive drives, forbidden desires, nameless fears and wishes, and traumatic childhood memories that are not available to the rational, conscious part of the mind. According to Freud, these unconscious desires, fears, and memories, although hidden from awareness, press upon the conscious mind and find expression in disguised or altered form, including dreams, mannerisms, slips of the tongue, and symptoms of mental illness, as well as in socially acceptable pursuits such as art and literature.

This **psychodynamic approach** to understanding behavior was as controversial at the turn of the twentieth century as Darwin's theory of evolution had been 25 years earlier. Many of Freud's Victorian contemporaries were shocked, not only by his emphasis on sexuality, but also by his suggestion that people often are unaware of their true motives and thus are not entirely in control of their thoughts and behavior. Conversely, members of the medical community in Vienna at that time generally held Freud's new theory in high regard, nominating him for the position of Professor Extraordinarious at the University of Vienna (Esterson, 2002).

Psychodynamic theory, as expanded and revised by Freud's colleagues and successors, laid the foundation for the study of personality and psychological disorders, which will be discussed in Chapters 10, 12, and 13. His revolutionary notion of the unconscious and his portrayal of human beings as constantly at war with themselves are taken for granted today, at least in literary and artistic circles. However, his theories and methods continue to inspire heated debate in part because much of Freud's theory is difficult or impossible to test scientifically.

■ THE EVOLUTIONARY/SOCIOBIOLOGICAL APPROACH

As seen earlier, Darwin believed that behaviors that contribute to the survival of a species will tend to persist while behaviors that are detrimental to survival will tend to disappear over time. Psychologists who take the **evolutionary/sociobiological approach** build on that foundation by exploring the ways in which human behavior patterns and mental processes have been beneficial to our emergence and survival as a distinct species (Buss, 2005). How did human beings get to be the way they are? In what ways might the roots of behavior serve to promote the survival of the species? For example, men the world over tend to prefer women with a waist-to-hip ratio of 0.7 (Streeter & McBurney, 2003). Moreover, a small waist-to-hip ratio is associated with a female's reproductive age and overall health (Singh, 1993). These preferences appear to be universal rather than the product of any particular society, so might they be considered "built in" because they have been adaptive for humans in the past?

Evolutionary psychologists study such diverse topics as perception, language, helping others (altruism), parenting, happiness, sexual attraction and mate selection, jealousy, and violence. By studying such phenomena in different species, in different habitats, in different cultures, and in males and females, evolutionary psychologists seek to understand how human beings are genetically preprogrammed to think and act in certain ways. In Chapter 2, we will discuss some of the insights that have arisen from this approach to understanding thinking and behavior.

■ THE SOCIOCULTURAL APPROACH

Through most of the twentieth century, psychology paid relatively little attention to human diversity. Psychology was a white male profession with a distinctly American accent (Strickland, 2000). The great majority of research studies were conducted by white male professors at American universities, using white male American college students as participants. In fact, one critical history of psychology during this period was titled *Even the Rat Was White!* (R. Guthrie, 1976). This arrangement was not the result of a conscious or deliberate decision to study just one particular group. As in the medical community and in other sciences and prestigious professions in Europe and North America, psychology took for granted that what was true of white Western males would be true for other people as well. We now know that was an invalid assumption.

Psychologists are now working to uncover and overcome biases in psychological research that are related to gender, race, and ethnicity. As a result, the field of psychology is broadening its scope to probe the full range and richness of human diversity, and this text mirrors that expansive and inclusive **sociocultural approach**. Psychologists have begun to look closely at the ways in which culture, gender, race, and ethnicity can affect virtually all aspects of human behavior and to question assumptions that are based explicitly on gender, race, and

To understand human behavior, we must appreciate the rich diversity of culture throughout the world.

culture. For example, the study of similarities and differences among men and women has become part of mainstream psychology. Psychologists in virtually every subfield conduct research to determine whether their findings apply equally to males and females, and if not, why not.

■ MULTIPLE PERSPECTIVES OF PSYCHOLOGY TODAY

Most contemporary psychologists tend to view these seven different approaches as complementary, with each one contributing to a more complete understanding of human behavior. When they study aggression, for example, psychologists no longer limit their explanations to the behavioral view (aggressive behavior is learned as a consequence of reward and punishment) or the Freudian perspective (aggression is an expression of unconscious hostility toward a parent). Instead, most contemporary psychologists trace aggression to a number of factors, including longstanding adaptations to the environment (evolutionary psychology) and the influences of culture, gender, and socioeconomic status on the way people perceive and interpret events—"That guy is making fun of me" or "She's asking for it"—(cognitive psychology). Similarly, physiological psychologists no longer limit themselves to identifying the genetic and biochemical roots of aggression. Instead, they study how biological processes interact with the environment to elicit aggressive behavior.

Sometimes, these theoretical perspectives mesh and enhance one another beautifully; at other times, adherents of one approach challenge their peers, arguing for one viewpoint over all the others. But all psychologists agree that the field advances only when new evidence is added to support or challenge existing theories.

Check Your Understanding

1. Which approach to psychology is reflected in the research article, "The Role of the Brain in Controlling Fear"?

a. The cognitive approach

b. The humanistic approach

c. The biological approach

d. The behavioral approach

2. Which approach to psychology is reflected in the research article, "The Effect of Prior Memories on New Memories"?

a. The cognitive approach

b. The evolutionary approach

c. The sociocultural approach

d. The psychodynamic approach

3. "Though we may explain away our behavior, the real reasons for our behavior are forever hidden from us." This statement most clearly reflects which approach to psychology?

a. The cognitive approach

b. The psychodynamic approach

c. The sociocultural approach

d. The humanistic approach

Enduring Issues in Psychology

Five "Enduring Issues" have their roots in ancient philosophy and persist today as topics of research and theorizing. The issues cut across the numerous approaches introduced in this chapter and cut to the core of what it means to be human. They will be encountered in every chapter of this book. Sometimes they will be pointed out; at other times, it will be left to the reader to realize that the discussion bears directly on one or more of these issues. In brief form, these five issues are discussed next.

▪ PERSON–SITUATION

To what extent is behavior caused by internal processes—thoughts, emotions, motives, attitudes, values, personality, and genes? In contrast, to what extent is behavior caused or triggered by external factors—incentives, environmental cues, and the presence of other people? Put another way, are people masters of their fate or victims of circumstances? These questions will be encountered directly as they relate to behavior genetics, learning, emotion and motivation, personality, and social psychology.

▪ NATURE–NURTURE

Is the individual we become a product of innate, inborn tendencies or a reflection of experiences and upbringing? This is the famous "nature versus nurture" debate that has been going on for thousands of years. Today, psychologists also debate the relative influence of heredity (genes) versus environment (experience) on thought and behavior. This issue surfaces most clearly in discussions of behavior genetics, intelligence, development, personality, and abnormal psychology.

▪ STABILITY–CHANGE

Are the characteristics a person develops in childhood more or less permanent, or do the characteristics change over the course of one's life? Is one's sense of self perhaps just a "fictional character" created to maintain a sense of inner continuity in the face of changes that result from varied, sometimes unpredictable, experiences? Developmental psychologists are interested especially in these and other questions, as are psychologists who specialize in personality, adjustment, abnormal psychology, and therapy.

▪ DIVERSITY–UNIVERSALITY

As humans, every person is similar to every other person in many specific ways. But in other ways, every person is similar only to certain other people. And in still other ways, everyone is unique and unlike any other person. Thus, similarity and diversity will exist wherever humans exist. Because people differ in how they look, feel, and behave, human diversity is necessarily a central concern for psychologists. As you read through this book, ask yourself: Does our understanding of human behavior apply equally well to every human being? Does it apply only to men or just to women or only to particular racial or ethnic groups or particular societies (especially our own)? Do we perhaps need "different psychologies" to account for the wide diversity of human behaviors?

▪ MIND–BODY

Finally, how are mind and body connected? Since the time of the ancient Greek philosophers, people have been fascinated by the relationship between *experience* (such as thoughts and feelings) and *biological processes* (such as activity in the nervous system). Contemporary psychologists use the scientific method and state-of-the-art tools to get closer to understanding the relationship between mind and body. This issue will be encountered most often in this book in discussions of the biological basis of behavior, sensation and perception, altered states of consciousness, emotion and motivation, adjustment and health psychology, and disorders and therapy.

Enduring Issues in Psychology

- Person–Situation _____
  _____
- Nature–Nurture _____
  _____
- Stability–Change _____
  _____
- Diversity–Universality _____
  _____
  _____
- Mind–Body_____
  _____

"I told my parents that if grades were so important they should have paid for a smarter egg donor."

Check Your Understanding

1. Match each of these enduring issues with its appropriate description.

_____ Person–Situation

_____ Nature–Nurture

_____ Stability–Change

_____ Diversity–Universality

_____ Mind–Body

a. How much do people stay the same as they develop, and how much do they change?

b. In what ways do people differ in how they think and act?

c. What is the relationship between one's internal experiences and his or her biological processes?

d. Is behavior caused more by inner traits or by external situations?

e. How do genes and experiences interact to influence people?

2. Caroline is interested in the question of whether people's personality characteristics are determined for life by genetics or whether these characteristics can be changed as a result of experiences in life. Which of the following enduring issues best describes Caroline's interests?

a. Mind–Body

b. Diversity–Universality

c. Nature–Nurture

d. Person–Situation

Psychology as Science

■ Psychologists rely on the scientific method to _____
_____
_____

■ As data are collected, psychologists propose _____
_____
_____

Psychology as Science

Earlier, we defined psychology as the science of behavior and mental processes. The key word in this definition is *science*. Psychologists rely on the **scientific method** when they seek to answer questions about behavior and mental processes. They collect data through careful, systematic observation; they attempt to explain what they have observed by developing theories; they make new predictions based on those theories; and they systematically test those predictions through additional observations and experiments to determine whether they are correct. Thus, as with all scientists, psychologists use the scientific method to *describe*, *explain*, *predict* and, eventually, achieve some measure of *control* over what they study.

Let's see what this means by looking at how psychologists would approach the question of whether there are sex differences in aggressiveness. Many people believe that males are naturally more aggressive than females. Others contend that boys learn to be aggressive because our society and culture encourages—indeed requires—males to be combative, even violent. Still others say there are no significant sex differences in aggression. How would psychologists approach this issue? First, they would want to find out whether in fact males and females actually

Males seem to be more physically aggressive than females. Different schools of psychology have different explanations for why this is true.

differ in aggressive behavior. Many research studies have addressed this question, and the evidence seems conclusive: Males are indeed more aggressive than females, particularly in terms of physical aggression (Knight, Fabes, & Higgins, 1996; Wright, 1994; Zimmer-Gembeck, Geiger, & Crick, 2005). Perhaps girls and women make nasty remarks or yell (Ostrov & Keating, 2004; Underwood, 2003), but boys and men are far more likely to fight physically.

Having established that sex differences in physical aggression do exist, and having *described* those differences, psychologists then seek to *explain* the differences. Psychologists who take the biological approach would be likely to ascribe the sex differences to genetics or body chemistry. Others taking the behavioral approach might look to the ways in which a child learns to behave "like a boy" or "like a girl." And from the sociocultural perspective, psychologists might explain the differences in terms of cultural norms that not only require males to "stand up for themselves" but also teach the notion that physical aggression is not "feminine."

Each of these explanations stands as a systematic explanation of a phenomenon, or **theory**, about the causes of sex differences in aggression. And each theory allows psychologists to make new **hypotheses**, or predictions, about the phenomena in question. For example, if gender differences in aggression arise because males have higher levels of testosterone than females, then one could predict that extremely violent men should have higher levels of testosterone than do men who are generally nonviolent. If sex differences in aggression stem from early training, then one could predict that there should be fewer sex differences in aggression in families in which parents did not stress gender differences. Finally, if sex differences in aggression reflect cultural norms, then one could predict that in societies that do not prohibit girls and women from fighting, or in those that consider physical aggression abnormal or improper for both sexes, the differences should be small.

Each of these predictions or hypotheses can be tested through research. If the research is done carefully, the results should indicate whether one theory is better than another at accounting for known facts and predicting new facts. In turn, if one or more of the theories is supported by research evidence, it should be possible to control aggressive behavior to a greater degree than was possible before.

How, then, do psychologists go about testing theories and hypotheses and gaining insight into behavior and mental processes?

Check Your Understanding

1. Indicate in the spaces below whether the following statements are true (T) or false (F).

   a. _____ Psychologists collect data through careful, systematic observation.

   b. _____ Psychologists attempt to explain their observations by developing theories.

   c. _____ Psychologists form hypotheses or predictions on the basis of theories.

   d. _____ Psychologists appeal to common sense in their arguments.

   e. _____ Psychologists systematically test hypotheses.

   f. _____ Psychologists base their conclusions on widely shared values.

Research Methods in Psychology

All sciences—including psychology, sociology, economics, political science, biology, medicine, and physics—require evidence based on careful observation and experimentation. To collect data systematically and objectively, psychologists use many different research methods, including naturalistic observation, case studies, surveys, correlational research, and experimental research.

■ DESCRIPTIVE METHODS

As we will see in the following section, several research methods are particularly appropriate for describing behavior.

The world-famous primatologist Jane Goodall has spent most of her adult life observing chimpanzees in their natural environment in Africa.

■ NATURALISTIC OBSERVATION

Many believe "telling it like it is" is a virtue. **Naturalistic observation** is basically a way of "*seeing* it like it is." Psychologists use this method to study human or animal behavior in its natural context instead of in the laboratory under artificial conditions. Most people use this method in everyday life without realizing it. When you watch dogs playing in the park or observe pedestrians crossing the street, you are using a form of naturalistic observation. A psychologist with this real-life orientation might observe behavior in a school or a factory; another might actually join a family to study the behavior of its members; still another might observe monkeys in the wild rather than viewing them in captivity. The primary advantage of naturalistic observation is that the behavior observed in everyday life is likely to be more natural, spontaneous, and varied than that observed in a laboratory.

For example, several researchers used naturalistic observation to understand why some people with a particular mental disorder were more likely to adjust successfully to the workplace than others (Hammen, Gitlin, & Altshuler, 2000). By carefully studying 52 people over a two-year period in their natural settings, these investigators found that the people who displayed the most successful work adjustment were those who also had strong supportive personal relationships with other people. Surprisingly, stressful life events did not seem to play an important role in how well these people adjusted to work. Because simulating a genuine workplace environment in a laboratory would have been extremely difficult (especially over an extended period of time), naturalistic observation provided a practical alternative with which to explore this issue.

Naturalistic observation is not without its drawbacks:

- Because naturalistic observation does not interfere with ongoing behavior, psychologists using this research method have to take behavior as it comes. They cannot suddenly yell, "Freeze!" when they want to study in more detail what is going on! Nor can psychologists tell people to stop what they are doing because it is not what the psychologists want to study.

- Psychologists may fail to observe or record behavior that seems to be irrelevant. Therefore, many observational studies employ teams of trained observers to pool their notes.

- Unlike laboratory experiments that can be repeated, each natural situation is a one-time-only occurrence. Therefore, psychologists prefer not to make general statements based solely on information from naturalistic studies. Instead, they would test the information under controlled laboratory conditions before they draw generalizations.

- But the main drawback in naturalistic observation is **observer bias**—expectations or biases by the observer that might distort or influence any interpretations made of what actually happened. As we will see in Chapter 6 (Memory), eyewitnesses to a crime often are unreliable sources of information. Even psychologists who are trained observers may subtly distort what they see to make it conform to what they were hoping to see. For this reason, contemporary researchers often use videotapes that can be analyzed and scored by other researchers who are not aware of the design and purpose of the study.

Despite the disadvantages, naturalistic observation is a valuable tool. After all, real-life behavior is what psychology is all about. Naturalistic observation often provides new ideas and suggests new theories, which then can be studied in the laboratory more systematically and in greater detail. This method also helps researchers maintain their perspective by reminding them of the larger world outside the lab.

Descriptive Methods

■ Naturalistic observation _____
_____
_____

■ Case studies _____
_____
_____

■ Surveys _____
_____
_____

■ CASE STUDIES

A second research method is the **case study**, which is a detailed description of one person or a few individuals. In some ways, this method is similar to naturalistic observation, but the researcher here uses various methods to collect information that will yield a detailed, in-depth portrait of the individual. A case study usually includes real-life observation, interviews, scores on various psychological tests, and whatever other measures the researcher considers revealing. For example, the Swiss psychologist Jean Piaget (1896–1980) developed a comprehensive theory of cognitive development by carefully studying each of his three children as they grew and changed during childhood (see Chapter 9: Life-Span Development).

Case studies can provide valuable insights and suggestions for further research (as does naturalistic observation as well), but they also can have significant drawbacks. Observer bias is as much a problem here as it is with naturalistic observation. Moreover, because each person is unique, no one can draw general conclusions confidently from a single case. Nevertheless, case studies figure prominently in psychological research. For example, the famous case of Phineas Gage, who suffered severe and unusual brain damage, led researchers to identify the front portion of the brain as important for the control of emotions and the ability to plan and carry out complex tasks (see Chapter 2: The Biological Basis of Behavior). The case study of another brain-damaged patient, known as "H. M.," focused on a patient who could remember events that preceded his injury but nothing that happened after it and prompted psychologists to suggest the existence of several distinct kinds of memory (Milner, 1959; see Chapter 6: Memory).

■ SURVEYS

In some respects, **survey research** addresses the shortcomings of naturalistic observation and case studies. In survey research, a carefully selected group of people is asked a set of predetermined questions in face-to-face interviews or in questionnaires. Surveys, even those with a low-response rate, can generate a great deal of interesting and useful information at relatively low cost, but for results to be accurate, researchers must pay close attention to the survey questions. In addition, the people surveyed must be selected with great care and be motivated to respond to the survey thoughtfully and carefully. For example, asking parents, "Do you ever use physical punishment to discipline your children?" may elicit the socially correct answer, "No." Asking "When was the last time you spanked your child?" or "In what situations do you feel it is necessary to spank your child?" is more likely to elicit honest responses. This is because the

Jean Piaget based his theory of cognitive development on case studies of children.

question is specific and implies that some parents use physical punishment; also, the researcher is merely asking when and why. At the same time, survey researchers must be careful not to ask leading questions, such as "Most Americans approve of physical punishment. Do you?" Guaranteeing anonymity to participants in a survey can also be valuable to the study's accuracy.

Naturalistic observations, case studies, and surveys can provide a rich set of raw data to describe behaviors, beliefs, opinions, and attitudes. But these research methods are not ideal for making predictions, explaining behavior, or determining the causes of behavior. For these purposes, psychologists use more powerful research methods, as described in the next sections.

■ CORRELATIONAL RESEARCH

Correlational Research

- This research technique is based on

_____

_____

- Correlational research can be used to

_____

_____

Suppose a psychologist wants to find out what makes a good pilot. Perhaps the Air Force has asked him to study this question because it costs thousands of dollars to train a single pilot, and each year many trainees wash out. An excellent approach to this problem would be **correlational research**. The psychologist might select several hundred trainees, give them a range of aptitude and personality tests, and compare the results with their performance in training school. This approach would tell the psychologist whether some characteristic or set of characteristics is closely related to, or correlated with, eventual success as a pilot.

Suppose that the psychologist finds that the most successful trainees score higher than the unsuccessful trainees on mechanical aptitude tests and that they are also cautious people who do not like to take unnecessary risks. The psychologist has discovered that there is a correlation, or relationship, between these traits and success as a pilot trainee: High scores on tests of mechanical aptitude and caution predict success as a pilot trainee. If these correlations are confirmed in new groups of trainees, then the psychologist could recommend with some confidence that the Air Force consider using these tests to select future trainees.

Correlational studies can identify relationships between two or more variables without giving psychologists an exact understanding as to why these relationships exist. This important distinction is often overlooked. Correlation simply means that two phenomena seem to be related: When one goes up, for whatever reason the other goes up (or down). For example, young people with high IQ scores usually earn higher grades in school than do students with average or below-average scores. Such a correlation allows researchers to predict that children with high IQ scores will do well on tests and in other academic work. But a conclusion cannot be drawn that high scores on IQ tests *cause* students to do better in school. That is certainly one interpretation (for example, children who learn they have high IQ scores might indeed work harder in school). But the reverse might also be true: Working hard in school might cause children to score higher on IQ tests. Or a third, unidentified factor might intervene. For example, growing up in a family that places a high value on education might cause both higher IQ scores and higher school grades. (See Appendix A for more on correlation.)

Recall the pilot trainee example: The psychologist discovered a relationship between skill as a pilot and two other characteristics. As a result, he is able to use those relationships to predict with some accuracy which trainees will and will not become skilled pilots. But he has no basis for drawing conclusions about cause and effect. Does the tendency to shy away from taking risks make a trainee a good pilot? Or is it the other way around: Learning to be a skillful pilot makes people cautious? Or is there some unknown factor that causes people to be both cautious and capable of acquiring the different skills needed in the cockpit? The psychologist does not know.

Despite limitations, correlational research often sheds light on important psychological phenomena. This book will address many examples of correlational research: People who are experiencing severe stress are more prone to develop physical illnesses than people who are not stressed; children whose parent(s) have schizophrenia are more likely to develop this disorder than are other children; and when someone needs help, the more bystanders there are, the less likely it is that any one of them will come forward to offer help. These interesting findings allow us to make some predictions about behavior, but ultimately, psychologists want to move beyond simply making predictions. They want to discover the root causes of psychological phenomena. They want to explain thoughts, feelings, and behavior. To do that, psychologists most often use the experimental method.

■ EXPERIMENTAL RESEARCH

A psychology instructor notices that on Monday mornings, most students in her class do not remember materials as well as they do later in the week. She has discovered a correlation between the day of the week and memory for course-related material. On the basis of this correlation, she could predict that next Monday and every Monday thereafter, the students in her class will not absorb material as well as on other days. But she wants to go beyond simply predicting her students' behavior. She wants to understand or explain why their memories are poorer on Mondays than on other days of the week.

As a result of her own experiences and some informal interviews with students, she suspects that students stay up late on weekends and that their difficulty in recalling facts and ideas presented on Mondays is due to lack of sleep. The psychologist then has a hypothesis that appears to make sense, but she wants to prove that it is correct and that all other possible explanations for the facts have been ruled out. To gather evidence that lack of sleep actually causes memory deficits, she turns to the **experimental method.**

Her first step is to select **participants**, people whom she can observe in a controlled setting. She decides to use student volunteers. To keep her results from being influenced by sex differences or intelligence levels, she chooses a group made up of equal numbers of men and women, all of whom scored between 520 and 550 on the verbal section of their college entrance exams.

The psychologist then needs to know which participants are sleep deprived. Simply asking people whether they have slept well is not ideal: Some may say "no," so that they will have an excuse for doing poorly on the test, and others may say "yes," because they do not want a psychologist to think that they have trouble sleeping. And two people who both say they "slept well" may not mean the same thing. So the psychologist decides to intervene—that is, to control the situation more closely—to determine which participants have sleep deficits. Everyone in the experiment, she decides, will spend the night in the same dormitory. They will be kept awake until 4:00 a.m. and awakened at 7:00 a.m. sharp. She and her colleagues will patrol the halls to make sure that no one falls asleep ahead of schedule. By manipulating the amount of time the participants sleep, the psychologist is introducing and controlling an essential element of the experimental method: an **independent variable**.

Next, she needs to know how well the students remember new information after they are deprived of sleep. For this, she designs a memory task. She needs something that none of her participants will know in advance. If she chooses a chapter in a history book, for example, she runs the risk that some of her participants are history buffs. Given the various possibilities, the psychologist decides to print a page of geometric shapes, each labeled with a nonsense word. Circles are "glucks," triangles are "rogs," and so on. She gives students half an hour to learn the names from this page, then takes it away and asks them to assign those same labels to geometric shapes on a new page. The psychologist believes that the students' ability to learn and remember labels for geometric shapes will depend on how much sleep they had the night before. Performance on the memory task (the number of correct answers) thus becomes the **dependent variable**. According to the psychologist's hypothesis, changing the independent variable (the amount of sleep) should also change the dependent variable (performance on the memory task). Her prediction is that these participants, who get no more than three hours of sleep, should do quite poorly on the memory test.

At this point, the experimenter begins looking for loopholes in her experimental design. How can she be sure that poor test results mean that the participants did less well than they would have done if they had more sleep? For example, their poor performance simply could be the result of knowing that they were being closely observed. To be sure that her experiment measures only the effects of inadequate sleep, the experimenter creates two groups that contain equal numbers of males and females of roughly the same age and college entrance exam scores. One of the groups, the **experimental group**, will be kept awake as described until 4:00 a.m. That is, they will be subjected to the experimenter's manipulation of the independent variable—amount of sleep. Members of the other group, the **control group**, will be allowed to go to sleep whenever they please. Finally, the psychologist questions her own objectivity. Because she believes that lack of sleep inhibits students' learning and memory, she does not want

---

Experimental Research

■ The experimental method can be used to _____ _____ _____

■ The experimental method involves the manipulation of a(n) _____ variable by the experimenter to determine whether it affects the _____ variable of interest.

■ Results from participants in the _____ group are compared to those in the _____ group to determine whether the _____ variable had the _____ effect.

SUMMARY TABLE   **Basic Methods of Research**

	RESEARCH METHOD	ADVANTAGES	LIMITATIONS
Naturalistic Observation	Behavior is observed in the environment in which it occurs naturally.	Provides a great deal of firsthand behavioral information that is more likely to be accurate than reports after the fact. The participants' behavior is more natural, spontaneous, and varied than behaviors taking place in the laboratory; a rich source of hypotheses as well.	The presence of an observer may alter the participants' behavior; the observer's recording of the behavior may reflect a preexisting bias; and it is often unclear whether the observations can be generalized to other settings and other people.
Case Studies	Behavior of one person or a few people is studied in depth.	Yields a great deal of detailed descriptive information; useful for forming hypotheses.	The case(s) studied may not be a representative sample. This method can be time consuming and expensive. Observer bias is a potential problem.
Surveys	Many participants are asked a standard set of questions.	Enables an immense amount of data to be gathered quickly and inexpensively.	Sampling biases can skew results. Poorly constructed questions can result in answers that are ambiguous, so data are not clear. Accuracy depends on ability and willingness of participants to answer questions honestly.
Correlational Research	Approach employs statistical methods to examine the relationship between two or more variables.	May clarify relationships between variables that cannot be examined by other research methods; allows prediction of behavior.	Method does not permit researchers to draw conclusions regarding cause-and-effect relationships.
Experimental Research	One or more variables are systematically manipulated, and the effect of that manipulation on other variables is studied.	Because of its strict control of variables, this approach offers researchers the opportunity to draw conclusions about cause-and-effect relationships.	The artificiality of the lab setting may influence participants' behavior; unexpected and uncontrolled variables may confound results; many variables cannot be controlled and manipulated.

to prejudice the results of her experiment; that is, she wants to avoid **experimenter bias.** So, she decides to ask a neutral person—someone who does not know which participants did or did not sleep all night—to score the tests.

   The experimenter reasons that if the only consistent difference between the two groups is the amount of sleep each gets, she can be much more confident that if the experimental group does relatively poorly on the memory task, her hypothesis gains support: Lack of sleep does indeed appear to cause memory deficit. But the psychologist will interpret even the most definitive findings with caution. Only after other researchers in other laboratories with other participants and other memory tasks have repeated her experiment and obtained the same results will she become confident that sleep deprivation hinders memory.

The experimental method is a powerful tool, but it, too, has limitations. First, many intriguing psychological variables, such as love, hatred, or grief, do not lend themselves to experimental manipulation readily. And even if it were possible to induce such strong emotions as part of a psychological experiment, this treatment would raise serious ethical questions. In some cases, psychologists may use animals rather than humans for experiments. But some subjects, such as the emergence of language in children or the expression of emotions, simply cannot be studied with other species. Second, because experiments are conducted in an artificial setting, participants—whether human or nonhuman animals—may behave differently than they would in real life. For example, because participants in laboratory research know that they are being observed by psychologists, they may try to appear especially healthy, normal, tolerant, and intelligent. In turn, this increases the difficulty of observing people's true responses to situations.

The accompanying Summary Table: Basic Methods of Research displays the main advantages and disadvantages of each research method just discussed. Because each method has strengths and weaknesses, psychologists often use more than one method to study a single problem.

■ MULTIMETHOD RESEARCH

The memory researcher might, for example, observe other classes at her college or university to see whether the "Monday morning memory deficit" shows up in those classes as well. That would be a form of *naturalistic observation*. She might discover that, indeed, the problem shows up in those classes as well. On the other hand, she might discover that the problem only shows up in certain subject areas and not others. In either case, her observations add to her understanding of the phenomenon. She also might study a few students in depth (for example, by asking them to keep a record of their sleep each night) and use interviews and scores on various psychological tests to determine whether she could gain additional insight into the problem. That would be an example of a *case study*. She might *survey* a large number of students to determine how much sleep they get on the weekend, how well they remember information on Monday morning, and whether they believe their sleep has an effect on their ability to remember. She also might ask a large number of students at different colleges and universities to report the amount of sleep they got on the weekend and then test their memory on Monday morning to see whether there is a consistent *correlation* between self-reported sleep and memory. Her findings at any point in this research program might prompt her to revise her memory test or her hypothesis—or they simply might give her added confidence that her hypothesis is correct. In fact, sleep deprivation does indeed hinder memory (Yoo, Hu, Gujar, Jolesz, & Walker, 2007).

■ IMPORTANCE OF SAMPLING

One obvious drawback to every form of research is that it usually is impossible, or at least impractical, to measure every single occurrence of a characteristic. No one could expect to measure the memory of every human being, to study the responses of all individuals who suffer from the irrational fears known as phobias, or to record the maternal behavior of all female monkeys. No matter what research method is used, researchers typically study only a small **sample**, or subset of the population, and use the results of that limited study to generalize cautiously about larger populations. For example, in her original experiment, the psychology instructor who studied the effect of lack of sleep on memory studied only student volunteers at her own college or university. When she discovered that sleep deprivation did indeed interfere with memory in those participants, she may have been tempted to assume that her results would apply to other students at her institution (past and future), to students at other colleges and universities around the world, and to people not of college age.

How realistic are such assumptions? How confident can researchers be that the results of research conducted on a relatively small sample of people apply to the much larger population from which the sample was drawn? Social scientists have developed several techniques to improve the generalizability of their results. One is to select participants at random from the larger population. For example, the researcher studying pilot trainees might begin with an alphabetical list of all trainees and select every third name or every fifth name on the list to be in

Multimethod Research

■ Psychologists often use more than one _____

_____

■ If the results from many studies that used different methods are in agreement, the researcher can _____

_____

_____

Importance of Sampling

■ Researchers typically study only a small sample, or _____

_____

■ To improve the generalizability of their results, researchers use _____

_____

_____

his study. These participants would constitute a **random sample** from the larger group of trainees because every trainee had an equal chance of being chosen for the study. Another approach is to pick a **representative sample** of the population being studied. For example, researchers looking for a representative cross-section of Americans would want to ensure that the proportion of males and females in the study matched the national proportion, that the number of participants from each state matched the national population distribution, and so on.

As a consumer of psychological research, you should adopt a critical attitude toward reports of psychological research. Ask yourself what kind of sample was used in the research and whether you are confident that results obtained from that sample are likely to apply to other populations. Determine whether the research used the experimental method with an independent variable, a dependent variable, an experimental group, and a control group. If not, be exceptionally cautious about drawing conclusions about cause and effect. On the other hand, if the report indicates that research was conducted on many different people or animals and used multiple methods (including controlled experiments), one can be more confident in the results. To get started, practice this kind of critical thinking as you read further in this book.

Check Your Understanding

1. A method of research known as _____ allows psychologists to study behavior as it occurs in real-life settings.

2. Psychologists use _____ research to examine relationships between two or more variables without manipulating any variable.

3. The method of research best suited to explaining behavior is _____ research.

4. The _____ variable in an experiment is manipulated to see how it affects a second variable; the _____ variable is the one observed for any possible effects.

5. To ensure that the results of a particular study apply to a larger population, researchers use _____ or _____ samples.

Ethical Principles That Guide Research in Psychology

■ Participants must be informed, in advance, about _____

_____

_____

■ Researchers who use nonhuman animals in research must _____

_____

_____

Ethics and Psychology

■ ETHICAL PRINCIPLES THAT GUIDE RESEARCH IN PSYCHOLOGY

At some point in your life, you probably will have a chance to participate in psychological research. It may be as simple as responding to a short survey, or it may require repeated trips to a psychological laboratory. You will be provided some information about the research, and you will be asked to give your consent to participate. To ensure that psychological research is carried out in an ethical manner, the American Psychological Association (1992, 2003) has approved a detailed code of ethics that is assessed annually and revised periodically to ensure that it protects participants in research studies adequately. The ethics code stipulates that:

- Participants must be informed of the nature of research in clearly understandable language.
- Informed consent must be documented.
- Risks, possible adverse effects, and limitations on confidentiality must be spelled out in advance.
- If participation is a condition of course credit, equitable alternative activities must be offered.
- Participants cannot be deceived about aspects of the research that would affect their willingness to participate, such as risks or unpleasant emotional experiences.
- Deception about the goals of the research can be used only when such deception absolutely is necessary to ensure the integrity of the research.

In addition, psychological researchers are required to follow the U.S. Code of Federal Regulations, which includes an extensive set of regulations concerning the protection of human participants in all kinds of research. Failure to abide by these federal regulations may result in the termination of federal funding for the researcher and penalties for the research institution.

Despite these formal ethical and legal guidelines, controversy still rages about the ethics of psychological research on humans. Some people contend that research procedures should never be emotionally or physically distressing. Others assert that ethical guidelines that are too strict may undermine the scientific value of research or cripple future research. Still others maintain that psychology, as a science, should base its ethical code on documented evidence about the effects of research procedures on participants, not on conjecture about what is "probably" a good way to conduct research.

In recent years, questions have also been raised about the ethics of using animals in psychological research. Psychologists study animal behavior to shed light on human behavior, particularly where it would be clearly unethical to use human participants—such as studies involving brain lesions (requiring cutting into the brain) or electric stimulation of parts of the brain. In fact, much of what is known currently about sensation, perception, drugs, emotional attachment, and the neural basis of behavior is derived from animal research (Carroll & Overmier, 2001; Dess & Foltin, 2005). Yet, many people question whether it is ethical to use nonhuman animals in research that would not be appropriate for human participants. Others point out that nonhuman animals cannot give their consent to participate in psychological research; thus they are unwilling (and unwitting) participants. Their opponents contend that the goals of psychological research—understanding thinking and behavior and, in many cases, reducing or eliminating human suffering—justify the means, even though they agree that animals should be made to suffer as little as possible. They point out that procedures already in place, including the use of anesthesia in many experiments, already minimize animal suffering.

The APA has addressed this issue as well in its ethical guidelines, noting that psychologists using animals in research must ensure "appropriate consideration of [the animal's] comfort, health, and humane treatment" (APA, 1992, 2003).

Now that you have an overview of the history of psychology, the methods used by psychologists to conduct research, and the protections provided for participants in psychological research, it is time to discover what psychologists have learned in their quest to understand mental and behavioral processes. The next chapter looks at what has been learned about the relationship between biology and psychology—the Mind–Body issue that has intrigued people since ancient times.

Check Your Understanding

1. Your classmate Jared says he does not need to be concerned about ethical standards for his naturalistic observation study. On the basis of what you have learned from this chapter, your reply should be:

   a. "You're right, because there are only ethical guidelines for the protection of animals."

   b. "You're right. Only laboratory experiments must conform to ethics standards."

   c. "That's incorrect. All psychological research is subject to ethical guidelines."

   d. "That's incorrect. Actually, naturalistic observation is the only kind of research subject to ethics rules."

2. Before anyone agrees to be in her experiment, Yolanda gives the participants a short description of what they will be asked to do in the study, the reasons she is conducting the study, and any risks or discomfort they might face. Yolanda is:

   a. Getting informed consent from her participants

   b. Mollycoddling her participants

   c. Deceiving her participants

   d. Not adhering to ethical guidelines for the treatment of human research participants

Chapter Review

www.psychologythecore.com

Psychology is the scientific study of behavior and mental processes. The roots of psychology can be found in the work of Greek philosophers (particularly Socrates, Plato, and Aristotle) who first began to speculate about how the mind works, about where thoughts and feelings come from, and about the relationship between the mind and behavior. From their thinking emerged the concept of **dualism**, which holds that thoughts and feelings (the mind) are distinct from the world of real objects and our bodies.

The Classical Roots of Psychology

In the seventeenth century, renewed interest in human thought and its relationship to behavior developed. René Descartes, John Locke, Thomas Hobbes, and Charles Darwin took very different positions on the nature of the mind, the source of knowledge, and the relationship between the mind and the brain. It was not until the late eighteenth century that the tools of science were applied to answering such questions.

The Rise of Scientific Psychology

Wilhelm Wundt established the first psychology laboratory in 1879 at the University of Leipzig in Germany. His use of experiment and measurement marked the beginning of psychology as a science. One of his students, Edward Titchener, established a perspective called **structuralism**, which was based on the belief that the role of psychology was to identify the basic elements of experience and discover how they combine. William James criticized structuralism, arguing that sensations cannot be separated from the mental associations that allow people to benefit from past experiences. James founded the school of **functionalism**, which held that the rich storehouse of human ideas and memories is what enables people to function in their environment. In a similar fashion, **Gestalt psychology** proposed that perception depends on the human tendency to see patterns, to distinguish objects from their backgrounds, and to complete pictures from a few clues. John Watson and B. F. Skinner took a very different view of psychology. They argued that one cannot have a science of the mind because thoughts and feelings are not observable and measurable. They proposed that psychology should concern itself instead with observable, measurable behavior. Thus, their approach became known as **behaviorism**. None of these early "schools" of psychology exist today as they did early in the twentieth century, but together they laid the groundwork for contemporary psychology.

Contemporary Approaches to Psychology

Contemporary psychologists apply several different approaches to understanding behavior and mental processes. Psychologists who adopt the **biological approach** study the relationship between biological processes and thoughts and behavior. Psychologists who take the **behavioral approach** follow in the footsteps of Watson and Skinner by focusing their attention on the ways in which specific events in the environment can shape behavior (also known as *behaviorism*). In sharp contrast, psychologists who take the **cognitive approach** believe that mental processes can and should be studied scientifically. As a result of this shift in focus, even the definition of psychology has changed. Psychology is still the study of human behavior, but psychologists' concept of "behavior" has expanded to include thinking, feeling, learning, remembering, making decisions and judgments, and so on. The **humanistic approach**, with its focus on meaning, values, and ethics, emphasizes the goal of reaching one's fullest potential. **Positive psychology** is a recent development that addresses some of the questions that humanistic psychologists first raised a half century ago, such as the origins and nurturance of mental wellness and understanding human strengths and virtues. The **psychodynamic approach** arose from the thinking of Sigmund Freud, his colleagues, and successors. They added another dimension to psychology: the idea that much of human behavior is governed by unconscious conflicts, motives, and desires. The **evolutionary approach** focuses on the functions and adaptive value of various human behaviors and the evolution of those behaviors. Finally, the

sociocultural approach emphasizes the importance of diversity and the important ways in which culture, gender, race, and ethnicity can affect virtually all aspects of human behavior. Most contemporary psychologists believe that these several different approaches can often complement one another and together enrich our understanding of human behavior.

Although psychology in the early twentieth century was dominated by men, women have contributed significantly from the beginning and are doing so in ever greater numbers. Today, most undergraduate and graduate degrees in psychology are awarded to women who are questioning some of the assumptions that have permeated the study of psychology and who are also greatly expanding the range of issues that psychologists address.

Enduring Issues in Psychology

From the very beginning, philosophers and psychologists, regardless of their approach, have grappled with five enduring issues or fundamental themes that are still the subject of study today:

Person–Situation: Is behavior caused more by inner traits or by external situations?

Nature–Nurture: How do genes and experiences interact to influence people?

Stability–Change: How much do people stay the same as they develop and how much do they change?

Diversity–Universality: In what ways do people differ in how they think and act?

Mind–Body: What is the relationship between one's internal experiences and one's biological processes?

Psychology as Science

As with the other sciences, psychology relies on the **scientific method** to find answers to questions. This method involves careful observation and collection of data, the development of **theories** about relationships and causes, and the systematic testing of **hypotheses** (or predictions) to disprove invalid theories.

Research Methods

Some psychologists use **naturalistic observation** to study behavior in natural settings where behavior is likely to be more accurate, spontaneous, and varied than behavior studied in a laboratory. Researchers using this method must be careful to avoid **observer bias**. Some researchers use **case studies** to investigate in depth the behavior of one person or a few persons. This method can yield a great deal of detailed, descriptive information that is useful for forming hypotheses but is vulnerable to observer bias and overgeneralization of results. Survey research generates a large amount of data quickly and inexpensively by presenting a standardized set of questions to a large number of people. Great care must be taken, however, in the wording of questions and in the selection of respondents.

Correlational research investigates the relationship, or correlation, between two or more variables. Although two variables may be related to each other, that does not imply that one causes the other. The **experimental method** is called for when a researcher wants to draw conclusions about cause and effect. In an experiment, the researcher varies one factor (the **independent variable**) and studies its effect on another factor (the **dependent variable**) while all other factors are held constant. Usually, an experiment includes an **experimental group** of **participants** and a **control group** for comparison purposes. Often, a neutral person records data and scores results, so **experimenter bias** is minimized. Many psychologists overcome the limitations of using a single research method by using numerous methods to study a single problem.

Regardless of the research method used, psychologists usually study a small **sample** of subjects and generalize their results to larger populations. Proper sampling is crucial for ensuring that results have broader application. **Random samples**, in which each potential participant has an equal chance of being chosen, and **representative samples**, in which subjects are chosen to reflect the general characteristics of the population as a whole, are two ways of doing this.

Ethics and Psychology

The American Psychological Association (APA) provides a code of ethics for conducting research involving human participants or animal subjects. Human subjects must be told in advance about the nature and possible risks of the research and must consent to participate in the research. Deception is permitted only when absolutely necessary. The APA has also issued a code of ethics for research using nonhumans, though use of animals continues to generate controversy.

Chapter 2
The Biological Basis of Behavior

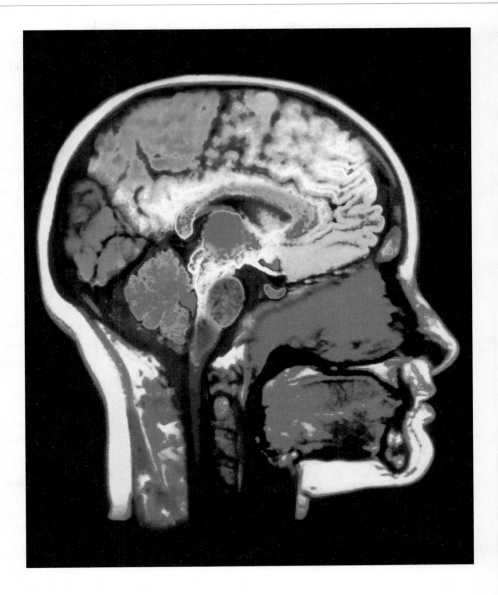

Go to *The Core Online* at **www.psychologythecore.com** to get the most up-to-date information for your introductory psychology course. The content online is an important part of what you are learning—the content there can help prepare you for your test! It includes up-to-date examples, simulations, video clips, and practice quizzes. Also be sure to check out the *Blog* to hear directly from the authors on what current events and latest research are most relevant to your course materials.

The first time you log in, you will need the access code packaged with your textbook. If you do not have a code, please go to **www.mypearsonstore.com** and enter the ISBN of your textbook **(0-13-603344-X)** to purchase the code.

Chapter 2 The Biological Basis of Behavior

2 1 Neurons: The Messengers

The Neural Impulse

- When at rest, the **neuron** is in a state of **polarization**.
- When stimulated, a neuron depolarizes (fires), and a **neural impulse** travels down the **axon**.
- Neurons either fire or they do not (the **all-or-none law**).

The Synapse

- The entire area composed of the axon terminals of one neuron, the **synaptic space**, and the **dendrites** and cell body of the next neuron is called the **synapse**.
- **Neurotransmitters** cross the synaptic space and lock into specific matching **receptor sites**.

2 2 The Central Nervous System

The Brain

- The **hindbrain**, which is just above the spinal cord, is responsible for basic life processes.
- The **midbrain** is important to several senses; also, it is the site of the **reticular formation** that governs alertness.
- The forebrain contains the **thalamus** (a sensory relay station), the **limbic system** (important for motivation, emotion, and memory), and the **cerebrum** (composed of two hemispheres covered by the **cerebral cortex**).
- Each cerebral hemisphere is composed of four lobes: **frontal lobe** (the site of many processes unique to humans as well as voluntary action), **occipital lobe** (vision), the **temporal lobe** (complex visual tasks and language), and the **parietal lobe** (processing sensory information, spatial abilities).

The Spinal Cord

- The **spinal cord** connects the brain to the rest of the nervous system.
- The spinal cord coordinates reflexes.

Hemispheric Specialization

- Cerebral hemispheres are connected by the **corpus callosum**.
- Language ability is concentrated primarily in the left hemisphere, which operates analytically and rationally.
- The right hemisphere excels at visual and spatial tasks, music, face recognition, and perception of emotions.
- Normally, the two hemispheres work together as a coordinated unit.

Neural Plasticity and Neurogenesis

- The brain changes structurally and chemically as a result of experience (**plasticity**).
- The brain is also capable of producing new brain cells (**neurogenesis**).

Tools for Studying the Brain

- Microelectrode techniques are used to study individual neurons.
- Macroelectrode techniques are used to study overall activity in specific brain areas.
- Structural imaging techniques produce three-dimensional images of the brain.
- Functional imaging techniques show the brain's activity.

2 3 The Peripheral Nervous System

- The peripheral nervous system connects the brain and spinal cord to every other part of the body.
- The **somatic nervous system** brings sensory messages to the brain and spinal cord via **afferent neurons** and sends messages from the brain and spinal cord to muscles and glands via **efferent neurons**.
- The **autonomic nervous system** is composed of the **sympathetic division** (which tells the body to prepare for an emergency and to get ready to act quickly or strenuously) and the **parasympathetic division** (returns the body to normal after arousal).

2 4 The Endocrine System

- Chemical messengers called **hormones** are produced by **endocrine glands** and are carried by the bloodstream throughout the body.
- Action of the endocrine system is slower, but longer lasting, than action of the nervous system.

2 5 Genes, Evolution, and Behavior

Genetics

- Humans have 23 pairs of **chromosomes** in every normal cell.
- In the nucleus of each chromosome are hundreds or thousands of **genes** composed primarily of **DNA (deoxyribonucleic acid)**.
- The 20,000 to 25,000 genes in each cell comprise a person's **genotype**.
- The most significant genetic traits are **polygenic** (the result of many genes).

Behavior Genetics

- This field of study focuses on how genes contribute to intelligence, temperament, talents, motivation, emotion, personality, and predispositions to psychological and neurological disorders.
- **Strain studies** and **selection studies** are used in nonhuman research.
- Human research uses **family studies**, **twin studies**, and **adoption studies**.

Evolutionary Psychology

- Evolutionary psychology focuses on the genetic roots of behavioral traits that people have in common and that give a species a survival advantage.

The journey through the body that you will take in this chapter is part of the branch of psychology known as **psychobiology**, the study of the biological foundations of behavior and mental processes. Psychobiology is related to virtually every other topic in this book, including learning, memory, thinking, problem solving, emotion, motivation, personality, and psychological disorders. This area of study overlaps with a much larger interdisciplinary field called **neuroscience**, which focuses specifically on the study of the brain and the nervous system.

The basic building blocks of the brain and nervous system are cells known as **neurons**. The electrical and chemical messages that neurons transmit are what allow people to react with speed and complexity to events around them. But neurons are only part of the story of how human behavior is controlled and coordinated. The endocrine system of glands, for example, provides for the secretion of chemical messages called *hormones* into the blood. Heredity, as well, has an influence on human behavior. These topics will be examined in this chapter.

ENDURING ISSUES in the Biological Basis of Behavior

As with the first chapter, all five "Enduring Issues" will be encountered. The core of this chapter—the notion that biological processes affect thoughts, emotions, and behavior—directly addresses the age-old debate about the relationship between human experience and biological processes (mind–body). It also sheds light on the extent to which behavior is caused by internal processes as opposed to environmental factors (person–situation). The section on genetics addresses the extent to which heredity affects behavior (nature–nurture). It may come as a surprise that the nervous system changes permanently as a result of experience (stability–change). Moreover, there are significant differences between men and women in the way the brain works and in the way they select their mates (diversity–universality).

Neurons: The Messengers

■ THE NEURAL IMPULSE

The brain of an average human being contains as many as a hundred billion nerve cells, or neurons. Billions more neurons are found in other parts of the nervous system. A typical neuron is shown in Figure 2–1. Neurons are cells and, like all other cells, have a cell body enclosed by a cell membrane and a nucleus (in which metabolism and respiration take place). Unlike other cells, however, neurons have tiny fibers extending from the cell body, the role of which is to pick up incoming messages from other neurons and transmit them to the cell body. No other cells in the body are equipped to do this.

The short fibers branching out around the cell body are called **dendrites**. The single long fiber extending from the cell body is an **axon**. The axon's job is to carry outgoing messages to neighboring neurons or to a muscle or gland. Axons vary in length from 1 to 2 millimeters (about the length of the word "or" in this sentence) to three feet. (In adults, a single axon may run all the way from the brain to the base of the spinal cord or from the spinal cord to the tip of the thumb.) A single neuron may have many hundreds of dendrites, and its axon may branch out in numerous directions so that it is in touch with hundreds or thousands of other cells at its input end (dendrites) and its output end (axon). When people speak of a **nerve** (or **tract**), they are referring to a group of axons bundled together as though tucked in an electrical cable.

The axon in Figure 2–1 is surrounded by a white, fatty covering called a **myelin sheath**. The myelin sheath is "pinched" at intervals, making the axon resemble a string of microscopic sausages (not all axons have this covering). Myelinated axons are found in all parts

---

The Neural Impulse

■ When at rest, the neuron is in a state of _____

_____

_____

■ When stimulated, a neuron depolarizes (fires), and _____

_____

_____

Neurons either fire or they do not (the

_____-_____-_____ law).

The Synapse

■ The entire area composed of the ___

_____

_____

■ Neurotransmitters cross _____

_____

_____

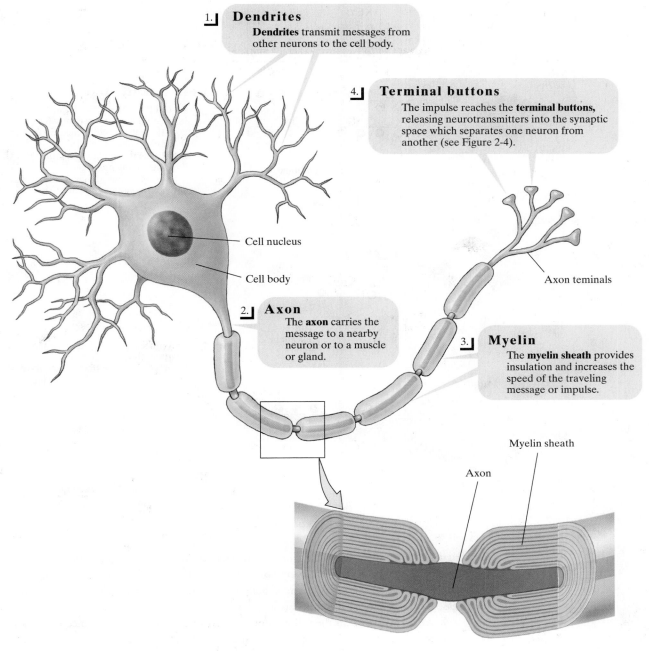

1. **Dendrites**
Dendrites transmit messages from
other neurons to the cell body.

4. **Terminal buttons**
The impulse reaches the **terminal buttons,**
releasing neurotransmitters into the synaptic
space which separates one neuron from
another (see Figure 2-4).

Cell nucleus

Cell body

Axon teminals

2. **Axon**
The **axon** carries the
message to a nearby
neuron or to a muscle
or gland.

3. **Myelin**
The **myelin sheath** provides
insulation and increases the
speed of the traveling
message or impulse.

Myelin sheath

Axon

FIGURE **2–1**

**This typical myelinated neuron shows the cell body, dendrites, axon, myelin sheath, and
terminal buttons.**

Source: Adapted from *Fundamentals of Human Neuropsychology* (4th ed.) by Brian Kolb and Ian Q. Whishaw. © 1980, 1985, 1990, 1996
by W. H. Freeman and Company. Reprinted with permission.

of the body. The myelin sheath has two functions: to provide insulation so that signals from
adjacent neurons do not interfere with one another and to increase the speed at which signals
are transmitted.

Neurons carry messages, but how do they "talk" to one another? What form do their
messages take? It turns out that neurons speak in a language that all cells in the body understand—in simple "yes/no" and "on/off" electrochemical impulses. Here's how it works. When a
neuron is at rest, the membrane surrounding the cell forms a partial barrier between the fluids
that are inside and outside the neuron. Both solutions contain electrically charged particles, or

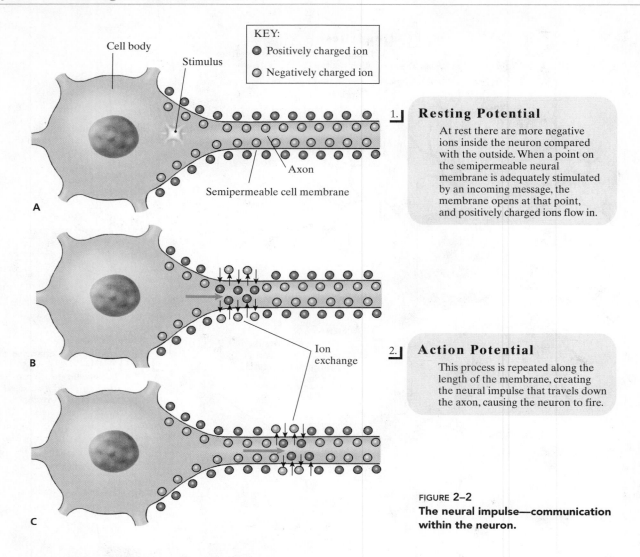

KEY:
● Positively charged ion
○ Negatively charged ion

Cell body

Stimulus

Axon

Semipermeable cell membrane

A

1. **Resting Potential**

At rest there are more negative ions inside the neuron compared with the outside. When a point on the semipermeable neural membrane is adequately stimulated by an incoming message, the membrane opens at that point, and positively charged ions flow in.

B

Ion exchange

2. **Action Potential**

This process is repeated along the length of the membrane, creating the neural impulse that travels down the axon, causing the neuron to fire.

C

FIGURE **2–2**
The neural impulse—communication within the neuron.

ions (Figure 2–2a). Because there are more negative ions inside the neuron than outside, there is a small electrical charge (called the **resting potential**) across the cell membrane. The resting neuron is said to be in a state of **polarization**, as though it were a spring that has been compressed but not released. All that is needed to generate a neuron's signal is the release of this tension.

When a small area on the cell membrane is adequately stimulated by incoming messages, the membrane at the stimulated area opens, allowing a sudden influx of positively charged ions (Figure 2–2b). This process is called *depolarization*; now, the inside of the neuron is positively charged relative to the outside. Depolarization sets off a chain reaction. As soon as the membrane allows positive ions to enter the neuron at one point, the next point on the membrane opens. More positive ions flow into the neuron at the second spot and depolarize this part of the neuron, and so on, along the entire length of the neuron. As a result, an electrical charge, called a **neural impulse** (or **action potential**), travels down the axon, as though it were a fuse burning from one end to the other (Figure 2–2c). When this happens, the neuron has "fired." The speed at which neurons carry impulses varies widely, from as fast as 400 feet per second on largely myelinated axons to as slow as about three feet per second on those with no myelin.

As a rule, single impulses received from neighboring neurons do not make a neuron fire. Rather, impulses from many neighboring neurons—or from a few neurons firing repeatedly—must exceed a certain minimum **threshold of excitation** before a neuron will fire. The process is similar to firing a gun: The trigger must be pulled far enough back before the gun will fire. Moreover, like a gun, neurons either fire or they do not, and every firing of a particular neuron produces an impulse of the same strength. This is called the **all-or-none law**. Immediately after firing, the neuron goes through an *absolute refractory period*. For about a thousandth of a second, the neuron will not fire again, no matter how strong the incoming messages may be. Following that is a *relative refractory period*, when the cell is returning to the resting state. During this period, the neuron will fire, but only when the incoming messages are considerably stronger than is normally necessary to make it fire. Finally, the neuron returns to its resting state, ready to fire again, as shown in Figure 2–3.

■ THE SYNAPSE

Neurons are not directly connected like links in a chain. Rather, they are separated by a tiny gap, called a **synaptic space**, or **synaptic cleft**, in which the axon terminals of one neuron nearly touch the dendrites or cell body of other neurons. The entire area composed of the axon terminals of one neuron, the synaptic space, and the dendrites and cell body of the next neuron is called the **synapse** (Figure 2–4). For the neural impulse to move on to the next neuron, it must somehow cross the synaptic space. It is tempting to imagine that the neural impulse simply leaps across the gap like an electrical spark, but in reality the transfer is made by chemicals.

   When a neuron fires, an impulse travels down the axon, moving outward through the axon terminals into a tiny swelling called a **terminal button**, or **synaptic knob**. Most terminal buttons contain numerous tiny oval sacs called **synaptic vesicles** (Figure 2–4). When the neural impulse reaches the end of the terminals, it causes these vesicles to release varying amounts of chemicals called **neurotransmitters** into the synaptic space. Each neurotransmitter has specific

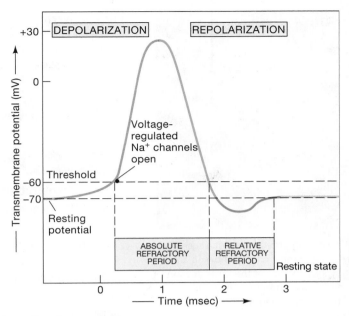

FIGURE 2–3
Electrical changes during the action potential.
The incoming message must be above a certain threshold to cause a neuron to fire. After it fires, the neuron is returned to its resting state. This process happens very quickly; and within a few thousandths of a second (msec), the neuron is ready to fire again.

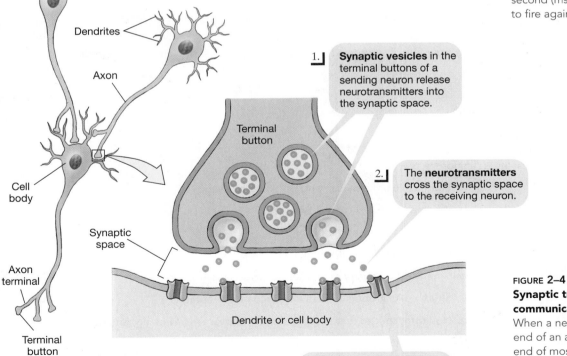

1. **Synaptic vesicles** in the terminal buttons of a sending neuron release neurotransmitters into the synaptic space.

2. The **neurotransmitters** cross the synaptic space to the receiving neuron.

3. After crossing the **synaptic space** the neurotransmitters fit into **receptor sites** located on the dendrites or cell body of the receiving neuron.

FIGURE 2–4
Synaptic transmission—communication between neurons.
When a neural impulse reaches the end of an axon, tiny oval sacs at the end of most axons (called *synaptic vesicles*) release varying amounts of chemical substances called *neurotransmitters*. These substances travel across the synaptic space and affect the next neuron.

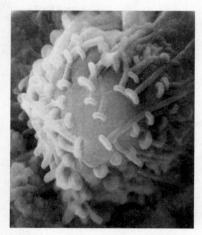

A photograph taken with a scanning electron microscope, showing the synaptic knobs at the ends of axons. Inside the knobs are the vesicles that contain neurotransmitters.

matching **receptor sites** on the other side of the synaptic space. Neurotransmitters fit into their corresponding receptor sites just as keys fit into locks. Some neurotransmitters "excite" the next neuron, making it more likely to fire. Other neurotransmitters have the opposite effect. The combination of excitatory and inhibitory neurotransmitters in the synaptic space at any given moment determines whether the next neuron will or will not fire. Once their job is over, neurotransmitters detach from the receptor site. In most cases, they are reabsorbed into the axon terminals to be used again, broken down and recycled to make new neurotransmitters, or disposed of as waste by the body. The result is that the synapse is now clear and back to its normal state.

ENDURING ISSUES   MIND/BODY

Neurotransmitters

Hundreds of neurotransmitters exist, and several are well known. *Acetylcholine (ACh)* is an excitatory neurotransmitter often found where neurons meet skeletal muscles. It also appears to play a crucial role in arousal, attention, memory, and motivation. *Dopamine* is an inhibitory neurotransmitter that affects voluntary movement, learning, memory, and emotions. *Serotonin* is popularly known as "the mood molecule" because it is often involved in emotional experiences. Serotonin is an example of a neurotransmitter that has widespread effects. Like a master key that opens many locks, it attaches to many receptor sites. Other brain chemicals regulate the sensitivity of large numbers of synapses, in effect "turning up" or "turning down" the activity level of whole portions of the nervous system. *Endorphins*, for example, appear to reduce pain by inhibiting, or "turning down," the neurons that transmit pain messages in the brain.

Chapter 4 (States of Consciousness) examines the effects of *psychoactive drugs* (such as heroin, cocaine, and marijuana) and the ways in which they alter synaptic transmission. Chapter 12 (Psychological Disorders) explores the imbalances in neurotransmitters and how they contribute to various types of mental illness. Schizophrenia, for example, has been associated with an abundance of, or hypersensitivity to, dopamine. A low supply of serotonin has been linked to depression and other disorders.

Check Your Understanding

Match each term with the appropriate definition.

_____ Neuron

_____ Dendrites

_____ Axons

_____ Neural impulse

_____ Resting potential

_____ Absolute refractory period

_____ Synapse

_____ Neurotransmitters

_____ Dopamine

_____ Serotonin

_____ All-or-none law

a. Long, cellular fibers carrying outgoing messages

b. When a nerve cell cannot fire again

c. Known as the "mood molecule"

d. Cell that transmits information

e. Chemicals that carry messages across synapses

f. Short, cellular fibers that pick up incoming messages

g. Neurotransmitter that affects voluntary movement, learning, and memory

h. Action potential

i. A neuron either fires at full strength or not at all

j. Terminal button, synaptic space, and dendrite of neighboring neuron

k. Electrical imbalance across a neural membrane at rest

The Central Nervous System

If the brain alone has more than a hundred billion neurons and each neuron can be "in touch" with hundreds or thousands of other neurons, then our bodies must contain hundreds of trillions of synapses through which each neuron is indirectly linked to every other neuron. It may be impossible to comprehend such an immense system of interconnected neurons, but there is some structure, some organization, to it all (Figure 2–5).

The nervous system usually is divided into two major parts: the **central nervous system (CNS)** and the **peripheral nervous system (PNS)**. The central nervous system includes the brain and spinal cord, which together contain more than 90% of the body's neurons. The peripheral nervous system connects the brain and spinal cord to every other part of the body, carrying messages back and forth between the central nervous system and the sense organs, muscles, and glands. Obviously, without the peripheral nervous system, the central nervous system could not do its job. What would it be like if the brain and spinal cord were isolated from the rest of the body? To answer this question, let's first try to understand what the central nervous system normally does.

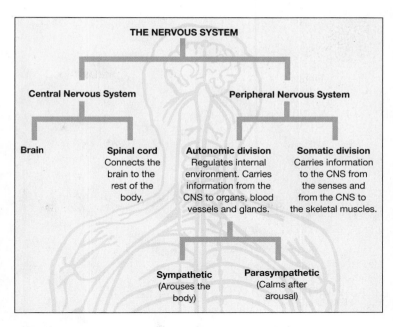

FIGURE **2–5**

A schematic diagram of the divisions of the nervous system and the various subparts.

■ THE BRAIN

The brain is the seat of awareness and reason; the place where learning, memory, and emotions are centered. It is the part of us that decides what to do and whether that decision was right or wrong, and it imagines how things might have turned out if we had acted differently. As soon as the brain begins to take shape in the human embryo, three distinct parts can be detected: the hindbrain, midbrain, and forebrain. These three parts are still present in the fully developed adult brain, though they are not so easily distinguished one from another. In this section, three basic divisions are used to describe the parts of the brain, what they do, and how they interact to influence human behavior (Figure 2–6).

The **hindbrain** is found in even the most primitive vertebrates. From that fact, one may rightly conclude that the hindbrain plays an essential role in basic life processes. The part of the hindbrain nearest to the spinal cord is the **medulla**, a narrow structure about 1.5 inches long. The medulla controls such bodily functions as breathing, heart rate, and blood pressure. The medulla is also the point at which many of the nerves from the body cross over on their way to and from the higher brain centers; nerves from the left part of the body cross to the right side of the brain and vice versa (a topic to be discussed in greater detail later). Near the medulla lies the **pons**, which produces chemicals that help maintain the sleep-wake cycle (Chapter 4: States of Consciousness). The medulla and the pons transmit messages to the upper areas of the brain.

The part of the hindbrain at the top and back of the brain stem is the **cerebellum**, which is sometimes called the "little brain"; however, appearances can be deceiving. Although the cerebellum takes up only a small space, its surface area is nearly two thirds that of the much larger cerebral cortex. It also contains more neurons than the rest of the brain. Clearly, the cerebellum plays many important roles. Specifically, is responsible for our sense of balance and for coordinating the body's actions to ensure that movements go together in efficient sequences. It is also involved in emotional control, attention, memory, and in coordinating sensory information. In addition, recent studies have indicated that numerous mental disorders, including autism, schizophrenia, and attention deficit disorder (ADD) may be associated with cerebellar dysfunction (Tamminga & Vogel, 2005).

The Brain

■ The hindbrain, which is just above the spinal cord, is responsible for

_____

■ The midbrain is important to

_____

■ The forebrain contains the

_____

■ Each cerebral hemisphere is composed of four lobes:

_____

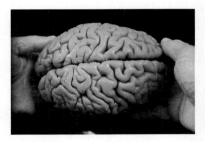

The human brain, viewed from the top. Its relatively small size belies its enormous complexity.

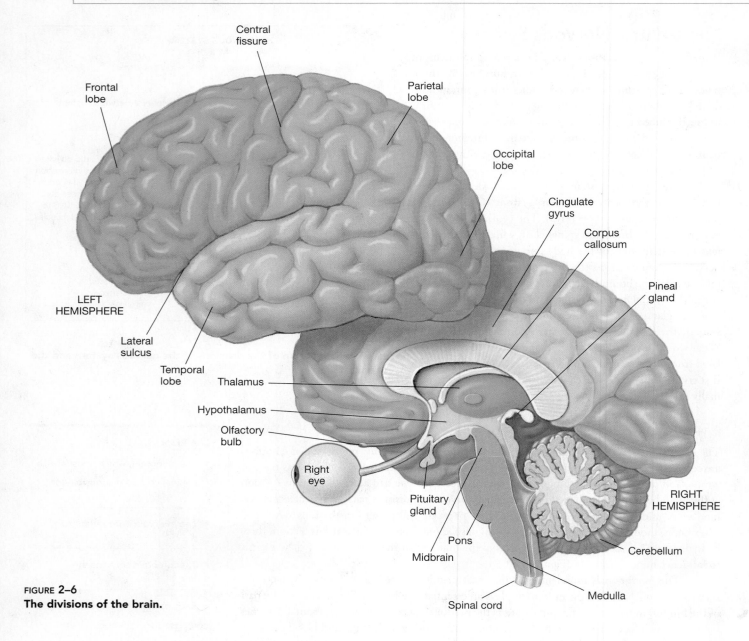

FIGURE **2–6**
The divisions of the brain.

Above the cerebellum and the pons is the **midbrain**. The midbrain is especially important for hearing and sight. It is also one of several places in the brain where pain is registered.
The midbrain is also the site of the **reticular formation (RF)**, a netlike system of neurons whose
main job is to send alert signals to the higher parts of the brain in response to incoming
messages. The RF can be subdued, however; during sleep, the RF is turned down. Anesthetics
work largely by temporarily shutting down this system, and permanent damage to the RF can
induce a coma.

Above the midbrain is the **forebrain**. In the center of it, more or less directly over the
brain stem, are the two egg-shaped structures that make up the **thalamus**. The thalamus is
often described as a relay station: Almost all sensory information passes through the thalamus
on the way to higher levels of the brain, where it is translated and routed to the appropriate
brain location. Surrounding the thalamus is a ring of loosely connected structures called the

SUMMARY TABLE	**Parts of the Brain and Their Functions**	
Central Core	Medulla	Regulates respiration, heart rate, blood pressure
	Pons	Regulates sleep-wake cycles
	Cerebellum	Regulates reflexes and balance; coordinates movement
	Reticular formation	Regulates attention and alertness
	Thalamus	Major sensory relay center; regulates higher brain centers and peripheral nervous system
	Hypothalamus	Influences emotion and motivation; governs stress reactions
Limbic System	Hippocampus	Regulates formation of new memories
	Amygdala	Governs emotions related to self-preservation
Cerebral Cortex	Frontal lobe	Goal-directed behavior; concentration; emotional control and temperament; voluntary movements; coordinates messages from other lobes; complex problem solving; involved in many aspects of personality
	Parietal lobe	Receives sensory information; visual–spatial abilities
	Occipital lobe	Receives and processes visual information
	Temporal lobe	Smell and hearing; balance and equilibrium; emotion and motivation; some language comprehension; complex visual processing and face recognition

limbic system (Figure 2–7). This system includes the *hypothalamus* which, despite its small size, governs hunger, thirst, sexual drive, and body temperature and is directly involved in emotional behavior such as experiencing rage, terror, or pleasure. Another part of the limbic system, the *hippocampus*, plays an essential role in the formation of new memories. People with severe damage to this area can still remember names, faces, and events that they recorded in memory before they were injured, but they cannot remember anything new. Another structure, the *amygdala* (working together with the hippocampus) is involved in governing and regulating emotions and in establishing emotional memories, particularly those related to fear and self-preservation. More will be discussed about the limbic system, particularly motivation and emotion, in Chapter 8.

Ballooning out, over, and around the brain stem and virtually hiding all the other portions of the brain from view is the **cerebrum**. This is what most people are thinking of when they talk about "the brain." It is the part of the brain that processes thought, vision, language, memory, and emotions. The cerebrum takes up most of the room inside the skull and accounts for about 80% of the weight of the human brain. Also, it contains about 70% of the neurons in existence in the entire central nervous system. The cerebrum is divided into two hemispheres and is covered by a thin layer of unmyelinated cells called the **cerebral cortex**. The cerebral cortex is more highly developed in humans than in any other animal. Spread out, the human cortex would cover two to three square feet. To fit inside the skull, the cerebrum in humans has developed intricate folds—hills and valleys called *convolutions* (Figures 2–6 and 2–8). In every person, these convolutions form a pattern that is as unique as a fingerprint.

Numerous landmarks on the cerebral cortex make it easier to identify distinct areas, each with different functions. The first is a deep cleft, running from front to back, that divides the cerebrum into right and left hemispheres. Each of these hemispheres can be divided into four lobes that are separated from one another by crevices, such as the central fissure and lateral sulcus shown in Figure 2–8. In addition, there are large areas on the cortex of all four lobes

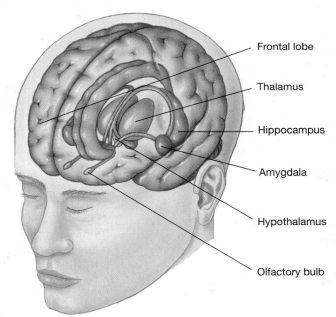

Frontal lobe

Thalamus

Hippocampus

Amygdala

Hypothalamus

Olfactory bulb

FIGURE **2–7**
The limbic system.
A system of brain structures, including the thalamus, hippocampus, amygdala, hypothalamus, and olfactory bulb. This system is primarily involved in regulating behaviors having to do with motivation and emotion.

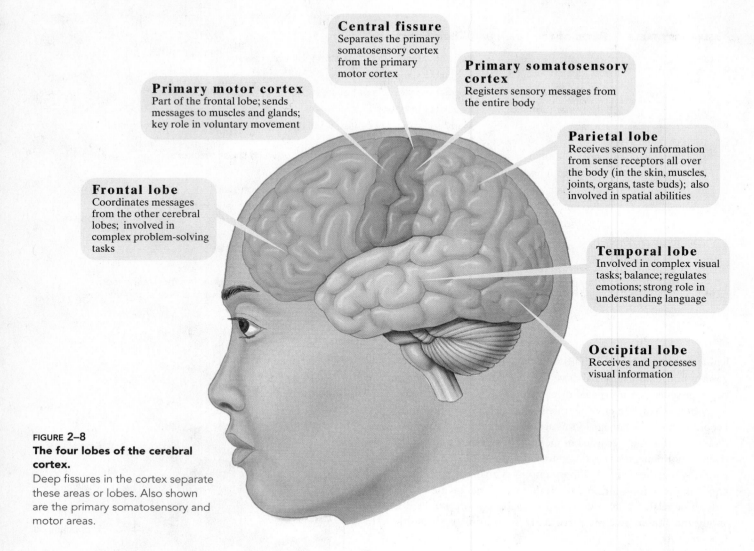

Central fissure
Separates the primary somatosensory cortex from the primary motor cortex

Primary somatosensory cortex
Registers sensory messages from the entire body

Primary motor cortex
Part of the frontal lobe; sends messages to muscles and glands; key role in voluntary movement

Parietal lobe
Receives sensory information from sense receptors all over the body (in the skin, muscles, joints, organs, taste buds); also involved in spatial abilities

Frontal lobe
Coordinates messages from the other cerebral lobes; involved in complex problem-solving tasks

Temporal lobe
Involved in complex visual tasks; balance; regulates emotions; strong role in understanding language

Occipital lobe
Receives and processes visual information

FIGURE 2–8
The four lobes of the cerebral cortex.
Deep fissures in the cortex separate these areas or lobes. Also shown are the primary somatosensory and motor areas.

called **association areas** that integrate information from diverse parts of the brain and are involved in several mental processes, including learning, thinking, and remembering.

The different lobes of the cerebral hemispheres are specialized for different functions (Figure 2–8). The **frontal lobe**, located just behind the forehead, accounts for about half the volume of the human brain yet it remains the most mysterious part of the brain. In part, this is because much of our knowledge of brain function comes from research on animals, whose frontal lobes are relatively undeveloped. Scientists do know, however, that the frontal lobe monitors and integrates the complex tasks that occur in the rest of the brain. The frontal lobe is also the site of many mental processes that are unique to human beings. These include self-awareness and goal-directed behavior, including the ability to plan and concentrate, control emotions, and conduct moral decision making. Finally, the section of the frontal lobe known as the **primary motor cortex**, which forms a band roughly from the top of the ear to the top of the head, plays a key role in voluntary action.

The **occipital lobe**, located at the very back of the head, receives and processes visual information. Damage to the occipital lobe can produce blindness and visual hallucinations. The **temporal lobe**, located in front of the occipital lobe (roughly behind the temple), plays an important role in complex visual tasks such as recognizing faces and interpreting the facial emotions of others. The temporal lobe also receives and processes information from the ears; contributes to balance and equilibrium; and regulates emotions and motivations such as anxiety, pleasure, and anger. In addition, the ability to understand and comprehend language is concentrated primarily in the rear portion of the temporal lobes.

The **parietal lobe** occupies the top back half of each hemisphere. Sensory information from all over the body—from sense receptors in the skin, muscles, joints, internal organs, and taste buds—goes to the **primary somatosensory cortex** at the front of the parietal lobe. The parietal lobe also seems to oversee spatial abilities, such as the ability to follow a map or to tell someone how to get from one place to another.

■ HEMISPHERIC SPECIALIZATION

The cerebrum, as noted earlier, consists of two separate hemispheres. Quite literally, humans have a "right half-brain" and a "left half-brain" that are connected at the bottom by a thick, ribbonlike band of nerve fibers called the **corpus callosum** (Figure 2–9). Under normal conditions, the two cerebral hemispheres are in close communication through the corpus callosum and work together as a coordinated unit. But careful research has shown that the cerebral hemispheres are not really equivalent. The most dramatic evidence comes from "split-brain" patients. In some cases of severe epilepsy, for example, surgeons cut the corpus callosum to

Hemispheric Specialization

■ Cerebral hemispheres are connected by the _____

_____

■ Language ability is concentrated primarily in the _____

_____

■ The right hemisphere excels at _____

_____

■ Normally, the two hemispheres

_____

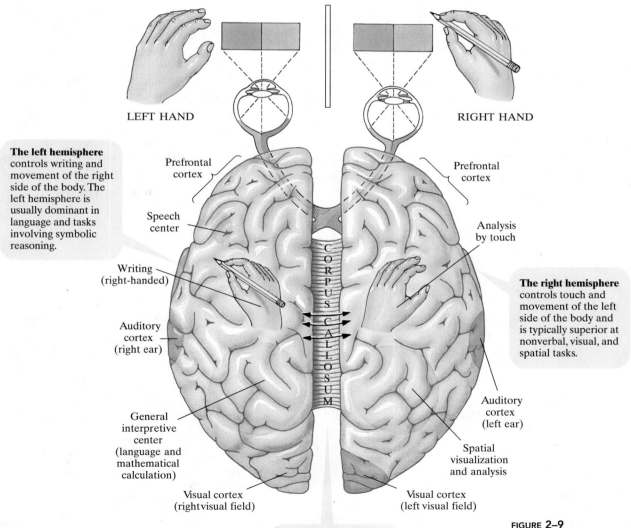

LEFT HAND

RIGHT HAND

The left hemisphere controls writing and movement of the right side of the body. The left hemisphere is usually dominant in language and tasks involving symbolic reasoning.

Prefrontal cortex

Prefrontal cortex

Speech center

Analysis by touch

Writing (right-handed)

The right hemisphere controls touch and movement of the left side of the body and is typically superior at nonverbal, visual, and spatial tasks.

Auditory cortex (right ear)

CORPUS CALLOSUM

Auditory cortex (left ear)

General interpretive center (language and mathematical calculation)

Spatial visualization and analysis

Visual cortex (right visual field)

Visual cortex (left visual field)

The corpus callosum permits the exchange of information between the two hemispheres.

FIGURE **2–9**
The two cerebral hemispheres.
Each hemisphere specializes in processing specific types of information, as shown in the diagram.

stop the spread of epileptic seizures from one hemisphere to the other. In general, this procedure is successful with the patients' seizures reduced and sometimes eliminated. Because sensory information typically is sent to both hemispheres, split-brain patients function quite normally in everyday life. But their two hemispheres are functionally isolated; in effect, their right brain does not know what their left brain is doing (and vice versa).

Roger Sperry received the Nobel Prize for developing a series of ingenious experiments for split-brain patients. These experiments revealed that for many people, language ability is concentrated primarily in the left hemisphere (Sperry, 1964, 1968, 1970). Specifically, one area toward the back of the left temporal lobe (Wernicke's area) is crucial in processing and understanding what others are saying. A second area, found in the left frontal lobe (Broca's area), is considered essential to our ability to talk (Figure 2–10). To oversimplify a bit, Wernicke's area seems to be important for listening and Broca's area seems to be important for talking. There is also some evidence that the left hemisphere operates more analytically, logically, rationally, and sequentially than the right hemisphere does (Kingstone, Enns, Mangun, & Gazzaniga, 1995). In contrast, the right hemisphere excels at visual and spatial tasks, music, face recognition, and the perception of emotions (Buklina, 2005; Steinke, 2003). Put another way, the left hemisphere specializes in analyzing sequences and details, whereas the right hemisphere specializes in holistic processing (Reuter-Lorenz & Miller, 1998), in solving problems that require insight or creative solutions (Bowden & Jung-Beeman, 2003), and in preserving one's sense of personal identity or "self" (Bower, 2006; Feinberg & Keenan, 2005; Uddin, Kaplan, Molnar-Szakacs, Zaidel, & Iacoboni, 2005).

Although such research is fascinating and fun to speculate about, one must be cautious when interpreting it. First, not everyone shows the same pattern of differences between the left and right hemispheres. In particular, the differences between the hemispheres may be greater in men than in women (Mucci et al., 2005). Second, it is easy to oversimplify and exaggerate differences between the two sides of the brain, but it is important to remember that under normal conditions, the right and left hemispheres are in close communication through the corpus callosum and so work together in a coordinated, integrated way. Third, hemispheric specialization is unrelated to handedness. With few exceptions, language is localized in the left hemisphere for the great majority of left- and right-handers. Finally, as will be seen in the next section, the brain is remarkably good at rewiring itself.

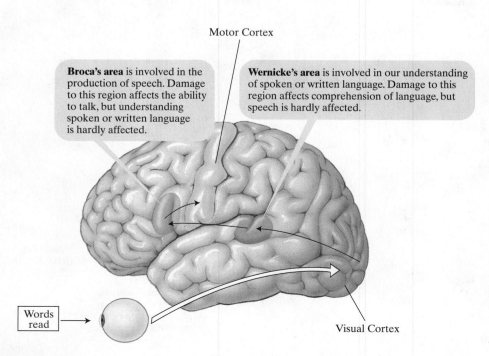

Motor Cortex

Broca's area is involved in the production of speech. Damage to this region affects the ability to talk, but understanding spoken or written language is hardly affected.

Wernicke's area is involved in our understanding of spoken or written language. Damage to this region affects comprehension of language, but speech is hardly affected.

Words read

Visual Cortex

FIGURE 2–10
Processing of speech and language.
Broca's and Wernicke's areas, generally found only on the left side of the brain, work together, enabling us to produce and understand speech and language.

■ NEURAL PLASTICITY AND NEUROGENESIS

ENDURING ISSUES   STABILITY/CHANGE

Neural Plasticity

The brain is the one organ in the body that is unique to each individual. From the beginning, your brain has been encoding experience and developing the patterns of emotion and thought that make you who you are. At the same time, your brain is continually changing as you learn new information and skills and adjusting to changing conditions. How do neurons perform this intricate balancing act of maintaining stability while adapting to change? Even more remarkably, how does the brain recover from injury or reorganize itself after surgery? The answer lies in **neural plasticity**, the ability of the brain to be changed structurally and chemically by experience.

Many experiments have shown that rats raised in enriched, stimulating environments, as well as those required to perform complex tasks, have larger neurons with more synaptic connections than those raised in less stimulating or demanding environments (Kleim, Vij, Ballard, & Greenough, 1997; Rosenzweig 1984, 1996; Ruifang & Danling, 2005); see Figure 2–11. But reorganization of the brain as a result of experience is not limited to rats. In deaf people, an area of the brain usually responsible for hearing rewires itself to read lips and sign language (Bosworth & Dobkins, 1999). Moreover, in blind people, the portion of the brain normally responsible for vision reorganizes to respond to touch and hearing (Amedi, Merabet, Bermpohl, & Pascual-Leone, 2005).

If experience can lead to dramatic changes in the number and complexity of synaptic connections in the brain, might it also produce new neurons? For many years, psychologists believed that organisms are born with all the brain cells they will ever have. However, we now know that adult brains are capable of **neurogenesis**, the production of new brain cells (Gage, 2003; Mohapel, Leanza, Kokaia, & Lindvall, 2006; Prickaerts, Koopmans, Blokland, & Scheepens, 2004). The discovery of lifelong neurogenesis has widespread implications for treating neurological disorders. Once the chemicals that regulate neurogenesis are understood more fully, it may be possible to increase the amounts of these substances in areas of the central nervous system where neural growth needs to occur. Specific treatments may take years to

Neural Plasticity and Neurogenesis

■ The brain changes _____

_____

_____

■ The brain is also capable of _____

_____

_____

FIGURE **2–11**

Brain growth and experience.

In Rosenzweig's experiment, young rats lived in two kinds of cages: "impoverished" with nothing to manipulate or explore and "enriched" with a variety of objects. When Rosenzweig examined the rats' brains, he found that the enriched group had larger neurons with more synaptic connections (shown as dendrites in the drawing) than had the rats that lived in the bare cages. Experience, then, can actually affect the structure of the brain.

Source: From "Brain changes in response to experience" by M. R. Rosenzweig, E. L. Bennett, and M. C. Diamond. © 1972, Scientific American, Inc. All rights reserved. Adapted with permission of the estate of Bunji Tagawa.

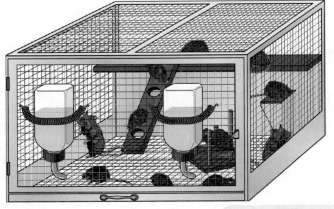

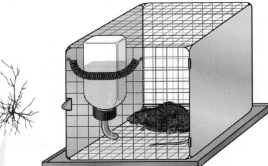

Dendrites of rats living in "enriched" cages showed more synaptic connections

Dendrites of rats living in bare cages

develop, but people suffering from such neurological disorders as Parkinson's and Alzheimer's diseases, as well as victims of spinal cord injuries and stroke, now have some hope of recovery.

■ TOOLS FOR STUDYING THE BRAIN

Psychologists cannot simply do brain surgery on humans whenever they want to learn something about how the brain works. For centuries, understanding the workings of the brain depended on observing people who had suffered brain injury or had endured brain surgery. One famous case, involving a bizarre accident, was reported in 1848. Phineas Gage, the foreman of a railroad construction gang, made a mistake while using some blasting powder. The explosion blew a nearly 4-foot-long tamping iron more than an inch thick into his cheek and all the way through the top of his head, severely damaging his frontal lobes. To the amazement of those who witnessed the accident, Gage remained conscious, walked part of the way to a doctor, and suffered few physical effects afterward. He did, however, suffer lasting psychological changes, including difficulty reasoning and making decisions, as well as difficulty controlling his emotions. These changes were so radical that, in the view of his friends, he was no longer the same man. A century later, neuroscientists using sophisticated research tools agree that the frontal lobes are essential to the ability to concentrate, make judgments, and control emotions.

Another approach that is still widely used is to remove or damage the brains of nonhuman animals and study the effects. But apart from ethical concerns (discussed in Chapter 1), the human brain is far more complicated than that of any other animal. How can scientists study the living, fully functioning human brain? Contemporary neuroscientists use four basic techniques—microelectrodes, macroelectrodes, structural imaging, and functional imaging.

Microelectrode Techniques   *Microelectrode* recording techniques are used to study the functions of single neurons. A microelectrode is a tiny glass or quartz pipette or tube (smaller in diameter than a human hair) that is filled with a conducting liquid. When technicians place the tip of this electrode inside a neuron, they can study changes in the electrical conditions of that neuron. Microelectrode techniques have been used to understand action potentials, the effects of drugs or toxins on neurons, and even processes that occur in the neural membrane.

Macroelectrode Techniques   *Macroelectrode* recording techniques are used to obtain an overall picture of the activity in particular regions of the brain, which may contain millions of neurons. The first such device—the *electroencephalograph* (EEG)—is still in use today. Flat electrodes, taped to the scalp, are linked by wires to a device that translates electrical activity into lines on a moving roll of paper (or, more recently, images on a computer screen). This graph of so-called "brain waves" provides an index of both the strength and the rhythm of neural activity. As will be seen in Chapter 4, this technique has given researchers valuable insights into changes in brain waves during sleep and dreaming. Macroelectrode techniques enable researchers to "listen" to what is going on in the brain, but the techniques do not allow scientists to look through the skull and see what is happening. Some newer techniques, however, do just that.

Structural Imaging   When researchers want to map the structures in a living human brain, they turn to two newer techniques. Computerized axial tomography (CAT or CT) scanning allows scientists to create three-dimensional images of a human brain without performing surgery. To produce a CAT scan, a radiographic (X-ray) unit rotates around the person, moving from the top of the head to the bottom; a computer then combines the resulting images. Magnetic resonance imaging (MRI) is even more successful at producing pictures of the inner regions of the brain, with all its ridges, folds, and fissures. With MRI, the person's head is surrounded by a magnetic field and the brain is exposed to radio waves, which causes hydrogen atoms in the brain to release energy. The energy released by different structures in the brain generates a three-dimensional image that appears on a computer screen.

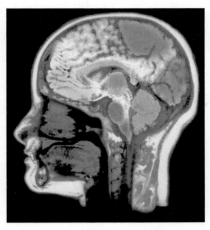

MRI image of the human head.

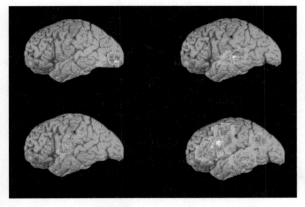

PET scans of a person at rest (top) and using language (bottom). The "hot" colors (red and yellow) indicate greater brain activity. These scans show that language activity is located primarily, but not exclusively, in the brain's left hemisphere.

Functional Imaging   In many cases, researchers are interested in more than structure; they want to look at the brain's activity as it actually reacts to sensory stimuli such as pain, tones, and words. Such is the goal of several *functional imaging* methods. In positron emission tomography (PET), a person first receives an injection of a radioactive substance. Brain structures that are especially active immediately after the injection absorb most of the substance. When the substance starts to decay, it releases subatomic particles. By studying where most of the particles come from, researchers can determine exactly which portions of the brain are most active. Functional magnetic resonance imaging (fMRI) measures the movement of blood molecules (which is related to neuron activity) in the brain, permitting neuroscientists to pinpoint specific sites and details of neuronal activity.

SUMMARY TABLE   Tools for Studying the Brain

Microelectrode Techniques	Used to study the functions of individual neurons
Macroelectrode Techniques	Used to obtain a picture of the activity in a particular region of the brain; the EEG is one such technique.
Structural Imaging	Family of techniques used to map structures in a living brain
Computerized axial tomography (CAT or CT)	Permits three-dimensional imaging of a living human brain
Magnetic resonance imaging (MRI)	Produces pictures of inner brain structures
Functional Imaging Techniques	Family of techniques that can image activity in the brain as it responds to various stimuli
EEG imaging	Measures brain activity on a millisecond-by-millisecond basis
Magnetoencephalography (MEG) *Magnetic source imaging (MSI)*	Two procedures that are similar to EEG imaging but have greater accuracy
Positron emission tomography (PET) scanning *Radioactive PET* *Single photon emission computed tomography (SPECT)*	Three techniques that use radioactive energy to map exact regions of brain activity
Functional magnetic resonance imaging (fMRI)	Measures the movement of blood molecules in the brain, pinpointing specific sites and details of neuronal activity

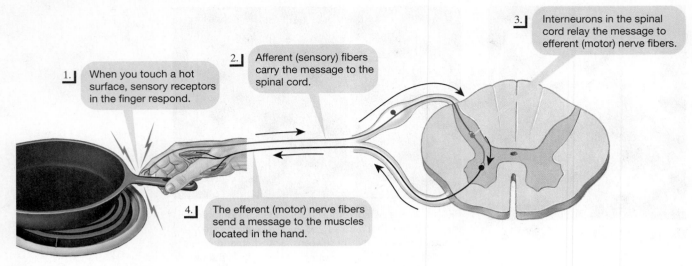

1. When you touch a hot surface, sensory receptors in the finger respond.

2. Afferent (sensory) fibers carry the message to the spinal cord.

3. Interneurons in the spinal cord relay the message to efferent (motor) nerve fibers.

4. The efferent (motor) nerve fibers send a message to the muscles located in the hand.

FIGURE **2–12**
The spinal cord and reflex action.

The Spinal Cord

■ The spinal cord connects the

brain to _____

_____

_____

■ The spinal cord coordinates _____

_____

_____

Severing the spinal cord at the neck typically causes paralysis of everything below the head because nerves connecting to the body's muscles no longer have a cable to the brain. The late actor Christopher Reeve suffered from paralysis of everything below the head when his spinal cord was severed after he was thrown from a horse; the nerves connected to his body's muscles no longer had a cable to the brain. Others with similar injuries may someday benefit from research on neurogenesis.

By combining these various techniques, neuroscientists simultaneously can observe anatomical structures (from CAT and MRI), sites of energy use (PET and MEG), blood and water movement (fMRI), and areas of electrical activity in the brain (EEG). Using tools such as these in the 1990s, sometimes called the "decade of the brain," neuropsychologists learned more about the brain than during the entire previous history of psychology. Many neuropsychologists believe that in the near future, through the use of these sophisticated tools, scientists will be able to describe the mind and even explain complex social behaviors, such as empathy, in biological terms.

■ THE SPINAL CORD

The brain is perhaps the most spectacular part of the central nervous system, but it would not be of much value without the spinal cord. The **spinal cord**, made up of long axons wrapped in myelin, is the human's communications superhighway. It has two basic functions: to permit some reflex movements and to connect the brain to most of the rest of the body. Without it, people would lose all sensation from the parts of the body that could no longer send information to higher brain areas, and they would no longer be able to control the movements of those body parts.

JOIN THE GOOD HOUS

If you believe the gover fund a search for a cure 200,000 Americans par of spinal cord injuries, f and mail it to Senator A PA), who chairs the Sen that decides how funding research within the Natio Health will be spent.

Senator Arlen Specte
ttee on Labor, H
Education
ffice Buildi
gton, DC :

To understand how the spinal cord works, consider the simple act of burning your finger on a hot pan (Figure 2–12). First, special sensory cells pick up the message that your finger is burned. They pass this information to **sensory (afferent) neurons** that carry the message to the spinal cord. In the spinal cord, **interneurons** (or **association neurons**) connect the message from the sensory neurons to **motor (efferent) neurons** that trigger a quick withdrawal of your hand without your thinking about it. (A similar reaction occurs when the doctor taps your knee with a rubber mallet.) But that quick, reflexive response is only the first in a series of reactions in your nervous system. The message is also sent up the spinal cord to the brain where it is interpreted and you decide what else, if anything, needs to be done: You feel pain, you look at the burn, perhaps you run cold water over your hand. Meanwhile, your body goes on "emergency alert": You breathe faster, your heart pounds, your entire body mobilizes itself against the wound. A simple, small burn, thus, triggers a complex, coordinated sequence of activities involving the central nervous system (the brain and spinal cord) and the peripheral nervous system—the subject of the next section.

Check Your Understanding

1. Match the lobes of the cerebral cortex with their functions.

_____ Frontal lobes   **a.** Process language and information from the ears

_____ Occipital lobes   **b.** Process body sensations and spatial information

_____ Temporal lobes   **c.** Plan goal-directed behavior

_____ Parietal lobes   **d.** Process visual information

2. Susan has a degenerative disease that causes her to lose her balance easily and to move in a jerky and uncoordinated way. She cannot drink from a glass without spilling it nor can she touch her toes without falling over. This disease is probably affecting her _____.

    a. Hypothalamus   **b.** Midbrain   **c.** Cerebellum   **d.** Reticular formation

The Peripheral Nervous System

The peripheral nervous system (PNS) carries messages to and from the central nervous system (CNS). Without the peripheral nervous system, no information could get to the spinal cord or brain nor could the brain give directions to the muscles and glands in the body. Even the simple reflex of pulling your hand away from a hot pan would not work: In the earlier example, the pain message was carried to the spinal cord on afferent (sensory) neurons that are part of the PNS and the instructions from your spinal cord to your hand were carried on efferent (motor) neurons that are also part of the PNS.

All the sensory neurons that carry information to the CNS and all the motor neurons that carry messages from the CNS to skeletal muscles belong to a part of the PNS called the **somatic nervous system**. All the things that register through your senses—sights, sounds, smells, temperature, pressure, and so on—travel to your brain via sensory neurons. Later chapters will show how the somatic nervous system affects our experience of the world both inside and outside our bodies. Every action one makes, from pedaling a bike to scratching a toe, involves motor neurons in the somatic nervous system.

The autonomic portion of the PNS is composed of all the neurons that carry messages between the CNS and internal organs of the body (glands and smooth muscles, such as the heart and digestive system). The **autonomic nervous system** is necessary to such vital body functions as breathing and blood flow. Because it is also important to the experience of emotions, psychologists take a special interest in it. To understand the workings of the autonomic nervous system, another distinction must be made. The autonomic nervous system consists of two branches: the **sympathetic division** and the **parasympathetic division** (Figure 2–13). These two divisions act in almost total opposition to each other, but both are directly involved in controlling and integrating the actions of the glands and the smooth muscles within the body.

The nerves in the sympathetic division are busiest when one is intensely aroused, such as when angry or frightened. These nerves carry messages that tell the body to prepare for an emergency and to get ready to act quickly or strenuously. In response, your heart begins to pound, your breathing quickens, your pupils enlarge, and your digestion stops. The sympathetic nervous system also tells the endocrine system to start pumping chemicals into the bloodstream

The Peripheral Nervous System

■ The peripheral nervous system connects the _____

_____

■ The somatic nervous system brings _____

_____

■ The autonomic nervous system is composed of the_____

_____

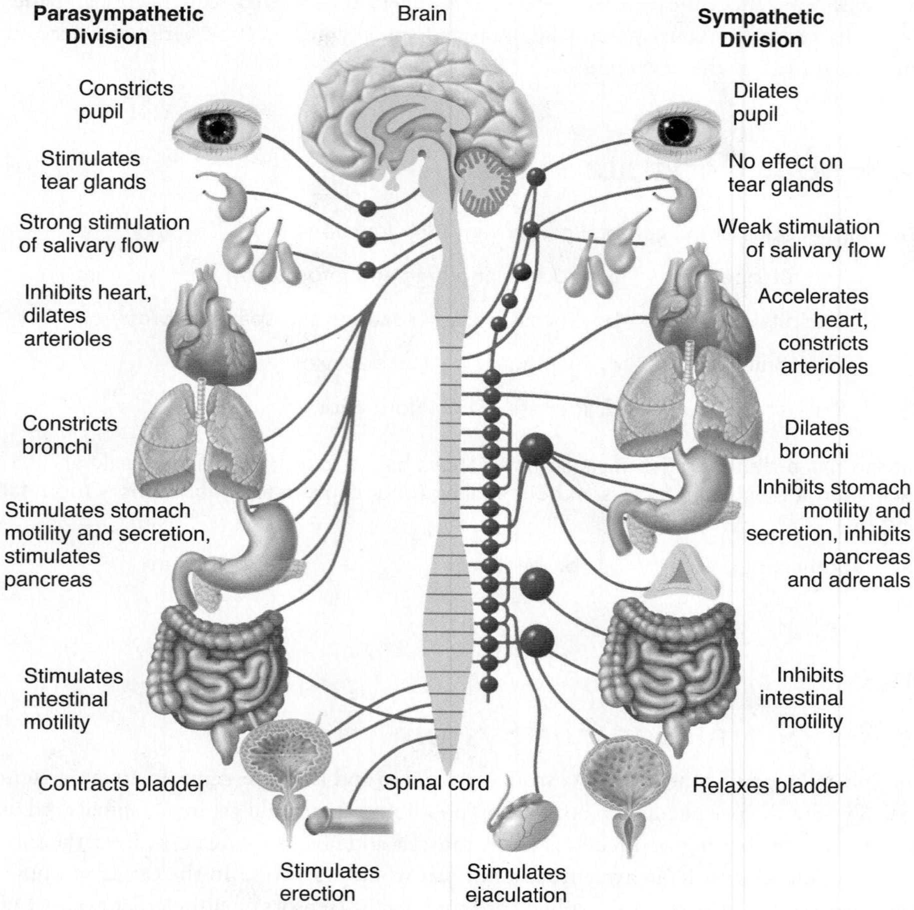

FIGURE 2–13

The sympathetic and parasympathetic divisions of the autonomic nervous system.
The sympathetic division generally acts to arouse the body, preparing it for "fight or flight." The parasympathetic follows with messages to relax.

Source: Adapted from *General Biology* (revised edition, 1st edition), by Willis Johnson, Richard A. Laubengayer, and Louis E. Delanney, © 1961. Reprinted with permission of Brooks/Cole, an imprint of the Wadsworth Group, a division of Thomson Learning.

to further strengthen reactions and improve reaction times. All these changes help direct energy and attention to the emergency at hand, giving one the keen senses, stamina, and strength needed to flee from the danger or to stand and fight it. Sympathetic nerve fibers connect to every internal organ in the body, which explains why the body's response to sudden stress is so widespread.

Although sympathetic reactions are often sustained even after danger is passed, eventually even the most intense sympathetic division reaction fades and the body calms down to normal. This calming effect is promoted by the parasympathetic division of the autonomic nervous system. Parasympathetic nerve fibers connect to the same organs as sympathetic nerve fibers do, but they cause the opposite reaction. The heart goes back to beating at its regular rate, the stomach muscles relax, digestion resumes, breathing slows, and the pupils contract.

Traditionally, the autonomic nervous system was regarded as the "automatic" part of the body's response mechanism. No one, it was believed, could tell the autonomic nervous system when to speed up or slow down the heartbeat or when to stop or start the digestive processes. However, research in the 1960s and 1970s showed that it is possible to exert some control over the autonomic nervous system. For example, people can learn to moderate the severity of high blood pressure (Buist, 2002) or migraine headaches (C. Hermann & Blanchard, 2002), and even to regulate their own heart rate and brain waves (Monastra, Monastra, & George, 2002). We will look more closely at autonomic control when we discuss biofeedback in Chapter 5 (Learning).

Check Your Understanding

1. Indicate whether each function is associated with the sympathetic (S) or the parasympathetic (P) division of the autonomic nervous system.

    a. _____ Heartbeat increases

    b. _____ Stomach starts digesting food

    c. _____ Breathing speeds up

    d. _____ Body recovers from an emergency situation

2. The heavy footsteps on the stairs get closer and closer. Slowly, the door to the bedroom creaks open. As a stranger lunges in, you let out an ear-piercing scream. Which of the following most accurately describes your nervous system at this point?

    a. Your sympathetic nervous system is more active than your parasympathetic nervous system.

    b. Your parasympathetic nervous system is more active than your sympathetic nervous system.

    c. Both your sympathetic and your parasympathetic nervous systems are extremely active.

    d. Neither your sympathetic nor your parasympathetic nervous systems are unusually active.

The Endocrine System

The nervous system is not the only mechanism that regulates the functioning of the human body. As noted throughout this chapter, the nervous system and the endocrine system work together in a constant chemical conversation. When you burn your finger, as seen in the example earlier, your response to the burn does not end with the nervous system. In addition, chemical substances called **hormones** are released into your bloodstream by internal organs called **endocrine glands**. These hormones are carried throughout your body, where they have widespread effects on various organs. Under less dramatic circumstances, hormones, acting either singly or together, affect such things as alertness or sleepiness, excitability, sexual behavior, ability to concentrate, aggressiveness, reactions to stress, even desire for companionship. Hormones can also have dramatic effects on mood, emotional reactivity, and ability to learn. Radical changes in some hormones may also contribute to serious psychological disorders, such as depression.

The locations of the endocrine glands are shown in Figure 2–14. This section focuses on those glands whose functions are best understood and that have the most impact on behavior and mental processes.

The pea-sized **pituitary gland**, which is located on the underside of the brain, is connected to the hypothalamus. The pituitary is often called the "master gland" because of its influential role in regulating other endocrine glands including the thyroid gland, adrenal gland, ovaries, and testes. The **thyroid gland**, located just below the larynx (or voice box), regulates the body's rate of metabolism and, thus, the degree to which people are alert and energetic. An overactive thyroid can cause excitability, insomnia, reduced attention span, agitation, out-of-character behavior, and snap decision making, as well as reduced concentration and difficulty focusing on a task. An underactive thyroid gland can cause constant fatigue. It is not surprising that thyroid problems are often misdiagnosed as depression or simply as "problems in living."

The two **adrenal glands**, located just above the kidneys, affect the body's reaction to stress. Imagine that you are crossing the street when you see a car bearing down on you at a high rate of speed. Your body reacts immediately. The hypothalamus secretes a hormone that causes the pituitary gland to release endorphins (the body's natural painkillers) and ACTH, a messenger hormone that goes to the adrenal cortex. Alerted by ACTH from the pituitary, the adrenal cortex in turn secretes hormones that increase the level of blood sugar, help to break down proteins, and help the body respond to injury. It also pours several hormones into the bloodstream: *Epinephrine* activates the sympathetic nervous system which, as we have seen, prepares the body to face an emergency. Another hormone, *norepinephrine*, not only raises

The Endocrine System

- Chemical messengers called hormones are produced by _____ _____ _____

- Action of the endocrine system is slower, but _____ _____ _____

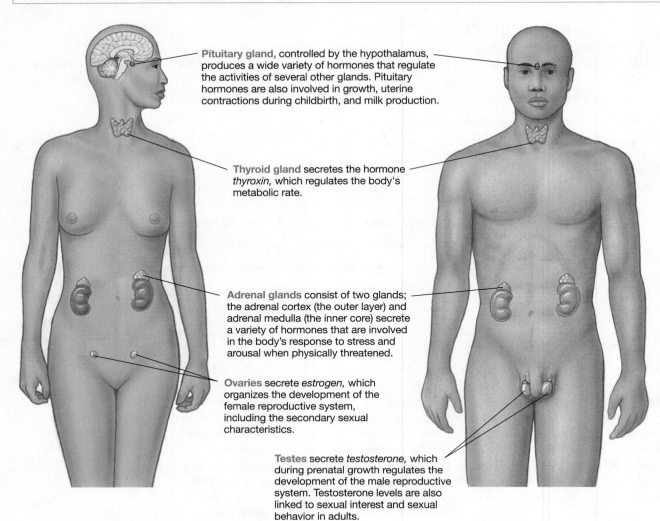

Pituitary gland, controlled by the hypothalamus, produces a wide variety of hormones that regulate the activities of several other glands. Pituitary hormones are also involved in growth, uterine contractions during childbirth, and milk production.

Thyroid gland secretes the hormone *thyroxin,* which regulates the body's metabolic rate.

Adrenal glands consist of two glands; the adrenal cortex (the outer layer) and adrenal medulla (the inner core) secrete a variety of hormones that are involved in the body's response to stress and arousal when physically threatened.

Ovaries secrete *estrogen,* which organizes the development of the female reproductive system, including the secondary sexual characteristics.

Testes secrete *testosterone,* which during prenatal growth regulates the development of the male reproductive system. Testosterone levels are also linked to sexual interest and sexual behavior in adults.

FIGURE **2–14**
The glands of the endocrine system.
Endocrine glands secrete hormones that produce widespread effects on the body.

blood pressure but also is carried by the bloodstream to the pituitary, where it triggers the release of still more ACTH, thus prolonging the response to stress. The complexity of this process explains why it takes time for the body to return to normal after extreme emotional excitement. (This interaction is seen in more detail in Chapter 8: Motivation and Emotion.)

The **gonads**—the *testes* in males and the *ovaries* in females—secrete hormones that traditionally have been classified as masculine (the androgens) and feminine (the estrogens). (Both sexes produce both types of hormone, but androgens predominate in males, whereas estrogens predominate in females.) At puberty, the gonads trigger the development of secondary sex characteristics, including breasts in females, a deeper voice in males, and pubic and underarm hair in both sexes. Testosterone, an androgen, also has long been linked to aggressive behavior.

The endocrine system plays a major role in helping to coordinate and integrate complex psychological reactions. In fact, the nervous system and the endocrine system work hand in hand, as will be seen in Chapter 8 (Motivation and Emotion) and in Chapter 11 (Stress and Health Psychology).

So far in this chapter we have seen that a very close connection exists between biology and psychology. Even the genes we inherit from our parents can affect important psychological processes, as we will now discover.

Check Your Understanding

1. Match each gland with its major function.

_____ Thyroid glands   **a.** Involved in stress response

_____ Pituitary glands   **b.** Produce androgens and estrogens

_____ Gonads   **c.** Regulate rate of metabolism

_____ Adrenal glands   **d.** The "master gland"

2. Mary has been under a great deal of stress lately. Her blood pressure has increased, she has lost her appetite, and her heart is beating faster than usual. These changes are most likely the result of:

a. Reduced activity in the thyroid gland

b. Reduced activity in the pancreas

c. Increased activity in the adrenal glands

Genes, Evolution, and Behavior

ENDURING ISSUES NATURE/NURTURE

Human Behavior Genetics

Charles Darwin (1809–1882) was one of the first to recognize the impact of heredity upon such psychological characteristics as intelligence, personality, and mental illness. In a discussion of gestures, he described the following case:

> A gentleman of considerable position was found by his wife to have the curious trick, when he lay fast asleep on his back in bed, of raising his right arm slowly in front of his face, up to his forehead, and then dropping it with a jerk so that the wrist fell heavily on the bridge of his nose. The trick did not occur every night, but occasionally. (Darwin, 1872, p. 34)

To protect the gentleman's nose, it was necessary to remove the buttons from the cuff of his nightgown. Years after the man's death, his son married a woman who observed precisely the same behavior in him. Their daughter, as well, exhibited the same gesture.

Darwin heard about this case from his half-cousin, Francis Galton (1822–1911), who was the first person to try to demonstrate systematically how behavior characteristics can be transmitted genetically. Galton was especially interested in the transmission of mental traits. To show that high mental ability is inherited, he identified about 1,000 men of eminence in Great Britain—judges, political leaders, scholars, scientists, artists, and so on—and found that they belonged to only 300 families. Because only

(Continued)

Genetics

- Humans have 23 pairs of _____ _____ _____

- In the nucleus of each chromosome are _____ _____ _____

- The 20,000 to 25,000 genes in each cell comprise a person's _____ _____ _____

- The most significant genetic traits are _____ _____ _____

one in 4,000 people in the population was "eminent," Galton concluded that eminence must be an inherited trait.

Galton's findings were challenged by others who claimed that environmental factors such as educational and social advantages could have accounted for the concentration of eminence in just a few hundred families. In the early twentieth century, Galton's assumptions about the inherited nature of behavioral traits came under more fundamental attack from the behaviorists. The founder of behaviorism, J. B. Watson, argued that:

> Give me a dozen healthy infants, well-formed, and my own specified world to bring them up in and I'll guarantee to take any one at random and train him to become any type of specialist I might select—doctor, lawyer, artist, merchant-chief, and yes, even beggerman and thief, regardless of his talents, penchants, tendencies, abilities, vocations and race of his ancestors. I am going beyond my facts and I admit it, but so have the advocates of the contrary and they have been doing it for many thousands of years. (Watson, 1924, p. 104)

The question of how much influence heredity has on various behaviors is at the heart of modern behavior genetics and, as will be seen, psychologists still disagree on the answer. To begin to appreciate the "nature–nurture controversy," it is important to become familiar with some of the basic mechanisms of inheritance.

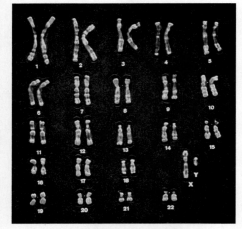

21

(*Above*) The 23 pairs of chromosomes found in every normal human cell. The two members of 22 of these pairs look exactly alike. The two members of the 23rd pair, the sex chromosomes, may or may not look alike. Females have equivalent X chromosomes, while males have one X and one Y chromosome, which look very different. (*Below*) The chromosome pattern that causes Down syndrome: the presence of three chromosomes in pair 21.

■ GENETICS

Genetics is the study of how living things pass on traits from one generation to the next. Selective breeding of plants and animals has been done for thousands of years, but it was Gregor Mendel (1822–1884), a Moravian monk, who gave modern genetics its beginnings in 1867 when he reported the results of his years of work systematically breeding peas. Mendel proposed that the basic characteristics of peas are controlled by elements passed on from one generation to the next. Offspring are not carbon copies or "clones" of their parents, yet some traits reappear from generation to generation in predictable patterns.

Around the beginning of the twentieth century, scientists named the basic units of inheritance **genes**. But they did not know what genes were or how they were transmitted. Today, however, scientists know much more about genes and the way they work. To understand more about these blueprints for development, let's take a look at some cellular components.

As shown in Figure 2–15, the nucleus of every cell contains **chromosomes**, each of which contains hundreds or thousands of genes in fixed locations. Chromosomes vary in size and shape, and they usually come in pairs. Each species has a constant number: Mice have 20 pairs, monkeys have 27, and peas have 7. In every normal cell except the sex cells (eggs and sperm), human beings have 46 chromosomes arranged as 23 pairs of chromosomes; the sex cells have only 23 single chromosomes. At fertilization, the 23 chromosomes from the father's sperm link to the 23 chromosomes from the mother's egg, creating a new cell that contains the normal 46 chromosomes arranged as 23 pairs. From that single, new cell spring the billions of other cells that eventually make up a fully grown adult. The 46 chromosomes in every normal cell, containing 20,000 to 25,000 genes, create a unique genetic "blueprint" or **genotype**.

Genes are composed primarily of **deoxyribonucleic acid (DNA)**, a complex organic molecule that resembles two chains twisted around each other in a double-helix

FIGURE **2–15**
The relationship among chromosomes, genes, and DNA.

Cell

1. The nucleus of each cell contains chromosomes. All cells, except the sperm and ovum, contain 46 chromosomes.

Chromosome

2. Each chromosome carries genes. The genes, which are the basic units of heredity, serve as the genetic blueprint for all of the various aspects of development.

Gene

3. Genes, in turn, are composed of dioxyribonucleic acid (DNA).

DNA

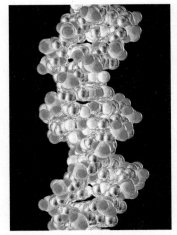

The twisted chain of the long DNA molecule contains the genetic code.

pattern. Like chromosomes, genes also occur in pairs, with one being dominant and one being recessive. For example, in the case of eye color, brown eyes are dominant; all other colors (blue, green, and hazel, for example) are recessive. As shown in Figure 2–16, a child who inherits the gene for blue eyes from both parents will have blue eyes. A sibling who inherits the gene for brown eyes from both parents will have brown eyes. And, because the brown-eye gene dominates, so will a sibling who inherits the gene for brown eyes from one parent and the gene for blue eyes from the other. Other examples of dominant genes include dark hair, dimples, freckles and even immunity to poison ivy.

Examples of a single-gene inheritance are relatively rare. Important characteristics, such as intelligence or a predisposition toward alcoholism or severe mental illness, cannot be traced back to a single gene. Rather, many different genes make a small contribution to the trait in question in a process known as **polygenic inheritance.** Similar to a symphony orchestra,

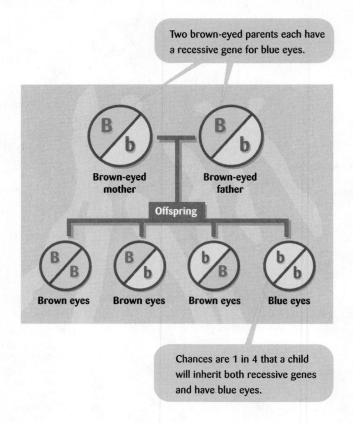

Two brown-eyed parents each have a recessive gene for blue eyes.

Brown-eyed mother

Brown-eyed father

Offspring

Brown eyes

Brown eyes

Brown eyes

Blue eyes

Chances are 1 in 4 that a child will inherit both recessive genes and have blue eyes.

FIGURE 2–16
Transmission of eye color by dominant (B) and recessive (b) genes.
This figure represents the four possible combinations of eye-color genes in these parents' offspring. Because three out of the four combinations result in brown-eyed children, the chance that any child will have brown eyes is 75%.

in which each instrument contributes separate notes to the total sound that reaches the audience, each of the genes in a polygenic system contributes separately to the total effect. Moreover, heredity need not be immediately or fully apparent. Even identical twins, who have the same genotype, differ in small ways that allow family members to tell them apart. In some cases, expression of a trait is delayed until later in life. For example, many men inherit "male-pattern baldness" that does not show up until middle age.

For the most part, the discussion has used physical characteristics as examples. In the next section, *behavior geneticists* apply the same basic principles to psychological characteristics.

ENDURING ISSUES   NATURE/NURTURE

Genetic Predispositions

Quite often, genes may *predispose* a person to developing a particular trait, but full expression of the characteristic depends on environmental factors. Given the same environment, for example, a person who inherits "tall" genes will be tall and a person who inherits "short" genes will be short. But if the first person is malnourished in childhood and the second person is well nourished as a child, they may be the same height as adults. Because an individual's genotype does not always correspond obviously or directly to what is expressed, the term **phenotype** is used when referring to the outward expression of a trait. For example, people with an inherited tendency to gain weight (genotype) may or may not become obese (phenotype), depending on their diet, exercise program, and overall health.

■ BEHAVIOR GENETICS

The goal of **behavior genetics** is to identify the ways in which genes contribute to intelligence, temperament, talents, motivation, emotion, personality, and predispositions toward psychological and neurological disorders. Of course, genes do not directly cause behavior. Rather, they affect the development and operation of the nervous system and the endocrine system, which, in turn, influence behavior and mental processes. The remainder of this chapter examines some of the methods used by behavior geneticists for animal studies and the techniques used to study behavior genetics in humans.

Animal Behavior Genetics   Much of what is known about behavior genetics comes from studies of nonhuman animals. In **strain studies**, close relatives (such as siblings) are intensively inbred over many generations to create strains of animals that are genetically similar to one another, but different from other strains. When animals from different strains are raised together in the same environment, differences between them largely reflect genetic differences in the strains. This method has shown that performance on learning tasks, as well as sense of smell and susceptibility to seizures, are affected by heredity.

Selection studies are another way to assess *heritability*, the degree to which a trait is inherited. If a trait is closely regulated by genes, when animals with the trait are interbred, their offspring should have more of the trait than one would find in the general population. Humans have practiced selective breeding for thousands of years to create breeds of dogs and other domesticated animals that have desirable physical and psychological traits.

Human Behavior Genetics   For obvious reasons, scientists cannot conduct strain or selection studies with human beings. But there are many ways to study behavioral techniques indirectly. **Family studies** are based on the assumption that if genes influence a trait, close relatives should share that trait more often than distant relatives because close relatives have more genes in common. For example, schizophrenia occurs in only 1 to 2% of the general population. But as you can see from Figure 2–17, the more closely people are related to someone with schizophrenia, the more likely they are to develop the disorder. Unfortunately, because people who are closely related share not only some genes but also similar environments, family studies alone cannot clearly distinguish the effects of heredity and environment.

To obtain a clearer picture of the influences of heredity and environment, psychologists often use **twin studies**. **Identical twins** develop from a single fertilized ovum and are, therefore, identical in genetic makeup at conception. Any differences between them must be the result of life experiences. **Fraternal twins**, however, develop from two separate fertilized egg cells and are no more similar genetically than are other brothers and sisters. If twin pairs grow up in similar environments and if identical twins are no more alike in a particular characteristic than fraternal twins, then heredity cannot be very important for that trait.

Referring again to Figure 2–17, when one identical twin develops schizophrenia, the chances that the other twin will develop the disorder are nearly 50%. For fraternal twins, the chances are about 15%. Thus, twin studies suggest that heredity plays a significant role in schizophrenia. Twin studies have also provided evidence for the heritability of a wide range of other behaviors, including verbal skills, mild intellectual impairment, aggressiveness, compulsive gambling, depression, anxiety, and eating disorders.

However, similarities between twins, even identical twins, cannot be attributed automatically to genes because twins usually grow up together. If they are more similar than nontwins, is it because of their inheritance or their shared environment? To minimize this problem, researchers attempt to locate identical twins who were separated at birth or in very early childhood and raised in different homes. For example, a University of Minnesota team led by Thomas Bouchard followed separated twins for more than 10 years (Bouchard, 1984, 1996;

Behavior Genetics

■ This field of study focuses on how genes contribute to _____

_____

■ Strain studies and selection studies are used in _____

_____

■ Human research uses _____

_____

_____

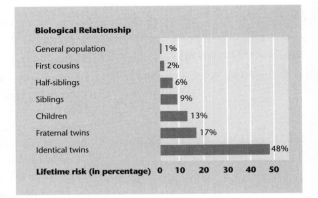

Biological Relationship

	Lifetime risk (in percentage)
General population	1%
First cousins	2%
Half-siblings	6%
Siblings	9%
Children	13%
Fraternal twins	17%
Identical twins	48%

Lifetime risk (in percentage) 0   10   20   30   40   50

FIGURE **2–17**

Average risk of schizophrenia among biological relatives of people with schizophrenia.

Source: Gill, M. (2004, October). Genetic approaches to the understanding of mental illness. Paper presented at the 12th World Congress on Psychiatric Genetics, Dublin, Ireland. Retrieved October 10, 2007, from http://www.medicine.tcd.ie/psychiatry/assets/docs/genes_mental_health.pdf.

Bouchard et al., 1990; W. Johnson, Bouchard, Segal, & Samuel, 2005). They confirmed that genetics plays a major role in mental retardation, schizophrenia, depression, reading skill, and intelligence. Bouchard and his colleagues have also found that complex personality traits, interests, and talents, and even the structure of brain waves, are guided by genetics.

But studies of twins reared apart are not without their own problems. Adoption agencies usually try to place twins in similar families, so even if the twins are reared apart, their environments may not be much different. And the number of twin pairs separated at birth is very small. For these reasons, scientists sometimes rely on other types of studies to investigate the influence of heredity.

Adoption studies focus on children who were adopted at birth and brought up by parents not related genetically to them. By comparing these children to their biological parents as opposed to their adoptive parents, it is possible to gain some additional insight into the role of genetics. Adoption studies have provided additional evidence for the heritability of intelligence and some forms of mental illness as well as some behaviors that were thought previously to be determined solely by environmental influences, such as smoking.

To complicate the picture a bit more, the environment is not just something "out there" that happens to people over which they have little control. People also shape their environments. For example, people tend to seek environments that promote a certain level of comfort. A shy child might prefer a quieter play group than would a child who is more outgoing. In addition, our own behavior causes others to respond in particular ways. A teacher's approach to correcting the behavior of a sensitive child might be quite different from how a more energetic child would be treated. Because genes and environments interact in so many intricate ways, trying to isolate the effects of heredity and environment is extraordinarily difficult.

The study of behavior genetics (and that of evolutionary psychology, which is discussed next) makes many people uneasy. Some fear that it may lead to the conclusion that who we are is written in some kind of permanent ink before we are born. Some people also fear that research in these fields could be used to undermine movements toward social equality. But far from finding human behavior to be genetically predetermined, behavior genetics studies show just how important the environment is in determining the genetic predispositions that get expressed and those that do not (Rutter, 1997). In other words, we may inherit predispositions but we do not inherit destinies. The emerging picture confirms that heredity *and* environment (nature *and* nurture) are woven together tightly and both shape most of our significant behaviors and traits.

■ EVOLUTIONARY PSYCHOLOGY

Evolutionary Psychology

■ Evolutionary psychology focuses on

_____

_____

Behavior geneticists attempt to discover the genetic causes of individual differences in human behavior, but *evolutionary* psychologists are more interested in the genetic roots of behavioral traits that people have in common. In particular, they focus on the ways in which the roots of behavior might serve to promote the survival of the species. The key to these shared characteristics, these psychologists assert, is the process of evolution by **natural selection**, which was first described by Charles Darwin in *On the Origin of Species* (1859). According to the principle of natural selection, those organisms that are best adapted to their environments are most likely to survive and reproduce. If the traits that give them a survival advantage are genetically based, those same genetic characteristics will be passed on to their offspring. Organisms that do not possess the adaptive traits tend to die off before they reproduce, and hence, the less-adaptive traits do not get passed along to future generations. If people in different cultures and different parts of the world share psychological characteristics, it is possible that those characteristics evolved because they have survival value.

Evolutionary psychologists cite language as a prime example. As Chapter 9 will show, all normal children acquire language without specific instruction; children in different cultures acquire language at about the same ages and in predictable stages; and the underlying structure of all human languages (nouns and verbs, subjects and objects, questions and conditional phrases, and so on) is basically the same. Taken as a whole, evolutionary psychologists argue, the evidence strongly suggests that our human brains have a built-in "program" for language. In support of this notion, scientists recently identified a specific gene, specific to humans, that may have played a pivotal role in stimulating the emergence of language among our early ancestors (Enard et al., 2002).

ENDURING ISSUES   DIVERSITY/UNIVERSALITY

Sex Differences in Mate Selection

Evolutionary psychologists cite mate selection as another example. In choosing a partner, males and females tend to pursue different strategies. Why? Evolutionary psychologists answer this way: Human females usually have only one child at a time. Women also invest more in each child than men do—going through pregnancy, caretaking, and providing nourishment. It would seem to be most adaptive for females to look for males who will provide the best genes, resources, and long-term parental care. Males, on the other hand, are limited only by the number of prospective mates they can attract, because sperm is plentiful and quickly replaced. It may be most adaptive for males to seek to mate with as many females as they can and to compete with other males for access to females. Studies analyzing human behaviors associated with sexual selection have found that men and women do indeed take different approaches to sexuality, mate choice, and aggression, as predicted by evolutionary psychology (Buss, 2000, 2004; Callahan, 2000; Chuang, 2002; Pawloski, Dunbar, & Lipowicz, 2000). In fact, comparing evolutionary explanations with more traditional social-learning explanations of sex differences in social behavior, it appears that evolutionary psychology does a much better job of accounting for overall patterns (Archer, 1996).

Evolutionary psychology is not without its critics. Some opponents argue that science is being used to justify perpetuating unjust social policies. These critics claim that simply by saying a trait is adaptive implies that it is both genetically determined and good. For example, the evolutionary theory of male–female differences in mate selection could be seen as endorsing male promiscuity, since it is biologically adaptive. In response, evolutionary psychologists are quick to point out that their aim is not to shape social policy, but to understand the origins of human behavior. They argue further that behaviors that may have contributed to our adaptive success during the early years of human evolution may no longer be adaptive in our current environment and, therefore, should not be viewed as good and right simply because at one time they may have once served an important adaptive function (Pinker, 2002).

Other critics chide evolutionary psychologists for too hastily explaining behaviors from an evolutionary perspective, rather than investigating other plausible origins of them. They argue that, just because a behavior occurs to some degree across many different cultures, it does not necessarily mean that it has evolutionary roots. Evolutionary psychologists answer that their goal is not to propose evolutionary theories that exclude all other possible explanations; instead, their aim is to offer an evolutionary perspective that may complement other points of view.

As a relatively new approach in psychology, the evolutionary perspective has yet to take its place among the most respected theoretical paradigms of the field. Only the results of empirical research, which compares evolutionary explanations with competing theoretical explanations of behavior, will determine the fate of this provocative and intriguing new perspective.

Check Your Understanding

1. Are the following statements true (T) or false (F)?

   a. _____ "Individual differences in intelligence, emotional reactivity, and susceptibility to schizophrenia and depression may all be influenced by genes."

   b. _____ Neuropsychology is the study of how traits are passed from one generation to another.

2. Imagine that psychologists document a long history of criminal behavior in a family: The children, their parents, their grandparents, and even their great-grandparents have long lists of convictions for crimes. Knowing only this, the most reasonable conclusion you can draw is that criminal behavior is most likely to the result of:

   a. Genetic factors

   b. Environmental factors

   c. A combination of genetic and environmental factors

Chapter Review

www.psychologythecore.com

Psychobiology deals with the biological processes in the nervous system and the endocrine system that are the basis of human thoughts, feelings, and actions. Psychobiology overlaps with **neuroscience**, which specifically focuses on the study of the brain and the nervous system.

Neurons: The Messengers

The basic building block of the nervous system is the **neuron**, or nerve cell. Neurons differ from other cells in two important ways: They receive messages from other neurons through short fibers called **dendrites,** and they send outgoing messages through a longer fiber, called an **axon**. A group of axons bundled together forms a **nerve** or **tract**. Some axons are covered with a fatty **myelin sheath** that increases neuron efficiency and provides insulation.

When a neuron is at rest, there is a small electrical charge (the **resting potential**) across the cell membrane and the membrane is said to be in a state of **polarization**. When stimulation from other neurons exceeds the **threshold of excitation**, this electrical imbalance changes abruptly. The membrane is depolarized and an **action potential (neural impulse)** travels down the axon. According to the **all-or-none law**, every firing of a particular neuron produces an impulse of equal strength. After firing, the neuron briefly goes through the absolute **refractory period**, when it will not fire again, followed by the **relative refractory period**, when firing will occur only when the incoming messages are much stronger than usual.

Neurotransmitters, released from **synaptic vesicles** in the axon **terminal buttons (synaptic knobs)**, cross the tiny **synaptic space** *(or* **cleft***)* between the axon of one neuron and the dendrites of other neurons. Here, they latch on to **receptor sites**, much as keys fit into locks, and pass on their excitatory or inhibitory messages. When their job is over, neurotransmitters detach from the receptor sites and are reabsorbed, broken down or recycled, or disposed of as waste by the body, with the result that the *synapse* is clear and back to its normal state.

The Central Nervous System

The human nervous system is organized into two parts: the **central nervous system (CNS)**, which consists of the brain and spinal cord, and the **peripheral nervous system (PNS)**, which connects the CNS to the rest of the body.

Physically, the brain has three more-or-less distinct areas: the hindbrain, the midbrain, and the forebrain. The **hindbrain** plays an essential role in basic life processes. It includes the **medulla**, which controls breathing, heart rate, and blood pressure, and the **pons**, which regulates the sleep-wake cycle. The **cerebellum** controls the sense of balance and coordinates the body's actions. It is also involved in controlling emotions, being attentive, recalling information, and coordinating sensory information. The cerebellum may also play a role in numerous mental disorders.

The **midbrain** is important for hearing and seeing and is an area where pain is registered. The **reticular formation** alerts the higher parts of the brain to incoming messages.

The **forebrain** includes the **thalamus** that relays sensory information to the higher levels of the brain. The forebrain also includes the **limbic system**, a ring of loosely connected structures including the hypothalamus (which is important to motivation and emotional behavior), the **hippocampus** (which is essential to the formation of new memories), and the **amygdala** (which is involved in emotions and emotional memories).

The **cerebrum** takes up most of the room inside the skull. It is composed of two separate hemispheres. The outer covering of the cerebral hemispheres is known as the **cerebral cortex**. Each cerebral hemisphere is divided into four lobes, delineated by deep fissures on the surface of the brain. In addition, large **association areas** spread throughout all four lobes integrate information from many different sources and are essential to such complex mental processes as learning, thinking, and remembering. The **frontal lobe** monitors and integrates the complex tasks that are going on in the rest of the brain. It is also the site of many mental processes that are unique to human beings, including self-awareness and goal-directed behavior and the ability to plan and concentrate, control emotions, and conduct moral decision making. One portion of the frontal lobe, the **primary motor cortex**, is responsible for voluntary movement. The **occipital lobe** receives and processes visual information. The **temporal lobe** helps people perform complex visual tasks, such as recognizing faces, hearing, and regulating emotions and motivations. The **parietal lobe** receives sensory information from all over the body and oversees spatial abilities. Messages from sensory receptors are registered in a portion of the parietal lobe known as the **primary somatosensory cortex**.

The two cerebral hemispheres are linked by the **corpus callosum**, through which they normally communicate and coordinate their activities. Despite this connection, each hemisphere appears to specialize in certain tasks. The right hemisphere excels at visual and spatial tasks and the perception of emotions, whereas the left hemisphere excels at language and analytical thinking.

The brain changes continuously in response to new information and skills. This is called **neural plasticity**. Human brains also are capable of **neurogenesis**—the production of new brain cells. The study of neurogenesis offers hope for the treatment of many neurological disorders, including spinal cord injury.

An increasingly sophisticated technology exists for investigating the brain. Among the most important tools are **microelectrode** techniques, **macroelectrode** techniques (such as the electroencephalograph or EEG), **structural imaging** (CT scanning and magnetic resonance imaging), and **functional imaging** (such as PET scans and functional MRI). Functional imaging techniques, PET scanning and fMRI, allow scientists to observe not only the structure, but also the functioning of parts of the brain. Scientists often combine these techniques to study brain activity in unprecedented detail—information that can help in the treatment of medical and psychological disorders.

The **spinal cord** is a complex cable of nerves that connects the brain to most of the rest of the body. It is made up of bundles of long axons wrapped in myelin and has two basic functions: to permit some reflex movements and to carry messages to and from the brain. **Sensory (afferent) neurons** carry messages to the spinal cord; *motor* **(efferent) neurons** carry messages away from the spinal cord. *Interneurons* connect sensory and motor neurons.

The Peripheral Nervous System

The peripheral nervous system (PNS) carries messages to and from the CNS. It is composed of two parts. All the sensory neurons that carry information to the CNS and all the motor neurons that carry messages from the CNS to skeletal muscles belong to the **somatic nervous system**. The **autonomic nervous system** consists of all the neurons that carry messages between the CNS and internal organs of the body (glands and smooth muscles, such as the heart and digestive system). The autonomic nervous system is itself divided into two parts: the sympathetic division, which acts primarily to arouse the body when it is faced with threat, and the parasympathetic division, which acts to calm the body down and restore it to normal levels of arousal. For decades, the autonomic nervous system was thought to be beyond control. But now, biofeedback techniques have shown that it can be controlled to some extent.

The Endocrine System

The endocrine system regulates the functioning of the human body. It is made up of endocrine glands that produce hormones, which are chemical substances released into the bloodstream that have widespread effects. The pituitary gland is often called the "master gland" because of its role in regulating other glands. The thyroid gland regulates the body's rate of metabolism. Symptoms of an overactive thyroid are agitation and tension, whereas an underactive thyroid produces lethargy. The two adrenal glands affect people's response to stress. One stress-related hormone of the adrenal medulla is epinephrine, which amplifies the effects of the sympathetic nervous system. The gonads—the testes in males and the ovaries in females—secrete hormones called androgens (including testosterone) and estrogens. Testosterone has long been linked to aggressive behavior.

Genes, Evolution, and Behavior

Genetics is the study of how traits are passed on from one generation to the next via genes. Genes are made up predominantly of a complex molecule called deoxyribonucleic acid (DNA) and are lined up on tiny threadlike bodies called chromosomes that usually come in pairs. Humans have 23 pairs of chromosomes. Each member of a gene pair will be dominant or recessive. In polygenic inheritance, several genes interact to produce a trait. The full complement of genes necessary to build a human body—approximately 20,000 to 25,000 genes—makes up each person's unique genotype. An individual's genotype does not always correspond to that person's phenotype, which is the outward expression of a trait.

The goal of behavior genetics is to identify the ways in which genes contribute to intelligence, temperament, talents, motivation, emotion, personality, and predispositions toward psychological and neurological disorders. Psychologists use various methods to study heritability; that is, the contribution of genes in determining variations in certain traits. Strain studies approach the problem by observing strains of highly inbred, genetically similar animals, whereas selection studies try to determine the extent to which an animal's traits can be passed on from one generation to another. In the study of humans, family studies tackle heritability by looking for similarities in traits as a function of biological closeness. Also useful in studying human heritability are twin studies (including identical and fraternal twins) and adoption studies.

Evolutionary psychologists are interested in the genetic roots of behavioral traits that people have in common; in particular, the ways in which the roots of behavior might serve to promote the survival of the species The theory of evolution by natural selection states that organisms best adapted to their environment tend to survive, transmitting their genetic characteristics to succeeding generations, whereas organisms with fewer adaptive characteristics tend to die off. Evolutionary psychology analyzes human behavioral tendencies by examining their adaptive value from an evolutionary perspective. Though not without its critics, evolutionary psychology has proved useful in helping to explain some of the commonalities in human behavior that occur across cultures.

Chapter 3
Sensation and Perception

Go to *The Core Online* at **www.psychologythecore.com** to get the most up-to-date information for your introductory psychology course. The content online is an important part of what you are learning—the content there can help prepare you for your test! It includes up-to-date examples, simulations, video clips, and practice quizzes. Also be sure to check out the *Blog* to hear directly from the authors on what current events and latest research are most relevant to your course materials.

The first time you log in, you will need the access code packaged with your textbook. If you do not have a code, please go to **www.mypearsonstore.com** and enter the ISBN of your textbook (**0-13-603344-X**) to purchase the code.

3 1 The Nature of Sensation

How Sensation Happens
- **Sensation** begins when energy stimulates a **receptor cell** in one of the sense organs.
- The process of converting physical energy, such as light or sound, into electrochemical codes is called **transduction**.

Sensory Thresholds
- The **absolute threshold** is the least amount of energy that can be detected 50% of the time.
- The **difference threshold** is the smallest change in energy that can be detected 50% of the time.

3 2 Vision

The Visual System
- Light enters through the **cornea** and **pupil** and is focused by the **lens** on the **retina**, where it activates **rods** and **cones** (visual receptor cells).
- Visual information is conveyed via the **bipolar cells** to **ganglion cells** that make up the **optic nerve**; these cells end up at the **occipital lobe** of the brain.

Color Vision
- The three characteristics of color vision are **hue**, **saturation**, and **brightness**.
- The **trichromatic theory** posits that there are three types of cones in the retina—some most sensitive to red light, others most sensitive to green light, and still others most sensitive to blue light.
- The **opponent-process theory** posits that there are three pairs of color receptors—yellow-blue, green-red, and black-white.
- Both theories are correct, but at different stages of the visual process.

3 3 Hearing

Sound
- **Sound** is an experience created by the brain in response to stimulation of the ear by **sound waves**.
- Frequency of sound waves is the primary determinant of **pitch**; the height of sound waves (**amplitude**), together with frequency, determines the perceived loudness of the sound (measured in **decibels**).

The Ear
- When sound waves reach the eardrum, they cause it to vibrate; the vibrations are carried to the **cochlea** where the **basilar membrane** ripples in response to the stimulation.
- The receptor cells for hearing are hair cells lying on top of the basilar membrane that transmit their messages via the **auditory nerve** to the brain.

Pitch Discrimination
- According to **frequency theory**, the vibration of the basilar membrane as a whole, up to about 1000 Hz, is translated into an equivalent frequency of nerve impulses between 1000 and 4000 Hz neurons that fire in sequence, one after another.
- According to **place theory**, a pitch higher than 4000 Hz is determined by the place on the basilar membrane where the vibration is strongest.

3 4 The Other Senses

Smell

- Airborne molecules stimulate the receptor cells for smell, located high in the nasal cavity; messages go from there directly to the **olfactory bulbs** that do some recoding and pass the messages along to the brain.

Taste

- The five basic taste qualities are sweet, sour, salty, bitter, and umami.
- The receptor cells for taste are contained in **taste buds** on the tongue that send messages to the parietal lobes of the brain and to the limbic system.

Kinesthetic and Vestibular Senses

- The **kinesthetic senses** provide information about muscle movement, changes in posture, and strain on muscles and joints.
- The **vestibular senses** provide information about our orientation, position, or movement in space.

The Skin Senses

- The skin contains the receptors for the sense of touch, but the brain draws on many other sources of information when interpreting messages from touch receptors.

Pain

- Damage to the body often causes pain; but pain sometimes can be experienced by the body without any injury at all.
- There is no simple relationship between pain receptors and the experience of pain.
- When the body is injured, information travels to the spinal cord where, according to the **gate-control theory**, the pain impulses are sent to the brain only when the gate in the spinal cord is open.

3 5 Perception

Perceptual Organization

- **Perception** is the brain's process of organizing and making sense of sensory information.
- *Gestalt psychologists* point out that the brain creates a coherent perceptual experience that is more than simply the sum of the available sensory information.
- Normally, people are able to distinguish a *figure* from the *ground* upon which it appears.
- People tend to perceive objects as belonging together when the objects are close to one another; of similar color, size, or shape; and continue a pattern or direction.

Perceptual Constancies

- **Perceptual constancy** refers to the tendency to perceive objects as relatively stable and unchanging despite changing sensory information.
- The major perceptual constancies include: **size, shape, color**, and **brightness constancy**.

Perception of Distance and Depth

- **Monocular cues** to distance and depth include **interposition, linear perspective, elevation, texture gradient, shadowing,** and **motion parallax**.
- **Binocular cues** to distance and depth include **retinal disparity** and **convergence**.

Visual Illusions

- Perceptual illusions occur because the stimulus contains misleading or ambiguous cues that give rise to inaccurate or impossible perceptions.
- In some cases, the stimulus contains misleading depth cues; in other cases, the sensory information is ambiguous.

Observer Characteristics

- Perceptual experiences are shaped by desires, needs, values, expectations, cognitive style, cultural background, experiences, and even personality.

How do you know when it is raining?

Perhaps you look out the window and see the falling raindrops; or lying in bed at night, perhaps you hear the rain falling on the roof. If you are outside, perhaps you feel the raindrops hitting your skin. Some people even say that they can smell rain. Vision, hearing, touch, and smell are just a few of the senses that give us a window on the world and that combine into a rich mosaic of awareness which forms the basis of consciousness.

We begin this chapter by examining the basic principles of *sensation*—how people acquire information from the external (and internal) world. The chapter looks at our various sense organs to see how each converts physical stimuli such as light waves, sound waves, or chemical molecules into nerve impulses. But this is only a starting point. To be meaningful, this kaleidoscope of sensory input must be organized and interpreted. Our eyes register only light, dark, and color; but our brains "perceive" distinctive visual objects—a tree, a branch, a leaf, a shimmering drop of rain—in three-dimensional space. Our ears are designed to detect the movement of vibrating air molecules, yet we distinguish between a baby's cry and a Bach concerto. *Perception* is the mental process of sorting, identifying, and arranging sensory data into coherent, meaningful patterns. In the last section of this chapter, we will explore the process of perception.

ENDURING ISSUES   in Sensation and Perception

You will encounter all five "Enduring Issues" in this chapter. Two key questions concern the extent to which our perceptual experiences accurately reflect what is in the outside world (person–situation) and the ways in which our experiences depend on biological processes (mind–body). The chapter also examines the extent to which people around the world perceive events in the same way (diversity–universality) and the ways that our experience of the outside world changes as a result of experience over the course of our lives (stability–change and nature–nurture).

The Nature of Sensation

How Sensation Happens

■ Sensation begins when _____

_____

_____

■ The process of converting physical energy, such as light or sound, into electrochemical codes is called

_____

_____

Sensation begins when energy, either from an external source or from inside the body, stimulates a **receptor cell** in one of the sense organs, such as the eye or the ear. Each receptor cell is specialized to respond to just one particular form of energy—light waves (in the case of vision) or vibration of air molecules (in the case of hearing). When there is sufficient energy, the receptor cell "fires" and sends to the brain a coded signal that varies according to the characteristics of the stimulus. The process of converting physical energy, such as light or sound, into electrochemical codes is called **transduction**. For instance, a very bright light might be coded by the rapid firing of a set of nerve cells, but a dim light would set off a much slower firing sequence. The neural signal is coded still further as it passes along the sensory nerves to the central nervous system, allowing the message that reaches the brain to be precise and detailed. As a result, the coded signal that the brain receives from a flashing red light differs significantly from the message signaling a soft yellow haze. And both of these signals are coded in a much different way than a loud, piercing noise. The specific sensation produced, then, depends on *how many* neurons fire, *which* neurons fire, and *how rapidly* these neurons fire.

ENDURING ISSUES   MIND/BODY

Sensory Experience

Each sensory experience—the color of a flower or the sound of a fire engine—is an illusion created in the brain by patterns of neural signals. The brain, isolated inside the skull, is bombarded by "impulses," or "firings," of coded neural signals arriving on millions of nerve fibers. The impulses on the optic nerve reliably produce an experience we call *vision*, just as impulses moving along an auditory nerve produce the experience of *hearing*, or audition. The one-to-one relationship between stimulation of a specific nerve and the resulting sensory experience is known as the *doctrine of specific nerve energies*. Even if the impulses on the optic nerve are caused by something other than light, the result is still a visual experience. Gentle pressure on an eye, for instance, results in signals from the optic nerve. And from these signals, the brain creates a visual experience—"seeing stars" when we're hit in the eye is so familiar that even cartoons depict it.

■ SENSORY THRESHOLDS

To produce any sensation at all, the physical energy reaching a receptor cell must achieve a minimum intensity, or **absolute threshold**. Any stimulation below the absolute threshold will not be experienced. But how much sensory stimulation is enough? How loud must a sound be, for example, for a person to hear it? How bright does a blip on a radar screen have to be for the operator to see it?

To answer such questions, psychologists present a stimulus at different intensities and ask people whether they sense anything. You might expect that there would come a point at which people would suddenly say, "Now I see the flash" or "Now I hear a sound." But actually, there is a range of intensities over which a person sometimes—but not always—can sense a stimulus. The absolute threshold is defined as the point at which a person can detect the stimulus 50% of the time that it is presented (Figure 3–1). Although there are differences among people—and from moment to moment, even for the same person—the absolute threshold for each of our senses is remarkably low. In very quiet conditions, for example, the tick of a watch can be heard from 20 feet away. On a clear, dark night, a candle flame can be seen from 30 miles.

Sensory Thresholds

■ The absolute threshold is _____

_____

_____

■ The difference threshold is _____

_____

_____

_____

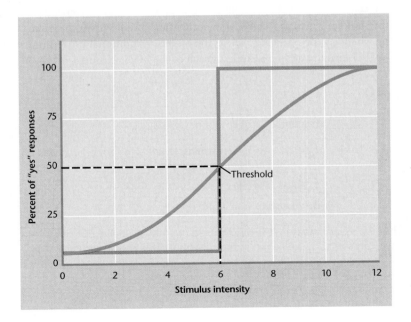

FIGURE **3–1**
Determining a sensory threshold. The red line represents an ideal case: At all intensities below the threshold, the person reports no sensation or no change in intensity; at all intensities above the threshold, the person reports a sensation or a change in intensity. In reality, however, we never come close to the ideal of the red line. The blue line shows the actual responses of a typical person. The threshold is taken as the point at which a person reports a sensation or a change in intensity 50% of the time.

Adding one pound to this barbell would not produce a noticeable difference because one pound would fall below the difference threshold for this amount of weight.

Under normal conditions, absolute thresholds vary according to the level and nature of ongoing sensory stimulation. For example, your threshold for the taste of salt is considerably higher after you eat salted peanuts; and your vision threshold is much higher in the middle of a sunny day than at midnight on a moonless night. In both cases, the absolute threshold rises because our senses automatically adjust to the overall level of stimulation in a particular setting. This process of sensory **adaptation** allows all of our senses to be keenly attuned to numerous environmental cues without getting overloaded. We can hear the breathing of a sleeping baby when we enter a quiet room; but if we are on a city street during rush hour, the traffic noise would be deafening if our ears did not become less sensitive to stimulation. Similarly, adaptation lets us go from a dark room into bright sunshine without experiencing great pain.

Imagine now that you can hear a particular sound. How much stronger must the sound become before you notice that it has grown louder? The smallest change in stimulation that you can detect 50% of the time is called the **difference threshold**, or the **just-noticeable difference (jnd)**. Like the absolute threshold, the difference threshold varies from person to person and from moment to moment for the same person. And, like absolute thresholds, difference thresholds reveal something about the flexibility of sensory systems. For example, adding one pound to a five-pound load will certainly be noticed, so one could conclude that the difference threshold must be considerably less than one pound. Yet adding one pound to a 100-pound load probably would not make much of a difference, so one could conclude that the difference threshold must be considerably more than one pound. But how can the difference threshold (jnd) be both less than and greater than one pound? It turns out that the difference threshold varies according to the strength or intensity of the original stimulus. The greater the stimulus, the greater the change necessary to produce a jnd.

In the 1830s, Ernst Weber (1795–1878) concluded that the difference threshold is a constant fraction or proportion of the original stimulus; his theory is known as **Weber's law.** It is important to note that the values of these fractions vary significantly for the different senses. Hearing, for example, is very sensitive: We can detect a change in sound of 0.3% (one third of 1%). By contrast, producing a jnd in taste requires a 20% change. To return to our earlier example of weight, a change in weight of 2% normally is necessary to produce a jnd. So, adding one pound to a 50-pound load would produce a noticeable difference half the time; adding one pound to a 100-pound load would rarely if ever be noticed.

So far, we have been talking about the general characteristics of sensation, but each of the body's sensory systems works a little differently. Individual sensory systems contain receptor cells that specialize in converting a particular kind of energy into neural signals. The threshold at which this conversion occurs varies from system to system, as do the mechanisms by which sensory data are sent to the brain for additional processing. In the following pages we'll discuss the unique features of each of the major sensory systems.

Check Your Understanding

1. A _____ _____ converts energy into a neural signal.

2. A psychologist who asked you to make a series of judgments to determine whether or not a light was present in an unlighted room would be trying to assess your _____ for perceiving light.

    a. Psychometric function

    c. Response bias

    b. Just-noticeable difference (jnd)

    d. Absolute threshold

3. When we leave bright daylight and enter a dark theater, it is hard to see anything initially. But our eyes slowly become more sensitive to light and, after a while, we can see fairly well even in the dim light. This process is known as _____.

    a. Transduction

    c. Adaptation

    b. The doctrine of specific nerve energies

    d. The difference threshold

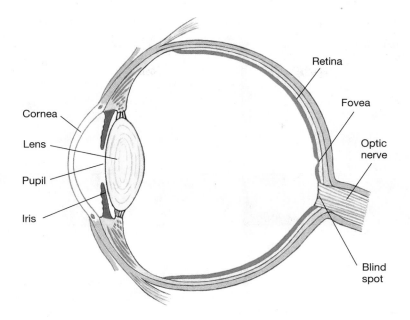

FIGURE 3–2
A cross-section of the human eye.
Light enters the eye through the cornea, passes through the pupil, and is focused by the lens onto the retina.
Source: Adapted from Hubel, 1963.

Vision

Different animal species depend more on some senses than on others. Dogs rely heavily on the sense of smell, bats on hearing, and some fish on taste. But for humans, vision is the most important sense; hence, it has received the most attention from psychologists. To understand vision, we need to look first at the parts of the visual system, beginning with the structure of the eye.

■ THE VISUAL SYSTEM

The structure of the human eye, including the cellular path to the brain, is shown in Figure 3–2. Light enters the eye through the **cornea**, the transparent protective coating over the front part of the eye. It then passes through the **pupil**, the opening in the center of the **iris**, the colored part of the eye. In very bright light, the muscles in the iris contract to make the pupil smaller and thus protect the eye from damage. This contraction also allows better vision in bright light. In dim light, the muscles relax to open the pupil wider and let in as much light as possible.

Inside the pupil, light moves through the **lens**, which focuses it onto the **retina**, the light-sensitive inner lining of the back of the eyeball. Normally, the lens is focused on a middle distance, and it changes shape to focus on objects that are closer or farther away. Directly behind the lens is a depressed spot in the retina called the **fovea**. The fovea occupies the center of the visual field. Images that pass through the lens are in sharpest focus here. Thus, the words you are now reading are hitting the fovea, while the rest of what you see—a desk, walls, or whatever—is striking other areas of the retina.

The Receptor Cells The retina contains the receptor cells responsible for vision. These cells are sensitive to only one small part of the spectrum of electromagnetic energy (Figure 3–3). The shortest wavelengths that can be seen are experienced as violet-blue colors; the longest appear as reds. There are two kinds of receptor cells in the retina—*rods* and *cones*—named for their characteristic shapes (Figure 3–4). **Rods** are receptors that respond only to varying degrees of light and dark. **Cones**, in contrast, allow us to see colors. Because cones are less sensitive to light than rods, they work best in relatively bright light. The more sensitive rods respond to much lower levels of illumination. Rods and cones also differ in the way they connect to the rest of the nervous system. Both rods and cones connect to specialized neurons called **bipolar cells**, so named because they have only one axon and one dendrite. Cones generally connect with only one bipolar cell—a sort of "private line" arrangement. In contrast, it is normal for several rods to share a single bipolar cell.

The Visual System

■ Light enters the eye through the

_____

_____

■ Visual information is conveyed to

the brain via _____

_____

_____

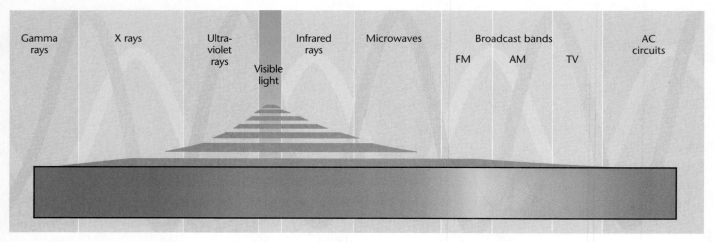

FIGURE 3–3
The electromagnetic spectrum.
The eye is sensitive to only a very small segment of the spectrum, known as visible light.

Taken together, these facts about rods and cones explain why, if one looks directly at a dim star at night, the star may seem to disappear. Because the fovea contains only relatively insensitive cones that connect to single bipolar neurons, it is not very responsive to dim light. If you shift your gaze slightly to the side, however, the light from the dim star falls just outside the fovea where the rods are most numerous. Because the rods are more sensitive to dim light and because they tend to combine with other rods in stimulating bipolar neurons, the area just outside the fovea is most sensitive to dim light.

Conversely, if we want to examine something closely and in detail, we move it into bright light and look directly at it. Stronger light stimulates more cones, which increases the likelihood that bipolar cells will respond. Because cones typically connect one-on-one with

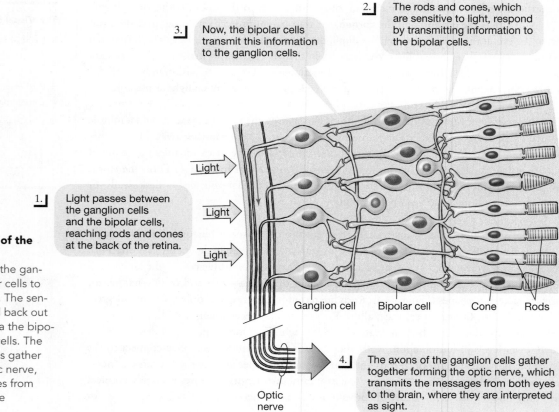

3. Now, the bipolar cells transmit this information to the ganglion cells.

2. The rods and cones, which are sensitive to light, respond by transmitting information to the bipolar cells.

1. Light passes between the ganglion cells and the bipolar cells, reaching rods and cones at the back of the retina.

FIGURE 3–4
A close-up of the layers of the retina.
Light must pass between the ganglion cells and the bipolar cells to reach the rods and cones. The sensory messages then travel back out from the receptor cells, via the bipolar cells, to the ganglion cells. The axons of the ganglion cells gather together to form the optic nerve, which carries the messages from both eyes to the brain (see Figure 3–2).

Ganglion cell   Bipolar cell   Cone   Rods

Optic nerve

4. The axons of the ganglion cells gather together forming the optic nerve, which transmits the messages from both eyes to the brain, where they are interpreted as sight.

SUMMARY TABLE **Rods and Cones**			
TYPE OF RECEPTOR CELL	**FEATURES AND FUNCTIONS**	**LOCATION**	**CONNECTIONS**
Rods	• Highly sensitive to light • Responsible for night vision • Responsible for perception of brightness	• Missing from the fovea • Concentrated just outside the fovea	Typically, many rods connect to a single bipolar cell.
Cones	• Moderately sensitive to light • Most useful in daylight • Responsible for color vision	• Located mainly in the fovea • Concentrated in the center of the fovea	In the fovea, typically, only a single cone connects to a single bipolar cell.

bipolar cells, the message they send to the brain can be quite precise. Thus, **visual acuity**—the ability to distinguish fine details visually—is greatest in the center of your field of vision. To see this for yourself, hold this book about 18 inches from your eyes and look at the "X" in the center of the following line:

This is a test to show how visual X acuity varies across the retina.

Your fovea picks up the "X" and about four letters to each side. This is the area of greatest visual acuity. Notice how your vision drops off for words and letters toward the left or right end of the line.

Adaptation   As we saw earlier in the chapter, *adaptation* is the process by which our senses adjust to different levels of stimulation. In the case of vision, adaptation occurs as the sensitivity of rods and cones changes according to the amount of light available. When you go from bright sunlight into a dimly lit theater, your cones and rods initially are fairly insensitive to light and you can see little as you look for a seat. Over a period of about 30 minutes, first the cones then the rods slowly adapt until they reach their maximum sensitivity. The process by which rods and cones become more sensitive to light in response to lowered levels of illumination is called **dark adaptation**. Problems with dark adaptation account in part for the much greater incidence of highway accidents at night. When people drive at night, their eyes shift from the darkened interior of the car to the road area illuminated by headlights to the darker areas at the side of the road. Unlike the situation in a darkened movie theater, these changing night-driving conditions do not permit complete adaptation to the rapidly changing light conditions.

In the reverse process known as **light adaptation**, the rods and cones become less sensitive to light. By the time you leave the movie theater, your rods and cones have grown very sensitive and all the neurons fire at once when you go into bright outdoor light. You squint and shield your eyes, and your irises contract—all of which reduces the amount of light entering your pupils and striking your retinas. As light adaptation proceeds, the rods and cones become less sensitive to stimulation by light. Within about a minute, rods and cones are fully adapted to the light and shielding your eyes is no longer necessary.

You can observe the effects of dark and light adaptation by staring continuously at the red dot in the center of Figure 3–5 for about 20 seconds. Then, shift your gaze to the dot in the blank white square. You will see a gray-and-white **afterimage** (if you blink your eyes, the illusion will last longer). The reason for the afterimage is that the parts of your retina that were exposed to the dark stripes of the upper square became more sensitive (they "dark adapted"), while the areas that were exposed to the white part of the upper square became less sensitive (they "light adapted"). When you shifted your eyes to the lower square, the less sensitive parts of your retina produced the sensation of gray rather than white and the hypersensitive parts of your retina produced a bright white sensation. This afterimage fades within a minute as the retina adapts again, this time to the solid white square.

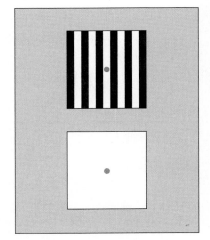

FIGURE **3–5**
An afterimage.
First, stare continuously at the center of the upper square for about 20 seconds, then look at the dot in the lower square. Within a moment, a gray-and-white afterimage should appear inside the lower square.

Consider for a moment what would happen if you were to stare for a long time at the upper square in Figure 3–5 and the image on your retina remained perfectly still. Gradually, all the receptors would adapt—the black and white lines would fade slowly and eventually, you would see nothing at all. If that is hard to imagine, go into a dark room with a penlight and shine the light into one of your eyes from above and to the side of your head. Something resembling the branches of a tree will appear. Those are the blood vessels that run across your retina in front of the rods and cones. Normally, the vessels are invisible because their shadows are held perfectly still on the retina, and the rods and cones behind them adapt completely to their presence. But when you shine the light from an unusual direction, the shadows shift slightly and fall on different rods and cones, which allows you to see the blood vessels.

In the real world, our eyes do not adapt completely because light stimulation is rarely focused on the same receptor cells long enough for them to become totally insensitive. Rather, small involuntary eye movements keep the image moving slightly on the retina, so the receptor cells never have time to adapt completely.

From Eye to Brain Messages from the eye must travel to the brain for a visual experience to occur. As Figure 3–4 shows, the series of connections between eye and brain is quite intricate. To begin with, rods and cones are connected to bipolar cells in many different numbers and combinations. In addition, *interneurons* link receptor cells to one another and bipolar cells to one another. Eventually, these bipolar cells hook up with the **ganglion cells**, leading out of the eye. The axons of the ganglion cells join to form the **optic nerve**, which carries messages from each eye to the brain. The place on the retina where the axons of all the ganglion cells join to form the optic nerve is called the **blind spot**. This area contains no receptor cells. Hence, even when light from a small object is focused directly on the blind spot, the object will not be seen (Figure 3–6).

The primary destination of the optic nerves is the occipital lobe at the back of the head (Figure 2–8). There, brain cells called **feature detectors** are highly specialized to detect particular elements of the visual field. Some detect horizontal or vertical lines. Others register more complex information such as movement, depth, or color. These different types of feature detectors send messages to nearby regions of the cerebral cortex that combine the various pieces of information into a meaningful image, as we will see later in the chapter.

■ COLOR VISION

Unlike many other animal species (such as dogs and cats), humans can see a wide range of colors. The following section discusses characteristics of color vision and considers how the eyes convert light energy into sensations of color.

Properties of Color What do you see when you look at the color solid in Figure 3–7? Most people report that they see some oranges, some yellows, some reds—a number of different colors. These different colors are called **hues**, and to a great extent, the hues you see depend on the wavelength of the light reaching your eyes (Figure 3–3).

Color Vision

■ The three characteristics of color vision are _____

_____

_____

■ The trichromatic theory posits that there are _____

_____

_____

■ The opponent-process theory posits that there are _____

_____

_____

■ Both theories are correct, but

_____

_____

_____

FIGURE **3–6**
Finding your blind spot.
To locate your blind spot, hold this book about a foot away from your eyes. Then, close your right eye, stare at the X, and slowly move the book toward you and away from you until the red dot disappears.

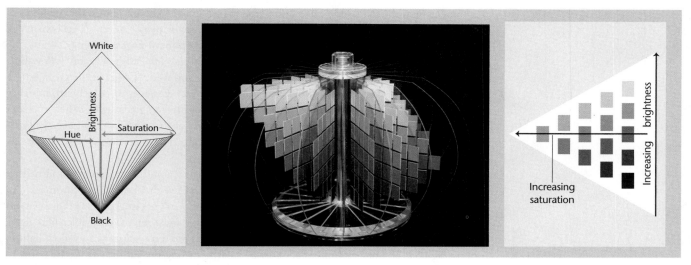

FIGURE 3–7
The color solid.
In the center portion of the figure, known as a color solid, the dimension of *hue* is represented around the circumference. *Saturation* ranges along the radius from the inside to the outside of the solid. *Brightness* varies along the vertical axis. The drawing at the left illustrates this arrangement schematically. The illustration at the right shows changes in saturation and brightness for the same hue.

Now look at the triangle of green colors on the right side of Figure 3–7. Although each color patch on the triangle is the same hue, the green color is purest toward the left side of the triangle. The purity of a hue is its **saturation**.

Look again at the color solid, but this time, squint your eyes so that you can barely see the colors. The colors appear darker; in fact, the colors toward the bottom of the color solid may look almost black. You have just reduced the **brightness** of the colors. The dimension of brightness depends largely on the strength of the light entering your eyes.

Hue, saturation, and brightness are three separate aspects of our color experience. Although we can distinguish only about 150 hues, gradations of saturation and brightness within those 150 hues allow us to see more than 2 million different colors. Some of this variety is captured in Figure 3–7.

Theories of Color Vision   For centuries, people have known that it is possible to produce all 150 hues simply by mixing together a few lights of different colors such as red, green and blue. In the nineteenth century, the German physiologist Hermann von Helmholtz (1821–1894) reasoned that the eye must contain three types of cones: some that are sensitive to red light, others that pick up green, and still others that respond most strongly to blue-violet. According to this view, color experiences come from mixing the signals from the three receptors. Helmholtz's explanation of color vision is known as **trichromatic** (three-color) **theory**. But this theory has some shortcomings. For example, people with the two most common forms of color blindness see the world in terms of only reds and greens or of only blues and yellows. Trichromatic theory does not clearly explain why that should be the case. Moreover, people with normal color vision never see "reddish green" or "yellowish blue." Why not? And what accounts for color afterimages such as that in Figure 3–8?

In 1872, another German scientist, Ewald Hering (1834–1918), proposed the existence of three pairs of color receptors: a yellow-blue pair and a red-green pair that determine the hue one sees; and a black-white pair that determines the brightness of the colors one sees. The yellow-blue pair can relay messages about yellow or blue, but not messages about yellow

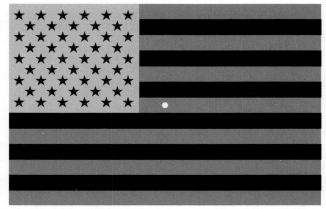

FIGURE 3–8
Afterimage.
Stare at the white spot in the center of the flag for about 30 seconds. Then, look at a blank piece of white paper and you will see an afterimage in complementary colors. Although the flag is printed in green, yellow, and black, its afterimage will appear in red, blue, and white.

and blue light at the same time; the same is true for red-green receptors. Thus, the members of each pair work in opposition to each other, which explains why people never see yellowish blue or reddish green. Hering's theory became known as the **opponent-process theory**.

Opponent-process theory does a good job of explaining red-green and yellow-blue color blindness. It also explains color afterimages. While you were looking at the green stripes in Figure 3–8, the red-green receptors were sending "green" messages to your brain, but they were also adapting to the stimulation by becoming less sensitive to green light. When you later looked at the white page (made up of light from all parts of the spectrum), the red-green receptors responded vigorously to wavelengths in the red portion of the spectrum, so you saw red stripes instead of green.

The two theories of color vision have coexisted for more than a century, and neither has succeeded in ousting the other. Today, psychologists believe that both the trichromatic and opponent-process theories are correct, but at different stages of the visual process. There are indeed three kinds of cones for color in the retina. Some are most sensitive to violet-blue light, others are most responsive to green light, and still others are most sensitive to yellow light— not red light, as Helmholtz contended. However, farther along the pathway from the retina to the brain (in the bipolar and ganglion cells) and in the brain itself, colors are processed in opponent process fashion.

Check Your Understanding

1. Match the terms with the appropriate definitions.

_____ Cornea   **a.** Colored part of the eye

_____ Pupil   **b.** Center of the visual field

_____ Iris   **c.** Opening in the iris through which light enters

_____ Lens   **d.** Protective layer over front part of the eye

_____ Fovea   **e.** Contains the receptor cells that respond to light

_____ Retina   **f.** Focuses light onto the retina

2. Imagine that you are wearing a multicolored shirt when you go out for a short walk on a dark night. During the walk, you look down and notice that all the colors look like patches of gray. The reason you no longer see the colors as different hues is that:

a. You are seeing primarily with the cones.

b. You are seeing primarily with the rods.

c. The image of your shirt is falling on your blind spot.

d. The colors have become saturated.

Hearing

If you had to make a choice, would you give up your sight or your hearing? Presented with this hypothetical choice, most people say they would give up hearing first. But the great teacher and activist Helen Keller, who was blind and deaf from infancy, regretted more than anything else her inability to hear.

> I am just as deaf as I am blind. The problems of deafness are deeper and more complex, if not more important than those of blindness. Deafness is a much worse misfortune. For it means the loss of the most vital stimulus—the sound of the voice that brings language, sets thoughts astir and keeps us in the intellectual company of man. (Keller, 1948; quoted in D. Ackerman, 1995, pp. 191–192)

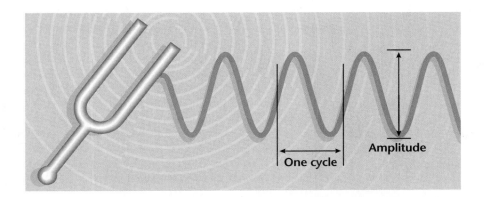

FIGURE **3–9**
Sound waves.
As the tuning fork vibrates, it alternately compresses and expands the molecules of air, creating a sound wave.

■ **SOUND**

An ancient question asks, "If a tree falls in the forest and no one is present, is there a sound?" One of the major themes of this chapter is that sights, sounds, and other sensations are *psychological experiences* created by the brain in response to stimulation. Put another way, psychologists distinguish between what happens in the environment, such as *sound waves*, and what people experience, such as **sound**—a psychological experience created by the brain in response to changes in air pressure received by the auditory system. Thus, a psychologist would answer, "No. There is no sound. The tree creates sound waves when it falls, but if no one is there to hear them, no sound is made."

Sound waves are changes in air pressure caused when molecules of air or fluid collide with one another and move apart. Sound waves that one hears as a pure tone can be pictured as the sine wave shown in Figure 3–9. The tuning fork vibrates, causing the molecules of air first to contract then to expand. The **frequency** of the waves is measured in cycles per second, expressed in a unit called **hertz** (Hz). Frequency primarily determines the **pitch** (highness or lowness) of the sound. The human ear responds to frequencies from approximately 20 Hz to 20,000 Hz. Cats can hear noises as high as 64,000 Hz, and mice apparently can hear sounds (and sing "songs") up to 100,000 Hz. A double bass can reach down to about 50 Hz; a piano can reach as high as 5000 Hz.

The height of the sound wave represents its **amplitude**, which, together with frequency, determines the perceived loudness of a sound. Loudness is measured by a unit called **decibel**, which is the smallest difference in sound level that the human ear can discern (Figure 3–10).

ENDURING ISSUES STABILITY/CHANGE

Aging

As people grow older, they lose some of their ability to hear soft sounds, but they often can hear loud sounds as well as ever. That is why when elderly people ask others to speak louder and the request is obeyed, they occasionally will respond with, "There's no need to shout!"

Like the other senses, hearing undergoes adaptation and can function optimally under a wide variety of conditions. City residents enjoying a weekend in the country, for example, may be struck at first by how quiet everything seems. But, after a while, they may find that the country starts to sound very noisy because they have adapted to the quieter environment.

Sound

■ Sound is an experience created by

■ Frequency of sound waves is the primary determinant of _____

The Ear

■ When sound waves reach the eardrum, _____

■ The receptor cells for hearing are

Pitch Discrimination

■ According to frequency theory, the vibration _____

■ According to place theory, a pitch

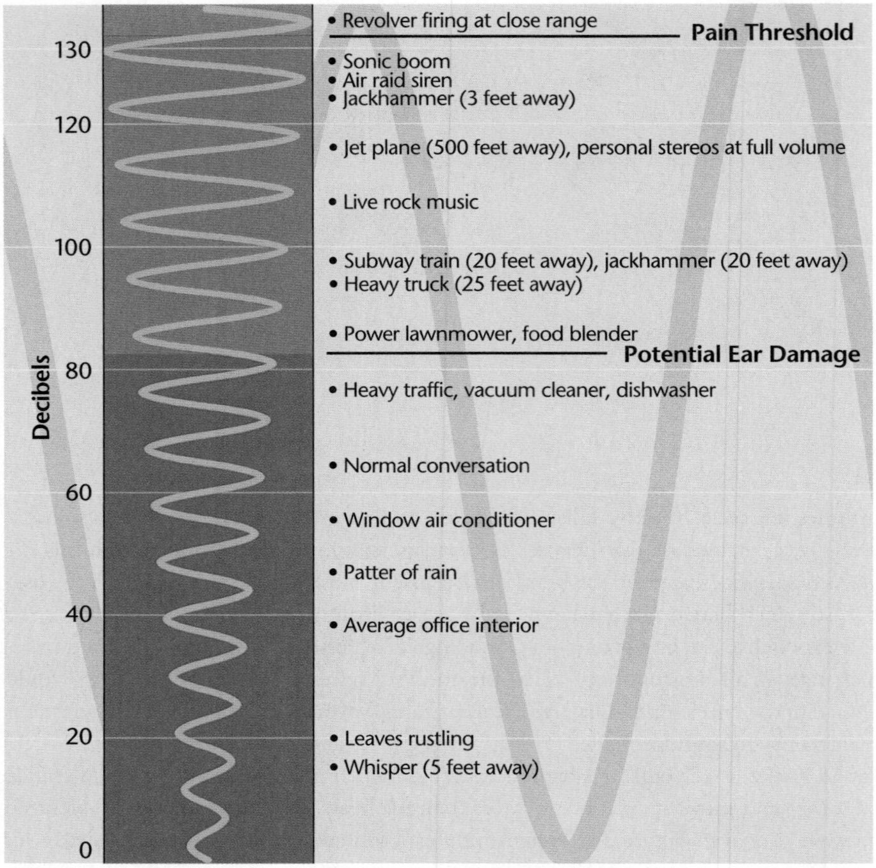

FIGURE 3–10
A decibel scale for several common sounds.
Prolonged exposure to sounds above 85 decibels can cause permanent damage to the ears, as can even brief exposure to sounds near the pain threshold.

Source: Adapted from T. Dunkle (1982, April). The sound of silence. *Science '82*, 30–33.

■ THE EAR

Hearing begins when sound waves are gathered by the outer ear and passed along to the eardrum (Figure 3–11), causing it to vibrate. The quivering of the eardrum prompts three tiny bones in the middle ear—the *hammer*, the *anvil*, and the *stirrup*—to hit each other in sequence and thus carry the vibrations to the inner ear. The last of these three bones, the stirrup, is attached to a membrane called the **oval window**. Vibrations of the oval window, in turn, are transmitted to the fluid inside a snail-shaped structure called the **cochlea**. The cochlea is divided lengthwise by the **basilar membrane**, which is stiff near the oval window but gradually becomes more flexible toward its other end. When the fluid in the cochlea begins to move, the basilar membrane ripples in response.

Lying on top of the basilar membrane and moving in sync with it is the **organ of Corti**. Here, the messages from the sound waves finally reach the receptor cells for the sense of hearing: thousands of tiny hair cells embedded in the organ of Corti. As shown in Figure 3–12, each hair cell is topped by a bundle of fibers. These fibers are pushed and pulled by the vibrations of the basilar membrane. When these fibers move, the receptor cells send a signal through the **auditory nerve** to the medulla, part of the brain stem (refer to Figure 2–6). The brain pools the information from thousands of hair cells to create sounds.

Neural Connections   The sense of hearing is truly bilateral: Each ear sends messages to both cerebral hemispheres. The switching station where the nerve fibers from the ears cross over is in the medulla (refer to Figure 2–7). From the medulla, other nerve fibers carry the messages from the ears to the higher parts of the brain. Some messages go to the brain centers that coordinate the movements of the eyes, head, and ears. Others travel through the reticular formation (which we examined in Chapter 2). But the primary destinations for these auditory messages are the auditory areas in the temporal lobes of the two cerebral hemispheres

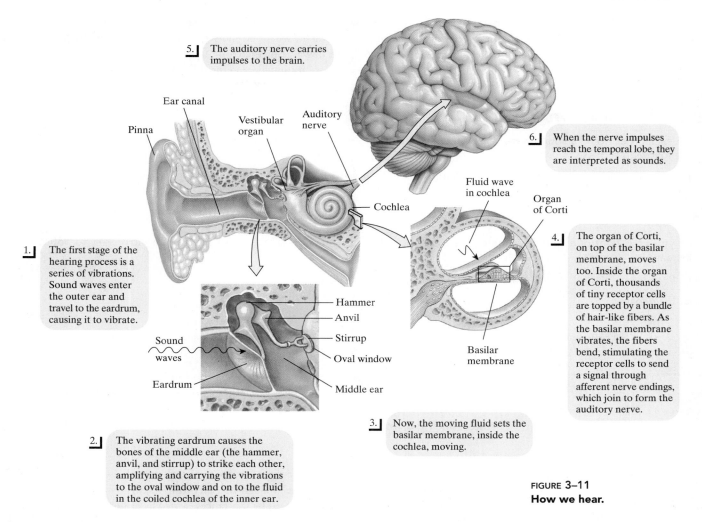

5. The auditory nerve carries impulses to the brain.

6. When the nerve impulses reach the temporal lobe, they are interpreted as sounds.

1. The first stage of the hearing process is a series of vibrations. Sound waves enter the outer ear and travel to the eardrum, causing it to vibrate.

4. The organ of Corti, on top of the basilar membrane, moves too. Inside the organ of Corti, thousands of tiny receptor cells are topped by a bundle of hair-like fibers. As the basilar membrane vibrates, the fibers bend, stimulating the receptor cells to send a signal through afferent nerve endings, which join to form the auditory nerve.

2. The vibrating eardrum causes the bones of the middle ear (the hammer, anvil, and stirrup) to strike each other, amplifying and carrying the vibrations to the oval window and on to the fluid in the coiled cochlea of the inner ear.

3. Now, the moving fluid sets the basilar membrane, inside the cochlea, moving.

FIGURE 3–11
How we hear.

(Figure 2–8). En route to the temporal lobes, auditory messages pass through at least four lower brain centers where auditory information becomes more precisely coded. One aspect of sound—loudness—seems to depend primarily on how many neurons are activated: The more cells that fire, the louder the sound seems to be. The coding of messages regarding pitch is more complicated.

■ PITCH DISCRIMINATION

For frequencies up to about 1000 Hz, the vibrations of the basilar membrane as a whole—not just parts of it—are translated into an equivalent frequency of nerve impulses. Neurons typically cannot fire more rapidly than a thousand times each second, and for sound waves between 1000 and 4000 Hz, auditory neurons must fire in sequence: One neuron fires, then a second one, and then a third. By then, the first neuron has had time to recover and can fire again. In this way, a set of neurons together, firing in sequence, can send a more rapid series of impulses to the brain than any single neuron could send by itself. This explanation of pitch discrimination is known as **frequency theory**.

For sound waves above about 4000 Hz, the experience of pitch depends on the place on the basilar membrane where the message is strongest (thus the name, **place theory**). High-frequency sounds cause the greatest vibration at the stiff base of the basilar membrane; low-frequency sounds resonate most strongly at the opposite end. The brain detects the location of the most intense nerve-cell activity and uses this to determine the pitch of a sound. Georg von

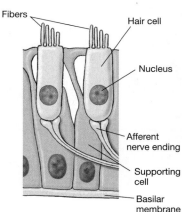

FIGURE 3–12
A detailed drawing of a hair cell.
At the top of each hair cell is a bundle of fibers. If the fibers bend as much as 100 trillionths of a meter, the receptor cells transmit a sensory message to the brain.

Source: Adapted from "The Hair Cells of the Inner Ear," by A. J. Hudspeth, © 1983. Illustrated by Bunji Tagawa for *Scientific American*. Adapted with permission from the Estate of Bunji Tagawa.

Bekesy (1899–1972), who was interested in telephone design, won the Nobel Prize in 1961 for a series of ingenious experiments in which he showed that at low frequencies, the entire basilar membrane moves up and down as predicted by frequency theory. But at higher frequencies, the pitch of sounds is more accurately accounted for by place theory.

Check Your Understanding

1. In which order would a sound wave reach the following structures when traveling from the outer ear to the inner ear? Number the following terms in the correct order.

   a. _____ Oval window   **d.** _____ Auditory nerve

   b. _____ Anvil   **e.** _____ Eardrum

   c. _____ Cochlea

2. As you sit in front of a sound generator, the frequency of the sound is gradually increased. You are most likely to notice an increase in:

   a. Pitch   **c.** Saturation

   b. Loudness   **d.** Overtones

The Other Senses

Psychologists have focused most of their attention on vision and hearing because humans rely primarily on these two senses to gather information about their environment. However, other senses are also at play, even when we are less conscious of them. Let's begin with the chemical senses—smell and taste.

Smell

- Airborne molecules stimulate the
  _____
  _____

■ SMELL

Unlike many lower animals that must use their noses to detect mates, predators, and prey, humans do not depend on their sense of smell for survival. Nevertheless, the sense of smell in humans is incredibly sensitive. Smell is activated by substances carried by airborne molecules that enter the nose. Certain substances that give off a large number of molecules and that dissolve easily in the moist, fatty tissues of the nose can be detected in incredibly small amounts. Decayed cabbage, lemons, and rotten eggs are examples.

The millions of receptors for smell are located high in each nasal cavity—in a patch of tissue about half the size of a postage stamp. The axons from these receptors carry messages directly to the **olfactory bulb** in each cerebral hemisphere (Figure 2–7). These fibers do not pass through the thalamus, as other sensory fibers do, thus the sense of smell's route to the cerebral cortex is the most direct. The olfactory bulbs do some recoding, and then the messages are routed to the brain, which results in our ability to recognize and remember nearly 10,000 different smells. Most mammals, including humans, have a second sensory system devoted to the sense of smell—which some animals use for communicating sexual, aggressive, or territorial signals. Receptors located in the roof of the nasal cavity detect chemicals called **pheromones**, which can have quite specific and powerful effects on behavior.

Taste

- The five basic taste qualities are
  _____
  _____

- The receptor cells for taste are
  contained in _____
  _____
  _____

■ TASTE

At the outset, *taste* must be distinguished from *flavor*, which is a complex interaction between taste and smell. When you were young and your parents insisted that you "Eat your vegetables," you may have resorted to the age-old trick of holding your nose while chewing. If so, hopefully you noticed that most of the food's flavor disappeared and you were able to experience only the five basic taste qualities: sweet, sour, salty, bitter and umami (umami accounts for our sensitivity to monosodium glutamate—MSG—and related proteins). The receptor cells for the sense of taste are housed in the **taste buds**, most of which are found on the tip, sides, and back of the tongue. The tip of the tongue is most sensitive to sweetness and saltiness;

Differences in Odor Sensitivity

Numerous studies confirm that women generally have a better sense of smell than do men (Dalton, Doolittle, & Breslin, 2002). Age also makes a difference: Generally, the ability to smell is sharpest during the early adult years—20 to 40 years of age (Doty, 1989; Schiffman, 1997). Of the people tested by Doty and his colleagues, one quarter of those over the age of 65 and half of those over the age of 80 had completely lost their ability to smell. In contrast, dogs have extraordinarily sharp senses of smell, in large part because they have more than 200 million smell receptors (compared with only about 10 million receptors in humans). Because the sense of smell adapts quickly, some differences between people are simply the result of adaptation. For example, people who live in a paper-mill town rarely notice the strong smell that is so obvious to visitors—not because their olfactory system works differently but simply because it has adapted to that particular smell. Similarly, people who eat a lot of garlic rarely notice the smell of garlic on their breath that is so quickly apparent to anyone standing near them.

the back, to bitterness; and the sides, to sourness (Figure 3–13). It is a fact that the number of taste buds decreases with age, which helps explain why older people often lose interest in food—they simply cannot taste it as well as they used to.

The taste buds are embedded in the tongue's papillae, which are the bumps on your tongue that you can see in the mirror. When you eat something, the chemical substances in the food dissolve in saliva and go into the crevices between the papillae, where they come into contact with the taste buds. In turn, your taste buds release a neurotransmitter that causes adjacent neurons to fire, sending a nerve impulse to the parietal lobes of the brain and to the limbic system.

Taste, as do the other senses, experiences adaptation. When you first start eating salted peanuts or potato chips, the saltiness is quite strong, but after a while it becomes less noticeable. Furthermore, exposure to one quality of taste can modify other taste sensations. Most of us would not choose to suck on a lemon just before eating chocolate—the sourness of the lemon would significantly alter the sweetness of the chocolate.

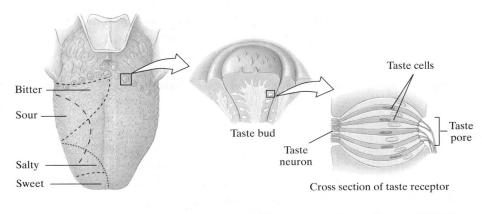

Bitter

Sour

Salty

Sweet

Taste bud

Taste neuron

Taste cells

Taste pore

Cross section of taste receptor

1. Different areas on the tongue are slightly more sensitive to different tastes.

2. When we eat, chemicals in the food dissolve in saliva and come into contact with the taste cells (receptors) within the taste buds.

3. Now, adjacent neurons fire, sending nerve impulses to the brain's parietal lobe, where the messages are perceived as taste.

FIGURE **3–13**
The structure of a taste bud.
The sensory receptors for taste are found primarily on the tongue. Taste cells can detect only sweet, sour, salty, bitter, and umami qualities. All other tastes result from different combinations of these taste sensations.

Kinesthetic and Vestibular Senses

- The kinesthetic senses provide information about _____

- The vestibular senses provide information about _____

The Skin Senses

- The skin contains the receptors for the _____, but the brain draws on many other _____ when interpreting messages from _____

Pain

- Damage to the body often causes _____

- There is no simple relationship between pain receptors and _____

- When the body is injured, information travels to the _____

This dancer is using information provided by her kinesthetic and vestibular senses. Her kinesthetic senses are relaying messages pertaining to muscle strain and movements; her vestibular senses are supplying feedback about her body position in space.

■ KINESTHETIC AND VESTIBULAR SENSES

The **kinesthetic senses** provide information about muscle movement, changes in posture, and strain on muscles and joints. Specialized nerve endings called *stretch receptors* are attached to muscle fibers. Different nerve endings called *Golgi tendon organs* are attached to the tendons, which connect muscle to bones. Together, these two types of receptors provide constant feedback from the stretching and contraction of individual muscles. The information from these receptors travels via the spinal cord to the cortex of the parietal lobes, the same brain area that perceives the sense of touch.

The **vestibular senses** provide information about one's orientation, position, or movement in space. As does hearing, the vestibular sense originates in the inner ear. As hair cells in the *semicircular canals* are moved to and fro, they send messages to the brain about the speed and direction of body rotation. Similarly, movement forward, backward, up, or down causes tiny crystals in the *vestibular sacs* (between the semicircular canals and the cochlea) to bend bundles of hair cells that, in turn, send a sensory message to the brain.

■ THE SKIN SENSES

Skin is our largest sense organ. For some perspective, a person 6 feet tall has about 21 square feet of skin. Skin contains receptors for the sense of touch, which plays an important role in human interaction and emotion. In most societies, hellos and good-byes are accompanied by shaking hands, hugging, and other gestures involving touch. And in most cultures, lovers express their affection by kissing, holding hands, and caressing. Touching and being touched by others bridges, at least momentarily, our isolation. Of all our senses, then, touch may be the most comforting.

The skin senses are remarkably sensitive. For example, skin displacement of as little as 0.00004 of an inch can result in a sensation of pressure. Moreover, various parts of the body differ greatly in their sensitivity to pressure: A person's face and fingertips are extremely sensitive, whereas the legs, feet, and back are much less so. Braille touch reading, which involves the identification of tiny raised dot patterns distributed over a very small area, is possible because of this remarkable sensitivity in the fingertips.

In a similar way as the other senses, the skin senses undergo various kinds of sensory adaptation. When we first get into a bath, it may be uncomfortably hot; but after a few minutes, our body adapts to the heat, just as our eyes adapt to darkness. Skin senses are also influenced by our expectations. Getting tickled by someone, for example, makes the skin senses respond with excitement, but when one tickles oneself, no similar effect is produced. Clearly, the brain draws on many sources of information when interpreting the sense of touch.

The skin's numerous nerve receptors, distributed in varying concentrations throughout its surface, send nerve fibers to the brain by two routes. Some information goes through the medulla and the thalamus, and from there, to the sensory cortex in the parietal lobe of the brain—which is where our experiences of touch, pressure, and so on arise (Figure 2–8). Other information goes through the thalamus then on to the reticular formation, which, as we saw in Chapter 2, is responsible for either arousing the nervous system or quieting it down.

■ PAIN

To a great extent, a full understanding of the sensation of pain remains a puzzle. An old adage holds that pain is nature's way of telling us that something is wrong; and it does seem reasonable to assume that damage to the body causes pain. But in many cases, actual physical injury is not accompanied by pain. Athletes injured during a game often feel no pain until the excitement of competition has passed. Many soldiers wounded during battle do not ask for painkillers. Conversely, some people feel pain without having been injured at all or only long after an injury has healed. Finally, there is no simple relationship between pain receptors and the experience of pain. In fact, scientists have had great difficulty even finding pain receptors.

When body tissue is damaged, information about the injury travels to the spinal cord where, according to the **gate control theory** of pain, a "neurological gate" in the spinal cord controls the transmission of pain impulses to the brain (Melzack, 1980; Melzack, & Katz,

2004). Pain is experienced more when the gate is open than when it is closed. Whether the gate is closed or open depends on a complex competition between two different types of sensory nerve fibers—when stimulated, large fibers "close the gate" and small fibers "open the gate," enabling the transmission of pain messages to the brain.

When the pain messages reach the brain, a complex series of reactions occurs. As we saw in Chapter 2, the sympathetic nervous system springs into action. The nervous system and endocrine system go on alert to help deal with the crisis. Meanwhile, chemicals to reduce or stop the pain messages may be released both in the brain and in the spinal cord. Certain areas of the brain stem also may reduce the flow of incoming pain information by sending signals to fibers in the spinal cord to partially or completely close the "gate." These processes account for the fact that, despite an injury, little or no pain may be experienced.

Glowing coals smolder under the feet of these participants in an annual ritual at Mt. Takao, Japan. How do they do it? Is it mind over matter—the human ability to sometimes "turn off" pain sensations? The secret in this case may actually lie more in the coals than in the men. Because wood is a poor conductor of heat, quickly walking over wood coals may not be that painful after all.

ENDURING ISSUES DIVERSITY/UNIVERSALITY

The Experience of Pain

Individuals vary widely both in their pain threshold (the amount of stimulation required to feel pain) and their pain tolerance (the amount of pain with which they can cope). Most people do experience pain, but there is no absolute correspondence between the perception of pain and the amount of tissue damage sustained. How, then, do psychologists explain why the experience of pain differs among individuals? According to the gate control theory, these differences are governed primarily by the number of small and large sensory nerve fibers in a person. Also, some people may have faulty neurological gates, resulting in a greater or lesser experience of pain than others. To the extent that these differences are hereditary, it follows that some people may be born with greater pain sensitivity than other people.

Check Your Understanding

1. The basic tastes are _____, _____, _____, _____, and _____.

2. Our _____ sense provides awareness of our body's position in space.

3. George suffers from chronic back pain. His doctor suggests that he try a form of therapy in which electrical stimulation is applied to his back. You recognize that this therapy is based on the idea that stimulating large sensory nerves in the spinal cord can prevent the sensation of pain, making it an application of the _____ theory of pain.

   a. Gate control

   b. Contrastimulation

   c. Free nerve ending

   d. Patterned firing

Perception

Our senses provide us with raw data about the external world. But unless this raw information is interpreted, it is nothing more than what William James (1890) called a "booming, buzzing confusion." The eye records patterns of lightness and darkness, but it does not "see" a bird flitting from branch to branch. The eardrum vibrates in a particular fashion, but it does not "hear" a symphony. Deciphering meaningful patterns in the jumble of sensory information is what is meant by perception. But how does perception differ from sensation?

FIGURE **3–14**
Perceiving a pattern.

Perception is the brain's process of organizing and interpreting sensory information to give it meaning. Look at Figure 3–14. At first glance, most people see only an assortment of black blotches. However, when they are told that the blotches represent a person riding a horse, suddenly their perceptual experience changes. What was meaningless sensory information now takes shape as a horse and rider. Figure 3–15 is similar. Yet another graphic illustration of the way perception transforms mere sensations into a meaningful whole can be seen in Figure 1–1. Although most viewers tend to perceive a white triangle in the center of the pattern, the sensory input consists only of three circles from which "pie slices" have been cut and three 60-degree angles. In each case, the brain creates perceptual experiences that go beyond what is sensed directly.

How do people see objects and shapes? Psychologists assume that perception begins with some real-world object with real-world properties "out there." Psychologists call that object, along with its important perceptual properties, the *distal stimulus*. People never experience the distal stimulus directly, however. Energy from it (or, in the case of the chemical senses, molecules from it) must activate the sensory system. The information that reaches our sensory receptors is called the *proximal stimulus*. Although the distal stimulus and the proximal stimulus are never the same thing, one's perception of the distal stimulus usually is very accurate. However, sometimes one can perceive things that could not possibly exist. The trident shown in Figure 3–16 exemplifies such an "impossible" figure; on closer inspection, the object that was "recognized" really is not there. In all these cases, the brain actively creates and organizes perceptual experiences out of raw sensory data—sometimes even from data we are not aware of receiving.

FIGURE **3–15**
Random dots or something more?
This pattern does not give us enough cues to allow us to easily distinguish the figure of the Dalmatian dog from the ground behind it.
Source: Gregory, 1970.

■ PERCEPTUAL ORGANIZATION

As Chapter 1 showed, Gestalt psychologists believe that the brain creates a coherent perceptual experience that is more than simply the sum of the available sensory information and that it does so in predictable ways. One important part of the perceptual process involves being able to distinguish *figures* from the *ground* against which they appear. A colorfully upholstered chair stands out from the bare walls of a room. A marble statue is perceived as a whole figure separate from the red brick wall behind it. The figure versus ground distinction pertains to all the senses, not just vision. One can distinguish a violin solo against the ground of a symphony orchestra, a single voice amid cocktail-party chatter, and the smell of roses in a florist's shop. In all these instances, some objects are perceived as "figures" and other sensory information is seen as "background."

Sometimes, however, there are not enough cues in a pattern to permit easy distinction between a figure and its ground. The horse and rider in Figure 3–14 illustrate this problem, as does the spotted dog investigating shadowy surroundings in Figure 3–15. It is hard to distinguish the dog because it has few visible contours of its own, and as a result, it seems to have no more form than the background. This is the principle behind camouflage: to make a figure blend into its background.

Sometimes, even a figure with clear contours can be perceived in two very different ways because it is unclear which part of the stimulus is the figure and which is the ground (see Figures 3–17 and 3–18). At first glance, one perceives figures against a specific background, but if the illustrations are stared at, the figures and the ground reverse, making for

FIGURE 3–16
An optical illusion.
In the case of the trident, we go beyond what is sensed (blue lines on flat white paper) to perceive a three-dimensional object that is not really there.

Perceptual Organization

■ Perception is the brain's process of
_____

■ Gestalt psychologists point out that
_____

■ Normally, people are able to distinguish _____
_____

■ People tend to perceive objects as belonging together when _____
_____

FIGURE 3–17
The reversible figure and ground in this M. C. Escher woodcut cause us first to see black devils then to see white angels in each of the rings.

FIGURE 3–18
Figure-ground relationship . . . How do you perceive this figure?
Do you see a goblet or the silhouettes of a man and a woman? Both interpretations are possible, but not at the same time. Reversible figures like this work because it is unclear which part of the stimulus is the figure and which is the neutral ground against which the figure is perceived.

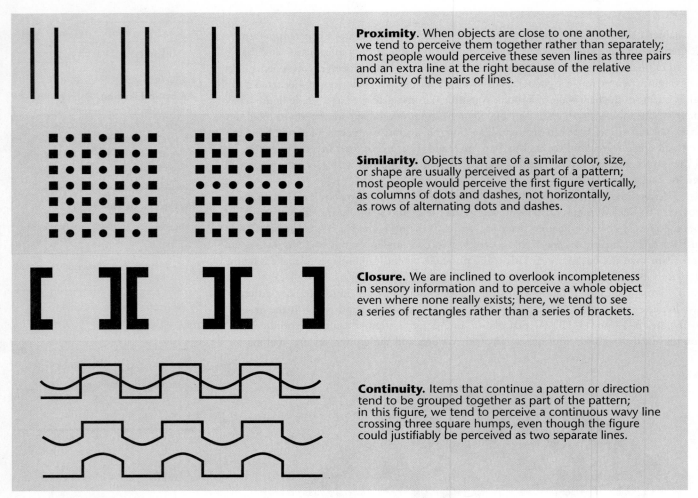

Proximity. When objects are close to one another, we tend to perceive them together rather than separately; most people would perceive these seven lines as three pairs and an extra line at the right because of the relative proximity of the pairs of lines.

Similarity. Objects that are of a similar color, size, or shape are usually perceived as part of a pattern; most people would perceive the first figure vertically, as columns of dots and dashes, not horizontally, as rows of alternating dots and dashes.

Closure. We are inclined to overlook incompleteness in sensory information and to perceive a whole object even where none really exists; here, we tend to see a series of rectangles rather than a series of brackets.

Continuity. Items that continue a pattern or direction tend to be grouped together as part of the pattern; in this figure, we tend to perceive a continuous wavy line crossing three square humps, even though the figure could justifiably be perceived as two separate lines.

FIGURE 3–19
Gestalt principles of perceptual organization.

two very different perceptions of the same illustration. The artwork or distal stimulus has not changed, but the perception of it has.

Figure 3–19 demonstrates some other important principles of perceptual organization. As the Gestalt psychologists suggested, sensory information is used to create a perception that is more than just the sum of the parts. Although this process sometimes can cause problems, the perceptual tendency to "fill in the blanks" usually broadens one's understanding of the world. In its search for meaning, the brain tries to fill in missing information, group various objects together, see whole objects, and hear meaningful sounds, rather than just accept random bits of raw sensory data.

■ PERCEPTUAL CONSTANCIES

Surprisingly, people often continue to have the same perceptual experience even as sensory data change. **Perceptual constancy** refers to this tendency to perceive objects as relatively stable and unchanging despite changing sensory information. Once a stable perception of an object has been formed, it can be recognized from almost any position, at almost any distance, and under almost any illumination. A white house looks like a white house by day or by night and from any angle, because, in part, the brain "sees" it as the same house. The sensory information may change as illumination and perspective change, but the object is perceived as constant. Without this ability, humans would find the world very confusing.

Perceptual Constancies

■ Perceptual constancy refers to the tendency to _____

_____

_____

■ The major perceptual constancies include_____

_____

_____

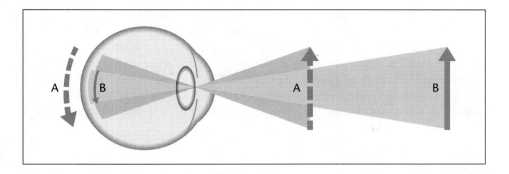

FIGURE **3–20**
The relationship between distance and the size of the retinal image.
Object A and object B are the same size, but A, being much closer to the eye, casts a much larger image on the retina.

People tend to perceive familiar objects at their true size, regardless of the size the image casts on the retina. As Figure 3–20 shows, the farther away an object is from the lens of the eye, the smaller the retinal image it casts. One might guess that a woman some distance away is 5 feet 4 inches tall when, in reality, she is 5 feet 8 inches. But hardly anyone would perceive her as being 3 feet tall, no matter how far away she is because experience has taught the brain that adults are seldom that short. **Size constancy** depends partly on experience—information about the relative sizes of objects stored in memory—and partly on distance cues.

Familiar objects also tend to be seen as having a constant shape, even though the retinal images they cast change as they are viewed from different angles. This is called **shape constancy**. A dinner plate is perceived as a circle even when it is tilted and the retinal image is oval. A rectangular door will project a rectangular image on the retina only when it is viewed directly from the front. From any other angle, it casts a trapezoidal image on the retina, but it is not perceived as suddenly having become a trapezoidal door (Figure 3–21).

Similarly, familiar objects are perceived as keeping their colors, regardless of the information that reaches the eye. If, for example, you own a red automobile, you will see it as red whether it is on a brightly lit street or in a dark garage, where the low light may send your eye a message that it is closer to brown or black than red. But **color constancy** does not always hold true. When objects are unfamiliar or there are no customary color cues to use as a guide, color constancy may be distorted—as when a woman buys a sweater in a brightly lit store only to discover that in ordinary daylight, it is not the shade she thought it was.

Brightness constancy means that even though the amount of light available to the eyes varies greatly over the course of a day, the perceived brightness of familiar objects hardly varies. A sheet of white paper is perceived as being brighter than a piece of coal whether these objects are viewed in candlelight or under bright sunlight. This may seem obvious, but bear in mind that coal in sunlight reflects more light than white paper in candlelight, yet people always see the white paper as brighter. The explanation for brightness constancy is that we do not base our judgment of brightness on the *absolute* amount of light that the object reflects. Rather, the brain assesses the *relative* reflection compared with the surrounding objects. Whether the white paper

FIGURE **3–21**
Examples of shape constancy.
Even though the image of the door on the retina changes greatly as the door opens, we still perceive the door as being rectangular.

Source: From *Foundations of Psychology* by E. G. Boring, H. S. Langfeld, & H. P. Weld (1976). Reprinted by permission of John Wiley & Sons.

FIGURE 3–22
Look again!
Context, hair style, and head shape lead us to believe that this is a picture of former President Clinton and former Vice President Gore when, in reality, Clinton's face is superimposed over the face of Gore.
Source: APA Monitor, 1997.

Perception of Distance and Depth

- Monocular cues to distance and depth include_____

    _____

    _____

- Binocular cues to distance and depth include_____

    _____

    _____

Visual Illusions

- Perceptual illusions occur because

    _____

    _____

- In some cases, the stimulus contains

    _____

    _____

    _____

Observer Characteristics

- Perceptual experiences are shaped by_____

    _____

    _____

---

and the dark coal are in candlelight or bright sunlight, the paper always reflects relatively more light than the dark coal and is, therefore, perceived as being brighter.

Memory and experience play important roles in perceptual constancy. If, in Figure 3–22, you see former President Bill Clinton and Vice President Al Gore, look again! Clinton's face has been superimposed over Gore's. Because people focus on the perceptual cues of head shape, hair style, and context (the microphones and the president are in front of the vice president, as protocol requires), they perceive the more likely image of the president and vice president standing together.

■ PERCEPTION OF DISTANCE AND DEPTH

We are constantly judging the distance between ourselves and other objects. When we walk through a classroom, our perception of distance helps us to avoid bumping into desks or tripping over the wastebasket. If we reach out to pick up a pencil, we automatically judge how far to extend our hand. We also assess the depth of objects—how much total space they occupy. We use many cues to determine the distance and the depth of objects. Some of these cues depend on visual messages that one eye alone can transmit; these are called **monocular cues**. Others, known as **binocular cues**, require the use of both eyes. Having two eyes allows us to make more accurate judgments about distance and depth, particularly when objects are relatively close. But monocular cues alone are often sufficient to allow us to judge distance and depth quite accurately.

Monocular Cues   One important monocular distance cue that provides information about relative position is called **interposition**. This occurs when one object partly blocks a second object. The first object is perceived as being closer, the second as more distant (Figure 3–23).

As art students learn, there are several ways in which perspective can help in estimating distance and depth. In **linear perspective**, two parallel lines that extend into the distance seem to come together at some point on the horizon. In **aerial perspective**, distant objects have a hazy appearance and a somewhat blurred outline. On a clear day, mountains often seem to be much closer than on a hazy day, when their outlines become blurred. The **elevation** of an object also serves as a perspective cue to depth: An object on a higher horizontal plane seems to be farther away than one on a lower plane (Figure 3–24).

Another very useful monocular cue to distance and depth is **texture gradient**. An object that is close seems to have a rough or detailed texture. As distance increases, the texture becomes finer, until finally the original texture cannot be distinguished clearly, if at all. For example, when

FIGURE 3–23
Interposition.
Because the King of Clubs appears to have been superimposed on the King of Spades, we perceive it to be closer to us.

FIGURE 3–24
Elevation as a visual cue.
Because of the higher elevation and the suggestion of depth provided by the road, the tree on the right is perceived as being more distant and about the same size as the tree at lower left. Actually, it is appreciably smaller, as you can see if you measure the heights of the two drawings.

standing on a pebbly beach, you can distinguish among the gray stones and the gravel in front of your feet. As you look down the beach, however, the stones appear to become smaller and finer until eventually you cannot make out individual stones at all (Figure 3–25). **Shadowing**—another important cue to the distance, depth, and solidity of an object—is illustrated in Figure 3–26.

Bus or train passengers often notice that nearby trees or telephone poles seem to flash past the windows, whereas buildings and other objects farther away seem to move slowly. These differences in the speeds of movement of images across the retina give an important cue to distance and depth. You can observe the same effect if you stand still and move your head from side to side as you focus your gaze on something in the middle distance: Objects close to you seem to move in the direction opposite to the direction in which your head is moving, whereas objects far away seem to move in the same direction as your head. This distance cue is known as **motion parallax**.

Binocular Cues   All the visual cues examined so far depend on the action of only one eye. Many animals—such as horses, deer, and fish—rely entirely on monocular cues. Although

FIGURE 3–25
Texture gradient.
Note how the nearby pebbles on this beach appear larger and clearer than the distant ones.

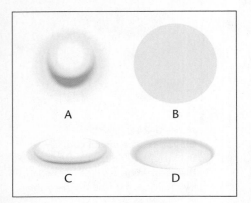

FIGURE 3–26
Shadowing.
Shadowing on the outer edges of a spherical object, such as a ball or globe, gives it a three-dimensional quality (A). Without shadowing (B), it might be perceived as a flat disk. Shadowing can also affect our perception of the direction of depth. In the absence of other cues, we tend to assume overhead lighting, so image C appears to be a bump because its top edge is lit, whereas image D appears to be a dent. If you turn this book upside down, the direction of depth is reversed.

they have two eyes, the two visual fields do not overlap, because their eyes are located on the sides of the head rather than in front. Humans, apes, and many predatory animals—such as lions, tigers, and wolves—have a distinct physical advantage over these other animals. Because both eyes are set in the front of the head, the visual fields overlap. The stereoscopic vision derived from combining the two retinal images—one from each eye—makes the perception of depth and distance much more accurate.

The average person's eyes are set approximately 2.5 inches apart, but each eye has a slightly different view of things. The difference between the two images received by the eyes is known as **retinal disparity**. The left eye receives more information about the left side of an object, and the right eye receives more information about the right side. Try this experiment to prove that each eye receives a different image. Close one eye and line up a finger with some vertical line, such as the edge of a door. Then, open that eye and close the other one. Your finger will appear to have moved a great distance. When you look at the finger with both eyes, however, the two different images become one.

Another important binocular cue to distance for objects that are relatively close comes from the muscles that control the **convergence** of the eyes. Our eyes tend to converge, or turn slightly inward toward each other, when objects are fairly close. The sensations from the muscles that control the movement of the eyes thus provide a cue to distance. If the object is very close, such as at the end of the nose, the eyes cannot converge and two separate images are perceived (Everyone who has ever looked cross-eyed at something is familiar with that experience). If the object is more than a few yards or meters away, the sight lines of the eyes are more or less parallel and convergence is no longer a useful cue to distance.

By combining all these sensory cues to distance and depth, the brain has a great deal of information with which to work. As a result, perception of distance and depth usually is quite accurate. However, sometimes the perceptual processes that work so well under normal conditions can be confusing, as can be seen in the next section.

■ VISUAL ILLUSIONS

Visual illusions graphically demonstrate the ways in which various sensory cues are used to create perceptual experiences that may (or may not) correspond to what is out there in the real world. Perceptual illusions occur because the stimulus contains misleading or ambiguous cues that give rise to inaccurate or impossible perceptions. The trident in Figure 3–16 is an example of such an illusion in which the brain, in attempting to create an accurate perception of "what must be out there," ends up creating an impossible object. Other impossible objects are shown in Figure 3–27. In each case, the sensory information contains false cues about depth that lead the brain to render a three-dimensional object that cannot possibly exist. The brain knows that the image is actually two dimensional, but it still responds as though the image were three dimensional and creates a perceptual experience that corresponds to "what must be out there" in order to give rise to those sensory cues. The illusion in Figure 3–28 also results from false and misleading depth cues. For example, in Figure 3–28, both monsters cast the same size image on the retina in our eyes. But the depth cues in the tunnel suggest that we are looking at a three-dimensional scene and that, therefore, the top monster must be much farther away. In the real world, this perception would mean that the top monster is actually much larger than the bottom monster. Therefore, we "correct" for the distance and actually perceive the top monster as larger, despite other cues to the contrary.

FIGURE 3–27
Visual illusions using misleading depth cues.
These visual illusions trick us through deceptive *depth cues*. For example, the odd triangle is drawn so that a false depth cue signals a three-dimensional object that cannot exist.
Source: Adapted from Gregory, 1978.

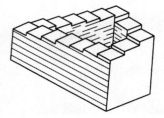
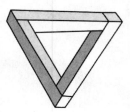
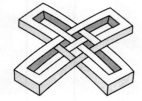

Other visual illusions arise because the sensory cues are ambiguous—it is not possible for the brain to favor one perception over another. In Figure 3–29a, is the cube facing to the left or the right? After staring at it for a minute, you will find that you first perceive it one way then suddenly your perception changes. Which way could you pass through the coils in Figure 3–29b—from the left or from the right? In Figure 3–29c, do you see a flight of stairs or an overhanging cornice? In each case, the more you stare at the figures, the more confusing they become—shifting first one way, then another. Reversible figures such as these show clearly that without adequate sensory information from the visual stimulus, the brain continually searches for the right interpretation. One perceptual experience gets shifted to a different one as though the brain were searching for the correct match between the sensory cues and the real world.

Artists rely on many of these perceptual phenomena both to represent reality accurately and to distort it deliberately (Figure 3–30). In paintings and sketches drawn on a two-dimensional surface, it is almost always necessary to distort objects in order for them to be perceived correctly by viewers. For example, in representational art, the railroad tracks, sidewalks, and tunnels are always drawn closer together in the distance. Three-dimensional movies also work on the principle that the brain can be deceived into seeing three dimensions if slightly different images are presented to the left and right eyes (working on the principle of retinal disparity). Thus, an understanding of perceptual illusions enables one to manipulate images for deliberate effect—and to delight in the results.

■ **OBSERVER CHARACTERISTICS**

FIGURE **3–28**
Misleading depth cues.
This shows how, through the use of misleading depth cues, we misjudge the size of objects.

Individual Differences in Perception

All normal human beings have the same sense organs and perceptual capacity. However, they draw on past experience and learning in creating perceptual experiences from sensory cues. Motivations, values, expectations, cognitive style, and cultural preconceptions can also affect perceptual experiences. While reading through the next section, consider the many ways in which one person's perceptual experiences can differ from another person's—even when both are in the same situation.

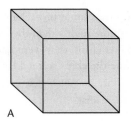

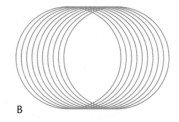

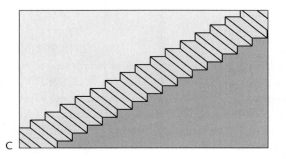

FIGURE **3–29**
Reversible figures.
Images A, B, and C are examples of reversible figures—drawings that we can perceive two different ways, but not at the same time.

FIGURE **3–30**
Perceptual illusion.
How has the artist, M.C. Escher, manipulated distance cues to create the perceptual illusion of water traveling uphill?

Motivation   Desires and needs shape everyone's perceptions. People in need are more likely to perceive something that they think will satisfy that need. The best known example of this, at least in fiction, is a mirage: People lost in the desert have visual fantasies of an oasis at the next dune. Research has found that when people have not eaten (16 hours seems to be a cut-off point), they perceive vague images or ambiguous pictures related to food (McClelland & Atkinson, 1948; Sanford, 1937). The effect of motivation on perception of ambiguous stimuli provides the rationale for *projective personality tests,* such as the Rorschach inkblot test (examined in Chapter 10).

Values   In an experiment that revealed how strongly perceptions can be affected by a person's values, nursery school children were shown a poker chip. Each child was asked to compare the size of the chip with the size of an adjustable circle of light until the children said that the chip and the circle of light were the same size. Then, they were brought to a machine with a crank that, when turned, produced a poker chip that could be exchanged for candy. Thus, the children were taught to value the poker chips more highly than they had before. After the children had been rewarded with candy for the poker chips, they were again asked to compare the size of the chips with a circle of light. This time the chips seemed larger to the children (Lambert, Solomon, & Watson, 1949).

Expectations   Preconceptions about what people are supposed to perceive can influence perception by causing them to delete, insert, transpose, or otherwise modify what they see. For example:

PARIS
IN THE
THE SPRING

Often, people tend to omit the "extra" words and to report seeing more familiar (and more normal) expressions, such as PARIS IN THE SPRING. This phenomenon reflects a strong tendency to see what we expect to see, even if our expectation conflicts with external reality. This process is the basis for the delightful pastime of lying on the ground, looking up at the clouds, and "seeing" familiar objects in the clouds. It is also the bane of authors who, despite their best efforts, occasionally miss typographical errors in their manuscripts because they see what they expect to see rather than what actually exists on the page.

FIGURE 3–31
Look first at the drawing on the left and ask a friend to look at the one on the right. When you both look at the drawing in the center, you will probably perceive it quite differently, because your expectations are different (from Leeper, 1935).

The effect of expectations can be demonstrated with the use of reversible figures. Consider Figure 3–31. Look first at the panel farthest to the left for a while, and then shift your gaze to the center panel. In all likelihood, you initially perceived the figure in the center panel as a young woman looking away. But the central panel can just as easily be seen as an old woman wrapped in a shawl. If you stare at the panel farthest right for a moment, then shift your gaze to the center, you most likely will see the old woman rather than the young woman. And if you stare steadily at the center panel, the figure likely will shift back and forth from the old woman to the young woman, as did the reversible figures discussed earlier.

Cognitive Style   As people mature, they develop a cognitive style—their own way of dealing with the environment—that also affects how they see the world. Some psychologists distinguish between two general approaches that people use in perceiving the world. People who adopt the *field-dependent* approach tend to perceive the environment as a whole and do not clearly delineate in their minds the shape, color, size, or other qualities of individual items. When field-dependent people are asked to draw a human figure, they generally draw it so that it blends into the background. By contrast, people who are *field independent* are more likely to perceive the elements of the environment as separate and distinct from one another and to draw each element as standing out from the background.

People also differ in the extent to which they are *levelers* or *sharpeners*—those who level out the distinctions among objects and those who magnify them. To investigate the differences between these two cognitive styles, Klein (1951) showed people sets of squares of varying sizes and asked them to estimate the size of each one. One group, the levelers, failed to perceive any differences in the size of the squares. The sharpeners, however, picked up the differences in the size of the squares and made their size estimates accordingly.

Experience and Culture   Cultural background also influences people's perceptions. As we will see in Chapter 7 (Cognition and Mental Abilities), the language that people speak affects the ways in which they perceive their surroundings. Cultural differences in people's experiences can also influence how they use perceptual cues. For example, East African Masai, who depend on herding animals for their living, are more perceptive about the characteristics of individual animals in their herd than are Westerners. Similarly, professional dog breeders see championship qualities in a pup that most people would not recognize. And wine experts can distinguish subtle differences in the flavor of different vintages that most people could not detect.

Personality   Several researchers have shown that individual personalities influence perception. When people with eating disorders are shown a series of words very quickly (for less than one-tenth of a second each), they are faster at identifying words that refer to foods they commonly think about than they are at identifying foods they rarely think about. Similarly, people who are depressed are faster at identifying words that describe personality traits they commonly think about (such as *quiet, withdrawn, hesitant,* and *timid*) than words that describe traits they rarely think about (such as *extroverted, lively,* and *bold*). A famous example of this is the fact that optimists tend to perceive a half-filled glass as half full, while pessimists tend to perceive the same glass as half empty. These findings and many others indicate that personality— along with the other factors explored in this chapter—can significantly influence perception.

ENDURING ISSUES   PERSON/SITUATION

Do Perceptual Experiences Reflect the Outside World?

Has this chapter changed any of your ideas about the relative importance of processes that occur inside the individual (such as thoughts, emotions, motives, attitudes, values, and personalities) as opposed to objects and events in the real world? If someone were to ask you whether perceptual experiences match more closely the image on the retina or the outside world, what would you say? What examples would you select from the chapter to make your point most effectively?

Check Your Understanding

1. Match the following principles of perception with the appropriate definitions.

_____ Similarity   **a.** Tendency to perceive a whole object even where none exists

_____ Continuity   **b.** Elements that continue a pattern likely are to be seen as part of the pattern

_____ Proximity   **c.** Objects similar to one another tending to be grouped together

_____ Closure   **d.** Elements found close together tending to be perceived as a unit

2. When studying a painting, you notice that a pathway in the painting is made up of stones that become smaller and smaller as you look "down the lane." The artist has used which of the following distance cues to create the impression of depth?

a. Interposition   **b.** Texture gradient   **c.** Elevation   **d.** Shadowing

Chapter Review

www.psychologythecore.com

The Nature of Sensation

Sensation begins when the body's sensory receptor cells are stimulated. Through the process of **transduction, receptor cells** then convert the stimulation into coded signals that vary according to the characteristics of the stimulus. Further coding occurs as the signal passes along sensory nerve fibers, so that the message finally reaching the brain is very detailed and precise.

The amount of physical energy that reaches sensory receptors must be of a minimal intensity to produce a detectable sensation. The least amount of energy needed to produce a sensation 50% of the time is called the *absolute threshold*. Absolute thresholds vary according to the level of stimulation present at any given time—a process called **adaptation**. People are very sensitive to changes in stimulus intensity. The **difference threshold** or *just-noticeable difference* (jnd) is the smallest change in stimulation that can be detected 50% of the time. According to **Weber's law**, the difference threshold is a constant fraction or proportion of the original stimulus. The greater the stimulus, the greater the change necessary to produce a jnd.

Light enters an eye through the **cornea** (a transparent protective coating) and passes through the **pupil** (the opening in the **iris**) as well as through the **lens**, which focuses it onto the eye's light-sensitive inner lining called the **retina**. Directly behind the lens, the **fovea** occupies the center of the visual field and is the place where sharpness of vision (**visual acuity**) is greatest. Neural impulses are generated in the retina by receptor cells known as **rods** and **cones**. Cones are responsible for our perception of color, while rods allow us to see varying degrees of brightness. Rods and cones connect to specialized neurons called **bipolar cells**, so named because they have only one axon and one dendrite. Cones generally connect with only one bipolar cell—a sort of "private line" arrangement. In contrast, it is normal for several rods to share a single bipolar cell. Rods and cones adapt to the overall level of stimulation, becoming more sensitive to light in lowered levels of illumination (**dark adaptation**) and less sensitive in bright light (**light adaptation**). Dark and light adaptation are responsible for some **afterimages**.

Bipolar cells, in turn, connect to **ganglion cells**. The axons of ganglion cells converge to form the **optic nerve**, which carries to the brain the neural impulses triggered in the retina. The place where the optic nerve leaves the eye is called the **blind spot**. The primary destination of the optic nerves is the occipital lobe where specialized brain cells called **feature detectors** detect particular elements of the visual field such as horizontal or vertical lines, movement, depth, or color.

Hue, **saturation**, and **brightness** are properties of color vision. The **trichromatic (three-color) theory** holds that the eyes contain three different kinds of color receptors, one of which is most responsive to yellow, another to green, and another to blue-violet. In contrast, the **opponent-process theory** of color vision maintains that receptors in the eyes are specialized to respond to one member of three basic color pairs: red-green, yellow-blue, and black-white (or light-dark). Each of these theories accounts for some, but not all, aspects of color vision. Today, psychologists believe that the trichromatic and opponent-process theories are correct, but at different stages of the visual process. There are indeed three kinds of color receptors in the retinas, but the messages they initiate are coded by other neurons into opponent-process form.

Hearing

The physical stimuli for the sense of hearing are **sound waves** that cause the experience of **sound**. The **frequency** of sound waves, the number of cycles per second (expressed in a unit called **hertz**, or **Hz**), is the primary determinant of **pitch**. The intensity or height of the sound wave represents its **amplitude** which, together with frequency, determines the perceived loudness of the sound wave (measured using a **decibel** scale). As with other senses, hearing adapts to the overall level of stimulation.

When sound waves strike the eardrum and cause it to vibrate, three bones in the middle ear—the hammer, the anvil, and the stirrup—are stimulated to vibrate in sequence. These vibrations are passed along to the **oval window** that, in turn, transmits the vibrations to the fluid inside the **cochlea**. Inside the cochlea, the **basilar membrane** ripples in response to the vibrations and those ripples in turn stimulate sensory receptors in the **organ of Corti**. This stimulation of the hair cells produces auditory signals that travel to the brain through the **auditory nerve** and go first to the medulla and, from there, to the temporal lobes of the brain.

The loudness of sounds is determined primarily by the number of receptors stimulated and thus the overall level of activity of the auditory nerve. Up to about 4000 Hz, pitch is determined by the vibrations of the basilar membrane as a whole (**frequency theory**). Above 4000 Hz, the brain determines pitch by noting the place on the basilar membrane at which the greatest stimulation is occurring (**place theory**).

The Other Senses

Smell and taste are designed to detect the presence of various chemical substances in the air and in food. Substances carried by airborne molecules into the nasal cavities activate highly specialized receptors for smell. From there, messages are carried directly to the **olfactory bulb** in the brain where they are recoded further before being sent to the cerebral hemispheres. Most animals have a second sensory system for smell through which they can detect **pheromones**—chemicals produced by organisms to communicate sexual, aggressive, or territorial signals to other animals.

Humans possess five basic tastes—sweet, sour, salty, bitter, and umami. The receptors for taste are housed in the **taste buds** on the tongue. When these receptors are activated by the chemical substances in food, their adjacent neurons fire, sending nerve impulses to the parietal lobes and to the limbic system. As with other senses, taste is subject to adaptation.

The **kinesthetic senses** provide information about muscle movement, changes in posture, and strain on muscles and joints. They rely on feedback from two sets of specialized nerve endings—stretch receptors, which are attached to muscle fibers, and Golgi tendon organs, which are attached to the tendons that connect muscle to bone.

The **vestibular senses** provide information about a person's orientation, position, or movement in space. The receptors for these senses are in two vestibular organs in the inner ear—the semicircular canals and the vestibular sacs.

Skin is the largest sense organ. Sensations that arise from the receptors embedded in it produce the sensation of touch. The skin senses are remarkably sensitive, but as do other senses they undergo adaptation. Some skin receptors send messages through the medulla and the thalamus and from there to the sensory cortex in the parietal lobe of the brain—which is where the experiences of touch, pressure, and so on arise. Other messages go through the thalamus, then on to the reticular formation.

A clear understanding of the experience of pain remains something of a scientific puzzle. There is no simple relationship between injury, or damage to the body, and pain. Moreover, people have varying degrees of sensitivity to pain based on their physiological makeup, current mental and emotional state, expectations, and cultural beliefs and values. However, there is a "neurological gate" in the spinal cord that controls the transmission of pain messages to the brain (the so-called **gate control theory** of pain). When the gate is open, more pain is experienced than when it is closed. Whether the gate is closed or open depends on a complex competition between two different types of sensory nerve fibers—large fibers that "close the gate" and small fibers that "open the gate" when they are stimulated, enabling transmission of pain messages to the brain.

Perception

Perception is the process of organizing, interpreting, and giving meaning to raw sensory data. Twentieth-century Gestalt psychologists demonstrated that the brain creates a coherent perceptual experience that is more than simply the sum of the available sensory data. In predictable ways, the brain imposes order on the data it receives partly by distinguishing patterns such as figure and ground, proximity, similarity, closure, and continuity. In fact, quite often people have the same perceptual experience despite changes in sensory data. **Perceptual constancy** refers to this tendency to perceive objects as unchanging even when many changes in sensory stimulation exist. Once a stable perception of something is formed, the brain perceives it as essentially the same regardless of differences in viewing angle, distance, lighting, and so forth. These **size**, **shape**, **brightness**, and **color constancies** help people better to relate to the world.

Distance and depth are perceived through **monocular cues** (from just one eye) and **binocular cues** (arising from the interaction of both eyes). Examples of monocular cues are **interposition** (in which one object partly covers another), **linear perspective**, **aerial perspective** (where distant objects appear more hazy and blurred), **elevation** (or closeness of something to the horizon), **texture gradient** (from coarser to finer depending on distance), *shadowing*, and **motion parallax** (differences in the relative movement of close and distant objects as the viewer changes position). An important binocular cue is stereoscopic vision, which is derived from the combination of two retinal images to produce a three-dimensional effect. Two other binocular cues are **retinal disparity** (the difference between the two separate images received by the eyes) and **convergence** of the eyes as viewing distance decreases.

Visual illusions occur when people use various sensory cues to create perceptual experiences that do not actually exist. Illusions most often occur because sensory information contains misleading depth cues. Other inaccurate perceptions arise because the sensory cues are ambiguous.

Perceptions are also influenced by motivation, values, expectations, cognitive style, experience, culture, and personality. Thus, there are many ways in which one person's perceptual experiences can differ from another's.

Chapter 4
States of Consciousness

Go to *The Core Online* at **www.psychologythecore.com** to get the most up-to-date information for your introductory psychology course. The content online is an important part of what you are learning—the content there can help prepare you for your test! It includes up-to-date examples, simulations, video clips, and practice quizzes. Also be sure to check out the *Blog* to hear directly from the authors on what current events and latest research are most relevant to your course materials.

The first time you log in, you will need the access code packaged with your textbook. If you do not have a code, please go to **www.mypearsonstore.com** and enter the ISBN of your textbook (**0-13-603344-X**) to purchase the code.

Chapter 4 States of Consciousness

4 1 Conscious Experience

Waking and Altered Consciousness
- The state of **waking consciousness** involves all the thoughts and feelings that occur when one is awake and reasonably alert; its hallmark is selective attention.
- **Altered states of consciousness** include mental states that differ noticeably from normal waking consciousness.

Daydreaming
- A daydreaming person makes apparently effortless, spontaneous shifts in attention away from the here and now into a private world of make-believe.
- **Daydreams** can serve some useful purposes, but they can be maladaptive when taken to an extreme.

4 2 Sleep

Circadian Cycles: The Biological Clock
- Sleep and waking follow a **circadian rhythm**, or biological clock, that repeats about every 24 hours.
- This clock is partially controlled by a tiny cluster of neurons in the hypothalamus that are responsive to light.

Rhythms of Sleep
- **Stage 1:** This stage is characterized by light sleep, with increasing relaxation; the person exhibits tight and low amplitude *alpha brain waves*.
- **Stage 2:** This stage is characterized by deeper sleep than Stage 1, with the person exhibiting short bursts of *sleep spindles* in the EEG.
- **Stage 3:** This stage is characterized by *delta waves* in the EEG; the person is very relaxed and hard to awaken.
- **Stage 4:** This stage is characterized by the deepest sleep of all; the person exhibits very slow delta waves in this stage, which is the first sleep to be made up after sleep is lost.
- **Stage 1 REM:** This stage is characterized by **rapid-eye movement (REM)**, or **paradoxical sleep**, in which physiological functions are similar to Stage 1, but the person is deeply asleep.

Sleep Disorders
- Sleepwalking and sleeptalking usually occur during Stage 4 sleep; waking a sleepwalker is not dangerous.
- **Nightmares** can occur during REM sleep.
- **Night terrors** usually occur during non-REM sleep.
- **Insomnia** is the inability to fall or remain asleep.
- **Apnea** is caused by breathing difficulties at night that interrupt sleep.
- **Narcolepsy** is a hereditary disorder that causes people to nod off without warning during the day.

4 3 Dreams

Nature of Dreams
- **Dreams** are visual and auditory experiences created by the mind during sleep.
- Dreams occur most often during the REM stage of sleep and last about 1 to 2 hours in an average night.
- Dreaming lasts about as long as the events would in real life.

Reasons for Dreaming
- Dreams are manifestations of unconscious wishes.
- Dreams allow the mind to process information.
- Dreams are altered extensions of the conscious concerns of daily life.
- Dreams are neural activity.

4 4 Drug-Altered Consciousness

Substance Use, Abuse, and Dependence

- **Substance abuse** is a pattern of drug use that diminishes a person's ability to fulfill responsibilities and results in repeated use of the drug in dangerous situations or leads to legal and relationship difficulties related to drug use.
- **Substance dependence**, or addiction, is the compulsive use of drugs that often leads to tolerance and withdrawal symptoms.

How Drug Effects Are Studied

- In a drug study, some participants are given the drug and others are given a **placebo**.
- A **double-blind** procedure is one in which neither researchers nor participants know who takes the placebo or who takes the drug.
- Sophisticated neuroimaging procedures have proved useful for studying drug effects.

Depressants: Alcohol, Barbiturates, and the Opiates

- **Depressants** slow down nervous system functioning and include **alcohol**, **barbiturates**, and opium derivatives.

Stimulants: Caffeine, Nicotine, Amphetamines, and Cocaine

- **Stimulants** speed up nervous system functioning and include **amphetamines**, **cocaine**, nicotine, and caffeine.

Hallucinogens and Marijuana

- Illegal drugs such as **LSD** and **marijuana** distort aspects of waking consciousness.

Explaining Abuse and Addiction

- Biological factors include a genetic basis for alcohol and nicotine abuse; disease model of addiction.
- Psychological, cultural, and social factors influence drug abuse and addiction; use and effects of a drug depend on a person's expectations, the social setting, and his or her cultural beliefs and values.

4 5 Meditation and Hypnosis

Meditation

- **Meditation** involves various methods of concentration, reflection, or focusing of thoughts to suppress activity of the sympathetic nervous system.

Hypnosis

- There is no simple definition of what it means to be hypnotized, but it is often described as a trancelike state.
- Regarding **hypnosis**, individuals vary in their susceptibility to hypnotic suggestions and post-hypnotic commands.

Consider the following scenario: You wake up and begin the day by deciding what to eat for breakfast and what to wear. After breakfast, you sit down to memorize some history facts for an upcoming exam, but after a while you find yourself daydreaming about last night's date or next summer's vacation. A deliberate focusing of attention may then be required before you can return to concentrating on your history test. During lunch, you drink a cup of coffee or tea to keep yourself alert. After lunch, you might spend some time reflecting on the meaning of life or pondering some other grand question; or perhaps you meditate for a short while to get rid of some of the anxiety that you feel about the upcoming test. If the day is Friday, perhaps you go out for dinner and have a glass of wine or beer with your meal. Finally, the day ends and, as you fall asleep, you begin to experience the first of several dreams you will have before waking in the morning.

This description of an imaginary day in your life demonstrates clearly the great variety of cognitive processes that occur in human beings: making decisions, remembering, daydreaming, concentrating, reflecting, sleeping, and dreaming are only a sample of the kinds of mental processes that people experience daily. Our awareness of these various mental processes is called **consciousness**.

Generally, psychologists divide the study of consciousness into two broad areas. **Waking consciousness**—or conscious awareness—includes all the thoughts and feelings that occur when we are awake and reasonably alert. But there are also times when we experience **altered states of consciousness (ASCs)**—times when our mental state differs noticeably from our experience when we are awake and alert. Some altered states (such as daydreaming, sleep, and dreaming) are quite normal and seem to occur spontaneously. Other ASCs (such as hypnosis, meditation, and intoxication) involve deliberate attempts to alter our normal consciousness.

Consciousness has important survival value. Throughout history, humans have compensated for their relative shortcomings in strength and speed by developing mental skills that enabled them to think, to reason, to remember, to plan, and to predict. Moreover, human beings appear to be unique in their development of self-consciousness—apparently, we are the only organism to have developed an awareness of our own existence.

As seen in Chapter 1, consciousness and self-awareness have been of interest to people for several thousand years. They were also important factors in the early development of psychology when Wilhelm Wundt set about studying thinking objectively and scientifically and William James drew attention to the constant flow of our thoughts as they start and stop and jump from one thing to another. James's concept of the "stream of consciousness" also had parallels in the art and literature of the time. For example, his novelist brother Henry James and, more notably, James Joyce wrote fiction that tried to capture the flow of subjective experiences in our conscious life.

Since the time of Wundt and James, the study of consciousness has passed in and out of favor among psychologists. Despite psychology's roots in the study of consciousness, in the early part of this century, behaviorists concluded that a truly scientific study of mental life could never succeed and so turned their attention elsewhere. Psychology, in the words of one observer, suffered a "loss of consciousness." However, in the 1950s and 1960s, psychology's interest in consciousness was reawakened. Aside from the commonsense observation that consciousness does indeed form a part of our psychological functioning, advances in technology made it possible to study indirectly various aspects of consciousness in ways that are far more scientific than the early method of introspection. For example, Chapter 2 showed that a wide range of techniques have made it possible to study with some precision the nature of brain activity during various states of consciousness. By linking data from those techniques to subjective reports of conscious processes, it is becoming possible to make tremendous strides in our understanding of consciousness.

Social and cultural events have also influenced psychology's renewed interest in consciousness. In the 1960s, many young people began experimenting with psychedelic, mind-altering drugs. Others became interested in Eastern religions—or mystical aspects of Western religion—as alternative means of insight into a reality not available to our normal, workday experience.

Technological and cultural developments continue to renew psychologists' interest in the study of consciousness. Throughout this book, various aspects of normal waking consciousness are examined. Such processes as sensation and perception, learning, memory, cognition, and intelligence are now so important in psychology that whole chapters are devoted to them. Because other chapters will address *normal* states of consciousness in great detail, the emphasis in this chapter will be on *altered* states of consciousness.

ENDURING ISSUES in States of Consciousness

In this chapter, you will quickly recognize several of the "Enduring Issues" that were introduced in Chapter 1. The *mind-body* relationship is central to this entire chapter because psychological states can affect biological processes and, conversely, biological changes can profoundly affect psychological experiences. In addition, the chapter explores several significant differences among people in their susceptibility to various altered states of consciousness (*diversity-universality*), and the settings in which consciousness-altering substances are taken can greatly alter their effects (*person-situation*). The ageless question of *nature-nurture* will become evident when hereditary factors influencing drug abuse and drug dependence are considered.

Conscious Experience

■ WAKING AND ALTERED CONSCIOUSNESS

In ordinary waking life, people are exposed continually to a variety of external and internal stimuli. External stimuli include sounds, sights, smells, and so on. Internal stimuli include thoughts, memories, and feelings associated with their bodies. However, they generally are not aware of all these competing stimuli at the same time. To survive and make sense of the environment, people must continually select only the most important information to attend to—and filter out everything else. Chapter 6 (Memory) will examine the ways in which people do this, but for now, it is sufficient to note that the hallmark of normal waking consciousness is the highly selective nature of attention.

People are subject to numerous processes, they undergo numerous experiences, and they perform numerous tasks without being consciously aware of them. For example, people usually are not aware of vital bodily processes such as control of blood pressure or respiration. And most people are able to walk down the street or ride a bicycle without consciously thinking about every movement—in fact, there are times when things go much better when we are *not* consciously aware of them. You probably have no trouble at all signing your name; you probably do it many times a day "without giving it a thought." In fact, if you think carefully about each movement of your pen or pencil, you will find that signing your name so that it looks normal becomes exceedingly difficult. Similarly, when you are driving along a familiar route (e.g., the way to work or school), the process can be so automatic that you remain largely unaware of your actions. Sigmund Freud (in Chapter 1) thought that many of the most important influences on human behavior are screened from one's consciousness and may be accessible only through states such as dreaming. With this in mind, let's start an exploration of states of consciousness with normal, everyday variations in consciousness.

■ DAYDREAMING

In James Thurber's classic short story, *The Secret Life of Walter Mitty* (Thurber, 1942), the meek, painfully shy central character spends much of his time weaving elaborate fantasies in which he stars as a bold, dashing adventurer. Daydreams are his reality—in comparison, his waking-conscious experience is boring. In the comic strip "Peanuts," Snoopy was well-known for his imaginary adventures as the archrival of the Red Baron. **Daydreams** are apparently effortless, spontaneous shifts in attention away from the here and now into a private world of make-believe.

Few people live in their imaginations to the extent that Walter Mitty does, but as with Snoopy, all of us have imagined ourselves being more heroic or talented or romantic or

Waking and Altered Consciousness

■ The state of waking consciousness involves _____

■ Altered states of consciousness include _____

Daydreaming

■ A daydreaming person makes _____

_____

■ Daydreams can serve some useful purposes, but _____

_____

_____

eloquent than we actually are. Typically, we daydream when we would rather be somewhere else or be doing something else—escaping from the demands of the real world for a moment. Some simply may reminisce pleasantly about last year's vacation; others may ponder leaving the daily grind behind or fantasizing about a future as a business tycoon. Other times, as in the case of Walter Mitty or Snoopy, we may project ourselves into fantastically unlikely adventures. Daydreams provide the opportunity to write, act in, and stage manage a private drama for which we are the only audience.

ENDURING ISSUES   DIVERSITY/UNIVERSALITY

Variations in Daydreaming

Although daydreaming may seem to be a random and effortless process, psychologists have discovered that people's daydreams tend to fall into a few distinct patterns and that different people tend to prefer different kinds of daydreams (Singer, 1975). People who score high on measures of anxiety tend to have fleeting, loosely connected daydreams related to worrying. They take little pleasure in their daydreaming. In contrast, people who are strongly achievement oriented tend to have daydreams that concern achievement, guilt, fear of failure, and hostility. These daydreams often reflect the self-doubt and competitive envy that accompanies great ambition. Still other people derive considerable enjoyment from their daydreams and use them to solve problems, think ahead, or distract themselves. These "happy daydreamers" tend to have pleasant fantasies uncomplicated by guilt or worry. And finally, some daydreamers display unusual curiosity about their environment and place great emphasis on objective thinking. These people tend to have daydreams whose contents are closely related to the objective world and are marked by controlled lines of thought. About 4 percent of people are considered *fantasy-prone*; that is, they spend more than half their time not just daydreaming but being lost in elaborate reveries. Studies of the fantasy-prone show that they are generally highly creative and able to become completely absorbed in their fantasies.

"Harry lives inside a beltway all his own."

If daydreaming is nearly universal, does it serve any useful function? Can Walter Mitty justify his fantasies on a practical basis? Some psychologists argue that daydreams have little or no positive or practical value. In fact, to the extent that daydreaming interferes with productive activities or substitutes for more direct and effective behavior, it can be maladaptive. In the extreme, people who have difficulty distinguishing between fantasy and reality and who begin replacing real-life relationships with imaginary family and friends need professional help (as will be seen in more detail in Chapter 12: Psychological Disorders).

By contrast, other psychologists have stressed the positive value of daydreaming and fantasy. Daydreams may provide a refreshing break from a stressful day and serve as reminders of neglected personal needs. Psychodynamic theorists tend to view simple daydreams as a harmless way of working through hostile feelings or satisfying guilty desires. Cognitive psychologists emphasize that daydreaming can build problem-solving and interpersonal skills, as well as encourage creativity. Moreover, daydreaming helps people endure difficult situations:

Prisoners of war have used fantasies to survive torture and deprivation. In sum, daydreaming and fantasy in moderation may provide welcome relief from unpleasant reality and reduce internal tension and external aggression.

Sleep

Humans spend about one third of their lives in the altered state of consciousness known as *sleep*. Throughout history, people have paid varying degrees of respect to sleep and to its product, dreams. Some societies have held that great universal truths are revealed in dreams, while others view sleep as an essential, but basically unproductive, activity. Sleep researchers have begun to shed some light on the fascinating complexity of sleep, its functions, and its influence on human activity.

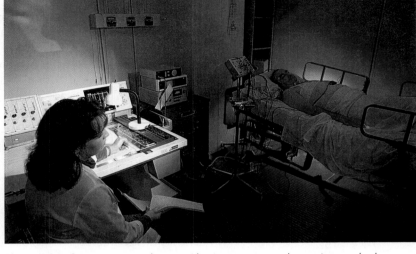

Sleep researchers monitor volunteers' brain waves, muscle tension, and other physiological changes during sleep.

When people are deprived of sleep, they crave sleep just as strongly as they would food or water after a period of deprivation. They will seize every opportunity to catch 40 winks. Yet nobody knows for sure why people need to sleep. Some evidence suggests that sleep may play an important restorative function, both physically and mentally. For instance, getting adequate sleep boosts the immune response, making people less susceptible to disease. In addition, considerable evidence shows that, with adequate sleep, people are able to experience enhanced creativity and problem-solving skills. Finally, sleep provides the platform for dreaming that seems to play an important role in memory. Although the function of sleep continues to be unclear, psychologists have learned a great deal about the nature of sleep and the dreams that accompany it.

■ CIRCADIAN CYCLES: THE BIOLOGICAL CLOCK

As with many other biological functions, sleep and waking follow a daily, or circadian, cycle (from the Latin expression *circa diem*, meaning "about a day"). **Circadian rhythms,** an ancient and fundamental adaptation to the 24-hour solar cycle of light and dark, are governed by a tiny cluster of neurons just above the optic chiasm in the lower region of the hypothalamus (Figure 2–7) known as the **suprachiasmatic nucleus (SCN).** The SCN receives information about the daily light and dark cycles via a direct pathway from the retina of the eye. In response to the light and dark cycles detected by the eye, the SCN releases specific neurotransmitters that control the body's temperature, metabolism, blood pressure, hormone levels, and hunger, which vary predictably through the course of the day. However, the SCN is not the only determinant of circadian rhythms—the biological clock can continue to function reasonably well even in the absence of external cues to the cycle of day and night.

Circadian rhythms are rarely noticed until they are disturbed. Jet lag is a familiar example. Travelers who cross several time zones in one day often feel "out of it" for several days. The reason for jet lag is not so much a lack of sleep as it is a desynchronization. Sleep-and-wake cycles adapt quickly, but hormones, body temperature, and digestive cycles change more slowly. As a result, bodily functions are out of sync. Likewise, shift workers often lose weight and suffer from irritability, insomnia, and extreme drowsiness for some time after changing to a new shift.

■ RHYTHMS OF SLEEP

"Going to sleep" means losing awareness and failing to respond to a stimulus that would produce a response in the waking state. As measured by an EEG, brain waves during this "twilight" state are characterized by irregular, low-voltage *alpha waves*. This brain-wave pattern mirrors the sense of relaxed wakefulness that is experienced when a person is lying on a beach

Circadian Cycles

■ Sleep and waking follow a _____ _____, or biological clock, that repeats about _____

■ This clock is partially controlled by _____ _____

Rhythms of Sleep

■ Stage 1 is characterized by

_____

■ Stage 2 is characterized by

_____

■ Stage 3 is characterized by

_____

■ Stage 4 is characterized by

_____

_____

■ Stage 1 REM is characterized by rapid-eye movement (REM), or

_____

_____

or in a hammock or when resting after a big meal. After this initial twilight phase, the sleeper enters Stage 1 of sleep. Stage 1 brain waves are tight and of very low amplitude (height), resembling those recorded when a person is alert or excited (Figure 4–1.) But, in contrast to normal waking consciousness, Stage 1 of the sleep cycle is marked by a slowing of the pulse, muscle relaxation, and side-to-side rolling movements of the eyes—the last being the most reliable indication of this first stage of sleep. Stage 1 usually lasts only a few moments. The sleeper is easily aroused at this stage and, once awake, may be unaware of having slept at all.

Stages 2 and 3 are characterized by progressively deeper sleep. During Stage 2, short rhythmic bursts of brain wave activity called *sleep spindles* periodically appear. In Stage 3, *delta waves*—slow waves with very high peaks—begin to emerge. During these stages, the sleeper will not easily awaken and does not respond to stimuli, such as noises or lights. Heart rate, blood pressure, and temperature continue to drop. In Stage 4 sleep, the brain emits very slow delta waves. Heart rate, breathing rate, blood pressure, and body temperature are as low as they will get during the night. In young adults, delta sleep occurs in 15- to 20-minute segments—interspersed with lighter sleep—mostly during the first half of the night. Delta sleep time lessens with age, but it continues to be the first sleep to be made up after sleep has been lost.

About an hour after falling asleep, the sleeper begins to ascend from Stage 4 sleep to Stage 3, Stage 2, and back to Stage 1—a process that takes about 40 minutes. The brain waves return to the low-amplitude, saw-toothed shape characteristic of Stage 1 sleep and waking alertness. Heart rate and blood pressure also increase, yet the muscles are more relaxed than at any other point in the sleep cycle and awakening the person will be very difficult. At this point, the eyes move rapidly under closed eyelids. This **rapid-eye movement (REM)** sleep stage is distinguished from all other stages of sleep, which are known as **non-REM** (or **NREM**) sleep, that precede and follow it.

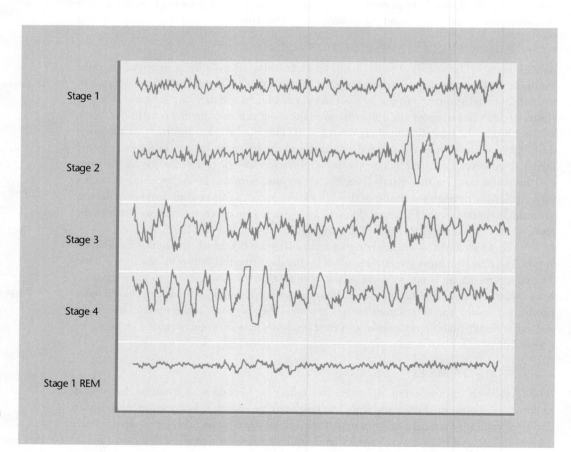

FIGURE **4–1**

The brain-wave patterns typical of the five stages of sleep.

The four NREM stages and the first REM stage. The brain waves in REM sleep closely resemble Stage 1 of NREM sleep, but the person in REM is very deeply asleep.

REM sleep is also called *paradoxical* sleep, because although measures of brain activity, heart rate, blood pressure, and other physiological functions closely resemble those recorded during waking consciousness, the person in this stage appears to be deeply asleep and is incapable of moving; the body's voluntary muscles are essentially paralyzed. Some research suggests that REM sleep is also the stage when most dreaming occurs, though dreams also take place during NREM sleep.

The first Stage 1 REM period lasts about 10 minutes and is followed by Stages 2, 3, and 4 of NREM sleep. This sequence of sleep stages repeats itself all night, averaging 90 minutes from Stage 1 REM to Stage 4 and back again. Normally, a night's sleep consists of 4 to 5 sleep cycles of this sort, but the pattern of sleep changes as the night progresses. At first, Stages 3 and 4 dominate; but as time passes, the Stage 1 REM periods gradually become longer, and Stages 3 and 4 become shorter, eventually disappearing altogether. Over the course of a night, then, about 45 to 50% of the sleeper's time is spent in Stage 2, whereas REM sleep takes up another 20 to 25% of the total.

ENDURING ISSUES DIVERSITY/UNIVERSALITY

Individual Differences in Sleep

Sleep requirements and patterns vary considerably from person to person. Some adults need hardly any sleep. Researchers have documented the cases of a Stanford University professor who slept for only 3 to 4 hours a night over the course of 50 years and a woman who lived a healthy life on only 1 hour of sleep per night (Rosenzweig & Leiman, 1982). As shown in Figure 4–2, sleep patterns also change with age. Infants sleep much longer than adults—13 to 16 hours during the first year—and much more of their sleep is REM sleep (Figure 4–3.)

Inadequate sleep has become a "national epidemic" in the United States. Between one third and one half of all adults regularly fail to get enough sleep. The resulting sleep deprivation affects the ability to pay attention and to remember things. Reaction time slows down, behavior becomes unpredictable, logical reasoning is impaired, and accidents and errors in judgment increase, while productivity and the ability to make decisions decline. These

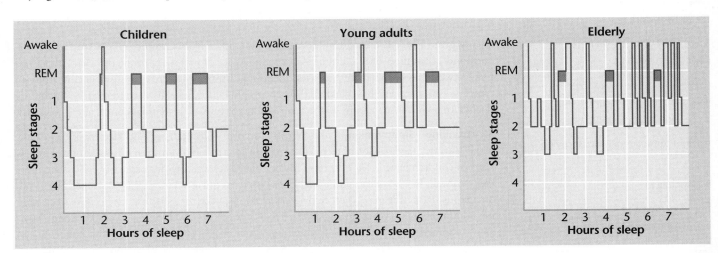

FIGURE 4–2

A night's sleep across the life span.

Sleep patterns change from childhood to young adulthood to old age. The red areas represent REM sleep, the stage of sleep that varies most dramatically across age groups.

Source: Adapted by permission of *The New England Journal of Medicine, 290*, p. 487, 1974. © 1974 Massachusetts Medical Society. All rights reserved.

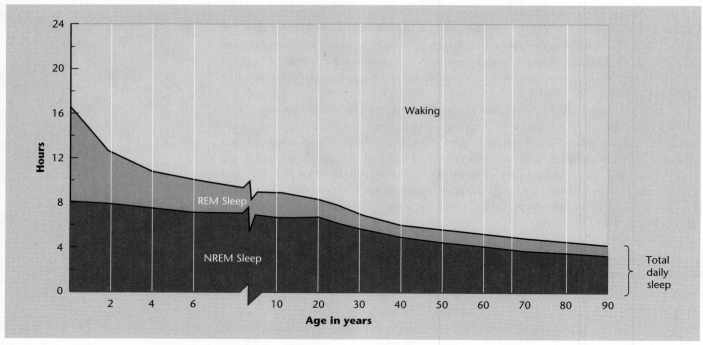

FIGURE 4–3
Changes in REM and NREM sleep.
The amount of REM sleep people need declines sharply during the first few years of life. New-borns spend about 8 hours, or almost half their total sleep time in REM sleep, whereas older children and adults spend just 1 to 2 hours or about 20 to 25% of their total sleep time in REM sleep.

Source: Adapted with permission from H. P. Roffwarg, "Ontogenetic Development of the Human Sleep-Dream Cycle," *Science, 152,* p. 604. © 1966 by the American Association for the Advancement of Science.

findings have important implications. For example, sleep loss is a contributing factor in several hundred thousand automobile accidents each year. Hospital residents who go without sleep for a long period of time without rest make a disproportionate amount of serious medical errors. Sleep deprivation is also clearly related to depression in high school and college students.

■ SLEEP DISORDERS

At any given time, at least 50 million Americans suffer from chronic, long-term sleep disorders; and 20 million other Americans experience occasional sleep problems. Also, there is a link between sleep and many diseases, including asthma and stroke. The scientific study of typical sleep patterns has yielded further insights into several sleep disorders, including sleeptalking and sleepwalking, nightmares and night terrors, insomnia, apnea, and narcolepsy.

Sleeptalking, Sleepwalking, and Night Terrors Sleeptalking and sleepwalking usually occur during Stage 4. Both are more common among children than adults: Approximately 20% of children have at least one episode of either sleepwalking or sleeptalking. Boys are more likely to walk in their sleep than girls. Contrary to popular belief, waking a sleepwalker is not dangerous (in fact, it may be more dangerous not to wake the person), but because sleepwalking commonly takes place during a very deep stage of sleep, waking a sleepwalker is not easy.

Sometimes, sleep can be frightening, when people experience nightmares or night terrors, also known as *sleep terrors*. **Nightmares** occur during REM sleep and often are remembered in the morning. These frightening dreams are also very common; virtually everyone young or old has had them. **Night terrors** often make the dreamer suddenly sit up in bed, sometimes screaming out in fear. People generally cannot be awakened from night terrors and will push away anyone trying to comfort them. Unlike nightmares, night terrors typically occur during NREM sleep, cannot be recalled the next morning, and are relatively rare among adults.

Sleep Disorders

■ Sleepwalking and sleeptalking usually occur during

_____

■ Nightmares can occur during

_____

■ Night terrors usually occur during

_____

■ Insomnia is

_____

■ Apnea is caused by

_____

■ Narcolepsy is a hereditary disorder that causes people to

_____

Insomnia, Apnea, and Narcolepsy   **Insomnia**, the inability to fall or remain asleep, afflicts as many as 35 million Americans. Most episodes of insomnia grow out of stressful events and are temporary; and many cases of insomnia yield to drug therapy or behavioral therapy. But for some sufferers, insomnia is a persistent disruption. Treatments can create problems as well. Some prescription medications for insomnia can cause anxiety, memory loss, hallucinations, and violent behavior.

The causes of insomnia vary for different individuals. For some people, insomnia is part of a larger psychological problem such as depression, so its cure requires treatment of the underlying disorder. Interpersonal difficulties, such as loneliness, can contribute to difficulty sleeping. For others, insomnia results from an overly aroused biological system. A physical predisposition to insomnia may combine with anxiety over chronic sleeplessness to create a cycle in which biological and emotional factors reinforce one another. People may worry so much about not sleeping that even simple "good sleep hygiene" bedtime rituals may unwittingly usher in anxiety, rather than set the stage for relaxation. Furthermore, bad sleep habits—such as varying bedtimes—and distracting sleep settings may aggravate or even cause insomnia.

Another sleep disorder, obstructive sleep **apnea**, affects 10 to 12 million Americans, many of whom have inherited the condition (Kadotani et al., 2001). Apnea is associated with breathing difficulties at night: In severe cases, the victim actually stops breathing after falling asleep. When the level of carbon dioxide in the blood rises to a certain point, apnea sufferers are spurred to a state of arousal just short of waking consciousness. Because this process may happen hundreds of times a night, apnea patients typically feel exhausted and fall asleep repeatedly the next day. They may also complain of depression, sexual dysfunction, difficulty concentrating, and headaches (El-Ad & Lavie, 2005; Strollo & Davé, 2005). Moreover, sleep-related breathing disorders have been shown to be related to hyperactivity, conduct disorders, and aggressiveness among children and adolescents (Chervin, Killion, Archbold, & Ruzicka, 2003). Depending on its severity, sleep apnea can also double or triple the risk of having a stroke or dying (Yaggi et al., 2005).

ENDURING ISSUES   **NATURE/NURTURE**

Narcolepsy

People suffering from insomnia and apnea may envy those who have no trouble sleeping. But too much sleep has serious repercussions as well. **Narcolepsy** is a hereditary disorder whose victims nod off without warning in the middle of a conversation or other alert activity. People with narcolepsy often experience a sudden loss of muscle tone upon expression of any sort of emotion. A joke, anger, sexual stimulation—all bring on the muscle paralysis associated with deep sleep. Suddenly, without warning, they collapse. Another symptom of the disorder is immediate entry into REM sleep, which produces frightening hallucinations that are, in fact, dreams that the person is experiencing while still partly awake. Narcolepsy is believed to arise from a hereditary defect in the central nervous system.

Check Your Understanding

1. The hallmark of waking consciousness is _____.

2. In humans, sleeping and waking follow a _____ cycle.

3. Rapid-eye movement sleep is also known as _____ sleep.

4. You are a psychologist studying an elderly person's sleep cycle. Compared with a younger person, you would expect to find that this person spends _____ time in Stage 3 and Stage 4 sleep.

   a. Less   **b.** More   **c.** About the same

Dfreams

■ NATURE OF DREAMS

Psychologists define **dreams** as visual and auditory experiences created by the mind during sleep. The average person has four or five dreams a night, accounting for about one to two hours of the total time spent sleeping. People awakened during REM sleep report graphic dreams about 80 to 85% of the time. Less-striking, dreamlike experiences that resemble normal wakeful consciousness are reported about 50% of the time during NREM sleep.

Most dreams last about as long as the events would in real life; they do not flash on your mental screen just before waking, as was once believed. Generally, dreams consist of a sequential story or a series of stories. External stimuli, such as a train whistle or a low-flying airplane, and internal stimuli, such as hunger pangs, may modify an ongoing dream, but they do not initiate dreams. Often, dreams are so vivid that it is difficult to distinguish them from reality.

■ REASONS FOR DREAMING

Dreams have been held in high regard throughout history. One example is the biblical story of a pharaoh's dreams of "fat and lean cattle," which Joseph interpreted as omens of 7 years of feast and 7 years of famine. Aristotle believed that dreams arose from the psychic activity of the sleeper. From ancient times, most people have felt that the content of their dreams was significant—even if they should not interpret it. Psychologists also have long been fascinated by dream activity and the contents of dreams, although they are not in agreement about the nature and causes of dreams.

Dreams as Unconscious Wishes   Sigmund Freud (1900), the first modern theorist to investigate this topic, called dreams the "royal road to the unconscious." Believing that dreams represent unfulfilled wishes, he asserted that people's dreams reflect the motives guiding their behavior—motives of which they may not be consciously aware. Freud distinguished between the *manifest* content, or *surface* content, of dreams and their *latent* content—the hidden, unconscious thoughts or desires that he believed were expressed indirectly through dreams.

In dreams, according to Freud, people permit themselves to express primitive desires that are relatively free of moral controls. For example, someone who is not consciously aware of hostile feelings toward another person may dream about murdering that person. However,

---

Nature of Dreams

■ Dreams are _____ created by the mind during sleep.

■ Dreams occur most often during the _____ stage of sleep and last about _____ to _____ hours in an average night.

Reasons for Dreaming

■ Dreams _____
■ Dreams _____
■ Dreams _____
■ Dreams _____

The fanciful images of Marc Chagall's paintings capture the quality of many of our dreams. Is a dream of an entwined man and woman floating high above a city symbolic of some subconscious sexual desire, as Freud would have suggested? Or is it just an illogical image caused by random brain-cell activity during sleep? Currently, psychologists have no conclusive answer. Perhaps both views have merit.

Source: Marc Chagall (Russian, 1887–1985), "Above the City." Tretyakov Gallery, Moscow, Russia. Super-Stock, Inc. © Artists Rights Society (ARS), New York.

even in a dream, such hostile feelings may be censored and transformed into a symbolic form. For example, the desire to do away with a person (the dream's latent content) may be recast into the dream image of seeing the person off at a train "terminal" (the dream's manifest content). According to Freud, this process of censorship and symbolic transformation accounts for the highly illogical nature of many dreams. Freud's pioneering work exploring the meaning of dreams paved the way for contemporary investigations of dream content.

Dreams and Information Processing A completely different explanation for dreaming emerged in the later part of the twentieth century with the advent of *information processing theory* (see Chapter 6, Memory). This view holds that in their dreams, people reprocess information gathered during the day as a way of strengthening memories of information that is crucial to survival. During the waking hours, the brain is bombarded with sensory data. People need a "time out" to decide what information is valuable, whether it should be filed in long-term memory, where it should be filed (with which older memories, ideas, desires, and anxieties), and what information should be erased to avoid a cluttering of neural pathways. According to this view, dreams seem illogical because the brain is rapidly scanning old files and comparing them with new, unsorted "clippings."

In support of this view, research has demonstrated that humans and nonhumans spend more time in REM sleep after learning difficult material; furthermore, interfering with REM sleep immediately after learning severely disrupts the memory for the newly learned material (C. T. Smith, Nixon, & Nader, 2004; Wetzel, Wagner, & Balschun, 2003). Brain-imaging studies have also demonstrated that the specific area of the brain most active while learning new material is also active during subsequent REM sleep (Maquet et al., 2000).

Other psychologists see dreams as a form of emotional processing. In dreams, emotionally significant events may be integrated with previous experiences. For example, children's first experience of a carnival or an amusement park is usually a blend of terror and excitement. Later in life, whenever they have experiences that are exciting, but also somewhat frightening, carnival rides or images may dominate their dreams. Some psychologists have suggested that people work through problems in their dreams—indeed, that dreams are part of the healing process after a divorce, the death of a loved one, or other emotional crisis.

Dreams and Waking Life Still another theory maintains that dreams are an extension of the conscious concerns of daily life in altered (but not disguised) form. Research has shown that what people dream about is generally similar to what they think about and do while awake. Most often, dream content reflects an individual's unique conceptions, interests, and concerns. For example, a parent having problems with a child may dream about earlier childhood confrontations with his or her own parents. Dream content is also related to where one is in the sleep cycle and what was done before sleep, as well as gender, age, and even socioeconomic status. For example, although the dreams of men and women have become more similar over the last several decades, men more often dream about weapons, unfamiliar characters, male characters, aggressive interactions, and failure outcomes, whereas women are more likely to dream about being the victims of aggression. Dream content also appears to be relatively "consistent" for most individuals, displaying similar themes across years and even decades.

Dreams and Neural Activity Research using advanced brain-imaging techniques has indicated that the limbic system, which is involved with emotions, motivations, and memories, is very active during dreams; so, to a lesser extent, are the visual and auditory areas of the forebrain that process sensory information. However, areas of the forebrain involved in working memory, attention, logic, and self-monitoring are relatively inactive during dreams. These facts may explain the highly emotional texture of dreams, as well as the bizarre imagery and the loss of critical insight, logic, and self-reflection experienced by the sleeper. This uncensored mixture of desires, fears, and memories comes very close to the psychoanalytic concept of unconscious wishes, suggesting that Freud may have come closer to the meaning of dreams than many contemporary psychologists have acknowledged.

Dreams are the most common alteration of normal consciousness, and they occur naturally under normal conditions. Altered states of consciousness can also be induced by drugs.

Check Your Understanding

1. Most vivid dreaming takes place during the _____ stage of sleep.

2. We normally spend about _____ hours each night dreaming.

3. Freud distinguished between the _____ and _____ content of dreams.

4. The amount of REM sleep changes over the life span. Which of the following people spend the least amount of time in REM sleep in an average day?

   a. 6-month-old infant   **c.** 20-year-old young adult

   b. 7-year-old child   **d.** 70-year-old adult

Drug-Altered Consciousness

Substance Use, Abuse, and Dependence

- Substance abuse is _____

_____

_____

- Substance dependence, or

addiction, is _____

_____

_____

How Drug Effects Are Studied

- In a drug study, some participants are given _____ and others are given _____.

- A double-blind procedure is one in which neither _____ nor _____ know who takes the placebo or who takes the drug.

- Sophisticated _____ _____ have proved useful for studying drug effects.

ENDURING ISSUES   MIND/BODY

Psychoactive Drugs

The use of **psychoactive drugs**—substances that change people's moods, perceptions, mental functioning, or behavior—is nearly universal. In almost every known culture throughout history, people have sought ways to alter waking consciousness. Many legal and illegal drugs currently available have been used for thousands of years. For example, marijuana is mentioned in the herbal recipe book of a Chinese emperor, dating from 2737 BC Natives of the Andes Mountains in South America chew leaves of the cocaine-containing coca plant as a stimulant—a custom dating back at least to the Inca Empire of the fifteenth century.

In the nineteenth century, Europeans began adding coca to wine, tea, and lozenges. Following this trend, in 1886, an Atlanta pharmacist combined crushed coca leaves from the Andes, caffeine-rich cola nuts from West Africa, cane sugar syrup, and carbonated water in a patent medicine he called "Coca-Cola." *Laudanum*—opium dissolved in alcohol—was also popular in the United States at that time and was used as a main ingredient in numerous over-the-counter (or patent) medicines.

Of all psychoactive substances, alcohol has the longest history of widespread use. Archaeological evidence suggests that Late Stone Age groups began producing mead (fermented honey flavored with sap or fruit) approximately 10,000 years ago. The Egyptians, Babylonians, Greeks, and Romans viewed wine as a "gift from the gods." Wine is mentioned often in the Bible and plays a sacramental role in several major religions. In the Middle Ages, alcohol earned the title *aqua vitae*, the "water of life," with good reason (Vallee, 1998). Wherever people settled, water supplies quickly became contaminated with waste products. As recently as the nineteenth century, most people in Western civilizations drank alcohol with every meal (including breakfast) and between meals, as a "pick-me-up," as well as on social and religious occasions.

Is today's drug problem different from the drug use in other societies and times? In many ways, the answer is yes. First, motives for using psychoactive drugs have changed. In most cultures, psychoactive substances have been used as part of religious rituals, as medicines and tonics, as nutrient beverages, or as culturally approved stimulants (such as coffee). By contrast, the use of alcohol and other drugs in contemporary society is primarily recreational. For the most part, people do not raise their glasses in praise of God or inhale hallucinogens to get in touch with the spirit world, but rather to relax, have fun with others, and get high. The French often drink wine with dinner, the Spanish are renowned not only for bullfights but for *tapas* bars, the British have their pubs, and Greeks have their festivals. Americans most often imbibe and inhale in settings specifically designed for recreation and inebriation: bars, clubs, beer parties, cocktail parties, "raves," and so-called crack houses. In addition, people use and abuse drugs privately and secretly in their homes, sometimes without the knowledge of their family and friends—leading to hidden addiction. Whether social or solitary, the use of psychoactive substances today is largely divorced from religious and family traditions.

Second, the drugs themselves have changed. Modern psychoactive substances often are stronger than those used in other cultures and times. For most of Western history, wine (12% alcohol) was often diluted with water. Hard liquor (40 to 75% alcohol) appeared only in the tenth century AD, and the heroin available on the streets today is stronger and more addictive than that available in the 1930s and 1940s. In addition, new, synthetic drugs appear regularly, with unpredictable consequences. In the 1990s, the National Institute for Drug Abuse created a new category it labeled "club drugs" for increasingly popular psychoactive substances manufactured in small laboratories or even home kitchens (often from recipes available on the Internet). Because the source, the psychoactive ingredients, and any possible contaminants are unknown, the symptoms, toxicity, and short- or long-term consequences are also unknown—making these drugs especially dangerous. The fact that they are often consumed with alcohol multiplies the risks.

Finally, scientists and the public know more about the effects of psychoactive drugs than in the past. Nicotine is an obvious example. The Surgeon General's Report issued in 1964 confirmed a direct link between smoking and heart disease, as well as lung cancer (Surgeon General's Report, 1964). Subsequent research establishing that cigarettes are harmful not only to smokers but also to people around them (secondhand smoke), as well as to their unborn babies, transformed a personal health decision into a moral issue. Nonetheless, tens of millions of Americans still smoke, and millions of others use drugs they know to be harmful.

■ SUBSTANCE USE, ABUSE, AND DEPENDENCE

If drugs are defined broadly to include caffeine, tobacco, and alcohol, then most people throughout the world use some type of drug on an occasional or a regular basis. Most of these people use such drugs in moderation and do not suffer ill effects. But for some, substance use escalates into **substance abuse**—pattern of drug use that diminishes the ability to fulfill responsibilities at home, work, or school and that results in repeated use of a drug in dangerous situations or that leads to legal difficulties related to drug use. The ongoing abuse of drugs, including alcohol, may lead to compulsive use of the substance, or **substance dependence**, also known as *addiction* (Table 4–1). Not everyone who abuses a substance develops a dependence, but dependence usually follows a period of abuse. Dependence often includes *tolerance*, the phenomenon whereby higher doses of the drug are required to produce its original effects or to prevent withdrawal symptoms (the unpleasant physical or psychological effects following discontinuance of the substance).

The causes of substance abuse and dependence are a complex combination of biological, psychological, and social factors that varies for each individual and for each substance. Also, the development of substance dependence does not follow an established timetable. One person might drink socially for years before abusing alcohol, whereas someone else might become addicted to cocaine in a matter of days. Before beginning the discussion of specific drugs and their effects, let's first look at how psychologists study drug-related behaviors.

TABLE 4–1 Signs of Substance Dependence

The most recent clinical definition of dependence (American Psychiatric Association, 2000; Anthony & Helzer, 2002) describes a broad pattern of drug-related behaviors characterized by at least three of the following seven symptoms over a 12-month period:

1. Developing tolerance; that is, needing increasing amounts of the substance to gain the desired effect or experiencing a diminished effect when using the same amount of the substance. For example, the person might have to drink an entire six-pack to get the same effect formerly experienced after drinking just one or two beers.

2. Experiencing withdrawal symptoms, which are physical and psychological problems that occur when the person tries to stop using the substance. Withdrawal symptoms range from anxiety and nausea to convulsions and hallucinations.

3. Using the substance for a longer period or in greater quantities than intended.

4. Having a persistent desire or making repeated efforts to cut back on the use of the substance.

5. Devoting a great deal of time to obtaining or using the substance.

6. Giving up or reducing social, occupational, or recreational activities because of drug use.

7. Continuing to use the substance even in the face of ongoing or recurring physical or psychological problems that are likely to be caused or made worse by the use of the substance.

■ HOW DRUG EFFECTS ARE STUDIED

The effects of particular drugs are studied under carefully controlled scientific conditions. In most cases, experimenters compare people's behavior before the administration of the drug with their behavior afterward, taking special precautions to ensure that any observed changes in behavior are because of the drug alone.

To eliminate research errors based on subject or researcher expectations, most drug experiments use the **double-blind procedure**, in which some participants receive the active drug and others are given a neutral, inactive substance called a **placebo**. In a double-blind scenario, neither the researchers nor the participants know who is taking the active drug and who is taking the placebo. If the behavior of the participants who actually receive the drug differs from the behavior of those who got the placebo, the cause is likely to be the active ingredient in the drug.

Studying drug-altered consciousness is complicated by the fact that most drugs not only affect different people in different ways, but they also produce different effects in the same person at different times or in different settings (S. Siegel, 2005). For example, some people are affected powerfully by even small amounts of alcohol, whereas others are not. And drinking alcohol in a convivial family setting usually produces somewhat different effects than does consuming alcohol under the watchful eyes of a scientist.

Recently, sophisticated neuroimaging procedures have proved useful for studying drug effects. Techniques such as PET imaging have enabled researchers to isolate specific differences between the brains of addicted and nonaddicted people. For example, the "addicted brain" has been found to differ qualitatively from the nonaddicted brain in many ways, including metabolically and in responsiveness to environmental cues. Investigators also have focused on the role played by neurotransmitters in the addictive process (see Chapter 2: The Biological Basis of Behavior). For example, every addictive drug causes dopamine levels in the brain to increase. These results may lead not only to better understanding of the biological basis of addiction, but also to more effective treatments.

In analyzing drugs and drug use, it is convenient to group psychoactive substances into three categories: depressants, stimulants, and hallucinogens. These categories are not rigid, as the same drug may have multiple effects or different effects on different users, but this division helps to organize our knowledge about drugs.

■ DEPRESSANTS: ALCOHOL, BARBITURATES, AND THE OPIATES

Depressants are chemicals that retard behavior and thinking by either speeding up or slowing down nerve impulses. Generally speaking, alcohol, barbiturates, and the opiates have depressant effects. People take depressants to reduce tension; to forget their troubles; or to relieve feelings of inadequacy, loneliness, or boredom.

Alcohol   In spite of, or perhaps because of, the fact that it is legal and socially approved, **alcohol** is America's number-one drug problem. A substantial percentage of high school seniors say they get drunk, and alcohol use is a significant problem among middle-school students (Johnston, O'Malley, Bachman, & Schulenbert, 2004). Alcohol is a highly addictive drug with potentially devastating long-term effects. At least 14 million Americans (more than 7% of the population ages 18 and older) have problems with drinking, including more than 8 million alcoholics.

Excessive, chronic alcohol use can harm virtually every organ in the body, beginning with the brain, and it is associated with impairments in perceptual-motor skills, visual-spatial processing, problem solving, and abstract reasoning. Alcohol is the leading cause of liver disease and kidney damage. It is also a major factor in cardiovascular disease; it increases the risk of certain cancers and can lead to sexual dysfunction and infertility. Alcohol is particularly damaging to the nervous system during the teenage years. Areas of the brain that are not fully developed until age 21 are especially susceptible to damage when exposed to high levels of alcohol.

The social costs of abusing alcohol are high as well. Alcohol is implicated in more than two thirds of all fatal automobile accidents, two thirds of all murders, two thirds of all spouse beatings, and more than half of all cases of violent child abuse. Moreover, the use of alcohol during pregnancy has been linked to a variety of birth defects, the most notable being fetal alcohol syndrome (see Chapter 9, Life-Span Development). More than 40% of all heavy drinkers die before the age of 65 (compared with less than 20% of nondrinkers). In addition, there is the untold cost in psychological trauma suffered by the nearly 30 million children of alcohol abusers.

What makes alcohol so powerful? Alcohol first affects the frontal lobes of the brain, which figure prominently in inhibitions, impulse control, reasoning, and judgment. As consumption continues, alcohol impairs functions of the cerebellum, the center of motor control and balance. Eventually, alcohol affects the spinal cord and medulla, which regulate such involuntary functions as breathing, body temperature, and heart rate. A blood-alcohol level of 0.25% or more may cause this part of the nervous system to shut down and severely impair functioning; slightly higher levels can cause death from alcohol poisoning (Table 4–2).

Even in moderate quantities, alcohol affects perception, motor processes, memory, and judgment and can diminish the ability to see clearly, to perceive depth accurately, and to distinguish the differences between bright lights and colors effectively. Also, it generally affects spatial-cognitive functioning—all of which is clearly necessary for driving a car safely. Alcohol also interferes with memory storage: Heavy drinkers may experience blackouts, making them unable to remember anything that occurred while they were drinking. Heavy drinkers have difficulty focusing on relevant information and ignoring inaccurate, irrelevant information, thus leading to poor judgments. Alcohol use is also associated with increases in aggression, hostility, violence, and abusive behavior. Thus, intoxication makes people less aware of and less concerned about the negative consequences of their actions, which increases their likelihood of engaging in risky behavior.

Depressants

■ Depressants slow down nervous system functioning and include _____

_____

_____

_____

TABLE 4–2   The Behavioral Effects of Blood-Alcohol Levels

LEVELS OF ALCOHOL IN THE BLOOD	BEHAVIORAL EFFECTS
0.05%	Feels good; less alert; reduced inhibitions
0.10%	Is slower to react; less cautious; slurred speech
0.15%	Reaction time is much slower
0.20%	Sensory-motor abilities are suppressed
0.25%	Is staggering (motor abilities severely impaired); perception is limited as well
0.30%	Is in semistupor; confused
0.35%	Is at level for anesthesia; death is possible
0.40%	Stupor
0.50%	Coma
0.60%	Respiratory paralysis and death

Source: Data from *Drugs, Society, and Human Behavior*, 10th ed., by Oakley Ray, 2003, New York: McGraw-Hill; U.S. National Library of Medicine. (2006). *Alcohol use*. Retrieved October 11, 2007, from http://www.nlm.nih.gov/medlineplus/ency/article/001944.htm.

ENDURING ISSUES DIVERSITY/UNIVERSALITY

Women and Alcohol

Women are especially vulnerable to the effects of alcohol (National Institute on Alcohol Abuse and Alcoholism [NIAAA], 2003). Because women generally weigh less than men, the same dose of alcohol has a stronger effect on the average woman than on the average man. Most women have lower levels of the stomach enzyme that regulates alcohol metabolism. The less of this enzyme in the stomach, the greater the amount of alcohol that passes into the bloodstream and spreads through the body. (This is the reason why drinking on an empty stomach has more pronounced effects than drinking with meals.) In addition, neuroimagining studies reveal that women's brains may also be more vulnerable to damage from alcohol consumption than male brains. As a rough measure, one drink is likely to have the same effects on a woman as two drinks have on a man.

The dangers of alcohol notwithstanding, alcohol continues to be popular because of its short-term effects. As a depressant, it calms the nervous system, much like a general anesthetic. Thus, people consume alcohol to relax or to enhance their mood. Although it is a depressant, it is often experienced as a stimulant because it inhibits centers in the brain that govern critical judgment and impulsive behavior. In low dosages, alcohol makes people feel more courageous, less inhibited, more spontaneous, and more entertaining.

Barbiturates Commonly known as "downers," **barbiturates** include such medications as Amytal, Nembutal, Seconal, and phenobarbital. Discovered about a century ago, this class of depressants was first prescribed for its sedative and anticonvulsant qualities. But after researchers recognized in the 1950s that barbiturates had potentially deadly effects—particularly in combination with alcohol—their use declined, though they still are sometimes prescribed to treat such diverse conditions as insomnia, anxiety, epilepsy, arthritis, and bed-wetting. Though barbiturates are often prescribed to help people sleep, they actually disrupt the body's natural sleep patterns and cause dependence when used for long periods.

The general effects of barbiturates are strikingly similar to those of alcohol: Taken on an empty stomach, a small dose causes light-headedness, silliness, and poor motor coordination, whereas larger doses may bring on slurred speech, loss of inhibition, and increases in aggression. When taken during pregnancy, barbiturates, like alcohol, produce such birth defects as a cleft palate and malformations of the heart, skeleton, and central nervous system.

Opiates Psychoactive substances derived from, or resembling, sap taken from the seedpod of the opium poppy, **opiates** have a long history of use—though not always abuse. A Sumerian tablet from 4000 BC refers to the "joy plant." Originating in Turkey, opium spread west around the Mediterranean and east through India into China where it was used in pill or liquid form in folk medicines for thousands of years. But changes in the way opium and its derivative, morphine, were used opened the door to abuse. In the mid-seventeenth century, when the emperor of China banned tobacco and the Chinese began to smoke opium, addiction quickly followed. During the American Civil War, physicians used a new invention, the hypodermic needle, to administer morphine, a much-needed painkiller for soldiers. In this form, morphine was far more addictive than smoking opium. Heroin—introduced in 1898 as a cure for morphine addiction—created an even stronger dependency.

Morphine compounds are still used in painkillers and other medications, such as codeine cough syrups. The nonmedicinal distribution of opiates was banned early in the twentieth century. After that, a black market for heroin developed. In the public mind, the heroin addict became synonymous with the "dope fiend," the embodiment of social evil.

Heroin and other opiates resemble endorphins, the natural painkillers produced by the body, and they occupy many of the same nerve-receptor sites (Chapter 2). Heroin users report a surge of euphoria soon after taking the drug, followed by a period of "nodding off" and clouded mental functioning. Regular use leads to tolerance; tolerance may lead to physical dependence. In advanced stages of addiction, heroin becomes primarily a painkiller to stave off withdrawal symptoms. These symptoms, which may begin within hours of the last dose, include profuse sweating; alternating hot flashes and chills with goose bumps resembling the texture of a plucked turkey (hence the term "cold turkey"); severe cramps, vomiting, and diarrhea; and convulsive shaking and kicking (as in "kicking the habit").

Heroin abuse is associated with serious health conditions, including fatal overdose, spontaneous abortion, collapsed veins, pulmonary problems, and infectious diseases, especially HIV/AIDS and hepatitis (as a result of sharing needles). The mortality rate of heroin users is nearly 15 times higher than that of nonusers.

■ STIMULANTS: CAFFEINE, NICOTINE, AMPHETAMINES, AND COCAINE

The drugs classified as **stimulants** have legitimate uses, but because they produce feelings of optimism and boundless energy, the potential for abuse is high.

Caffeine Caffeine, which occurs naturally in coffee, tea, and cocoa, belongs to a class of drugs known as *xanthine stimulants*. The primary ingredient in most over-the-counter stimulants, caffeine is popularly believed to maintain wakefulness and alertness, but many of its stimulant effects are illusory. In one study, research participants performing motor and perceptual tasks believed they were doing better when they were on caffeine, but their actual performance was no better than without it. In terms of wakefulness, caffeine reduces the total number of sleep minutes and increases the time it takes to fall asleep. It is the only stimulant that does not appear to alter sleep stages, making it much safer than amphetamines.

Caffeine is found in many beverages and nonprescription medications, including pain relievers and cold and allergy remedies (Figure 4–4.) It is generally considered a benign drug, although large doses—more than five or six cups of strong coffee per day, for example—may cause caffeinism, or "coffee nerves": anxiety, headaches, heart palpitations, insomnia, and diarrhea. Caffeine interferes with prescribed medications, such as tranquilizers and sedatives, and appears to aggravate the symptoms of many psychiatric disorders. It is not clear what percentage of coffee drinkers are dependent on caffeine. Those who are dependent experience tolerance, difficulty

Stimulants

■ Stimulants speed up nervous system functioning and include _____

_____

_____

_____

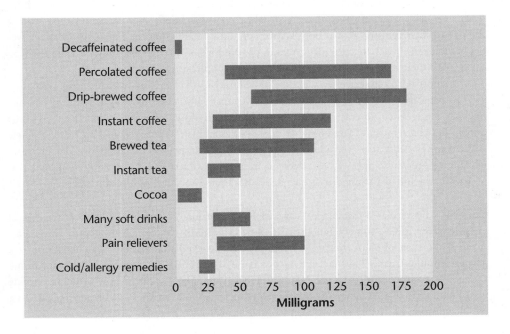

FIGURE 4–4
The amount of caffeine in some common preparations.
Caffeine occurs in varying amounts in coffee, tea, soft drinks, and many nonprescription medications. On average, Americans consume about 200 mg of caffeine each day.
Source: Blakeslee, 1991.

in giving it up, and physical and psychological distress, such as headaches, lethargy, and depression, whether the caffeine is in soda, coffee, or tea.

Nicotine   Nicotine, the psychoactive ingredient in tobacco, is probably the most dangerous and addictive stimulant in legal use today. Recent studies have found that the neurochemical properties of nicotine are similar to those of cocaine, amphetamines, and morphine. When smoked, nicotine tends to arrive at the brain all at once following each puff—a rush similar to the "high" experienced by heroin users. The smoker's heart rate increases and blood vessels constrict, causing dull skin and cold hands and accelerating the process of wrinkling and aging. Nicotine affects levels of several neurotransmitters, including norepinephrine, dopamine, and serotonin. Depending on the time, the amount smoked, and other factors, it may have either sedating or stimulating effects. Symptoms of withdrawal from nicotine include nervousness, difficulty concentrating, insomnia and drowsiness, headaches, irritability, and intense craving, all of which continue for weeks and may recur months or even years after a smoker has quit.

Amphetamines   Amphetamines are powerful synthetic stimulants, first marketed in the 1930s as a nasal spray to relieve symptoms of asthma. At the chemical level, amphetamines resemble epinephrine, a hormone that stimulates the sympathetic nervous system (Chapter 2, The Biological Basis of Behavior). During World War II, the military routinely gave soldiers amphetamines in pill form to relieve fatigue. After the war, the demand for "pep pills" grew among night workers, truck drivers, students, and athletes. Because amphetamines tend to suppress the appetite, they were widely prescribed as "diet pills." Today, the only legitimate medical uses for amphetamines are to treat narcolepsy and attention deficit disorder (ADD). They are, however, widely used for nonmedical, "recreational" reasons.

Amphetamines not only increase alertness, but also produce feelings of competence and well-being. People who inject amphetamines intravenously report a "rush" of euphoria. After the drug's effects wear off, however, users may "crash" into a state of exhaustion and depression. Amphetamines are habit forming: Users may come to believe that they cannot function without them. High doses can cause sweating, tremors, heart palpitations, anxiety, and insomnia—which may lead people to take barbiturates or drugs to counteract these effects. Excessive use of amphetamines may cause personality changes, including paranoia, homicidal and suicidal thoughts, and aggressive, violent behavior. Chronic users may develop *amphetamine psychosis*, which resembles paranoid schizophrenia and is characterized by delusions, hallucinations, and paranoia.

Methamphetamine—known on the street as "speed" and "fire," or in a crystal, smokable form as "ice," "crystal," and "crank"—is easily produced in clandestine laboratories from readily available ingredients. Ecstasy, a variation that was briefly popular around the turn of the twenty-first century, acts as both a stimulant and a hallucinogen. The name "Ecstasy" reflects the users' belief that the drug makes people love and trust one another, puts them in touch with their own emotions, and heightens sexual pleasure.

Short-term physical effects include involuntary teeth clenching (which is why users often wear baby pacifiers around their neck or suck lollipops), faintness, and chills or sweating. Animal research going back several decades shows that high doses of methamphetamine damage dopamine- and serotonin-containing neurons (National Institute on Drug Abuse, 2005). There is also some evidence that even a low dose of methamphetamine can lead to increased aggression, while longer-term use may lead to a decrease in intelligence test scores and a decline in memory. Moreover, the use of Ecstasy during pregnancy has been associated with birth defects.

Cocaine   First isolated from cocoa leaves in 1885, **cocaine** came to be used widely as a topical anesthetic for minor surgery (and still is, for example, in the dental anesthetic Novocain). Around the turn of the century, many physicians believed that cocaine was beneficial as a general stimulant, as well as a cure for excessive use of alcohol and morphine addiction. Among the more famous cocaine users was Sigmund Freud. When he discovered how addictive cocaine was, Freud campaigned against it, as did many of his contemporaries, and ingesting the drug fell into disrepute.

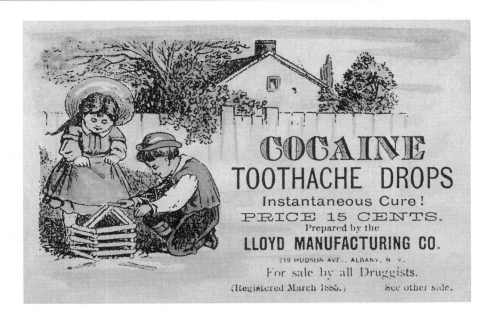

An 1885 American advertisement for Cocaine Toothache Drops, obviously intended for young children, as well as adults. The addition of cocaine to everyday products, including Coca-Cola, was quite common in the nine-teenth century.

Cocaine made a comeback in the 1970s in such unlikely places as Wall Street, among investment bankers who found that the drug not only made them high, but also allowed them to wheel and deal around the clock with little sleep. In the white-powdered form that is snorted (street names include "coke" and "snow"), it became a status drug, the amphetamine of the wealthy. In the 1980s, a cheaper, smokable, crystallized form known as "crack" (made from the by-products of cocaine extraction) appeared in inner-city neighborhoods. Crack reaches the brain in less than 10 seconds, producing a high that lasts from 5 to 20 minutes, followed by a swift and equally intense depression. Users report that crack leads to almost instantaneous addiction. Addiction to powdered cocaine, which has longer effects, is not inevitable, but is likely. Babies born to women addicted to crack and cocaine often are premature or have low birth weight, may have withdrawal symptoms, and may enter school with subtle to profound deficits in intelligence and language skills.

On the biochemical level, cocaine blocks the reabsorption of the neurotransmitter dopamine, which is associated with awareness, motivation, and, most significantly, pleasure. From an evolutionary perspective, dopamine rewards such survival-related activities as eating, drinking, and engaging in sex. Excess dopamine intensifies and prolongs feelings of pleasure—hence the cocaine user's feelings of euphoria. Normally, dopamine is reabsorbed, leading to feelings of satiety or satisfaction; dopamine reabsorption tells the body, "That's enough." But cocaine short-circuits this feeling of satisfaction, in effect telling the body, "More!" The addictive potential of cocaine may be related to the fact that it damages the brain cells that produce dopamine, thus increasing the amount of cocaine needed to get the same high in the future.

■ HALLUCINOGENS AND MARIJUANA

Certain natural or synthetic drugs can cause striking shifts in perception of the outside world or, in some cases, can cause their users to experience imaginary landscapes, settings, and beings that may seem more real than the outside world. Because such experiences resemble hallucinations, the drugs causing them are known as **hallucinogens**. The hallucinogens include **lysergic acid diethylamide (LSD)**, also known as "acid"; mescaline; peyote; and psilocybin. Marijuana is sometimes included in this group, although its effects are normally less powerful. How many cultural groups have used hallucinogens is not known. Historians believe that Native Americans have used mescaline, a psychedelic substance found in the mushroom-shaped tops or "buttons" of peyote cactus, for at least 8,000 years.

Hallucinogens and Marijuana

■ Illegal drugs such as LSD and marijuana _____

_____

_____

LSD   About an hour after ingesting lysergic acid diethylamide (LSD), people begin to experience an intensification of sensory perception, loss of control over their thoughts and emotions, and feelings of depersonalization and detachment, as though they were watching themselves from a distance. Some LSD users say that things never looked or sounded or smelled so beautiful; others have terrifying, nightmarish visions. Some users experience a sense of extraordinary mental lucidity; others become so confused that they fear they are losing their minds. The effects of LSD are highly variable, even for the same person on different occasions. "Bad trips," or unpleasant experiences, may be set off by a change in dosage or an alteration in setting or mood. During a bad trip, the user may not realize that the experiences are being caused by the drug and thus may panic. Flashbacks, or recurrences of hallucinations, may occur weeks after ingesting the drug. Other consequences of frequent use may include memory loss, paranoia, panic attacks, nightmares, and aggression.

Unlike depressants and stimulants, LSD and the other hallucinogens do not appear to produce withdrawal effects. If LSD is taken repeatedly, tolerance builds up rapidly: After a few days, no amount of the drug will produce its usual effects, until its use is suspended for about a week. This effect acts as a built-in deterrent to continuous use, which helps explain why LSD is generally taken episodically, rather than habitually. After a time, users seem to get tired of the experience and so decrease or discontinue their use of the drug, at least for a period of time.

Marijuana   **Marijuana** is a mixture of dried, shredded flowers and leaves of the hemp plant Cannabis sativa (which is also a source of fiber for rope and fabrics). Unlike LSD, marijuana usage has a long history. In China, cannabis has been cultivated for at least 5,000 years. The ancient Greeks knew about its psychoactive effects; and it has been used as an intoxicant in India for centuries. But only in the twentieth century did marijuana become popular in the United States. Today, marijuana is the most frequently used illegal drug in the United States and the fourth most popular drug among students (after alcohol, caffeine, and nicotine). Marijuana smokers report feelings of relaxation; heightened enjoyment of food, music, and sex; a loss of awareness of time; and on occasion, dreamlike experiences. As with LSD, experiences are varied. Many users experience a sense of well-being and feel euphoric, but others become suspicious, anxious, and depressed.

Marijuana has direct physiological effects, including dilation of the blood vessels in the eyes, making the eyes appear bloodshot; a dry mouth and coughing (because it is generally smoked); increased thirst and hunger; and mild muscular weakness, often in the form of drooping eyelids. The major physiological dangers of marijuana are potential respiratory and cardiovascular damage, including triggering heart attacks. Among the drug's psychological effects is a distortion of time, which appears to be related to the impact marijuana has on specific regions of the brain—feelings that minutes occur in slow motion or that hours flash by in seconds are common. In addition, marijuana may produce alterations in short-term memory and attention.

While under the influence of marijuana, people often lose the ability to remember and coordinate information, a phenomenon known as *temporal disintegration*. For instance, someone who is "high" on marijuana may forget what he or she was talking about in midsentence. Such memory lapses may trigger anxiety and panic. While high, marijuana users have shortened attention spans and delayed reactions, which contribute to concerns about their ability to drive a car or to study or work effectively.

Is marijuana a "dangerous" drug? This question is the subject of much debate in scientific circles as well as public forums. On one hand are those who contend that marijuana can be psychologically if not physiologically addictive (Haney et al., 2004; F. R. Levin et al., 2004); that frequent, long-term use has a negative impact on learning and motivation; and that legal prohibitions against marijuana should be continued. The evidence for cognitive or psychological damage is mixed. On the other hand are those who maintain that marijuana is less harmful than the legal drugs (alcohol and nicotine), and they argue that the criminalization of marijuana forces people to buy unregulated cannabis from illegal sources, which means that they might smoke "pot" contaminated with more harmful substances. Moreover, some evidence indicates that marijuana can relieve some of the unpleasant side effects of chemotherapy and can reduce suffering among terminal cancer patients. In short, the jury is still out, and the debate over marijuana is likely to continue.

■ EXPLAINING ABUSE AND ADDICTION

Some people drink socially and never develop a problem with alcohol, whereas others become dependent or addicted. Some experiment with crack, which is known to be almost instantly addictive, or use "club drugs," which are known to be dangerous. Others "just say no." Each year, millions of Americans stop smoking cigarettes while millions more continue. Why do some people abuse drugs and others do not?

The causes of substance abuse and dependence are complex, the result of a combination of biological, psychological, social, and cultural factors that vary from person to person. Causes also depend, in part, on the specific drug. In short, there is no "one-size-fits-all" explanation. But psychologists have identified a number of factors that, especially in combination, make substance abuse more likely to occur.

ENDURING ISSUES   NATURE/NURTURE

Genetics and Drug Abuse

There is substantial evidence for a genetic basis for alcohol abuse. People whose biological parents have alcohol-abuse problems are more likely to abuse alcohol—even if they are adopted and are raised by people who do not abuse alcohol. Identical twins also are far more likely to have similar patterns relating to alcohol use than are fraternal twins. There is also evidence that suggests a hereditary contribution to tobacco use.

Biological Factors   To the extent that heredity plays a role in drug addiction, is drug addiction then a disease like diabetes or high blood pressure? Alcoholics Anonymous (AA), the oldest and probably the most successful self-help organization in this country, has long endorsed this view. According to the disease model, alcoholism is not a moral issue, but a medical one; and rather than being a sign of character flaws, alcohol abuse is a symptom of a physiological condition. An important aspect of the disease model is that, regardless of the initial source of the addiction, addictive substances dramatically change the brain. Those changes can take months or years to reverse and, during that time, cravings to use the drug can be intense. The disease model has been applied to many addictions. In fact, to a degree, the disease model has become part of conventional wisdom: Many Americans view substance abuse as a biological problem that requires medical treatment. Not all psychologists agree, however, in part because drug use and abuse is also linked to psychological, social, and cultural factors as well. Many researchers believe that a full understanding of the causes of alcoholism and other drug addictions will not be achieved unless a wide variety of factors—heredity, personality, social setting, and culture—are taken into account.

Psychological, Social, and Cultural Factors   Whether a person uses a psychoactive drug and what effects that drug has depends, in part, on the person's expectations, the social setting, and cultural beliefs and values. Numerous studies have shown that people use or abuse alcohol because they expect that drinking will help them to feel better. During the 1960s and 1970s, members of the counterculture held similar expectations for marijuana, as do a significant number of young people today.

The family in which a child grows up also shapes attitudes and beliefs about drugs. For example, children whose parents do not use alcohol tend to abstain or to drink only moderately; children whose parents abuse alcohol tend to drink heavily. Such children are most likely to abuse alcohol whenever their family tolerates deviance in general or encourages excitement and pleasure seeking. Moreover, adolescents who have been physically assaulted or sexually abused in their homes are at increased risk for drug abuse. Parents are not the only family influence; some research indicates that siblings' and peers' attitudes and behavior have as much or more impact on young people than parents do (J. R. Harris, 1998).

Explaining Abuse and Addiction

■ Biological factors include a

_____

for alcohol and nicotine abuse.

■ _____,

_____, and

_____ factors

influence drug abuse and addiction;

use and effects of a drug depend

on _____,

_____, and

_____.

Factors Affecting Drug Effects

The setting in which drugs are taken is another powerful determinant of their effects. Every year thousands of hospital patients are given opiate-based painkillers before and after surgery. They may have experiences that a heroin or cocaine user would label as a "high," but they are more likely to consider them confusing than pleasant. In this setting, psychoactive substances are defined as medicine, dosage is supervised by physicians, and patients take them to get well, not to get high. In contrast, at teenage raves, college beer parties, and all-night clubs, people drink specifically to get drunk and take other drugs to get high. But even in these settings, some individuals participate without using or abusing drugs, and motives for using drugs vary. People who drink or smoke marijuana because they think that they need a drug to overcome social inhibitions and to be accepted are more likely to slip into abuse than people who use the same substances in the same amounts because they want to have more fun.

Culture, too, may steer people toward or away from alcoholism. Parents and spouses may introduce people by example to a pattern of heavy drinking. Alcohol is also more acceptable in some ethnic cultures than in others. For example, many religious groups frown on the excessive use of alcohol, including Muslims, Mormons, conservative Baptists, and Seventh-Day Adventists, who prohibit it altogether.

Many different psychoactive drugs may alter consciousness, often with negative consequences such as abuse and addiction. The next section examines meditation and hypnosis, two procedures that have been used for centuries to promote positive outcomes through altered states of consciousness without the use of drugs.

Check Your Understanding

1. Indicate whether the following statements are true (T) or false (F).

a. _____ Caffeine is not addictive.

b. _____ Many users become dependent on crack cocaine almost immediately after beginning to use it.

c. _____ Recurring hallucinations are common among users of hallucinogens.

d. _____ Marijuana interferes with short-term memory.

2. Even though you know that alcohol is a central nervous system depressant, your friend says it is actually a stimulant because he does things that he would not otherwise do after having a couple of drinks. He also feels less inhibited, more spontaneous, and more entertaining. The reason your friend experiences alcohol as a stimulant is that

a. Alcohol has the same effect on the nervous system as amphetamines.

b. Alcohol has a strong placebo effect.

c. The effects of alcohol depend almost entirely on the expectations of the user.

d. Alcohol depresses areas in the brain responsible for critical judgment and impulsiveness.

Meditation and Hypnosis

At one time, Western scientists viewed meditation and hypnosis with great skepticism. However, research has shown that these techniques can produce alterations in consciousness that can be measured through such sophisticated methods as brain imaging.

■ MEDITATION

For centuries, people have used various forms of **meditation** to experience an alteration in consciousness. Generally speaking, the goal of meditation is to attain a restful, yet fully alert state that enables the self-regulation of one's emotions. Each form of meditation focuses the meditator's attention in a slightly different way. Zen meditation concentrates on respiration, for example, whereas Sufism relies on frenzied dancing and prayer. In transcendental meditation (TM), practitioners intone a mantra, which is a sound, specially selected for each person to keep all other images and problems at bay and to allow the meditator to relax more deeply.

In all its forms, meditation suppresses the activity of the sympathetic nervous system which, as noted in Chapter 2, is the part of the nervous system that prepares the body for strenuous activity during an emergency. Meditation also lowers the rate of metabolism, reduces heart and respiratory rates, and decreases blood lactate, a chemical linked to stress. Alpha brain waves (which accompany relaxed wakefulness) increase noticeably during meditation. Not surprisingly, brain-imagining studies indicate that practicing meditation activates brain centers involved in attention and regulation of the autonomic nervous system activity.

Meditation has been used to treat certain medical problems, especially so-called functional complaints (those for which no physical cause can be found). For example, stress often leads to muscle tension and, sometimes, to pressure on nerves—and pain. In other cases, pain leads to muscle tension, which makes the pain worse. Relaxation techniques such as meditation may bring relief of such physical symptoms. Studies have also found that for some people, meditating reduces or eliminates the need to use or abuse drugs. There is even some evidence that meditation may increase the effectiveness of the immune system (Davidson et al., 2003). In addition to physiological benefits, people who regularly practice some form of meditation report emotional and even spiritual gains, including increased sensory awareness and a sense of timelessness, well-being, and being at peace with oneself and the universe.

Meditation can help relieve anxiety and promote peace of mind and a sense of well-being.

■ HYPNOSIS

In mid-eighteenth-century Europe, Franz (Anton) Mesmer (1734–1815), a Viennese physician, fascinated audiences by putting patients into trances to cure their illnesses. Mesmerism—now known as **hypnosis**—was initially discredited by a French commission chaired by Benjamin Franklin. But some respectable nineteenth-century physicians revived interest in hypnosis when they discovered that it could be used to treat certain forms of mental illness. Nevertheless, even today, considerable disagreement persists about how to define hypnosis.

One reason for the controversy is that there is no simple definition of exactly what it means to be hypnotized. Different people who have undergone hypnosis describe their experiences in very different ways. Thus, some researchers who study hypnosis still debate whether or not it should be characterized as a state of altered consciousness at all. However, other researchers stress that studying the phenomena that characterize a hypnotic state, such as the social interactions and the neurophysiological changes, is of more importance than reaching a consensus on whether hypnosis is an altered state.

Individuals also vary in their susceptibility to hypnosis. Several studies have shown that although susceptibility to hypnosis is not related to personal characteristics such as trust, gullibility, submissiveness, and social compliance, it is related to the ability of an individual to become absorbed in reading, music, and daydreaming. One measure of susceptibility is whether people respond to *hypnotic suggestion*. Some people under hypnosis who are told that they cannot move their arms or that their pain has vanished do, in fact, experience paralysis or anesthesia. If told that they are hearing a certain piece of music or are unable to hear anything, they may hallucinate or become deaf temporarily. When hypnotized subjects are told, "You will remember nothing that happened under hypnosis until I tell you," some people do indeed experience amnesia. But, contrary to rumors, hypnotic suggestion cannot force people to do something foolish and embarrassing—or dangerous—against their will.

Meditation

■ Meditation involves various methods of _____, _____, or _____ to suppress activity of the _____.

Hypnosis

■ There is no simple definition of what it means to be hypnotized, but it is often described as _____.

■ Regarding hypnosis, individuals vary in their susceptibility to _____ and _____

Another measure of susceptibility to hypnosis is whether people respond to posthypnotic commands. For example, under hypnosis, a person suffering from back pain may be instructed that when he feels a twinge, he will imagine that he is floating on a cloud, his body is weightless, and the pain will stop—a technique also called "imaging." A runner may be told that when she pulls on her ear, she will block out the noise of the crowd and the runners on either side of her to heighten her concentration.

ENDURING ISSUES   MIND/BODY

Clinical Applications of Hypnosis

Because hypnotic susceptibility varies significantly from one person to another, its value in clinical and therapeutic settings is difficult to assess. Nevertheless, hypnosis is used in a variety of medical and counseling situations. Some research indicates that it can enhance the effectiveness of traditional forms of psychotherapy (Chapman, 2006; Kirsch, Montgomery, & Sapirstein, 1995), especially when it is used to treat anxiety disorders (Lynn & Kirsch, 2006a), and posttraumatic stress disorder (Lynn & Kirsch, 2006b). Hypnosis has been shown to be effective in controlling various types of physical pain (Lynn, Kirsch, & Koby, 2006; D. R. Patterson & Jensen, 2003; D. R. Patterson & Ptacek, 1997). Dentists have used it as an anesthetic for years. Hypnosis has also been used to alleviate pain in children with leukemia who have to undergo repeated bone-marrow biopsies (Hilgard, Hilgard, & Kaufmann, 1983). Moreover, it also has a role in treating some medical conditions, such as irritable bowel syndrome (Gonsalkorale, Miller, Afzal, & Whorwell, 2003).

Can hypnosis make someone change or eliminate bad habits? In some cases, posthypnotic commands temporarily diminish a person's desire to smoke or overeat (Elkins & Rajab, 2004; Green & Lynn, 2000; Lynn & Kirsch, 2006c). But even certified hypnotists agree that this treatment is effective only when people are motivated to change their behavior. Hypnosis may shore up their will, but so might joining a support group, such as Nicotine Anonymous or Weight Watchers.

Check Your Understanding

1. Match the following terms with the appropriate description.

_____ Meditation   **a.** Individuals vary greatly in this

_____ Hypnosis   **b.** Is a controversial altered state of consciousness

_____ Hypnotic susceptibility   **c.** Suppresses the sympathetic nervous system

2. You overhear some people discussing the effects of hypnosis. On the basis of what you have learned in this chapter, you agree with everything they say EXCEPT:

a. "Some people can be hypnotized easily and some people can't."

b. "If you tell someone under hypnosis to forget everything that happens, some people will actually do that."

c. "Under hypnosis, people can be forced to do foolish or embarrassing things against their will."

d. "Hypnosis can actually be used to control some kinds of pain."

Chapter Review

www.psychologythecore.com

Conscious Experience

Consciousness is our awareness of various cognitive processes that operate in our daily lives such as sleeping, dreaming, concentrating, and making decisions. Psychologists divide consciousness into two broad areas: **waking consciousness**, which includes thoughts, feelings, and perceptions that arise when we are awake and reasonably alert; and **altered states of consciousness**, during which our mental state differs noticeably from normal waking consciousness.

The temporary escape offered by **daydreaming** occurs without effort when we spontaneously shift our attention away from the demands of the real world. Some psychologists see no positive or practical value in this activity. Others contend daydreams let us process hidden desires without guilt or anxiety. Daydreams may also build cognitive and creative skills that help us survive difficult situations or help to relieve tension.

Sleep

Nobody knows exactly why we need to sleep, although evidence has begun to accumulate that sleep may play an important restorative function, physically and mentally. As with many other biological functions, sleep and waking follow a daily biological cycle known as a **circadian rhythm**. The human biological clock is governed by a tiny cluster of neurons in the brain known as the **suprachiasmatic nucleus (SCN)** that regulates proteins related to metabolism and alertness. Normally, the rhythms and chemistry of the body's cycles interact smoothly; but when we cross several time zones in one day, hormonal, temperature, and digestive cycles become desynchronized, which leads to jet lag.

Normal sleep consists of several stages. During Stage 1, the pulse slows, muscles relax, and the eyes move from side to side. The sleeper is easily awakened from Stage 1 sleep. In Stages 2 and 3, the sleeper is hard to awaken and does not respond to noise or light. Heart rate, blood pressure, and temperature continue to drop. During Stage 4 sleep, heart and breathing rates, blood pressure, and body temperature are at their lowest points of the night. About an hour after first falling asleep, the sleeper begins to ascend through the stages back to Stage 1—a process that takes about 40 minutes. At this stage in the sleep cycle, heart rate and blood pressure increase, the muscles become more relaxed than at any other time in the cycle, and the eyes move rapidly under closed eyelids. This stage of sleep is known as **rapid-eye movement (REM)** or **paradoxical sleep**. REM sleep is called *paradoxical* sleep because although measures of brain activity, heart rate, blood pressure, and other physiological functions closely resemble those recorded during waking consciousness, the person in this stage appears to be deeply asleep and is incapable of moving; the body's voluntary muscles are essentially paralyzed. REM sleep is also the stage when most dreaming occurs, though dreams also take place during **non-REM (NREM) sleep**. Insufficient sleep has become a "national epidemic" in the United States, causing difficulty in paying attention and remembering things, impairment of logical reasoning, and an increase in accidents and errors of judgment.

Sleep disorders include sleeptalking, sleepwalking, **night terrors**, **insomnia**, **apnea**, and **narcolepsy**. Most episodes of sleeptalking and sleepwalking occur during a deep stage of sleep. Unlike **nightmares**, night terrors most often occur during REM sleep and are often remembered. Also, they are more common among children than adults, prove difficult to be awakened from, and are rarely remembered the next morning. Insomnia is characterized by difficulty in falling asleep or remaining asleep throughout the night. Some prescription medicines can cause anxiety, memory loss, hallucinations, and violent behavior. Apnea is marked by breathing difficulties during the night and feelings of exhaustion during the day. Narcolepsy is a hereditary sleep disorder characterized by sudden nodding off during the day and sudden loss of muscle tone following moments of emotional excitement.

Dreams

Dreams are visual or auditory experiences that occur primarily during REM periods of sleep. Less vivid experiences that resemble conscious thinking tend to occur during NREM sleep.

Several theories have been developed to explain the nature and content of dreams. According to Freud, dreams have two kinds of contents: manifest (the surface content of the dream itself) and latent (the disguised, unconscious meaning of the dream). According to a more recent hypothesis, dreams arise out of the mind's reprocessing of daytime information that is important to the survival of the organism. With this hypothesis, dreaming thus strengthens our memories of important information.

Drug-Altered Consciousness

Chemical substances that change moods and perceptions are known as **psychoactive drugs**. Although many of the psychoactive drugs available today have been used for thousands of years, the motivation for using drugs is different today. Traditionally, these drugs were used in religious rituals, as nutrient beverages, or as culturally approved stimulants. Today, most psychoactive drug use is recreational, divorced from religious or family traditions.

Substance abuse is a pattern of drug use that diminishes the person's ability to fulfill responsibilities at home, work, or school and that results in repeated use of a drug in dangerous situations or that leads to legal difficulties related to drug use. Continued abuse over time can lead to **substance dependence**, a pattern of compulsive drug taking that is much more serious than substance abuse. It is often marked by tolerance, the need to take higher doses of a drug to produce its original effects or to prevent withdrawal symptoms. Withdrawal symptoms are the unpleasant physical or psychological effects that follow discontinuance of the psychoactive substance. When studying drug effects, most researchers use the **double-blind** procedure in which none of the researchers knows which participants will receive the active drug and those who will receive a neutral, inactive substance called a **placebo**.

Depressants are chemicals that slow down behavior or cognitive processes. **Alcohol** calms down the nervous system, working like a general anesthetic. It is often experienced subjectively as a stimulant because it inhibits centers in the brain that govern critical judgment and impulsive behavior. This accounts, in part, for its involvement in a substantial proportion of violent and accidental deaths. **Barbiturates** are potentially deadly depressants, first used for their sedative and anticonvulsant properties, but today their use is limited to the treatment of such conditions as epilepsy and arthritis. **Opiates** are highly addictive drugs such as opium, morphine, and heroin that dull the senses and induce feelings of euphoria, well-being, and relaxation. Morphine and heroin are derivatives of opium.

Stimulants are drugs that stimulate the sympathetic nervous system and produce feelings of optimism and boundless energy, making the potential for their abuse significant. Caffeine occurs naturally in coffee, tea, and cocoa. Considered a benign drug, in large doses caffeine can cause anxiety, insomnia, and other unpleasant conditions. Nicotine occurs naturally only in tobacco. Although it is a stimulant, it acts like a depressant when taken in large doses. **Amphetamines** are stimulants that initially produce "rushes" of euphoria often followed by sudden "crashes" and, sometimes, depression. **Cocaine** brings on a sense of euphoria by stimulating the sympathetic nervous system, but it can also cause anxiety, depression, and addictive cravings. Its crystalline form—crack—is highly addictive.

Hallucinogens include drugs such as **lysergic acid diethylamide (LSD)**, psilocybin, and mescaline that distort visual and auditory perception. **Marijuana** is a mild hallucinogen capable of producing feelings of euphoria, a sense of well-being, and swings in mood from gaiety to relaxation to paranoia. Though similar to hallucinogens in certain respects, marijuana is far less potent, and its effects on consciousness are far less profound. Marijuana can disrupt memory, distort the experience of time, and alter short-term memory and attention.

The causes of substance abuse and dependence are complex, the result of a combination of biological, psychological, social, and cultural factors that varies from person to person. There is evidence of a genetic basis for alcohol and tobacco abuse; however, there is disagreement about whether this means that abuse of these and other drugs is a disease. Expectations, the social setting, and cultural beliefs and values also affect the drug experience and the likelihood of drug abuse and dependence.

Meditation and Hypnosis

Meditation refers to any of several methods of concentration, reflection, or focusing of thoughts intended to suppress the activity of the sympathetic nervous system. Meditation not only lowers the metabolic rate but also reduces heart and respiratory rates. Brain activity during meditation resembles that experienced during relaxed wakefulness; and the accompanying decrease in blood lactate reduces stress.

Hypnosis is a trancelike state in which the hypnotized person responds readily to suggestions. Susceptibility to hypnosis depends on how easily people can become absorbed in concentration. Hypnosis can ease the pain of certain medical conditions and can help people stop smoking and break other habits.

Chapter 5
Learning

Go to *The Core Online* at **www.psychologythecore.com** to get the most up-to-date information for your introductory psychology course. The content online is an important part of what you are learning—the content there can help prepare you for your test! It includes up-to-date examples, simulations, video clips, and practice quizzes. Also be sure to check out the *Blog* to hear directly from the authors on what current events and latest research are most relevant to your course materials.

The first time you log in, you will need the access code packaged with your textbook. If you do not have a code, please go to **www.mypearsonstore.com** and enter the ISBN of your textbook (**0-13-603344-X**) to purchase the code.

5 1 Classical Conditioning

Elements of Classical Conditioning

- **Classical conditioning** is the type of learning in which a response naturally elicited by one stimulus comes to be elicited by a different, formerly neutral, stimulus.
- An **unconditioned stimulus** is a stimulus that invariably causes an organism to respond in a specific way.
- A **conditioned stimulus** is an originally neutral stimulus.
- An **unconditioned response** is a response that takes place in an organism whenever an unconditioned stimulus occurs.
- A **conditioned response** is a response that, after conditioning, an organism produces when a conditioned stimulus is presented.

Establishing a Classically Conditioned Response

- To establish a classically conditioned response, repeated pairings of US and CS are required and spaced moderately apart.
- Intermittent pairing reduces the rate of learning and final strength of the UR.
- Eventually, learning reaches a point of diminishing returns.

Classical Conditioning Is Selective

- **Preparedness** is a kind of classical conditioning that is much easier to establish.
- **Conditioned taste aversions** are acquired very swiftly.

5 2 Operant Conditioning

Elements of Operant Conditioning

- **Operant conditioning** refers to a change in behavior resulting from the consequences of that behavior.
- The **law of effect (principle of reinforcement)** states that **reinforcers** increase the likelihood that a behavior will be repeated and **punishers** decrease the likelihood that a behavior will be repeated.

Establishing an Operantly Conditioned Response

- To establish an operantly conditioned response, wait until the desired response occurs, then reinforce it.
- Alternatively, reinforce successive approximations to the desired response (**shaping**).
- Eventually, operant conditioning reaches a point of diminishing returns.

A Closer Look at Reinforcement

- **Positive reinforcers** add something rewarding.
- **Negative reinforcers** remove something unpleasant.
- Positive and negative reinforcers strengthen behavior.
- Accidental or random reinforcement can lead to superstitious behaviors.

Punishment

- To be effective, punishment must be swift, sufficient, and consistent and, preferably, paired with reinforcement for a more desirable behavior.
- Disadvantages of punishment are that it merely suppresses undesirable behavior, can impede the learning of more desirable behavior, teaches the learner that punishment works, and often creates anger and aggression.
- Often, the threat of punishment is sufficient to change behavior (**avoidance training**).

Learned Helplessness

- When punishment is unavoidable, a "giving up" response may be learned.
- Once established, learned helplessness can generalize to new situations and can be very persistent.

Shaping Behavioral Change Through Feedback

- Operant conditioning can be used to control certain biological functions, such as blood pressure, skin temperature, heart rate (**biofeedback**), and even brain waves (**neurofeedback**).
- Biofeedback and neurofeedback treatments take considerable time, effort, patience, and discipline, and do not work for everyone.

5 3 Factors Shared by Classical and Operant Conditioning

Basic Similarities

- Both classical conditioning and operant conditioning involve the learning of associations.
- In both kinds of conditioning, responses are under the control of stimuli in the environment.

Importance of Contingencies

- Both classical conditioning and operant conditioning involve perceived **contingencies**.
- In classical conditioning, the CS comes to be viewed as a signal that the US is about to happen.
- In operant conditioning, the learner must perceive a connection between performing a certain voluntary action and receiving a certain reward or punishment.
  — Partial or intermittent reinforcement results in long-lasting behavior.
  — **Schedules of reinforcement** include:
    - **Fixed-interval**
    - **Fixed-ratio**
    - **Variable-interval**
    - **Variable-ratio**

Extinction and Spontaneous Recovery

- In classical conditioning and operant conditioning, learned responses eventually may disappear (**extinction**) and spontaneously reappear (**spontaneous recovery**).
- Failing to pair the US and CS eventually will cause the extinction of the CR, while presenting the CS once again may elicit the CR briefly at reduced strength.
- In operant conditioning, withholding reinforcement eventually will lead to the extinction of the learned response. However, the response may appear again briefly at some future time.

Generalization and Discrimination

- In both classical and operant conditioning, the learner may respond to cues that are merely similar (but not identical) to the ones that prevailed during the original learning (**stimulus generalization**).
- In operant conditioning, the learned response may generalize to other, similar responses (**response generalization**).
- Discrimination training can be used to prevent stimulus and response generalization.

New Learning Based on Original Learning

- In classical and operant conditioning, original learning can serve as the basis for new learning (**higher-order conditioning**).

5 4 Cognitive Learning

Latent Learning and Cognitive Maps

- **Cognitive learning** is impossible to observe and measure directly, but it can be inferred from behavior.
- Some learning need not be reflected immediately in a behavior change (**latent learning**).
- One kind of latent learning is the formation of a mental image of a spatial environment that can be used to navigate that environment in the future (**cognitive map**).

Insight and Learning Sets

- **Insight** is learning that occurs rapidly as a result of understanding all the elements of a problem.
- A **learning set** refers to the ability to become increasingly more effective in solving problems as more problems are solved (learning to learn).

Learning by Observing

- **Observational** (or **vicarious**) **learning** is the act of learning by observing the behavior of other people.
- **Social learning theorists** are psychologists who emphasize the ability to learn by observing a model or by receiving instructions, without firsthand experience by the learner.
- **Vicarious reinforcement** (or **punishment**) refers to reinforcement or punishment experienced by models that affects the willingness of others to perform the behaviors they learned by observing those models.

W|hat do the following anecdotes have in common?

- In Mozambique, a giant pouched rat the size of a cat scurries across a field, pauses, sniffs the air, turns, sniffs again, then begins to scratch at the ground with her forepaws. She has discovered yet another land mine buried a few inches underground. After a brief break for a bit of banana and a pat or two from her handler, she scurries off again to find more land mines.

- In the middle of a winter night, Adrian Cole—four years old and three feet tall—put on his jacket and boots and drove his mother's car to a nearby video store. When he found the store closed, he drove back home. Because he was driving very slowly with the lights off and weaving a bit, he understandably attracted the attention of police officers who followed him. When he got home, he collided with two parked cars and backed into the police cruiser! When the police asked him how he learned to drive, he explained that his mother would put him on her lap while she drove, and he just watched what she did.

- While driving along a congested boulevard, a middle-aged man glances at a park bench, and, for a moment, his heart pounds as he experiences a warm feeling throughout his body. At first, he does not understand why passing this spot has evoked such a strong emotion. Then he remembers—it was the meeting place he once shared with his high school sweetheart more than 20 years ago.

The common element in all these stories—and the topic of this chapter—is learning. Most people associate learning with classrooms and studying for tests, but psychologists define it more broadly. To them, **learning** occurs whenever experience or practice results in a relatively permanent change in behavior or in potential behavior. This definition includes all the examples mentioned previously, plus a great many more. When you remember which way to put the key into your front-door lock, when you recall how to park a car, or when you recall where the library water fountain is located, you are showing a tiny part of your enormous capacity for learning.

Human life would be impossible without learning, which is involved in virtually everything people do. If you were unable to learn, you could not communicate with other people, recognize yourself as human, or even know what substances are appropriate to eat. This chapter explores several kinds of learning. One type of learning involves associating one event with another. When rats associate the smell of TNT with receiving food or when people associate a certain place with a specific strong emotion, they are engaging in two forms of learning called *operant conditioning* and *classical conditioning*. Psychologists have studied these forms of learning extensively, so much of this chapter is devoted to them. But making associations is not all there is to human learning. Learning also involves the formation of concepts, theories, ideas, and other mental abstractions. Psychologists call this *cognitive learning*, a process we will discuss later in this chapter.

Our tour of learning begins in another time and place—the laboratory of a Nobel-Prize–winning Russian scientist at the turn of the twentieth century. His name is Ivan Pavlov, and his work is helping to revolutionize the study of learning. He has discovered **classical conditioning**, a form of learning in which a response elicited by a stimulus becomes elicited by a previously neutral stimulus.

ENDURING ISSUES   in Learning

This chapter addresses how humans and other animals acquire new behaviors because of their experiences. Thus, this chapter bears directly on the enduring issue of the extent to which organisms change over the course of their lives (stability-change). The events that shape learning not only vary among different individuals (diversity-universality), but the events are influenced by an organism's inborn characteristics (nature-nurture). Finally, some types of learning can affect a person's physical health by influencing how the body responds to disease (mind-body).

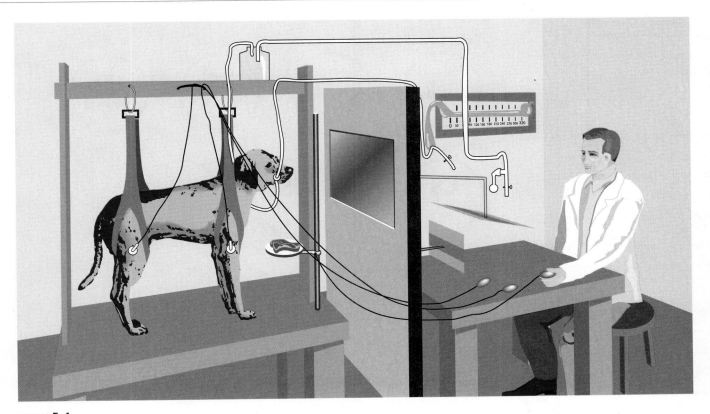

FIGURE 5–1
Pavlov's apparatus for classically conditioning a dog to salivate.
The experimenter sits behind a one-way mirror and controls the presentation of the conditioned stimulus (touch applied to the leg) and the unconditioned stimulus (food). A tube runs from the dog's salivary glands to a vial, where the drops of saliva are collected as a way of measuring the strength of the dog's response.

Classical Conditioning

As we saw in Chapter 1, Pavlov was studying digestion, which begins when saliva mixes with food in the mouth (Figure 5–1). While measuring the amount of saliva dogs produce when given food, he noticed that they began to salivate even before they tasted the food. The mere sight of food made them drool. In fact, they even drooled at the sound of the experimenter's footsteps. This aroused Pavlov's curiosity. What was causing these responses? How had the dogs learned to salivate to sights and sounds?

To answer this question, Pavlov sounded a bell just before presenting his dogs with food. A ringing bell does not usually make a dog's mouth water, but after hearing the bell many times right before getting fed, Pavlov's dogs began to salivate as soon as the bell rang. It was as though they had learned that the bell signaled the appearance of food; indeed, their mouths watered on cue even when no food followed. The dogs had been *conditioned* to salivate in response to a new stimulus, the bell, which normally would not have prompted salivation (Pavlov, 1927).

■ ELEMENTS OF CLASSICAL CONDITIONING

In Figure 5–2, the four basic elements in classical conditioning are diagrammed: the unconditioned stimulus, the unconditioned response, the conditioned stimulus, and the conditioned response. The **unconditioned stimulus (US)** is an event that automatically elicits a certain reflex reaction, which is the **unconditioned response (UR)**. In Pavlov's studies, food in the mouth was the unconditioned stimulus, and salivation to it was the unconditioned response. The third element in classical conditioning, the **conditioned stimulus (CS)**, is an event that is paired repeatedly with the unconditioned stimulus. At first, the conditioned stimulus does not

Elements of Classical Conditioning

■ Classical conditioning is the type of learning in which _____ _____ _____

■ An unconditioned stimulus is a stimulus that_____ _____

■ A conditioned stimulus is_____ _____ _____

■ An unconditioned response is _____ _____

■ A conditioned response is_____ _____ _____

(Continued)

Establishing a Classically Conditioned Response

- To establish a classically conditioned response,_____

_____

_____

- Intermittent pairing reduces the rate of _____ and final strength of the _____.
- Eventually, _____ reaches a point of_____.

Classical Conditioning Is Selective

- Preparedness is _____

_____

_____

- Conditioned taste aversions are

_____

_____

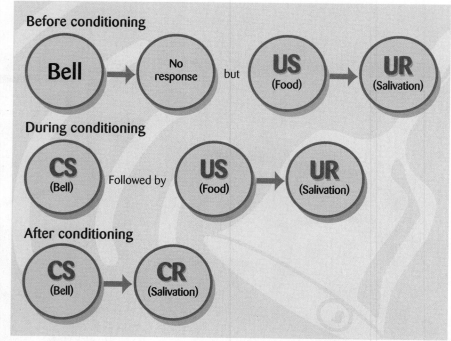

FIGURE 5–2

A model of the classical conditioning process.

elicit the desired response. But eventually, after being paired repeatedly with the unconditioned stimulus, the conditioned stimulus alone comes to trigger a reaction similar to the unconditioned response. This learned reaction is the **conditioned response (CR)**.

Classical conditioning has been demonstrated in virtually every animal species, even cockroaches, bees, squid, and spiders (Abramson & Aquino, 2002; Hidehiro & Makato, 2006; Krasne & Glanzman, 1995; Watanabe, Kobayashi, Sakura, Matsumoto, & Mizunami, 2003). Many people inadvertently have classically conditioned their own pets. For example, a cat may begin to purr when it hears the sound of an electric can opener running. For the cat, the taste and smell of food are unconditioned stimuli for a purring response. By repeatedly pairing the can opener whirring with the delivery of food, the cat's owner has turned this sound into a conditioned stimulus that triggers a conditioned response.

■ ESTABLISHING A CLASSICALLY CONDITIONED RESPONSE

As shown in Figure 5–3, repeated pairings of the conditioned stimulus with the unconditioned stimulus are needed before the unconditioned response can become a conditioned response. The likelihood or strength of the conditioned response increases each time the two stimuli are paired. This learning, however, eventually reaches a point of diminishing returns. The amount of each increase gradually becomes smaller, until finally, no further learning occurs. The conditioned response is now fully established.

The spacing of pairings is also important in establishing a classically conditioned response. When pairings of the CS and US follow each other very rapidly, or when they are very far apart, learning the association is slower. If the spacing of pairings is moderate—neither too far apart nor too close together—learning occurs more quickly. It is also important that the CS and US rarely, if ever, occur alone. Pairing the CS and US only once in a while, or **intermittent pairing**, reduces both the rate of learning and the final strength of the learned response.

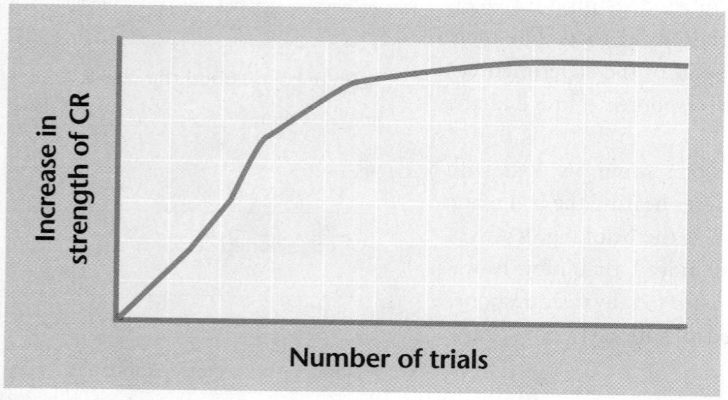

FIGURE 5–3

Response acquisition.

At first, each pairing of the US and CS increases the strength of the response. After many trials, learning begins to level off; eventually, it reaches a point of diminishing returns.

Increase in strength of CR

Number of trials

■ CLASSICAL CONDITIONING IN HUMANS

Classical conditioning is as common in humans as it is in other animals. The story at the beginning of the chapter about the sight of a park bench triggering a strong emotion is an example of classical conditioning. Movie buffs probably are aware that music in a film is chosen carefully to create an emotional state appropriate to what is happening on the screen. Scary music accompanies scary scenes; light music accompanies happy scenes. In fact, sometimes conditioning works the other way, too: After seeing the classic movie *Jaws*, some people become nervous whenever they hear the theme song from the film. Long after seeing the film *Titanic*, some people are still brought to tears whenever they hear the tragic love song "My Heart Will Go On" from the movie.

Also, classical conditioning has been used as a treatment for certain kinds of anxiety. Since people cannot be fearful and relaxed at the same time, if they are taught to relax in fearful or anxious situations, their anxiety in those situations should disappear. As we will see in Chapter 13 (Therapies), this technique is indeed effective in treating a variety of disorders, including phobias and posttraumatic stress disorder (PTSD).

ENDURING ISSUES MIND/BODY

Classical Conditioning and the Immune System

In another example of classical conditioning in humans, researchers have devised a novel way to treat autoimmune disorders, which cause the immune system to attack healthy organs or tissues. Although powerful drugs can be used to suppress the immune system and thus reduce the impact of the autoimmune disorder, these drugs often have dangerous side effects and must be administered sparingly. The challenge, then, was to find a treatment that could suppress the immune system without damaging vital organs. Researchers discovered that they could use formerly neutral stimuli either to increase or to suppress the activity of the immune system (Hollis, 1997; Markovic, Dimitrijevic, & Jankovic, 1993). It works like this: As US, the researchers use immune-suppressing drugs and pair them with a specific CS, such as a distinctive smell or taste. After only a few pairings of the drug (US) with the smell or taste (CS), the CS alone suppresses the immune system (the CR) without any dangerous side effects. In this case, classical conditioning works on the mind but, ultimately, affects the body. The use of classical conditioning to treat autoimmune disorders shows promise, but additional research is still necessary to validate its effectiveness and evaluate its potential application as a therapy to treat these disorders (Bovbjerg, 2003; G. E. Miller & Cohen, 2001).

■ CLASSICAL CONDITIONING IS SELECTIVE

Some kinds of classical conditioning are much easier to establish than others. This phenomenon is called **preparedness**. One example is **conditioned taste aversion**, a learned association between the taste of a certain food and a feeling of nausea and revulsion. Conditioned taste aversions are acquired very quickly: For example, often only one pairing of a distinctive flavor (say, eating sushi for the first time) with subsequent illness (nausea or vomiting) is needed to develop a learned aversion to the taste of it. The biological preparedness to learn taste aversions is so strong that even when people know a certain food did not cause illness, this knowledge still does not spare them from developing a conditioned taste aversion.

Readily learning connections between distinctive flavors and illness has clear benefits. If we can learn quickly which foods are poisonous and avoid those foods in the future, we greatly increase our chances of survival. Other animals with a well-developed sense of taste, such as rats and mice, also readily develop conditioned taste aversions.

A bird's nervous system is adapted to remember sight-illness combinations, such as the distinctive color of a certain berry and subsequent food poisoning. In mammals, by contrast, taste-illness combinations are learned quickly and powerfully.

Check Your Understanding

1. The simplest type of learning is called _____ _____. It refers to the establishment of fairly predictable behavior in the presence of well-defined stimuli.

2. Match the following in Pavlov's experiment with dogs.

   _____ Unconditioned stimulus   **a.** Bell

   _____ Unconditioned response   **b.** Food

   _____ Conditioned stimulus   **c.** Salivating to bell

   _____ Conditioned response   **d.** Salivating to food

3. Which of the following are examples of classical conditioning?

   a. Eating when not hungry just because we know it is lunchtime

   b. A specific smell triggering a bad memory

   c. A cat running into the kitchen to the sound of a can opener

   d. All of the above

Operant Conditioning

Around the turn of the twentieth century, while Pavlov was busy with his dogs, the American psychologist Edward Lee Thorndike (1874–1949) was using a simple wooden cage, or "puzzle box," to study how cats learn (Thorndike, 1898). As illustrated in Figure 5–4, Thorndike confined a hungry cat in the puzzle box and placed food just outside where the cat could see and smell it. To get to the food, the cat had to figure out how to open the latch on the box door, a process that Thorndike timed. In the beginning, it took the cat quite a while to discover how to open the door. But on each trial, it took the cat less time, until eventually, it could escape from the box in very little time at all. Thorndike was a pioneer in studying the kind of learning that involves a change in behavior resulting from its consequences. This form of learning

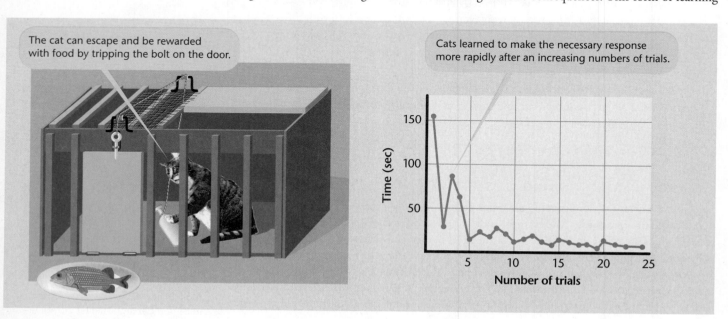

The cat can escape and be rewarded with food by tripping the bolt on the door.

Cats learned to make the necessary response more rapidly after an increasing numbers of trials.

FIGURE 5–4

A cat in a Thorndike "puzzle box."

The cat can escape and be rewarded with food by tripping the bolt on the door. As the graph shows, Thorndike's cats learned to make the necessary response more rapidly after an increasing number of trials.

has come to be called **operant** (or **instrumental**) **conditioning**. The pouched rat described earlier in the chapter learned to find land mines through operant conditioning.

■ ELEMENTS OF OPERANT CONDITIONING

In classical conditioning, eliciting the desired response is relatively easy. All Pavlov had to do when he wanted his dogs to salivate was to put food (the unconditioned stimulus) in their mouths, and they salivated (the unconditioned response). But operant behavior does not automatically follow from a stimulus. Pouched rats do not naturally sniff for buried land mines. Circus tigers do not naturally jump through flaming hoops. People do not naturally put money into machines for a chance to win a prize. And children do not naturally pick up their toys when they are through playing. These and similar actions are developed over time, because they lead to desirable consequences. Thus, **operant behaviors** involve "operating" on the environment.

The consequences that follow a behavior are critical for operant conditioning to occur. Thorndike's cats gained freedom and a piece of fish for escaping from the puzzle boxes; your dog may receive a food treat for sitting on command; a child may receive praise for picking up toys; the mine-sniffing rat received a bit of banana and a few pats after discovering a hidden mine. Consequences that increase the likelihood that a behavior will be repeated are called **reinforcers**. In contrast, consequences that decrease the chances that a behavior will be repeated are called **punishers**. Imagine how Thorndike's cats might have acted had they been greeted by a large, snarling dog when they escaped from the puzzle boxes. Or consider what might happen if a dog that sits on command is scolded for doing so, or if a child who has picked up his toys is sent to sit in a "time-out" corner. Thorndike summarized the influence of consequences in his **law of effect**: Behavior that brings about a satisfying effect (reinforcement) likely will be performed again, whereas behavior that brings about a negative effect (punishment) likely will be suppressed. Contemporary psychologists often refer to this as the **principle of reinforcement**, rather than the law of effect, but the two terms mean the same thing.

■ ESTABLISHING AN OPERANTLY CONDITIONED RESPONSE

Because operant behavior does not automatically follow a stimulus, how is it possible to get the desired response to occur? Sometimes, the answer is simply to wait for this action to happen. But one would have to wait a very long time before a tiger would suddenly decide to jump through a flaming hoop to be rewarded. One way to speed up the process is to increase *motivation*, as Thorndike did by allowing his cats to become hungry. A hungry animal is more

Elements of Operant Conditioning

■ Operant conditioning refers to

_____

_____

■ The law of effect (principle of reinforcement) states that _____ _____ increase(s) the likelihood that _____ will be repeated and _____ _____ decrease(s) the likelihood.

Establishing an Operantly Conditioned Response

■ To establish an operantly conditioned response, _____ _____ _____

■ Alternatively, reinforce _____ to the _____ (shaping).

■ Eventually, _____ reaches a point of _____.

S. GROSS

FIGURE 5–5
A rat in a Skinner box.
By pressing the bar, the rat releases food pellets into the box; this procedure reinforces its bar-pressing behavior.

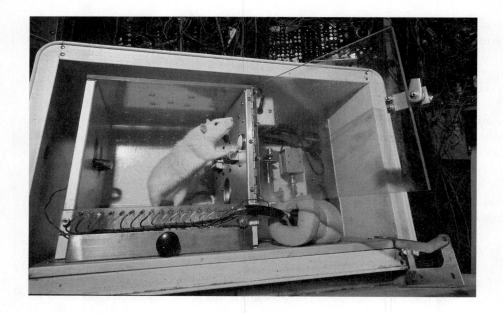

active than a well-fed one, and so, is more likely, just by chance, to make the response being sought. Another way to speed up the process is to reduce opportunities for irrelevant responses, as Thorndike did by making his puzzle boxes small and bare and by putting the lever that opened the latch on the floor where the cat would be likely, eventually, to step on it. Today, some researchers do the same thing by using Skinner boxes to train small animals. A **Skinner box**, named after B. F. Skinner who was another pioneer in the study of operant conditioning, is a small, solid-wall cage that is relatively empty except for a food cup and an activating device, typically a bar or a button (Figure 5–5). In this simple environment, an active, hungry rat or pigeon will take very little time to press the bar or peck the button that releases food into the cup, thereby reinforcing the behavior.

Usually, however, the environment cannot be controlled so easily. In such a case, one can reinforce successive approximations of the desired behavior. This approach is called **shaping**. The circus is a wonderful place to see the results of shaping. To teach a tiger to jump through a flaming hoop, the trainer might first reinforce the animal simply for jumping up on a pedestal. After that behavior has been learned, the tiger might be reinforced only for leaping from that pedestal to another. Next, the tiger might be required to jump through a hoop between the pedestals to gain a reward. And finally, the hoop is set on fire, and the tiger must leap through it to be rewarded.

As in classical conditioning, the learning of an operantly conditioned response eventually reaches a point of diminishing returns. Refer to Figure 5–4 and notice that the first few reinforcements produced quite large improvements in performance, as indicated by the rapid drop in time required to escape from the puzzle box. But each successive reinforcement produced less of an effect until, eventually, continued reinforcement brought no evidence of further learning. After 25 trials, for example, Thorndike's cats were escaping from the box no more quickly than they had been after 15 trials. The operantly conditioned response had, by then, been fully established.

■ A CLOSER LOOK AT REINFORCEMENT

We have been talking about reinforcement as though all reinforcers are alike, but this is not the case. Think about the kinds of consequences that would encourage you to perform some behavior. Certainly these include consequences that give you something positive, such as praise, recognition, or money. But the removal of some negative stimulus is also a good reinforcer of behavior. When new parents discover that rocking a baby will stop the infant's persistent crying, they sit down and rock the baby deep into the night; the removal of the infant's crying is a powerful reinforcer.

These examples show that there are two kinds of reinforcers. **Positive reinforcers**, such as food, praise, or money, add something rewarding to a situation, whereas **negative reinforcers**, such as stopping an aversive noise, subtract something unpleasant. Animals will learn to press bars and open doors not only to obtain food and water (positive reinforcement), but also to turn off a loud buzzer or to avoid an electric shock (negative reinforcement).

Positive reinforcement and negative reinforcement result in the learning of new behaviors or the strengthening of existing ones. Remember, in everyday conversation when we say that we have "reinforced" something, we mean that we have strengthened it. The addition of steel rods or steel mesh strengthens "reinforced concrete"; generals strengthen their armies by sending in "reinforcements"; and facts that "reinforce" an argument make it stronger. Similarly, in operant conditioning, reinforcement—whether positive or negative—always strengthens or encourages a behavior. A child might practice the piano because she or he receives praise for practicing (positive reinforcement) or because it gives her or him a break from doing tedious homework (negative reinforcement). In either case, the result is a higher incidence of piano playing.

But what if a particular behavior is reinforced *accidentally* just because, by chance, it happens to be followed by some rewarding incident? Will the behavior still be more likely to occur again? B. F. Skinner (1948) showed that the answer is yes. He put a hungry pigeon in a cage containing only a food hopper. At random intervals, he dropped a few grains of food into the hopper. The pigeon began repeating whatever it had been doing just prior to the food being given—standing on one foot, hopping around, or strutting with its neck stretched out. None of these actions had anything to do with getting the food, of course, but the bird repeated them nonetheless. Skinner called the bird's behavior "superstitious," because the behavior had been learned in a way that is similar to how some superstitions are learned. If you happened to have been wearing an Albert Einstein T-shirt when you got your first A on an exam, you might have come to believe that wearing that shirt had been a factor in your success. Even though the connection was purely coincidental, you might still keep wearing your "lucky" shirt to every test thereafter.

■ PUNISHMENT

Everyone hates to be subjected to it, but **punishment** is a powerful controller of behavior. After a person receives a heavy fine for failing to report extra income to the IRS, he or she is less likely to make that mistake again. After rudely being turned down when asking someone for a favor, most of us would be less likely to ask that person for another favor. In both cases, an unpleasant consequence reduces the likelihood that the behavior will be repeated. This is the definition of punishment.

Punishment is different from negative reinforcement. Reinforcement of whatever kind *strengthens* (reinforces) behavior. Negative reinforcement *strengthens* behavior by removing something unpleasant from the environment. In contrast, punishment adds something unpleasant to the environment; and as a result, it tends to *weaken* the behavior that caused it. If going skiing during the weekend rather than studying for a test results in getting an F, the F is an unpleasant consequence (a punisher) that makes you less likely to skip homework for ski time again.

Is punishment effective? There are plenty of instances to show that it does not always work. Children often continue to misbehave even after they have been punished repeatedly for that particular misbehavior. Some drivers persist in driving recklessly despite receiving repeated fines. The family dog may sleep on the couch at night despite being punished for being on the couch every morning. Why are there these seeming exceptions to the law of effect? Why, in these cases, doesn't punishment have the result it is supposed to have?

For punishment to be effective, it must be imposed properly. First, punishment should be *swift*. If it is delayed, it does not work as well. Sending a misbehaving child immediately to a time-out seat (even when it is not convenient to do so) is much more effective than waiting for a "better" time to punish. Punishment should also be *sufficient* without being cruel. If a parent briefly scolds a child for hitting other children, the effect probably will be less pronounced than

A Closer Look at Reinforcement

- _____ add(s) something rewarding.

- _____
_____ remove(s) something unpleasant.

- Positive and negative reinforcers
_____

- _____ or _____ reinforcement can lead to _____ behaviors.

Punishment

- To be effective, punishment must be _____, _____, and _____ and, preferably, paired with _____ for a more desirable behavior.

- Disadvantages of punishment are that it _____, can _____, teaches the learner _____, and often creates _____ and _____.

- Often, the _____ of punishment is sufficient to change behavior (avoidance training).

Learned Helplessness

- When punishment is unavoidable, a _____ response may be learned.

- Once established, learned helplessness can
_____

if the child is sent to his or her room for the day. At the same time, punishment should be *consistent*. It should be imposed for all infractions of a rule, not just for some. If parents allow some acts of aggression to go unpunished, hitting and bullying other children are likely to persist.

Punishment is particularly useful in situations in which a behavior is dangerous and must be changed quickly. A child who likes to poke things into electric outlets must be stopped immediately, so punishment may be the best course of action. But even in situations like these, punishment has drawbacks. First, it only *suppresses* the undesired behavior; it does not prompt someone to "unlearn" the behavior, and it does not teach a more desirable one. If the threat of punishment is removed, the negative behavior is likely to recur. Second, punishment often stirs up negative feelings (such as frustration, resentment, self-doubt) that can impede the learning of new, more desirable behaviors. Third, harsh punishment teaches an unintended lesson—the learner may copy that same harsh and aggressive behavior with other people. In addition, punishment often makes people angry, and angry people frequently become more aggressive and hostile.

Because of these drawbacks, punishment should be used carefully, and always together with reinforcement of desirable behavior. Once a more desirable response is established, punishment should be removed so that the new behavior is negatively reinforced. Positive reinforcement (such as praise and rewards) should also be used to strengthen the desired behavior. This approach is more productive than punishment alone, because it teaches an alternative behavior to replace the punished one. Positive reinforcement also makes the learning environment less threatening.

Sometimes, after punishment has been administered a few times, it does not need to be continued. This is because the mere threat of punishment is enough to induce the desired behavior. How many times did your parents say, "If you don't eat your vegetables, you won't get any dessert"? Psychologists call this **avoidance training**, because the person is learning to avoid the possibility of a punishing consequence. Avoidance training is responsible for many everyday behaviors. You learn to carry an umbrella when the sky turns gray to avoid the punishment of getting wet. You also learn to keep your hand away from a hot iron to avoid the punishment of a burn. Avoidance training, however, does not always work in our favor. For instance, if you have learned not to run on a particular street because there is a vicious dog in one of the yards, you may never discover that the people in that house have moved and the dog is no longer there. Someone who has a bad experience in a high school science class may avoid science classes in the future, even though science might be for that person an immensely rewarding subject to study. So, avoidance learning comes with a potential cost.

ENDURING ISSUES DIVERSITY/UNIVERSALITY

What Is Punishment?

We do not know whether something is reinforcing or punishing until we see whether it increases or decreases the occurrence of a response. We might assume that candy, for example, is a reinforcer for children, but some children do not like candy. We also might assume that having to work alone, rather than in a group of peers would be punishing, but some children prefer to work alone. Teachers must understand the children in their classes as individuals before they decide how to reward or punish them. Similarly, something that might be reinforcing for men may not be reinforcing for women, and something reinforcing for people in one culture might not have the same effect for people in other cultures.

In addition, an event or object might not remain rewarding or punishing over time. So, even if candy is initially reinforcing for some children, if they eat large amounts of it, it can become neutral or even punishing. Therefore, caution is required when labeling items or events as "reinforcers" or "punishers."

■ LEARNED HELPLESSNESS

Have you ever met someone who has decided he will never be good at science or perhaps has determined that he will never find someone to fall in love with? Through avoidance training, people learn to prevent themselves from being punished. But, what happens when such avoidance of punishment is not possible? The answer is often a "giving-up" response that can generalize to other situations. This response is known as **learned helplessness**.

Martin Seligman and his colleagues first studied learned helplessness in experiments with dogs (Seligman & Maier, 1967). They placed two groups of dogs in chambers that delivered a series of electric shocks to the dogs' feet at random intervals. The dogs in the control group could turn off (escape) the shock by pushing a panel with their nose. The dogs in the experimental group could not turn off the shock—they were, in effect, helpless. Next, the experimental and the control animals were placed in a different situation, one in which they could escape shock by jumping over a hurdle. A warning light always came on 10 seconds before each 50-second shock was given. The dogs in the control group quickly learned to jump the hurdle as soon as the warning light flashed, but the dogs in the experimental group did not. These dogs, having previously experienced unavoidable shocks, did not even jump the hurdle *after* the shock started. They just laid there and accepted the shocks.

Many subsequent studies have shown that learned helplessness can occur in animals *and* in humans. Once established, the condition generalizes to new situations and can be very persistent. For example, children raised in an abusive family, where punishment is unrelated to behavior, often develop a feeling of helplessness. Even in relatively normal settings outside their home, they often appear listless, passive, and indifferent. They make little attempt either to seek rewards or to avoid discomfort.

■ SHAPING BEHAVIORAL CHANGE THROUGH FEEDBACK

Operant conditioning can be used to control certain biological functions, such as blood pressure, skin temperature, heart rate (**biofeedback**), and even brain waves (**neurofeedback**). Variations in the biological functions are converted into a light, a tone, or some other signal. Through shaping, the person can learn to control the signal and thus the underlying biological function. Biofeedback and neurofeedback have become well-established treatments for a number of medical problems, including migraine headaches, hypertension, asthma, irritable bowel conditions, and panic attacks. Biofeedback has also been used by athletes, musicians, and other performers to control the anxiety that can interfere with their performance. Marathon runners use it to help overcome the tight shoulders and shallow breathing that can prevent them from finishing races. Biofeedback has even been used in space: NASA has used biofeedback as part of a program to reduce the motion sickness astronauts experience at zero gravity.

Biofeedback treatment does have some drawbacks. Learning the technique takes considerable time, effort, patience, and discipline. And it does not work for everyone. But it gives many patients control of their treatment, a major advantage over other treatment options, and it has achieved impressive results in alleviating certain medical problems.

Shaping Behavioral Change Through Feedback

■ Operant conditioning can be used to control _____
_____

■ Biofeedback and neurofeedback treatment takes considerable _____
_____
_____

Check Your Understanding

1. An event whose reduction or termination increases the likelihood that ongoing behavior will recur is called _____ reinforcement, whereas any event whose presence increases the likelihood that ongoing behavior will recur is called _____ reinforcement.

2. When a threat of punishment induces a change to more desirable behavior, it is called _____ _____.

3. Any stimulus that follows a behavior and decreases the likelihood that the behavior will be repeated is called a _____.

4. Imagine that you want to teach a child to make his or her bed. What kind of reinforcement could you use to do that?
   a. Punishment
   b. Positive reinforcement
   c. Negative reinforcement
   d. Both B and C would work

Factors Shared by Classical and Operant Conditioning

Despite the differences between classical and operant conditioning, these two forms of learning have many things in common. First, they both involve the learning of associations. In classical conditioning, it is a learned association between one stimulus and another (between food and a bell, for instance), whereas in operant conditioning, it is a learned association between some action and a consequence (reinforcement or punishment). Second, the responses in both classical and operant conditioning are under the control of stimuli in the environment. A classically conditioned fear response might be triggered by the scary soundtrack in a movie; an operantly conditioned jump might be cued by the flash of a red light. And as we are about to see, neither classically nor operantly conditioned responses will last forever if they are not periodically renewed. Moreover, in both kinds of learning, new behaviors can build on previously established ones.

■ IMPORTANCE OF CONTINGENCIES

Because classical conditioning and operant conditioning are forms of associative learning, both involve perceived contingencies. A **contingency** is a relationship in which one event *depends* on another. Graduating from college is *contingent* on passing a certain number of courses. Earning a paycheck is *contingent* on having a job. In both classical and operant conditioning, perceived contingencies are very important.

Contingencies in Classical Conditioning   In classical conditioning, the CS comes to be viewed as a signal that the US is about to happen. This is why, in classical conditioning, the CS not only must occur in close proximity to the US, but also should precede the US and provide predictive information about it.

Imagine an experiment in which animals are exposed to a tone (the CS) and a mild electric shock (the US). One group always hears the tone a fraction of a second before it is shocked. Another group sometimes hears the tone first, but other times the shock comes before the tone, and still other times the tone and shock occur together. Soon, the first group will show a fear response upon hearing the tone alone, but the second group will not. This is because the first group has learned a contingency between the tone and the shock: The tone has always preceded the shock, so it has come to mean that the shock is about to be given. For the second group, in contrast, the tone has signaled little or nothing about the shock. Sometimes, the tone has meant that a shock is coming; sometimes, it has meant that the shock is here; and sometimes, it has meant that the shock is over and "the coast is clear." Because the meaning of the tone has been ambiguous for this group, its members do not develop a conditioned fear response to it.

What if the tone (the CS) *always* follows the shock (the US)? This process is called *backward conditioning*. After a while, the learner shows a conditioned *relaxation* response to the sound of the tone, because the tone has served as a signal that the shock is over and will not occur again for some time. Again, the importance of contingency learning can be seen—the learner responds to the tone on the basis of the information that it provides about what will happen next.

Contingencies in Operant Conditioning   Contingencies also figure prominently in operant conditioning. The learner must come to perceive a connection between performing a certain voluntary action and receiving a certain reward or punishment. If no contingency is perceived, there is no reason to increase or decrease the behavior.

But once a contingency is perceived, does it matter how often a consequence is actually delivered? When it comes to rewards, the answer is "Yes." Fewer rewards are often better than more. In the language of operant conditioning, *partial* or *intermittent reinforcement* results in behavior that will persist longer than behavior learned by *continuous reinforcement*. Why would this be the case? The answer has to do with expectations. When people receive only

---

Basic Similarities

■ _____
involve(s) the learning of associations.

■ _____
is/are under the control of stimuli in the environment.

Importance of Contingencies

■ _____
involve(s) perceived contingencies.

■ In classical conditioning, the
_____ comes
to be viewed as a signal that the
_____ is
about to happen.

■ In operant conditioning, the
_____ must
perceive a connection between
performing a certain
_____ and
receiving a certain
_____.

■ _____
reinforcement results in long-lasting
behavior.

■ Schedules of reinforcement include:

_____

_____

occasional reinforcement, they learn not to expect reinforcement with every response, so they continue responding in the hopes that eventually they will gain the desired reward. Vending machines and slot machines illustrate these different effects of continuous versus partial reinforcement. A vending machine offers continuous reinforcement. Each time you put in the right amount of money, you get something desired in return (reinforcement). If a vending machine is broken and you receive nothing for your coins, you are unlikely to put more money in it. In contrast, a casino slot machine pays off intermittently; only occasionally do you get something back for your investment. This intermittent payoff has a compelling effect on behavior. You might continue putting coins into a slot machine for a very long time even though you are getting nothing in return.

Psychologists refer to a pattern of reward payoffs as a **schedule of reinforcement**. Partial or intermittent reinforcement schedules are either fixed or variable, and they may be based on either the number of correct responses or the time elapsed between correct responses. Table 5–1 gives some everyday examples of different reinforcement schedules.

On a **fixed-interval schedule**, learners have to wait for a set period before they will be reinforced again. With a fixed-interval schedule, performance tends to fall off immediately after each reinforcement and then tends to pick up again as the time for the next reinforcement draws near (Figure 5–6). For example, when exams are given at fixed intervals—such as midterms and finals—students tend to decrease their studying right after one test is over and increase their studying as the next test approaches.

A **variable-interval schedule** reinforces correct responses after varying lengths of time following the last reinforcement. One reinforcement might be given after 6 minutes, the next after 4 minutes, the next after 5 minutes, and the next after 3 minutes. The learner typically

TABLE 5–1 Examples of Reinforcement in Everyday Life

Continuous reinforcement (reinforcement every time the response is made)	Putting money in a parking meter to avoid getting a ticket. Putting coins in a vending machine to get candy or soda.
Fixed-ratio schedule (reinforcement after a fixed number of responses)	Being paid on a piecework basis. In the garment industry, for example, workers may be paid a fee per 100 dresses sewn.
Variable-ratio schedule (reinforcement after a varying number of responses)	Playing a slot machine. The machine is programmed to pay off after a certain number of responses have been made, but that number keeps changing. This type of schedule creates a steady rate of responding because players know that if they play long enough, they will win.
	Sales commissions. You have to talk to many customers before you make a sale, and you never know whether the next one will buy. The number of sales calls you make, not how much time passes, will determine when you are reinforced by a sale, and the number of sales calls will vary.
Fixed-interval schedule (reinforcement of first response after a fixed amount of time has passed)	You have an exam coming up, and as time goes by and you have not studied, you have to make up for it all by a certain time, and that means cramming.
	Picking up a salary check, which you receive every week or every two weeks.
Variable-interval response (reinforcement of first response after varying amounts of time)	Surprise quizzes in a course cause a steady rate of studying because you never know when they will occur; you have to be prepared all the time.
	Watching a football game; waiting for a touchdown. It could happen anytime. If you leave the room, you may miss it, so you have to keep watching continuously.

Source: From Landy, 1987, p. 212. Adapted by permission.

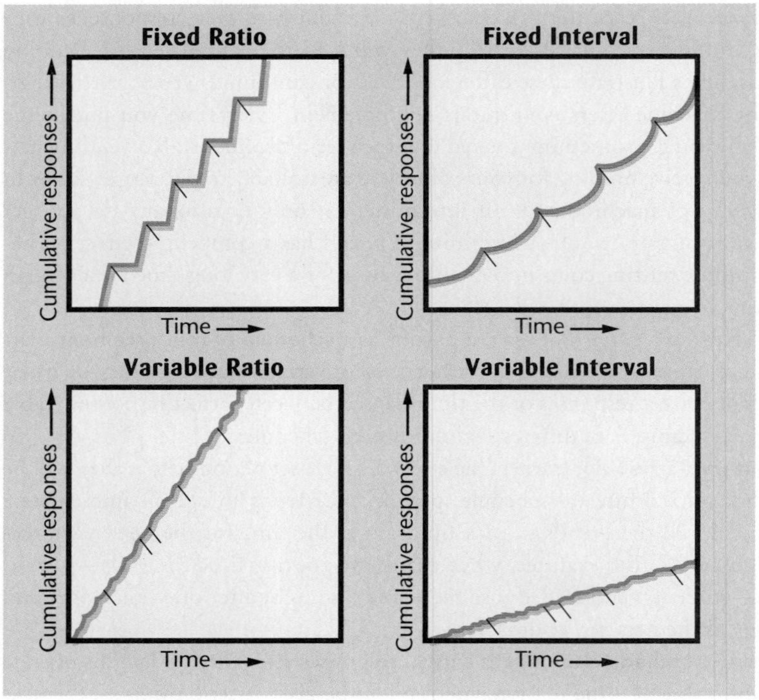

FIGURE 5–6
Response patterns to schedules of reinforcement.
On a fixed-interval schedule, as the time for reinforcement approaches, the number of responses increases and the slope becomes steeper. On a variable-interval schedule, the response rate is moderate and relatively constant. Notice that each tick mark on the graph represents one reinforcement. The fixed-ratio schedule is characterized by a high rate of response and a pause after each reinforcement. A variable-ratio schedule produces a high rate of response with little or no pause after each reinforcement.

Extinction and Spontaneous Recovery

■ In classical and operant conditioning, learned responses eventually may _____ (extinction) and spontaneously _____ (spontaneous recovery).

■ Failing to pair the _____ and _____ eventually will cause the extinction of the _____, while presenting the _____ once again may elicit the _____ briefly at reduced strength.

■ In operant conditioning, withholding _____ eventually will lead to the _____ of the learned response. However, the response may _____ again briefly at some future time.

gives a slow, steady pattern of responses, being careful not to be so slow as to miss all the rewards. For example, when exams are given during a semester at unpredictable intervals, students have to keep studying at a steady rate because, on any given day, there might be a test.

On a **fixed-ratio schedule**, a certain number of correct responses must occur before reinforcement is provided, resulting in a high response rate, since making many responses in a short time yields more rewards. Being paid on a piecework basis is an example of a fixed-ratio schedule. Farm workers might get $3 for every 10 baskets of cherries they pick. The more they pick, the more money they make. Under a fixed-ratio schedule, a brief pause after reinforcement is followed by a rapid and steady response rate until the next reinforcement.

On a **variable-ratio schedule**, the number of correct responses needed to gain reinforcement is not constant. The casino slot machine is a good example of a variable-ratio schedule. It will eventually pay off, but you have no idea when. Because there is always a chance of hitting the jackpot, the temptation to keep playing is great. Learners on a variable-ratio schedule tend not to pause after reinforcement, and they exhibit a high rate of response over a long period of time. Because they never know when reinforcement may come, they keep on testing for a reward.

■ **EXTINCTION AND SPONTANEOUS RECOVERY**

Another factor shared by classical and operant conditioning is that learned responses sometimes weaken and may even disappear. If a CS and a US are never paired again or if a consequence never follows a certain behavior, the learned association will begin to fade until, eventually, the effects of prior learning are no longer seen. This outcome is called **extinction** of a conditioned response.

Extinction and Spontaneous Recovery in Classical Conditioning   Pavlov's dogs, having learned to salivate upon hearing a bell, provide an example of extinction in classical conditioning. When the dogs heard the bell (the CS) but food (the US) was no longer given, the conditioned response to the bell—salivation—gradually decreased until, eventually, it stopped altogether. Extinction had taken place.

Once such a response has been extinguished, is the learning gone forever? Pavlov trained his dogs to salivate when they heard a bell, then he extinguished this conditioned

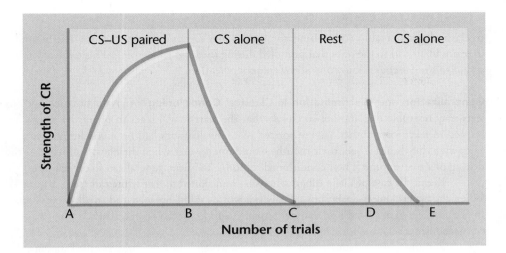

FIGURE 5–7
Response acquisition and extinction in classical conditioning.
From point A to point B, the conditioned stimulus and the unconditioned stimulus were paired and learning increased steadily. From B to C, however, the conditioned stimulus was presented alone. By point C, the response had been extinguished. After a rest period from C to D, spontaneous recovery occurred—the learned response reappeared at about half the strength that it had at point B. When the conditioned stimulus again was presented alone, the response extinguished rapidly (point E).

response. A few days later, the dogs were exposed to the bell again in the laboratory setting. As soon as they heard it, their mouths began to water. The response that had been learned and later extinguished reappeared on its own with no retraining. This phenomenon is known as **spontaneous recovery**. The dogs' response was now only about half as strong as it had been before extinction, and it was very easy to extinguish a second time. Nevertheless, the fact that the response occurred at all indicated that the original learning was not forgotten completely (Figure 5–7).

How can extinguished behavior disappear then reappear later? The explanation is that extinction does not erase learning. Rather, extinction occurs because new learning interferes with a previously learned response. For example, if you take a break from watching the latest horror movies in theaters and, instead, watch reruns of classic horror films on television, these classic films may seem so amateurish that they make you laugh rather than scare you. Here, you are learning to associate the scary music in such films with laughter rather than with fear. The result is extinction of the fear response. But if you return to the theater to see the latest Stephen King movie, when the scary music first starts, the conditioned response of fear may suddenly reappear. The fact that you are back in a theater and watching a scary movie serves as a reminder of your earlier learning and renews your previous classically conditioned response.

Extinction and Spontaneous Recovery in Operant Conditioning Extinction and spontaneous recovery also occur in operant conditioning. In operant conditioning, extinction happens as a result of withholding reinforcement. The effect usually is not immediate. In fact, when reinforcement is discontinued, first there is often a brief *increase* in the strength or frequency of responding before a decline sets in. For instance, if you put coins in a vending machine and it fails to deliver the goods, you may push the button more forcefully and in rapid succession before you finally give up.

Just as in classical conditioning, extinction in operant conditioning does not completely erase what has been learned. Even though much time has passed since a behavior was last rewarded and the behavior seems extinguished, it may suddenly reappear. This spontaneous recovery may again be understood in terms of interference from new behaviors. If a cat is no longer reinforced for pressing a lever that opens a latch providing access to food, it will start to engage in other behaviors—turning away from the lever, pawing at the walls of the box, attempting to escape, and so on. These new behaviors will interfere with the operant response of lever pressing, causing it to extinguish. Spontaneous recovery is a brief victory of the original learning over interfering responses. The cat, in effect, decides to give the previous "reward" lever one more try, as though testing again for a reward.

When reinforcement has been frequent, a learned behavior tends to be retained even after reinforcement is reduced. A dog "shaking hands" is an excellent example. Many previous rewards for this response tend to keep the dog offering people its paw even when no reward follows.

■ GENERALIZATION AND DISCRIMINATION

In classical and operant conditioning, the learner may respond to cues that are merely similar (but not identical) to the ones that prevailed during the original learning. This tendency to respond to similar cues is known as **stimulus generalization**.

Generalization and Discrimination in Classical Conditioning   Certain situations or objects may resemble one another so closely that the learner will react to one as he or she has learned to react to the other. Pavlov noticed that after his dogs had been conditioned to salivate when they heard a bell, their mouths would often water when they heard a buzzer or the ticking of a metronome. Their conditioned response had been generalized to other noises.

Recall the case of Little Albert who was conditioned to fear white rats (see Chapter 1). When the experimenters later showed Albert a white rabbit, he cried and tried to crawl away. In fact, his fear generalized to a number of white, furry objects—cotton balls, a fur coat, even a bearded Santa Claus mask.

Stimulus generalization is not inevitable, however. Through a process called **stimulus discrimination**, learners can be trained not to generalize, but rather to make a conditioned response only to a single specific stimulus. This process involves presenting several similar stimuli, only one of which is followed by the unconditioned stimulus. For instance, Albert might have been shown a rat, a rabbit, cotton balls, and other white, furry objects, but only the rat would be followed by a loud noise (the US). Given this procedure, Albert would have learned to discriminate the white rat from the other objects and the fear response would not have generalized as it did.

Learning to discriminate is essential in everyday life. For example, most children learn not to fear *every* loud noise, *every* insect, *every* dog, and so forth, but rather only those that are potentially harmful. Through stimulus discrimination, behavior becomes tuned more finely to the demands of the environment.

Generalization and Discrimination in Operant Conditioning   Stimulus generalization also occurs in operant conditioning. A baby who is hugged and kissed for saying "Mama" when he sees his mother may begin to call everyone "Mama"—males and females alike. Although the person whom the baby sees—the stimulus—changes, he responds with the same word. In operant conditioning, responses also can be generalized. For example, the baby who calls everyone "Mama" may also call people "Nana." His learning has generalized to other sounds that are similar to the correct response, "Mama." This is called **response generalization**. Response generalization does not occur in classical conditioning. If a dog is taught to salivate when it hears a high-pitched tone, it will salivate less when it hears a low-pitched tone (stimulus generalization), but the response is still salivation.

Just as discrimination is useful in classical conditioning, it is also useful in operant conditioning. Learning *what* to do has little value if one does not know *when* to do it. Learning that a response is triggered is pointless if the person does not know which response is right. Discrimination training in operant conditioning consists of reinforcing *only* a specific, desired response and *only* in the presence of a specific stimulus. With this procedure, pigeons have been trained to peck at a red disk, but not at a green one. First, they are taught to peck at a disk. Then, they are presented with two disks, one red and one green. They get food when they peck at the red one, but not when they peck at the green. Eventually, they learn to discriminate between the two colors, pecking only at the red. In much the same way, children learn to listen to exactly what the teacher is asking before they raise their hands.

■ NEW LEARNING BASED ON ORIGINAL LEARNING

Original learning can serve as the basis for new learning in other ways besides stimulus generalization and discrimination. In classical conditioning, an existing conditioned stimulus can be paired with a new stimulus to produce a new conditioned response. This is called **higher-order conditioning**. In operant conditioning, objects that have no intrinsic value can nevertheless become reinforcers because of their association with other, more basic, reinforcers. These learned reinforcers are called *secondary reinforcers*.

Higher-Order Conditioning   Pavlov demonstrated higher-order conditioning with his dogs. After the dogs had learned to salivate when they heard a bell, Pavlov used the bell (*without* food) to teach the dogs to salivate at the sight of a black square. Instead of showing them the square and following it with food, he showed them the square and followed it with the bell until the dogs learned to salivate when they saw the square alone. This procedure is known as *higher-order conditioning,* not because it is more complex than other types of conditioning or because it incorporates any new principles, but simply because it is conditioning based on previous learning.

Higher-order conditioning is difficult to achieve because it is battling against extinction of the original conditioned response. In Pavlov's case, the unconditioned stimulus (food) no longer followed the original conditioned stimulus (the bell), which is precisely the way to extinguish a classically conditioned response. Thus, the square became a signal that the bell would not precede food, and soon, all salivation stopped. For higher-order conditioning to succeed, the unconditioned stimulus must be reintroduced occasionally. Once in a while, Pavlov had to provide food after the bell rang so that the dogs would continue to salivate when they heard the bell.

Secondary Reinforcers   Some reinforcers, such as food, water, and sex, are intrinsically rewarding in and of themselves. These are called **primary reinforcers**. No prior learning is required to make them reinforcing. Other reinforcers have no intrinsic value. They have acquired value only through association with primary reinforcers. These are the **secondary reinforcers** mentioned earlier. They are called secondary not because they are less important but because prior learning is needed before they will function as reinforcers. Suppose a rat learns to get food by pressing a bar; then a buzzer is sounded every time food drops into the dish. Even if the rat stops getting the food, it will continue to press the bar for a while just to hear the buzzer. Although the buzzer by itself has no intrinsic value to the rat, it has become a secondary reinforcer through association with food, a primary reinforcer.

Note how, in creating a secondary reinforcer, classical conditioning is involved. Because it has been paired with an intrinsically pleasurable stimulus, a formerly neutral stimulus comes to elicit pleasure as well. This stimulus then can serve as a reinforcer to establish an operantly conditioned response.

For humans, money is one of the best examples of a secondary reinforcer. Although money is just paper or metal, through its exchange value for food, clothing, and other primary reinforcers, it becomes a powerful reinforcer. Children come to value money only after they learn that it will buy such things as candy (a primary reinforcer). Then, the money becomes a secondary reinforcer, and, through the principles of higher-order conditioning, stimuli paired with a secondary reinforcer can acquire reinforcing properties.

■ BRINGING THE TWO TOGETHER

Classical conditioning and operant conditioning entail forming associations between stimuli and responses, and perceiving contingencies between one event and another. Both are subject to extinction and spontaneous recovery, as well as to stimulus control, generalization, and discrimination. The main difference between the two is that in classical conditioning, the learner is passive and the behavior involved is usually involuntary; whereas, in operant conditioning, the learner is active and the behavior involved is usually voluntary.

Some psychologists downplay these differences, however, suggesting that classical and operant conditioning are simply two different ways of bringing about the same kind of learning. For example, classical conditioning can be used to shape voluntary movements and operant conditioning can be used to shape involuntary responses such as heart rate, blood pressure, and brain waves. In addition, once an operant response becomes linked to a stimulus, it looks very much like a conditioned response in classical conditioning. If you have been reinforced repeatedly for stepping on the brake when a traffic light turns red, the red light comes to elicit braking just as the sound of a bell elicited salivation in Pavlov's dogs. Classical and operant conditioning, then, may simply be two different procedures for achieving the same end. If so, psychologists may have overstressed the differences between them and paid too little attention to what they have in common.

Check Your Understanding

1. After extinction and a period of rest, a conditioned response may suddenly reappear. This phenomenon is called _____ _____.

2. The process by which a learned response to a specific stimulus comes to be associated with different, but similar stimuli is known as _____ _____.

3. On the first day of class, your instructor tells you that there will be unscheduled quizzes *on average* about every 2 weeks throughout the term, but not exactly every 2 weeks. This is an example of a _____ reinforcement schedule.

   a. Continuous   **c.** Fixed-ratio

   b. Fixed-interval   **d.** Variable-interval

4. In the situation in question 3, what study pattern is the instructor most likely trying to encourage?

   a. Slow, steady rates of studying

   b. Cramming the night before quizzes

   c. Studying a lot right before quizzes, then stopping for a while right after them

Cognitive Learning

Some psychologists insist that because classical conditioning and operant conditioning can be *observed* and *measured*, they are the only legitimate kinds of learning to study scientifically. But others contend that mental activities are crucial to learning, and so, they cannot be ignored. How do you grasp the layout of a building from someone else's description of it? How do you know how to hold a tennis racket just from watching a game of tennis being played? How do you enter into memory abstract concepts such as *conditioning* and *reinforcement*? You do all these things, and many others, through **cognitive learning**—the mental processes that go on inside everyone when we learn. Cognitive learning is impossible to observe and measure directly, but it can be *inferred* from behavior, and so, it is also a legitimate topic for scientific study.

■ LATENT LEARNING AND COGNITIVE MAPS

Latent Learning and Cognitive Maps

■ Cognitive learning is impossible to _____ and _____ directly, but it can be _____ from behavior.

■ Some learning need not be reflected immediately in a _____ (latent learning).

■ One kind of latent learning is the formation of a _____ of a spatial environment that can be used to _____ that environment in the future (cognitive map).

Interest in cognitive learning began shortly after the earliest work in classical and operant conditioning. In the 1930s, Edward Chace Tolman (1886–1959) argued that people do not need to show their learning in order for learning to have occurred. Tolman called learning that is not apparent **latent learning**, because it is not yet demonstrated.

Tolman studied latent learning in a famous experiment (Tolman & Honzik, 1930). Two groups of hungry rats were placed in a maze and allowed to find their way from a start box to an end box. The first group found food pellets (a reward) in the end box; the second group found nothing there. According to the principles of operant conditioning, the first group would learn the maze better than the second group—which is, indeed, what happened. But when Tolman took some of the rats from the second, unreinforced group and started to give them food at the goal box, almost immediately they ran the maze as well as the rats in the first group (Figure 5–8). Tolman argued that the unrewarded rats actually had learned a great deal about the maze as they wandered around inside it. In fact, they may have even learned *more* about it than the rats that had been trained with food rewards, but their learning was *latent*—stored internally but not yet reflected in their behavior. It was not until they were given a motivation to run the maze that they put their latent learning to use.

Since Tolman's time, much work has been done on the nature of latent learning regarding spatial layouts and relationships. From studies of how animals or humans find their way around a maze, a building, or a neighborhood with many available routes, psychologists have proposed that this kind of learning is stored in the form of a mental image, or **cognitive map**. When the proper time comes, the learner can call up the stored image and put it to use. More recent research confirms this picture of cognitive spatial learning. Even in rats, learning involves more than just a new behavior "stamped in" through reinforcement. It also involves the formation of new mental images and constructs that may be reflected in future behavior.

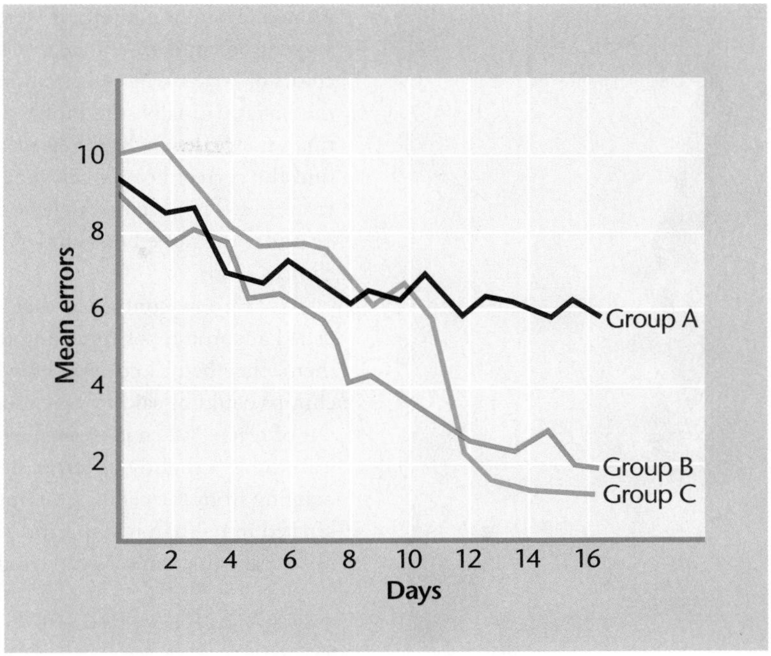

■ INSIGHT AND LEARNING SETS

During World War I, the German Gestalt psychologist Wolfgang Köhler (1887–1967) conducted a classic series of studies into another aspect of cognitive learning: sudden **insight** into a problem's solution. Outside a chimpanzee's cage, Köhler placed a banana on the ground, not quite within the animal's reach. When the chimp realized that it could not reach the banana, it reacted with frustration. But then it started looking at what was in the cage, including a stick left there by Köhler. Sometimes, quite suddenly, the chimp would grab the stick, poke it through the bars of the cage, and drag the banana within reach. The same kind of sudden insight occurred when the banana was hung from the roof of the cage, too high for the chimp to grasp. This time the cage contained some boxes, which the chimp quickly learned to stack up under the banana so that it could climb up to pull the fruit down. Subsequent studies have shown that even pigeons can solve the box-and-banana problem through insight when they are motivated properly, given the right tools, and taught how to use them.

FIGURE 5–8
Graph showing the results of the Tolman and Honzik study.
The results of the classic Tolman and Honzik study are revealed in the graph. Group A never received a food reward. Group B was rewarded each day. Group C was not rewarded until Day 11, but note the significant change in the rats' behavior on Day 12. The results suggest that Group C had been learning all along, although this learning was not reflected in their performance until they were rewarded with food for demonstrating the desired behaviors.
Source: Tolman & Honzik, 1930.

ENDURING ISSUES STABILITY/CHANGE

Human Insight

Insightful learning is particularly important in humans, who must learn not only where to obtain food and how to escape from predators but also to grasp such complex ethical and cultural ideas as the value of hard work, helping others, overcoming addictions, or dealing with a life crisis. Chapter 7 (Cognition and Mental Abilities) explores the role of insight in creative problem solving. There are times when all other problem-solving techniques fail to produce a solution; in such cases, it is not unusual for the solution to suddenly "pop up" in a moment of insight. Moreover, to the extent that people gain insight into their own behavior, they should be capable of changing significantly over the course of their lives. Indeed, as Chapter 13 (Therapies) reveals, the common goal of the various insight therapies, such as psychoanalysis, is to give people a better awareness and understanding of their feelings, motivations, and actions in the hope that this will lead to better adjustment.

Insight and Learning Sets

■ Insight is _____

_____

_____

■ A learning set refers to _____

_____

_____

Previous learning often can be used to help solve problems through insight. This was demonstrated by Harry Harlow (1905–1981) in a series of studies with rhesus monkeys (Harlow, 1949). Harlow presented each monkey with two boxes—for example, a round green box on the left side of a tray and a square red box on the right side. A morsel of food was put under one of the boxes. The monkey was permitted to lift just one box; if it chose the correct box, it got the food. On the next trial, the food was put under the same box (which had been moved to a new position), and the monkey again got to choose just one box. Each monkey had six trials to figure out that the same box covered the food no matter where that box was

Köhler's experiments with chimpanzees illustrate learning through insight. In this photo, one of the chimps has arranged a stack of boxes to reach bananas hanging from the ceiling. Insights gained in this problem-solving situation may transfer to similar ones.

Learning by Observing

- Observational (or vicarious) learning is _____

_____

- Social learning theorists are _____

_____

- _____ (or punishment) refers to _____

_____

located. Then, the monkeys were given a new set of choices—for example, between a blue triangular box and an orange oval one—and another six trials, and so on with other shapes and colors of boxes. The solution was always the same: The food invariably was under only one of the boxes. Initially, the monkeys chose boxes randomly, sometimes finding the food, sometimes not. After a while, however, their behavior changed: In just one or two trials, they would find the correct box, which they chose consistently thereafter until the experimenter changed the boxes. They seemed to have learned the underlying principle—that the food would always be under the same box—and they used that learning to solve almost instantly each new set of choices given.

Harlow concluded that the monkeys "learned how to learn"; that is, they had established a **learning set** regarding this problem. Within the limited range of choices available to them, they had discovered how to tell which box would give the reward. Similarly, Köhler's chimps could be said to have established a learning set regarding how to get food that was just out of reach. When presented with a new version of the problem, they simply called upon past learning in a slightly different situation (reaching a banana on the ground versus reaching one hanging from the ceiling). In both Harlow's and Köhler's studies, the animals seemed to have learned more than just specific behaviors: They apparently had learned *how* to learn. Whether this means that animals can think is an issue still being debated.

■ LEARNING BY OBSERVING

The first time you drove a car, you successfully turned the key in the ignition, put the car in gear, and pressed the gas pedal without having ever done any of those things before. How were you able to do that without step-by-step shaping of the correct behaviors? The answer is that like Adrian Cole, the four-year-old driver described at the start of the chapter, you had often watched other people driving, a practice that made all the difference. People learn countless things by watching other people and listening to what they say. This process is called **observational (or vicarious) learning** because although learning is taking place, no one has to do the learned behaviors firsthand; the modeled behavior merely has been observed. Observational learning is a form of "social learning," in that it involves interaction with other people. Psychologists who study it are known as **social learning theorists**.

Observational learning is very common. In fact, young children often "over imitate"—slavishly following what they are shown to do, even when that is not the most effective way to behave. By watching other people who model new behavior, others can learn how to start a lawn mower, how to saw wood, and much more. People also can learn how to show love, respect, or concern, as well as how to show hostility and aggression. They can even learn bad habits, such as smoking. When the Federal Communications Commission (FCC) banned cigarette commercials on television, it was acting on the belief that providing models of smokers would prompt people to imitate smoking. The FCC removed the models to discourage the behavior.

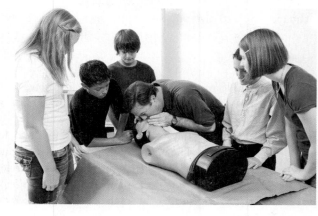

In observational or vicarious learning, we learn by watching a model perform a particular action and then trying to imitate that action correctly. Some actions would be very difficult to master without observational learning.

Of course, people do not imitate *everything* that other people do. Why are people selective in their imitation? There are several reasons: First, people cannot pay attention to everything going on around them. The behaviors people are most likely to imitate are those that are modeled by someone who commands their attention (for example, a famous or attractive person, or an expert). Second, a model does certain things to imitate it. If a behavior is not memorable, it will not be learned. Third, an effort must be made to convert into action what people see. If no motivation exists to perform an observed behavior, no one probably will show what has been learned. This distinction between *learning* and *performance* is crucial to social learning theorists.

One important motivation for acting is the kind of consequences associated with an observed behavior; that is, the rewards or punishments it appears to bring. These consequences do not necessarily have to happen to the observer. They may happen simply to the other people whom the observer is watching. This is called **vicarious reinforcement** (or **vicarious punishment**), because the learner does not experience the consequences firsthand: The consequences are experienced *through* other people. If a young teenager sees adults drinking and determines that they seem to be having a great deal of fun, the teenager is experiencing vicarious reinforcement of drinking and is more likely to imitate it.

The foremost proponent of social learning theory is Albert Bandura (1925–), who refers to his perspective as a *social cognitive theory* (Bandura, 1986, 2004). In a classic experiment, Bandura (1965) showed that people can learn a behavior without being reinforced directly for it and that learning a behavior and performing it are not the same thing. Three groups of nursery school children watched a film in which an adult model walked up to an adult-size plastic inflated doll and ordered it to move out of the way. When the doll failed to obey, the model became aggressive, pushing the doll on its side, punching it in the nose, hitting it with a rubber mallet, kicking it around the room, and throwing rubber balls at it. However, each group of children saw a film with a different ending. Those in the *model-rewarded condition* saw the model showered with candies, soft drinks, and praise by a second

After watching an adult behave aggressively toward an inflated doll, the children in Bandura's study imitated many of the aggressive acts of the adult model.

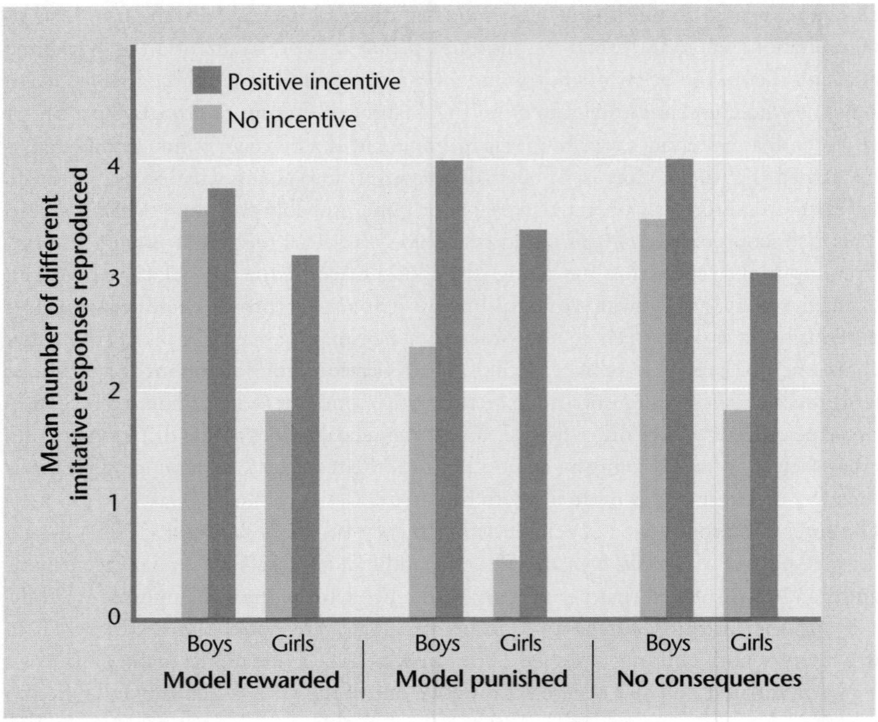

FIGURE 5–9
Results of Bandura's study.
As the graph shows, even though all the children in Bandura's study of imitative aggression learned the model's behavior, they performed differently depending on whether the model they saw was rewarded or punished.
Source: Bandura, 1965.

adult (vicarious reinforcement). Those in the *model-punished condition* saw the second adult shaking a finger at the model, scolding, and spanking him (vicarious punishment). And those in the *no-consequences condition* saw nothing happen to the model as a result of his aggressive behavior.

Immediately after seeing the film, the children were escorted individually into another room where they found the same large inflated doll, rubber balls, and mallet, as well as many other toys. Each child played alone for 10 minutes, while observers behind a one-way mirror recorded the number of imitated aggressive behaviors that the child spontaneously performed in the absence of any direct reinforcement for those actions. After 10 minutes, an experimenter entered the room and offered the child treats in return for imitating things the model had done. This was a measure of how much the child had previously learned from watching the model, but perhaps had not yet displayed.

The green bars in Figure 5–9 show that *all* the children had learned aggressive actions from watching the model, even though they were not reinforced overtly for that learning. When later offered treats to copy the model's actions, they all did so quite accurately. In addition, the yellow bars in the figure show that the children tended to suppress their inclination spontaneously to imitate an aggressive model when they had seen that model punished for aggression. This result was especially true of girls. Apparently, vicarious punishment provided the children with information about what might happen to them if they copied the "bad" behavior. Vicarious reinforcement similarly provides information about likely consequences, but in this study, its effects were not large. For children of this age (at least those not worried about punishment), imitating aggressive behavior toward a doll seems to have been considered "fun" in its own right, even without being associated with praise and candy. This outcome was especially true for boys.

This study has important implications regarding how not to teach aggression unintentionally to children. Suppose that you want to get a child to stop hitting other children. You might think that slapping the child as punishment would change the behavior, and it probably would suppress it to some extent. But slapping the child also demonstrates that hitting is an effective means of getting one's way. So slapping not only provides a model of aggression; it also provides a model associated with vicarious reinforcement. You and the child would be better off if the punishment given for hitting was not a similar form of aggression and if the child also could be rewarded for showing appropriate interactions with others.

Social learning theory's emphasis on expectations, insights, and information broadens our understanding of how people learn. According to social learning theory, humans use their powers of observation and thought to interpret their own experiences and those of others when deciding how to act. Moreover, Bandura stresses that human beings are capable of setting performance standards for themselves and rewarding (or punishing) themselves for achieving or failing to achieve those standards as a way to regulate their own behavior. This important perspective can be applied to the learning of many different things, from skills and behavioral tendencies to attitudes, values, and ideas.

Check Your Understanding

1. Match the following terms with the appropriate definition.

_____ Latent learning   **a.** A new, suddenly occurring idea to solve a problem

_____ Insight   **b.** Learning by watching a model

_____ Observational learning   **c.** Learning that has not yet been demonstrated in behavior

2. Indicate whether the following statements are true (T) or false (F).

a. _____ "Social learning theory broadens our understanding of how people learn skills and gain abilities by emphasizing expectations, insight, information, self-satisfaction, and self-criticism."

b. _____ "Social learning theory supports spanking as an effective way to teach children not to hit."

Chapter Review

 www.psychologythecore.com

Classical Conditioning

Learning is the process by which experience or practice produces a relatively permanent change in behavior or potential behavior. One basic form of learning involves learning to associate one event with another. **Classical conditioning** is a type of associative learning that Pavlov discovered while studying digestion. Pavlov trained a dog to salivate at the sound of a bell when the bell was rung just before food was given. The dog learned to associate the bell with food and began to salivate at the sound of the bell alone. Food is an **unconditioned stimulus (US)** that automatically evokes the **unconditioned response (UR)** of salivation. By repeatedly pairing food with a second, initially neutral stimulus (such as a bell), the second stimulus eventually became a **conditioned stimulus (CS)** eliciting a **conditioned response (CR)** of salivation.

Establishing a classically conditioned response usually is easier when the US and CS are paired with each other repeatedly, rather than at a single time or even once in a while (**intermittent pairing**). It is also important that the spacing of pairings be neither too far apart nor too close together.

The concept of **preparedness** accounts for the fact that certain conditioned responses are acquired very easily. The ease with which one develops **conditioned taste aversions** illustrates preparedness. Because animals are biologically prepared to learn them, conditioned taste aversions can occur with only one pairing of the taste of a tainted food and later illness, even when there is a lengthy interval between eating the food and becoming ill.

Operant Conditioning

Operant or **instrumental conditioning** is learning to make or withhold a certain response because of its consequences. **Operant behaviors** are different from the responses involved in classical conditioning because they are emitted voluntarily; whereas, those involved in classical conditioning are elicited by stimuli.

A key element in operant conditioning is the consequence associated with that behavior. When a consequence increases the likelihood of an operant behavior's being emitted, it is called a **reinforcer**. When a consequence decreases the likelihood of an operant behavior, it is called a **punisher**. These relationships are the basis of the **law of effect**, or **principle of reinforcement**: Consistently rewarded behaviors likely will be repeated; whereas, consistently punished behaviors likely will be suppressed.

To speed up operant conditioning, one can increase motivation and reduce the number of potential responses by restricting the environment (for example, by using a **Skinner box**). For behaviors outside the laboratory, which cannot be controlled so conveniently, the process of **shaping** is often useful. In shaping, reinforcement is given for successive approximations to the desired response.

Several kinds of reinforcers strengthen or increase the likelihood of behavior. **Positive reinforcers** (such as food) add something rewarding to a situation. **Negative reinforcers** (for example, stopping an electric shock) subtract something unpleasant. When an action is followed closely by a reinforcer, people tend to repeat the action, even when the action did not actually produce the reinforcement. Such behaviors are called *superstitious*.

Punishment is any unpleasant consequence that decreases the likelihood that the preceding behavior will recur. Although punishment can be effective, it also can stir up negative feelings and serve to model aggressive behavior. Also, rather than teaching a more desirable response, it only suppresses an undesirable one. Sometimes, after punishment has been administered a few times, it does not need to be continued. This is because the mere threat of punishment is enough to induce the desired behavior. With this process, called **avoidance training**, people learn to avoid the possibility of a punishing consequence.

When people or other animals are unable to escape from a punishing situation, they may acquire a "giving-up" response, called **learned helplessness**. Learned helplessness can generalize to new situations, causing resignation in the face of unpleasant outcomes, even when the outcomes can be avoided. A college student who gives up trying to do well in school after a few poor grades on tests is exhibiting learned helplessness.

Operant conditioning that is used to control biological functions, such as blood pressure or heart rate, is referred to as **biofeedback**. When it is used to control brain waves it is called **neurofeedback**. Biofeedback and neurofeedback have been applied successfully to a variety of medical problems, including migraine headaches, hypertension, and asthma. Athletes and musicians have used biofeedback to improve their performance and to control anxiety.

Factors Shared by Classical and Operant Conditioning

Despite the differences between classical and operant conditioning, these two forms of learning have many things in common: (1) Both cases involve learned associations; (2) in both cases, responses come under control of stimuli in the environment; (3) in both cases, the responses will gradually disappear if they are not periodically renewed; and (4) in both cases, new behaviors can build upon previously established ones.

In classical and operant conditioning, an "if-then" relationship, or **contingency**, exists either between two stimuli or between a stimulus and a response. In both kinds of learning, perceived contingencies are very important. In classical conditioning, the contingency is between the CS and the US. The CS comes to be viewed as a signal that the US is about to happen. For that reason, the CS must not only occur in proximity to the US, but must also precede the US and provide predictive information about it. If the CS occurs *after* the US, it will come to serve as a signal that the US is over, not that the US is imminent. In operant conditioning, contingencies exist between responses and consequences. Contingencies between responses and rewards are called **schedules of reinforcement**. *Partial reinforcement*, in which rewards are given only for some correct responses, generates behavior that persists longer than that learned by *continuous reinforcement*. A **fixed-interval schedule**, by which reinforcement is given for the first correct response after a fixed time period, tends to result in a flurry of responding right before a reward is due. A **variable-interval schedule**, which reinforces the first correct response after an unpredictable period of time, tends to result in a slow, but steady, pattern of responding. In a **fixed-ratio schedule**, behavior is rewarded after a fixed number of correct responses occurs, so the result usually is a high rate of responding. Finally, a **variable-ratio schedule** provides reinforcement after a varying number of correct responses occurs. It encourages a high rate of response that is especially persistent.

Learned responses sometimes weaken and may even disappear, which is a phenomenon called **extinction**. The learning is not necessarily forgotten completely, however. Sometimes, **spontaneous recovery** occurs, in which the learned response suddenly reappears on its own, with no retraining.

Extinction is produced in classical conditioning by failure to continue pairing the CS and the US. The CS no longer serves as a signal that the US is about to happen, and so, the conditioned response dies out. Often, an important contributing factor is new, learned associations that interfere with the old one. In situations in which one is reminded of the old association, spontaneous recovery may occur.

Extinction occurs in operant conditioning when reinforcement is withheld until the learned response is no longer emitted. The ease with which an operantly conditioned behavior is extinguished varies according to several factors: the strength of the original learning, the variety of settings in which learning took place, and the schedule of reinforcement used during conditioning.

The tendency to respond to cues that are similar, but not identical, to those that prevailed during the original learning is known as **stimulus generalization**. **Stimulus discrimination** enables learners to perceive differences among cues so as not to respond to all of them.

In operant conditioning, learners may generalize their responses by performing behaviors that are similar to the ones that were reinforced originally. This result is called **response generalization**. Discrimination in operant conditioning is taught by reinforcing only a certain response and only in the presence of a certain stimulus.

In classical and operant conditioning, original learning serves as a building block for new learning. In classical conditioning, an earlier CS can be used as a US for further training. For example, Pavlov used the bell to condition his dogs to salivate at the sight of a black square. This effect, which is called **higher-order conditioning**, is difficult to achieve because of extinction. The initial conditioned response will die out, unless the original unconditioned stimulus is presented occasionally.

In operant conditioning, initially neutral stimuli can become reinforcers by being associated with other reinforcers. A **primary reinforcer** is one that, like food and water, is rewarding in and of itself. A **secondary reinforcer** is one whose value is learned through its association with primary reinforcers or with other secondary reinforcers. Money is such a good secondary reinforcer because it can be exchanged for so many different primary and secondary rewards.

Classical and operant conditioning share so many similarities that many psychologists now wonder whether classical and operant conditioning are not just two ways of bringing about the same kind of learning.

Cognitive Learning

Cognitive learning refers to the mental processes that go on inside people when they learn. Although cognitive learning is impossible to observe and measure directly, it can be *inferred* from behavior, and so, it is a legitimate topic for scientific study.

Latent learning is learning that has not yet been demonstrated in behavior. One kind of latent learning is knowledge of spatial layouts and relationships, which is usually stored in the form of a **cognitive map.** Rewards or punishments are not essential for latent learning to take place. You did not need rewards and punishments to learn the layout of your campus, for example. You acquired this cognitive map simply by storing your visual perceptions.

A **learning set** is a concept or procedure that provides a key to solving a problem even when its demands are slightly different from those of problems one has solved in the past. As a student, you probably have a learning set for writing a term paper that allows you successfully to develop papers on many different topics. A learning set can sometimes encourage **insight** or the sudden perception of a solution, even to a problem that at first seemed totally new. In this case, you are perceiving similarities between old and new problems that were not initially apparent.

Social learning theorists argue that we learn much both by observing other people who model a behavior or by simply hearing about something. This process is called **observational** (or **vicarious**) **learning.** It would be harder to learn to drive a car without ever having been in one because you would lack a model of "driving behavior." It is hard for deaf children to learn spoken language because they have no auditory model of correct speech. The extent to which people imitate behaviors that are learned through observation depends on the motivation to do so. One important motivation is the reward or punishment that has come with the behavior. When a consequence is not experienced firsthand, but only occurs to other people, it is called **vicarious reinforcement** or **vicarious punishment.**

Chapter 6
Memory

Go to *The Core Online* at **www.psychologythecore.com** to get the most up-to-date information for your introductory psychology course. The content online is an important part of what you are learning—the content there can help prepare you for your test! It includes up-to-date examples, simulations, video clips, and practice quizzes. Also be sure to check out the *Blog* to hear directly from the authors on what current events and latest research are most relevant to your course materials.

The first time you log in, you will need the access code packaged with your textbook. If you do not have a code, please go to **www.mypearsonstore.com** and enter the ISBN of your textbook (**0-13-603344-X**) to purchase the code.

6.1 The Sensory Registers

Visual and Auditory Registers
- The **information-processing model of memory** states that memory involves encoding, storing, and retrieving information.
- **Sensory registers** temporarily hold data from the senses.

Attention
- **Attention** involves selectively looking at, listening to, smelling, tasting, or feeling what we deem to be important.
- Background information is "toned down," but it receives at least some processing so that we can quickly shift attention if appropriate.

6.2 Short-Term Memory

Short-term memory (STM or *working memory*) stores new information briefly while processing information that is being attended to.

Capacity of STM
- Capacity of STM is limited to information that can be repeated or rehearsed in 1.5 to 2 seconds.
- **Chunking** refers to grouping information into larger meaningful units for processing in STM.

Encoding in STM
- Verbal information is encoded by sound.
- Information can also be coded visually or based on meaning.

Maintaining STM
- **Rote rehearsal** (maintenance rehearsal) keeps information in STM.
- Mere repetition without an intent to remember does not promote long-term memories.

6.3 Long-Term Memory

Long-term memory (LTM) contains everything a person knows.

Capacity of LTM
- LTM can store a vast amount of information for many years.

Encoding in LTM
- Most information is coded according to its meaning.

Maintaining LTM
- **Rote rehearsal** with the intent to remember is useful for remembering conceptually meaningless material.
- **Elaborative rehearsal** is more effective for meaningful information that can be linked to other content already in LTM.
- Memory techniques that rely on elaborative processing are called **mnemonics**.

Serial Position Effect
- Items toward the end of a long list tend to be remembered well because they are the most likely to be in STM (*recency effect*).
- Items toward the beginning of a long list tend to be remembered well because they received some elaborative processing (*primacy effect*).

Types of LTM
- **Episodic memories** are memories of events experienced in a specific time and place.
- **Semantic memories** are memories of facts and concepts not linked to a specific time or place (general knowledge).
- **Procedural memories** are motor skills and habits.
- **Emotional memories** are learned emotional responses.

Explicit and Implicit Memory
- **Explicit memories** are memories that one is aware of (typically semantic and episodic memories).
- **Implicit memories** are memories about information that was not intentionally committed to LTM or is retrieved without effort from LTM (often procedural and emotional memories).
- **Tip-of-the tongue phenomenon** refers to knowing a word but not quite being able to recall it.

6 4 The Biology of Memory

Memory Storage

- **Long-term potentiation** is the process by which memories are stored in the chemistry and structure of neurons.
- Short-term memories are located primarily in the prefrontal cortex and the temporal lobe.
- Semantic and episodic memories are located primarily in the frontal and temporal lobes of the cortex.
- Procedural memories are located primarily in the cerebellum and motor cortex.
- The hippocampus is important in the formation of semantic, episodic, and procedural memories.
- The amygdala is important in the formation of emotional memories.

6 5 Forgetting

The Biology of Forgetting

- **Decay theory** states that memories deteriorate simply as a result of the passage of time.
- Disruption of the storage process can also cause forgetting as in **retrograde amnesia**.
- Severe memory loss is invariably a result of brain damage.

Experience and Forgetting

- Forgetting can be caused by a lack of attention being paid to critical cues.
- Forgetting can be caused by insufficient rehearsal.
- Learning itself can cause forgetting because of interference.
  - **Retroactive interference** refers to the interference created when the learning of new information interferes with information already in LTM.
  - **Proactive interference** refers to the interference created when information already in LTM interferes with the formation of new memories.
- The absence of environmental cues present during learning or a change in one's physiological state can reduce recall.
- **Reconstruction** is the process by which memories change over time while they are being stored in LTM.

6 6 Special Topics in Memory

Cultural Influences

- Cultural values and customs profoundly affect what people remember and how easily they recall information.

Autobiographical Memory

- **Autobiographical memory** refers to the recollection of events from one's life.
- **Childhood (infantile) amnesia** is the inability to recall events before about the age of 2.

Extraordinary Memory

- **Eidetic imagery**, often called *photographic memory*, refers to the extraordinarily accurate and vivid recall of visual images.
- **Mnemonists** are people skilled in the use of memory techniques.

Flashbulb Memories

- **Flashbulb memories** refer to vivid memories of an event and incidents surrounding it.
- Despite the vividness of flashbulb memories, they may not be accurate or stable.

Eyewitness Testimony

- Because of the reconstructive nature of LTM, eyewitness testimony often does not accurately reflect what actually occurred.

Recovered Memories

- **Recovered memories** are recollections of an event despite having no prior memory of the event's occurrence.
- Recovered memories are highly controversial because there is no scientifically reliable way to distinguish real memories from false ones.

Rajan Mahadevan, an Indian psychologist, has always had a knack for remembering numbers. At age 5, he became intrigued by the license plate numbers on the cars of some 50 guests at a party given by his parents. Quickly memorizing all the plates, he flabbergasted everyone by reciting the numbers in the order in which the cars were parked. Similarly, in fourth grade, Rajan astonished his teacher with a long list of memorized statistics on railroad accidents in India during the previous decade. His teacher had insisted Indian railways were safe; and Rajan wanted to prove him incorrect. But what landed Rajan in the *Guinness Book of World Records* was his memorization of the constant *pi*. In 1981, at the age of 24, he recited from memory the value of *pi* to 31,810 decimal places. Yet when Rajan was tested for retention of material other than digits, such as recalling a complex story or reproducing from memory an intricate geometric design, his performance fell to average (C. P. Thompson, Cowan, & Frieman, 1993).

How does Rajan do it? Basically, he divides the numbers into groups of 10, learns each 10-digit unit largely by rote memorization, then strings them together. Occasionally, he attaches meaning to a 3- or 4-digit string of numbers, enabling him to recall that string as a single chunk. For example, he remembers the string 312 as the area code for Chicago and the string 1865 as the year Lincoln died. But for Rajan, this strategy is only incidental.

Accounts of people with extraordinary memories raise many questions about the nature of **memory** itself: Why are some people so much better at remembering things than are others? Are they simply born with this ability or could any person learn to remember as much as they do? And why is it that remembering sometimes can be so easy (think how effortlessly baseball fans remember the batting averages of their favorite players) and other times so difficult (as when students grope for answers on an exam)? Why do some people find it hard to remember an event that happened only a few months back, yet they can recall in vivid detail some other event that happened 10, 20, or even 30 years ago? Just how does memory work and what makes it fail? This chapter explores these and other questions about memory.

ENDURING ISSUES in Memory

The "Enduring Issues" in psychology for this chapter include the biological basis of memory (mind-body), the ways in which memory differs among people and across cultures (diversity-universality), and the ways in which memory changes in the first few years of life (stability-change). Chapter 6 also considers whether people with extraordinary memory are born with special skills (nature-nurture), and it explores the extent to which memories can be affected by events outside the person (person-situation).

Most contemporary psychologists perceive memory as a series of steps the brain follows to process information, much as a computer stores and retrieves data. Together, these steps form the **information-processing model** of memory. Because far more information bombards the senses than a person can possibly process, the first stage of information processing involves selecting the material to think about and remember. Therefore, let's turn first to the sensory registers and to attention, the process that allows people to select incoming information for further processing.

The Sensory Registers

Look slowly around the room. At each glance, you are taking in enormous amounts of visual information, including colors, shapes, textures, relative brightness, and shadows. At the same time, you are picking up sounds, smells, and other sensory data. All this raw information then flows from your senses into the **sensory registers**, which are like waiting rooms into which information enters and stays for only a short time. Whether any of the information is remembered depends on which operations are performed on it. There are registers for each of the senses, but the visual and auditory registers have been studied more extensively.

■ VISUAL AND AUDITORY REGISTERS

Although the sensory registers have virtually unlimited capacity, information disappears from them quite rapidly. A simple experiment can demonstrate how much visual information is taken in—and how quickly it is lost. Bring a digital camera into a darkened room, then take a photograph with a flash. During the split second that the room is lit up by the flash, your visual register will absorb a surprising amount of information about the room and its contents. Try to hold on to that visual image, or *icon*, as long as you can. You will find that in a few seconds, it is gone. Then, compare your remembered image of the room with what you actually saw, as captured in the photograph. You will discover that your visual register took in far more information than you were able to retain for even a few seconds.

Classic experiments by George Sperling (1960) clearly demonstrate how quickly information disappears from the visual register. Sperling flashed groups of letters, organized into three rows, on a screen for just a fraction of a second. When the letters were gone, he sounded a tone to tell his participants which row of letters to recall: A high-pitched tone indicated that they should try to remember the top row of letters, a low-pitched tone meant that they should recall the bottom row, and a medium-pitched tone signaled them to recall the middle row. Using this *partial-report technique*, Sperling found that if he sounded the tone immediately after the letters were flashed, people could usually recall three or four of the letters in *any* of the three rows; that is, they seemed to have at least nine of the original 12 letters in their visual registers. But if he waited for even one second before sounding the tone, his participants were able to recall only one or two letters from any single row—in just one second, then, all but four or five of the original set of 12 letters had vanished from their visual registers.

Visual information often disappears from the visual register even more rapidly than Sperling thought. In everyday life, new visual information keeps coming into the register; and the new information replaces the old information almost immediately, a process often called *masking*. This is just as well; otherwise, the visual information would simply pile up in the sensory register and get hopelessly scrambled. Under normal viewing conditions, visual information is erased from the sensory register in about a quarter of a second as it is replaced by new information, long before it has a chance to simply fade out by itself.

Auditory information fades more slowly than visual information. The auditory equivalent of the icon, the *echo*, tends to last for several seconds, which, given the nature of speech, is certainly a lucky thing. Otherwise, "*You* did it!" would be indistinguishable from "You *did* it!" because the emphasis on the first words would not be remembered by the time the last words were registered.

■ ATTENTION

If information disappears from the sensory registers so rapidly, how do we remember anything for more than a second or two? The answer is that we select some of the incoming information for further processing by means of attention (Figure 6–1). **Attention** is the process of selectively looking, listening, smelling, tasting, and feeling. At the same time, meaning is given to the information coming in. Look at the page in front of you. You will see a series of black lines on a white page. Until you recognize these lines as letters and words, they are just meaningless marks. For you to make sense of this jumble of data, you must process the information for meaning. As discussed in Chapter 3 (Sensation and Perception), you must convert raw sensory information into meaningful perceptual experiences.

Suppose you are sitting at a desk reading this book. Your roommate is listening to a talk show on the radio. There are traffic sounds outside. The water you are heating to make tea begins to boil. In situations such as this, how do you select the sensory information to pay attention to? In 1958, the British psychologist Donald Broadbent (1926–1993) suggested that a filtering process at the entrance to the nervous system allows information to pass through the filter and draw a person's attention when it stands out because of its physical properties—loudness, size,

---

Visual and Auditory Registers

■ The information-processing model of memory states that memory involves _____, _____, and _____.

■ Sensory registers temporarily _____ _____

Attention

■ Attention involves _____ _____ _____

■ Background information is "toned down," but it receives _____ _____ _____

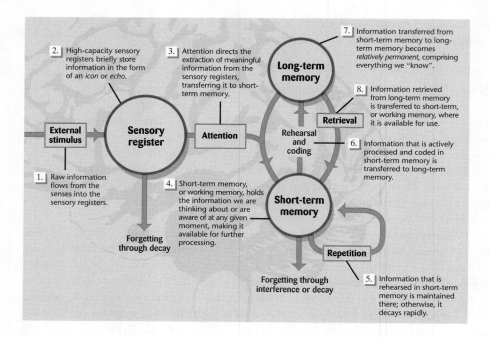

FIGURE 6–1
The sequence of information processing.

color, sudden start or stop. Imagine that you and a friend are sitting in a restaurant talking. You filter out all other conversations taking place around you, a process known as the *cocktail-party phenomenon* (Cherry, 1966). Although you later might be able to describe certain characteristics of those other conversations, such as whether the people speaking were men or women and whether the words were spoken loudly or softly, according to Broadbent, you normally could not recall what was being discussed, even at neighboring tables. Because you filtered out those other conversations, the processing of that information did not proceed far enough for you to understand what you heard.

Broadbent's filtering theory helps explain some aspects of attention. To continue the restaurant example, if a sudden loud noise or bright flash occurs or if the lights suddenly go out, your attention will shift to those events. But if someone nearby were to mention your name in a normal conversational voice, your attention probably would shift to that conversation also, not because it was especially loud but because the information was *meaningful*. Anne Treisman (1960, 1964, 2004) modified the filter theory to account for phenomena such as that. She contended that the filter is not a simple on-and-off switch, but rather a variable control—like the volume control on a radio that can "turn down" unwanted signals without rejecting them entirely. Although people generally pay attention to only some incoming sensory information, they monitor other information at a low level and give it at least some minimal processing. Thus, they can shift their attention when they pick up something particularly meaningful. This explains why parents often wake up immediately when they hear their baby crying, but sleep through other, much louder but less meaningful noises. The information the senses attend to enters the person's short-term memory, a process that will be examined next.

Check Your Understanding

1. Indicate whether the following statements are true (T) or false (F).

a. _____ The sensory registers have virtually unlimited capacity.

b. _____ Some kinds of information are stored permanently in the sensory registers.

c. _____ Auditory information fades from the sensory registers more quickly than visual information does.

d. _____ The filter theory as modified by Treisman holds that attention is similar to an on-and-off switch.

2. You are in a large, noisy group in which everyone seems to be talking at once. To concentrate on the conversation you are having with one of the people, you "tune out" all the other conversations going on around you. A few minutes later, someone nearby turns to you and says, "Did you hear what I was saying to John?" You have to admit that even though you were standing right next to her, you do not know what she said. Your failure to remember that other conversation is an example of

   a. Partial-report technique

   b. Cocktail-party phenomenon

   c. Masking

Short-Term Memory

The information that people think about or are aware of at any given moment is held in **short-term memory (STM)**. In Chapter 4 (States of Consciousness), this is referred to as normal *waking consciousness*. Short-term memory has two primary tasks: to store new information briefly and to work on that (and other) information. Short-term memory sometimes is called *working memory*, to emphasize the active or working component of this memory system.

■ **CAPACITY OF STM**

Video-game fanatics are oblivious to the outside world. Chess masters at tournaments demand complete silence while they ponder their next move. Students shut themselves in a quiet room to study for final exams. As these examples illustrate, STM can handle only so much information at any given moment. Research suggests that STM can hold about as much information as can be repeated or rehearsed in 1.5 to 2 seconds (Baddeley, 1986, 2002).

To get a better idea of the limits of STM, read the first row of letters in the list that follows just once. Then, close your eyes and try to remember the letters in the correct sequence. Repeat the procedure for each subsequent row.

1. C X W
2. M N K T Y
3. R P J H B Z S
4. G B M P V Q F J D
5. E G Q W J P B R H K A F

Like most other people, you probably found rows 1 and 2 fairly easy, row 3 a bit harder, row 4 extremely difficult, and row 5 impossible to remember after just one reading. Now try reading through the following set of 12 letters just once and see whether you can repeat them:

TJYFAVMCFKIB

How many letters were you able to recall? In all likelihood, not all 12. But what if you had been asked to remember the following 12 letters instead?

TV FBI JFK YMCA

Could you remember them? Almost certainly the answer is yes. These are the same 12 letters as before, but here they are grouped into four separate "words." This way of grouping and organizing information so that it fits into meaningful units is called **chunking**. The 12 letters have been chunked into four meaningful elements that can be handled readily by STM—they can be repeated in less than 2 seconds. By chunking words into sentences or sentence fragments, people can process an even greater amount of information in STM. For example, suppose that you want to remember the following list of words: *tree, song, hat, sparrow, lilac, cat*. One strategy would be to cluster as many of them as possible into phrases or sentences: "The *sparrow* in the *tree* wears a *lilac hat* while warbling a *song* to the *cat*." Take a minute now to imagine this scene and think about how silly it would look and sound. Using this technique, many people can remember very long lists. But is there a limit to this strategy? Would five sentences be as easy to remember for a short time as five single words? No. As the size of

Chess players demand complete silence as they consider their next move. This is because there is a definite limit to the amount of information STM can handle at any given moment.

Short-Term Memory

■ Short-term memory (STM or _____ memory) stores _____ briefly while

_____

Capacity of STM

■ Capacity of STM is limited to

_____

■ Chunking refers to _____

_____

Encoding in STM

■ _____

is encoded by sound.

■ Information can also be coded

_____

Maintaining STM

■ Rote rehearsal (maintenance rehearsal) _____

_____

■ Mere repetition without an intent to remember does not promote

_____.

"Hold on a second, Bob. I'm putting you on a stickie."

any individual chunk increases, the number of chunks that can be held in STM declines. STM can easily handle five unrelated letters or words at once, but five unrelated sentences are much harder to remember.

■ ENCODING IN STM

Verbal information is encoded for storage in STM *phonologically*—that is, according to how it sounds. This is true even when people see the word, letter, or number on a page, rather than hear it spoken. Numerous experiments have shown that when people try to retrieve material from STM, they generally mix up items that sound alike. A list of words that includes *mad, man, mat,* and *cap* is harder for most people to recall accurately than a list that includes *pit, day, cow,* and *bar.*

But not all material in short-term memory is stored phonologically. At least some material is stored in visual form, and other information is retained on the basis of its meaning. For example, people do not have to convert visual data such as maps, diagrams, and paintings into sound before they can think about them. In fact, research has shown that memory for images is generally better than memory for words because images very often are stored both phonologically and as images, while words often are stored only phonologically (Paivio, 1986). The *dual coding* of images accounts for the fact that forming a mental picture of something one is trying to learn can be very helpful.

■ MAINTAINING STM

Short-term memories are fleeting, generally lasting a matter of seconds. However, people can hold information in STM for longer periods through rote rehearsal, also called *maintenance rehearsal.* **Rote rehearsal** consists of repeating information, silently or audibly. It may not be the most efficient way to remember something permanently, but it can be quite effective for a short time.

Remembering a small amount of information for a short period is important, but a person's ability to store vast quantities of information for indefinite periods is essential for mastering complex skills, acquiring an education, or remembering the personal experiences that contribute to one's identity. The next section explores how memories that often last a lifetime are stored.

Check Your Understanding

1. _____ memory is what we are thinking about at any given moment. Its function is to store new information for a brief time and to work on that and other information.

2. You try to remember the letters CNOXNPEHFOBSN in sequence, but despite your best efforts, you cannot seem to remember more than half of them. Then, you are told that the letters can be rearranged as CNN FOX HBO ESPN (four television channels). After that, you are able to remember all the letters even weeks later. Rearranging the letters into groups that are easier to retain in memory is known as

   a. Shadowing   **c.** Rote rehearsal

   b. Chunking   **d.** Cueing

3. Your sister looks up a phone number in the phone book, but then cannot find the phone. By the time she finds it, she has forgotten the number. While she was looking for the phone, she apparently failed to engage in

   a. Rote rehearsal   **c.** Phonological coding

   b. Parallel processing **d.** Categorizing

Long-Term Memory

Everything a person learns is stored in **long-term memory (LTM)**—the words to a popular song, the results of the last election, the meaning of justice, the way to roller skate or draw a face, the enjoyment of opera or disgust at the sight of raw oysters, and the thing you are supposed to be doing tomorrow at 4:00 p.m.

■ CAPACITY OF LTM

In contrast to short-term memory, long-term memory can store a vast amount of information for many years. Under the proper circumstances, a person can often dredge up an astonishing amount of information from LTM. In one study, for example, adults who had graduated from high school more than 40 years earlier were still able to recognize the names of 75% of their classmates (Bahrick, Bahrick, & Wittlinger, 1974). And some people who can remember their Spanish from high school after 50 years can do so even with little or no opportunity to practice it (Bahrick, 1984).

■ ENCODING IN LTM

Can you picture the shape of Florida? Do you know what a trumpet sounds like? Can you imagine the smell of a rose or the taste of coffee? When you answer the telephone, can you sometimes identify the caller immediately, just from the sound of the voice? Your ability to do most of these things means that at least some long-term memories are coded in terms of nonverbal images: shapes, sounds, smells, tastes, and so on.

Yet, most of the information in LTM seems to be encoded in terms of *meaning*. If material is especially familiar (the words of the national anthem, say, or the opening of the Gettysburg Address), you may have stored it verbatim in LTM and you can often retrieve it word for word when you need it. Generally speaking, however, people do not use verbatim storage in LTM. When someone tells you a long, rambling story, you may listen to every word but will not likely try to remember the story verbatim. Instead, you will normally extract the main points of the story and try to remember those. Even simple sentences usually are encoded in terms of their meaning. Thus, when people are asked to remember that "Tom called John," they often find it impossible to remember later whether they were told "Tom called John" or "John was called by Tom." They usually remember the *meaning* of the message, rather than the exact words.

■ MAINTAINING LTM

Have you ever been in a group in which people were taking turns speaking up—perhaps on the first day of class when all present are asked to introduce themselves briefly or at the beginning

---

Long-Term Memory

■ Long-term memory (LTM) contains

_____

_____

Capacity of LTM

■ LTM can store _____

_____

_____

Encoding in LTM

■ Most information is coded

according to its _____

_____

Maintaining LTM

■ Rote rehearsal with the intent to

remember is useful for _____

_____

■ Elaborative rehearsal is more

effective for _____

_____

■ Memory techniques that rely on

elaborative processing are called

_____

of a panel discussion when the speakers are asked to do the same in front of a large audience? Did you notice that you forgot virtually everything that was said by the person who spoke just before you did? That person's comments simply "went in one ear and out the other" while you were preoccupied with thinking about your own remarks. To prevent forgetting, we must attend to and process information we wish to remember. Two kinds of processing are key to long-term memory: rote rehearsal and elaborative rehearsal.

Rote Rehearsal   Rote rehearsal, the principal tool for holding information in STM, is also useful for holding information in LTM. The old saying "practice makes perfect" has some merit. Rajan's remarkable memory for the digits in *pi* was based largely on rote memory. Millions of students have learned the alphabet and multiplication tables by doggedly repeating letters and numbers. And rote rehearsal is the normal method of storing conceptually meaningless material, such as phone numbers, social security numbers, security codes, computer passwords, birth dates, and people's names.

However, it is important to distinguish rote rehearsal from mere repetition. Repetition without any intention to learn generally has little effect on subsequent recall. You can probably prove this phenomenon to yourself: Stop here and try to imagine from memory the front side of a U.S. penny. Now look at Figure 6–2 and pick the illustration that matches your memory. For most people, this task is surprisingly difficult: Despite seeing thousands of pennies and being able to recognize them quickly, most people cannot accurately draw one or even pick one out from among other, similar objects (Nickerson & Adams, 1979).

Elaborative Rehearsal   For getting meaningful information into LTM, **elaborative rehearsal** is far more effective than rote rehearsal. Through elaborative rehearsal, one extracts the meaning of the new information and links it to as much of the material already in LTM as possible. The more links or associations that are made, the more likely the person is to remember the new information later. Think back to the "sparrow in the tree" mentioned earlier in this chapter. Can you remember what the sparrow was wearing? And what was it doing? If you stopped to imagine that silly scene when you first read about it, in all likelihood you can remember all those details (and perhaps some details that were not provided, such as whether the tree had leaves and what kind of cat was being serenaded).

Special techniques called **mnemonics** (pronounced *nee-MON-iks*) may help you to tie new material to information already in LTM. Some of the simplest mnemonic techniques are the rhymes and jingles many use to remember dates and other facts. For example, "Thirty days hath September, April, June, and November . . ." enables us to recall how many days are in a month. Other simple mnemonic devices can be words or sentences made out of the material to be recalled. The colors of the visible spectrum—red, orange, yellow, green, blue, indigo, and violet—can be remembered simply by forming their first letters into the acronym ROY G. BIV. In addition, when a mnemonic device is related to personal information, such as a hobby or interest, people are even more likely to be able to recall it later. Making up a story with vivid imagery (such as the sparrow in the tree) also can serve to enhance long-term memory. Using mnemonics can be helpful in many different situations.

■ SERIAL POSITION EFFECT

When people are given a long list of items to remember, they tend to do better at recalling the first items (*primacy effect*) and the last items (*recency effect*) in the list (Figure 6–3). The explanation for

---

Serial Position Effect

■ Items toward the end of a long list tend to be remembered well because

_____

_____

■ Items toward the beginning of a long list tend to be remembered well because _____

_____

_____

FIGURE 6–2
A penny for your thoughts.
Which of these accurately illustrates a real U.S. penny? The answer is on page 157.

this **serial position effect** resides in understanding how short- and long-term memory work together. The recency effect occurs because the last items that were presented are still contained in STM and thus are available for recall. The primacy effect, on the other hand, reflects the opportunity to rehearse the first few items in the list—increasing their likelihood of being transferred to LTM. Poor performance occurs on the items in the middle of the list because they were presented too long ago to still be in STM, and because so many items requiring attention were presented before and after them, there was little opportunity for rehearsal.

In summary, LTM offers a vast storage space for information. Its capacity is immense, and material stored there may endure, more or less intact, for decades. By comparison, STM has a sharply limited capacity; information may disappear quickly from it because it fades or simply because the storage space is full. To keep information in STM, it must be refreshed constantly through rote rehearsal. To retain information for a long time, one must transfer it to LTM, usually through rote or elaborative rehearsal. The sensory registers can take in an enormous volume of less permanent information, but they have no ability to process memories. Together, these three stages of memory—the sensory registers, STM, and LTM—comprise the information-processing view of memory, as reviewed in the Summary Table: Memory as an Information-Processing System. (The answer to the question on page 156 is: The accurate illustration of a penny in Figure 6–3 is the third from the left.)

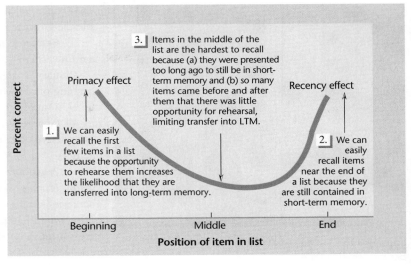

FIGURE 6–3
The serial position effect.
The serial position effect demonstrates how short-term and long-term memory work together.

■ TYPES OF LTM

The information stored in LTM can take many forms. However, most long-term memories can be classified into one of several types: episodic, semantic, procedural, and emotional memories.

Episodic memories are memories of events experienced in a specific time and place. These are *personal* memories, rather than historical facts. If you can recall what you ate for dinner last night, what presents you got at your sixteenth birthday party, or how you learned to ride a bike

Types of LTM

■ Episodic memories are memories of

_____

■ Semantic memories are memories of

_____

■ Procedural memories are

_____

■ Emotional memories are

_____

SUMMARY TABLE	**Memory as an Information-Processing System**					
SYSTEM	MEANS BY WHICH INFORMATION IS STORED	FORM IN WHICH INFORMATION IS STORED	STORAGE ORGANIZATION	STORAGE DURATION	MEANS BY WHICH INFORMATION IS RETRIEVED	FACTORS IN FORGETTING
Sensory Register	Visual and auditory registers	Raw sensory data	None	From less than 1 second to only a few seconds	Reconsideration of registered information	Decay or masking
Short-Term Memory	Rote or maintenance rehearsal	Visual and phonological representation	None	Usually 15 to 20 seconds	Rote or maintenance rehearsal	Interference or decay
Long-Term Memory	Rote rehearsal, elaborative rehearsal, schemata	Some nonverbal representations, mostly stored by meaning	Logical frameworks, such as hierarchies or categories	Perhaps for an entire lifetime	Retrieval cues linked to organized information	Retrieval failure or interference

Looking into a bakery window, perhaps smelling the aromas of the cakes inside, may prime the memory and trigger distinct memories associated with those sights and smells that may have formed many years earlier.

Explicit and Implicit Memory

■ Explicit memories are memories that _____

_____

■ Implicit memories are memories about _____

_____

■ Tip-of-the-tongue phenomenon refers to _____

_____

_____

when you were little, then you are calling up episodic memories. Think of episodic memory as a diary or daily journal that lets you "go back in time."

Semantic memories are facts and concepts not linked to a particular time. If episodic memory is like a daily journal, semantic memory is like a dictionary or an encyclopedia, filled with facts and concepts, such as the meaning of the word *semantic*, the name of the inventor of the light bulb, the location of the Empire State Building, the value of 2×7, and the identity of George Washington. Memory for sequences of numbers, such as those described at the beginning of the chapter, is an example of semantic memory.

Procedural memories are motor skills and habits. They are not memories *about* skills and habits; they *are* the skills and habits. Procedural memories have to do with knowing *how*: how to ride a bicycle, swim, play a violin, type a letter, make coffee, write your name, send a text message, walk across a room, or slam on a car's brakes. The information involved usually consists of a precise sequence of coordinated movements that often are difficult to describe in words. Repetition, and in many cases, deliberate practice, are often required to master skills and habits. But once learned, they are rarely completely lost. The saying "You never forget how to ride a bicycle" illustrates the durability of procedural memories.

Emotional memories are learned emotional responses to various stimuli such as all our loves and hates, our rational and irrational fears, and our feelings of disgust and anxiety. If you are afraid of flying insects, become enraged at the sight of a Nazi flag, or are ashamed of something you did, you have emotional memories.

■ EXPLICIT AND IMPLICIT MEMORY

Consider the case of H. M., a young man who had severe, uncontrollable epileptic seizures (Milner, Corkin, & Teuber, 1968). The seizures became life threatening, so as a last resort, surgeons removed most of the afflicted area of his brain. The surgery greatly reduced the frequency and severity of seizures, but it left behind a new problem: H. M. apparently could no longer form new memories. He could meet someone again and again, but each time it was as though he were meeting the person for the first time. He could read the same magazine day after day and not recall ever having seen it before. Old memories were intact: He could remember things he had learned long before the operation, but he could not learn anything new. Or so it seemed.

One day Milner asked H. M. to trace the outline of a star while looking in a mirror. This simple task is surprisingly difficult, but with practice most people show steady progress. Surprisingly, so did H. M. Each day he got better and better at tracing the star, just as a person with an undamaged brain would do—yet each day he had no recollection of ever having attempted the task. H. M.'s performance demonstrated not only that he could learn new things, but also that there are different kinds of memories. Some are **explicit**: We know things, we intended to remember them, and we know that we know them. Other memories are **implicit**: We know things, but in many cases, we had no intention of remembering them, and the knowledge may be outside our awareness. H. M. was unable to form and retrieve new explicit memories, but he clearly was able to form and retrieve new implicit memories (in his case, procedural memory for drawing the star). See Table 6–1 for a summary of implicit and explicit memory.

Priming Research on a phenomenon called *priming* also demonstrates the distinction between explicit and implicit memory. In priming, a person is exposed to a stimulus, usually a word or picture. Later, the person is shown a fragment of a stimulus (a few letters of a word or a piece of a picture) and is asked to complete it. For example: You are shown a list of words, including the word *tour*, and later on, you are shown a list of word fragments that include ___*ou*___. Then, you are asked to fill in the blanks to make a word. Typically, people are more

TABLE 6–1   Types of Memories

EXPLICIT		IMPLICIT	
SEMANTIC	**EPISODIC**	**PROCEDURAL**	**EMOTIONAL**
Memories of facts and concepts	Memories of personally experienced events	Motor skills and habits	Learned emotional reactions
Example: recalling that Albany is the capital of New York	*Example:* recalling a trip to Albany	*Example:* ice skating	*Example:* recoiling at the sight of a rat

able to complete fragments with items seen earlier than they are with other, equally plausible items they have not seen before. In this example, if you saw the list with the word *tour*, you are far more likely to write *tour* than *four*, *pour*, or *sour*, all of which are just as acceptable as *tour*. Mere exposure to *tour* primes you to write that word even though you may not recall having seen that word on the list.

The Tip-of-the-Tongue Phenomenon   Everyone has had the experience of knowing a word but not quite being able to recall it. This is called the **tip-of-the-tongue phenomenon**, or **TOT** (Brown & McNeil, 1966). Although everyone experiences TOTs, these experiences become more frequent during stressful situations and as people get older. Moreover, other words— usually with a sound or meaning similar to the word you are seeking—occur to you while you are in the TOT state and these words interfere with and sabotage your attempt to recall the desired word. The harder you try, the worse the TOT state gets. The best way to recall a blocked word, then, is to stop trying to recall it. Most of the time, the word you were searching for will pop into your head, minutes or even hours after you stopped consciously searching for it. (If you want to experience TOT yourself, try naming Snow White's seven dwarfs.)

The distinction between explicit and implicit memories means that some knowledge is literally unconscious. Moreover, explicit and implicit memories also seem to involve different neural structures and pathways. However, memories typically work together. When we remember going to a Chinese restaurant, we recall not only when and where we ate and who was with us (episodic memory), but also the nature of the food we ate (semantic memory), the skills we learned such as eating with chopsticks (procedural memory), and the embarrassment we felt when we spilled the tea (emotional memory). When we recall events, we typically do not experience these kinds of memories as distinct and separate; rather, they are integrally connected, just as the original experiences were. Whether we will continue to remember the experiences accurately in the future depends to a large extent on what happens in our brain, as will be seen in the next section.

Check Your Understanding

1. The primacy effect accounts for why we remember items at the _____ of a list, while the recency effect accounts for why we remember items at the _____ of the list.

2. You run into an old friend who gives you his phone number and asks you to call. You want to be sure to remember the phone number, so you relate the number to things that you already know. 555 is the same as the combination to your bicycle lock. 12 is your brother's age. And 34 is the size of your belt. This technique for getting information into long-term memory is called

   a. Rote rehearsal   **c.** Elaborative rehearsal

   b. Relational rehearsal   **d.** Episodic rehearsal

3. *He:* "We've been to this restaurant before."

She: "I don't think so."

He: "Didn't we eat here last summer with your brother?"

She: "That was a different restaurant, and I think it was last fall, not last summer."

This couple is trying to remember an event they shared and, obviously, their memories differ. The information they are seeking is most likely stored in

a. Procedural memory   **c.** Semantic memory

b. Emotional memory   **d.** Episodic memory

The Biology of Memory

Research on the biology of memory focuses mainly on the question of how and where are memories stored. The question may sound simple, but it has proved enormously difficult to answer—and the answers are still not entirely complete.

Memory Storage

■ Long-term potentiation is the process by which _____

_____

■ Short-term memories are located primarily in _____

_____

■ Semantic and episodic memories are located primarily in _____

_____

■ Procedural memories are located primarily in _____

_____

■ The hippocampus is important in the formation of _____

_____

■ The amygdala is important in the formation of _____

_____

ENDURING ISSUES   MIND/BODY

Long-Term Potentiation

Current research indicates that memories consist of changes in the synaptic connections among neurons (Kandel, 2001; Squire & Kandel, 1999). When people learn new things, new connections are formed in the brain; when they review or practice previously learned things, old connections are strengthened. These chemical and structural changes can continue over a period of months or years, during which the number of connections among neurons increases as does the likelihood that cells will excite one another through electrical discharges, a process known as **long-term potentiation (LTP)**.

■ MEMORY STORAGE

There is no single place in the brain where memories are stored (Figure 6–4). Short-term memories seem to be located primarily in the prefrontal cortex and the temporal lobe (Rainer & Miller, 2002; Rolls, Tovee, & Panzeri, 1999; Scheibel & Levin, 2004; Szatkowska, Grabowska, & Szymanska, 2001). Long-term semantic memories seem to be located primarily in the frontal and temporal lobes of the cortex, which also play a prominent role in consciousness and awareness. Episodic memories also find their home in the frontal and temporal lobes (Jackson, 2004; Nyberg et al., 2003; Wheeler, Stuss, & Tulving, 1997). Procedural memories appear to be located primarily in the cerebellum (an area required for balance and motor coordination) and in the motor cortex (Gabrieli, 1998; Hermann et al., 2004).

Subcortical structures also play a role in long-term memory. For example, the hippocampus has been implicated in the formation of new long-term semantic and episodic memories (Eichenbaum & Fortin, 2003; Manns, Hopkins, & Squire, 2003; Rolls, 2000), as well as being involved in the ability to remember spatial relationships (Astur, Taylor, Marnelak, Philpott, & Sutherland, 2002; Bilkey & Clearwater, 2005). If the hippocampus is damaged, people can remember events that have just occurred (and are still in STM), but their long-term recall of those same events is impaired. The amygdala, a structure that lies near the hippocampus, seems to play a role in emotional memory that is similar to the role the hippocampus plays in episodic, semantic, and procedural memory (Cahill & McGaugh, 1998; Pare, Collins, & Guillaume, 2002; Vermetten & Bremner, 2002).

Clearly, psychologists have a long way to go before they will fully understand the biology of memory, but progress is being made in this fascinating area. Another question that is beginning to come under scientific scrutiny is, why do we forget?

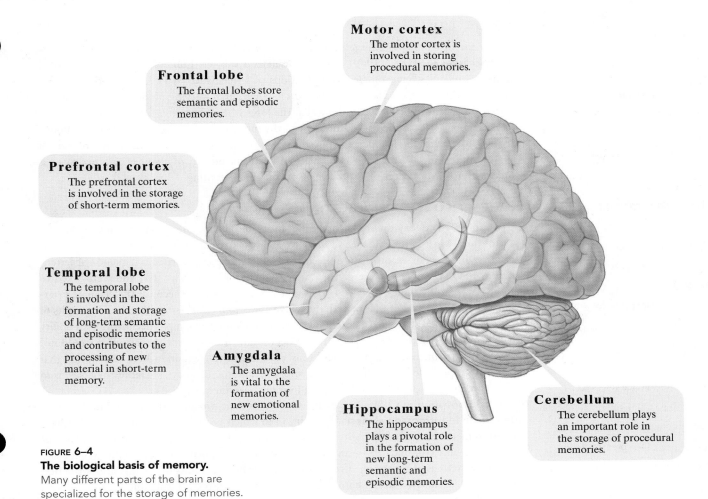

Motor cortex
The motor cortex is involved in storing procedural memories.

Frontal lobe
The frontal lobes store semantic and episodic memories.

Prefrontal cortex
The prefrontal cortex is involved in the storage of short-term memories.

Temporal lobe
The temporal lobe is involved in the formation and storage of long-term semantic and episodic memories and contributes to the processing of new material in short-term memory.

Amygdala
The amygdala is vital to the formation of new emotional memories.

Hippocampus
The hippocampus plays a pivotal role in the formation of new long-term semantic and episodic memories.

Cerebellum
The cerebellum plays an important role in the storage of procedural memories.

FIGURE 6–4
The biological basis of memory.
Many different parts of the brain are specialized for the storage of memories.

Check Your Understanding

1. Oliver Sacks, the author of *The Man Who Mistook His Wife for a Hat*, describes Jimmie G., who was an otherwise healthy 49-year-old man whose long-term memory stopped changing when he was 19. New information in his short-term memory simply never got stored in long-term memory. Which part of his brain was most likely not working correctly?

   a. Prefrontal cortex

   b. Hippocampus

   c. Broca's area

   d. Occipital lobe

2. Imagine now that you encounter someone like Jimmie G., but in this case, the person cannot form new emotional memories. He has emotional reactions to things he encountered early in his life, but he has no such reactions to things he encountered more recently—no new loves or hates, no new fears, no new sources of anger or happiness. Which part of his brain is most likely not working correctly?

   a. Amygdala

   b. Temporal lobe

   c. Prefrontal cortex

   d. Cerebellum

The Biology of Forgetting

- Decay theory states that _____

_____

- Disruption of the storage process

can also cause forgetting as in

_____

- Severe memory loss invariably is a

result of _____

Experience and Forgetting

- Forgetting can be caused by a lack

of _____

- Forgetting can be caused by

insufficient _____

- Learning itself can cause forgetting

because of _____

- Retroactive interference refers to

_____

- Proactive interference refers to

_____

- The absence of _____

_____ present during

learning or a change in one's

_____

can reduce recall.

- _____

_____ is the process by

which memories change over time

while they are being stored in LTM.

Forgetting

Among the first to explore forgetting was the nineteenth-century German psychologist Hermann Ebbinghaus (1850–1909). Using himself as a subject, Ebbinghaus composed lists of "nonsense syllables," meaningless combinations of letters, such as PIB, WOL, or TEB. He memorized lists of 13 nonsense syllables each. Then, after varying amounts of time, he relearned each list of syllables. He found that the longer he waited after first learning a list, the longer it took to learn the list again. Most of the information was lost in the first few hours. Ebbinghaus's research left open the question of why memories, once formed, do not remain forever in the brain. Part of the answer has to do with the biology of memory; another part has to do with the experiences that we have before and after learning.

■ THE BIOLOGY OF FORGETTING

According to the **decay theory** of forgetting, memories deteriorate simply because of the passage of time. Most of the evidence supporting decay theory comes from experiments known as *distractor studies*. For example, in one experiment, participants learned a sequence of letters, such as PSQ. Then, they were given a three-digit number, such as 167, and were asked to count backward by threes: 167, 164, 161, and so on, for up to 18 seconds (Peterson & Peterson, 1959). At the end of that period, they were asked to recall the three letters. The results of this test astonished the experimenters. The participants showed a rapid decline in their ability to remember the letters. Because the researchers assumed that counting backward would not *interfere* with remembering, they could only account for the forgotten letters by noting that they had simply faded from short-term memory in a matter of seconds. Decay, then, seems to be at least partly responsible for forgetting in short-term memory.

Information in LTM also can be lost if the storage process is disrupted. Head injuries often result in **retrograde amnesia**, a condition in which people cannot remember what happened to them shortly before their injury. In such cases, forgetting may occur because memories are not fully consolidated in the brain. The problem is analogous to something that every computer user has experienced: A momentary power outage results in the loss of information that has not been saved to the hard drive. At one moment, the information is clearly present and readily accessed; in the next, it is gone.

Severe memory loss invariably is traced to brain damage caused by accidents, surgery, poor diet, or disease. For example, chronic alcoholism can lead to a form of amnesia called *Korsakoff's syndrome* caused by a vitamin deficiency in the nutritionally poor diet that is typical of people who abuse alcohol. Brain scans also reveal hippocampus damage in people suffering from *Alzheimer's disease*, a neurological disorder that causes severe memory loss (see Chapter 9 for more information about Alzheimer's disease). Alzheimer's may also involve below-normal levels of the neurotransmitter acetylcholine in the brain. Indeed, some research suggests that drugs and surgical procedures that increase acetylcholine levels may serve as effective treatments for age-related memory problems (Smith, Roberts, Gage, & Tuszynski, 1999; McIntyre, Marriott, & Gold, 2003).

■ EXPERIENCE AND FORGETTING

Although sometimes caused by biological factors, forgetting can also result from inadequate learning. A lack of attention to critical cues, for example, is a cause of the forgetting commonly referred to as *absentmindedness*. For example, if you cannot remember where you parked your car, most likely you cannot remember because you did not pay attention to where you parked it in the first place.

EDY (DRAMA (VIDEOS YOU'VE FORGOTTEN YOU'VE SEEN ALREADY (ACTION

Forgetting also occurs because, although we attended to the matter to be recalled, we did not rehearse the material enough. As seen earlier in this chapter, merely "going through the motions" of rehearsal does little good. Prolonged, intense practice results in less forgetting than a few, halfhearted repetitions with little or no intent to remember. By now it should be clear that elaborative rehearsal can help make new memories more durable. When you park your car in space G-47, you are more likely to remember its location if you think, "G-47. My uncle *George* is about *47* years old." In short, it is more difficult to remember information for long periods if the information is not learned well in the first place.

Interference   Inadequate learning accounts for many memory failures, but learning itself can cause forgetting. It is true that learning one thing can interfere with learning another. Information gets mixed up with or is pushed aside by other information and thus becomes harder to remember. Such forgetting is said to be the result of *interference*. As portrayed in Figure 6–5, there are two kinds of interference. In **retroactive interference**, new material interferes with information already in long-term memory. Retroactive interference occurs every day. For example, once you learn a new telephone number, you may find it difficult to recall your old number, even though you used that old number for years.

In the second kind of interference, **proactive interference**, old material interferes with new material being learned. As with retroactive interference, proactive interference is an everyday phenomenon. Suppose you always park your car in the lot behind the building where you work, but one day all those spaces are full, so you have to park across the street. When you leave for the day, you are likely to head for the lot behind the building—and may even be surprised at first that your car is not there. Learning to look for your car behind the building has interfered with your memory that today you parked the car across the street.

The most important factor in determining the degree of interference is the similarity of the competing items. Learning to swing a golf club may interfere with your ability to hit a baseball, but it probably will not affect your ability to make a free throw on a basketball court. The more dissimilar something is from other things that you have already learned, the less likely it will be to mingle and interfere with other material in memory.

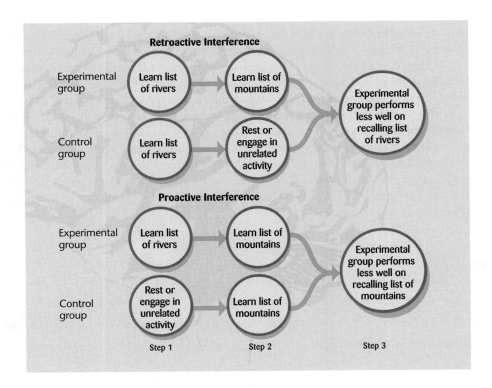

FIGURE **6–5**
Diagram of experiments measuring retroactive and proactive interference.
In retroactive interference, the experimental group usually does not perform as well on tests of recall as those in the control group, who experience no retroactive interference from a list of words in Step 2. In proactive interference, people in the experimental group suffer the effects of proactive interference from the list in Step 1. When asked to recall the list from Step 2, they perform less well than those in the control group.

ENDURING ISSUES PERSON/SITUATION

Contextual Cues and State-Dependent Memory

Whenever people try to memorize something, they are also unintentionally picking up information about the context in which the learning is taking place. That information becomes useful when the person later tries to retrieve the corresponding information from LTM. If the environmental cues are absent when the person tries to recall what was learned, the effort to remember is often unsuccessful. The effects of *context-dependent memory* tend to be small, so studying in the same classroom where you are scheduled to take an exam probably will not do too much to improve your grade. Nevertheless, contextual cues occasionally are used by police who sometimes take witnesses back to the scene of a crime with the hope that they will recall crucial details that could be used to solve the crime.

The ability of people to recall information accurately is also affected by internal cues, a phenomenon known as *state-dependent memory*. Researchers have found that people who learn material in a particular physiological state tend to recall that material better whenever they return to the same state they were in during learning. For example, if people learn material while under the influence of caffeine, recall of the material is improved slightly when they are again under the influence of caffeine. Similarly, if you discovered a bakery with scrumptious pastries on a day when you were really hungry, finding your way there again may be easier when you're hungry than when you are full.

The Reconstructive Process In the early part of the twentieth century, the British psychologist Sir Frederic C. Bartlett (1886–1969) discovered some intriguing facts about long-term memory. Bartlett had people read a story or examine a drawing, then recount the story or describe the drawing at various intervals. In some experiments, he had one person tell a story to another, who told it to another, and so on. He discovered that memories of the stories or drawings were transformed over time. For example, people tended to drop out or alter details of the stories, especially details with which they were not familiar. Specific facts (such as the presence of a "canoe") often were transformed into more general terms ("boat"). Activities such as "hunting seals" often were changed into simply "fishing," a much more familiar activity.

In a similar fashion, people are unable sometimes to tell the difference between what actually happened and what they merely heard or imagined. This is because they have unknowingly combined the elements of real and imagined events or have "rewritten" past events to fit their current image or their desired image of themselves. Each time they recall information, they unconsciously may make subtle changes in their memories to better fit their view of the world or themselves. In some cases, these changes become such an integral part of their memory for the event that they are more likely to recall things that never happened than what actually took place. Clearly, reconstruction of memories can lead to huge errors. This fact is critically important in criminal trials, in which a person's guilt or innocence may depend on the testimony of an eyewitness.

Check Your Understanding

1. Match the following terms with their appropriate definitions.

_____ Retrograde amnesia **a.** Forgetting because new information makes it harder to remember information already in memory

_____ Retroactive interference **b.** Forgetting because old information in memory makes it harder to learn new information

_____ Proactive interference **c.** Can result from head injury or electroconvulsive therapy

2. You are trying to explain to someone that "forgetting" sometimes occurs because of the reconstructive nature of long-term memory. Which of the following would be an example that you might use to support your position?

    a. People can distinguish between real and fictional accounts in narratives.

    b. People who learn material in a particular setting tend to recall that material better whenever they return to that same setting.

    c. Rote rehearsal with no intention to remember has little effect on long-term memory.

    d. People often rewrite their memories of past events to fit their current view or desired view of themselves.

Special Topics in Memory

Having reviewed the various types of memory and how memory for different events is stored in the brain, let's look at some special factors that affect memory.

■ CULTURAL INFLUENCES

Remembering has practical consequences for daily life and takes place within a particular context. It is not surprising, then, that the values and customs of a given culture can have a profound effect on what and how easily people remember. In many Western cultures, for example, being able to recite a long list of words or numbers, to repeat the details of a scene, and to provide facts and figures about historical events are all signs of a "good memory." In fact, tasks such as these often are used to test people's memory abilities. However, these kinds of memory tasks do not necessarily reflect the type of learning, memorization, and categorization skills taught in non-Western schools. Members of other cultures often perform poorly on such memory tests, because the exercises seem so odd to them.

In contrast, consider the memory skills of a person living in a society in which cultural information is passed on from one generation to the next through a rich oral tradition. Such an individual may be able to recite the deeds of the culture's heroes in verse or rattle off the lines of descent of families, larger lineage groups, and elders. Or perhaps the individual has a storehouse of information about the migration of animals or the life cycles of plants that help people to obtain food and to know when to harvest crops.

ENDURING ISSUES   DIVERSITY/UNIVERSALITY

Memory and Culture

Sir Frederic Bartlett, whose work on memory was discussed earlier in this chapter, anticipated the intertwining of memory and culture long ago. Bartlett (1932) related a tale of a Swazi cowherd who had a prodigious memory for facts and figures about cattle. The cowherd could recite, with virtually no error, the selling price, type of cattle bought, and circumstances of the sale for purchases dating back several years. These skills are not surprising when one realizes that, in Swazi culture, the care and keeping of cattle are very important in daily life, and many cultural practices focus on the economic and social importance of cattle. In contrast, Bartlett reported, Swazi children did no better than his young European participants in recalling a 25-word message. Stripped of its cultural significance, their memory performance was not exceptional. More recent research showed that college students in Ghana, a culture with a strong oral tradition, were much better than college students in New York at remembering a short story they had heard (Matsumoto, 2000).

■ AUTOBIOGRAPHICAL MEMORY

Autobiographical memory refers to the recollection of events that happened in one's life and when those events took place; as such, it is a form of episodic memory. Autobiographical

---

Cultural Influences

■ Cultural values and customs profoundly affect _____ and_____

Autobiographical Memory

■ Autobiographical memory refers to

_____

■ Childhood (infantile) amnesia is

_____

Extraordinary Memory

■ Eidetic imagery, often called

_____,

refers to the extraordinarily accurate and vivid recall of _____.

■ _____ are people skilled in the use of memory techniques.

Flashbulb Memories

■ Flashbulb memories refer to

_____

■ Despite the vividness of flashbulb memories, they _____

_____

Eyewitness Testimony

■ Because of the _____ nature of LTM, eyewitness testimony often _____

Recovered Memories

■ Recovered memories are

_____

■ Recovered memories are highly controversial because

_____

Look carefully at these cows and try to notice significant distinguishing characteristics of each animal. Is this task difficult for you? It probably is, unless you have been working closely with cattle all your life, as these two people have.

memories are of fundamental importance. Indeed, Conway (1996, p. 295) contends that "autobiographical memory is central to self, to identity, to emotional experience, and to all those attributes that define an individual."

ENDURING ISSUES   STABILITY/CHANGE

Childhood Amnesia

Despite the richness of our autobiographical memories, research shows that people rarely, if ever, recall events that occurred before they were 2 years old. This phenomenon is called **childhood amnesia**, or infantile amnesia.

Exactly why people have difficulty remembering events from their first years of life is not well understood, although several explanations have been advanced. One hypothesis holds that childhood amnesia is a result of the child's brain not being fully developed at birth. An immature brain structure, such as the prefrontal cortex, may be incapable of efficiently processing and storing information in memory. In fact, the hippocampus, which is so important in the formation of episodic and semantic memories, is not fully formed until about age 2 (Jacobs & Nadel, 1997).

Childhood amnesia may also occur because young children lack a clear sense of self (Wheeler et al., 1997). According to this theory, without a sense of one's self, very young children find it difficult to organize and integrate their experiences into a coherent autobiographical memory scheme. However, with the emergence of self-concept and self-awareness near the end of the second year, childhood amnesia would be expected to lessen—which it does (Howe & Courage, 1993). Also, childhood amnesia may be linked to language skills: Young children do not have the language skills necessary to strengthen and consolidate early experiences (Hudson & Sheffield, 1998; Simcock & Hayne, 2002). Other research suggests that age-related changes in encoding, retention, and retrieval processes that accompany the transition from infancy to early childhood account for childhood amnesia (Hayne, 2004).

In a twist on these theories, Patricia Bauer (1996) has shown that infants as young as 13 months can construct and maintain memories of specific events. Bauer contends that appropriate cues and repetition are the primary influences on efficient recall, not age. However, childhood amnesia has to do with the inability of *adults* to remember early experiences, especially before the age of 2. And that, argue many psychologists, is a real phenomenon that needs to be explained (Eacott, 1999; Newcombe, Drummey, Fox, Lie, & Ottinger-Alberts, 2000).

■ EXTRAORDINARY MEMORY

As seen at the beginning of this chapter, some people are able to perform truly amazing feats of memory. From time to time, the newspaper will carry a report of a person with a "photographic memory." Such people can apparently create unusually sharp and detailed visual images of something they have seen—a picture, a scene, a page of text. This phenomenon, called **eidetic imagery**, enables people to see the features of an image in minute detail, sometimes even to recite an entire page of a book they read only once. One of the most famous documented cases of extraordinary memory comes from the work of the distinguished psychologist Alexander Luria (1902–1977). For more than 20 years, Luria studied a Russian newspaper reporter named Shereshevskii ("S"). In *The Mind of a Mnemonist* (1968), Luria described how "S" could recall masses of senseless trivia as well as detailed mathematical formulas and complex arrays of numbers. He could easily repeat lists of up to 70 words or numbers after having heard or seen them only once.

ENDURING ISSUES | NATURE/NURTURE

Exceptional Memories

"S" and other people with exceptional memories are not born with a special gift for remembering things. Rather, they have carefully developed memory techniques using certain principles. For example, Luria discovered that when "S" studied long lists of words, he would form an image for every item. When reading a long and random list of words, for example, "S" might visualize a well-known street, specifically associating each word with some object along the way. When asked to recite the lists of words, he would take an imaginary walk down that street, recalling each object and the word associated with it. By organizing his data in a way that was meaningful to him, he could more easily link them to existing material in his long-term memory. In turn, this connection provided him with many more retrieval cues than he would have had for isolated, meaningless facts.

Developing an exceptional memory takes time and effort. **Mnemonists** (pronounced *nee-MON-ists*) are people who are highly skilled at using memory techniques, and they frequently have compelling reasons for developing their memories. "S" used his memory skills to his advantage as a newspaper reporter. Chess masters sometimes display astonishing recall of meaningful chessboard configurations. In fact, some master chess players are able to recall the position of every single piece on the board after only a five-second exposure to a particular pattern. Yet when these same masters view a totally random and meaningless array of chess pieces, their recall is no better than yours or mine.

■ FLASHBULB MEMORIES

"We were on the phone together when the first building fell, and the two of us were just screaming—oh my god, oh my god, oh my god."

"The images of the towers burning and crashing—and the most bizarre thing is that this woman who I went to her house, just had a baby. And the baby's crib was right next to the television. Just to see the devastation of what was happening in New York, and to see this baby completely innocent laying right next to the television and completely oblivious, asleep to the history that was happening, it was one of the most surreal moments I've ever lived through in my life."

"I don't want to see another image of the plane going into that building. I've seen it enough in my nightmares. . . ."

From PRI, Public Radio International, Gray Matters, Produced in Association with the Dana Alliance for Brain Initiatives.

A **flashbulb memory** is the experience of vividly remembering a certain event and the incidents surrounding it even after a long time has passed. People often remember events that are shocking or otherwise highly significant in this way. The death of a close relative, a birth, a graduation, or a wedding day may all elicit flashbulb memories. As in the example, people can recall dramatic events in which they were not involved personally, such as the attacks on the World Trade Center and the Pentagon on September 11, 2001. In fact, 97% of Americans surveyed one year after the September 11 attacks claimed they could remember exactly where they were and what they were doing when they first heard about the attacks (Pew Research Center for the People and the Press, 2002).

However, all may not be as it seems. First, photos of startling major events are replayed over and over and people watch them intently. It is not surprising that memories of those

Millions of people will forever have a vivid flashbulb memory of planes flying into the twin towers of the World Trade Center in New York City on September 11, 2001.

events seem much sharper than memories of less dramatic events. Second, flashbulb memories are not always accurate. For example, psychologist Ulric Neisser vividly recalled what he was doing on the day in 1941 when the Japanese bombed Pearl Harbor. He clearly remembered that he was listening to a professional baseball game on the radio, which was interrupted by the shocking announcement. But professional baseball is not played in December, when the attack took place, so this vivid flashbulb memory was simply incorrect (Neisser, 1982).

Finally, even when an event is registered accurately, it may undergo periodic revision, just like other long-term memories. We are bound to discuss and rethink a major event many times, and we probably also hear a great deal of additional information about that event in the weeks and months after it occurs. As a result, the flashbulb memory may change as a result of reconstruction, in some cases becoming less accurate over time until it bears little or no resemblance to what actually happened even though it seems just as vivid as when it was first formed.

■ EYEWITNESS TESTIMONY

"I know what I saw!" When an eyewitness to a crime gives evidence in court, that testimony often overwhelms evidence to the contrary. Faced with conflicting or ambiguous testimony, jurors tend to put their faith in people who saw an event with their own eyes. However, there is now compelling evidence that this faith in eyewitnesses is often misplaced. Whereas eyewitness accounts are essential to courtroom testimony, studies clearly show that people who say, "I know what I saw," often do not know.

For several decades, Elizabeth Loftus (1993; Loftus & Hoffman, 1989; Loftus & Pickrell, 1995) has been the most influential researcher in the area of eyewitness memory. In a classic study, Loftus and Palmer (1974) showed experimental participants a film depicting a traffic accident. Some of the participants were asked, "About how fast were the cars going when they hit each other?" Other participants were asked the same question, but with the words "smashed into," "collided with," "bumped into," or "contacted" in place of "hit." The researchers discovered that people's reports of the cars' speed depended on the word that was inserted in the question. Those asked about cars that "smashed into" each other reported that the cars were going faster than those who were asked about cars that "contacted" each other.

Why do eyewitnesses make mistakes? Some research suggests that the problem may be *source error.* People are sometimes unable to tell the difference between what they witnessed and what they merely heard about or imagined (Garry & Polaschek, 2000; Henkel, Franklin, & Johnson, 2000; Mazzoni & Memon, 2003). This is especially true for young children. Similarly, if you hear information about an event you witnessed, you may later confuse your memory of that information with your memory of the original event. The impact of subsequent information seems to be particularly strong when it is repeated several times (Zaragoza & Mitchell, 1996), as is often the case with extensive media coverage or when it comes from an authority figure such as a police officer (Roper & Shewan, 2002).

■ RECOVERED MEMORIES

In recent years, a controversy has raged, both within the academic community and in society at large, about the validity of *recovered* memories (Cerri, 2005; Gerkens, 2005; McNally, 2003a, 2003b). The idea is that people experience an event, then lose all memory of it, and later recall it, often in the course of psychotherapy or under hypnosis. Frequently, the recovered memories concern physical or sexual abuse during childhood. The issue is important not only for theoretical reasons, but also because of the fact that people have been imprisoned for abuse solely on the basis of the recovered memories of their "victims." No one denies the reality of childhood abuse or the damage that such experiences cause. But are the recovered memories real? Did the remembered abuse really occur?

The answer is by no means obvious. There is ample evidence that people can be induced to "remember" events that never happened. For example, when Loftus and her colleagues told people that relatives had mentioned an event in their lives, a fourth of the participants "remembered" those events even though they had never actually happened (Loftus,

Coan, & Pickrell, 1996; Loftus & Pickrell, 1995). And as we have seen, simply imagining that something happened can increase the likelihood that people will "remember" that the event actually happened. Other research confirms that it is relatively easy to implant memories of an experience merely by asking about it. The more times that people are asked about the event, the more likely they are to "remember" it. Sometimes these memories become quite real to the participant. In one experiment, 25% of adults "remembered" fictitious events by the third time they were interviewed about them. One of the fictitious events involved knocking over a punch bowl onto the parents of the bride at a wedding reception. At the first interview, one participant said that she had no recollection whatsoever of the event; by the second interview, she "remembered" that the reception was outdoors and that she had knocked over the bowl while running around. Some people even "remembered" details about the event, such as what people looked like and what they wore. Yet, the researchers documented that these events never happened (Hyman, Husband, & Billings, 1995). Other research shows that people can even become convinced that they remember experiences from infancy that never happened (Spanos, 1996; Spanos, Burgess, Burgess, Samuels, & Blois, 1997).

The implication of this and similar research is that it is quite possible for people to "recover" memories for events that never happened. And indeed some people who have "recovered" abuse memories have later realized that the events never occurred. However, not all recovered memories are merely the products of suggestion. There are numerous case studies of people who have lived through traumatic experiences, including natural disasters, accidents, combat, assault, and rape, who apparently forgot these events for many years but later remembered them (Arrigo & Pezdek, 1997). For example, Wilbur J. Scott, a sociologist, claimed to remember nothing of his tour of duty in Vietnam during 1968–1969, but during a divorce in 1983, he discovered his medals and souvenirs from Vietnam, and the memories then came back to him (Arrigo & Pezdek, 1997).

What is needed is a reliable way of separating real memories from false ones, but so far no such test exists. The sincerity and conviction of the person who "remembers" long-forgotten events is no indication of the reality of those events. We are left with the conclusion that recovered memories are not, in themselves, sufficiently trustworthy to justify criminal convictions. There must also be corroborative evidence, because without corroboration, there is no way that even the most experienced examiner can separate real memories from false ones (Loftus, 1997).

Check Your Understanding

1. Indicate whether the following statement is true (T) or false (F).

_____ Research demonstrates that it is nearly impossible to change a person's memory once that memory has been stored.

2. You are talking with someone from a different culture who is not very good at remembering long lists of random words or numbers, but who can recite from memory all of his ancestors going back hundreds of years. What is the most likely explanation for this difference in memory skills?

   a. The values and customs of a given culture have a profound effect on what people remember.

   b. The person's autobiographical memory is stronger than his semantic memory.

   c. The list of his ancestors has been stored in flashbulb memory.

   d. The list of his ancestors is an example of a "recovered memory."

3. Your mother is reminiscing about your first birthday party and asks you, "Do you remember when Aunt Mary dropped her piece of cake in your lap?" Try as you might, you can't recall that incident. This most likely is an example of

   a. Memory decay   **c.** Infantile amnesia

   b. Retrograde amnesia   **d.** Proactive interference

Chapter Review

 **www.psychologythecore.com**

The Sensory Registers

Many psychologists view **memory** as a series of steps in which people encode, store, and retrieve information, much as a computer does. This is called the **information-processing** model of memory. The first step in the model is inputting data through the senses into temporary holding bins, called **sensory registers**. These registers provide a brief moment to decide whether something deserves attention.

Information entering a sensory register disappears very quickly when it is not processed further. Information in the visual register lasts for only about a quarter of a second before it is replaced by new information. If sounds faded from our auditory register as rapidly as this, spoken language would be more difficult to understand. Luckily, information in the auditory register can linger for several seconds.

The next step in the memory process is **attention**—selectively looking at, listening to, smelling, tasting, or feeling what is deemed important. To some extent, the nervous system filters out peripheral information, allowing one to zero in on what is essential at a particular time (the *cocktail-party phenomenon*). However, unattended information receives at least some processing so that one can quickly shift attention to it if it suddenly becomes significant.

Short-Term Memory

Short-term memory (**STM**), also called *working memory*, holds whatever information a person is actively attending to at any given time. Its two primary tasks are to store new information briefly and to "work" on information that is currently in mind. People can process more information in STM by grouping it into larger meaningful units, a process called **chunking**.

Information can be stored in STM according to its sound, its look, or its meaning. Verbal information is encoded by sound, even when it is written rather than heard. The capacity for visual encoding in STM is greater than for encoding by sound.

Through **rote rehearsal**, or maintenance rehearsal, people retain information in STM for a minute or two by repeating it over and over again. However, simple repetition without an intent to remember does not promote long-term memory.

Long-Term Memory

Long-term memory (**LTM**) can store a vast amount of information for many years. Most of the information in LTM seems to be encoded according to its meaning. The way in which we encode material for storage in LTM affects the ease with which we can retrieve it later on. Rote rehearsal with the intent of remembering is particularly useful for holding conceptually meaningless material, such as phone numbers, in LTM. Through the deeper and more meaningful mechanism of **elaborative rehearsal**, one extracts the meaning of information and links it to as much material as possible that is already in LTM. Memory techniques such as **mnemonics** rely on elaborative processing.

Short- and long-term memory together explain the **serial position effect**, in which people tend to recall the first and last items in a list better than items in the middle. Items at the end of the list are likely still to be held in STM (*recency effect*), while items near the beginning of the list are most likely to have gone through elaborative rehearsal (*primacy effect*).

There are several kinds of long-term memories. **Episodic memories** are memories for events experienced in a specific time and place. **Semantic memories** are facts and concepts not linked to a particular time. **Procedural memories** are motor skills and habits. **Emotional memories** are learned emotional responses to various stimuli.

Explicit memories are memories that people are aware of, including many episodic and semantic memories. **Implicit memory** refers to memories for information that either was not intentionally committed to LTM or is retrieved without effort from LTM, including many procedural and emotional memories. This distinction is illustrated by research on priming, in which people are more likely to complete fragments of stimuli with items seen earlier than with other, equally plausible items. The **tip-of-the-tongue phenomenon** (**TOT**) refers to the experience of knowing a word but not quite being able to recall it.

The Biology of Memory

Memories are stored in the chemistry and structure of neurons. The process by which these changes occur is called **long-term potentiation** (**LTP**). There is no single place in the brain where memories are stored. Short-term memories seem to be located primarily in the pre-frontal cortex and temporal lobe. Long-term memories seem to involve both subcortical and cortical structures. Semantic and episodic memories seem to be located primarily in the frontal and temporal lobes of the cortex, and procedural memories appear to be located primarily in the cerebellum and motor cortex. The hippocampus seems especially important in the formation of semantic, episodic, and procedural memories. Emotional memories are dependent on the amygdala.

Forgetting

Biological and experiential factors can contribute to one's inability to recall information. According to the **decay theory**, memories deteriorate simply because of the passage of time. Information in LTM also can be lost if the storage process is disrupted. For example, head injuries can cause **retrograde amnesia**, the inability of people to remember what happened shortly before they were injured. Severe memory loss invariably is traced to brain damage caused by accidents, surgery, poor diet, or disease.

To the extent that information is apparently lost from LTM, the cause is most likely to be either inadequate learning or interference from competing information. Interference may come from two directions: In **retroactive interference**, new information interferes with old information already in LTM; **proactive interference** refers to the process by which old information already in LTM interferes with new information.

Retrieving information from memory is affected by internal and external cues. When environmental cues present during learning are absent during recall, *context-dependent* forgetting may occur. The ability to recall information is affected by one's physiological state when the material was learned; this process is known as *state-dependent memory*.

Finally, memories change over time while they are being stored. Often details are lost and specific facts are transformed into more general facts. Memories can also be "rewritten" to fit people's current or desired image of themselves. This process of memory reconstruction is especially important in eyewitness testimony.

Special Topics in Memory

Cultural values and customs profoundly affect what people remember and how easily they recall it. Many Western schools stress being able to recall long lists of words, facts, and figures that are divorced from everyday life. In contrast, societies in which cultural information is passed on through a rich oral tradition may instead emphasize memory for events that directly affect people's lives.

Autobiographical memory refers to the recollection of events from one's life. Not all of these events are recalled with equal clarity, of course, and some are not recalled at all. In particular, people generally cannot remember events that occurred before age 2, a phenomenon called **childhood** (or **infantile**) **amnesia**. Childhood amnesia may result from the incomplete development of brain structures before age 2, from the infants' lack of a clear sense of self, or from the lack of language skills used to consolidate early experience.

Some people have truly exceptional memories. With the possible exception of **eidetic imagery** (often called *photographic memory*), people with exceptional memories have carefully developed memory techniques. **Mnemonists** are individuals who are highly skilled at using those techniques.

Years after a dramatic or significant event occurs, people often report having vivid memories of that event as well as the incidents surrounding it. These memories are known as

flashbulb memories. Research has shown that even vivid flashbulb memories are not necessarily accurate or stable.

Although eyewitness testimony is often compelling, there is a great deal of evidence that faith in eyewitnesses is often misplaced. Because of the reconstructive nature of long-term memory, eyewitnesses sometimes are unable to tell the difference between what they witnessed and what they merely heard about or imagined. The result is that eyewitness testimony often does not accurately describe what actually occurred.

There are many examples of people who have no memory of an event but who later recall it, often vividly. Such *recovered memories* are highly controversial, because research shows that people can be induced to "remember" events that never happened. So far, there is no clear, scientifically reliable way to distinguish real recovered memories from false ones.

Chapter 7
Cognition and Mental Abilities

Go to *The Core Online* at **www.psychologythecore.com** to get the most up-to-date information for your introductory psychology course. The content online is an important part of what you are learning—the content there can help prepare you for your test! It includes up-to-date examples, simulations, video clips, and practice quizzes. Also be sure to check out the *Blog* to hear directly from the authors on what current events and latest research are most relevant to your course materials.

The first time you log in, you will need the access code packaged with your textbook. If you do not have a code, please go to **www.mypearsonstore.com** and enter the ISBN of your textbook (**0-13-603344-X**) to purchase the code.

Chapter 7 Cognition and Mental Abilities

7 1 Building Blocks of Thought

Language
- **Language** is a flexible system of symbols that allows us to communicate ideas to others.
- Basic sounds (**phonemes**) combine to make meaningful units (**morphemes**) that can be put into words, phrases, and sentences following the rules of **grammar**.

Images
- **Images** are mental representations of sensory experiences.

Concepts
- **Concepts** are categories for classifying objects, people, and experiences based on their common elements.

7 2 Language, Thought, and Culture

- Whorf's **linguistic relativity hypothesis** is an example of **linguistic determinism**: The language people speak determines the pattern of their thinking and their view of the world. However, thought and experience can also shape and change a language.

7 3 Nonhuman Thought and Language

Animal Cognition
- Some animals have humanlike cognitive capacities.
- Nonhuman animals communicate primarily through **signs**.

The Question of Language
- No other species has its own language.

7 4 Problem Solving

Interpreting Problems
- **Problem representation**—defining or interpreting the problem—is the first step in problem solving.
  - **Divergent thinking** involves many different possible answers and is often required for problems with no single correct solution.
  - **Convergent thinking** involves narrowing one's focus and is best applied to problems with a limited number of solutions.

Implementing Strategies and Evaluating Progress
- Problem-solving strategies include:
  - Trial and error
  - Information retrieval based on similar problems
  - Step-by-step procedures guaranteed to work (an **algorithm**)
  - Rule-of-thumb approaches (**heuristics**) that include **hill climbing**, creation of **subgoals**, **means-end analysis**, and **working backward**

Obstacles to Solving Problems
- Strong **mental sets** (such as **functional fixedness**) can interfere with problem solving.
- **Brainstorming** involves generating many ideas before evaluating them.

7 5 Decision Making

Compensatory Decision Making
- Rate each available choice in terms of weighted criteria, then total the ratings for each choice.

Decision-Making Heuristics
- Decision-making heuristics can save a great deal of time and effort, but are prone to errors.
  - **Representativeness** heuristic: Making decisions based on information that matches the model of the "typical" member of a category
  - **Availability** heuristic: Making decisions based on whatever information that can be most easily retrieved
  - **Confirmation bias**: Seeking evidence in support of existing beliefs and ignoring contradictory evidence

Explaining One's Decisions
- **Framing:** Refers to the perspective or phrasing that is used to make a decision
- **Hindsight bias:** Tendency to view outcomes as inevitable or predictable
- **Counterfactual thinking:** Revisiting decisions by considering "what if" alternatives

7 6 Intelligence and Mental Abilities

Theories of Intelligence
- **Intelligence**: General term referring to the ability or abilities involved in learning and adaptive behavior
- Most theorists believe that intelligence is composed of many separate abilities:
  —Sternberg's **triarchic theory of intelligence**
  —Gardner's **theory of multiple intelligences**
- Goleman's theory of **emotional intelligence**: Emphasizes skill in social relationships and awareness of others' and one's own emotions

Intelligence Tests
- Individual tests
  —Binet–Simon Scale
  —Stanford–Binet Intelligence Scale
  —Wechsler Adult Intelligence Scale
  —Wechsler Intelligence Scale for Children
- Group tests   ■ Performance tests   ■ Culture-fair tests
- **Intelligence quotient (IQ)**: Numerical score for intelligence

What Makes a Good Test?
- **Reliability**: Ability of a test to produce consistent and stable scores
- **Validity**: Ability of a test to measure what it has been designed to measure
- Reliability of IQ tests is seldom questioned; validity is open to question.

7 7 Heredity, Environment, and Intelligence

Heredity
- Identical twins raised in different families tend to have very similar intelligence test scores.
- Adopted children have IQ scores that are more similar to their biological mothers than to their adoptive mothers.

Environment
- In impoverished families, heredity has little or no bearing on intelligence.
- Development of mental capacities depends on nutrition, attention, and environmental stimulation.

Heredity and Environment
- Approximately half of the variability in IQ test scores is due to genetics; the other half is due to differences in experiences including environmental stimulation, education, and nutrition.

Mental Abilities and Human Diversity: Gender and Culture
- Gender differences in mental abilities are virtually nonexistent.
- The achievement gap between American and Asian students is due to culturally influenced views of the relative importance of effort and innate ability.

Extremes of Intelligence
- **Mental retardation**: Significantly subaverage general intellectual functioning that is accompanied by significant limitations in adaptive functioning and that appears before the age of 21
  —In most cases, causes are unknown.
  —About 25% of cases can be traced to genetic or biological disorders.
  —Mental retardation can be moderated through education and training.
- **Giftedness**: Exceptional mental abilities, as measured by scores on standard intelligence tests

7 8 Creativity

Creativity: The ability to produce novel and socially valued ideas or objects

Intelligence and Creativity
- A minimum level of intelligence is needed for creativity, but above that threshold level, greater intelligence does not necessarily make for greater creativity.

Creativity Tests
- Creativity is difficult to measure.
- The validity of most creativity tests is not particularly high.

If someone asked you "What is **cognition**, or thinking?" you might respond with something as broad as "Thinking is what goes on inside your head." And indeed this is not a bad answer. Cognitive processes play a role in many psychological functions. A clue to the vast range of things involved in thinking can be found in the different ways the word is used. "I've given it some thought" implies reflection or meditation. "I think this town is like the one I grew up in" indicates conceptualization. "What does she think of all this?" is a way of asking for an evaluation. "Aha! I think I have the answer!" reflects problem solving and insight. "I think I'll buy the red one" indicates a decision. These are examples of thinking. Thinking includes the processing and retrieval of information from memory. But, in addition, it requires manipulation of information in various ways.

In previous chapters, we have seen that thinking is relevant to such diverse processes as attention, sensation and perception, learning, memory, and forgetting. Later in this book we will see that cognition also plays a crucial role in coping and adjustment, abnormal behavior, and interpersonal relations. This chapter examines the building blocks of thought—the kinds of things people think about—and shows the ways these building blocks are used in problem solving and decision making. The last section of the chapter looks at two key mental abilities: intelligence and creativity.

ENDURING ISSUES in Cognition and Mental Abilities

The "Enduring Issues" sections in this chapter are highlighted in four prominent places. The diversity-universality theme is encountered when the differences and similarities in the way people process information are discussed and again when exceptional abilities are explored. Two additional enduring issues are raised with the discussion about the stability–change of intelligence test scores over time and the measures of intelligence and performance that sometimes vary as a function of expectations and situations (person–situation).

Building Blocks of Thought

When you think about a close friend, you may have in mind some complex statements about her, such as "I'd like to talk to her soon" or "I wish I could be more like her." You may also have an image of her—probably her face, but perhaps the sound of her voice as well. Or you may think of your friend by using various concepts or categories such as *woman*, *kind*, *strong*, *dynamic*, and *gentle*. When we think, we make use of all these things—language, images, and concepts—often simultaneously. These are the three most important building blocks of thought.

■ LANGUAGE

Human **language** is a flexible system of symbols that enables us to communicate our ideas, thoughts, and feelings. One way to understand the uniquely human system of language is to consider its basic structure. Spoken language is based on units of sound called **phonemes**. The sounds of *t*, *th*, and *k*, for instance, are all phonemes in English. There are about 45 phonemes in the English language and as many as 85 in some other languages. By themselves, phonemes are meaningless and seldom play an important role in helping people to think. The sound *b*, for example, has no inherent meaning. But phonemes can be grouped together to form words, prefixes (such as *un-* and *pre-*), and suffixes (such as *-ed* and *-ing*). These meaningful combinations of phonemes are known as **morphemes**—the smallest meaningful units in a language. Morphemes play a key role in human thought. They can represent important ideas such as "red" or "calm" or "hot." The suffix *-ed* captures the idea of "in the past" (as in *visited* or *liked*). The prefix *pre-* conveys the idea of "before" or "prior to" (as in *preview* or *predetermined*).

Morphemes can be combined to create words that represent quite complex ideas, such as *pre-exist-ing*, *un-excell-ed*, *psycho-logy*. In turn, words can be joined to reflect even more complex thoughts. Just as there are rules for combining phonemes and morphemes, there are

Building Blocks of Thought

Language

■ Language is a flexible system of

_____

_____

■ Basic sounds (phonemes) combine

to make _____

_____

_____

Images

■ Images are _____

_____

_____

Concepts

■ Concepts are categories for

_____

_____

also rules for structuring sentences and their meaning. These rules are what linguists call **grammar**. The two major components of grammar are *syntax* and *semantics*. *Syntax* is the system of rules that governs how words are combined to form meaningful phrases and sentences. For example, in English and many other languages, the meaning of a sentence is often determined by word order. "Sally hit the car" means one thing; "The car hit Sally" means something quite different; and "Hit Sally car the" is meaningless.

Semantics describes how people assign meaning to morphemes, words, phrases, and sentences—in other words, the content of language. When we are thinking about something—say, the ocean—our ideas usually consist of phrases and sentences, such as "The ocean is unusually calm tonight." Sentences have both a *surface structure*—the particular words and phrases—and a *deep structure*—the underlying meaning. The same deep structure can be conveyed by different surface structures:

> The ocean is unusually calm tonight.
> Tonight, the ocean is particularly calm.
> Compared with most other nights, tonight the ocean is calm.

Alternatively, the same surface structure can convey different meanings or deep structures, but a knowledge of language permits one to know what is meant within a given context:

Surface Structure	Might Mean . . . or . . .
Flying planes can be dangerous.	An airborne plane . . . The profession of pilot . . .
Visiting relatives can be a nuisance.	Relatives who are visiting . . . The obligation to visit relatives . . .
The chicken is ready to eat.	Food has been cooked sufficiently . . . The bird is hungry . . .

Syntax and semantics enable speakers and listeners to perform what linguist Noam Chomsky calls *transformations* between the surface structure and the deep structure. According to Chomsky (1957; Chomsky, Place, & Schoneberger, 2000), when you want to communicate an idea, you start with a thought, then you choose words and phrases that will express the idea, and finally, you produce the speech sounds that make up those words and phrases, as shown by the left arrow in Figure 7–1. When you want to understand a sentence, your task is reversed. You must start with speech sounds and work your way up to the meaning of those sounds, as represented by the right arrow in Figure 7–1.

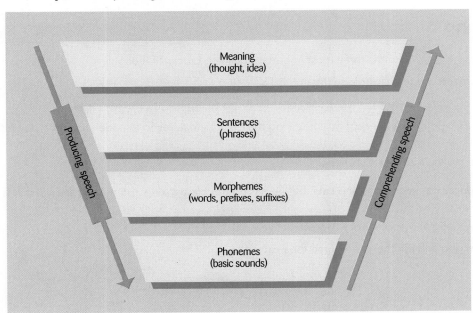

FIGURE **7–1**
The direction of movement in speech production and comprehension.
Producing a sentence involves movement from thoughts and ideas to basic sounds; comprehending a sentence requires movement from basic sounds back to the underlying thoughts and ideas.

■ IMAGES

Think for a moment about Abraham Lincoln. Your thoughts of Lincoln may have included such phrases as "wrote the Gettysburg Address," "president during the Civil War," and "assassinated by John Wilkes Booth." You probably also had some mental images about him: bearded face, lanky body, or log cabin. Now imagine being outside in a summer thunderstorm. You probably formed mental images of wind, rain, and lightning—perhaps even the sound of thunder or the smell of wet leaves and earth. An **image** is a mental representation of some sensory experience. We can visualize the Statue of Liberty; we can smell Thanksgiving dinner or the scent of a Christmas tree; we can hear Martin Luther King Jr., saying, "I have a dream!" In short, we can think by using images. In fact, images also allow us to think about complex and abstract ideas that would be hard to capture in words, as when newspapers use pie charts and graphs to illustrate how people voted in an election. Albert Einstein relied heavily on his powers of visualization to understand phenomena he would later describe by using complex mathematical formulas. This great thinker believed his extraordinary genius resulted in part from his skill in visualizing possibilities (Kosslyn, 2002).

■ CONCEPTS

Concepts are mental categories for classifying specific people, things, or events. *Dogs*, *books*, *fast*, and *beautiful* are all concepts. When you think about a specific thing—say, Mt. Everest—you may think of the concepts that apply to it, such as *highest* and *dangerous to climb*. It is tempting to think of concepts as simple and clear-cut, but most of the concepts people use are rather "fuzzy": They overlap one another and often are poorly defined. For example, most people can tell a mouse from a rat, but listing the critical differences between the two would be difficult (Rosch, 1973, 2002).

If we cannot readily explain the difference between mouse and rat, how can we use these *fuzzy concepts* in our thinking? The answer is that we usually construct a **prototype**, or **model**, of a representative mouse and one of a representative rat, then we use those prototypes in our thinking (Rosch, 1978, 1998, 2002). For example, most people have a model bird, or prototype, in mind—such as a robin or a sparrow—that captures for them the essence of *bird*. When new objects are encountered, people compare them with this prototype to determine whether they are, in fact, birds. And when people think about birds, they usually think about their prototypical bird.

Concepts, then, like words and images, help people formulate thoughts. But human cognition involves more than just passively thinking about things. It also involves actively using words, images, and concepts to fashion an understanding of the world, to solve problems, and to make decisions. Let's turn now to an examination of how this is done.

Check Your Understanding

1. _____, _____, and _____ are the three most important building blocks of thought.

2. Indicate whether the following statements are true (T) or false (F).

a. _____ Images help us to think about things because images use concrete forms to represent complex ideas.

b. _____ People decide which objects belong to a concept by comparing the object's features to a model or prototype of the concept.

c. _____ Concepts help people give meaning to new experiences.

3. Harry cannot list the essential differences between dogs and cats, but he has no trouble thinking about dogs and cats. This is most likely because he

a. Has a prototype of a representative dog and another of a representative cat

b. Has developed a morpheme for a dog and another morpheme for a cat

c. Is exhibiting functional fixedness

d. Is using heuristics

Language, Thought, and Culture

ENDURING ISSUES DIVERSITY/UNIVERSALITY

Do We All Think Alike?

For at least 100 years, psychologists and philosophers assumed that the basic processes of human cognition were universal. They accepted that cultural differences affect thought—thus Masai elders in the Serengeti count their wealth in heads of cattle, whereas Wall Street bankers measure theirs in stocks and bonds. But habits of thought—the ways people process information—were assumed to be the same everywhere. The tendency to categorize objects and experiences, the ability to reason logically, and the desire to understand situations in terms of cause and effect were believed to be part of human nature, regardless of cultural setting (Goode, 2000). This section examines the validity of these viewpoints.

Language, Thought, and Culture

■ Whorf's linguistic relativity hypothesis is an example of linguistic determinism: _____

_____

_____

Do people from different cultures perceive and think about the world in different ways? A series of experiments suggests that they do (Nisbett & Norenzayan, 2002; Nisbett, Peng, Choi, & Norenzayan, 2001; Peng & Nisbett, 1999). When American and Japanese students were shown an underwater scene and asked to describe what they saw, most Japanese students described the scene as a whole, beginning with the background; by contrast, most American students described the biggest, brightest, fastest fish. (In psychological terms, the Japanese were "field dependent" and the Americans, "field independent"; see Chapter 3: Sensation and Perception). Similar differences emerged in social perception and styles of reasoning. Nisbett and his colleagues concluded these studies reflect fundamental, qualitative differences in how Easterners and Westerners perceive and think about the world. They also emphasized that the origin of these differences is cultural rather than genetic, because the cognitive approach of U.S.-born Asian Americans is indistinguishable from that of European Americans.

Can language also influence how we think and what we can think about? Benjamin Whorf (1956) strongly believed that it does. According to Whorf's **linguistic relativity hypothesis**, the language people speak determines the pattern of their thinking and their view of the world—a position known more generally as **linguistic determinism**. For Whorf, when a language lacks a particular expression, the corresponding thought probably will not occur to speakers of that language.

Think for a moment about how linguistic relativity might apply to what you are learning in this course. Phrases such as "linguistic relativity hypothesis" or "surface structure" and "deep structure" capture very complex ideas. To the extent that you understand those terms, you probably do find it easier to think about the relationship between language and thought, or between words and sentences and their underlying meaning. The technical vocabulary of any field of study permits people to think and communicate more easily, more precisely, and in more complex ways about the content of that field. But this example also illustrates some of the criticisms of Whorf's hypothesis. The idea of *deep structure* occurred before someone thought up that particular phrase. Similarly, you were able to identify and think about the basic speech sounds before you learned that they are called *phonemes*. And you certainly recognize the difference between what someone says and what that person means without having to know that these are called *surface structure* and *deep structure* respectively.

In the same vein, some critics of the linguistic relativity hypothesis point out that it is more likely that the need to think about things differently changes a language than vice versa. For example, English-speaking skiers, realizing that different textures of snow can affect their downhill run, refer to snow as *powder, corn*, and *ice*. The growth of personal computers and the

Internet has inspired a vocabulary of its own, such as *RAM*, *gigabyte*, *online*, *CPU*, and *blogs*. In short, people create new words when they need them.

Psychologists have not dismissed the Whorf hypothesis altogether, but rather have softened it, recognizing that language, thought, and culture are intertwined. Basically, people create words to capture important aspects of their experiences; and to some extent, words shape how people think and what they think about. But people also can think about things for which they have no words. Experience shapes language; and language, in turn, affects subsequent experience.

Check Your Understanding

1. Cross-cultural studies indicate that people from different cultures with very different languages nonetheless perceive and are able to think about things such as colors in very similar ways even when their language contains no words for these things.

   These data _____ Whorf's theory.

   a. Support

   b. Contradict

   c. Neither support nor contradict

2. Indicate whether the following statements are true (T) or false (F).

   a. _____ Many words in our language correspond to concepts.

   b. _____ Experience shapes language.

   c. _____ Thoughts are limited to the words in the language that a person speaks.

Nonhuman Thought and Language

Animal Cognition

- Some animals have _____

  _____

- Nonhuman animals communicate

  primarily _____

  _____

The Question of Language

- No other species has its own _____

  _____

  _____

Nonhuman Thought and Language

Can animals think? Pet owners almost certainly will answer yes—and may even regale listeners with stories about a cat that jumped out of a car miles from home and yet found its way back, or tell of a dog that saved its owner's life, or share some amazing fact or feat. From someone who does not own or like pets, however, the question may elicit a sarcastic reply such as, "Does a bullfrog have wings?" Ask a psychologist, and the most likely response will be a thoughtful pause, then, "That's a difficult question."

■ ANIMAL COGNITION

Numerous studies indicate that other animals can form and use concepts, one of the building blocks of thought. For example, researchers have taught dolphins to select which of two objects is identical to a sample object—the basis of the concepts *same* and *different* (Harley, Roitblat, & Nachtigall, 1996; Roitblat, Penner, & Nachtigall, 1990)—and to respond accurately to numerical concepts such as *more* and *less* (Jaakkola, Fellner, Erb, Rodriguez, & Guarino, 2005). More than this, rhesus monkeys can learn the concept of *numeration* (the capacity to use numbers) and *serialization* (the ability to place objects in a specific order based on a concept) (Brannon & Terrace, 1998; Terrace, Son, & Brannon, 2003).

The great apes—chimpanzees, gorillas, and orangutans—have demonstrated sophisticated problem-solving skills. Recall from Chapter 5: Learning, that chimpanzees figured out various ways to retrieve a bunch of bananas that was positioned out of their reach. In other studies, chimpanzees have learned to use computer keyboards to make and respond to complex requests (Premack, 1971, 1976), to identify and categorize objects, and to place objects in a given order (Kawai & Matsuzawa, 2000).

But do chimps, dolphins, and other animals know what they know? Do nonhuman animals have a *sense of self*? George Gallup (1985, 1998) noticed that after a few days' exposure, captive chimpanzees began making faces in front of a mirror and used the mirror to examine and groom parts of their bodies they had never seen before. To test whether the animals understood that they were seeing themselves, Gallup anesthetized them and painted a bright red mark above the eyebrow ridge and on the top of one ear. The first time the chimps looked at the mirror after awakening, they reached up and touched the red marks, presumably recognizing themselves. Hundreds of researchers have used the mirror test with many other animals. Only two nonhuman species—chimpanzees and orangutans—consistently show signs of self-awareness, even after extended exposure to mirrors. For that matter, even human infants do not demonstrate mirror-recognition until 18 to 24 months of age.

If chimpanzees possess self-awareness, do they understand that others have information, thoughts, and emotions that may differ from their own? Observational studies suggest they do have at least a limited sense of other-awareness (Goodall, 1971; Parr, 2003; Savage-Rumbaugh & Fields, 2000). One measure of other-awareness is *deception*. For example, if a chimpanzee were to discover a hidden store of food and another chimpanzee happened along, the first may begin idly grooming himself. Presumably, the first chimpanzee recognizes that the second (a) is equally interested in food and (b) will interpret the grooming behavior as meaning there is nothing interesting nearby. In the wild and in captive colonies, chimpanzees frequently practice deception in matters of food, receptive females, and power or dominance.

■ THE QUESTION OF LANGUAGE

Although the forms of animal communication vary widely, all animals communicate. Birds do it, bees do it, whales and chimpanzees do it (to paraphrase Cole Porter). Honeybees enact an intricate waggle dance that tells their hive mates not only exactly where to find pollen, but also the quality of that pollen. Humpback whales perform long, haunting solos ranging from deep bass rumblings to high soprano squeaks. The technical term for such messages is **signs**, general or global statements about the animal's *current* state. Research shows clearly that apes can learn signs without intensive training or rewards from human trainers. Whether they can grasp the deep structure of language is less clear. Moreover, at best, apes have reached the linguistic level of a 2- to 2-1/2-year-old child. Critics see this as evidence of severe limitations, whereas others view it as an extraordinary accomplishment.

The distinguishing features of language are *meaningfulness* (or semantics), *displacement* (talking or thinking about the past or the future), and *productivity* (the ability to produce and understand new and unique words and expressions, such as slang terms). Using these criteria, as far as we know no other species has its own language.

So far, the discussion has been about *what* humans and nonhumans think about. As the next section shows, cognitive psychologists are equally interested in *how* people use thinking to solve problems and make decisions.

Check Your Understanding

1. Chimpanzees and orangutans are the only two nonhuman species to consistently show

   a. Self-awareness

   b. Problem-solving ability

   c. Numeration comprehension

2. Humans use language to communicate. What is the nonhuman animal equivalent of language?

   a. Grunts   **b.** Squeaks   **c.** Signs

FIGURE **7–2**
Figure for Problem 1.

FIGURE **7–3**
Figure for Problem 2.

Interpreting Problems

- Problem representation _____

_____

_____

  - Divergent thinking involves

_____

  - Convergent thinking involves

_____

Problem Solving

Solve the following problems. Answers to these problems may be found in the Answer Key at the back of this book:

Problem 1   You have three measuring spoons (Figure 7–2). One is filled with eight teaspoons of salt; the other two are empty, but each has a capacity of two teaspoons each. Divide the salt among the spoons so that only four teaspoons of salt remain in the largest spoon.

Most people find this problem very easy. But now try solving a more elaborate version of the same problem:

Problem 2   You have three measuring spoons (Figure 7–3). One (spoon A) is filled with eight teaspoons of salt. The second and third spoons are empty. The second spoon (spoon B) can hold five teaspoons, and the third (spoon C) can hold three teaspoons. Divide the salt among the spoons so that spoon A and spoon B each have exactly four teaspoons of salt and spoon C is empty.

Most people find problem 2 much more difficult than the first one. Why? The answer lies in interpretation, strategy, and evaluation. Problem 1 is considered trivial because interpreting what is needed is so easy, the strategies for solving it are simple, and the steps required to move closer to a solution can be verified effortlessly. Problem 2, by contrast, requires some thought to interpret what is needed; the strategies for solving it are not immediately apparent; and the steps required to see actual progress toward your goal are harder to evaluate. These three aspects of problem solving—interpretation, strategy, and evaluation—provide a useful framework for investigating this topic.

■ INTERPRETING PROBLEMS

The first step in solving a problem is called **problem representation**, which means interpreting or defining the problem. It is tempting to leap ahead and try to solve a problem just as it is presented, but this impulse often leads to poor solutions. For example, if your business is losing money, you might define the problem as cutting costs. But by defining the problem so narrowly, you have ruled out other options. A better representation of this problem would be to figure out ways to boost profits—by cutting costs, by increasing income, or both. Problems that have no single correct solution and that require a flexible, inventive approach often call for **divergent thinking**—or thinking that involves generating many different possible answers. By contrast, **convergent thinking** is thinking that narrows its focus in a particular direction and assumes that there is only one solution (or at most a limited number of right solutions).

To see the importance of problem representation, consider the following problem:

Problem 3   You have four pieces of chain, each of which is made up of three links (Figure 7–4). All links are closed at the beginning of the problem. It costs two cents to open a link and three cents to close a link. How can you join all 12 links together into a single, continuous circle without paying more than 15 cents?

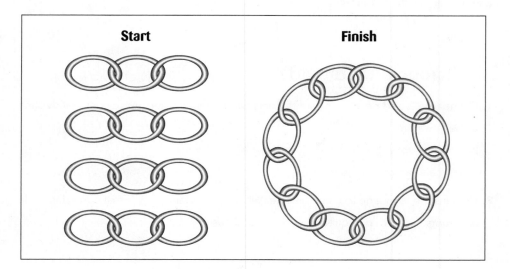

FIGURE **7–4**
Figure for Problem 3.

Problem 3 is difficult because most people assume that the best way to proceed is to open and close the end links on the pieces of chain. As long as they persist with this "conceptual block," they will be unable to solve the problem. If the problem is represented differently, the solution is obvious almost immediately (see Answer Key for solution).

If you have successfully interpreted Problem 3, give Problem 4 a try:

Problem 4 A monk wishes to get to a retreat at the top of a mountain. He starts climbing the mountain at sunrise and arrives at the top at sunset of the same day. During the course of his ascent, he travels at various speeds and stops often to rest. He spends the night engaged in meditation. The next day, he starts his descent at sunrise, following the same narrow path that he used to climb the mountain. As before, he travels at various speeds and stops often to rest. Because he takes great care not to trip and fall on the way down, the descent takes as long as the ascent and he does not arrive at the bottom until sunset. Prove that there is one place on the path that the monk passes at exactly the same time of day on the ascent and on the descent.

This problem is extremely difficult to solve when it is represented verbally or mathematically. It is considerably easier to solve when it is represented visually, as you can see from the explanation that appears in the Answer Key.

Another aspect of successfully representing a problem is determining the category into which the problem belongs. Properly categorizing a problem can provide clues about how to solve it. In fact, once a problem has been categorized properly, its solution may be very easy. Quite often, people who seem to have a knack for solving problems are actually just very skilled at categorizing them in effective ways. Star chess players, for example, can readily categorize a game situation by comparing it with various standard situations stored in their long-term memories. This strategy helps them interpret the current pattern of chess pieces with greater speed and precision than a novice chess player. Similarly, a seasoned football coach may quickly call for a particular play because he has interpreted a situation on the field in terms of familiar categories. Gaining expertise in any field, from football to physics, consists primarily of increasing your ability to represent and categorize problems so that they can be solved quickly and effectively.

■ IMPLEMENTING STRATEGIES AND EVALUATING PROGRESS

Once you have interpreted a problem properly, the next steps are to select a solution strategy and evaluate progress toward your goal. A solution strategy can be anything from simple trial and error, to information retrieval based on similar problems, to a set of step-by-step procedures guaranteed to work (called an *algorithm*), to rule-of-thumb approaches known as *heuristics*.

Trial and Error Trial and error is a strategy that works best when choices are limited. For example, if you have only three or four keys from which to choose, trial and error is the best way to determine the one that unlocks your friend's front door. In most cases, however, trial and error wastes time because there are so many different options to test. It is better to eliminate unproductive approaches and to zero in on a more functional one. Let's consider some alternative strategies.

Information Retrieval One approach is to retrieve information from long-term memory about how such a problem was solved in the past. Information retrieval is an especially important option when a solution is needed quickly. For example, pilots simply memorize the slowest speed at which a particular airplane can fly before it stalls.

Algorithms Complex problems require more complex strategies. An **algorithm** is a problem-solving method that guarantees a solution when it is appropriate for the problem and executed properly. For example, to calculate the product of 323 and 546, multiply the numbers according to the rules of multiplication (the algorithm). If that is done accurately, the right answer is guaranteed. Similarly, to convert temperatures from Fahrenheit to Celsius, use the algorithm $C = 5/9 (F - 32)$.

Heuristics Because algorithms do not exist for every kind of problem, **heuristics**, or rules of thumb, are used. Heuristics do not guarantee a solution, but they may bring it within reach. The challenge is to decide which heuristic is most appropriate for a given problem.

Implementing Strategies and Evaluating Progress

- Problem-solving strategies include:

    - _____

    - Information retrieval based on ___
      _____

    - Step-by-step _____
    - Rule-of-thumb approaches
      (heuristics) that include _____
      _____

A very simple heuristic is **hill climbing**: We try to move continually closer to our goal without going backward. At each step, we evaluate how far "up the hill" we have come, how far we still have to go, and precisely what the next step should be. On a multiple-choice test, for example, one useful hill-climbing strategy for answering a question is first to eliminate the obviously incorrect alternatives. Or imagine taking a long road trip—say from Los Angeles to New York. You'll be implementing a hill-climbing strategy if, whenever you come to a fork in the road, you always choose to take the road that goes more directly east.

Another problem-solving heuristic is to create **subgoals**, which involves breaking a problem into smaller, more manageable pieces that are easier to solve individually than the problem as a whole. Consider the problem of the hobbits and the orcs:

Problem 5 Three hobbits and three orcs are on the bank of a river. They all want to get to the other side, but their boat will carry only two creatures at a time. Moreover, if at any time the orcs outnumber the hobbits, the orcs will attack the hobbits. How can all the creatures get across the river without endangering the hobbits?

The solution to this problem can be found by thinking of the situation in terms of a series of **subgoals**. What has to be done to get just one or two creatures across the river safely, temporarily leaving aside the main goal of getting everyone across? Two of the orcs could be sent across and one of them be allowed to return. That gets one orc across the river. Now the next trip can be contemplated. It is clear that we cannot send a single hobbit across with an orc, because the hobbit would be outnumbered as soon as the boat landed. Therefore, either two hobbits or two orcs must go across. By working on the problem in this fashion—concentrating on subgoals—everyone eventually can be brought across.

Once you have solved problem 5, try problem 6, which is considerably more difficult:

Problem 6 This problem is identical to problem 5, except that there are five hobbits and five orcs, and the boat can carry only three creatures at a time.

Subgoals are often helpful in solving a variety of everyday problems. According to Henry Ford (1863–1947), who invented assembly-line manufacturing of affordable automobiles in the early 1900s, "Nothing is particularly hard if you divide it into small steps." For example, a student whose goal is to write a term paper might set subgoals by breaking the project into a series of separate tasks: choosing a topic, doing research and taking notes, preparing an outline, writing the first draft, editing, rewriting, and so on. Even the subgoals can sometimes be broken down into separate tasks: Writing the first draft of the paper might break down into the subgoals of writing the introduction, describing the position to be taken, supporting the position with evidence, drawing conclusions, writing a summary, and writing a bibliography. Subgoals make problem solving more manageable because they free us from the burden of having to "get to the other side of the river" all at once. Although the overall purpose of setting subgoals is still to solve the larger problem, this tactic allows us to set our sights on closer, more manageable objectives.

One of the most frequently used heuristics, called **means-end analysis**, combines hill climbing and subgoals. Like hill climbing, means-end analysis involves analyzing the difference between the current situation and the desired end, then doing something to reduce that difference. But in contrast to hill climbing—which does not permit detours away from the final goal to solve the problem—means-end analysis takes into account the entire problem situation. It formulates subgoals in such a way as to allow us temporarily to take a step that appears to be backward to reach our goal in the end. One example is the pitcher's strategy in a baseball game when confronted with the best batter in the league. The pitcher might opt to walk this batter intentionally even though doing so moves away from the major subgoal of keeping runners off base. Intentional walking might enable the pitcher to keep a run from scoring and so contribute to the ultimate goal of winning the game. This flexibility in thinking is a major benefit of means-end analysis.

But means-end analysis also poses the danger of straying so far from the end goal that the goal disappears altogether. One way of avoiding this situation is to use the heuristic of **working backward**. With this strategy, the search for a solution begins at the goal and works backward toward the "givens." Working backward is often used when the goal has more information than the givens and when the operations involved can work in two directions. For example, if you wanted to spend exactly $100 on clothing, it would be difficult to reach that goal simply by buying some items and hoping that they totaled exactly $100. A better strategy would be to buy one item, subtract its cost from $100 to determine how much money you have left, then purchase another item, subtract its cost, and so on, until you have spent $100.

■ OBSTACLES TO SOLVING PROBLEMS

In everyday life, many factors can either help or hinder problem solving. One factor is a person's level of motivation, or emotional arousal. Generally, people must generate a certain surge of excitement to motivate themselves to solve a problem, yet too much arousal can hamper the ability to find a solution (refer to Chapter 8: Motivation and Emotion).

Another factor that can either help or hinder problem solving is **mental set**—the tendency to perceive and to approach problems in certain ways. Set determines which information people tend to retrieve from memory to help them find a solution. Set can be helpful when a person has learned operations that he or she can apply to the present situation. Much of our formal education involves learning sets and ways to solve problems; that is, learning heuristics and algorithms. But sets can also create obstacles, especially when a novel approach is needed. The most successful problem solvers can choose from many different sets and can judge when to change sets or when to abandon them entirely. Great ideas and inventions come out of such flexibility.

One type of set that can seriously hinder problem solving is called **functional fixedness**. Consider Figure 7–5. Do you see a way to mount the candle on the wall? If not, you probably are stymied by functional fixedness (see Answer Key for the solution). The more you use an object in only one way, the harder it is to see new uses for it, because you have "assigned" the object to a fixed function. To some extent, part of the learning process is to assign correct functions to objects—this is how people form concepts. But for effective problem solving, it is important to be aware that many objects can be used for an entirely different purposes.

The value of looking for new ways to represent a difficult problem cannot be overstated. Being open to potential solutions that at first seem unproductive is often important. This is the rationale behind the technique called **brainstorming**, which involves generating lots of ideas before reviewing and evaluating them.

Obstacles to Solving Problems

- Strong mental sets (such as functional fixedness) can _____

_____

- Brainstorming involves _____

_____

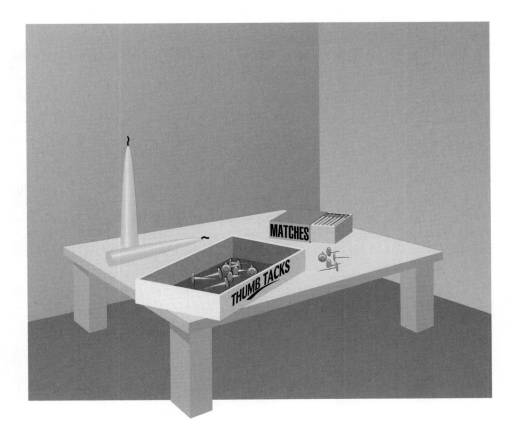

FIGURE **7–5**
To test the effects of functional fixedness, participants might be given the items shown on the table and asked to mount a candle on the wall.

Check Your Understanding

1. Match each problem-solving strategy with the appropriate definition.

_____ Algorithm

_____ Heuristic

_____ Hill climbing

_____ Means-end analysis

_____ Working backward

_____ Subgoal creation

a. Rule-of-thumb approach that helps in simplifying and solving problems, although it does not guarantee a correct solution

b. Strategy in which each step moves one closer to a solution

c. Step-by-step method that guarantees a solution

d. Strategy in which one moves from the goal to the starting point

e. Strategy that aims to reduce the discrepancy between the current situation and the desired goal at a number of intermediate points

f. Breaking down the solution to a larger problem into a set of smaller, more manageable steps

2. You are at a football game when rain starts to pour down heavily. As you get soaked, you see the people next to you pull folded plastic garbage bags out of their pockets to use as a temporary "raincoat." Your failure to realize that the garbage bag might also be used as rain protection is an example of

a. An algorithm

b. A heuristic

c. Means-end analysis

d. Functional fixedness

Decision Making

Compensatory Decision Making

■ Rate each available choice in terms of _____ criteria, then

_____

Decision-Making Heuristics

■ Decision-making heuristics can save a great deal of time and effort, but are prone to _____

■ Representativeness heuristic:

_____

■ Availability heuristic: _____

_____

■ Confirmation bias: _____

_____

Explaining One's Decisions

■ Framing: Refers to _____

_____

■ Hindsight bias: Tendency to _____

_____

■ Counterfactual thinking: _____

_____

Decision Making

Decision making is a special kind of problem solving in which one already knows all the possible solutions or choices. The task is not to come up with new solutions, but rather to identify the best one based on various criteria. This process might sound fairly simple, but sometimes people are faced with many possible choices and a large, complex set of criteria. For example, suppose you are looking for an apartment among hundreds available. A reasonable rent is important to you, but so are good neighbors, a good location, a low noise level, and cleanliness. If you find an inexpensive, noisy apartment with undesirable neighbors, should you take it? Is it a better choice than a more expensive, less noisy apartment in a better location? How can you weigh the various criteria and make the best choice?

■ COMPENSATORY DECISION MAKING

The logical way to make a decision is to rate each of the available choices on all the criteria you are using, arriving at some overall measure of the extent to which each choice matches your criteria. For each choice, the attractive features can offset or compensate for the unattractive features. This approach to decision making is, therefore, called a **compensatory model**.

Table 7–1 illustrates one of the most useful compensatory models applied to a car-buying decision. The buyer's three criteria are weighted in terms of importance: price (not weighted heavily), gas mileage, and service record (both weighted more heavily). Next, each car is rated from 1 (poor) to 5 (excellent) on each of the criteria. Car 1 has an excellent price (5) but relatively poor gas mileage (2) and service record (1); Car 2 has a less desirable price but fairly good mileage

TABLE **7–1**	Compensatory Decision Table for Purchase of a New Car			
	PRICE (WEIGHT = 4)	GAS MILEAGE (WEIGHT = 8)	SERVICE RECORD (WEIGHT = 10)	WEIGHTED TOTAL
Car 1	5 (20)	2 (16)	1 (10)	(46)
Car 2	1 (4)	4 (32)	4 (40)	(76)
Ratings: 5 = Excellent; 1 = Poor				

and service record. Each rating is then multiplied by the weight for that criterion (e.g., for Car 1, the price rating of 5 is multiplied by the weight of 4, and the result is put in parentheses next to the rating). Finally, ratings are totaled for each car. Clearly, Car 2 is the better choice: It is more expensive, but that disadvantage is offset by its better mileage and service record; and these two criteria are more important than price to this particular buyer.

Although most people would agree that using such a table is a good way to decide which car to buy, at times people will abandon the compensatory decision-making process in the face of more vivid anecdotal information. For example, if a friend had previously bought Car 2 and found it to be a lemon, you might choose Car 1 despite the well-thought-out advantages of Car 2. Moreover, as the next section shows, it is often not possible or desirable to rate every choice on all criteria. In such situations, people typically use heuristics that have worked well in the past to simplify decision making, even though such heuristics may lead to less-than-optimal decision making.

■ DECISION-MAKING HEURISTICS

Research has identified several common heuristics that people use to make decisions. We use the **representativeness** heuristic whenever we make a decision on the basis of certain information that matches our model of the typical member of a category. For example, if every time you went shopping you bought the least expensive items and if all of these items turned out to be poorly made, you might eventually decide not to buy anything that seems typical of the category "very cheap."

Another common heuristic is **availability**. In the absence of full and accurate information, people will often base decisions on whatever information is most readily available, even though this information may not be accurate. For example, it seems to be a law of nature that when you are driving at the speed limit, everyone else is going faster or slower than you are. Based on that information, you might decide that you should speed up or slow down to keep up with the flow of traffic. The problem here is that you don't see all the cars that are going the same speed you are. Since you don't pass them and they don't pass you, their presence isn't as obvious as the cars that are going faster or slower.

Another heuristic, closely related to availability, is **confirmation bias**—the tendency to notice and remember evidence that supports one's beliefs and to ignore evidence that contradicts them. For example, individuals who believe that AIDS is something that happens to "other people" (homosexual men and intravenous drug users, not middle-class heterosexuals) are more likely to remember articles about rates of HIV infection in these groups or in third-world countries than articles about AIDS cases among people similar to themselves (Fischhoff & Downs, 1997). Convinced that HIV is not something they personally need to worry about, they ignore evidence to the contrary.

A related phenomenon is our tendency to see connections or patterns of cause and effect where none exist (Kahneman & Tversky, 1996; Rottenstreich & Tversky, 1997). For example, many people still believe that consuming chocolate will cause acne to flare up in susceptible teenagers, yet this myth was disproved nearly half a century ago. Many parents strongly believe that sugar may cause hyperactivity in children and that arthritis pain is related to weather—despite research evidence to the contrary. The list of commonsense beliefs that persist in the face of contrary evidence is long (Redelmeier & Tversky, 2004).

■ EXPLAINING ONE'S DECISIONS

Framing For the most part, people are reasonably satisfied with the decisions they make in the real world. However, these decisions intentionally or inadvertently can be swayed by the way the information provided to make the decision is presented, or framed. Psychologists use the term **framing** to refer to the perspective or phrasing of information that is used to make a decision. Numerous studies have shown that subtle changes in the way information is presented can dramatically affect the final decision (Mann, Sherman, & Updegraff, 2004). A classic study (B. J. McNeil, Pauker, Sox, & Tversky, 1982) illustrates how framing may influence a medical decision. In this study, experimental participants were asked to choose between surgery and radiation therapy to treat lung cancer. However, the framing of information provided to make this choice was manipulated. In the *survival frame*, participants were given the statistical outcomes of both procedures in the form of survival statistics, thus emphasizing the 1- and 5-year *survival* rates after treatment. In the *mortality frame*, the participants were given the same information, presented (or framed) according to death rates after 1 year and after 5 years. Although the actual number of deaths and survivors associated with each procedure was identical in both the survival and mortality frames, the percentage of participants who chose one procedure over another varied dramatically depending on how the information was framed. Probably most surprising was that this framing effect was found even when 424 experienced radiologists served as the experimental participants.

Hindsight   Whether a choice is exceptionally good, extraordinarily foolish, or somewhere in between, most people think about their decisions after the fact. The term **hindsight bias** refers to the tendency to view outcomes as inevitable and predictable after individuals know the outcome and to believe that they could have predicted what happened, or perhaps that they did. For example, research shows that physicians remember being more confident about their diagnoses when they learn that they were correct than at the time they were making the actual diagnoses.

Psychologists have long viewed the hindsight bias as a cognitive flaw—a way of explaining away bad decisions and maintaining a sense of confidence. A team of researchers in Berlin, however, argues that the hindsight bias serves a useful function (Hoffrage, Hertwig, & Gigerenzer, 2000). "Correcting" memory is a quick and efficient way to replace misinformation or faulty assumptions, so that our future decisions and judgments will be closer to the mark. In a sense, hindsight functions like the "find and replace" function in a word processing program, eliminating extra, time-consuming keystrokes and mental effort.

"If Only"   At times, everyone imagines alternatives to reality and mentally plays out the consequences. Psychologists refer such thoughts about things that never happened as **counterfactual thinking**—in which thoughts are counter to the facts. Counterfactual thinking often takes the form of "If only" constructions, in which people mentally revise the events or actions that led to a particular outcome: "If only I had studied harder"; "If only I had said no"; "If only I had driven straight home." Research shows that counterfactual thinking usually centers around a small number of themes: reversing a course of events that led to a negative experience, explaining unusual events by assigning responsibility to someone or something, and regaining a sense of personal control (Roese, 1997).

Any discussion of cognition, problem solving, or decision making inevitably raises the question of how individuals differ in intelligence, where the question of individual differences in reasoning and problem solving is of central importance.

Check Your Understanding

1. Match each decision-making heuristic with the appropriate definition.

_____ Representativeness heuristic

_____ Availability heuristic

_____ Confirmation bias

a. Making judgments on the basis of whatever information can be most readily retrieved from memory

b. Attending to evidence that supports your existing beliefs and ignoring other evidence

c. Making decisions on the basis of information that matches your model of what is "typical" of a certain category

2. In deciding where to go on vacation, you decide you want a place where you can relax, a place that is warm, and a place that you can reach inexpensively. But you will not consider any place that is more than 1,000 miles away. What kind of decision-making model are you using?

a. Visualization

b. Brainstorming

c. Noncompensatory

d. Compensatory

3. You are driving down the highway at the posted speed limit. After a while, you mention to your passenger, "It sure looks like everyone is either going slower or faster than the speed limit. Hardly anyone seems to be going the same speed as I am." In fact, most of the cars on the highway are also traveling at the speed limit. Your erroneous conclusion is most likely because of

    a. Framing   **c.** Mental set

    b. Hindsight bias   **d.** The availability heuristic

Intelligence and Mental Abilities

In many societies, one of the nicest things you can say is "You're smart"; and one of the most insulting is "You're stupid." Intelligence is so basic to our view of human nature that any characterization of a person that neglects to mention that person's intelligence is considered incomplete. Our mental capabilities affect our success in school, the kind of work we do, the kinds of recreation we enjoy, and even our choice of friends.

    Psychologists have studied intelligence almost since psychology first emerged as a science, yet they still struggle to understand this complex and elusive concept. Throughout the next few sections, you may come to appreciate the difficulty of their task. Toward that end, we begin by asking you some questions intended to measure intelligence:

    1. Describe the difference between *laziness* and *idleness*.
    2. Which direction would you have to face so that your right ear would be facing north?
    3. What does *obliterate* mean?
    4. Name the way in which an hour and a week are alike.
    5. Choose the lettered block that best completes the pattern in the following figure:

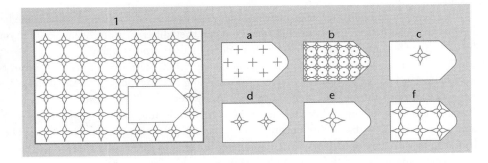

    6. If three pencils cost 25 cents, how many pencils can you buy for 75 cents?
    7. Select the lettered pair that best expresses a relationship similar to that expressed in the original pair:

        Crutch: locomotion
        a. Paddle: canoe   **d.** Spectacles: vision
        b. Hero: worship   **e.** Statement: contention
        c. Horse: carriage

    8. Decide how the first two items in the following figure are related to each other. Then, find the one item at the right that goes with the third item in the same way that the second item goes with the first.

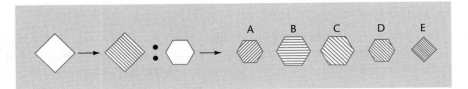

9. For each item in the figure shown, decide whether it can be completely covered by using some or all of the given pieces without overlapping any.

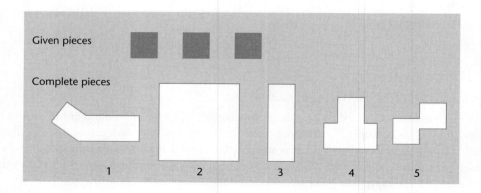

These questions were taken from various tests of **intelligence**, or mental ability (see Answer Key for solutions). Because the complex mental processes involved in intelligent thinking are unable to be seen, the subject of intelligence has to be approached indirectly—primarily, by watching what people do when situations require the use of intelligence. But what do tests of intelligence actually reveal? Do they reflect all the abilities that make up intelligence? And what exactly *is* intelligence? How is it related to creativity? If a person does well on tests of intelligence, will he or she be more successful in school, in a job, or in life than someone else who does less well? To address these and other questions, let's look at what is meant by intelligence.

Before reading further, take a few minutes to write down on a sheet of paper some behaviors that you believe reflect intelligence. How are they different from behaviors that you believe reflect less intelligence? When you have done that, continue reading.

Robert Sternberg and his associates (Sternberg, 1982; Sternberg, Conway, Ketron, & Bernstein, 1981) discovered that people with no training in psychology generally think of intelligence as a mix of practical problem-solving ability, verbal ability, and social competence. Practical problem-solving ability includes using logic, connecting ideas, and viewing a problem in its entirety. Verbal ability encompasses using and understanding written and spoken language in well-developed ways. Social competence refers to interacting well with others—being open-minded about different kinds of people and showing interest in a variety of topics. When Sternberg and his colleagues asked psychologists who specialize in the area of intelligence for their ideas about intelligence, they generally agreed that it includes verbal and problem-solving abilities, but they did not agree that it includes social competence. Instead, they said that practical intelligence is an important component of overall intelligence (Table 7–2). In addition, many experts now list creativity and the ability to adapt to the environment as crucial components of intelligence.

Compare your own description of intelligent behaviors with those listed in Table 7–2. Was your description closer to that of the laypersons or the experts? Which of the characteristics of intelligence do you think are most important? Why do you think so?

The next section takes a closer at the ways in which psychologists think about intelligence and how those formal theories of intelligence affect the content of intelligence tests.

■ **THEORIES OF INTELLIGENCE**

For more than a century, psychologists have argued about what constitutes general intelligence—or even if "general" intelligence actually exists. One of their most basic questions is whether intelligence is a single, general mental ability or whether it is composed of many separate abilities.

Theories of Intelligence

■ Intelligence: General term referring to _____

_____

■ Most theorists believe that intelligence is composed of _____

_____:

   ■ Sternberg's _____ theory of intelligence

   ■ Gardner's theory of _____

■ Goleman's theory of emotional intelligence: _____

_____

_____

TABLE 7–2   Some Characteristics of Intelligence as Seen by Laypersons and Experts

LAYPERSONS

Practical problem-solving ability: reasons logically, makes connections among ideas, can see all sides of a problem, keeps an open mind, responds thoughtfully to the ideas of others, is good at sizing up situations, interprets information accurately, makes good decisions, goes to original source for basic information, has good source of ideas, perceives implied assumptions, deals with problems in a resourceful way.

Verbal ability: speaks articulately, converses well, is knowledgeable about a particular field, studies hard, reads widely, writes without difficulty, has a good vocabulary, tries new things.

Social competence: accepts others as they are, admits mistakes, shows interest in the world at large, arrives on time for appointments, has social conscience, thinks before speaking and acting, shows curiosity, avoids snap judgments, makes fair judgments, assesses the relevance of information to the problem at hand, is sensitive to others, is frank and honest with self and others, shows interest in the immediate environment.

EXPERTS

Problem-solving ability: makes good decisions, displays common sense, shows objectivity, is good at solving problems, plans ahead, has good intuition, gets to the heart of problems, appreciates truth, considers the results of actions, approaches problems thoughtfully.

Verbal intelligence: has a good vocabulary, reads with high comprehension, is intellectually curious, sees all sides of a problem, learns rapidly, shows alertness, thinks deeply, shows creativity, converses easily on a wide range of subjects, reads widely, sees connections among ideas.

Practical intelligence: sizes up situations well, determines how best to achieve goals, shows awareness of world around him or her, shows interest in the world at large, uses self-knowledge of own motives to select the tasks that will best accomplish own goals.

Source: Sternberg, 1982; Wagner & Sternberg, 1986.

Early Theorists Charles Spearman (1863–1945), an early twentieth-century British psychologist, maintained that intelligence is quite general—a kind of well or spring of mental energy that flows through every action. Spearman believed that people who are bright in one area are often bright in other areas as well. The American psychologist L. L. Thurstone (1887–1955) disagreed with Spearman. Thurstone argued that intelligence is composed of seven distinct kinds of mental abilities (Thurstone, 1938): spatial ability, memory, perceptual speed, word fluency, numerical ability, reasoning, and verbal meaning. Unlike Spearman, Thurstone believed that these abilities are relatively independent of one another. Thus, a person with exceptional spatial ability (the ability to perceive distance, recognize shapes, and so on) might lack word fluency.

Contemporary Theorists Contemporary psychologists have considerably broadened the concept of intelligence and reexamined how it can best be measured. For example, Robert Sternberg (1986, 2003) has proposed a **triarchic theory of intelligence**. Sternberg argues that human intelligence encompasses a broad range of skills that are just as important as the more limited skills assessed by traditional intelligence tests. *Analytical intelligence* refers to the mental processes emphasized by most theories of intelligence, such as the ability to learn how to do things, acquire new knowledge, solve problems, and carry out tasks effectively. According to Sternberg, this is the aspect of intelligence assessed by most intelligence tests. *Creative intelligence* is the ability to adjust to new tasks, use new concepts, respond effectively in new situations, gain insight, and adapt creatively. *Practical intelligence* is the ability to find solutions to practical and personal problems.

Another contemporary theory of intelligence is the **theory of multiple intelligences** advanced by Howard Gardner and his associates at Harvard (J.-Q. Chen & Gardner, 2005; Gardner, 1983, 2004). Gardner, like Thurstone, believes that intelligence is made up of several distinct abilities, each of which is relatively independent of the others. Precisely how many separate intelligences might exist is difficult to determine, but Gardner lists eight: logical-mathematical, linguistic, spatial, musical, bodily-kinesthetic, interpersonal, intrapersonal, and naturalistic. The first four are self-explanatory. Bodily-kinesthetic intelligence is the

SUMMARY TABLE	Comparing Gardner's, Sternberg's, and Goleman's Theories of Intelligence	
GARDENER'S MULTIPLE INTELLIGENCES	STERNBERG'S TRIARCHIC INTELLIGENCES	GOLEMAN'S EMOTIONAL INTELLIGENCE
Logical-mathematical Linguistic	Analytical	
Spatial Musical Bodily-kinesthetic	Creative	
Interpersonal	Practical	Recognizing emotions in others and managing relationships
Intrapersonal Naturalistic		Knowing yourself and motivating yourself with emotions

ability to manipulate one's body in space; a skilled athlete shows high levels of this kind of intelligence. People who are extraordinarily talented at understanding and communicating with others, such as exceptional teachers and parents, have strong interpersonal intelligence. Intrapersonal intelligence reflects the ancient adage, "Know thyself." People who understand themselves and who use this knowledge effectively to attain their goals rank high in intrapersonal intelligence. Finally, naturalistic intelligence reflects an individual's ability to understand, relate to, and interact with the world of nature.

Finally, Daniel Goleman (1997) has proposed a theory of **emotional intelligence**, which refers to how effectively people perceive and understand their own emotions and the emotions of others and can manage their emotional behavior. Goleman contends that one of the reasons IQ tests sometimes fail to predict success accurately is that they do not take into account an individual's emotional competence.

The Summary Table displays the contemporary theories described here. These theories shape the content of intelligence tests and other measures that evaluate the abilities of millions of people.

■ INTELLIGENCE TESTS

The Stanford–Binet Intelligence Scale   The first test developed to measure intelligence was designed by two Frenchmen, Alfred Binet (1857–1911) and Théodore Simon (1872–1971). The test, first used in Paris in 1905, was designed to identify children who might have difficulty in school.

The first Binet–Simon scale consisted of 30 tests arranged in order of increasing difficulty. With each child, the examiner started with the easiest tests and worked down the list until the child could no longer answer questions. A well-known adaptation of the Binet–Simon scale, the Stanford–Binet Intelligence Scale, was prepared at Stanford University in 1916 by Lewis Terman (1877–1956). Updated repeatedly since then, the current Stanford–Binet Intelligence Scale is designed to measure four virtually universal abilities related to traditional views of intelligence: verbal reasoning, abstract/visual reasoning, quantitative reasoning, and short-term memory. The Stanford–Binet test is given individually by a trained examiner. It is best suited for children, adolescents, and very young adults. Questions 1 and 2 on page 189 were drawn from an early version of the Stanford–Binet scale.

Terman also introduced the now-famous term **intelligence quotient (IQ)** to establish a numerical value of intelligence, setting the score of 100 for a person of average intelligence. Figure 7–6 shows an approximate distribution of IQ scores in the population.

Intelligence Tests

■ Individual tests

  ■ _____

  ■ _____

  ■ _____

  ■ _____

■ Group tests

■ Performance tests

■ Culture-fair tests

■ Intelligence quotient (IQ): _____

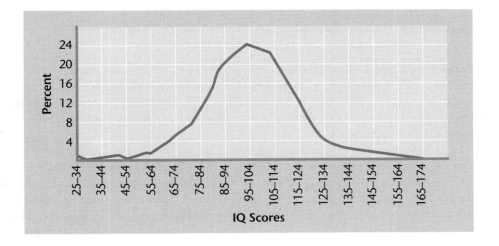

FIGURE **7–6**
The approximate distribution of IQ scores in the population.
Note that the greatest percentage of scores fall around 100; very low percentages of people score at the two extremes of the curve.

The Wechsler Intelligence Scales   The most commonly used individual test of intelligence for adults is the **Wechsler Adult Intelligence Scale—Third Edition (WAIS-III)**, which was developed in the late 1930s by psychologist David Wechsler (1896–1981). The Stanford–Binet emphasizes verbal skills, but Wechsler believed adult intelligence consists more of the ability to handle life situations than to solve verbal and abstract problems.

The WAIS-III is divided into two parts: one stresses verbal skills, the other focuses on performance skills. The verbal scale includes tests of information, simple arithmetic, and comprehension. The performance scale measures routine tasks such as asking people to "find the missing part" (buttonholes in a coat, for example), to copy patterns, and to arrange three to five pictures so that they tell a story.

Although the content of the WAIS-III is somewhat more sophisticated than that of the Stanford–Binet, Wechsler's chief innovation was in scoring. His test gives separate verbal and performance scores as well as an overall IQ score. Moreover, on some items, one or two extra points can be earned, depending on the complexity of the answer given. This unique scoring system gives credit for the reflective qualities that one would expect to find in intelligent adults. Finally, on some questions, speed and accuracy affect the score. Questions 3 and 4 on page 189 resemble questions on the WAIS-III.

Wechsler also developed a similar intelligence test for use with school-age children. As with the WAIS-III, the **Wechsler Intelligence Scale for Children—Third Edition (WISC-III)** yields separate verbal and performance scores as well as an overall IQ score.

Group Tests   With the Stanford–Binet, the WAIS-III, and the WISC-III, an examiner takes a single person to an isolated room, spreads the materials on a table, and spends from 30 to 90 minutes administering the test. The examiner may then take another hour or so to score the test according to detailed instructions in the manual. This is a time-consuming, costly operation; and under some circumstances, the examiner's behavior can influence the score. For these reasons, test makers have devised **group tests**, which a single examiner can administer to many people at once. Instead of sitting across the table from a person who asks you questions, you receive a test booklet that contains questions for you to answer in writing within a certain amount of time.

Group tests have some distinct advantages over individualized tests. They eliminate bias on the part of the examiner, answer sheets can be scored quickly and objectively, and it is possible to collect data from large numbers of test takers. But group tests also have some distinct disadvantages. The examiner is less likely to notice whether a person is tired, ill, or confused by the directions. People who are not used to being tested tend to do less well on group tests than on individual tests. Finally, emotionally disturbed children and children with

The Wechsler Intelligence Scales, developed by David Wechsler, are individual intelligence tests administered to one person at a time. There are versions of the Wechsler Scales for both adults and children. Here, a child is being asked to copy a pattern using blocks.

learning disabilities often do better on individual tests than on group tests. Questions 5–9 on pages 189–190 are drawn from group tests.

Performance and Culture-Fair Tests To perform well on the intelligence tests that have been discussed, people must be adept at the language in which the test is given. How, then, can a test examine non-native English speakers in English-speaking countries? Psychologists have designed two general forms of tests for such situations: performance tests and culture-fair tests.

Performance tests consist of problems that minimize or eliminate the use of words. One of the earliest performance tests, the Seguin Form Board, is essentially a puzzle. The examiner removes specifically designed cutouts, stacks them in a predetermined order, and asks the person to replace them as quickly as possible. A more recent performance test, the Porteus Maze, consists of a series of increasingly difficult printed mazes. People trace their way through the maze without lifting the pencil from the paper. Such tests require the test taker to pay close attention to a task for an extended period and continuously to plan ahead to make the correct choices.

Culture-fair tests, like performance tests, minimize or eliminate the use of language (Ortiz & Dynda, 2005). But they also try to downplay skills and values—such as the need for speed—that vary from culture to culture. In the Goodenough–Harris Drawing Test, for example, people are asked to draw to the best of their ability a picture of a person. Drawings are scored for proportions, correct and complete representation of the parts of the body, detail in clothing, and so on. An example of a culture-fair item from the Progressive Matrices is Question 5 on page 189. This test consists of 60 designs, each with a missing part. The test taker is given six to eight possible choices to replace the part.

■ WHAT MAKES A GOOD TEST?

How can we tell whether intelligence tests will produce consistent results no matter when they are given? And how can we tell whether they really measure what they claim to measure? Psychologists address these questions by referring to a test's reliability and validity. Issues of reliability and validity apply equally to all psychological tests, not just to tests of mental abilities. In Chapter 10, for example, we will reexamine these issues as they apply to personality assessment.

Reliability By **reliability**, psychologists mean the dependability and consistency of the scores that a test yields. If your alarm clock is set for 8:15 a.m. and it goes off at that time every morning, it is reliable. But if it is set for 8:15 and rings at 8:00 one morning and 8:40 the next, you cannot depend on it; it is unreliable. Similarly, a test has reliability when it yields consistent results.

How do we know whether a test is reliable? The simplest way to find out is to give the test to a group and, after a time, give the same people the same test again. If they obtain similar scores each time, the test is said to have high *test-retest reliability*. For example, Table 7–3 shows the IQ scores of eight people who were tested one year apart using the same test. Although the scores did change slightly, none changed by more than six points. That is a highly reliable test.

There is a drawback, however. How do we know that people have not simply remembered the answers from the first testing and repeated them the second time around? To avoid this possibility, psychologists prefer to give two equivalent tests designed to measure the same thing. If people score the same on both forms, the tests are considered reliable. One way to create alternate forms is to split a single test into two parts—for example, to assign odd-numbered items to one part and even-numbered items to the other. If scores on the two halves agree, the test has **split-half reliability**. Most intelligence tests do, in fact, have alternate equivalent forms, just as each college admission test often has many versions.

What Makes a Good Test?

■ Reliability: Ability of a test to

_____

■ Validity: Ability of a test to _____

_____

■ Reliability of IQ tests is seldom questioned; validity is _____

_____

TABLE 7–3 IQ Scores on the Same Test Given One Year Apart

PERSON	FIRST TESTING	SECOND TESTING
A	130	127
B	123	127
C	121	119
D	116	122
E	109	108
F	107	112
G	95	93
H	89	94

ENDURING ISSUES STABILITY/CHANGE

Test Reliability and Changes in Intelligence

If a person takes an intelligence test on Monday and obtains an IQ score of 90 then retakes the test on Tuesday and scores 130, clearly something is amiss. But what? Is the test at fault or do the differences in scores accurately reflect changes in performance?

People vary from moment to moment and day to day. Changes in health and motivation can affect test results even with the most reliable tests. And although IQ scores tend to be remarkably stable after the age of 5 or 6, intellectual ability does sometimes change dramatically—for better or worse. One person's mental ability may decline substantially after a mild head injury; another person's scores on intelligence tests may rise after years of diligent intellectual study.

Because scores on even the best tests vary somewhat from one day to the next, many testing services now report a person's score along with a range of scores that allows for variations. For example, a score of 110 might be reported with a range of 104–116. This implies that the true score is most likely within a few points of 110, but almost certainly does not fall lower than 104 or higher than 116.

These methods of testing reliability can be very effective. But psychological science demands more precise descriptions than "very reliable" or "fairly reliable." Psychologists express reliability in terms of **correlation coefficients**, which measure the relationship between two sets of scores (Appendix A). If test scores on one occasion are absolutely consistent with those on another occasion, the correlation coefficient is 1.0. If there is no relationship between the scores, the correlation coefficient is zero. In Table 7–3, where there is a very close but not perfect, relationship between the two sets of scores, the correlation coefficient is .96.

How reliable are intelligence tests? In general, people's IQ scores on most intelligence tests are quite stable. Performance and culture-fair tests are somewhat less reliable. However, as discussed, scores on even the best tests vary somewhat from one day to another.

Validity   Do intelligence tests really measure "intelligence"? When psychologists ask this question, they are concerned with test validity. **Validity** refers to a test's ability to measure what it has been designed to measure. How do we know whether a given test actually measures what it claims to measure?

One measure of validity is known as **content validity**—whether the test contains an adequate sample of the skills or knowledge that it is supposed to measure. Most widely used intelligence tests, such as those from which the questions at the beginning of this chapter were taken, seem to measure many of the mental abilities that we think of as part of intelligence although they may not adequately sample all aspects of intelligence equally well.

Another way to measure a test's validity is to see whether a person's score on that test closely matches his or her score on another test designed to measure the same thing. The two different scores should be very similar if they are measures of the same ability. Various intelligence tests seem to show this kind of validity as well. Despite differences in test content, people who score high on one intelligence test tend to score high on others. Still, this outcome does not necessarily mean that the two tests measure intelligence. Conceivably, they could both be measuring the same thing, but that thing is not necessarily intelligence. For example, the tests may simply be measuring the ability to take tests. This fact alone could explain why people who do well on one IQ test also tend to do well on other tests.

To demonstrate that intelligence tests are valid, an independent measure of intelligence is needed against which to compare test scores. Determining test validity in this way is called **criterion-related validity**. Ever since Binet invented the intelligence test, the main criterion against which intelligence test scores have been compared has been school achievement. Even the strongest critics agree that IQ tests predict school achievement well (Aiken & Groth-Marnat, 2005; Anastasi & Urbina, 1997).

Criticisms of IQ Tests What is it about IQ tests, then, that makes them controversial? One major criticism concerns the narrowness of their content. Most intelligence tests assess only a limited set of skills, though as we have seen most psychologists today believe that intelligence is not a single entity but rather a combination of abilities required for living effectively in the real world. Another criticism is that a test score is a very simplistic way of summing up an extremely complex set of abilities. Maloney and Ward (1976) point out that we do not describe a person's personality by using a two- or three-digit number. So why should we try to sum up something as complex as intelligence by labeling someone "90" or "110"?

Another major criticism of IQ tests is that their content and administration do not take into account cultural differences. High scores on most IQ tests require considerable mastery of standard English, thus biasing the tests in favor of middle- and upper-class white people (Ortiz & Dynda, 2005). Moreover, white middle-class examiners may not be familiar with the speech patterns of lower-income African American children or children from homes in which English is not the primary language, a complication that can hamper good test performance (Sattler, 2005). In addition, certain questions may have very different meanings for children of different social classes. The WISC-III, for instance, asks, "What are you supposed to do if a child younger than you hits you?" The "correct" answer is "Walk away." But for a child who lives in an environment where survival depends on being tough, the "correct" answer might be "Hit him back." This answer, however, receives zero credit.

ENDURING ISSUES PERSON/SITUATION

Tracking the Future

Tracking, the practice of assigning students who "test low" to special classes for slow learners, can work to the student's disadvantage if the test results do not reflect the student's true abilities. However, the opposite mistake may sometimes work to the student's advantage: A student of mediocre ability who is identified early on as above average may receive special attention, encouragement, and tutoring that would otherwise have been considered "wasted effort" on the part of teachers. In either case, intelligence test scores can set up a self-fulfilling prophecy, so that students defined as slow become slow and those defined as quick become quick. In this way, intelligence tests may not only predict achievement but also help determine it (Rosenthal, 2002a).

IQ and Success As seen earlier, IQ scores predict success in school with some accuracy. No one should be surprised that scores on these tests correlate well with academic achievement, since both of these involve intellectual activity and stress verbal ability. Moreover, both academic achievement and high IQ scores require similar kinds of motivation, attention, perseverance, and test-taking ability.

IQ tests also tend to predict success after people finish their schooling. People with high IQ scores tend to enter high-status occupations, and high grades and intelligence test scores do predict occupational success and performance on the job. Critics point out, however, that this pattern can be explained in various ways. For one thing, because people with higher IQs tend to do better in school, they stay in school longer and earn advanced degrees, thereby opening the door to high-status jobs. Moreover, children from wealthy families generally grow up in environments that encourage academic success and reward good performance on tests. In addition, they are more likely to have financial resources for postgraduate education or advanced occupational training, as well as family connections that pave the way to occupational success.

Psychologists continue to look for better ways to predict academic and job success. Although there is much more research to be done, it seems reasonable that abilities beyond those measured by intelligence tests contribute to success on the job and to success in school. For example, job performance may be better predicted by tests of tacit knowledge—the kind of practical knowledge that people need to be able to perform their jobs effectively. One approach to expanding the usefulness of intelligence testing in schools is to use IQ scores in conjunction with other kinds of information that help interpret what these scores mean. One such approach is the System of Multicultural Pluralistic Adjustment (SOMPA), which involves collecting a wide range of data on a child, such as overall health status and socioeconomic background. This information on the student's characteristics and his or her environment is used to provide a context within which intelligence test scores can be interpreted.

Check Your Understanding

1. Indicate whether the following statements are true (T) or false (F).

   a. _____ Intelligence is synonymous with problem-solving ability.

   b. _____ The early American psychologist L. L. Thurstone maintained that intelligence was quite general and should not be thought of as several distinct abilities.

   c. _____ Intrapersonal intelligence reflects the adage, "Know thyself."

   d. _____ Sternberg's and Gardner's theories of intelligence emphasize practical abilities.

2. In 1916, the Stanford psychologist L. M. Terman introduced the term _____ _____, or _____, and set the score of _____ for a person of average intelligence.

Heredity, Environment, and Intelligence

Is intelligence inherited or is it the product of the environment? Sorting out the importance of each factor as it contributes to intelligence is a complex task.

■ HEREDITY

As Chapter 2: The Biological Basis of Behavior revealed, scientists can use studies of identical twins to measure the effects of heredity in humans. Twin studies of intelligence begin by comparing the IQ scores of identical twins who have been raised together. As Figure 7–7 shows, the correlation between their IQ scores is very high. In addition to identical genes, however, these twins grew up in very similar environments: They shared parents, home, teachers, vacations, and probably friends. These common experiences could explain their similar IQ scores. To check this possibility, researchers have tested identical twins who were separated early in life—generally before they were 6 months old—and raised in different families. As Figure 7–7 shows, even when identical twins are raised in different families, they tend to have very similar test scores; in fact, the similarity is much greater than that between non-twin siblings who grow up in the *same* environment.

These findings make a strong case for the heritability of intelligence. Although, for reasons identified in Chapter 2, twin studies do not constitute "final proof," other evidence also demonstrates the role of heredity. For example, adopted children have been found to have IQ scores that are more similar to those of their biological mothers than to those of the mothers who are raising them. Researcher John Loehlin finds these results particularly interesting because "[they] reflect genetic resemblance in the absence of shared environment: These birth mothers had no contact with their children after the first few days of life" (Loehlin, Horn, & Willerman, 1997, p. 113). Do psychologists, then, conclude that intelligence is an inherited trait and that environment plays little, if any, role?

Heredity

■ Identical twins raised in different families tend to _____

_____

_____

■ Adopted children have IQ scores that are more similar to their _____ mothers than to their _____ mothers.

Environment

■ In impoverished families, heredity _____

■ Development of mental capacities depends on _____,

_____, and

_____

(Continued)

FIGURE 7–7

Correlations of IQ scores and family relationships.

Identical twins who grow up in the same household have IQ scores that are almost identical to each other. Even when they are reared apart, their scores are highly correlated.

Source: Adapted from "Genetics and Intelligence: A Review," by L. Erienmeyer-Kimling and L. F. Jarvik 1963, *Science, 142,* pp. 1477–1479. © 1963 by the American Association for the Advancement of Science. Reprinted with permission of the author.

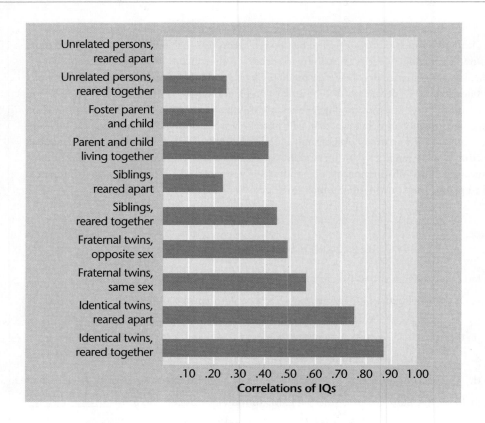

Heredity and Environment

■ Approximately half of the variability in IQ test scores is due to

_____ ; the other half is due to

_____

Mental Abilities and Human Diversity: Gender and Culture

■ Gender differences in mental abilities are _____

■ The achievement gap between American and Asian students is due to

_____

■ ENVIRONMENT

Probably no psychologist denies that genes play a role in determining intelligence, but most believe that genes only provide a base or starting point. All of us inherit a certain body build from our parents, but our actual weight is determined greatly by what we eat and how much we exercise. Similarly, we may inherit certain mental capacities, but their development depends on what we see around us as infants, how our parents respond to our first attempts to talk, what schools we attend, which books we read, which television programs we watch—even what we eat (Sternberg & Grigorenko, 2001). Moreover, recent evidence indicates that the role of heredity varies with social economic status: In impoverished families, heredity appears to have little or no bearing on intelligence; in affluent families, its influence appears to be stronger (Turkheimer, Haley, Waldron, D'Onofrio, & Gottesman, 2003).

Nutrition appears to have a significant effect on measured intelligence. In one study of economically deprived pregnant women, half were given a dietary supplement and half were given placebos. At ages 3 and 4, the children of the mothers who had taken the supplement while pregnant scored significantly higher on intelligence tests than the other children (Harrell, Woodyard, & Gates, 1955). During infancy, malnutrition can lower IQ test scores by an average of 20 points (Stock & Smythe, 1963). Conversely, vitamin supplements can increase young children's IQ test scores, possibly even among well-nourished children (Benton & Roberts, 1988; Schoenthaler, Amos, Eysenck, Peritz, & Yudkin, 1991).

Attention and environmental stimulation also can have a profound effect on intelligence. While investigating orphanages for the state of Iowa, psychologist Harold Skeels observed that the children lived in very overcrowded wards and that the few adults there had almost no time to play with the children, to talk to them, or to read them stories. Many of these children were classified as "subnormal" in intelligence. Skeels followed the cases of two girls who, after 18 months in an orphanage, were sent to a ward for women with severe retardation. Originally, the girls' IQ scores were in the range of retardation, but after a year on the adult ward, as if by magic, their scores had risen to normal (Skeels, 1938). Skeels regarded this fact as quite remarkable—after all, the women with whom the girls had lived were themselves severely retarded. When he placed 13 other "slow" children as houseguests in such adult wards, within 18 months, their mean IQ scores rose from 64 to 92 (within the normal range)—all because they had had someone (even someone of below-normal intelligence) to play with them, to read to them, to cheer them on when they took their first steps, and to encourage them to talk (Skeels, 1942). During the same period, the mean IQ scores of a group of children who had been left in orphanages dropped from 86 to 61. Thirty years later, Skeels found that all 13 of the children raised on adult wards were self-supporting, their occupations ranging from waiting on tables to real-estate sales. Of the contrasting group, half were unemployed, four were still in institutions, and of those who had jobs, all were dishwashers (Skeels, 1966).

■ HEREDITY AND ENVIRONMENT

Heredity and environment have important effects on individual differences in intelligence. But is one of these factors more important than the other? The answer depends on what you are comparing. A useful analogy comes from studies of plants (Turkheimer, 1991). Suppose that you grow one group of randomly assigned plants in enriched soil and another group in poor soil. The enriched group will grow to be taller and stronger than the nonenriched group; the difference between the two groups in this case is entirely the result of differences in their environment. *Within* each group of plants, however, differences among individual plants are likely to be primarily the result of genetics, because all plants in the same group share essentially the same environment. Thus, the height and strength of any single plant reflects heredity *and* environment.

Similarly, group differences in IQ scores might result from environmental factors, but differences among people *within* groups could be caused primarily by genetics. At the same time, the IQ scores of particular people would reflect the effects of heredity *and* environment. Robert Plomin, an influential researcher in the field of human intelligence, concludes that "the world's literature suggests that about half of the total variance in IQ scores can be accounted for by genetic variance" (Plomin, 1997, p. 89). This finding means that environment accounts for the other half. Both heredity and environment contribute to human differences.

■ MENTAL ABILITIES AND HUMAN DIVERSITY: GENDER AND CULTURE

Are there differences in mental abilities between males and females or among people from different cultures? Many people assume, for example, that males are naturally better at mathematics and that females excel in verbal skills. Others believe that the sexes basically are alike in mental abilities. Similarly, how is the superior academic performance by students from certain countries and certain cultural backgrounds accounted for? Research offers some interesting insights into these controversial issues.

Gender   Many occupations are dominated by one gender or the other. Engineering, for example, has traditionally been almost exclusively a male domain. Is it possible that this occupational difference and others like it reflect underlying gender differences in mental abilities?

In 1974, psychologists Eleanor Maccoby and Carol Jacklin published a review of psychological research on gender differences (Maccoby & Jacklin, 1974). They found no differences at all between males and females in most of the studies they examined. However, a few differences did appear in cognitive abilities: Girls tended to display greater verbal ability, and boys tended to exhibit stronger spatial and mathematical abilities. Largely because of this research, gender differences in verbal, spatial, and mathematical abilities became so widely accepted that they were cited often as one of the established facts of psychological research.

Yet, a closer examination of the research literature, including more recent work, indicates that gender differences in math and verbal ability may be virtually nonexistent. For example, Janet Shibley Hyde and her colleagues analyzed 165 research studies, involving more than a million people, in which gender differences in verbal ability were examined. They

Individual differences in intelligence can be explained partly by differences in environmental stimulation and encouragement. The specific forms of stimulation given vary from culture to culture. Because our culture assigns importance to developing academic skills, the stimulation of reading and exploring information in books can give children an edge over those who are not so encouraged.

Research shows there are only negligible differences between men and women in mathematical ability.

concluded that "there are no gender differences in verbal ability, at least at this time, in American culture, in the standard ways that verbal ability has been measured" (Hyde & Linn, 1988, p. 62). In a similar analysis of studies examining mathematical ability, Hyde and her colleagues concluded that "females outperformed males by only a negligible amount . . . . Females are superior in computation, there are no gender differences in understanding of mathematical concepts, and gender differences favoring males do not emerge until the high school years" (Hyde, Fennema, & Lamon, 1990, pp. 139, 151).

Males apparently do have an advantage over females in spatial ability, however. Spatial tasks include mentally rotating an object and estimating horizontal and vertical dimensions. These skills are particularly useful in solving certain engineering, architecture, and geometry problems. They are also handy in deciding how to arrange furniture inside a new apartment or how to fit a load of suitcases into the trunk of a car.

Men also differ from women in another way: They are much more likely than women to fall at the extremes of the intelligence range. In one review of several large studies, Hedges and Nowell (1995) found that males accounted for seven of eight people with extremely high IQ scores. These authors also reported that males represented an almost equally large proportion of the IQ scores within the range of mental retardation.

What can be concluded from these findings? First, the cognitive differences between males and females appear to be restricted to specific cognitive skills. Scores on tests such as the Stanford–Binet or the WAIS reveal no gender differences in general intelligence. Second, gender differences in specific cognitive abilities typically are small and, in some cases, appear to be diminishing. Finally, no one knows whether the differences that do exist result from biological or cultural factors.

Culture   For years, U.S. media have been reporting an achievement gap, especially in math, between American and Asian students. Recent media reports suggest even broader differences. According to one report: "The United States is now behind, or has lost ground, on several important education measures among countries in the OECD, an economic- and social-policy organization of 30 industrialized countries" (Gehring, 2001).

Psychological research reveals something about the causes of these achievement gaps. Two decades ago, a team of researchers led by Harold Stevenson (1925–2005) began to study the performance of first- and fifth-grade children in American, Chinese, and Japanese elementary schools (Stevenson, Lee, & Stigler, 1986). At that time, the American students at both grade levels lagged far behind the other two countries in math and came in second in reading. A decade later, when the study was repeated with a new group of fifth-graders, the researchers discovered that the American students performed even worse than they had earlier. In 1990, the research team also studied the original first-graders from all three cultures, who were now in the eleventh grade. The result? The American students retained their low standing in mathematics compared with the Asian students (Stevenson, 1992, 1993; Stevenson, Chen, & Lee, 1993).

The next question was: Why? Stevenson's team wondered whether cultural attitudes toward ability and effort might, in part, explain the differences. To test this hypothesis, the researchers asked students, their parents, and their teachers in all three countries whether they thought effort or ability had a greater impact on academic performance. From first through eleventh-grade, American students, on the whole, disagreed with the statement that "everyone in my class has about the same natural ability in math." In other words, the Americans thought that "studying hard" has little to do with performance. Their responses appear to reflect a belief that mathematical skill is primarily a function of innate ability. American mothers expressed a similar view. Moreover, 41% of the American eleventh-grade teachers believed that "innate intelligence" was the most important factor in mathematics performance. By contrast, Asian students, parents, and teachers believed that effort and "studying hard" determine success in math.

Such culturally influenced views of the relative importance of effort and innate ability may have profound consequences for the way that children, their parents, and their teachers approach the task of learning. Students who believe that learning is based on natural ability see little value in working hard to learn a difficult subject. By contrast, students who believe that academic success comes from studying are more likely to work hard. Indeed, even the brightest students will not get far without making an effort. Although many Americans no doubt believe in the value of effort and hard work, our widespread perception that innate ability is the key to academic success may be affecting the performance of U.S. students (Stevenson, Lee, & Mu, 2000).

In short, while Stevenson's research confirms the existence of significant differences in student performance across various cultures, the evidence suggests that these differences reflect cultural attitudes toward the importance of ability and effort, rather than an underlying difference in intelligence across the cultures.

■ EXTREMES OF INTELLIGENCE

The average IQ score on intelligence tests is 100. Nearly 70% of all people have IQ scores between 85 and 115, and all but 5% of the population has IQ scores between 70 and 130. The next section focuses on people who score at the two extremes of intelligence—those with mental retardation and those who are intellectually gifted.

Mental Retardation   Mental retardation encompasses a vast array of mental deficits and exhibits a wide variety of causes, treatments, and outcomes. The American Psychiatric Association (1994) defines mental retardation as "significantly subaverage general intellectual functioning . . . that is accompanied by significant limitations in adaptive functioning" and that appears before the age of 21 (p. 39). There are also various degrees of mental retardation. Mild retardation corresponds to Stanford–Binet IQ scores ranging from a high of about 70 to a low near 50. Moderate retardation corresponds to IQ scores from the low 50s to the middle 30s. People with IQ scores between the middle 30s and 20 are considered severely retarded, and the profoundly retarded are those whose scores are below 20 (Table 7–4).

But a low IQ test score is not in itself sufficient for diagnosing mental retardation. The person must also be unable to perform the daily tasks needed to function independently.

Extremes of Intelligence

■ Mental retardation: _____
_____

■ In most cases, causes are _____
■ About 25% of cases can be
traced to _____
■ Mental retardation can be
moderated through _____
■ Giftedness: _____
_____

TABLE 7–4   Levels of Mental Retardation

TYPE OF RETARDATION	IQ RANGE	ATTAINABLE SKILL LEVEL
Mild Retardation	Low 50s to low 70s	People may be able to function adequately in society and learn skills comparable to a sixth-grader, but they need special help at times of unusual stress.
Moderate Retardation	Mid-30s to low 50s	People profit from vocational training and may be able to travel alone. They learn on a second-grade level and perform skilled work in a sheltered workshop under supervision.
Severe Retardation	Low 20s to mid-30s	People do not learn to talk or to practice basic hygiene until after age 6. They cannot learn vocational skills but can perform simple tasks under supervision.
Profound Retardation	Below 20 or 25	Constant care is needed. Usually, people have a diagnosed neurological disorder.

Source: Based on APA, *DSM-IV*, 1994.

Down syndrome is a common biological cause of mental retardation, affecting one in 600 newborns. The prognosis for Down syndrome children today is much better than it was in the past. With adequate support, many children with the affliction can participate in regular classrooms and other childhood activities.

Therefore, to fully assess individuals and to place them in appropriate treatment and educational programs, mental health professionals need information on physical health and on emotional and social adjustment.

Moreover, people with mental retardation sometimes display exceptional skills in areas other than general intelligence. Probably the most dramatic and intriguing examples involve *savant* performance. Some people with mental retardation (or other mental handicaps) exhibit remarkable abilities in highly specialized areas, such as numerical computation, memory, art, or music. Savant performances include mentally calculating large numbers almost instantly, determining the day of the week for any date over many centuries, and playing back a long musical composition after hearing it played only once.

What causes mental retardation? In most cases, the causes are unknown—especially in cases of mild retardation, which account for nearly 90% of all retardation. When causes can be identified, most often they stem from a wide variety of genetic, environmental, social, nutritional, and other risk factors (A. A. Baumeister & Baumeister, 2000).

About 25% of cases—especially the more severe forms of retardation—appear to involve genetic or biological disorders. Scientists have identified more than 100 forms of mental retardation caused by single defective genes (Plomin, 1997). One is the genetically based disease phenylketonuria, or PKU, which occurs in about one person out of 25,000. In people suffering from PKU, the liver fails to produce an enzyme necessary for early brain development. Fortunately, placing a PKU baby on a special diet can prevent mental retardation from developing. Another form of hereditary mental retardation is fragile-X syndrome, which affects about 1 in every 1,250 males and 1 in every 2,500 females. A defect in the X chromosome, passed on between generations, seems to be caused by a specific gene. In the disorder known as Down syndrome (or trisomy 21), which affects 1 in 600 newborns, an extra twenty-first chromosome is the cause. Down syndrome, named for the British physician John Langdon Down (1828–1896) who first described its symptoms, is marked by moderate to severe mental retardation.

Biologically caused mental retardation can be moderated through education and training. The prognosis for those cases that have no underlying physical causes is even better. People whose retardation results from a history of social and educational deprivation may respond dramatically to appropriate interventions. Today, most children with physical or mental disabilities are educated in local school systems, in *inclusion* arrangements (previously known as *mainstreaming*), which help these students to socialize with their nondisabled peers. The principle of mainstreaming has also been applied to adults with mental retardation, by taking them out of large, impersonal institutions and placing them in smaller community homes that provide more normal life experiences.

Giftedness   At the other extreme of the intelligence scale are "the gifted"—those with exceptional mental abilities, as measured by scores on standard intelligence tests. As with mental retardation, the causes of **giftedness** are largely unknown.

In the early 1920s, Lewis Terman and his colleagues began the first, and now classic, study of giftedness. They defined giftedness in terms of academic talent and measured it by an IQ score in the top 2 percentile (Terman, 1925). More recently, some experts have sought to broaden the definition of giftedness to include, in addition to above-average intelligence, things such as exceptional creativity and high levels of commitment (Renzulli, 1978).

A common view of gifted people is that they have poor social skills and are emotionally maladjusted. However, research does not support this stereotype (Richards, Encel, & Shute, 2003; Robinson & Clinkenbeard, 1998). Indeed, one review (Janos & Robinson, 1985) concluded that "being intellectually gifted, at least at moderate levels of ability, is clearly an asset in terms of psychosocial adjustment in most situations" (p. 181). Nevertheless, children who are exceptionally gifted sometimes do experience difficulty "fitting in" with their peers.

ENDURING ISSUES DIVERSITY/UNIVERSALITY

Not Everyone Wants to Be Special

Because gifted children sometimes become bored and socially isolated in regular classrooms, some experts recommend that special programs be offered to them. Special classes for the gifted would seem to be something the gifted themselves would want, but this is not always the case. Special *classes* and, even more, special *schools*, can separate gifted students from their friends and neighbors. And stereotypes about the gifted may mean that, once identified as gifted, the student is less likely to be invited to participate in certain school activities, such as dances, plays, and sports. Gifted students also sometimes object to being set apart, labeled "brains," and pressured to perform beyond the ordinary.

Any discussion of giftedness inevitably leads to the topic of creativity. The two topics are, indeed, closely related, as we shall see in the next section.

Check Your Understanding

1. Indicate whether the following statements are true (T) or false (F).

   a. _____ When identical twins are raised apart, their IQ scores are not highly correlated.

   b. _____ Environmental stimulation has little, if any, effect on IQ.

2. Imagine that an adoption agency separates identical twins at birth and places them randomly in very different kinds of homes. Thirty years later, a researcher discovers that the pairs of twins have almost identical scores on IQ tests. Which of the following conclusions is most consistent with that finding?

   a. Heredity has a significant effect on intelligence.

   b. Environment has a significant effect on intelligence.

   c. Heredity provides a starting point, but environment determines our ultimate intelligence.

   d. Because the twins were placed in very different environments, it is not possible to draw any conclusions.

3. Ten-year-old John has an IQ score of 60 on the Wechsler Intelligence Scale for Children. Which of the following would you need to know before you could determine whether John is mildly retarded?

   a. Whether his score on the Stanford–Binet Intelligence Scale is also below 70

   b. Whether he can perform the daily tasks needed to function independently

   c. Whether he has a genetic defect in the X chromosome

   d. Whether he suffered from malnutrition before birth

Creativity

Creativity is the ability to produce novel and socially valued ideas or objects ranging from philosophy to painting, from music to mousetraps. As seen earlier in this chapter, Sternberg included creativity and insight as important elements in human intelligence. Most IQ tests, however, do not measure creativity, and many researchers would argue that intelligence and creativity are not the same thing. What, then, is the relationship between intelligence and creativity? Are people who score high on IQ tests likely to be more creative than those who score low?

Creativity

■ Creativity: The ability to _____

_____

_____

Intelligence and Creativity

■ A minimum level of intelligence is needed for _____, but above that threshold level, greater intelligence does not necessarily make for

_____

Creativity Tests

■ Creativity tests are difficult to _____

_____

■ The validity of most creativity tests is

_____

■ INTELLIGENCE AND CREATIVITY

Early studies typically found little or no relationship between tests of creativity and tests of intelligence (for example, Getzels & Jackson, 1962; Wing, 1969), but those studies were concerned only with very bright students. Other studies, using people with a wider range of intelligence test scores, have found that creativity and intelligence are indeed linked but only until intelligence test scores reach a certain threshold level. After that, higher intelligence test scores are not associated with higher creativity test scores (Barron, 1963; Yamamoto & Chimbidis, 1966). It makes sense that a certain minimum level of intelligence might be needed for creativity to develop and be expressed, but other factors appear to underlie creativity as well.

■ CREATIVITY TESTS

Measuring creativity poses special problems. Because creativity involves original responses to situations, questions that can be answered as True or False or A or B are not effective measures. Open-ended tests are better. Instead of asking for one predetermined answer to a problem, the examiner asks the test takers to let their imaginations run free. Scores are based on the originality of a person's answers and often on the number of responses, too.

In one such test, the Torrance Test of Creative Thinking, people must explain what is happening in a picture, how the scene came about, and what its consequences are likely to be. In the Christensen–Guilford Test, they are to list as many words containing a given letter as possible, to name things belonging to a certain category (such as liquids that will burn), and to write four-word sentences beginning with the letters RDLS—"Rainy days look sad, Red dogs like soup, Renaissance dramas lack symmetry," and so on. One of the most widely used creativity tests, Sarnoff Mednick's (1962) Remote Associates Test (RAT), asks people to relate three apparently unrelated words. For example, the three stimulus words might be *poke*, *go*, and *molasses*, and one response is to relate them through the word *slow*: "Slowpoke, go slow, slow as molasses." In the newer Wallach and Kogan Creative Battery, people form associative groupings. For instance, children are asked to "name all the round things you can think of" and to find similarities between objects, such as between a *potato* and a *carrot*. Although these tests appear to tap into some of the mental processes associated with creativity, in general, current tests of creativity do not show a high degree of validity (Clapham, 2004; Feldhusen & Goh, 1995), so scores derived from them must be interpreted with caution.

Check Your Understanding

1. You are discussing creativity and intelligence with a friend who says, "Those are two different things. There's no relationship between being intelligent and being creative." Based on what you have learned in this chapter, which of the following would be the most accurate reply?

   a. "You're right. There is no evidence of a relationship between creativity and intelligence."

   b. "You're wrong. The higher a person's intelligence, the more creative he or she is likely to be."

   c. "That's apparently true only among very bright people. For most people, creativity and intelligence tend to go together."

   d. "That's true for people with IQ scores below about 100, but above that point, intelligence and creativity tend to go together."

Chapter Review  www.psychologythecore.com

Building Blocks of Thought

The three most important building blocks of thought are language, images, and concepts. As people think, they use words, sensory "snapshots," and categories that classify things.

Language is a flexible system of symbols that allows people to communicate ideas to others. When we express thoughts as statements, we must conform to our language's rules.

Every language has rules indicating which sounds (or **phonemes**) are part of that particular language, how those sounds can be combined into meaningful units (or **morphemes**), and how those meaningful units can be ordered into phrases and sentences (rules of **grammar**). To communicate an idea, we start with a thought and then choose sounds, words, and phrases that will express the idea clearly. To understand the speech of others, the task is reversed.

Images are mental representations of sensory experiences. Visual images in particular can be powerful aids in thinking about the relationships between things. Picturing things in our mind's eye can sometimes help us solve problems.

Concepts are categories for classifying objects, people, and experiences based on their common elements. Many concepts are "fuzzy," lacking clear-cut boundaries. Therefore, we often use **prototypes**, mental **models** of the most typical examples of a concept, to classify new objects.

Language, Thought, and Culture

According to Benjamin Whorf's **linguistic relativity hypothesis**, the language people speak determines the pattern of their thinking and their view of the world—a position known more generally as **linguistic determinism**. But critics contend that thought and experience can shape and change a language as much as a language can shape and change thought.

Nonhuman Thought and Language

Research indicates that some animals have humanlike cognitive capacities, such as the ability to form concepts and to reason. Apes have demonstrated sophisticated problem-solving skills. However, only chimpanzees and orangutans consistently show signs of self-awareness. Nonhuman animals communicate primarily though **signs**: general or global statements about the animal's current state. Using the distinguishing features of language, which include semantics, displacement, and productivity as criteria, no other species has its own language.

Problem Solving

Interpreting a problem, formulating a strategy, and evaluating progress toward a solution are three general aspects of the problem-solving process. Each in its own way is critical to success at the task.

Problem representation—defining or interpreting the problem—is the first step in problem solving. We must decide whether to view the problem verbally, mathematically, or visually; and to get clues about how to solve it we must categorize it. Some problems require **convergent thinking**, or searching for a single correct solution, while others call for **divergent thinking**, or generating many possible solutions. Representing a problem in an unproductive way can block progress completely.

Selecting a solution strategy and evaluating progress toward the goal are also important steps in the problem-solving process. A solution strategy can range from trial and error, to information retrieval based on similar problems, to a set of step-by-step procedures guaranteed to work (an **algorithm**), to rule-of-thumb approaches known as **heuristics**. An algorithm is often preferable over trial and error because it guarantees a solution and does not waste time. But because we lack algorithms for so many things, heuristics are vital to human problem solving. Some useful heuristics are **hill climbing**, creating **subgoals**, **means-end analysis**, and **working backward**.

A **mental set** is a tendency to perceive and approach a problem in a certain way. Although sets can enable people to draw on past experience to help solve problems, a strong set can also prevent them from using essential new approaches. One set that can seriously hamper problem solving is **functional fixedness**—the tendency to perceive only traditional uses for an object. One way to minimize mental sets is the technique of **brainstorming** in which an individual or group collects numerous ideas and evaluates them only after all possible ideas have been collected.

Decision Making

Decision making is a special kind of problem solving in which all possible solutions or choices are known. The task is not to come up with new solutions, but rather to identify the best one available based on various criteria.

The logical way to make a decision is to rate each available choice in terms of weighted criteria, then to total the ratings for each choice. This approach is called a **compensatory model** because heavily weighted attractive features can compensate for lightly weighted unattractive ones.

Heuristics can save a great deal of time and effort, but they do not always result in the best choices. Errors in judgment may occur based on the **representativeness** heuristic, which involves making decisions based on information that matches our model of the "typical" member of a category. Other examples are overreliance on the **availability** heuristic (making choices based on whatever information we can most easily retrieve from memory, even though it may not be accurate) and the **confirmation bias** (the tendency to seek evidence in support of our existing beliefs and to ignore evidence that contradicts them).

Framing, or the perspective in which a problem is presented, can affect the outcome of a decision. Regardless of whether a decision proves to be good or bad, after we know the outcome there is a tendency to view outcomes as inevitable or predictable and to "correct" our memories so that the decision seems to be a good one (a process known as **hindsight bias**). **Counterfactual thinking** involves revisiting our decisions by considering "what if" alternatives.

Intelligence and Mental Abilities

Psychologists who study **intelligence** explore the nature of intelligence and the ways to measure it. Some theorists believe that intelligence is quite general and that it affects all aspects of cognitive functioning. Thus, people who are bright in one area should be bright in other areas as well. Spearman's view of intelligence is an example of this perspective. Most theorists, however, believe that intelligence is composed of many separate abilities. Thus, a person strong in one area will not necessarily be strong in others. Thurstone's theory is an example of this view, as are Sternberg's **triarchic theory of intelligence** and Gardner's **theory of multiple intelligences**. Goleman's theory of **emotional intelligence** emphasizes skill in social relationships and awareness of others' and one's own emotions.

The Binet–Simon scale, developed in France by Alfred Binet and Théodore Simon, was the first test intended to measure intelligence. Later, it was adapted by Stanford University's L. M. Terman to create the Stanford–Binet Intelligence Scale. Terman also created the term **intelligence quotient (IQ)** to provide a numerical score for intelligence. The **Wechsler Adult Intelligence Scale** and the **Wechsler Intelligence Scale for Children** were the first intelligence tests to yield both a verbal and performance IQ score as well as an overall IQ score. In contrast to these individual intelligence tests, **group tests** of intelligence are administered by one examiner to many people at a time. Alternatives to traditional IQ tests include **performance tests** of mental abilities that exclude the use of language and **culture-fair tests** that reduce cultural bias in a variety of ways.

A good test must be reliable and valid. **Reliability** refers to the ability of a test to produce consistent and stable scores. Often, reliability is determined by splitting a test into two parts and determining whether scores on the two halves are consistent, referred to as **split-half reliability**. Psychologists express reliability in terms of **correlation coefficients**, which measure the relationship between two sets of scores. In general, contemporary intelligence tests are quite reliable. **Validity** is the ability of a test to measure what it has been designed to measure. **Content validity** exists when a test contains an adequate sample of questions relating to the skills or knowledge the test is supposed to measure. **Criterion-related validity** refers to the relationship between test scores and whatever the test is designed to measure. In the case of intelligence, the most common independent measure is academic achievement and intelligence tests do indeed predict school achievement well.

Although the reliability of IQ tests is seldom questioned, their validity is questioned. Critics charge that these tests assess a very limited set of mental skills and that assigning a single score to something as complex as intelligence is simplistic. In addition, most intelligence tests do not take into account cultural differences. Intelligence tests can set up a self-fulfilling prophecy so that students become what their IQ tests say they should be. Finally, although IQ tests tend to predict occupational success and performance on the job after college, the relationship may be the result of factors other than intelligence.

Heredity, Environment, and Intelligence

Although there has been extended debate about the extent to which heredity and environment contribute to intelligence, research generally indicates that approximately 50% of the variability in IQ test scores results from genetics and the other half results from differences in experiences including environmental stimulation, education, and nutrition.

Research indicates that gender differences in mental abilities are virtually nonexistent. Women have a slight advantage over men in the area of mathematical computation, while men have a slight advantage in spatial skills. Men are also more likely than women to fall at the extremes of the intelligence range. There is an achievement gap between American and Asian students, but research indicates that it is not because of genetic differences in intelligence. Rather the gap results from culturally influenced views of the relative importance of effort and innate ability.

The IQ scores of nearly 70% of the population fall between 85 and 115; and all but 5% have IQ scores between 70 and 130. **Mental retardation** and **giftedness** are the two extremes of intelligence. About 25% of cases of mental retardation can be traced to biological causes, including Down syndrome, but causes of the remaining 75% are not fully understood; nor are the causes of giftedness. Gifted people do not necessarily excel in all mental abilities.

Creativity

Creativity is the ability to produce novel and socially valued ideas or objects. It appears that a minimum level of intelligence is needed for creativity, but above that threshold level, higher intelligence does not necessarily make for greater creativity. Apparently, factors other than intelligence contribute to creativity.

By its very nature, creativity is difficult to test. Some tests encourage people to exercise their imagination. Others call for finding relationships between words or objects that initially seem to be unrelated. However, the validity of most creativity tests is not particularly high.

Chapter 8
Motivation and Emotion

Go to *The Core Online* at **www.psychologythecore.com** to get the most up-to-date information for your introductory psychology course. The content online is an important part of what you are learning—the content there can help prepare you for your test! It includes up-to-date examples, simulations, video clips, and practice quizzes. Also be sure to check out the *Blog* to hear directly from the authors on what current events and latest research are most relevant to your course materials.

The first time you log in, you will need the access code packaged with your textbook. If you do not have a code, please go to **www.mypearsonstore.com** and enter the ISBN of your textbook (**0-13-603344-X**) to purchase the code.

8 1 Perspectives on Motivation

Motive: A specific need or desire that arouses the organism and directs its behavior toward a goal

Instincts
- **Instincts**: Specific, inborn behavior patterns characteristic of an entire species
- Early explanation for all motivated behavior, no longer accepted

Drive-Reduction Theory
- **Drive-reduction theory** holds that motivated behavior is an attempt to reduce an unpleasant state of tension in the body (**drive**) and return the body to a state of balance (**homeostasis**).
- **Primary drives**: Unlearned motives found in all animals
- **Secondary drives**: Motives acquired through learning

Arousal Theory
- **Arousal theory** holds that behavior is motivated by the desire to maintain an optimum level of arousal.

Intrinsic and Extrinsic Motivation
- **Intrinsic motivation**: Motivation provided by an activity itself
- **Extrinsic motivation**: Motivation that derives from the consequences of an activity

A Hierarchy of Motives
- According to Maslow, motives can be arranged in a **hierarchy of needs** from lower to higher.
- Higher motives emerge only after more basic needs have been largely satisfied.

8 2 Hunger and Thirst

Biological and Environmental Factors
- Hunger is regulated by several centers within the brain that monitor levels of **glucose**, fats, carbohydrates, **insulin**, **leptin**, and **ghrelin**.
- Thirst is controlled by two regulators that monitor the level of fluids inside and outside the cells.
- Hunger and thirst can be triggered by environmental cues (**incentives**).

Eating Disorders and Obesity
- Eating disorders include **anorexia nervosa** and **bulimia nervosa**.
- **Body mass index (BMI)** can be used to determine the risk of diseases associated with obesity.
- **Set point theory** holds that our bodies are genetically set to maintain a target weight.

8 3 Sex

Biological Factors
- Hormones (**testosterone**) and pheromones are important in nonhuman sexual motivation, but less important in human sexual motivation.
- The human **sexual response cycle** has four phases: excitement, plateau, orgasm, and resolution.

Cultural and Environmental Factors
- Human sexual motivation depends more on experience and learning than on biology.
- Culture also influences sexual attractiveness.

Patterns of Sexual Behavior Among Americans
- Most Americans are conservative in their sex lives.

Sexual Orientation
- **Sexual orientation**: Direction of an individual's sexual interest—heterosexual, homosexual, or bisexual
- Sexual orientation is determined by genetic and environmental factors.

8 4 Other Important Motives

Contact
- The importance of physical contact has been demonstrated in nonhuman primates and premature human infants.

Aggression
- **Aggression**: Any behavior intended to inflict physical or psychological harm on others
- According to Freud, aggression is an innate drive that builds up until it is released.
- Others believe it is an unlearned instinct triggered by pain or frustration.
- Most psychologists today believe that it is a learned motive that is greatly affected by experience and by culture.

Achievement
- **Achievement motive**: Desire for achievement for its own sake

Affiliation
- **Affiliation motive**: Desire to be around other people

8 5 Emotions

Emotion: The experience of feelings such as fear, joy, surprise, and anger

Basic Emotions
- Primary emotions: Evident in all cultures, contribute to survival, associated with distinct facial expressions, and evident in nonhuman primates; basic emotions include fear, anger, and pleasure, possibly also disgust, sadness, surprise, and love
- Secondary emotions: Not found in all cultures

Theories of Emotion
- The **James-Lange theory** holds that stimuli cause biological changes that cause emotions.
- The **Cannon-Bard theory** holds that stimuli simultaneously cause biological changes and emotions.
- The **Cognitive theory** holds that stimuli cause biological changes that are interpreted, then an appropriate emotion is experienced.
- Izard's theory holds that situations trigger unlearned facial movement and body postures that, in turn, give rise to emotional experiences.

8 6 Communicating Emotion

Voice Quality and Facial Expression
- Some emotional expression is verbal, but much more is conveyed in facial expressions.

Body Language, Personal Space, and Gestures
- Body language, personal space, gestures, and explicit acts can also be used to express emotions.

Gender and Emotion
- Women are more likely than men to express emotions and seek help in dealing with emotional issues.
- Men and women also often react to the same situation with very different emotions.
- Women are better than men at interpreting emotions in others.

Culture and Emotion
- At least some emotional expressions are inborn and universal.
- Other emotional expressions are influenced by language, familiarity, majority or minority status within a culture, cultural learning, and expressive style, among others.
- **Display rules**: Culturally determined rules concernng the circumstances under which emotions should be expressed.

Classic detective stories are usually studies of motivation and emotion. At the beginning, all anyone knows is that a murder has been committed: After eating dinner with her family, sweet old Amanda Jones collapses and dies of strychnine poisoning. "Now, why would anyone do a thing like that?" everybody wonders. The police ask the same question, in different terms: "Who had a motive for killing Miss Jones?" In a good mystery, the answer is "Practically everybody."

There is, for example, the younger sister—although she is 75 years old, she still bristles when she thinks of that tragic day 50 years ago when Amanda stole her sweetheart. And there is the next-door neighbor, who was heard saying that if Miss Jones's poodle trampled his peonies one more time, there would be consequences. Then, there is the spendthrift nephew who stands to inherit a fortune from the deceased. Finally, the parlor maid has a guilty secret that Miss Jones knew and had threatened to reveal. All four suspects were in the house on the night of the murder, had access to the poison (which was used to kill rats in the basement), and had strong feelings about Amanda Jones. All of them had a motive for killing her.

In this story, motivation and emotion are so closely intertwined that drawing distinctions between them is difficult. However, psychologists do try to separate them. A **motive** is a specific need or desire that arouses the organism and directs its behavior toward a goal. All motives are triggered by some kind of stimulus: a bodily condition (such as low levels of blood sugar or dehydration), a cue in the environment (such as a sale sign), or a feeling (such as loneliness, guilt, or anger). When a stimulus induces goal-directed behavior, it has motivated the person.

Emotion refers to the experience of feelings such as fear, joy, surprise, and anger. Like motives, emotions also activate and affect behavior, but predicting the kind of behavior that a particular emotion will prompt is difficult. If a man is hungry, for example, it is reasonable to assume that he will seek food. If, however, the man experiences a feeling of joy or surprise, it cannot be known with certainty how he will act.

The important thing to remember about motives and emotions is that they push people to take some kind of action—from an act as drastic as murder to a habit as mundane as drumming fingers on a table when one is nervous. Motivation occurs whether or not we are aware of it. People do not need to think about feeling hungry to make a beeline for the refrigerator or to focus on their need for achievement to study for an exam. Similarly, they do not have to recognize consciously that they are afraid before stepping back from a growling dog or to know that they are angry before raising their voice at someone. Moreover, the same motivation or emotion may produce different behaviors in different people. Ambition might motivate one person to go to law school and another to join a crime ring. Feeling sad might lead one person to cry alone and another to seek out a friend. On the other hand, the same behavior might arise from different motives or emotions: You may go to a movie because you are happy, bored, or lonely. In short, the workings of motives and emotions are very complex.

This chapter first examines some specific motives that play important roles in human behavior. It then addresses emotions and the various ways they are expressed.

ENDURING ISSUES in Motivation and Emotion

Motives and emotions affect behavior and, in turn, are affected by the external environment (person–situation). In addition to covering these key issues, this chapter will explore the question of whether sexual orientation is inborn or acquired (nature–nurture) and will consider the extent to which individuals differ in their motives and emotions (diversity–universality), including the ways in which motives and emotions arise from and, in turn, affect biological processes (mind–body).

Perspectives on Motivation
■ INSTINCTS

Early in the twentieth century, psychologists generally attributed motivated behavior to **instincts**—specific, inborn behavior patterns characteristic of an entire species. Just as instincts motivate salmon to swim upstream to spawn and spiders to spin webs, instincts were thought to explain much of human behavior. In 1890, William James compiled a list of human instincts that included hunting, rivalry, fear, curiosity, shyness, love, shame, and resentment. Thirty years later, after thousands of human instincts had been identified, instinct theory began to fall out of favor for several reasons: (1) Most important human behavior is learned; (2) human behavior is rarely rigid, inflexible, unchanging, and found throughout the species, as is the case with instincts; and (3) ascribing every conceivable human behavior to a corresponding instinct explains nothing (calling a person's propensity to be alone an "antisocial instinct," for example, merely names the behavior without pinpointing its origins). After World War I, psychologists started looking for more credible explanations of human behavior.

■ DRIVE-REDUCTION THEORY

An alternative view of motivation holds that bodily needs (such as the need for food or the need for water) create a state of tension or arousal called a **drive** (such as hunger or thirst). According to **drive-reduction theory**, motivated behavior is an attempt to reduce this unpleasant state of tension in the body and to return the body to a state of **homeostasis**, or balance. When people are hungry, they look for food to reduce the hunger drive. When they are tired, they find a place to rest. When they are thirsty, they find something to drink. In each of these cases, behavior is directed toward reducing a state of bodily tension or arousal.

ENDURING ISSUES   NATURE/NURTURE

Primary and Secondary Drives

According to drive-reduction theory, drives can be divided into two general categories. **Primary drives** are unlearned and are found in all animals (including humans). Also, they motivate behavior that is vital to the survival of the individual or species. Primary drives include hunger, thirst, and sex. **Secondary drives** are acquired through learning. For example, no one is born with a drive to acquire great wealth, yet many people are driven to acquire money. Other secondary drives include getting good grades in school and enjoying a successful career.

■ AROUSAL THEORY

Drive-reduction theory is appealing, but it cannot explain all kinds of behavior. For example, when people are bored, they may seek out activities that actually *increase* tension and arousal. They will go to horror movies, jog, skydive, and take on all kinds of new challenges. To others, it can be difficult to see how these motivated behaviors reduce states of arousal.

Arousal theory suggests that individuals have an optimum level of arousal that varies over the course of the day. According to this theory, behavior is motivated by the desire to maintain an optimum level of arousal. Sometimes, behavior seems to be motivated by a desire to reduce the state of arousal. For example, when you are sleepy, you are likely to turn off the

---

Perspectives on Motivation
- Motive: _____
_____

Instincts
- Instincts: _____
- Early explanation for all _____

Drive-Reduction Theory
- Drive-reduction theory holds that _____
- Primary drives: _____
- Secondary drives: _____

Arousal Theory
- Arousal theory holds that behavior is motivated by _____

Intrinsic and Extrinsic Motivation
- Intrinsic motivation: _____
- Extrinsic motivation: _____

A Hierarchy of Motives
- According to Maslow, motives can be arranged in a _____
- Higher motives emerge only_____
_____

television and turn off the light. Other times, behavior appears to be motivated by a desire to increase the state of arousal. For example, when you are bored, you may turn on the television, take a walk, or call a friend.

Arousal theory has some advantages over drive-reduction theory, but neither one can readily account for some kinds of behavior. For example, many people today participate in activities that are stimulating in the extreme: rock climbing, skydiving, bungee jumping, and hang gliding. Such thrill-seeking activities do not seem to be drive-reducing and do not seem to be done in pursuit of an optimal level of arousal. Zuckerman (1979, 1994, 2000, 2005) accounts for such activities by suggesting that *sensation seeking* is itself a basic motivation, at least some aspects of which are inherited and neurologically based.

■ INTRINSIC AND EXTRINSIC MOTIVATION

Some psychologists further distinguish between intrinsic and extrinsic motivation. **Intrinsic motivation** refers to motivation provided by an activity itself. Play is a good example. Children typically climb trees, finger paint, and play games for no other reason than the fun they get from the activity itself. In the same way, many adults solve crossword puzzles, play golf, and tinker in a workshop largely for the enjoyment they get from the activity. **Extrinsic motivation** refers to motivation that derives from the consequences of an activity. For example, a child may do chores not because he enjoys them but because doing so earns an allowance, and an adult who hates golf may play a round with a client because doing so may help close a sale.

Whether behavior is intrinsically or extrinsically motivated can have important consequences. For example, if parents offer a reward to their young daughter for writing to her grandparents, the likelihood of her writing to them when rewards are no longer available may actually decrease. One analysis of some 128 studies that examined the effect of extrinsic rewards on the behavior of children, adolescents, and adults found that when extrinsic rewards are offered for a behavior, intrinsic motivation and sense of personal responsibility for that behavior are likely to decrease, at least for a short time (Deci, Koestner, & Ryan, 1999, 2001). However, unexpected (as opposed to contractual) rewards do not necessarily reduce intrinsic motivation, and positive feedback (including praise) may actually increase intrinsic motivation (Chance, 1992; Deci et al., 1999; Reiss, 2005).

■ A HIERARCHY OF MOTIVES

Humanistic psychologist Abraham Maslow (1908–1970) arranged motives in a hierarchy, from lower to higher (Maslow, 1954). The lower motives spring from physiological needs that must be satisfied. As one moves higher in Maslow's **hierarchy of needs**, the motives have more subtle origins: the desire to live as safely as possible, to connect meaningfully with other human beings, and to make the best possible impression on others. Maslow believed that the highest motive in the hierarchy is self-actualization—the drive to realize one's full potential. Maslow's hierarchy of motives is illustrated in Figure 8–1. According to Maslow's theory, higher motives emerge only after the more basic ones have been largely satisfied: A person who is starving does not care what people think of her table manners.

Research has challenged the universality of Maslow's model. Maslow's thinking was influenced heavily by observations of historical figures, famous living individuals, and even friends whom he greatly admired. However, most of these people were white males living in Western society. In many simpler societies, people often live on the very edge of survival, yet they form strong and meaningful social ties and possess a firm sense of self-esteem (Neher, 1991; Wubbolding, 2005). In fact, difficulty in meeting basic needs can actually foster the satisfaction of higher needs: A couple struggling financially to raise a family may grow closer as a result of the experience. Because of this, many psychologists now view Maslow's model with a measure of skepticism, although it continues to offer an appealing way to organize the wide range of human motives into a coherent structure.

With these basic concepts in mind, let's turn our attention to specific motives.

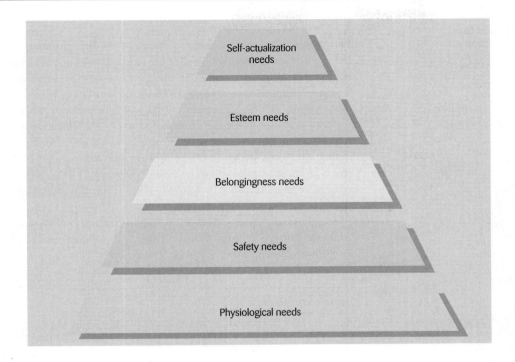

FIGURE **8–1**

A pyramid representing Maslow's hierarchy of needs.
From bottom to top, the stages correspond to how fundamental the motive is for survival and how early it appears in both the evolution of the species and the development of the individual. According to Maslow, the more basic needs must largely be satisfied before higher motives can emerge.

Source: After A. H. Maslow (1954). *Motivation and personality.* New York: Harper & Row.

Check Your Understanding

Match the following terms with the appropriate definitions.

_____ Drive

_____ Drive reduction

_____ Homeostasis

_____ Self-actualization

_____ Intrinsic motivation

_____ Extrinsic motivation

a. Drive to realize one's full potential

b. State of balance in which the organism functions effectively

c. Theory that motivated behavior is focused on reducing bodily tension

d. Tending to perform behavior to receive some external reward or avoid punishment

e. State of tension brought on by biological needs

f. Motivation arising from behavior itself

Hunger and Thirst

When you are hungry, you eat. If you do not eat, your need for food will continue to increase, but your hunger may not. Suppose that you decide to skip lunch to study at the library. Your need for food will increase throughout the day, but your hunger will come and go. You will probably be hungry around lunchtime; then, your hunger will likely abate while you are at the library. By dinnertime, no concern will seem as pressing as eating. The psychological state of hunger, then, is not the same as the biological need for food, although that need often sets the psychological state in motion.

Internally, thirst is controlled by two regulators that monitor the level of fluids inside and outside the cells. These regulators stimulate thirst when fluid levels are too low. But as with hunger, the psychological state of being thirsty is not necessarily the same as the biological need for water. In summertime, managers of grocery stores often place coolers full of ice cold soft drinks near the checkout lanes as gentle "reminders" that shoppers might want to have a drink. And in extremely hot climates, people are reminded to drink lots of water to meet biological needs even if they do not feel particularly thirsty.

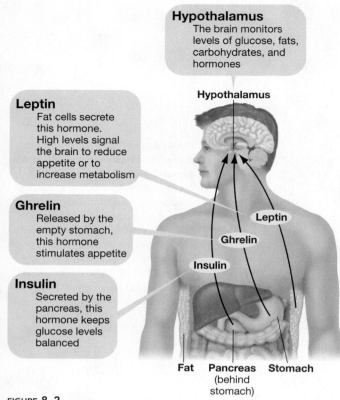

Hypothalamus
The brain monitors levels of glucose, fats, carbohydrates, and hormones

Hypothalamus

Leptin
Fat cells secrete this hormone. High levels signal the brain to reduce appetite or to increase metabolism

Ghrelin
Released by the empty stomach, this hormone stimulates appetite

Insulin
Secreted by the pancreas, this hormone keeps glucose levels balanced

Leptin

Ghrelin

Insulin

Fat Pancreas Stomach
(behind stomach)

FIGURE 8–2
Physiological factors regulating appetite and body weight.
A variety of chemical messengers interact to stimulate and suppress appetite. Among these are insulin, leptin, and ghrelin.

Biological and Environmental Factors

■ Hunger is regulated by several centers within the brain that monitor levels of _____, _____, _____, _____, _____, and _____.

■ Thirst is controlled by _____
_____

■ Hunger and thirst can be triggered by _____ (incentives).

Eating Disorders and Obesity

■ Eating disorders include _____ and _____.

■ _____ can be used to determine the risk of diseases associated with obesity.

■ Set point theory holds that _____
_____

■ BIOLOGICAL AND ENVIRONMENTAL FACTORS

Early research established the importance of the hypothalamus as the brain center involved in hunger and eating. Initially, researchers identified two regions in the hypothalamus that appeared to control hunger. One center seemed to turn on eating while the other turned it off. Subsequent research challenged this simple "on-off" explanation for the control of eating by showing that numerous other areas of the brain are also involved (Hinton et al., 2004). Moreover, the connections among brain centers that control hunger are now known to be considerably more complex than were once thought (Flier & Maratos-Flier, 1998; Woods, Seeley, Porte, & Schwartz, 1998).

How do these various areas of the brain know when to stimulate hunger? It turns out that the brain monitors the blood levels of **glucose** (a simple sugar used by the body for energy), fats, and carbohydrates, as well as the hormones **insulin** and **leptin** (Figure 8–2). Changes in the blood levels of these substances signal the need for food.

The brain also monitors the amount of food you have eaten. Specialized cells in the stomach and the upper part of the small intestine sense the volume of food in the digestive system. When only a small quantity of food is present, these cells release a hormone called **ghrelin** into the bloodstream, which travels to the brain where it stimulates appetite and focuses our thoughts and imagination on food.

■ EATING DISORDERS AND OBESITY

Anorexia Nervosa and Bulimia Nervosa "When people told me I looked like someone from Auschwitz [the Nazi concentration camp], I thought that was the highest compliment anyone could give me." This confession comes from a young woman who as a teenager suffered from a serious eating disorder known as **anorexia nervosa.** She was 18 years old, stood 5 feet 3 inches tall, and weighed 68 pounds. This young woman was lucky. She managed to overcome the disorder and has since maintained normal body weight. Many others are less fortunate.

The following four symptoms are considered in the diagnosis of anorexia nervosa (American Psychiatric Association, 2000):

1. Intense fear of becoming obese, which does not diminish as weight loss progresses
2. Disturbance of body image (for example, claiming to "feel fat" even when emaciated)
3. Refusal to maintain body weight at or above a minimum normal weight for age and height
4. In females, the absence of at least three consecutive menstrual cycles

Anorexia is frequently compounded by another eating disorder known as **bulimia nervosa.** The following criteria are used for its diagnosis (American Psychiatric Association, 2000):

1. Recurrent episodes of binge eating (rapid consumption of a large amount of food, usually in less than 2 hours)
2. Recurrent inappropriate behaviors to try to prevent weight gain, such as self-induced vomiting
3. Binge eating and compensatory behaviors occurring at least twice a week for three months
4. Body shape and weight excessively influencing the person's self-image
5. Occurrence of the just-mentioned behaviors at least sometimes in the absence of anorexia

Because anorexia and bulimia are much more prevalent among females than males, research into the causes of these eating disorders has focused primarily on women. Among adolescent women, several factors appear likely to contribute to eating disorders. On one hand, the

ENDURING ISSUES | **PERSON/SITUATION**

Control of Hunger and Thirst

As noted earlier, a biological need for food or water does not always result in hunger or thirst. The sensation of hunger is the product not only of things going on in the body, but also of things going on outside the body. The smell of a cake baking in the oven, for example, may trigger the desire to eat whether the body needs fuel or not. Sometimes just looking at the clock and realizing that it is dinner-time can make people feel hungry. In fact, people tend to eat more when they are with others, especially when the others are eating a lot (Herman, Roth, & Polivy, 2003). One intriguing line of research suggests that such external cues may set off internal biological processes that mimic those associated with the need for food. For example, the mere sight, smell, or thought of food causes an increase in insulin production, which, in turn, lowers glucose levels in the body's cells, mirroring the body's response to a physical need for food. Thus, the aroma from a nearby restaurant may serve as more than an **incentive** to eat; it may actually trigger an apparent need for food. Similarly, numerous studies with humans and nonhuman animals have shown that regularly eating at particular times during the day leads to the release at those times of the hormones and neurotransmitters that cause hunger (Woods, Schwartz, Baskin, & Seeley, 2000). In other words, when a person regularly gets hungry around noon, it is partly because the body has "learned" that noon is the time to eat.

Just as people can become hungry in response to external cues, the experience of thirst can also be affected by environmental factors. We may get thirsty when we see a TV commercial featuring people savoring tall, cool drinks in a lush, tropical setting. Seasonal customs and weather conditions also affect our thirst-quenching habits: Ice-cold lemonade is a summer staple, whereas hot chocolate warms us on cold winter nights.

Thus, the psychological experiences of hunger and thirst are the products of complex interactions between biological processes and environmental cues.

How and when you satisfy hunger and thirst depends on social, psychological, environmental, and cultural influences as well as on physiological needs. For example, the Japanese tea ceremony (*below*) is concerned more with restoring inner harmony than with satisfying thirst. Do you think the office worker (*right*) is drinking coffee because she is thirsty?

BMI	Weight Status
Below 18.5	Underweight
18.5 – 24.9	Normal
25.0 – 29.9	Overweight
30.0 and above	Obese

FIGURE 8–3
Body Mass Index.
The standard weight status categories associated with BMI ranges for adults.

mass media promote the idea that females must be thin to be attractive. In addition, females with bulimia commonly have low self-esteem, are hypersensitive to social interactions, and are more likely to come from families where negative comments are often made about weight. Many also display clinical depression or obsessive–compulsive disorder (see Chapter 12: Psychological Disorders) and engage or have engaged in self-injurious behaviors such as cutting themselves. Finally, growing evidence suggests that genetics plays a role in anorexia nervosa and bulimia nervosa among men and women, although the two eating disorders may have a very different genetic basis (Jacobi, Hayward, de Zwaan, Kraemer, & Agras, 2004; Keel & Klump, 2003).

Anorexia and bulimia are notoriously hard to treat. In fact, some psychologists doubt that these eating disorders will ever be eradicated in a culture that bombards its population with the message that "thin is in." Regrettably, in many developing countries such as Taiwan, Singapore, and China, where dieting is becoming a fad, eating disorders, once little known, are now becoming a serious problem (Hsu, 1996; Lee, Chan, & Hsu, 2003).

Obesity and Weight Control   Arguably, obesity is the most pressing health problem in America: More than two thirds of Americans are either overweight or obese. *Obesity* refers to an excess of body fat in relation to lean body mass, while *overweight* refers to weighing more than a desirable standard, whether from high amounts of fat or being very muscular. One screening tool used to identify weight issues is **body mass index (BMI)**, a numerical index calculated from a person's height and weight that is used to indicate health status and predict disease risk (Figure 8–3). Body mass index is correlated with body fat, although variations exist by sex, race, and age. Elevated BMI is associated with increased risk for hypertension, stroke, coronary heart disease, Type II diabetes, and sleep apnea, among other conditions. Calculate your BMI by using the following formula:

$$\text{BMI} = 703 \times \text{weight(lb)}/\text{height(in)}^2$$

BMI is not applicable to everyone, however. For example, competitive athletes often have a high BMI because of their large proportion of muscle mass.

Adding to the medical difficulties accompanying obesity, overweight people often face ridicule and discrimination resulting in significant economic, social, and educational loss (D. Carr & Friedman, 2005; Maranto & Stenoien, 2000). Despite federal laws prohibiting employment bias against overweight people, studies show discrimination is still a problem. For example, overweight women have reported lowered self-confidence owing to victimization in school and at work because of their weight (C. Johnson, 2002; Rothblum, Brand, Miller, & Oetjen, 1990). Obese male lawyers earn less than male lawyers of normal weight (Saporta & Halpern, 2002). Even children who are overweight display increased rates of behavior problems, including aggression, lack of discipline, immaturity, anxiety, and depression when compared with their peers of "normal" weight (Yang & Chen, 2001).

Many factors contribute to overeating and obesity. Some people inherit a tendency to be overweight: Children born to two obese parents are seven times more likely to become obese than children born to parents of normal weight. A sedentary lifestyle contributes to the problem as do the abundant opportunities to overeat in American culture. Moreover, it appears that our bodies are genetically "set" to maintain a certain weight (Hallschmid, Benedict, Born, Fehm, & Kern, 2004; Wade, 2004). According to this **set point theory**, if a person consumes more calories than needed for that weight, the person's metabolic rate will increase and he or she will feel an increase in energy that will prompt a desire for greater activity, thereby burning more calories. If, however, one eats fewer calories than needed to maintain current weight, metabolic rate will decrease and the person will feel tired and become less active, thereby burning fewer calories. This mechanism was no doubt helpful during the thousands of years that our species lived literally hand to mouth, but it is less helpful in places where food is abundant, as is the case in modern industrialized nations.

Given these multiple contributors to obesity, it is understandable that no quick fixes to weight loss exist. Any successful weight-control program must be long term and must work with, rather than against, the body's normal tendency to maintain weight. Such a program should be undertaken only after consultation with a doctor.

Check Your Understanding

1. You are on your way to a play, and you notice that you are hungry. While you are watching the play, you no longer feel hungry. But when the play is over, you notice that you are hungry again. This demonstrates that

   a. The biological need for food causes hunger.

   b. If you are distracted, primary drives (but not secondary drives) will decrease.

   c. Hunger does not necessarily correspond to a biological need for food.

   d. Primary drives are unlearned and are essential to survival of the individual or species.

2. You've noticed that when you are hungry, eating a carrot does not satisfy you, but eating a chocolate bar does. This is probably because the chocolate bar, to a greater extent than the carrot

   a. Increases the amount of glucose in your bloodstream, which in turn reduces hunger

   b. Reduces your biological need for food

   c. Is an extrinsic motivator

   d. Serves as an incentive

Sex

Sex is the primary drive that motivates reproductive behavior. Like the other primary drives, it can be turned on and off by biological conditions in the body and by environmental cues. The human sexual response is affected also by social experience, sexual experience, nutrition, emotions (particularly feelings about one's sex partner), and age. In fact, just thinking about, viewing, or having fantasies about sex can lead to sexual arousal in humans. Sex differs from other primary drives in one important way: Hunger and thirst are vital to the survival of the individual, but sex is vital only to the survival of the species.

■ BIOLOGICAL FACTORS

Biology clearly plays a major role in sexual motivation, but the exact details are less clear than one might expect. In part, this is because sexual activity in lower animals is controlled largely by hormones and the female's reproductive cycle. At one time, the level of hormones such as **testosterone**—the male sex hormone—was believed to determine human sexual motivation as well. Today, scientists recognize that hormonal influences on human sexual arousal are considerably more complex and much less powerful than in nonhumans. For example, moment-to-moment fluctuations in testosterone levels are not closely linked to sex drive in humans. In fact, adult males who have been castrated (resulting in a significant decrease in testosterone levels) often report little decrease in sex drive (Persky, 1983).

In addition, many animals secrete substances called *pheromones* that promote sexual readiness in potential partners (refer to Chapter 3: Sensation and Perception). There is some indirect evidence that humans, too, may secrete pheromones in the sweat glands of the armpits and in the genitals. But here too the effect on human sexual motivation is much more mild and subtle than in nonhumans.

The brain clearly exerts a powerful influence on the sex drive in humans and nonhumans. In particular, the limbic system, located deep within the brain, appears to play an especially important role in sexual excitement (see Chapter 2: The Biological Basis of Behavior). But research on the role of the limbic system in human sexuality is necessarily quite limited by ethical concerns.

The result is that the biology of sexual behavior is better understood than that of the sex drive itself. Sex researchers William Masters (1915–2001) and Virginia Johnson long ago

Biological Factors

■ _____ and _____ are important in nonhuman sexual motivation, but less important in human sexual motivation.

■ The human sexual response cycle has four phases: _____, _____, _____, and _____.

Cultural and Environmental Factors

■ Human sexual motivation depends more on _____ and _____ than on _____.

■ _____ also influences sexual attractiveness.

Patterns of Sexual Behavior Among Americans

■ Most Americans are_____ in their sex lives.

Sexual Orientation

■ Sexual orientation: _____

■ Sexual orientation is determined by _____ and _____ factors.

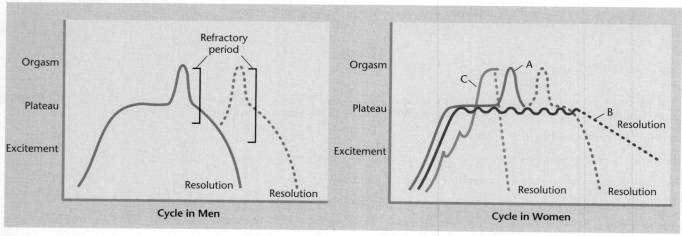

FIGURE 8–4

The sexual response cycle in males and females.

As the illustration shows, males typically go through one complete response cycle and are then capable of becoming excited again after a refractory period. Females have three characteristic patterns: one similar to the male cycle, with the added possibility of multiple orgasms (A); one that includes a lengthy plateau phase with no orgasm (B); and a rapid cycle including several increases and decreases of excitement before reaching orgasm (C).

Source: Adapted from Masters & Johnson, 1966. Reprinted by permission of The Masters and Johnson Institute.

identified a **sexual response cycle** that consists of four phases: excitement, plateau, orgasm, and resolution (Masters & Johnson, 1966). In the *excitement phase,* the genitals become engorged with blood. In the male, this causes erection of the penis; in the female, it causes erection of the clitoris and nipples. This engorgement of the sexual organs continues into the *plateau phase,* in which sexual tension levels off. During this phase, breathing becomes more rapid and genital secretions and muscle tension increase. During *orgasm,* the male ejaculates and the woman's uterus contracts rhythmically; and both men and women experience some loss of muscle control. Following orgasm, males experience a *refractory period,* which can last from a few minutes to several hours, during which time they cannot have another orgasm. Women do not have a refractory period, and, if stimulation is reinitiated, may experience another orgasm almost immediately. The *resolution phase* is one of relaxation, in which muscle tension decreases and the engorged genitals return to normal. Heart rate, breathing, and blood pressure also return to normal. Figure 8–4 displays the pattern of sexual responses for men and women.

■ CULTURAL AND ENVIRONMENTAL FACTORS

Although hormones and the nervous system do figure in the sex drive, human sexual motivation, especially in the early stages of excitement and arousal, depends much more on experience and learning than on biology.

What kind of stimuli activates the sex drive? It need not be anything as immediate as a sexual partner. The sight of one's lover, as well as the smell of perfume or aftershave lotion, can stimulate sexual excitement. Soft lights and music often have an aphrodisiacal effect. One person may be unmoved by an explicit pornographic movie but aroused by a romantic love story, whereas another may respond in just the opposite way. Ideas about what is moral, appropriate, and pleasurable also influence human sexual behavior. Finally, as shown in Figure 8–5, one global survey of reported sexual activity indicated the rate at which couples have sex varies dramatically around the world (Durex Global Sex Survey, 2005). This survey also revealed that the frequency of sexual activity varies by age, with 35- to 44-year-olds reportedly having sex an average of 112 times a year, 25- to 34-year-olds having sex an average of 108 times per year, and 16- to 20-year-olds having sex 90 times a year.

Just as society dictates standards for sexual conduct, culture guides our views of sexual attractiveness. Culture and experience may influence the extent to which people find particular articles of clothing or body shapes sexually arousing. In some cultures, most men prefer women with very large breasts, but in other cultures, small and delicate breasts are preferred. Among some African cultures, elongated earlobes are considered very attractive. In many Western cultures, attractiveness often depends on the styles of the time.

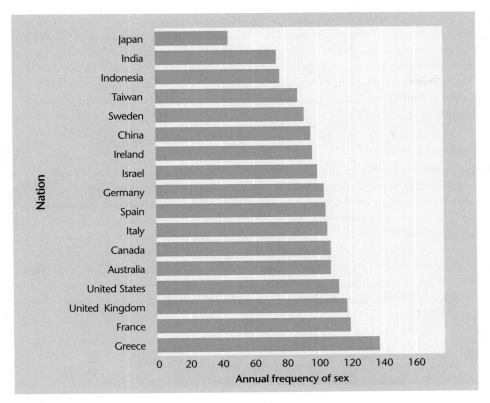

FIGURE 8–5
Frequency (annual) of sexual behavior around the world.
A global survey of reported sexual activity indicates the frequency that couples have sex varies dramatically by country.
Source: http://www.durex.com/cm/gss2005result.pdf

■ PATTERNS OF SEXUAL BEHAVIOR AMONG AMERICANS

Contrary to portrayals in the media that often depict Americans as oversexed and unwilling to commit to long-term relationships, research indicates that most people are far more conservative in their sex lives. One carefully designed study (Michael, Gagnon, Laumann, & Kolata, 1994) of 3,432 randomly selected people between the ages of 18 and 59 revealed the following patterns in the sexual activity of American men and women:

- About one third of those sampled had sex twice a week or more, one third had sex a few times a month, and the remaining third had sex a few times a year or not at all.

- The overwhelming majority of respondents did not engage in kinky sex. Instead, vaginal intercourse was the preferred form of sex for more than 90% of those sampled. Watching their partner undress was ranked second, and oral sex, third.

- Married couples reported having sex more often—and being more satisfied with their sex lives—than did unmarried persons.

- The average duration of sexual intercourse reported by most people was approximately 15 minutes.

- The median number of partners over the lifetime for males was 6 and for females 2 (17% of the men and 3% of the women reported having sex with more than 20 partners).

- About 25% of the men and 15% of the women had committed adultery.

Do his elongated earlobes and other bodily adornments enhance this young man's sexual attractiveness? It all depends on your cultural point of view. In the Samburu society of Kenya in which he lives, these particular adornments are considered highly attractive.

Homosexual activity is common among animals. For example, male giraffes often engage in extreme necking, entwining, and rubbing, becoming sexually aroused as they do.

Extensive research has also documented at least four significant differences in sexuality between American men and women: (1) Men are more interested in sex than are women; (2) women are more likely than men to link sex to a close, committed relationship; (3) aggression, power, dominance, and assertiveness are more closely linked to sex among men than among women; and (4) women's sexuality is more malleable—that is, more open to change over time and more closely associated with things such as level of education and religion (Peplau, 2003).

■ SEXUAL ORIENTATION

Sexual orientation refers to the direction of an individual's sexual interest. People with a *heterosexual* orientation are sexually attracted to members of the opposite sex; those with a *homosexual* orientation are sexually attracted to members of their own sex; and *bisexuals* are attracted to members of both sexes. About 3% of males and just under 2% of females have a homosexual orientation (Ellis, Robb, & Burke, 2005). Among other animals, homosexual activity occurs with some degree of regularity. Among pygmy chimpanzees, for example, nearly 50% of all observed sexual activity is between members of the same sex. Even male giraffes commonly entwine their necks until both become sexually stimulated. And among some birds, such as greylag geese, homosexual unions have been found to last up to 15 years (Bagemihl, 2000).

ENDURING ISSUES NATURE/NURTURE

What Determines Sexual Orientation?

The determinants of sexual orientation have been argued for decades. Those on the nature side hold that sexual orientation is rooted in biology and is influenced primarily by genetics. They point out that homosexual men and women generally know before puberty that they are "different" and often remain "in the closet" regarding their sexual orientation for fear of recrimination (Lippa, 2005). Evidence from family and twin studies shows a higher incidence of male homosexuality in families with other gay men (Camperio-Ciani, Corna, & Capiluppi, 2004), and a higher rate of homosexuality among men with a homosexual twin even when the twins were raised separately (LeVay & Hamer, 1994). And they point out that if homosexuality were the result of early learning and socialization, children raised by gay or lesbian parents would be more likely to become homosexual. Research, however, has clearly demonstrated that this is not the case (C. J. Patterson, 2000). The nature position also derives support from studies revealing anatomical and physiological differences between the brains of homosexual and heterosexual men.

Those on the nurture side argue that sexual orientation is primarily a learned behavior, influenced by early experience. They criticize research supporting the biological position as methodologically flawed—sometimes confusing what causes homosexuality with what results from homosexuality (Byne, 1994). They find some support for their position from cross-cultural studies that show sexual orientations occurring at different frequencies in various cultures.

To date, neither the biological nor the socialization theory has provided a completely satisfactory explanation for the origin of sexual orientation. As with most complex behaviors, a more likely explanation probably involves a combination of these two positions (Garnets, 2002; Hammack, 2005).

Check Your Understanding

1. Match the following terms with the appropriate definitions.

_____ Pheromones   **a.** Brain center involved in sexual excitement

_____ Testosterone   **b.** Hormone that influences some aspects of sexual development

_____ Limbic system   **c.** Scents that may cause sexual attraction

2. You are reading an article in the newspaper when you come across the following statement: "The extent to which a male is interested in sex is determined by the level of the hormone testosterone at that moment." Based on what you have learned in this chapter, which of the following would be an accurate response?

a. "That would be true only for adolescent and young adult males, not older adults."

b. "Actually, there is very little relationship between moment-to-moment levels of testosterone and sex drive in males."

c. "That's true, but testosterone is a pheromone, not a hormone."

d. "That's true, but only during the excitement phase of the sexual response cycle."

Other Important Motives

So far, we have moved from motives that depend on biological needs (hunger and thirst) to a motive that is far more sensitive to external cues—sex. Let's now consider motives that are even more responsive to environmental stimuli. These motives include contact, aggression, achievement, and affiliation.

■ CONTACT

In a classic series of experiments, Harry Harlow demonstrated the importance of the need for contact (Harlow, 1958; Harlow & Zimmerman, 1959). Newborn baby monkeys were separated from their mothers and given two "surrogate mothers." Both surrogate mothers were the same shape, but one was made of wire mesh and had no soft surfaces. The other was cuddly—layered with foam rubber and covered with terry cloth. Both surrogate mothers were warmed by means of an electric light placed inside them, but only the wire-mesh mother was equipped with a nursing bottle. Thus, the wire-mesh mother fulfilled two physiological needs for the infant monkeys: the need for food and the need for warmth. But baby monkeys most often gravitated to the terry-cloth mother, which did not provide food. When they were frightened, they would run and cling to it as they would to a real mother. Because both surrogate mothers were warm, the researchers concluded that the need for closeness goes deeper than a need for mere warmth. The importance of contact has also been demonstrated with premature infants. Babies with low birth weight who are held and massaged gain weight faster, stay calmer, and display more advanced sensory and motor skills at 1 year than those who are seldom touched (Field, 1986; Weiss, Wilson, & Morrison, 2004).

■ AGGRESSION

Human **aggression** encompasses all behavior that is intended to inflict physical or psychological harm on others. Intent is a key element of aggression. Accidentally hitting a pedestrian with your car is not an act of aggression—whereas deliberately running down a person would be.

Why are people aggressive? Freud considered aggression an innate drive, similar to hunger and thirst, that builds up until it is released. According to Freud, one important function of society is to channel the aggressive drive into constructive and socially acceptable avenues, such as sports, debate, and other forms of competition. If Freud's analysis is correct, then expressing aggression should reduce the aggressive drive. Research shows, however, that under some circumstances, venting one's anger is more likely to increase than to reduce future aggression (Bushman, 2002).

Contact
■ The importance of physical contact has been demonstrated in _____ and _____.

Aggression
■ Aggression: Any behavior intended to _____
■ According to Freud, _____ is an innate drive that builds up until it is released.
■ Others believe it is an unlearned instinct triggered by _____ or _____.
■ Most psychologists today believe that it is a(n) _____ motive that is greatly affected by _____ and by _____.

Achievement
■ Achievement motive: _____

Affiliation
■ Affiliation motive: _____

An infant monkey with Harlow's surrogate "mothers"—one made of bare wire, the other covered with soft terry cloth. The baby monkey clings to the terry-cloth mother, even though the wire mother is heated and dispenses food. Apparently, there is contact comfort in the cuddly terry cloth that the bare wire mother cannot provide.

Another view is that aggression is an unlearned instinct, a vestige of our past triggered by pain or frustration. There is some evidence that, in fact, pain and frustration can motivate aggressive behavior. For example, in one experiment, Kulik and Brown (1979) divided people into two groups and told those in each group that they could earn money by soliciting charitable contributions over the telephone. One group was told that previous callers had been quite successful in eliciting pledges; the other group was told that its predecessors had been quite unsuccessful. Each group was given a list of prospective donors, all of whom were accomplices with instructions to refuse to pledge any money. The people who had been led to expect a high rate of success tended to express considerable anger, exchanging harsh words with their respondents and even slamming down the receiver.

However, research shows that almost any unpleasant event can lead to aggression. Foul odors, high room temperatures, frightening information, and irritating cigarette smoke have been shown to increase hostility in humans. Thus, frustration is only one of many types of unpleasant experiences that can provoke aggression. Moreover, frustration does not always produce aggression—in fact, aggression is unlikely to manifest itself whenever frustration does not generate anger (Berkowitz & Harmon-Jones, 2004). Finally, people react to frustration in different ways: Some seek help and support, others withdraw from the source of frustration, some become aggressive, and some choose to escape into drugs or alcohol. There is some evidence that frustration is most likely to cause aggression in those people who have learned to be aggressive as a means of coping with unpleasant situations (Tremblay, Hartup, & Archer, 2005).

Faced with evidence that aggression in humans is not an innate response to pain or frustration, along with evidence that there is no aggressive drive that periodically builds up until it is released, most psychologists today take a somewhat different view of human aggression than did Freud and believe that it is largely a learned response. One way people learn aggression is by observing aggressive models, especially those who get what they want (and avoid punishment) when they behave aggressively. For example, in contact sports, acts of aggression often are applauded. In professional hockey, fistfights between players may elicit as much fan fervor as the scoring of goals. But what if the aggressive model does not come out ahead or is punished for aggressive actions? The ancient custom of public executions and painful punishments, such as being flogged and getting locked in the stocks, arose from the notion that punishing a person for aggressive acts would deter others from committing those acts. Observers usually will avoid imitating a model's behavior when such behavior brings negative consequences. However, as seen in Chapter 5, children who viewed aggressive behavior learned aggressive behavior, regardless of whether the aggressive model was rewarded or punished. Moreover, research shows that exposure to cinematic violence of any sort causes a small to moderate increase in aggressive behavior among children and adolescents (Wood, Wong, & Chachere, 1991).

Aggression and Culture   Culture also affects aggressiveness. For example, cultures as diverse as the Semai of the Malaysian rain forest, the Tahitian Islanders of the Pacific, the Zuni and Blackfoot nations in North America, the Pygmies of Africa, and the residents of Japan and the Scandinavian nations place a premium on resolving conflicts peacefully. They tend to withdraw from confrontations rather than risk open conflict. In contrast, cultures such as the Yanomanö of South America, the Truk Islanders of Micronesia, and the Simbu of New Guinea encourage aggressive behavior, particularly among males. Actually, one need not travel to exotic, faraway lands to find such diversity. Within the United States, subcultures such as the Quakers, the Amish, the Mennonites, and the Hutterites traditionally have valued nonviolence and peaceful coexistence. This outlook contrasts markedly with attitudes and practices in mainstream American culture.

Cultural differences in aggressiveness are reflected in statistics on violent crimes. In the United States, violent-crime rates are shockingly high compared with those of other nations. The murder rate in Norway, for example, is less than 1 per 100,000 people; in England and Wales, it is 1.5; and in France it is 1.6. In contrast, in the United States, the 2004 murder rate was 5.5 per 100,000 people (Federal Bureau of Investigation, 2005). Indeed, the murder rate in the United States is the highest among the industrialized nations of the world (Geen, 1998). The United States also reports higher rates of rape and vandalism.

These striking cultural differences suggest that aggressiveness is influenced greatly by learning. The same is true for gender differences in aggression, which are examined next.

Gender and Aggression   Across cultures and at every age, males are more likely than females to behave aggressively. Research consistently shows that males are more aggressive than females both verbally (i.e., with taunts, insults, and threats) and, in particular, physically (i.e., with hitting, kicking, and fighting) (Bettencourt & Miller, 1996; Eagly & Steffen, 1986; Hyde, 1986). These gender differences tend to be greater in natural settings than in controlled laboratory settings and appear to be remarkably stable. Even historical data that go back to sixteenth-century Europe show that males committed more than three times as many violent crimes as females (Ellis & Coontz, 1990).

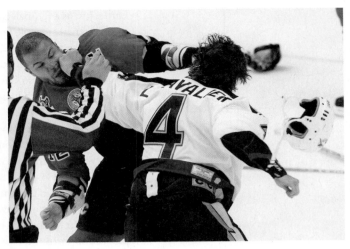

Some psychologists believe that aggression is largely a learned behavior. Professional athletes in contact sports often serve as models of aggressive behavior.

Is the origin of gender difference in aggression biological or social? As might be expected, the answer is not simple. On the one hand, certain biological factors appear to contribute to aggressive behavior. As seen in Chapter 2, the hormone testosterone is associated with aggressiveness. Even exposure to high levels of testosterone during prenatal development is associated with increased aggressiveness (Reinisch, Ziemba-Davis, & Sanders, 1991). At the same time, our society clearly tolerates and even encourages greater aggressiveness in boys than in girls. For example, we are more likely to give boys toy guns and to reward them for behaving aggressively; girls are more likely than boys to be taught to feel guilty for behaving aggressively or to expect parental disapproval for their aggressive behavior.

Taken together, the data support the idea that aggression is primarily a learned motive. Several other important social motives, including achievement and affiliation, also seem to be learned.

■ ACHIEVEMENT

Climbing Mount Everest, sending rockets into space, making the dean's list, rising to the top of a giant corporation—all are actions that may have mixed underlying motives. But in all of them, there is a desire to excel, "to overcome obstacles, to exercise power, to strive to do something difficult as well and as quickly as possible" (H. A. Murray, 1938, pp. 80–81). It is this desire for achievement for its own sake that leads psychologists to suggest that there is an **achievement motive**.

As with all learned motives, need for achievement varies widely from person to person. From psychological tests and personal histories, psychologists have developed a profile of people with high achievement motivation. These people are fast learners. They relish the opportunity to develop new strategies for unique and challenging tasks, whereas people with a low need for achievement rarely deviate from methods that worked for them in the past. Driven less by the desire for fame or fortune than by the need to live up to a high, self-imposed standard of performance (M. Carr, Borkowski, & Maxwell, 1991), they are self-confident, are willing to take on responsibility, and do not bow readily to outside social pressures. They are energetic and do not allow many things to stand in the way of their goals, but they are apt to be tense and to suffer from stress-related ailments, such as headaches. They may also feel like impostors even—or especially—when they achieve their goals.

■ AFFILIATION

Sometimes, everyone wants to get away from it all—to spend an evening or a weekend just reading, thinking, or being alone. But generally, people have a need for affiliation, a need to be with other people. Why do people tend to seek out one another?

For one thing, the **affiliation motive** is aroused when people feel threatened. Cues that signal danger, such as illness or catastrophe, appear to increase the desire to be with others. *Esprit de corps*—the feeling of being part of a sympathetic group—is crucial among troops going into battle, just as a football coach's pregame pep talk fuels team spirit. Both of these examples are designed to make people feel they are working for a common cause or against a common foe.

Sometimes, affiliation behavior results from another motive entirely. For example, you may give a party to celebrate getting a job because you want to be praised for your achievements. Fear and anxiety also can be tied to the affiliation motive. When rats, monkeys, or humans are placed in anxiety-producing situations, the presence of a member of the same species who remains calm will reduce the fear experienced by the anxious ones. Patients with critical illnesses tend to prefer being with healthy people, rather than with other seriously ill patients or by themselves (Rofe, Hoffman, & Lewin, 1985). In the same way, if you are nervous on a plane during a bumpy flight, you may strike up a conversation with the calm-looking woman sitting next to you.

On the basis of these facts, some theorists have argued that the human need for affiliation has an evolutionary basis (Ainsworth, 1989; R. F. Baumeister & Leary, 2000; Buss, 1990, 1991). In this view, forming and maintaining social bonds provided our ancestors with survival and reproductive benefits. Social groups can share resources such as food and shelter, provide opportunities for reproduction, and assist in the care of offspring. Children who chose to stay with adults were probably more likely to survive (and ultimately reproduce) than those who wandered away from their groups. Thus, it is understandable that people in general tend to seek out other people.

In any given case, affiliation behavior (as does most behavior) usually stems from a subtle interplay of biological and environmental factors. Deciding to strike up a conversation with the person sitting next to you on a bumpy airplane flight depends on how friendly you normally are, on what is considered proper behavior in your culture, and on how scared you feel at the moment, how calm your neighbor appears to be, and how turbulent the flight is, among other things.

Check Your Understanding

1. A person who is willing to contend with the high risks of a career in sales is probably motivated by a high _____ motive.

2. You are watching a children's show on television in which the "bad guys" eventually are punished for their aggressive behavior. Your friend says, "It's a good thing the bad guys always lose. Otherwise, kids would learn to be aggressive from watching shows like this." You think about that for a minute and then, on the basis of what you have learned in this chapter, you reply with

   a. "Actually, seeing an aggressor punished for his or her actions leads to more aggression than seeing no aggression at all."

   b. "You're right. Seeing aggressors punished for their actions is a good way to reduce the amount of aggressiveness in children."

   c. "Aggression is an instinctual response to frustration, so it really doesn't matter what children see on TV. If they are frustrated, they will respond with aggression."

Emotions

Ancient Greek rationalists believed that emotions, if not held in check, would wreak havoc on higher mental abilities such as rational thought and decision making. In the past, psychologists, too, often viewed emotions as a "base instinct"—a vestige of an evolutionary heritage that needed to be repressed. Not surprisingly, emotions received very little attention from researchers.

More recently, however, scientists have begun to see emotions in a more positive light. Today, emotions are considered essential to survival and are seen as a major source of personal enrichment and resilience. Emotions are linked to variations in immune function and, thereby, to health (see Chapter 11: Stress and Health Psychology). As seen in Chapter 7, emotions may also influence how successful a person becomes (Goleman, 1997; Goleman, Boyatzis, & McKee, 2002). It is clear, then, that if one is to understand human behavior, he or she must understand emotions. Unfortunately, that task is easier said than done. It is very difficult to begin to even identify how many emotions there are.

■ BASIC EMOTIONS

One of the most influential attempts to identify and classify emotions was made by Robert Plutchik (1980). He proposed that there are eight basic emotions: fear, surprise, sadness, disgust, anger, anticipation, joy, and acceptance. Each of these emotions helps people adjust to the demands of their environment, albeit in different ways. Fear, for example, underlies flight, which helps protect animals from their enemies; anger propels animals to attack or destroy.

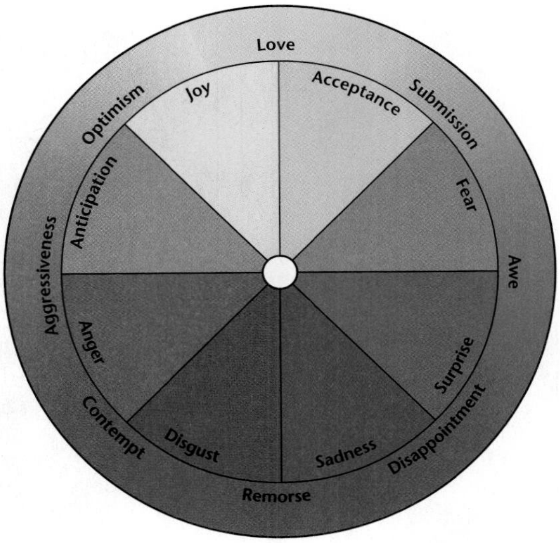

Emotions adjacent to each other on Plutchik's emotion "circle" (Figure 8–6) are more alike than those situated opposite each other or that are farther away from each other. Surprise is more closely related to fear than to anger; joy and acceptance are more similar to each other than either is to disgust. Moreover, according to Plutchik's model, different emotions may combine to produce an even wider and richer spectrum of experience. Occurring together, anticipation and joy, for example, yield optimism; joy and acceptance fuse into love; and surprise and sadness make for disappointment. Within any of Plutchik's eight categories, emotions vary in intensity. Thus, fear is a less intense emotion than terror, but it is more intense than apprehension.

FIGURE 8–6
Plutchik's eight basic categories of emotion.

Source: R. Plutchik (1980). *Emotion: A psychoevolutionary synthesis.* New York: Harper & Row.

ENDURING ISSUES   DIVERSITY/UNIVERSALITY

Are Emotions Universal?

Some scientists challenge Plutchik's model, noting that it may apply only to the emotional experience of English-speaking people. Anthropologists report enormous differences in the ways that other cultures view and categorize emotions. Some languages, in fact, do not even have a word for "emotion." Languages also differ in the number of words that they have to name emotions. English includes more than 2,000 words to describe emotional experiences, but Taiwanese Chinese has only 750 such descriptive words. One tribal language has only seven words that could be translated into categories of emotion. Some cultures lack words for "anxiety" or "depression" or "guilt." Samoans have only one word to encompass love, sympathy, pity, and liking—all of which are distinct emotions in our own culture (Frijda, Markam, & Sato, 1995; Russell, 1991).

Because of the differences in emotions from one culture to another, the tendency now is to distinguish between primary and secondary emotions. Primary emotions are those that are evident in all cultures, that contribute to survival, that are associated with a distinct facial expression, and that are evident in nonhuman primates. Currently, no consensus exists about what emotions qualify as primary, but the number is small, very likely no more than a dozen. They include, at a minimum, fear, anger, and pleasure, but may also include sadness, disgust, surprise, and possibly a few others.

Secondary emotions, which are not found in all cultures, may be thought of as subtle amalgamations of the primary emotions. There are many more secondary emotions than primary ones, but there is, again, no consensus about what those emotions are or how many they number.

Emotions

■ Emotion: _____

Basic Emotions

■ Primary emotions: _____ in all cultures, contribute to _____, associated with distinct _____, and evident in nonhuman primates; basic emotions include _____, _____, and _____, possibly also _____, _____, _____, and _____.

■ Secondary emotions: Not found in all _____

Theories of Emotion

■ The James-Lange theory holds that _____

_____

■ The Cannon-Bard theory holds that _____

_____

■ The cognitive theory holds that _____

_____

■ Izard's theory holds that situations trigger _____

_____

FIGURE 8–7
Name that face.
Dr. Paul Ekman believes that facial expressions are distinct, predictable, and easy to read for someone who has studied them. His research involved breaking the expressions down into their specific muscular components and developing programs to help train people to become more accurate observers of the feelings that flit briefly across others' faces. Here, he demonstrates six emotional states. How many of them can you match to the pictures?

a. Fear
b. Neutral (no emotion)
c. Sadness
d. Anger
e. Surprise
f. Disgust

Source: *New York Times*, 2003.

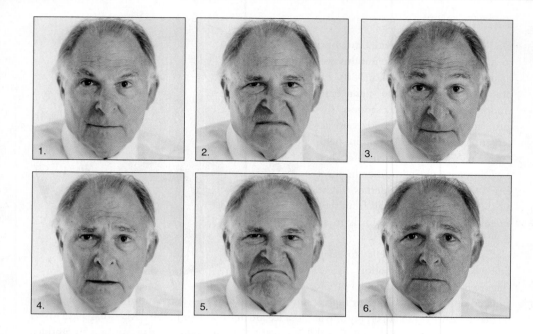

Attempts to identify primary emotions have generally used cross-cultural studies. For example, one group of researchers asked participants from 10 countries to interpret photographs depicting various facial expressions of emotions (Ekman et al., 1987). The percentage of participants from each country who correctly identified the emotions ranged from 60 to 98% (Figure 8–7). The researchers used this and other evidence to argue for the existence of six primary emotions—happiness, surprise, sadness, fear, disgust, and anger. Notice that love is not included in this list. Although Ekman did not find a universally recognized facial expression for love, many psychologists nevertheless hold that love is a primary emotion (Hendrick & Hendrick, 2003; Sabini & Silver, 2005). Its outward expression, however, may vary greatly across cultures.

■ THEORIES OF EMOTION

Why do people feel on top of the world one minute and down in the dumps the next? What causes emotional experiences?

In the 1880s, the American psychologist William James formulated the first modern theory of emotion. At almost the same time, the Danish psychologist Carl Lange (1834–1900) reached the same conclusions. According to the **James-Lange theory**, stimuli in the environment (say, seeing a large growling dog running toward you) cause physiological changes in the body (accelerated heart rate, enlarged pupils, deeper or shallower breathing, increased perspiration, and goose bumps), and emotions arise from those physiological changes. The emotion of *fear*, then, would simply be the almost instantaneous and automatic awareness of physiological changes.

There is some supporting evidence for this theory, but if you think back to the biology of the nervous system in Chapter 2, you should be able to identify a major flaw in the James-Lange theory. Recall that sensory information about bodily changes flows to the brain through the spinal cord. If bodily changes are the source of emotions, then people with severe spinal cord injuries should experience fewer and less intense emotions, but this is not the case (Chwalisz, Diener, & Gallagher, 1988). Moreover, most emotions are accompanied by very similar physiological changes. All strong emotions, for example, are accompanied by a rapid pulse rate. But a rapid pulse rate does not tell you which strong emotion you are feeling. Therefore, bodily changes triggered by the sympathetic nervous system do not cause specific emotions and may not even be necessary for emotional experience.

Recognizing these facts, the **Cannon-Bard theory** holds that people *mentally* process emotions and *physically* respond simultaneously, not one after another. When you see the

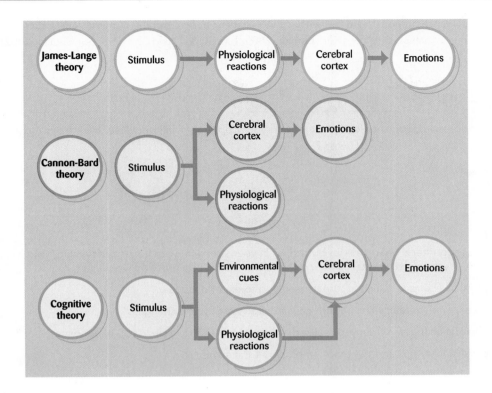

FIGURE **8–8**
The three major theories of emotion.
According to the James-Lange theory, the body first responds physiologically to a stimulus, then the cerebral cortex determines that emotion is being experienced. The Cannon-Bard theory holds that impulses are sent simultaneously to the cerebral cortex and the peripheral nervous system; thus, the response to the stimulus and the processing of the emotion are experienced at the same time, but independently. Cognitive theorists assert that the cerebral cortex interprets physiological changes in the light of information about the situation to determine which emotions we feel.

threatening dog, you experience fear. At the same time, your sympathetic nervous system causes various physiological changes, but neither one depends on the other. Emotions and physiological reactions occur simultaneously and independently.

Cognitive Theories of Emotion   Cognitive psychologists have taken Cannon-Bard's theory a step further. They argue that one's emotional experience depends on *both* physiological changes and one's perception of a situation (Ellsworth, 2002; Lazarus, 1991a, 1991b, 1991c; Scherer, Schorr, & Johnstone, 2001). According to the **cognitive theory** of emotion, the situation reveals clues as to how one should interpret biological states. According to Schachter and Singer's *Two-Factor Theory of Emotion*, when you see a threatening dog, you indeed experience bodily changes; but you then use information about the situation to tell you how to experience and respond to those changes. Only when you cognitively recognize that you are in danger do you experience the accompanying bodily changes, such as fear, and respond appropriately (Schachter & Singer, 1962, 2001). See Figure 8–8 for a comparison of these three theories of emotion.

Challenges to Cognitive Theory   Although cognitive theories of emotion make a lot of sense, some critics reject the idea that feelings always stem from cognitions. For example, a rabbit does not evaluate the possibilities that might account for a rustle in the bushes before it runs away. All animals, human and nonhuman alike, have the ability to respond instantaneously to situations without taking time to interpret and evaluate them. Moreover, Carroll Izard argues that some emotions can be experienced without the intervention of cognition at all (Izard, 1971, 1994). He suggests that a situation such as separation or pain provokes a unique pattern of unlearned facial movements and body postures. When information about our facial expressions and posture reaches the brain, we automatically experience the corresponding emotion. According to Izard, then, the James-Lange theory was essentially right in suggesting that emotional experience arises from bodily reactions. But Izard's theory stresses facial expression and body posture as being crucial to the experience of emotion, whereas the James-Lange theory emphasized the role of the sympathetic nervous system. Considerable evidence supports Izard's view that a key element in determining our emotional experience is our own expressive behavior (Ekman, 2003; Ekman & Davidson, 1993; Soussignan, 2002).

Check Your Understanding

1. Ralph believes that when you feel depressed, you should smile a lot and your depression will decrease. His view is most consistent with

   a. Izard's theory

   b. The Schachter-Singer theory

   c. The James-Lange theory

   d. The Cannon-Bard theory

2. You are on a camping trip when you encounter a bear. You get butterflies in your stomach, your heart starts racing, your mouth gets dry, and you start to perspire. A psychologist who takes the cognitive perspective on emotion would say,

   a. "Seeing the bear caused the physical changes, which in turn caused you to experience fear."

   b. "Seeing the bear caused you to experience fear, which in turn caused all those physical changes."

   c. "Seeing the bear caused the physical changes. When you realized they were caused by a bear, you experienced fear."

   d. "Seeing the bear caused the physical changes and the emotion of fear at the same time."

Communicating Emotion

Sometimes you are vaguely aware that a person makes you feel uncomfortable. When pressed to be more precise, you might say, "You never know what she is thinking." It probably would be more accurate to say that you do not know what she is feeling. Nearly everyone conceals their emotions to some extent, but usually people can tell what others are feeling by using clues such as voice quality, facial expression, body language, personal space, and explicit acts.

■ VOICE QUALITY AND FACIAL EXPRESSION

If your roommate is washing the dishes and says acidly, "I *hope* you're enjoying your novel," the literal meaning of his words is quite clear, but you probably know very well that he is not expressing a concern about your reading pleasure. He is really saying, "I am annoyed that you are not helping to clean up." Similarly, if you receive a phone call from someone who has had very good or very bad news, you will probably know how she feels before she has told you what happened. In the same way, we can hear fear in a person's voice, as we do when we listen to a nervous student give an oral report. Much of the emotional information people convey is not contained in the words they use, but in the way those words are expressed.

The muscles in the face, while complex, allow facial expressions to communicate very specific feelings, and we can tell a good deal about another person's emotional state by observing whether that person is laughing, crying, smiling, or frowning. Moreover, there is considerable evidence that many facial expressions are innate, not learned. Charles Darwin first advanced the idea that most animals share a common pattern of muscular facial movements. For example, dogs, tigers, and humans all bare their teeth in rage. Children who are born deaf and blind use the same facial expressions as do other children to express the same emotions. Finally, adults are quite adept at interpreting infant nonverbal communications, such as whether they are looking at a new or familiar object, just by observing their facial expressions (Camras et al., 2002). (See Figure 8–9.)

FIGURE 8–9
People throughout the world use the "brow-raise" greeting when a friend approaches.

Source: Eibl-Eibesfeldt, 1972.

■ BODY LANGUAGE, PERSONAL SPACE, AND GESTURES

Body language is another way that we communicate emotional messages nonverbally. How we hold our back, for example, communicates a great deal. When we are relaxed, we tend to stretch back into a chair; when we are tense, we sit more stiffly with our feet together.

The distance we maintain between ourselves and others is called *personal space*. This distance varies, depending on the nature of the activity and the emotions felt. If someone stands closer to you than is customary, that proximity may indicate either anger or affection; if farther away than usual, it may indicate fear or dislike. The normal conversing distance between people varies from culture to culture. Two Swedes conversing would ordinarily stand much farther apart than would two Arabs or Greeks.

Explicit acts, of course, can also serve as nonverbal clues to emotions. A slammed door may reveal that the person who just left the room is angry. If friends drop in for a visit and you invite them into your living room, you probably are less at ease with them than with friends who generally sit down with you at the kitchen table. Gestures, such as a slap on the back or an embrace, can also indicate feelings. Whether people shake your hand briefly or for a long time, firmly or limply, reveals something about how they feel about you.

Nonverbal communication of emotions is certainly an important concept, but a word of caution is needed here. Although it may offer a clue to a person's feelings, nonverbal behavior is not an *infallible* clue. Laughing and crying can sound alike, yet crying may signal sorrow, joy, anger, or nostalgia—or that you are slicing an onion. Moreover, as with verbal reports, people sometimes "say" things nonverbally that they do not mean. We all have done things thoughtlessly—turned our backs, frowned when thinking about something else, or laughed at the wrong time—that have given offense because our actions were interpreted as an expression of an emotion that we were not, in fact, feeling.

Also, many of us overestimate our ability to interpret nonverbal cues. For example, in one study of several hundred "professional lie catchers," including members of the Secret Service, government lie detector experts, judges, police officers, and psychiatrists, every group except for the psychiatrists rated themselves above average in their ability to tell whether another person was lying. Only the Secret Service agents managed to identify the liars at a better-than-chance rate (Ekman & O'Sullivan, 1991). Similar results have been obtained with other groups of people (Frank, 2006). In part, the reason seems to be that many behaviors that might seem to be associated with lying (such as avoiding eye contact, rapid blinking, or shrugs) are not actually associated with lying; and other behaviors that are indeed associated with lying (such as tenseness and fidgeting) also occur frequently when people are not lying (DePaulo et al., 2003). Thus, even the best nonverbal cues only indicate that a person *may* be lying.

■ GENDER AND EMOTION

Men are often said to be less emotional than women. But do men feel less emotion, or are they simply less likely to express the emotions they feel? And are there some emotions that men are more likely to express than women?

Research sheds some light on these issues. Numerous studies show that men are more likely than women to inhibit the expression of sympathy, sadness, empathy, and distress, which are often considered "unmanly" emotions in Western culture (L. Brody & Hall, 2000). Men are also much less likely than women to seek help in dealing with emotional issues (Komiya, Good, & Sherrod, 2000). Moreover, women tend to have stronger emotional reactions to self-generated thoughts and memories (R. Carter, 1998). See Figure 8–10.

Men and women are likely to react with very different emotions to the same situation. For example, being betrayed or criticized by another person tends to elicit anger in males, whereas females are more likely to feel hurt, sad, or disappointed (L. Brody & Hall, 2000; Fischer, Rodriguez-Mosquera, van-Vianen, & Manstead, 2004). And, when men get angry, they generally turn their anger outward, against other people and against the situation in which they find themselves. Women are more likely to see themselves as the source of the problem and to turn their anger inward, against themselves. These gender-specific reactions

Voice Quality and Facial Expression

■ Some emotional expression is verbal, but much more is conveyed in _____.

Body Language, Personal Space, and Gestures

■ _____, _____, _____, and _____ can also be used to express emotion.

Gender and Emotion

■ Women are more likely than men to _____ and _____ in dealing with emotional issues.

■ Men and women also often react to the same situation with very _____ emotions.

■ Women are better than men at _____ emotions in others.

Culture and Emotion

■ At least some emotional expressions are _____ and _____.

■ Other emotional expressions are influenced by _____, _____, _____, _____, and _____, among others.

■ Display rules: Culturally determined _____ concerning the _____ under which emotions should be expressed

are consistent with the fact that men are four times more likely than women to become violent in the face of life crises; women, by contrast, are much more likely to become depressed.

When having a conversation, most people of Middle-Eastern descent stand closer to one another than most Americans do. In our society, two men would not usually stand as close together as these two Arabs unless they were very aggressively arguing with each other (a baseball player heatedly arguing with an umpire, for example).

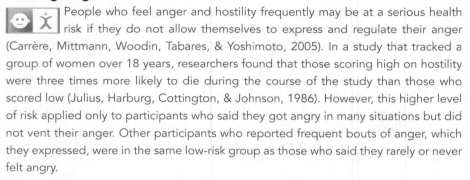

ENDURING ISSUES MIND/BODY

Holding Anger In

People who feel anger and hostility frequently may be at a serious health risk if they do not allow themselves to express and regulate their anger (Carrère, Mittmann, Woodin, Tabares, & Yoshimoto, 2005). In a study that tracked a group of women over 18 years, researchers found that those scoring high on hostility were three times more likely to die during the course of the study than those who scored low (Julius, Harburg, Cottington, & Johnson, 1986). However, this higher level of risk applied only to participants who said they got angry in many situations but did not vent their anger. Other participants who reported frequent bouts of anger, which they expressed, were in the same low-risk group as those who said they rarely or never felt angry.

Men and women also differ in their ability to interpret nonverbal cues of emotion. For example, women and young girls are more skilled than men or young boys at decoding the facial expressions, body cues, and vocal tones of others. How can these differences be explained? One possibility is that because women tend to be the primary caregivers for preverbal infants, they need to become more attuned than men to the subtleties of emotional expressions. Some psychologists have even suggested that this skill may be genetically programmed into females. Another explanation of gender differences in emotional sensitivity is based on the relative power of women and men. Because women historically have occupied less powerful positions, they may have felt the need to become acutely attuned to the emotional displays of others, particularly those in more powerful positions (namely, men).

■ CULTURE AND EMOTION

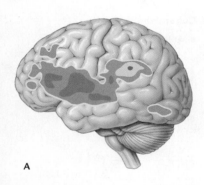

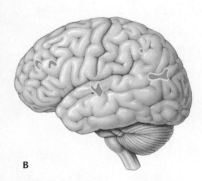

FIGURE 8–10
Emotion and brain activity in men and women.
When asked to think of something sad, women (A) generate more activity in their brains than men (B).
Source: R. Carter, 1998, p. 100. Shading added.

As we have seen, Ekman and his colleagues have concluded from cross-cultural studies that at least six emotions are accompanied by universal facial expressions: happiness, sadness, anger, surprise, fear, and disgust. Carroll Izard (1980) conducted similar studies in England, Germany, Switzerland, France, Sweden, Greece, and Japan with similar results. These studies appear to support the *universalist* position that holds that facial expressions are innate, not learned. However, all the participants in these studies were members of developed countries and likely had been exposed to one another through movies, magazines, and tourism. Thus, they simply might have become familiar with the facial expressions seen in other cultures. A stronger test was needed that reduced or eliminated the possibility that facial expressions of emotion are learned (the *culture-learning* view).

Such a test was made possible by the discovery of several contemporary cultures that had been totally isolated from Western culture for most of their existence. Members of the Fore and the Dani cultures of New Guinea, for example, had their first contact with anthropologists only a few years before Ekman's research took place. They provided a nearly perfect opportunity to test the universalist/culture-learning debate. If members of these cultures gave the same interpretation of facial expressions and produced the same expressions on their own faces as did people in Western cultures, there would be much stronger evidence for the universality of facial expressions of emotion. Ekman and his colleagues presented members of the Fore culture with three photographs of people from outside their culture and asked them to point to the picture that represented how they would feel in a certain situation. For example, if a participant was told "Your child has died, and you feel very sad," he or she would have the opportunity to choose which of the three pictures most closely corresponded to sadness. The results indicated very high rates of agreement on facial expressions of emotions (Ekman &

Friesen, 1971; Ekman, Sorenson, & Friesen, 1969). Moreover, when photographs of the Fore and Dani posing the primary emotions were shown to college students in the United States, the same high agreement was found (Ekman & Friesen, 1975). This finding provides strong support for the notion that at least some emotional expressions are inborn and universal.

If this is true, why are people so often confused about the emotions being expressed by people in other cultures? Part of the explanation involves **display rules** that concern the circumstances under which it is appropriate for people to show emotion (Ekman & Friesen, 1975). Display rules differ substantially from culture to culture. For example, the Japanese are taught not to display strong negative emotion in the presence of a respected elder. Americans typically do not honor this display rule; hence, they are more likely to express negative emotions regardless of whom they are with. However, display rules do not tell the whole story. In a comprehensive review of the literature, Elfenbein and Ambady (2002, 2003) have demonstrated that differences in language, familiarity, majority or minority status within a culture, cultural learning, expressive style, and numerous other factors may also account for the fact that "we understand emotions more accurately when they are expressed by members of our own cultural or subcultural group" (p. 228). Clearly, as the world becomes increasingly multicultural, the ability to correctly identify emotions of people from different cultures will become increasingly important.

Check Your Understanding

1. Research shows that some _____ _____ are recognized universally.

2. _____ _____ define the circumstances under which it is appropriate to show emotions.

3. Which of the following probably would be best at "reading" nonverbal emotional cues?

   a. A young man

   b. An older woman

   c. An older man

   d. All would be equally accurate because gender is not related to the ability to understand nonverbal cues to emotion.

Chapter Review

 www.psychologythecore.com

A **motive** is a specific need or desire that arouses the organism and directs its behavior toward a goal. **Emotion** refers to the experience of feelings such as fear, joy, surprise, and anger. Motives and emotions push people to take some kind of action.

Perspectives on Motivation

The idea that motivated behavior reflects **instincts** was popular in the early twentieth century, but it has since has fallen out of favor. An alternative view of motivation, **drive-reduction theory**, holds that a state of tension or arousal (a **drive**) motivates behavior directed toward returning the body to a state of **homeostasis**, or balance. **Primary drives** (such as hunger and thirst) are unlearned, while **secondary drives** are acquired through learning. In contrast, **arousal theory** suggests that behavior stems from a desire to maintain an optimal level of arousal. Some motivation derives from the activity itself **(intrinsic motivation)**, while other motivation arises from the consequence of the activity **(extrinsic motivation)**.

Abraham Maslow suggested human motives can be arranged in a **hierarchy of needs**, with primitive ones based on physical needs positioned at the bottom and higher ones such as self-esteem positioned toward the top. Maslow believed that the higher motives do not emerge until the more basic ones have been met, but recent research challenges his view.

Hunger and Thirst

Hunger is regulated by several centers within the brain. These centers are stimulated by receptors that monitor blood levels of **glucose**, fats, and carbohydrates as well as the hormones **insulin**, **leptin**, and **ghrelin**. In the absence of a biological need for food, hunger can be triggered by **incentives** such as cooking aromas and by emotional, cultural, and social factors. Thirst is controlled by two regulators that monitor the level of fluids inside and outside the cells. Both of these regulators stimulate thirst when fluid levels are too low. But as with hunger, the psychological state of being thirsty can be triggered by environmental cues quite apart from the biological need for water.

Eating disorders, particularly **anorexia nervosa** and **bulimia nervosa**, are more prevalent among females than among males. These disorders are characterized by extreme preoccupation with body image and weight. Another food-related problem, *obesity*, affects millions of Americans. Obesity has complex causes and negative consequences particularly for obese children, who are likely to have health problems as adults. **Body mass index (BMI)** can be used to determine the risk of diseases that are associated with obesity. To some extent, our bodies are genetically "set" to maintain a certain weight (**set point theory**), which makes it difficult to maintain significant weight changes over time.

Sex

Sex is a primary drive that gives rise to reproductive behavior that is essential for the survival of the species. The biological basis of the sex drive in humans is not well understood. Although hormones (such as **testosterone)** and pheromones are involved in human sexual responses, they do not play as dominant a role as they do in some other species. The human **sexual response cycle**, which differs somewhat for males and females, has four stages—excitement, plateau, orgasm, and resolution.

Although hormones and the nervous system do figure in the sex drive, human sexual motivation, especially in the early stages of excitement and arousal, depends much more on experience and learning than on biology. Sexual attractiveness is also influenced by culture. Research suggests a more conservative pattern of sexual behavior in the United States than is portrayed in popular media.

Sexual orientation refers to the direction of an individual's sexual interest. People with a heterosexual orientation are sexually attracted to members of the opposite sex; those with a homosexual orientation are sexually attracted to members of their own sex. Bisexuals are attracted to members of both sexes. Research has shown that both biological and environmental factors play a role in explaining sexual orientation.

Other Important Motives

An important motive in humans and other primates is to seek various forms of tactile stimulation or contact. The importance of contact has been demonstrated in nonhuman animal studies as well as in premature human infants.

Any behavior intended to inflict physical or psychological harm on others is an act of **aggression**. Freud saw aggression as an innate drive in humans that must be channeled toward constructive ends. Another view is that aggression is an unlearned instinct, a vestige of an evolutionary past, that is triggered by pain or frustration. But frustration is only one of many types of unpleasant experiences that can provoke aggression. Moreover, frustration does not always produce aggression. Most contemporary psychologists view aggression more as a learned response that is influenced greatly by modeling, norms, and values. Significant differences in aggression across cultures support the latter view. Interaction of nature and nurture accounts for the fact that almost universally, males are more inclined than females to behave aggressively.

People who display a desire to excel, to overcome obstacles, and to accomplish difficult things well and quickly score high in **achievement motive**. As with all learned motives, the need for achievement varies widely from person to person.

The **affiliation motive**, or need to be with other people, is especially pronounced when one feels threatened or anxious. Affiliation with others in such situations can counteract fear and bolster spirits.

Emotions

Robert Plutchik's classification system encompasses eight basic emotions. The vast array of human emotional experiences can be traced to the fact that different emotions can combine to produce other emotions, and emotions also vary in intensity. Cross-cultural research suggests that happiness, surprise, sadness, fear, disgust, and anger are "primary" emotions that are universally recognized through facial expressions. Many psychologists add *love* to this list, although there is no universally recognized facial expression that expresses love.

According to the **James-Lange theory**, environmental stimuli cause physiological changes; emotions then arise from our awareness of those changes. In contrast, the **Cannon-Bard theory** holds that emotions and bodily responses occur simultaneously and independently. A third perspective, the **cognitive theory** of emotion, holds that the situation provides clues as to how we should interpret biological states. Yet another view holds that emotional situations provoke unique patterns of unlearned facial movements and body postures. When information about those facial expressions and posture reaches the brain, we automatically experience the corresponding emotion.

Communicating Emotion

People express emotions verbally through words, tone of voice, exclamations, and other sounds. Facial expressions are also excellent indicators of emotion. Other indicators involve body language—our posture, the way we move, our preferred personal distance from others when talking to them, our degree of eye contact, and the like. Explicit acts, such as slamming a door, express emotions, too. People vary in their skill at reading these nonverbal cues.

Research confirms some gender differences in expressing and perceiving emotions. Women are more likely than men to express sympathy, sadness, empathy, and distress. Also, being betrayed or criticized tends to elicit anger in men versus disappointment and hurt in women. Women generally are better than men at reading other people's emotions.

Regardless of a person's cultural background, the facial expressions associated with some basic emotions appear to be universal. This is not to say that there are no cultural differences in emotional expression, however. Overlaying the universal expression of certain emotions are culturally varying **display rules** that govern when it is appropriate to show emotion—to whom, by whom, and under what circumstances.

Chapter 9
Life-Span Development

Go to *The Core Online* at **www.psychologythecore.com** to get the most up-to-date information for your introductory psychology course. The content online is an important part of what you are learning—the content there can help prepare you for your test! It includes up-to-date examples, simulations, video clips, and practice quizzes. Also be sure to check out the *Blog* to hear directly from the authors on what current events and latest research are most relevant to your course materials.

The first time you log in, you will need the access code packaged with your textbook. If you do not have a code, please go to **www.mypearsonstore.com** and enter the ISBN of your textbook (**0-13-603344-X**) to purchase the code.

9 1 Research Methods in Developmental Psychology

- **Cross-sectional studies** observe people of different ages at the same point in time.
- **Longitudinal studies** observe the same people as they grow older.
- **Biographical** (or **retrospective**) **studies** gather data about people's past.

9 2 Prenatal Development

- Lasts from the moment of conception to birth.
- During **critical periods**, substances that pass through the placenta can cause irreparable harm to the **embryo** or **fetus**, including **fetal alcohol syndrome (FAS)**.

9 3 The Newborn

Reflexes
- **Neonates** (newborn babies) have a number of useful reflexes: rooting, sucking, swallowing, grasping, and stepping.

Temperament
- Neonates have unique **temperaments**, including easy, difficult, slow to warm up, and shy.

Perceptual Abilities
- Sight, hearing, taste, smell, and touch function at birth.

9 4 Infancy and Childhood

Neurological Development
- Interconnections between neurons increase dramatically.
- Growth of myelin sheaths increases the speed of transmission.

Physical Development
- First year: Rapid height and weight gain and marked changes in proportion
- Second year: Growth slows down

Motor Development
- **Developmental norms:** Average ages at which skills are achieved
- **Maturation:** Biological processes that unfold as a person grows older

Cognitive Development
- Piaget's stages of cognitive development include:
  —**Sensory-Motor Stage** (birth to 2 years)
  —**Preoperational Stage** (2 to 7 years)
  —**Concrete-Operational Stage** (7 to 11 years)
  —**Formal-Operational Stage** (adolescence through adulthood)

Moral Development
- According to Kohlberg, moral development progresses through the following stages: preconventional, conventional, and postconventional.

Language Development
- Cooing gives way to **babbling**; first word usually appears at about 12 months, followed by **holophrases**. Second year of life: naming. Third year: short sentences.
- Most linguists assert that an inborn **language acquisition device** or **language instinct** is required.

Social Development
- **Imprinting:** Forming a strong bond to the first moving object; characteristic of young animals of many species
- **Attachment:** In humans, emotional bonds to caretakers are typically evident by age 6 months, followed by stranger anxiety that peaks at 12 months.
- Erikson's psychosocial stages:
  —Birth to 1 year: Trust versus Mistrust
  —1 to 3 years: Autonomy versus Shame and Doubt
  —3 to 6 years: Initiative versus Guilt
  —7 to 11 years: Industry versus Inferiority
- Peer relationships start with siblings and expand to include **peer groups** and other **nonshared environments** specific to each child.

Sex-Role Development
- Gender identity
- Gender constancy
- Gender-role awareness
- Gender stereotypes
- Sex-typed behavior

9 5 Adolescence

Physical Changes
- **Growth spurt**: Rapid increase in height and weight
- **Puberty**: Onset of sexual maturation

Cognitive Changes
- **Formal-operational thought**: Ability to understand and manipulate abstract concepts

Personality and Social Development
- Erikson's psychosocial stages:
  —Identity versus role confusion
- **Identity crisis**: Period of intense self-exploration

Some Problems of Adolescence
- Low self-esteem resulting from dissatisfaction with appearance (especially girls)
- High suicide rate

9 6 Adulthood

Love, Partnerships, and Parenting
- Intimacy versus Isolation: The major challenge of young adulthood according to Erikson
- Nearly all adults form a long-term, loving partnership with another adult at some point in their lives.
- For most parents, children are a source of fulfillment.

The World of Work
- Initial career choice is determined as much by personality, interests, and values as abilities.
- Process of occupational choice is lifelong
- While the percentage of women in the paid labor force has increased dramatically, many women bear more than half the responsibility for housework and child care.

Cognitive Changes
- Vocabulary and verbal memory increase steadily through the sixth decade of life; perceptual speed and ability to perform mathematical computations decline the most over the life span.

Midlife
- According to Erikson, the major challenge of midlife involves generativity versus stagnation.
- **Midlife crisis** is not typical; most people go through a less dramatic **midlife transition**.
- Two significant physical changes occur in midlife: **menopause** in women and a drop in testosterone and male fertility in men.

9 7 Late Adulthood

Physical Changes
- Significant changes in physical appearance and biological processes occur in late adulthood.

Social Development
- Most people over age 65 live outside nursing homes.
- The majority of older adults enjoy sex.

Cognitive Changes
- For many older adults, cognitive abilities remain largely intact.
- **Alzheimer's disease** causes profound changes in mental abilities and personality.

Facing the End of Life
- According to Kübler-Ross, American culture is *death denying* rather than *death affirming*.
- Five stages occur in reacting to one's impending death: denial, anger, bargaining, depression, and acceptance.

How does Oprah Winfrey's life illustrate several key issues in developmental psychology?

In 1954, a girl was born in a rundown Mississippi farmhouse. When her mother moved north in search of work, the girl remained in Mississippi with her grandmother, helping to tend the pigs and chickens and hauling water from the well to the house, which lacked indoor plumbing. Without neighborhood friends to play with, the child entertained herself by talking to the animals, delighting in making speeches to the cows. Extremely gifted in language and encouraged by her grandmother, who highly valued education, she learned to read and write at the age of 3.

But the precocious child's life took a turn for the worse when she went to Milwaukee to live with her mother in a shabby rooming house. Her mother belittled her daughter's deep love of books. Neglected and often inadequately supervised, the girl was raped and sexually abused by a string of men. Soon, she blamed herself for what was happening to her. She also began to lie, steal, and run away. Her mother tried but failed to have her placed in a home for delinquent teenagers. Instead, the now-pregnant 14-year-old girl went to live with her father in Tennessee.

Her father and his wife were able to provide love, stability, and discipline. They also encouraged the teenager to study hard and cultivate her talent for public speaking. Winning a speech contest earned her a four-year scholarship to college. Soon, she was hired as a newscaster, an event that led, in turn, to hosting several popular morning talk shows. Audiences loved her personal touch and the way she often shared her innermost thoughts and feelings on "The Oprah Winfrey Show."

The study of how and why people change over the course of the life span is called **developmental psychology**. Because virtually everything about a person changes over the life span, developmental psychology includes all the other topics that psychologists study, such as thinking, language, intelligence, emotions, and social behavior. But developmental psychologists focus only on the changes that occur as people grow older. To what extent and for what reasons has your own development differed from that of your friends or your siblings? And why does the course of a person's development sometimes change direction markedly, as Oprah's did? These are some of the fascinating topics explored in this chapter.

Research

- Cross-sectional studies observe _____ at the same point in time.

- Longitudinal studies observe _____ as _____

- Biographical (or retrospective) studies gather _____ about _____

Research Methods in Developmental Psychology

As developmental psychologists study growth and change across the life span, they use the same research methods used by psychologists in other specialized areas: naturalistic observations, case studies, correlational studies, and experiments (see Chapter 1). But because developmental psychologists are interested in processes of change over time, they use these methods in three special types of studies: cross-sectional, longitudinal, and biographical.

In a **cross-sectional study**, researchers examine developmental change by observing or testing people of different ages at the same time. For example, they might study the development of mathematical ability by testing a group of 20-year-olds and a group of 70-year-olds, looking for similarities and differences between the two age groups. However, one problem with cross-sectional studies is that they do not distinguish age differences from cohort differences. A **cohort** is a group of people born and raised during the same period of history. For example, all Americans born in 1940 form a cohort. If we were to find that the 20-year-olds were able to solve harder math problems than the 70-year-olds, we would not know whether this difference was the result of better cognitive ability in younger people (an age difference) or improvements in math education over the past 50 years (a cohort difference).

Longitudinal studies address this problem by testing the same people repeatedly as they grow older. For instance, researchers who are interested in the development of logical thought might begin their study by testing a group of 6-year-olds, then wait 3 years and test the same children again at age 9, then wait another 3 years to test them again at age 12. But longitudinal studies can take a long time. Imagine studying mathematical ability in 20-year-olds and having to wait 50 years to study them again when they are 70-year-olds!

ENDURING ISSUES in Development Psychology

In trying to understand the "what" and the "why" of human development, psychologists focus especially on three of the "Enduring Issues" first introduced in Chapter 1:

1. **Individual characteristics versus shared human traits (diversity–universality)**— Although human development is characterized by many common patterns, each person's development is also unique. Oprah Winfrey's life illustrates this well. As with other women, she progressed through the stages of childhood, adolescence, and adulthood; she embarked on a career, developed a number of close friendships, and dealt with the normal challenges of growing up to become a mature adult. All these are common developmental milestones. Yet in other ways, Oprah's development was not like that of everyone else. Not every woman is born into such a poor family, lacking neighborhood friends, surviving sexual assault as a child, or achieving such professional heights. This combination of shared and distinctive elements is common to human development. All of us take essentially the same developmental journey, but each of us travels a different road and experiences events in different ways.

2. **Stability versus change (stability–change)**—Human development is characterized by major life transitions *and* by continuities with the past. Again, Oprah Winfrey's life is an excellent example. The move to live with her mother was certainly a major turning point in her development, as was her subsequent move to live with her father. And yet, with all the changes that these transitions brought, she still had a connection with the person she had been before. We still see many of the qualities she displayed as a young child in Mississippi.

3. **Heredity versus environment (nature–nurture)**—This issue is central to developmental psychology. Human development can be explained by a combination of biological forces and environmental experiences. These two elements constantly interact to shape human growth. What made Oprah Winfrey into the person she has become? She was gifted in language, but that gift might have gone undeveloped had her grandmother not encouraged literacy at a very early age and had her father and his wife not encouraged her to study hard and cultivate her talent for public speaking. How different might she have been had she been born into a different family or had she chosen a different life's work?

To avoid some of these problems, researchers have devised a third way of studying development: the **biographical (or retrospective) study**. With this approach, the researcher might start with some 70-year-olds and pursue their lives backward; that is, the researchers would try to reconstruct their subjects' past by interviewing them and consulting various other sources. Biographical data are less trustworthy than either longitudinal or cross-sectional data because people's recollections of the past may be inaccurate. Moreover, the desired data may not be available. For example, how many 70-year-olds can put their hands on the results of mathematical tests they took 50 years earlier?

Each of these approaches to studying development has its own strengths and weaknesses (see the Summary Table: Advantages and Disadvantages of Different Types of Developmental Research Methods). Often, developmental psychologists will use data gathered from all of them. These converging data are then combined to provide a fuller picture than any one method could afford. In this chapter, you will see examples of all these research methods as they are used to help us understand psychological development.

METHOD	PROCEDURE	ADVANTAGES	DISADVANTAGES
Cross-Sectional	Studies development by observing people of different ages at the same point in time	• Inexpensive • Takes relatively little time to complete • Avoids high attrition rate (dropout of participants from study)	• Different age groups are not necessarily very much alike • Differences across age groups may result from cohort differences rather than age
Longitudinal	Studies development by observing the same people at two or more times as they grow older	• Generates detailed information about individuals • Allows for the study of developmental change in great detail • Eliminates cohort differences	• Expensive and time consuming • Potential for high attrition rate—participants may drop out over a long period of time • Differences over time may result from differences in assessment tools rather than age
Biographical or Retrospective	Studies development by interviewing people about past experiences	• Generates rich detail about one individual's life • Allows for in-depth study of one individual	• Individual's recall often untrustworthy • Can be very time consuming and expensive

SUMMARY TABLE   Advantages and Disadvantages of Different Types of Developmental Research Methods

Check Your Understanding

1. You are conducting a study looking at the effects of aging on mathematical ability. You administer a math test to a large group of 20-year-olds, then retest them when they are 40 and again when they are 60 years old. Which research method are you using?

a. Naturalistic observation   **b.** Cross-sectional approach   **c.** Longitudinal approach   **d.** Case study approach

2. Distinguishing between age differences and cohort differences is a serious problem in

a. Longitudinal studies   **b.** Generational studies   **c.** Cross-sectional studies   **d.** Biographical studies

Prenatal Development

- Lasts from _____
- During _____, substances that pass through the placenta can cause irreparable harm to the embryo or fetus, including
_____

Prenatal Development

Scientists once thought that the development of the child before birth was simply a process of physical growth. Only at birth, they believed, did experience and learning begin to influence psychological development. Today, it is well known that the unborn baby is affected profoundly by its environment. Some psychologists believe that this period of **prenatal development**—the stage of development from conception to birth—may be the single most important developmental period of a person's life. Although most experts do not go quite that far, they do agree that much more is going on during the prenatal period than mere physical growth.

Immediately after conception, the fertilized egg divides many times, embarking on the process that will transform it, in just nine months, from a one-celled organism into a complex human being. The dividing cells form a hollow ball that implants itself in the uterine wall. Two weeks after conception, the cells begin to specialize: Some will form the baby's internal organs, others will form muscles and bones, and still others will form the skin and the nervous system. No longer an undifferentiated mass of cells, the developing organism is now called an **embryo**. If all goes well, by the end of this stage of development the organism will be recognizably human and become referred to as a **fetus**. The fetal period begins in the eighth week after conception and lasts until birth.

From the second week after conception until birth, the baby is linked to its mother, and thus to the outside world, through the *placenta*. The placenta transmits nutritive substances to the baby and carries waste products away from it. Although the mother's blood never actually mingles with that of her unborn child, **teratogens**, or toxic agents that she eats, drinks, or inhales, are capable of crossing the placenta and compromising the baby's development (Newland & Rasmussen, 2003).

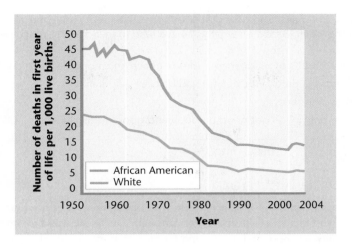

FIGURE 9–1
Mortality rates for white and African American infants.

Source: National Center for Health Statistics, 1995 (through 1990); http://www.BlackHealthCare.com, 2000 (for 1991–1996); Centers for Disease Control (for 2000); Kochanek, K. D., Murphy, S. L., Anderson, R. N., & Scott, C. (2004). Deaths: Final data for 2002. *National Vital Statistics Reports, 53*(5), 1–115 (for 2002); Miniño, A. M., Heron, M., & Smith, B. L. (2006). Deaths: Preliminary data for 2004. Retrieved June 8, 2006, from http://www.cdc.gov/nchs/products/pubs/pubd/hestats/prelimdeaths04/preliminarydeaths04.htm (for 2003–2004).

There is a **critical period** during development when many substances are most likely to have a major effect on the fetus. At other times, the same substance may have no effect at all. For example, if a woman contracts rubella (German measles) during the first 3 months of pregnancy, the effects can range from death of the fetus to a child who is born deaf. The reason is that the first 3 months are the critical period for the formation of major body parts. If the mother gets rubella during the final 3 months of pregnancy, however, severe damage to the fetus is unlikely.

Good nutrition is at least as important for the fetus as it is for the mother. Yet, many mothers, especially in developing countries, subsist on diets that are not substantial enough to nourish them or their babies properly. Malnutrition in the prenatal period can result in seriously deprived babies and often permanent damage. Even in the United States, the diets of expectant mothers often are inadequate, a fact that helps to explain why the infant death rate in the United States is more than twice as high for African Americans as it is for Caucasians (Figure 9–1). A much higher percentage of African Americans live in poverty, and poor pregnant women have a much harder time getting proper nutrition and seeing a doctor regularly.

Besides malnutrition, drugs constitute a particular threat to the unborn child. Alcohol is the drug most often abused by pregnant women, and devastating consequences can result. Even small amounts of alcohol can cause neurological problems; large amounts of alcohol can cause **fetal alcohol syndrome (FAS)**, a condition characterized by facial deformities, heart defects, stunted growth, and cognitive impairments. For these reasons, doctors recommend that pregnant women and those who are trying to become pregnant abstain from drinking alcohol altogether.

Pregnant women are also wise not to smoke. Smoking restricts the oxygen supply to the fetus, slows its breathing, and disrupts the regular rhythm of the fetal heartbeat. These changes are associated with a significantly increased risk of miscarriage. In the United States alone, smoking may be the cause of more than 100,000 miscarriages per year. Babies of mothers who smoke are also more likely to suffer low birth weight, setting the stage for other developmental problems.

The mother's level of psychological stress during pregnancy and the way she copes with it also appear to be related to the health of a newborn. In one study (Rini, Dunkel-Schetter, Wadhwa, & Sandman, 1999), researchers found that the risks of premature birth and low birth weight were higher in mothers with low self-esteem who felt pessimistic, stressed, and anxious during pregnancy.

Children born with fetal alcohol syndrome often exhibit facial deformities, heart defects, stunted growth, and cognitive impairments that can last throughout life. The syndrome is entirely preventable, but not curable.

Check Your Understanding

1. Match each of the following terms with the appropriate definition.

_____ Fetus
_____ Prenatal development
_____ Critical periods
_____ Placenta

a. Times at which harmful agents can do major damage to the fetus
b. The developing organism, after 3 months
c. The period from conception to birth
d. The organ that nourishes the fetus

2. Sue has just discovered that she is pregnant. She asks you whether you think it would be all right if she drinks a beer or two with her friends at the end of the week. Based on what you have read in this chapter, which of the following would be the most appropriate reply?

a. "Don't drink during the first three months of pregnancy, and don't have any more than one drink a week thereafter."

b. "Don't drink during the last six months of pregnancy, but it would be okay before that."

c. "Avoid alcohol at all times during pregnancy."

d. "Only one drink a week, and then only if you get good nutrition and good medical care."

Reflexes

■ Neonates (newborn babies) have a number of useful reflexes: _____, _____, _____, _____, and _____.

Temperament

■ Neonates have unique temperaments, including _____, _____, _____, and _____.

Perceptual Abilities

■ _____, _____, _____, _____ and _____ function at birth.

The Newborn

Research has disproved the old idea that **neonates**, or newborn babies, are passive creatures who merely eat, sleep, and remain oblivious to the world around them. In fact, newborn babies see, hear, and understand far more than previously thought. Most of their senses operate fairly well at birth or shortly thereafter. They absorb and process information from the outside world almost as soon as they are born—and, in some cases, perhaps even before. They learn quickly who takes care of them, and they begin to form close attachments to those individuals. It is true that newborns can sleep up to 20 hours a day, but when awake, they are much more aware and competent than they may seem at first glance.

■ REFLEXES

Newborns come equipped with a number of useful reflexes. The baby's tendency to turn his or her head toward anything that touches the cheek, called the *rooting reflex*, helps the baby find the mother's nipple. The *sucking reflex* is the tendency to suck on anything that enters the mouth; and the *swallowing reflex* enables the baby to swallow milk and other liquids without choking. The *grasping reflex* is the tendency to cling vigorously to an adult's finger or to any other object placed in the baby's hands. The *stepping reflex* refers to the fact that very young babies take what looks like walking steps when they are held upright with their feet just touching a flat surface.

Infants are also capable of imitating the facial expressions of adults. If an adult opens his or her mouth or sticks out his or her tongue, newborn babies often respond by opening their mouths or sticking out their tongues. Nearly all newborns respond to the human face, the human voice, and the human touch. This behavior improves their chances of survival. And from the very beginning, they have a means of communicating their needs: They can cry. And very soon—in only about 6 weeks—they have an even better method of communication, one that serves as a thank you to the people who are working so hard to keep them happy: They can smile.

■ TEMPERAMENT

So far, we have talked about neonates as though they were all the same, but from the very start babies display individual differences in **temperament**. Some cry much more than others; some are much more active. Some babies love to be cuddled; others seem to wriggle uncomfortably when held. Some are highly reactive to stimuli around them, whereas others are quite placid no matter what they see or hear.

These differences in temperament are quite stable over time. In one study that asked mothers to describe their children's temperaments, characteristics such as degree of irritability, flexibility, and persistence were relatively stable from infancy through age 8 (Pedlow, Sanson, Prior, & Oberklaid, 1993). Other studies have found that fussy or difficult infants are likely to become "problem children" who are aggressive and have difficulties in school (Guérin, 1994; Persson-Blennow & McNeil, 1988). And longitudinal studies have shown that most shy infants continue to be relatively shy and inhibited, just as most uninhibited infants remained relatively outgoing and bold (Kagan & Snidman, 2004).

A combination of biological and environmental factors generally contributes to this stability in behavior. For instance, if a newborn has an innate predisposition to cry often and react negatively to things, the parents may find themselves tired, frustrated, and often angry.

ENDURING ISSUES DIVERSITY/UNIVERSALITY

Different From Birth

In a classic study of infant temperament, child psychiatrists Alexander Thomas (1914–2003) and Stella Chess (1914–2007) identified three types of babies: "easy," "difficult," and "slow to warm up" (Thomas & Chess, 1977).

- "Easy" babies are good-natured and adaptable, easy to care for and to please.
- "Difficult" babies are moody and intense, with strong, negative reactions to new people and situations.
- "Slow to warm up" babies are relatively inactive and slow to respond to new things; when they do react, their reactions are mild.

To these three types, Jerome Kagan and his associates (Kagan, Reznick, Snidman, Gibbons, & Johnson, 1988; Kagan & Snidman, 1991) have added a fourth: the "shy child." Shy children are timid and inhibited, fearful of anything new or strange. Their nervous systems react to stimuli in a characteristically hypersensitive way (Kagan, 1994).

These reactions in the parents may serve to reinforce the baby's difficult behaviors, and so they tend to endure. However, even if children are born with a particular temperament, they need not have that temperament for life. Each child's predispositions interact with his or her experiences, and how the child turns out is the result of that interaction.

■ PERCEPTUAL ABILITIES

Vision   Unlike puppies and kittens, human babies are born with their eyes open and functioning, even though the world looks a bit fuzzy to them at first. Visual acuity (the clarity of vision) improves rapidly, however, and so does the ability to focus on objects at different distances. By 6 or 8 months of age, babies can see nearly as well as the average college student, though their visual system takes another 3 or 4 years to develop fully.

Very young babies already have visual preferences. They would rather look at a new picture or pattern than one they have seen many times before. If given a choice between two pictures or patterns, both of which are new to them, they generally prefer the one with the clearer contrasts and simpler patterns. Infants also find human faces and voices particularly interesting (Flavell, 1999; Turati, 2004). They not only like to look at another person's face, but almost from the moment of birth, they will follow the other person's gaze (Farroni, Massaccesi, Pividori, & Johnson, 2004).

Other Senses   Even before babies are born, their ears are in working order. Fetuses can hear sounds and will startle at a sudden, loud noise in the uterine environment. After birth, babies show signs that they remember sounds they heard in the womb. For example, immediately after birth, newborns prefer the sound of their mother's voice to that of an unfamiliar female voice (Kisilevsky et al., 2003). In some ways, young infants are better at distinguishing speech sounds than are older children and adults. As children grow older, they often lose their ability to hear the difference between two very similar speech sounds that are not distinguished in their native language (Werker & Desjardins, 1995). For example, young Japanese infants have no trouble hearing the difference between "ra" and "la," sounds that are not distinguished in the Japanese language. By the time they are 1 year old, however, Japanese infants can no longer tell these two sounds apart (Werker, 1989).

With regard to taste and smell, newborns have clear-cut likes and dislikes. They like sweet flavors, a preference that persists through childhood. Babies only a few hours old will show pleasure at the taste of sweetened water but will screw up their faces in disgust at the taste of lemon juice.

Check Your Understanding

1. What are the four types of temperament?

2. You show a 6-month-old baby a checkerboard pattern with big, bright red and white squares. The baby seems fascinated and stares at the pattern for a long time but eventually turns her attention to other things. You then show her two patterns: the familiar checkerboard and a new pattern. Which pattern is she likely to look at more?

a. The familiar checkerboard

b. The new pattern

c. There should be no difference because 6-month-olds do not have visual preferences.

d. There should be no difference because 6-month-olds cannot yet see patterns.

Infancy and Childhood

During the first dozen or so years of life, a helpless baby becomes a competent member of society. Many important changes occur during these early years, all of which are discussed in this section, including neurological, physical, and motor changes as well as cognitive and social ones.

■ NEUROLOGICAL DEVELOPMENT

The normal sequence of motor development. At birth, babies have grasping and stepping reflexes. At about 2 months, they can lift their head and shoulders. They can sit up by themselves at about 6 1/2 months and can stand (while holding on to something) at about 9 months. Crawling begins, on average, at 10 months, and walking at 1 year.

The human brain changes dramatically during infancy and early childhood. Though infants are born with a full complement of neurons, the number of connections between neurons immediately after birth is relatively small. During the first 2 years of life however, dendrites begin to bloom and branch out, the number of interconnections between neurons increases dramatically, rapid growth of myelin sheaths around many neurons occurs, and the density of synaptic connections increases dramatically. With this rapid growth in the number of connections and the speed of neural conduction, the developing brain has an enhanced potential to respond to new and varied experiences, which in turn further increases the number of connections between neurons (refer to Figure 2–5.)

■ PHYSICAL DEVELOPMENT

Certainly one of the most visible changes during infancy and childhood is physical growth. The child increases in size, of course: During the first year of life, the average baby grows 10 inches and gains 15 pounds. But there are also marked changes in body proportion. The body becomes longer, and the head proportionally smaller, so that the child's overall shape becomes more like that of an adult. During the second year, physical growth slows considerably. Rapid increases in height and weight will not occur again until early adolescence.

■ MOTOR DEVELOPMENT

Motor development refers to the acquisition of skills involving movement, such as grasping, crawling, and walking. The *average ages* at which such skills are achieved are called *developmental norms*. By about 9 months, for example, the average infant can stand up while holding onto something. Crawling occurs, on average, at 10 months, and walking occurs at about 1 year. However, some normal infants develop much faster than average, whereas others develop more slowly.

Motor development proceeds in a *proximodistal* fashion—that is, from nearest the center of the body (proximal) to farthest from the center (distal). For example, the infant initially has much greater control over gross arm movements than over movements of the fingers. Babies start batting at nearby objects as early as 1 month, but they cannot reach accurately until they are about 4 months old. It takes them another month or two before they are consistently successful in grasping objects. At first, they grasp with the whole hand, but by the end of the first year, they can pick up a tiny object with the thumb and forefinger.

ENDURING ISSUES   NATURE/NURTURE

Maturation

Maturation refers to biological processes that unfold as a person grows older and that contribute to orderly sequences of developmental changes, such as the progression from crawling to toddling to walking. Psychologists used to believe that maturation of the central nervous system largely accounted for many of the changes in early motor skills—that environment and experience played only a minor part in their emergence. But this view has been changing. Many researchers now see early motor development as arising from a combination of factors both within and outside the child. The child plays an active part in the process by exploring, discovering, and selecting solutions to the demands of new tasks. A baby who is learning to crawl, for example, must figure out how to position the body with belly off the ground and to coordinate arm and leg movements to maintain balance while managing to proceed forward (Bertenthal, Campos, & Kermoian, 1994). What does not work must be discarded or adapted; what does work must be remembered and called on for future use. This process is a far cry from seeing the baby as one day starting to crawl simply because he or she has reached the point of maturational "readiness." Moreover, to some extent parents can accelerate the acquisition of motor skills in children by providing them with ample training, encouragement, and practice. Differences in these factors seem to account for most of the cross-cultural differences in the average age at which children reach certain milestones in motor development (Hopkins & Westra, 1990; Nixon-Cave, 2001).

As coordination improves, children learn to run, skip, and climb. At ages 3 and 4, they begin to use their hands for increasingly complex tasks, learning how to put on mittens and shoes, then grappling with buttons, zippers, shoelaces, and pencils. Gradually, through a combination of practice and the physical maturation of the body and the brain, they acquire increasingly complex motor abilities, such as bike riding, rollerblading, and swimming. By the age of about 11, some children begin to be highly skilled at such tasks (Gallahue & Ozmun, 2006).

■ COGNITIVE DEVELOPMENT

The most influential theorist in the area of cognitive development was the Swiss psychologist Jean Piaget (1896–1980). Piaget observed and studied children, including his own three. He watched them play games, solve problems, and perform everyday tasks, and he asked them questions and devised tests to learn how they thought. As a result of his observations, Piaget believed that cognitive development is a way of adapting to the environment. In Piaget's view, children are intrinsically motivated to explore and understand things. As they do so, according to Piaget, they progress through four basic stages of cognitive development. These are outlined in the Summary Table.

Neurological Development

- Interconnections between neurons _____ dramatically.
- Growth of myelin sheaths _____ _____ of transmission.

Physical Development

- First year: _____
- Second year: _____

Motor Development

- Developmental norms:_____
- Maturation:_____

Cognitive Development

- Piaget's stages of cognitive development include:

_____ (_____ to _____)

_____ (_____ to _____)

_____ (_____ to _____)

_____ (_____ through _____)

SUMMARY TABLE	**Piaget's Stages of Cognitive Development**	
STAGE	APPROXIMATE AGE	KEY FEATURES
Sensory-motor	0–2 years	Object permanence Mental representations
Preoperational	2–7 years	Representational thought Fantasy play Symbolic gestures Egocentrism
Concrete-operational	7–11 years	Conservation Complex classification
Formal-operational	Adolescence-adulthood	Abstract and hypothetical thought

Sensory-Motor Stage (Birth to 2 Years) According to Piaget, babies spend the first 2 years of life in the **sensory-motor stage** of development. They start out by simply applying the skills with which they were born—primarily sucking and grasping reflexes—to a broad range of activities. As they gain experience, they begin to distinguish between things that make noise and things that do not, between things that are suckable and those that are not. In this way, infants begin to organize their experiences, fitting them into rudimentary categories such as "suckable" and "not suckable," "noise making," and "not noise making."

Another important outcome of the sensory-motor stage, according to Piaget, is the development of **object permanence**, an awareness that objects continue to exist even when out of sight. For newborns, objects that disappear simply cease to exist—"out of sight, out of mind." But by the time they are 18 to 24 months old, infants can imagine the movement of an object that they do not actually see move. This last skill depends on the ability to form **mental representations** of objects and to manipulate those representations in their heads. This is a major achievement of the late sensory-motor stage, as is the capacity for self-recognition—toddlers are able to recognize the child in a mirror as "myself."

In Piaget's famous experiment, the child has to judge which glass holds more liquid: the tall, thin one or the short, wide one. Although both glasses hold the same amount, children in the preoperational stage say that the taller glass holds more, because they focus their attention on only one thing—the height of the column of liquid.

Preoperational Stage (2 to 7 Years) When children enter the **preoperational stage** of cognitive development, their thought is still tightly bound to their physical and perceptual experiences. But their increasing ability to use mental representations lays the groundwork for the development of language which, as we saw in Chapter 7: Cognition and Mental Abilities, is one of the building blocks of thought (more about language development shortly). Representational thought also lays the groundwork for two other hallmarks of this stage—engaging in *fantasy play* (a cardboard box becomes a castle) and using *symbolic gestures* (slashing the air with an imaginary sword to slay an imaginary dragon).

Although children of this age have made advances over sensory-motor thought, in many ways they do not yet think as do older children and adults. For example, preschool children are **egocentric**. They have difficulty seeing things from another person's point of view or putting themselves in someone else's place. An illustration of egocentric behavior can sometimes be seen during the game of hide-and-seek, when young children cover their own eyes to prevent others from seeing them.

Also, children of this age are easily misled by appearances. They tend to concentrate on the most outstanding aspect of a display or an event, ignoring everything else. In a famous experiment, Piaget showed preoperational children two identical glasses, filled to the same level with juice. The children were asked which glass held more juice, and they replied (correctly) that both had the same amount. Then, Piaget poured the juice from one glass into a taller, narrower glass (accompanying photo). Again, the children were asked which glass held more juice. They looked at the two glasses, saw that the level of the juice in the tall, narrow one was much higher, and replied that the narrow glass had more. According to Piaget, children at this stage cannot consider the past (Piaget simply poured all the juice from one container into another) or the future (if he poured it back again, the levels of juice would be identical). Nor can they consider a container's height and width at the same time. Thus, they cannot understand how an increase in one dimension (height) might be offset by a decrease in another dimension (width).

Concrete-Operational Stage (7 to 11 Years)   During the **concrete-operational stage**, children become more flexible in their thinking. They learn to consider more than one dimension of a problem at a time and to look at a situation from someone else's viewpoint. At this stage, they become able to grasp **principles of conservation**, such as the idea that the volume of a liquid stays the same regardless of the size and shape of the container into which it is poured. Other related conservation concepts have to do with number, length, area, and mass. All involve an understanding that basic amounts remain constant despite superficial changes in appearance, which can always be reversed.

Another accomplishment of this stage is the ability to grasp complex classification schemes such as those involving superordinate and subordinate classes. For instance, if you were to show a preschooler four toy dogs and two toy cats and ask whether there are more dogs or more animals, the child would almost always answer "more dogs." It is not until age 7 or 8 that children are able to think about objects as being simultaneously members of two classes, one more inclusive than the other. Yet even well into the elementary school years, children's thinking is still very much stuck in the "here and now." Often, they are unable to solve problems without concrete reference points that they can handle or imagine handling.

Formal-Operational Stage (Adolescence Through Adulthood)   The limitation just described is overcome in the **formal-operational stage** of cognitive development, which is often reached during adolescence. Youngsters at this stage are able to think in abstract terms. They can formulate hypotheses, test them mentally, and accept or reject them according to the outcome of mental experiments. Therefore, they are capable of going beyond the here and now to understand things in terms of cause and effect; to consider possibilities as well as realities; and to develop and use general rules, principles, and theories.

Criticisms of Piaget's Theory   Piaget's work has been extraordinarily influential, but over the years it has also produced a great deal of controversy. Many question his assumption that there are distinct stages in cognitive development that always progress in an orderly, sequential way, and that a child must pass through one stage before entering the next. Moreover, when young babies are allowed to reveal their understanding of object permanence without being required to conduct a search for a missing object, they often seem to know perfectly well that objects continue to exist when hidden by other objects (Baillargeon, 1994). They also show other quite sophisticated knowledge of the world that Piaget believed they lacked, such as a rudimentary grasp of numbers (Wynn, 1995). At older ages, too, milestone cognitive achievements seem to be reached much sooner than Piaget believed (Gopnik, 1996).

Despite these criticisms, Piaget's theory provides a useful schematic road map of cognitive development. Moreover, Piaget profoundly impacted our understanding with his observation that children play an active role in the learning process, his description of qualitative changes in the way children think at various ages, and his emphasis on "readiness to learn."

▪ MORAL DEVELOPMENT

One of the important changes in thinking that occurs during childhood and adolescence is the development of moral reasoning. Lawrence Kohlberg (1927–1987) studied this kind of development by telling his participants stories that illustrate complex moral issues (Kohlberg, 1979, 1981). The "Heinz dilemma" is the best known of these stories:

Moral Development

▪ According to Kohlberg, moral development progresses through the following stages:

_____

_____

_____

In Europe, a woman was near death from cancer. One drug might save her, a form of radium that a druggist in the same town had recently discovered. The druggist was charging $2,000, ten times what the drug cost him to make. The sick woman's husband, Heinz, went to everyone he knew to borrow the money, but he could only get together about half of what it cost. He told the druggist that his wife was dying and asked him to sell it cheaper or let him pay later. But the druggist said, "No." The husband got desperate and broke into the man's store to steal the drug for his wife. (Kohlberg, 1969, p. 379)

The children and adolescents who heard this story were asked, "Should the husband have done that? Why?"

On the basis of his participants' replies to these questions (particularly the second one, "Why?"), Kohlberg theorized that moral reasoning develops in stages, much like Piaget's account of cognitive development:

- *Preconventional level*—Preadolescent children tend to interpret behavior in terms of its concrete consequences: whether behavior is rewarded or punished, whether or not it satisfies needs (particularly their own).

- *Conventional level*—With the arrival of adolescence and the shift to formal-operational thought, children begin to define right behavior as that which pleases or helps others and is approved by them. Around mid-adolescence, there is a further shift toward considering various abstract social virtues, such as being a "good citizen" and respecting authority. Both forms of conventional moral reasoning require an ability to think about such abstract values as "duty" and "social order," to consider the intentions that lie behind behavior, and to put oneself in the "other person's shoes."

- *Postconventional level*—The third level of moral reasoning requires a still more abstract form of thought. This level is marked by an emphasis on abstract principles such as justice, liberty, and equality. Personal and strongly felt moral standards become the guideposts for deciding what is right and wrong. Whether these decisions correspond to the rules and laws of a particular society at a particular time is irrelevant. For the first time, people may become aware of discrepancies between what they judge to be moral and what society has determined to be legal.

Kohlberg's views have not gone without criticism. First, research indicates that many people in our society, adults as well as adolescents, never progress beyond the conventional level of moral reasoning (Conger & Petersen, 1991). Does this finding mean that these people are morally "underdeveloped," as Kohlberg's theory implies?

Second, Kohlberg's theory does not take account of cultural differences in moral values. Kohlberg put considerations of "justice" at the highest level of moral reasoning. In Nepal, however, researchers discovered that a group of adolescent Buddhist monks placed the highest moral value on alleviating suffering and showing compassion (Huebner, Garrod, & Snarey, 1990).

Finally, Kohlberg's theory has been criticized as sexist. According to Carol Gilligan (1982, 1992), boys are more inclined to base their moral judgments on the abstract concept of justice while girls tend to base theirs more on the criteria of caring about other people and the importance of maintaining personal relationships. In Gilligan's view, there is no valid reason to assume that one of these perspectives is morally superior to the other. Subsequent research on Gilligan's theory of sex differences in moral reasoning has been mixed (J. L. Murray, Feuerstein, & Adams, 2006). In addition, other research has found that gender differences in moral thinking tend to diminish in adulthood (Cohn, 1991). However, concerns about gender bias in Kohlberg's theory still remain.

More recent research on moral development has moved in the direction of broadening Kohlberg's focus on changes in moral reasoning. These researchers are interested in the factors that influence moral choices in everyday life and the extent to which those choices are actually put into action. In other words, they want to understand moral behavior as much as moral thinking (Tappan, 2006).

■ LANGUAGE DEVELOPMENT

The development of language follows a predictable pattern. At about 2 months of age, an infant begins to *coo* (a nondescript word for nondescript sounds). In another month or two, the infant enters the **babbling** stage and starts to repeat sounds such as "da" or even meaningless sounds that developmental psychologists refer to as "grunts"; these sounds are the building blocks for later language development. A few months later, the infant may string together the same sound, as in "dadadada." Finally, the baby will form combinations of different sounds, as in "dabamaga."

Even deaf babies with deaf parents who communicate with sign language engage in a form of babbling. Like hearing infants, these babies begin to babble before they are 10 months old—but they babble with their hands. Just as hearing infants utter sounds repeatedly, deaf babies make repetitive movements of their hands, like those of sign language (Morgan, 2005).

Gradually, an infant's babbling takes on certain features of adult language. At about age 4 to 6 months, the infant's vocalizations begin to show signs of *intonation*, the rising and lowering of pitch that allows adults to distinguish, for example, between questions ("You're tired?") and statements ("You're tired."). Also around this time, babies learn the basic sounds of their native language and can distinguish them from the sounds of other languages. By 6 months, they may recognize commonly used words, such as their own names and the words "mommy" and "daddy."

All this preparation leads up to the first word at about 12 months, usually "dada." During the next 6 to 8 months, children build a vocabulary of one-word sentences called **holophrases**: "Up!," "Out!," or "More!" Children may also use compound words such as "awgone" [all gone]. To these holophrases, they add words used to address people: "bye-bye"—a favorite—and a few exclamations, such as "ouch!"

In the second year of life, children begin to distinguish between themselves and others. Possessive words become a big part of the vocabulary: [The shoes are] "Daddy's." But the overwhelming passion of children from 12 to 24 months old is naming. With little or no prompting, they will name virtually everything they see, though not always correctly.

During the third year of life, children begin to form two- and three-word sentences such as "See Daddy," "Baby cry," "My ball," and "Dog go woof woof." Typically at this age, children omit auxiliary verbs and verb endings ([Can] "I have that?"; "I [am] eat[ing] it up"), as well as prepositions and articles ("It [is] time [for] Sarah [to] take [a] nap"). Apparently, children at this age seize on the most important parts of speech—those that contain the most meaning.

After 3 years of age, children begin to fill in their sentences ("Nick school" becomes "Nick goes to school"), and language production increases dramatically. Children start to use the past tense as well as the present. Sometimes, they *overregularize* the past tense, by applying the regular form when an irregular one is called for (saying "Alex goed" instead of "Alex went," for example). Such mistakes are signs that the child has implicitly grasped the basic rules of language. Preschoolers also ask more questions and learn to employ "Why?" effectively (sometimes monotonously so). By the age of 5 or 6, most children have a vocabulary of more than 2,500 words and can construct sentences of 6 to 8 words.

Theories of Language Development   Two very different theories explain how language develops. B. F. Skinner (1957) believed that parents and other people listen to the infant's cooing and babbling and reinforce those sounds that most resemble adult speech. If the infant says something that sounds like "mama," mommy reinforces this behavior with smiles and attention. As children get older, the things they say must sound more and more like adult speech to be reinforced (a process called *shaping*, as seen in Chapter 5: Learning). Children who call the wrong person "mama" are less likely to receive a smile; they are praised only when they use the word appropriately. Skinner believed that an understanding of grammar, word construction, and so on are acquired in much the same way.

Most psychologists and linguists now believe that learning alone cannot explain the speed, accuracy, and originality with which children learn to use language. Noam Chomsky, in particular, argues that children are born with a **language acquisition device**, an internal mechanism that is "wired into" the human brain, facilitating language learning and making it universal (Chomsky, 1986, 1998). This language acquisition device is like an internal "map" of

Language Development

■ Cooing gives way to _____; first word usually appears at about _____, followed by _____.

Second year of life: _____

Third year: _____

■ Most linguists assert that an inborn _____ or _____ is required.

Social Development

- Imprinting: _____
- Attachment: _____
- Erikson's psychosocial stages:
  Birth to 1 year: _____
  1 to 3 years: _____
  3 to 6 years: _____
  7 to 11 years: _____
- Peer relationships start with siblings and expand to include _____
  _____

Konrad Lorenz discovered that goslings will follow the first moving object they see, regardless of whether it is their mother, a mechanical toy, or a human. Here, Lorenz is trailed by ducklings that have imprinted on him.

language: All the child has to do is to fill in the blanks with information supplied by the environment. An American child fills in the blanks with English words, a Mexican child with Spanish words, and so on. A more recent theory advanced by Steven Pinker (1994, 1999, 2002) holds that, to a large extent, evolutionary forces may have shaped language, providing humans with what he calls a *language instinct*.

■ SOCIAL DEVELOPMENT

Learning to interact with others is an important aspect of development in childhood. Early in life, children's most important relationships are with their parents and other caregivers. But by the time they are 3 years old, their important relationships have usually expanded to include siblings, playmates, and other adults outside the family. Their social world expands further when they start school. Social development involves ongoing relationships as well as new or changing ones.

Parent–Child Relationships in Infancy: Development of Attachment Young animals of many species follow their mothers around because of **imprinting**. Perhaps the most familiar example of imprinting is seen in baby ducklings following their mother. Shortly after they are born or hatched, they form a strong bond to the first moving object they see. In nature, this object is most often the mother, the first source of nurturance and protection. Human newborns do not imprint on first-seen moving objects, but they do gradually form an **attachment**, or emotional bond, to the people who take care of them (regardless of the caregiver's gender). Signs of attachment are evident by the age of 6 months or even earlier. The baby will react with smiles and coos at the caregiver's appearance and with whimpers and doleful looks when the caregiver goes away. At around 7 months, attachment behavior becomes more intense. The infant will reach out to be picked up by the caregiver and will cling to the caregiver, especially when tired, frightened, or hurt. The baby will also begin to display **stranger anxiety**, often reacting with loud wails at even the friendliest approach by an unfamiliar person. If separated from the caregiver even for a few minutes in an unfamiliar place, the baby will usually become quite upset. Stranger anxiety usually begins around 7 months, reaching its peak at 12 months then declining during the second year of life. Parents often are puzzled by this new behavior in their previously nonchalant infants, but it is perfectly normal.

Ideally, infants learn in their first year of life that their primary caregivers can be counted on to be there when needed. Psychologist Erik Erikson (1902–1994) called this the development of *basic trust* (see the Summary Table: Stages of Development). They develop faith in other people and also in themselves. They see the world as a secure, dependable place and have optimism about the future. In contrast, babies whose needs are not usually met, perhaps because of an unresponsive or often-absent caregiver, develop what Erikson referred to as *mistrust*. They grow to be fearful and overly anxious about their own security.

As infants develop basic trust, they are freed from preoccupation with the availability of the caregiver. They come to discover that there are other things of interest in the world. Cautiously at first, then more boldly, they venture away from the caregiver to investigate objects and other people around them. This exploration is a first indication that the child is developing **autonomy**, or a sense of independence. Autonomy and attachment may seem to be opposites, but they are actually closely related. The child who has formed a secure attachment to a caregiver can explore the environment without fear. Such a child knows that the caregiver will be there when really needed, and so the caregiver serves as a "secure base" from which to venture forth (Ainsworth, 1977).

At about 2 years of age, children begin to assert their growing independence, becoming very negative when interfered with by parents. They refuse everything: getting dressed ("No!"), going to sleep ("No!"), using the potty ("No!"). The usual outcome of these first declarations of independence is that the parents begin to discipline the child. Children are told they have to eat and go to bed at a particular time, they must not pull the cat's tail or kick their sister, and they must respect other people's rights. The conflict between the parents' need for peace and order and the child's desire for autonomy often creates difficulties. But it is an essential first step in **socialization**, the process by which children learn the behaviors and attitudes appropriate to their family and their culture.

SUMMARY TABLE   Stages of Development: Erikson and Freud

STAGE	AGE	CHALLENGE	FREUDIAN PSYCHOSEXUAL STAGE
Trust versus Mistrust	Birth to 1 year	Developing a sense that the world is safe and good	Oral
Autonomy versus Shame and Doubt	1–3 years	Realizing that one is an independent person with the ability to make decisions	Anal
Initiative versus Guilt	3–6 years	Developing a willingness to try new things and to handle failure	Phallic
Industry versus Inferiority	6 years to adolescence	Learning competence in basic skills and to cooperate with others	Latency
Identity versus Role Confusion	Adolescence	Developing a coherent, integrated sense of inner self	Genital
Intimacy versus Isolation	Young adulthood	Establishing ties to another in a trusting, loving relationship	
Generativity versus Stagnation	Middle adulthood	Finding meaning in career, family, and community via productive work	
Ego Integrity versus Despair	Late life	Viewing one's life as satisfactory and worth living	

Erikson saw two possible outcomes of this early conflict: *autonomy* or *shame and doubt*. If a toddler fails to acquire a sense of independence and separateness from others, self-doubt may take root. The child may begin to question his or her own ability to act effectively in the world. If parents and other adults belittle a toddler's efforts, the child may also begin to feel ashamed. The need for both autonomy and socialization can be met if parents allow the child a reasonable amount of independence, while insisting that the child follow certain rules.

Parent–Child Relationships in Childhood   As children grow older, their social worlds expand. They play with siblings and friends, they go off to nursery school or day care, and they eventually enter kindergarten. Erikson saw the stage between ages 3 and 6 as one of growing initiative, surrounded by a potential for guilt (*initiative versus guilt*). Children of this age become increasingly involved in independent efforts to accomplish goals—making plans, undertaking projects, mastering new skills—from bike riding to table setting to drawing, painting, and writing simple words. Parental encouragement of these initiatives leads to a sense of joy in taking on new tasks. But if children are criticized repeatedly and scolded for things they do wrong, they may develop strong feelings of unworthiness, resentment, and guilt. In Erikson's view, avoiding these negative feelings is the major challenge of this stage.

The effect of parenting style on a child's outlook and behavior has been the subject of extensive research. For example, Diana Baumrind (1972, 1991, 1996) identified four basic parenting styles:

- *Authoritarian*—These parents control their children's behavior rigidly and insist on unquestioning obedience. Authoritarian parents are likely to produce children who generally have poor communication skills and are moody, withdrawn, and distrustful.

- *Permissive-indifferent*—These parents exert too little control, failing to set limits on their children's behavior. They are also neglectful and inattentive, providing little emotional support to their children. The children of permissive-indifferent parents tend to be overly dependent and lacking in social skills and self-control.

According to Erik Erikson, children around age 2 are struggling to establish autonomy from their parents.

- *Permissive-indulgent*—These parents are very supportive of their children, but they fail to set appropriate limits on their behavior. The children of permissive-indulgent parents tend to be immature, disrespectful, impulsive, and out of control.
- *Authoritative*—These parents, according to Baumrind, represent the most successful parenting style. Authoritative parents provide firm structure and guidance without being overly controlling. They listen to their children's opinions and give explanations for their decisions, but it is clear that they are the ones who make and enforce the rules. Parents who use this approach are most likely to have children who are self-reliant and socially responsible. Moreover, the positive effects of authoritative parenting have been demonstrated across different ethnic groups (Querido, Warner, & Eyberg, 2002).

Although many studies show a relationship between parental behavior and child development, conclusions about cause and effect must be drawn with caution. Children influence the behavior of their caregivers at the same time that the caregivers are influencing them. Moreover, parents do not act the same way toward every child in the family (even though they may try to), because each child is a different individual.

As seen so far, parents can have a profound effect on the development of their children. The next section examines the extent to which peers also influence development.

Relationships With Other Children   At a very early age, infants begin to show an interest in other children, but the social skills required to play with them develop only gradually. Among the first peers that most children encounter are their siblings. The quality of sibling relationships can have a major impact on how children learn to relate to other peers. Once children enter school, peer influences outside the family increase greatly. Children come under a great deal of pressure to be part of a **peer group** of friends. In peer groups, children learn many valuable things, such as how to engage in cooperative activities aimed at collective goals and how to negotiate the social roles of leader and follower. Conversely, inability to get along well with classmates can have long-lasting negative consequences.

Successfully making friends is one of the tasks that Erikson saw as centrally important to children between the ages of 7 and 11, the stage of *industry versus inferiority*. At this age, children must master many increasingly difficult skills, social interaction with peers being only one of them. Others have to do with mastering academic skills at school, meeting growing responsibilities placed on them at home, and learning to do various tasks that they will need as independent-living adults. In Erikson's view, if children become stifled in their efforts to prepare themselves for the adult world, they may conclude that they are inadequate or inferior and lose faith in their power to become self-sufficient. Those whose industry is rewarded are likely to develop a sense of competence and self-assurance.

Nonshared Environments   Most developmental psychologists believe that peer influence is just one example of a much broader class of environmental factors called the **nonshared environment** (Plomin, 1999; Rose et al., 2003; Turkheimer & Waldron, 2000). Even children who grow up in the same home, with the same parents, are likely to have very different day-to-day human relationships, and this nonshared environment can have a significant effect on their development. "The message is not that family experiences are unimportant," concludes one review of the research. Instead, the crucial environmental influences that shape personality development are "specific to each child, rather than general to an entire family" (Plomin & Rende, 1991, p. 180).

Children in dual-career families are especially likely to have nonshared environments because they usually spend a sizable portion of their waking hours in child-care settings, which are not usually the same for all their siblings. Some psychologists have expressed concern that being entrusted to caregivers outside the immediate family may interfere with the development of secure attachments and put children at greater risk for emotional maladjustment. However, research data show that the critical variable is *quality* of care (Brobert, Wessels, Lamb, & Hwang, 1997; Scarr, 1999; Votruba-Drzal, Coley, & Chase-Lansdale, 2004). Children of working mothers who are placed in a quality day care, even at very early ages, are no more likely to develop behavior problems or have problems with their self-esteem than children reared at home (Harvey, 1999). In fact, some research shows clear benefits for the children of mothers who work, even if the children are still very young. For example, children of employed mothers tend to be more independent and self-confident and have fewer stereotyped views of males and females (Clarke-Stewart, Christian, & Fitzgerald, 1994). The next section discusses how children learn gender stereotypes.

■ SEX-ROLE DEVELOPMENT

By about age 3, boys and girls have developed a **gender identity**—that is, a little girl knows that she is a girl and a little boy knows that he is a boy. At this point, however, children have little understanding of what that means. A 3-year-old boy might think that he could grow up to be a mommy or that if you put a dress on him and a bow in his hair, he will turn into a girl. By the age of 4 or 5, most children know that gender depends on what kind of genitals a person has. They have also acquired **gender constancy**, the realization that gender cannot be changed.

At quite a young age, children also start to acquire **gender-role awareness**, a knowledge of the behaviors expected of males and of females in their society. As a result, they develop **gender stereotypes**, oversimplified beliefs about what the "typical" male and female are like. At the same time, children develop their own **sex-typed behavior**: Girls play with dolls, and boys play with trucks; girls put on pretty clothes and fuss with their hair, and boys run around and wrestle with one another. Although the behavioral differences between boys and girls are minimal in infancy, quite major differences tend to develop as children grow older. Boys become more active and physically aggressive, and they tend to play in larger groups. Girls talk more, shove less, and tend to interact in pairs. The source of such sex-typed behavior is a matter of considerable debate.

By school age, boys and girls tend to play by the rules of sex-typed behavior. Typically, girls play nonaggressive games, in pairs or small groups, whereas boys prefer more active group games.

ENDURING ISSUES NATURE/NURTURE

Sex-Typed Behavior

Because gender-related differences in styles of interaction appear very early in development (even before the age of 3), some specialists in this area believe that they are at least partly biological in origin. In addition to the influence of genes, some evidence suggests that prenatal exposure to hormones plays a part (Collaer & Hines, 1995). But psychologist Eleanor Maccoby believes that biologically based differences are small at first and later become exaggerated because of the different kinds of socialization experienced by boys and girls. She suggests that a lot of gender-typical behavior is the product of children playing with others of their sex (Maccoby, 1998). Undoubtedly, popular culture—especially as portrayed on television—also influences the norms of gender-appropriate behavior that develop in children's peer groups. And parents, too, can sometimes add input, especially during critical transitions in the child's life when parents feel it is important to behave in more sex-stereotyped ways (Fagot, 1994). The result is substantial sex-typed behavior by middle childhood. Research on this topic continues, but the growing consensus is that both biology and experience contribute to gender differences in behavior (Collaer & Hines, 1995; Collins, Maccoby, Steinberg, Hetherington, & Bornstein, 2000).

Sex-Role Development
- Gender identity: _____
- Gender constancy: _____
- Gender-role awareness: _____
- Gender stereotypes: _____
- Sex-typed behavior: _____

In the rest of this chapter, we will explore the ways in which adolescents and adults grow and change—physically, intellectually, and socially. Adolescence, adulthood, and old age bring significant changes in the way people think. People react to physical change and to their sexuality in many ways, and changes in social relationships and personality occur throughout the life span. Let's begin the discussion at the end of childhood and the start of adolescence, the period of life roughly between the ages of 10 and 20, when a person transforms from a child into a young adult.

Check Your Understanding

1. Match each phase of childhood with its major challenge, according to Erik Erikson's theory.

_____ Infancy

_____ Toddlerhood

_____ Preschool years

_____ Elementary school years

a. Industry versus inferiority

b. Trust versus mistrust

c. Autonomy versus shame and doubt

d. Initiative versus guilt

2. Three preschoolers of different ages are sitting in a room watching a playful puppy. Child 1 exclaims, "I play puppy tail." Child 2 reaches for the dog and cries out, "Gimme!" Child 3 asks, "Who left the puppy here?" On the basis of your knowledge of language development, which child is most likely to be the youngest and which is most likely to be the oldest?

a. Child 3 is youngest, child 1 is oldest.

b. Child 3 is youngest, child 2 is oldest.

c. Child 2 is youngest, child 3 is oldest.

d. Child 1 is youngest, child 3 is oldest.

Adolescence

ENDURING ISSUES STABILITY/CHANGE

Life-Span Development

William James, the nineteenth-century American psychologist and philosopher, believed that a person's character is "set like plaster" by the age of 30. Since James's day, psychologists have suggested ever earlier ages as the point at which development is more or less finished. In fact, until recently, many psychologists believed that most important developmental changes occurred in early childhood. Although it was acknowledged that people did change throughout life, these changes were considered routine and predictable—such as the physical changes of middle and old age.

However, research has demonstrated that significant developmental changes occur throughout the life span. We now know that adolescence and adulthood are important developmental periods for human beings—not just years during which people simply play out their lives according to the patterns established in early childhood.

Physical Changes

■ Growth spurt: _____

■ Puberty: _____

Cognitive Changes

■ Formal-operational thought: _____

Personality and Social Development

■ Erikson's psychosocial stages:

■ Identity versus _____

■ Identity crisis: _____

Some Problems of Adolescence

■ Low self-esteem resulting from ____

_____

■ _____ suicide rate

■ PHYSICAL CHANGES

A series of dramatic physical milestones ushers in adolescence. The most obvious is the **growth spurt**, a rapid increase in height and weight that begins, on average, at about 10.5 years of age in girls and 12.5 in boys, and reaches its peak at ages 12 and 14, respectively. Typical adolescents attain their adult height about 6 years after the start of the growth spurt.

Teenagers are acutely aware of the changes taking place in their bodies. Many become anxious about whether they are the "right" shape or size and may obsessively compare themselves to the models and actors they see on television and in magazines. Because few adolescents can match these ideals, it is not surprising that when asked what they most dislike about themselves, physical appearance is mentioned most often.

Sexual Development The visible signs of **puberty**—the onset of sexual maturation—occur in a different sequence for boys and girls. In boys, the initial sign is growth of the testes. This starts, on average, at around 11.5 years old, nearly a year before the beginning of the growth spurt in height. Along with the growth spurt comes enlargement of the penis. Development of pubic hair takes a little longer, followed by development of facial hair. Deepening of the voice is one of the last noticeable changes of male maturation.

In females, the beginning of the growth spurt is typically the first sign of approaching puberty. Shortly thereafter, the breasts begin to develop; pubic hair appears around the same time. **Menarche**, the first menstrual period, occurs about a year or so later—at 12.5 years of age for the average girl in the United States. The onset of menstruation does not necessarily mean that a girl is biologically capable of becoming a mother. It is uncommon (though not unheard of) for a girl to become pregnant during her first few menstrual cycles. Female fertility increases gradually during the first year after menarche. The same is true of male fertility.

Achieving the capacity to reproduce is probably the single most important development in adolescence. But sexuality is a confusing issue for adolescents in the United States. Fifty years ago, young people were expected to postpone expressing their sexual needs until they were responsible, married adults. Since then, major changes have occurred in sexual customs. Three fourths of all males and more than half of all females between the ages of 15 and 19 have had intercourse.

The United States has the highest teen birth rate in the industrialized world: nearly six times the rate in France and 13 times the rate in Japan (UNICEF, 2001). One reason for this may be ignorance of basic facts concerning reproduction. In countries such as Norway, Sweden, and the Netherlands, which have extensive sex education programs, teenage pregnancy rates are much lower. Another explanation for some unwanted teenage pregnancies may be the adolescent tendency to believe that "nothing bad will happen to me." This sense of invulnerability, in the absence of sex education, may blind some teenagers to the possibility of pregnancy.

Whatever the causes of unmarried teenage pregnancy and teen childbearing, its consequences can be devastating. The entire future of a young unmarried mother is in jeopardy, particularly if she has no parental support or is living in poverty. She is less likely to graduate from high school, less likely to improve her economic status, and less likely to get married and stay married than a girl who postpones childbearing (Coley & Chase-Lansdale, 1998). The babies of teen mothers are apt to suffer too. They are more likely to have low birth weight, which is associated with learning disabilities and later academic problems, childhood illnesses, and neurological problems (Furstenberg, Brooks-Gunn, & Chase-Lansdale, 1989; Moore, Morrison, & Greene, 1997). In addition, children of teenage mothers are more likely to be neglected and abused than are children of older mothers (Coley & Chase-Lansdale, 1998; George & Lee, 1997).

■ COGNITIVE CHANGES

Just as bodies mature during adolescence, so do patterns of thought. Piaget (1969) saw the cognitive advances of adolescence as an increased ability to reason abstractly, called *formal-operational thought* (see Summary Table: Piaget's Stages of Cognitive Development on p. 248). Adolescents can understand and manipulate abstract concepts, can speculate about alternative possibilities, and can reason in hypothetical terms. This process allows them to debate such problematic issues as abortion, sexual behavior, and AIDS. Of course, not all adolescents reach the stage of formal operations, and many of those who do, fail to apply formal-operational thinking to the everyday problems they face. Younger adolescents especially are unlikely to be objective about matters concerning themselves and lack a deep understanding of the difficulties involved in moral judgments. The achievement of formal-operational thinking has its hazards, including overconfidence in new mental abilities and a tendency to place too much importance on one's own thoughts. Some adolescents also fail to realize that not everyone thinks the way they do and that other people may hold different views. Piaget called these tendencies the "egocentrism of formal operations" (Piaget, 1969).

■ PERSONALITY AND SOCIAL DEVELOPMENT

Adolescents are eager to establish independence from their parents, but simultaneously, they fear the responsibilities of adulthood. They see they have many important tasks and decisions ahead of them. Particularly in a technologically advanced society, this period of development is bound to involve some stress.

The "Storm and Stress" of Adolescence   Early in the twentieth century, many people saw adolescence as a time of great instability and strong emotions. For example, G. Stanley Hall (1844–1924), one of the first developmental psychologists, portrayed adolescence as a period of "storm and stress," fraught with suffering, passion, and rebellion against adult authority (G. S. Hall, 1904). Research, however, indicates that the storm-and-stress view greatly exaggerates the experiences of most teenagers. Adolescence inevitably is accompanied by some difficult stress related to school, family, and peers. However, the great majority of adolescents do not describe their lives as rent by turmoil and chaos (Eccles et al., 1993). For instance, a cross-cultural study of adolescents from 10 countries, including the United States, found that more than 75% enjoyed a healthy self-image, felt generally happy, and valued the time they spent at school and at work (Offer, Ostrov, Howard, & Atkinson, 1988).

Forming an Identity   To make the transition from dependence on parents to dependence on oneself, the adolescent must develop a stable sense of self. This process is called **identity formation**, a term derived from Erik Erikson's theory, that sees the major challenge of this stage of life as *identity versus role confusion*. The overwhelming question for the young person becomes "Who am I?" In Erikson's view, the answer comes by integrating a number of different roles—say, talented math student, athlete, and artist, or political liberal and aspiring architect—into a coherent whole that "fits" comfortably. Erikson believed that failure to form this coherent sense of identity leads to confusion about roles.

James Marcia (1980) took this idea one step further by suggesting that finding an identity requires a period of intense self-exploration called an **identity crisis**. He described four possible outcomes of this process:

- *Identity achievement*—Success in making personal choices about one's beliefs and goals and feeling comfortable with those choices
- *Identity foreclosure*—Prematurely settling on an identity chosen by others; becoming what others want
- *Moratorium*—Being in the process of actively exploring various role options, but not yet committing to any of them
- *Identity diffusion*—Avoiding considering role options in any conscious way; some who are dissatisfied with this condition but are unable to start a search to "find themselves" resort to escapist activities such as drug or alcohol abuse

Relationships With Peers   For most adolescents, the peer group provides a network of social and emotional support that enables both greater independence from adults and the search for personal identity. But peer relationships change during the adolescent years. Friendship groups in early adolescence tend to be small unisex groups, called **cliques**, of three to nine members. Especially among girls, these unisex friendships increasingly deepen and become more mutually self-disclosing as the teens develop the cognitive abilities better to understand themselves and one another. Then, in mid-adolescence, unisex cliques generally give way to mixed-sex groups. These, in turn, usually are replaced by groups consisting of couples. At first, adolescents tend to have short-term heterosexual relationships within the group that fulfill short-term needs without exacting the commitment of "going steady." Such relationships do not demand love and can dissolve overnight. But between the ages of 16 and 19, most adolescents settle into more stable dating patterns.

Relationships With Parents   While they are still searching for their own identity, striving toward independence, and learning to think through the long-term consequences of their actions, adolescents require guidance and structure from adults, especially their parents. In their struggle for independence, adolescents question everything and test every rule. Unlike young children who believe that their parents know everything and are all-powerful and good, adolescents are all too aware of their parents' shortcomings. It takes many years for adolescents to see their mothers and fathers as real people with their own needs and strengths as well as weaknesses.

The low point of parent–child relationships generally occurs in early adolescence, when the physical changes of puberty are occurring. Then, the warmth of the parent–child relationship ebbs and conflict rises. Warm and caring relationships with adults outside the home, such as those at school or at a supervised community center, are valuable to adolescents during this period. However, conflicts with parents tend to be over minor issues and usually are not intense. In only a small minority of families does the relationship between parents and children markedly deteriorate in adolescence (Paikoff & Brooks-Gunn, 1991).

■ SOME PROBLEMS OF ADOLESCENCE

Adolescence is a time of experimentation and risk taking, whether with sex, drugs, hair color, body piercing, or various kinds of rule breaking. It is also a time when certain kinds of developmental problems are apt to arise, especially problems that have to do with self-perceptions, feelings about the self, and negative emotions in general.

"Is everything all right, Jeffrey? You never call me 'dude' anymore."

Declines in Self-Esteem   As discussed earlier, adolescents are especially likely to be dissatisfied with their appearance. Satisfaction with one's appearance tends to be tied to satisfaction with oneself. Thus, adolescents who are least satisfied with their physical appearance tend also to have low self-esteem (Altabe & Thompson, 1994). Because adolescent girls are especially likely to be dissatisfied with their appearance and because perceived attractiveness and self-esteem are more closely related for females than for males (Allgood-Merten, Lewinsohn, & Hops, 1990), it is no surprise that adolescent girls have significantly lower self-esteem than do adolescent boys, for whom there is little or no decline in self-esteem during adolescence (Kling, Hyde, Showers, & Buswell, 1999).

Depression and Suicide   The rate of suicide among adolescents has increased more than 600% since 1950, though there are signs that since the mid-1990s, it has begun to decrease, at least among males. Suicide is the third leading cause of death among adolescents, after accidents and homicides (National Mental Health Association, 2007). Although successful suicide is much more common in males than in females, twice as many females *attempt* suicide (National Adolescent Health Information Center, 2004).

Research shows that suicidal behavior (thoughts and attempts) in adolescents is often linked to other psychological problems, such as depression, drug abuse, and disruptive behaviors (Andrews & Lewinsohn, 1992; Studer, 2000). A history of physical or sexual abuse and poor family communication skills are also associated with suicide and suicide attempts. Although these data allow us to identify people at risk, it is hard to tell which higher-than-average risk adolescents will actually attempt suicide. For example, depression in and of itself rarely leads to suicide: Although 3% of adolescents suffer severe depression at any one time, the suicide rate among adolescents is less than .01% (National Adolescent Health Information Center, 2004). Apparently, a combination of depression and other risk factors makes suicide more likely, but exactly which factors are most important and what kinds of intervention might reduce adolescent suicides are still unclear.

Youth Violence   Virginia Tech. The University of Texas. Columbine High School. Each of these academic settings was the site of a massacre carried out by adolescents. Why did the massacres happen? What causes children to kill other people and, equally often, to kill themselves? It is tempting to look for simple answers to these questions, but the causes of youth violence are quite complex.

ENDURING ISSUES MIND/BODY

Youth Violence

Biology definitely plays a role, although its influence is certain to be much more complex than simply identifying a "murderer gene." More likely, the genetic component, if any, is related to a lack of compassion or an inability to control strong emotions. Apart from genetics, the constant interplay between the brain and the environment actually "rewires" the brain, sometimes with disastrous effects (Niehoff, 1999). Research suggests that repeated stress during the first 3 years of life may give rise to a steady flow of "stress chemicals," with two consequences. First, the normal "fight or flight" response may go on "hair-trigger alert," which can result in impulsive aggression. Alternatively, the person may become unresponsive and unfeeling, leading in turn to a lack of empathy and an unresponsiveness to punishment (Perry & Pollard, 1998; Read, Perry, Moskowitz, & Connolly, 2001). Other research has found that early trauma may cause a brain structure to become hyperactive, causing obsession with a single thought (such as violence); at the same time the prefrontal cortex becomes less able to control impulsive behavior (Amen, Stubblefield, Carmicheal, & Thisted, 1996; Schmahl, Vermetten, Elzinga, & Bremmer, 2004).

Environment also plays a role. Most psychologists believe that the "gun culture" in which most of the youthful murderers were raised is an important factor, along with the relatively easy availability of guns (Bushman & Baumeister, 1998; Cooke, 2004). Most youthful killers have had extensive experience with guns.

Severe neglect, rejection, or both contribute as well. All the young killers involved the school shootings mentioned earlier indicated that they felt isolated from their family and from girls, outcast and abandoned by those who should have loved them. In turn, this condition led to feelings of powerlessness and injustice (Leary, Kowalski, Smith, & Phillips, 2003). In other cases, the youths lacked adult supervision and support, often having no real attachment to even one loving and reliable adult (Garbarino, 1999).

What are the warning signs that might alert family and friends to potential violence? Lack of social connection, masking of emotions, withdrawal (being habitually secretive and antisocial), silence, rage, increased lying, trouble with friends, hypervigilance, and cruelty toward other children and animals—these factors should all be a cause for concern. This is especially true when they are exhibited by a boy who comes from a family with a history of criminal violence, who has been abused, who belongs to a gang, who abuses drugs or alcohol, who has previously been arrested, or who has experienced problems at school (Leschied & Cummings, 2002).

Check Your Understanding

1. The most obvious indication that adolescence is starting is a rapid increase in height and weight, known as the _____ _____. This is combined with a series of physical changes leading to sexual maturation, the onset of which is called _____.

2. Erikson's view of the major challenge in adolescence is one of _____ versus _____.

3. List the four identity statuses described by James Marcia.

4. True (T) or false (F): The most difficult time in the relationship between a teenager and his or her parents is usually in late adolescence, when the young person is anxious to leave the family "nest."

Adulthood

During adulthood, development is much less predictable than that during adolescence, in that it is much more a function of decisions, circumstances, and even luck. Although developmental milestones do not occur at particular ages, certain experiences and changes eventually occur in nearly every adult's life; and most adults try to fulfill certain needs, including nurturing partnerships and satisfying work.

■ LOVE, PARTNERSHIPS, AND PARENTING

Nearly all adults form a long-term, loving partnership with another adult at some point in their lives. Such a partnership can happen at any stage in the life course, but it is especially common in young adulthood. According to Erik Erikson, the major challenge of young adulthood is *intimacy versus isolation*. Failure to form an intimate partnership with someone else can cause a young adult to feel painfully lonely and incomplete. Erikson believed that a person is not ready to commit to an intimate relationship until he or she has developed a firm sense of personal identity, the task of the preceding stage of life.

Forming Partnerships   Nearly 90% of Americans eventually get married, but those who marry are waiting longer to do so. This postponement of marriage is even greater among African Americans than among whites (Benokraitis, 2004). Although heterosexual marriage is still the statistical norm in the United States, other types of partnerships exist. Cohabiting relationships are one example. About one third of all American adults aged 30 to 49 have lived in a cohabiting relationship. Contrary to popular belief, more than 1 million older adults are also cohabiting outside of marriage in the United States. Among elderly widows and widowers, cohabitation is increasingly seen as a way of enjoying a life together without financial complications and tax penalties.

Homosexual couples are another example of nontraditional intimate partnerships. Studies show that most gays and lesbians seek the same loving, committed, and meaningful partnerships as their heterosexual counterparts (Kurdek, 2005). Moreover, successful homosexual relationships share the same characteristics as successful heterosexual ones: high levels of mutual trust, respect, and appreciation; shared decision making; good communication; and good conflict-resolution skills (Kurdek, 2005; Laird, 2003).

Parenthood   For most parents, loving and being loved by their children is an unparalleled source of fulfillment. However, the birth of the first child is also a major turning point in a couple's relationship, one that requires many adjustments. Romance and fun often give way to duty and obligations. Because young children demand a lot of time and energy, parents may be left with little time or energy for each other.

Parenthood may also heighten conflicts between pursuit of careers and responsibilities at home. This outcome is especially likely among women who have had an active career outside the home. They may be torn between feelings of loss and resentment at the prospect of leaving their job and anxiety or guilt over the idea of continuing to work. This conflict is in addition to the usual worries about being an adequate wife and mother. It is no wonder that women feel the need for their partner's cooperation more strongly during this period of life than men do (Kendall-Tackett, 2001).

Although homosexual couples as a group believe more strongly in equally dividing household duties than heterosexual couples do, homosexuals tend to make an exception when it comes to child rearing. After the arrival of a child (through adoption or artificial insemination), child-care responsibilities tend to fall more heavily on one member of a homosexual couple, whereas the other spends more time in paid employment (Peplau & Beals, 2004).

Love, Partnerships, and Parenting
- Intimacy versus isolation: _____

- Nearly all adults form a _____ _____ with another adult at some point in their lives.

- For most parents, children are a source of _____

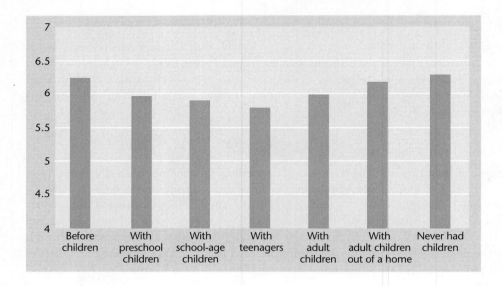

FIGURE 9–2
Marital satisfaction.
This graph shows when married people are most and least content with their marriage, on a scale of 1 (very unhappy) to 7 (very happy).

Source: American Sociological Association. Adapted from *USA Today*, August 12, 1997, p. D1.

Given the demands of child rearing, it is not surprising that marital satisfaction tends to decline after the arrival of the first child (Figure 9–2). But once children leave home, many parents experience renewed satisfaction in their relationship as a couple. Rather than lamenting over their "empty nests," many women experience an increase in positive mood and well-being (Dennerstein, Dudley, & Guthrie, 2002; Owen, 2005). For the first time in years, the husband and wife can be alone together and enjoy each other's company.

Ending a Relationship   Intimate relationships frequently end. Although this is the case for all types of couples (married and unmarried, heterosexual and homosexual), most research on relationships that end has focused on married, heterosexual couples. Nearly half of American marriages eventually end in divorce. Rarely is the decision to separate a mutual one. Most often, one partner takes the initiative in ending the relationship after a long period of slowly increasing unhappiness. Making the decision does not necessarily bring relief. In the short term, it often brings turmoil, animosity, and apprehension. However, in the longer term, friendships between divorced mothers often grow very strong and, in turn, help them to cope more effectively with divorce (Albeck & Kaydare, 2002).

Divorce can have serious and far-reaching effects on children—especially on their school performance, self-esteem, gender-role development, emotional adjustment, relationships with others, and attitudes toward marriage (Collins et al., 2000; Greene, Anderson, Doyle, & Riedelbach, 2006). Children who have been involved in several divorces are at even greater risk (Kurdek, Fine, & Sinclair, 1995). Children adapt more successfully to divorce when they have good support systems, when the divorcing parents maintain a good relationship, and when sufficient financial resources are made available to them. The effects of divorce also vary with the children themselves: Those who have easygoing temperaments and who generally were well behaved before the divorce usually have an easier time adjusting (Hetherington, Bridges, & Insabella, 1998; Storksen, Roysamb, & Holmen, 2006).

■ **THE WORLD OF WORK**

Choosing the job or career of one's life was not always an important concern in early adulthood. Years ago, men followed in their fathers' footsteps or took whatever apprenticeships were available in their communities. Women stayed home and raised families. Today, the choices are far more numerous for men and women. In turn, this increases the stress experienced by many adolescents since the educational achievements and training obtained during the late teens and early twenties often have a profound effect on income and occupational status for the remainder of adult life.

The World of Work

■ Initial career choice is determined as much by _____, _____, and _____ as _____.

■ Process of occupational choice is _____.

■ While the percentage of women in the paid labor force has _____ dramatically, many women bear more than half the responsibility for _____ and _____.

How does one choose a career? Before 1950, it was assumed that at a given point in time, an individual simply assessed his or her personal abilities, surveyed the employment opportunities available, and selected the job that offered the greatest chances for satisfaction and success. However, during the 1950s, alternative theories began to appear that were more concerned with *why* and *how* people choose one career over another. Two common threads run through all these theories. First, personality, interests, and values are at least as important as ability in selecting a career. Second, while initial career choices are made during late adolescence and early adulthood, for many people the process of occupational choice goes on throughout life as interests change, new abilities are discovered, and new job opportunities become available.

The Effects of Work   Once a career has been chosen, what effect does working have on adults? Studies of job satisfaction indicate that the vast majority of workers, in virtually all occupations, are moderately or highly satisfied with their jobs and would continue to work even if they did not have to do so because work gives meaning to their lives. This meaning varies, of course, just as jobs vary. For some adults, jobs are a way of passing time or of obtaining economic independence. For others, the job is a source of self-respect or respect from others and provides a life purpose. And people in all occupational groups say that they value the peer group relationships they experience as a result of work. Moreover, increases in job status during adulthood contribute to feelings of self-esteem.

However, in dual-career families, the picture is not universally bright, especially for women. Over the last 50 years, the percentage of women in the paid labor force has increased dramatically from 36% in 1960 to 56% in 2003 (U.S. Bureau of the Census, 2007a). The change is even greater for married women (32 to 61%) (U.S. Bureau of the Census, 2007b). This increasing role of women as economic providers is a worldwide trend (Elloy & Mackie, 2002). Of employed women, 74% worked full-time; the rest worked part-time. The largest percentage of employed women (38%) worked in management, professional, and related occupations, while 35% worked in sales and office occupations (Figure 9–3).

However, even when the wife has a full-time job outside the home, she is likely to end up doing far more than half of the housework and child care. She is also likely to be aware of this imbalance and to resent it. The "double shift"—one paying job at work outside the home and another unpaid job at household labor—is the common experience of millions of women throughout the world. As a result, according to a report from the Pew Research Center (2007), the majority of working mothers with children at home say they would prefer part-time rather than full-time employment and approximately 20% say they would prefer no paid employment at all. Nearly half the mothers with children at home and without outside employment say that is the ideal situation for them. In contrast, fathers with children at home overwhelmingly say full-time employment is the ideal situation. Despite the pressures associated with the double shift, most women report increases in self-esteem when they have a paid job (Elliott, 1996). They also tend to experience less anxiety and depression than childless working women do (Barnett, Brennan, & Marshall, 1994). Most also say that they would continue to work even if they did not need the money (Schwartz, 1994).

■ COGNITIVE CHANGES

As noted earlier in this chapter, Piaget's model of cognitive development stops with the acquisition of formal operations in adolescence. Piaget (1969) hinted that there might be further changes in styles of thinking during adulthood, but only recently have several investigators begun to explore the ways in which an adult's thinking may differ from that of an adolescent.

The ability to think in abstractions allows adolescents to operate in a world of possibility, thus contributing to their increased flexibility. The tasks of adulthood, however, involve making commitments. Careers must be started, bonds of intimacy formed, and children

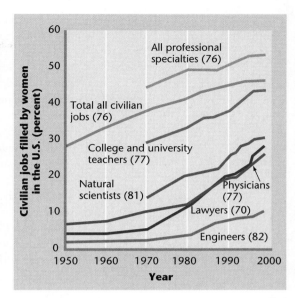

FIGURE 9–3
Percentage of selected jobs filled by women in the United States, 1950–2000.
This graph shows the percentage of each job filled by women. The figures in parentheses indicate women's earnings as a percentage of men's in the given field.

Source: © 2000 Rodger Doyle. Reprinted with permission.

Cognitive Changes

■ Vocabulary and verbal memory
_____ steadily through the sixth decade of life; _____
and ability to perform _____ decline the most over the life span.

raised. From a multitude of possible alternatives, adults must restrict their courses of action. The ability to make choices and commitments is one mark of cognitive maturity.

In many other respects as well, adult thinking differs appreciably from that of adolescents. The acquisition of knowledge is often less important in adulthood than knowing how to apply knowledge to the solution of social problems. Many adults are also better at identifying new problems rather than simply solving problems posed by others. Some investigators feel that becoming aware of the genuine complexity of our social system is another hallmark of adult thinking. Moreover, mature adults see many problems as open-ended and ambiguous with no single "correct" solution, and they realize that the best approach to such problems is likely to be an effort to reduce ambiguity.

It has been suggested that these changes in adult thinking occur as a result of experience with the kinds of complex problems that arise in adult life. Thinking within social contexts requires movement away from the literal, formal, and somewhat rigid thinking of young adulthood. Executive thinking, for example, involves goal-setting, self-regulation, and self-actualization; it also involves give-and-take, participation with others in planning, and anticipating what others will think. Of necessity, adults come to recognize the limitations of pure reasoning for solving problems that need to be viewed from many different perspectives, and so formal reasoning gives way to complex social reasoning.

Most measurable cognitive changes during adulthood do not simply involve a rise or fall in general ability. Instead, for most people, such cognitive skills as vocabulary and verbal memory increase steadily through the sixth decade of life. Other cognitive skills, such as reasoning and spatial orientation generally peak during the 40s, falling off only slightly with increasing age. Perceptual speed (the ability to make quick and accurate visual discriminations) and the ability to perform mathematical computations show the largest decrease with age, with the former beginning to decline as early as age 25, and the latter starting to decline around age 40 (Schaie & Willis, 2001; Willis & Shaie, 1999).

And just as physical exercise is necessary for optimal physical development, so mental exercise is necessary for optimal cognitive development. Although some decline in cognitive skills is inevitable as people age, the decline can be minimized for people who stay mentally active (Wilson et al., 2003).

■ MIDLIFE

Midlife

■ According to Erikson, the major challenge of midlife involves

_____ versus _____.

■ Midlife crisis is not typical; most people go through a less dramatic

_____.

■ Two significant physical changes occur in midlife: _____

in women and _____ in men.

Psychological health generally improves in adulthood. Men and women tend to become less self-centered, and they develop better coping skills with age. One longitudinal study found that people are more sympathetic, giving, productive, and dependable at 45 than they were at 20 (Block, 1971). Another found that people in their middle years feel an increasing commitment to and responsibility for others, develop new ways of adapting, and feel more comfortable in interpersonal relationships (Vaillant, 1977). Such findings suggest that the majority of people are successfully meeting what Erik Erikson saw as the major challenge of middle adulthood: *generativity versus stagnation*. Generativity refers to the ability to continue being productive and creative, especially in ways that guide and encourage future generations. For those who fail to achieve this state, life becomes a drab and meaningless routine and the person feels stagnant and bored.

Feelings of boredom and stagnation in middle adulthood may be part of what is called a **midlife crisis**. The person in midlife crisis feels painfully unfulfilled and ready for a radical, abrupt shift in career, personal relationships, or lifestyle. Research shows, however, that the midlife crisis is not typical; most people do not make sudden dramatic changes in their lives in mid-adulthood (Lachman, 2004). In one study, in fact, only about 10% reported experiencing a midlife crisis (Brim, 1999). Furthermore, a large-scale study found that the majority of middle-aged adults reported lower levels of anxiety and worry than young adults and generally felt positively about their lives. Daniel Levinson (1920–1994), who studied personality development in men and women throughout their adulthood, preferred the term **midlife transition** for the period when people tend to take stock of their lives (Levinson, 1978, 1986, 1987). Many of the men and women in his studies, when confronted with the first signs of aging, began to think about the finite nature of life. They realized that they may never accomplish all that they had hoped to, and they questioned the value of some of the things they had accomplished so far, wondering how meaningful those things were. As a result, some gradually reset their life priorities, establishing new goals based on their new insights.

ENDURING ISSUES   STABILITY/CHANGE

The "Change of Life"

A decline in reproductive function occurs during middle age both in men and in women. In women, the amount of estrogen produced by the ovaries drops sharply at around age 45, although the exact age varies considerably. Breasts, genital tissues, and the uterus begin to shrink; and menstrual periods become irregular, ceasing altogether at around age 50. The cessation of menstruation is called **menopause**.

Experts disagree about whether a "male menopause" exists. Men never experience as severe a drop in testosterone as women do with estrogen. Instead, studies have found a more gradual decline—perhaps 30 to 40%—in testosterone in men between the ages of 48 and 70 (Brody, 2004; Crooks & Bauer, 2002). Recent evidence also confirms that with increasing age, male fertility slowly decreases as well (Ford et al., 2000).

Check Your Understanding

1. According to Erik Erikson, the major challenge of young adulthood is _____ versus _____, whereas the major challenge of middle adulthood is _____ versus _____.

2. If you were to poll a group of older couples, you would expect to find that most of them say that their marital satisfaction
   a. Has steadily decreased over the years
   b. Has not changed over the years
   c. Declined during the child-rearing years, but has increased since then
   d. Has steadily increased over the years

Late Adulthood

Older adults constitute the fastest-growing segment of the U.S. population. Indeed, during the twentieth century, the percentage of Americans over 65 more than tripled; and those over 85 now represent the fastest-growing segment of the population (National Institute on Aging, 2006). In the 2000 census, 35 million Americans were over age 65 (U.S. Bureau of the Census, 2001); by the year 2030, more than 70 million are expected to be in this age group. This dramatic rise stems from the aging of the large baby-boom generation, coupled with increases in life expectancy primarily because of better health care and nutrition (Figure 9–4).

However, a sizable gender gap exists in life expectancy. The average American woman today enjoys a life span that is 5.2 years longer than that of the average American man. The reasons for this gender gap are still unclear, but likely factors include differences in hormones, exposure to stress, health-related behaviors, and genetic makeup.

Because older adults are becoming an increasingly visible part of American society, it is important to understand their development. Unfortunately, our views of older adults often are

FIGURE **9–4**

Population age structure, 2000.
The U.S. population will continue to age over the next several decades, as the huge baby-boom generation (shown in orange) matures.

Source: U.S. Census Bureau. Retrieved June 8, 2006, from http://www.census.gov/cgi-bin/ipc/idbpyrs.pl?cty=US&out=s&ymax=250.

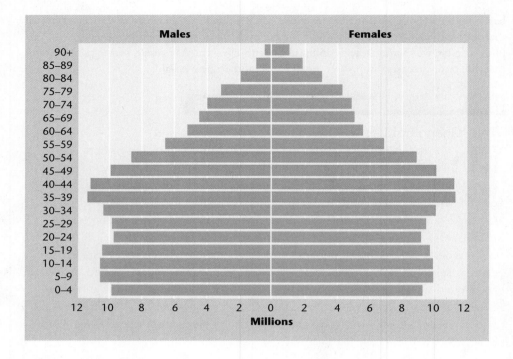

heavily colored by myths. For example, many people believe that most elderly people are lonely, poor, and troubled by ill health. Even health-care professionals sometimes assume that it is natural for elderly people to feel ill. As a result, symptoms considered treatable in younger people sometimes are interpreted as inevitable signs of decay in elderly people and consequently are left untreated. The false belief that "senility" is inevitable in old age is another damaging myth, as is the belief that most older adults are helpless and dependent on their families for care and financial support. All the research on late adulthood contradicts these stereotypes. Increasingly, people age 65 and over are healthy, productive, and able.

■ PHYSICAL CHANGES

In middle adulthood and continuing through late adulthood, physical appearance changes, as does the functioning of every organ in the body. The hair thins and turns white or gray. The skin wrinkles. Bones become more fragile. Muscles lose power; and joints stiffen or deteriorate. Circulation slows and blood pressure rises, and because the lungs hold less oxygen, the older adult has less energy. Body shape and posture change, and the reproductive organs atrophy. Difficulties in falling asleep and staying asleep become more common, and reaction times are slower. The senses of sight, hearing, and smell become less acute.

Given these noticeable changes, it is curious that researchers do not yet know why physical aging happens. However, several theories exist:

- *Genetics*—One theory suggests that genes may program cells to deteriorate over time and die. According to this theory of aging, the body is directed genetically to age and deteriorate just as maturation shapes early growth and development. The role of inheritance in aging is supported by a recent finding of a gene that appears to be related to exceptional longevity (Puca et al., 2001).

- *Telomeres*—According to a second theory, *telomeres* (special protective structures located on chromosomal tips) become shorter with each replication (Saretzki & Zglinicki, 2002). After about 100 replications, the size of the telomeres is reduced so significantly that cells no longer are capable of precise replication. Some research indicates that telomeres may also be shortened by increased stress (Epel et al., 2006).

- *Free radicals*—This recent and widely accepted theory of aging contends that unstable oxygen molecules ricochet within cells and damage the cellular components

Physical Changes

■ Significant changes in _____ and _____ occur in late adulthood.

Social Development

■ Most people over age 65 live _____ nursing homes.

■ The _____ of older adults enjoy sex.

Cognitive Changes

■ For many older adults, cognitive abilities _____.

■ _____ causes profound changes in mental abilities and personality.

(including DNA) over time, causing them to age (De la Fuente, 2002). Damage from the continued bombardment of oxygen molecules may lead to the wide range of disorders accompanying aging, including arthritis, cancer, and cognitive decline (Berr, 2002; J. A. Knight, 2000; Leborgne, Maziere & Andrejak, 2002; McGeer, Klegeris, & McGeer, 2005).

Whatever the ultimate explanation for physical decline, many factors affect adults' physical well-being. Among these are things they can control—particularly, diet, exercise, health care, smoking, drug use, and overexposure to sun. Attitudes and interests also matter. People who have a continuing sense of usefulness, who maintain old ties, who investigate new ideas, who take up new activities, and who feel in control of their lives have the lowest rates of disease and the highest survival rates. Indeed, in a survey of 2,724 people aged 25 to 74, older adults reported experiencing more positive emotions than did younger adults during the previous month (Mroczek & Kolarz, 1998). So there is a good deal of truth in the saying: "You're only as old as you feel." In fact, psychologists are starting to use functional or psychological age, instead of chronological age, to predict an older adult's adaptability to life's demands.

Although physical changes are inevitable during late adulthood, how people respond to these changes has a major effect on their quality of life.

■ SOCIAL DEVELOPMENT

Far from being weak and dependent, most men and women over age 65 live apart from their children and outside nursing homes; and most are very satisfied with their autonomous lifestyles. Moreover, those who remain physically and mentally active, travel, exercise, and attend meetings are more likely to report being happier and more satisfied with their lives than those who stay at home (George, 2001).

Still, gradual social changes do take place in late adulthood. In general, older people interact with fewer people and perform fewer social roles. Behavior becomes less influenced by social rules and expectations than it was earlier in life. Most older people step back and assess life, realize there is a limit to their capacity for social involvement, and learn to live comfortably within those restrictions. This process does not necessarily entail a psychological "disengagement" from the social world, as some researchers have contended. Rather, older people simply make sensible decisions that suit their more limited time frames and physical capabilities.

Retirement   In late adulthood, most people retire from paid employment. Individual reactions to this major change vary widely, partly because society has no clear idea of what retirees are supposed to do. Should they sit in rocking chairs and watch life go by or should they play golf, become foster grandparents, or study Greek? The advantage to this lack of clear social expectations is that older adults have the flexibility to structure their retirement as they please. Men and women often go about this process differently. Men generally see retirement as a time to slow down and do less, whereas women often view it as a time to learn new things and explore new possibilities (Helgesen, 1998). This difference can cause obvious problems for retired couples.

Of course, the nature and quality of retired life depend in part on financial status. If retirement means a major decline in a person's standard of living, that person will be less eager to retire and will lead a more limited life after retirement. Another factor in people's attitudes toward retirement is their feelings about work. People who are fulfilled by their jobs usually are less interested in retiring than people whose jobs are unrewarding. Similarly, people who have very ambitious, hard-driving personalities tend to want to stay at work longer than those who are more relaxed.

Sexual Behavior   A common misconception is that elderly people have outlived their sexuality. Although the sexual response of older people is slower and they are less sexually active than younger people, the majority can enjoy sex and have orgasms. One survey revealed that 37% of married people over the age of 60 have sex at least once a week, 20% have sex outdoors, and 17% swim in the nude (Woodward & Springen, 1992). Another study of people age 65 to 97 found that about half the men still viewed sex as important; and slightly more than half of those in committed relationships were satisfied with the quality of their sex lives (Clements, 1996).

■ COGNITIVE CHANGES

Healthy people who remain intellectually active maintain a high level of mental functioning in old age. Far from the common myth that the brain cells of elderly people are rapidly dying, brain size shrinks an average of only about 10% between the ages of 20 and 70 (Peters, 2005). For a sizable number of older adults, therefore, cognitive abilities remain largely intact. Because the aging mind works a little more slowly, certain types of memories are a little more difficult to store and retrieve and the ability to process and attend to information does gradually decline. For the most part, however, these changes do not interfere significantly with the ability to enjoy an active, independent life. Moreover, older adults who stay both mentally and physically active generally experience significantly less cognitive decline than those who do not (Bosma, van Boxtel, Ponds, Houx, & Jolles, 2003; Colcombe & Kramer, 2003; Vaillant, 2003). Training and practice on cognitive tasks can also help to greatly reduce the decline in cognitive performance in later adulthood, though the benefits of training are often limited only to the skills that are practiced (Kramer & Willis, 2002).

Alzheimer's Disease　For people suffering from **Alzheimer's disease**, the picture is quite different. They forget the names of their children or are unable to find their way home from the store. Some even fail to recognize their lifelong partners. Named for the German neurologist Alois Alzheimer (1864–1915), the disease causes brain changes resulting in the progressive loss of the ability to communicate and reason.

For many years, Alzheimer's disease was considered rare and was diagnosed only in people under age 60 who developed symptoms of memory loss and confusion. But now Alzheimer's is recognized as a common disorder in older people formerly described as "senile." According to current estimates, about 10% of adults over age 65 and nearly half of adults over age 85 suffer from Alzheimer's disease (Alzheimer's Association, 2006). Risk factors include having a genetic predisposition, having a family history of *dementia* (a general decline in physical and cognitive abilities), having Down syndrome or Parkinson's disease, having been born to a woman over age 40, and suffering a head trauma (especially one that caused unconsciousness). In addition, people who are not active (physically and intellectually) during their middle years increase their risk for developing Alzheimer's disease (Friedland et al., 2001; Vaillant, 2003; Wilson & Bennett, 2003).

Alzheimer's usually begins with minor memory losses, such as difficulty in recalling words and names or in remembering where something was placed. As it progresses—a process that may take anywhere from 2 to 20 years—personality changes are also likely. First, people may become emotionally withdrawn or flat. Later, they may suffer from delusions, such as thinking that relatives are stealing from them. These people become confused and may not know where they are or what time of day it is. Eventually, they lose the ability to speak, to care for themselves, and to recognize family members. If they do not die of other causes, Alzheimer's will be fatal eventually (Wolfson et al., 2001).

■ FACING THE END OF LIFE

Fear of death is seldom a central concern for people in later adulthood. In fact, such fear seems to be a greater problem in young adulthood or in middle age, when the first awareness of mortality coincides with a greater interest in living (Tomer, 2000). But elderly people do have some major fears associated with dying. They fear the pain, indignity, and depersonalization they might experience during a terminal illness, as well as the possibility of dying alone. They also worry about burdening their relatives with the expenses of their hospitalization or nursing care. Sometimes, too, relatives are not able to provide much support for the elderly as they

Because people with Alzheimer's disease suffer memory loss, signs can remind them to perform ordinary activities.

decline, either because they live too far away or because they may be unable to cope either with the pain of watching a loved one die or with their own fears of mortality.

Stages of Dying   In her classic work, the late psychiatrist Elisabeth Kübler-Ross (1926–2004) interviewed more than 200 dying people of all ages to try to understand the psychological aspects of death. From these interviews, she described a sequence of five stages people pass through as they react to their own impending death (Kübler-Ross, 1969):

1. *Denial*—The person denies the diagnosis, refuses to believe that death is approaching, insists that an error has been made, and seeks other, more acceptable opinions or alternatives.
2. *Anger*—The person now accepts the reality of the situation but expresses envy and resentment toward those who will live to fulfill a plan or dream. The question becomes "Why me?" Anger may be directed at the doctor or directed randomly. The patience and understanding of other people are particularly important at this stage.
3. *Bargaining*—The person desperately tries to buy time, negotiating with doctors, family members, clergy, and God in a healthy attempt to cope with the realization of death.
4. *Depression*—As bargaining fails and time is running out, the person may succumb to depression, lamenting failures and mistakes that can no longer be corrected.
5. *Acceptance*—Tired and weak, the person at last enters a state of "quiet expectation," submitting to fate.

According to Kübler-Ross, Americans have a greater problem coping with death than people in some other cultures. She observed that some cultures are *death affirming*. For example, the Trukese of Micronesia start preparing for death at age 40. Alaskan Indians also begin preparing for death at an early age, and the whole community participates in the process. In contrast, American culture is *death denying*: "We are reluctant to reveal our age; we spend fortunes to hide our wrinkles; we prefer to send our old people to nursing homes" (1975, p. 28). We also shelter children from knowledge of death and dying. By trying to protect them from these unpleasant realities, however, we actually may make them more fearful of death.

It is worth noting that Kübler-Ross studied only a relatively small sample of people and provided little information about how they were selected and how often they were interviewed. Also, all her patients were suffering from cancer. Does her model apply as well to people dying from other causes? We do not yet know. And does her model apply well to people in other cultures? Again, we do not yet know. Despite these legitimate questions, there is nearly universal agreement that Kübler-Ross deserves credit for pioneering the study of the transitions that people undergo during the dying process. She was the first to investigate an area long considered taboo; and her research has made dying a more "understandable" experience, perhaps one that is easier to deal with.

Death of a Spouse   The death of one's spouse may be the most severe challenge of late adulthood. Especially if the death was unexpected, people often respond with initial disbelief, followed by numbness. Only later is the full impact of the loss felt, and this impact can be severe. Not surprisingly, the incidence of depression rises significantly following the death of a spouse (Bonanno, Wortman, & Nesse, 2004; Nakao, Kashiwagi, & Yano, 2005). One long-term study revealed that older widows and widowers had a higher incidence of dying within 6 months after the death of their spouse than other married persons of their age.

For somewhat different reasons, then, the burden of widowhood is heavy for men and women. Perhaps because they are not as accustomed to taking care of themselves, men seem to suffer more than women from the loss of a mate. But because women have a longer life expectancy, there are many more widows than widowers. Thus, men have a better chance of remarrying. More than half the women over 65 who are widowed will live another 15 years without remarrying.

Facing the End of Life

- According to Kübler-Ross, American culture is _____ rather than _____.
- Five stages occur in reacting to one's impending death:

_____, _____, _____, _____, and _____.

Check Your Understanding

1. Indicate whether the following statements are true (T) or false (F).

   a. _____ The average man lives as long as the average woman.

   b. _____ The physical changes of aging inevitably become incapacitating.

   c. _____ Most elderly people are dependent on their adult children.

   d. _____ Healthy people who remain intellectually involved maintain a high level of mental functioning in old age.

2. In a discussion about cognitive changes in late adulthood, you hear people make several claims. Based on what you have learned in this chapter, you agree with all the following claims *except*:

   a. "If you are healthy and remain intellectually active, you are likely to maintain a high level of mental functioning in old age."

   b. "As you get older, it will become more difficult to process and attend to information."

   c. "If you practice mental tasks, you can help to minimize the decline in those skills."

   d. "As you get older, you will become increasingly confused, gradually lose the ability to speak, and eventually be unable to recognize friends and family."

Chapter Review

 www.psychologythecore.com

The study of how and why people change over the course of the life span is called **developmental psychology**.

Research Methods in Developmental Psychology

Cross-sectional studies involve studying different age groups of people at the same time, whereas **longitudinal studies** involve the same group of individuals at different times in their lives. Longitudinal studies are more time consuming, but they do account for **cohort** differences in the typical experiences of members of different generations. **Biographical**, or **retrospective**, **studies** involve reconstructing a person's past through interviews. Each of these approaches to studying development has its own strengths and weaknesses. Thus, developmental psychologists often use data gathered from all of them.

Prenatal Development

The period of development from conception to birth is called **prenatal development**. During this time, **teratogens** (disease-producing organisms or potentially harmful substances, such as drugs) can pass through the placenta and cause irreparable harm to the **embryo** or **fetus**. This harm is greatest when the drug or other substance is introduced at the same time that a major developmental process is occurring. If the same substance is introduced outside this **critical period**, little or even no harm may result. Pregnant women who consume alcohol, even in small amounts, may give birth to children who exhibit the symptoms of **fetal alcohol syndrome (FAS)**.

The Newborn

Although **neonates** (newborn babies) appear helpless, they are much more competent and aware than they seem. Newborns see and hear. They also come equipped with a number of useful reflexes. And they are distinctly unique in their underlying **temperaments**. Often a baby's temperament remains quite stable over time because of a combination of genetic and environmental influences, but stability in temperament is not inevitable. Your own temperament may be similar to and different from the temperament you displayed as a newborn.

All senses are functioning at birth: sight, hearing, taste, smell, and touch. Newborns seem particularly adept at discriminating speech sounds, suggesting that their hearing is quite keen. Their least developed sense is probably vision, which takes 6 to 8 months to become as good as that of the average college student.

Infancy and Childhood

During the first dozen years of life, a helpless infant becomes a competent older child. This transformation encompasses many important kinds of changes, including physical, motor, cognitive, and social developments.

During the first 3 years of life, there are rapid increases in the number of connections between neurons in the brain, the speed of conduction between neurons, and the density of synaptic connections. Growth of the body is most rapid during the first year, with the average baby growing approximately 10 inches and gaining about 15 pounds. It then slows down considerably until early adolescence.

Babies tend to reach the major milestones in early motor development at broadly similar ages. The average ages are called *developmental norms*. Some perfectly normal infants develop much faster than average, whereas others develop more slowly. **Maturation**, the biological process that leads to developmental changes, also is shaped by experiences with the environment.

According to Swiss psychologist Jean Piaget, children undergo qualitative cognitive changes as they grow older. During the **sensory-motor stage** (birth to age 2), children acquire **object permanence**, the understanding that things continue to exist even when they are out of sight. Late in the sensory-motor stage, infants develop the ability to form **mental representations** of objects and to manipulate those representations in their heads. In the **preoperational stage** (ages 2 to 7), they become increasingly adept at using mental representations, and language assumes an important role in describing, remembering, and reasoning about the world. Children at this age are **egocentric** in that they have difficulty appreciating others' viewpoints. In the **concrete-operational stage** (ages 7 to 11), children are able to pay attention to more than one factor at a time, grasp **principles of conservation**, and understand the viewpoints of others. Finally, in the **formal-operational stage** (adolescence through adulthood), teenagers acquire the ability to think abstractly and to test ideas mentally using logic. Piaget's work has been extraordinarily influential, but over the years, it has also produced a great deal of controversy.

Lawrence Kohlberg's stage theory of cognition focused exclusively on moral thinking. He proposed that children at different levels of moral reasoning base their moral choices on different factors: first, a concern about physical consequences, next, a concern about what other people think, and finally a concern about abstract principles. Kohlberg's theory, as with Piaget's, has experienced its share of criticism. More recent research on moral development has focused less on moral thinking and more on the factors that influence moral choices in everyday life and the extent to which those choices are actually put into action.

Language begins with cooing and progresses to **babbling**, the repetition of speechlike sounds. The first word usually is uttered at about 12 months. During the next 6 to 8 months, children build a vocabulary of one-word sentences called **holophrases**. Skinner believed that language develops as a result of reinforcement for making sounds that resemble adult speech. In contrast, Chomsky proposed that children are born with a **language acquisition device**, an innate mechanism that enables them to build a vocabulary, master the rules of grammar, and form intelligible sentences.

Young animals of many species form a strong bond to the first moving object they see, a process known as **imprinting**. In contrast, human newborns only gradually form a secure **attachment**, or emotional bond, with their caregivers. One consequence of attachment is that around 7 months of age, an infant will begin to display **stranger anxiety**. One important achievement during early infancy is the development of *basic trust* (seeing the world as a secure, dependable place). As infants develop basic trust, they become more able to investigate the environment around them. This exploration is a first indication of children's developing **autonomy**. The inevitable conflict between the parents' need for peace and order and the child's desire for autonomy often creates difficulties. But it is an essential first step in **socialization**, the process by which children learn the behaviors and attitudes appropriate to their family and their culture. As children grow older, their social worlds expand. The years between the ages of 3 and 6 are characterized by growing *initiative* on the part of the child—a desire to do things on their own. Parental encouragement of these initiatives leads to a sense of joy in taking on new tasks.

Parenting style affects children's behavior and self-image. The most successful parenting style is authoritative, in which parents provide firm guidance but are willing to listen to the child's opinions. However, parents do not act the same way toward every child in the family because children are different from each other and elicit different parental responses.

As children get older, they develop a deeper understanding of the meaning of friendship and come under the influence of a **peer group**. Successfully making friends is one of the tasks that Erikson saw as centrally important to children between the ages of 7 and 11, the stage of *industry versus inferiority*.

Peer influence is just one example of a much broader class of environmental factors called the **nonshared environment**. Even children who grow up in the same home, with the same parents, are likely to have very different day-to-day human relationships in part because children influence the behavior of their caregivers at the same time that the caregivers are influencing them. Moreover, parents do not act the same way toward every child in the family because children are different from one another and elicit different parental responses.

By age 3, a child has developed a **gender identity**: a girl's knowledge that she is a girl and a boy's knowledge that he is a boy. But children of this age have little idea of what it means to be a particular gender. By 4 or 5, most children develop **gender constancy**, the realization that gender depends on the kind of genitals one has and that one's gender cannot be changed. Children develop **sex-typed behavior**, or behavior appropriate to their gender, through a process of **gender-role awareness** and the formation of **gender stereotypes** reflected in their culture.

Adolescence

The **growth spurt** is a rapid increase in height and weight that begins, on average, at about age 10.5 in girls and 12.5 in boys, and reaches its peak at age 12 in girls and 14 in boys. These physical changes of adolescence are just part of the transformation that occurs during this period. The child turns into an adult, not only physically but also cognitively, socially, and emotionally. Signs of **puberty**—the onset of sexual maturation—begin around 11.5 years of age in boys. In girls, **menarche**, the first menstrual period, occurs at 12.5 years of age for the average girl in the United States. But individuals vary widely in when they go through puberty. The United States has the highest teen birth rate in the industrialized world.

In terms of cognitive development, teenagers often reach the level of *formal-operational thought*, in which they can reason abstractly and speculate about alternatives. These newfound abilities may make them overconfident that their own ideas are right, turning adolescence into a time of cognitive egocentrism.

Adolescence inevitably is accompanied by some difficult stress related to school, family, and peers. However, research evidence indicates that it is not normally a period of great "storm and stress" as was originally thought. To make the transition from dependence on parents to dependence on oneself, the adolescent must develop a stable sense of self. **Identity formation** may follow an intense period of self-exploration called an **identity crisis**.

Most adolescents rely on a peer group for social and emotional support, often rigidly conforming to the values of their friends. From small unisex **cliques** in early adolescence, friendship groups change to mixed-sex groups in which short-lived romantic interests are common. Later, stable dating patterns emerge. Parent–child relationships may become temporarily rocky during adolescence as teenagers become aware of their parents' faults and question parental rules.

Developmental problems often emerge for the first time during adolescence. Adolescents are especially likely to be dissatisfied with their appearance. This, in turn, can lead to low self-esteem. Some adolescents think about committing suicide; a much smaller number attempt it. However, suicide is the third leading cause of death among adolescents. A handful of adolescents turn to extreme violence.

Adulthood

Reaching developmental milestones in adulthood is much less predictable than in earlier years; it is much more a function of the individual's decisions, circumstances, and even luck. Still, certain experiences and changes eventually take place and nearly every adult tries to fulfill certain needs.

Nearly every adult forms a long-term loving partnership with at least one other adult at some point in life. According to Erik Erikson, the task of finding intimacy versus being isolated and lonely is especially important during young adulthood. Erikson believed that people are not ready for love until they have formed a firm sense of identity.

Although heterosexual marriage is still the statistical norm in the United States, cohabitation and homosexual partnerships are also common. For most parents, loving and being loved by their children is an unparalleled source of fulfillment. However, the birth of the first child is also a major turning point in a couple's relationship—one that requires many adjustments. Marital satisfaction tends to decline after the arrival of the first child. But once children leave home, many parents experience renewed satisfaction in their relationship as a couple.

Almost half of American marriages eventually end in divorce. At least in the short term, this often brings turmoil, animosity, and apprehension. Divorce can also have serious and far-reaching effects on children.

In the world of work, the numerous career choices for men and women contribute to the stress experienced by many adolescents. Personality, interests, and values are at least as important as ability in selecting a career. Initial career choices are made during late adolescence and early adulthood, but for many people, the process of occupational choice goes on throughout life. The great majority of adults are moderately or highly satisfied with their jobs and would continue to work even if they did not need to do so for financial reasons. Balancing the demands of job and family is often difficult, however, especially for women, because they tend to have most of the responsibility for housework and child care. Yet, despite this stress of a "double shift," most women report increases in self-esteem when they have a job outside the home.

In many respects, adult thinking differs appreciably from that of adolescents. The ability to make choices and commitments is one mark of cognitive maturity. Acquiring knowledge is often less important in adulthood than knowing how to apply knowledge to the solution of social problems. Many adults are also better at identifying new problems rather than simply solving problems posed by others. Whereas adolescents search for the one "correct" solution to a problem, adults are more likely to recognize the limitations of pure reasoning for solving problems that need to be viewed from many different perspectives, and so formal reasoning gives way to complex social reasoning.

As people grow older, they tend to become less self-centered and more comfortable in interpersonal relationships. They also develop better coping skills and new ways of adapting. By middle age, many adults feel an increasing commitment to, and responsibility for, others. This suggests that many adults are successfully meeting what Erik Erikson saw as the major challenge of middle adulthood: *generativity* (the ability to continue being productive and creative, especially in ways that guide and encourage future generations) *versus stagnation* (a sense of boredom or lack of fulfillment, sometimes called a **midlife crisis**). Most adults, however, do not experience dramatic upheaval in their middle years, so this period may be thought of more appropriately as one of **midlife transition**.

Middle adulthood brings a decline in the functioning of the reproductive organs. In women, this is marked by **menopause**, the cessation of menstruation, accompanied by a sharp drop in estrogen levels. Men experience a slower decline in testosterone levels.

Late Adulthood

Over the past century, life expectancy in America has increased mainly because of improved health care and nutrition. There is, however, a sizable gender gap, with women living an average of 5.2 years longer than men. Unfortunately, our views of older adults are often heavily colored by myths. Most elderly people are not lonely, poor, and troubled by ill health, nor is "senility" inevitable in old age. Increasingly, people age 65 and over are healthy, productive, and able.

The physical changes of late adulthood affect outward appearance and the functioning of every organ. It is not yet known why these changes happen. One possibility is that genes program cells to eventually deteriorate and die. It is also possible that genetic instructions simply degrade over time. Another possible explanation is that body parts wear out after repeated use, with environmental toxins contributing to the wearing-out process. Whatever the reason, physical aging is inevitable, although it can be slowed by a healthy lifestyle.

Far from being weak and dependent, most men and women over age 65 live apart from their children and outside nursing homes; and most are very satisfied with their autonomous lifestyles. In late adulthood, most people retire from paid employment. Individual reactions to this major change vary widely. Moreover, although their sexual responses may be slowed, most older adults continue to enjoy sex beyond their seventies. Still, gradual social changes occur in late adulthood. Older adults interact with fewer people and perform fewer social roles. They may also become less influenced by social rules and expectations. Realizing that there is a limit to the capacity for social involvement, they learn to live with some restrictions.

Healthy people who remain intellectually active maintain a high level of mental functioning in old age. It is true that the aging mind works a little more slowly and certain kinds of memories are more difficult to store and retrieve, but these changes generally are not extensive enough to interfere with most everyday tasks. Healthy older adults who engage in intellectually stimulating activities usually maintain a high level of mental functioning. However, some older adults develop **Alzheimer's disease,** a progressive neurological condition characterized by losses of memory and cognition and changes in personality.

Most elderly people fear death less than younger people fear it. They do fear the pain, indignity, depersonalization, and loneliness associated with a terminal illness. They also worry about becoming a financial burden to their families. Elizabeth Kübler-Ross believed that American culture is "death denying" rather than "death affirming." As a result of her observations of people dying of cancer, she proposed a sequence of five stages that people go through when they are dying: *denial, anger, bargaining, depression,* and *acceptance.* Whether those stages apply to people dying from other causes and to other cultures is unknown.

The death of a spouse is perhaps the most severe challenge faced by the elderly. Especially if the death was unexpected, people often respond with initial disbelief, followed by numbness. Not surprisingly, the incidence of depression and death rises significantly among widows and widowers. Men seem to suffer more than women from the loss of a mate.

Chapter 10
Personality

Go to *The Core Online* at
www.psychologythecore.com
to get the most up-to-date information
for your introductory psychology course.
The content online is an important part
of what you are learning—the content
there can help prepare you for your test!
It includes up-to-date examples, simulations, video clips, and practice quizzes.
Also be sure to check out the *Blog* to
hear directly from the authors on what
current events and latest research are
most relevant to your course materials.

The first time you log in, you will need
the access code packaged with your textbook. If you do not have a code, please
go to **www.mypearsonstore.com**
and enter the ISBN of your textbook
(**0-13-603344-X**) to purchase the code.

275

10 1 Personality Traits

Personality:
An individual's unique pattern of thoughts, feelings, and behaviors that persists over time and across situations

Personality traits:
Ways in which personalities can differ

The Big Five
- Extraversion, agreeableness, conscientiousness, emotional stability, and openness to experience

Evaluating the Trait Approach
- Provides a way of classifying personalities
- Does not explain why personality develops

10 2 The Psychodynamic Approach

Psychodynamic theories: Emphasize unconscious factors and personal life experience

Sigmund Freud
- **Psychoanalysis:** Freud's theory and approach to therapy
- Personality is composed of three structures:
  - **Id:** Unconscious urges and desires; operates according to the pleasure principle
  - **Ego:** Controls all thinking and reasoning; operates according to the **reality principle**
  - **Superego:** Conscience; moral standards; **ego ideal**
- **Libido:** Energy generated by the sexual instinct
- **Fixation:** Sexual energy permanently tied to a part of the body
- Psychosexual stages of development:
  - **Oral Stage** (birth to 18 months)
  - **Anal Stage** (18 months to 3.5 years)
  - **Phallic Stage** (3 to 5 or 6 years)
  - **Latency Period** (5 or 6 years to age 12 or 13)
  - **Genital Stage** (adolescence through adulthood)

Other Psychodynamic Theorists
- Carl Jung
  - Libido represents all life forces.
  - **Personal unconscious:** Repressed thoughts, forgotten experiences, and undeveloped ideas
  - **Collective unconscious:** Collective memories inherited from past generations; includes **archetypes** (thought forms shared by all human beings)
- Alfred Adler
  - **Compensation:** Efforts to overcome physical weakness or feelings of inadequacy
  - Fixation on feelings of personal inferiority that results in emotional and social paralysis is called an **inferiority complex**.
  - Later theory: Strivings for superiority and perfection
- Karen Horney
  - Feelings of insecurity and anxiety are more important than sexuality.
  - Neurotic lifestyles: submissive type, aggressive type, detached type
  - Biology is not destiny.
  - Gender differences are derived from culture, not anatomy.
- Erik Erikson
  - Empasized the quality of parent-child relationships
  - According to Erikson, only when children feel competent and valuable, in their own eyes and in society's, will they develop a secure sense of identity.

Evaluating the Psychodynamic Approach
- Difficult to translate psychodynamic personality theories into hypotheses that can be tested scientifically
- Five propositions, central to all psychodynamic theories, have withstood the tests of time:
  - Much of mental life is unconscious.
  - Mental processes operate in parallel; may lead to conflicting feelings.
  - Stable personality patterns begin to form in childhood; early experiences strongly affect personality development.
  - Our mental representations of ourselves, of others, and of our relationships tend to guide our interactions with other people.
  - Personality development involves learning to regulate sexual and aggressive feelings as well as to become socially interdependent rather than dependent.

10 3 The Humanistic Approach

Humanistic personality theory: Emphasizes positive motivation, progress toward higher levels of functioning, potential for growth and change, personal responsibility

Carl Rogers
- **Actualizing tendency:** Biological push toward fulfillment of innate capacities, capabilities, potentialities
- **Self-actualizing tendency:** Attempt to fulfill one's self-concept
- **Fully functioning person:** One whose self-concept closely matches inborn capacities
- **Unconditional positive regard:** Acceptance and love by others regardless of one's feelings, attitudes, and behaviors
- **Conditional positive regard:** Acceptance and love conditional on fulfilling expectations and demands of others

Evaluating the Humanistic Approach
- Central tenet (self-actualization) is difficult, if not impossible, to test scientifically
- Some support for specific predictions from theories
- Perhaps overly optimistic view of human nature
- Reflects Western values of individual achievement

10 4 The Cognitive–Social Learning Approach

Cognitive–social learning theories: Hold that people internally organize their expectancies and values to guide their own behavior

Expectancies, Self-Efficacy, and Locus of Control
- **Performance standards:** Individually determined measures of excellence by which people judge their own behavior
- **Self-efficacy:** Attitude that results from meeting one's own internal performance standards
- **Locus of control:** Belief that hard work, skill, and training versus chance, luck, and behavior determine success

Evaluating the Cognitive–Social Learning Approach
- Key concepts defined and studied scientifically
- Accounts for inconsistencies in behavior across situations
- Already has numerous practical applications

10 5 Personality Assessment

The Personal Interview
- Unstructured interview: Relatively free-flowing interview
- Structured interview: Fixed order and content of questions; preferred method for most research

Direct Observation
- Observe behavior in everyday situations over a long period
- Method tends to be expensive and time consuming
- Behavior may be affected by presence of observer

Objective Tests
- **Objective tests** (personality inventories): Usually written tests administered and scored according to a standard procedure
- Rely on self report
- **Sixteen Personality Factor Questionnaire (16PF):** Measures Cattell's personality traits
- **NEO-PI-R:** Measures Big Five personality traits
- **Minnesota Multiphasic Personality Inventory (MMPI-2):** Provides scores on a number of clinical scales as well as nonclinical personality characteristics

Projective Tests
- **Projective tests:** Simple, ambiguous stimuli that can elicit an unlimited number of responses
- **Rorschach Test:** Test consisting of ambiguous inkblots
- **Thematic Apperception Test (TAT):** Twenty cards picturing one or more human figures in ambiguous situations
- Flexible; difficult to fake; may reflect motives, events, or feelings of which the person is unaware
- Depend heavily on the skill of the examiner; uncertain validity and reliability, especially in cross-cultural settings

It is easy to talk about aspects or traits of personality without defining the term itself. And people often do: Words such as "honest," "irritable," "outgoing," "modest," "friendly," "self-conscious," and "curious" are used to describe themselves and others. But defining personality is difficult, partly because it is not just one characteristic or ability, but a whole range of them. Even psychologists have a hard time agreeing on a single definition of personality. One current definition, and the one used in this book, is that **personality** is the "pattern of characteristic thoughts, feelings, and behaviors that persists over time and situations and that distinguishes one person from another" (Phares, 1984, p. 673).

While that is quite a mouthful, let's look at two important parts of the definition. First, personality refers to those aspects that distinguish a person from everybody else. In this sense, personality is both characteristic of and unique to a particular person. Second, personality persists over time and across situations. When we say "Anne is friendly," we imply that she tends to be friendly in a variety of situations and from one day to the next. In fact, if Anne is suddenly unfriendly, we suspect that something is wrong.

It was only a century ago that scientists began to make systematic scientific observations of personality and to draw conclusions from them. As this chapter will reveal, some theorists emphasize early childhood experiences as determinants of personality. Other theorists stress the role of heredity. Some researchers even question just how consistent people actually are. This chapter explores these views and examines some representative ways to assess personality.

ENDURING ISSUES in Personality

The very concept of personality implies that people differ from one another in significant ways (diversity–universality), that personality tends to be stable across time (stability–change), and that a person's behavior should not vary greatly from one situation to another (person–situation). Nonetheless, as will be seen, there is considerable debate over exactly *how* unique and stable personality is, as well as the extent to which personality is shaped by heredity (nature–nurture).

Personality Traits

Personality Traits

- Personality:_____

- Personality traits:_____

The Big Five

- _____, _____, _____, _____, and _____

Evaluating the Trait Approach

- Provides a way of classifying _____

- Does not explain _____

If someone consistently throws parties, goes to great lengths to make friends, and travels in groups, it might be safe to conclude that this person possesses a high degree of *sociability*. If someone is trustworthy, dependable, and competent, one could conclude that they are *responsible*. Sociability and responsibility are examples of **personality traits**. They describe just two ways in which people often differ from one another. How many other personality traits might there be? To answer that question, Gordon Allport (1897–1967) and his colleague H. S. Odbert turned to the dictionary where they found nearly 18,000 entries that might refer to personality traits (Allport & Odbert, 1936). Only about 2,800 of the words on Allport and Odbert's list concern the kinds of stable or enduring characteristics that most psychologists would call personality traits; and when synonyms and near-synonyms are removed, the number of possible personality traits drops to around 200—which is still a formidable list. Psychologist Raymond Cattell (1905–1998), using a statistical technique called **factor analysis,** found that those 200 traits tend to cluster in groups (R. B. Cattell, 1965). Thus, a person who is described as persevering or determined is also likely to be thought of as responsible, ordered, attentive, and stable and probably would not be described as frivolous, neglectful, and changeable. On the basis of extensive research, Cattell originally concluded that just 16 traits account for the complexity of human personality; later he suggested that it might be necessary to add another seven traits to the list (R. B. Cattell & Kline, 1977).

Other researchers believe that Cattell used too many traits to describe personality. Hans Eysenck (1916–1997) argued that personality could be reduced to three basic dimensions: *emotional stability*, *introversion-extraversion*, and *psychoticism* (Eysenck, 1976). According to Eysenck, *emotional stability* refers to how well a person controls emotions. On a continuum, individuals at one end of this trait would be seen as poised, calm, and composed, whereas people at the other end might be described as anxious, nervous, and excitable. *Introversion-extraversion* refers to the degree to which a person is inwardly or outwardly oriented. At one end of this dimension would be the socially outgoing, talkative, and affectionate people, known as *extraverts*. *Introverts*—generally described as reserved, silent, shy, and socially withdrawn—would be at the other extreme. Eysenck used the term *psychoticism* to describe people characterized by insensitivity and uncooperativeness at one end and warmth, tenderness, and helpfulness at the other end.

■ THE BIG FIVE

Contemporary researchers have boiled down personality traits to five basic dimensions: *extraversion*, *agreeableness*, *conscientiousness*, *emotional stability*, and *culture* (Costa & McCrae, 2006; Wiggins, 1996). There is a growing consensus today that these **Big Five** personality dimensions, also known as the *five-factor model*, capture the most salient dimensions of human personality, although there is some disagreement about whether the fifth dimension should be called "culture" or "openness to experience" or "intellect." Each of the Big Five traits has been shown to have at least six *facets*, or components, as shown in Table 10–1. The 30 identified facets are not an exhaustive listing of all aspects of personality; rather, they represent a broad sample of important traits (Costa & McCrae, 2006; Paunonen & Ashton, 2001).

Most studies of the Big Five have been conducted in the United States. Would the same five personality dimensions be evident in other cultures? The answer appears to be yes. Costa and McCrae (1992) measured the Big Five personality dimensions by developing a test, which has since been translated into German, Portuguese, Hebrew, Chinese, Korean, Japanese, and others. McCrae and Costa (1997) then compared the results from the various questionnaires in an effort to determine whether the same Big Five personality dimensions would emerge. The results from the six non-American cultures were virtually identical to the data from American samples: The Big Five personality dimensions were clearly evident. Other researchers have reached the same conclusions using quite different techniques (Salgado, Moscoso & Lado, 2003; Williams, Satterwhite, & Saiz, 1998).

TABLE 10–1   The "Big Five" Dimensions of Personality

TRAITS	FACETS OF EACH BIG FIVE TRAIT
Extraversion	Warmth, gregariousness, assertiveness, activity, excitement seeking, positive emotions
Agreeableness	Trust, straightforwardness, altruism, compliance, modesty, tender mindedness
Conscientiousness/ Dependability	Competence, order, dutifulness, achievement-striving, self-discipline, deliberation
Emotional Stability	Anxiety, hostility, depression, self-consciousness, impulsiveness, vulnerability
Openness to Experience/ Culture/Intellect	Fantasy, aesthetics, feelings, actions, ideas, values

Source: Adapted from Jang, K. L., Livesley, W. J., McCrae, R. R., Angleitner, A., & Riemann, R. (1998). Heritability of facet-level traits in a cross-cultural twin sample: Support for a hierarchical model of personality. *Journal of Personality and Social Psychology*, 74, 1556–1565. Table 3, p. 1560. © 1998 by the American Psychological Association. Adapted with permission.

PETER WAS A BORN WORRIER ...

I HOPE THIS GUY KNOWS WHAT HE'S DOING.

Source: © Tee and Charles Addams Foundation.

ENDURING ISSUES NATURE/NURTURE

Is Personality Inherited?

Surprisingly, many of the Big Five personality traits apparently exist in a number of species besides humans. Studies have found that the Big Five, with the two added factors of dominance and activity, could be used to rate and describe personality characteristics in species including gorillas, chimpanzees, rhesus and vervet monkeys, hyenas, dogs, cats, and pigs (Gosling & John, 1999; King, Weiss, & Farmer, 2005). These findings, and those from cross-cultural research, suggest that there is some kind of common genetic basis for the Big Five personality traits that cuts across cultures and species. Indeed, recent evidence shows that not only the Big Five but also many of their individual facets are strongly influenced by heredity (W. Johnson, & Krueger, 2004; Livesley, Jang, & Vernon, 2003; Loehlin, McCrae, Costa, & John, 1998).

There are several implications of these findings. It appears that the Big Five traits and their facets are, to some extent, hardwired into the human species (and some nonhuman species as well) and are not simply cultural artifacts. However, saying a particular trait such as extraversion has a genetic component does *not* mean that researchers have found a *gene* for extraversion. Many genes—perhaps thousands of them—surely work in combination to account for such complex traits. Finally, because heredity explains only part of the variability in the Big Five traits, it is clear that experience also plays a significant role in determining the expression of personality traits in any given individual.

■ EVALUATING THE TRAIT APPROACH

Traits are the language that people commonly use to describe others, such as when we say someone is shy or insecure or arrogant. Thus, the trait view of personality has considerable common-sense appeal. But the trait approach has several shortcomings. First, while traits describe the basic dimensions of personality, aside from heredity, we are left wondering why one person is high on a particular trait while another is not. In short, trait theories tell us little about why people are the way they are. Second, there is a legitimate question about whether human diversity can be reduced to just a few dozen characteristics. Finally, although the Big Five model is well supported by research, there continues to be some disagreement about whether the Big Five traits are the *best* way to describe the basic traits of personality.

ENDURING ISSUES STABILITY/CHANGE

How Stable Is Personality Over Time?

Are "agreeable" people at age 20 still agreeable at age 60? As we saw in Chapter 9, Life-Span Development, numerous research studies have shown that temperament remains quite stable over time. Similarly, the Big Five dimensions of personality show considerable stability during early childhood and appear to be "essentially fixed by age 30" (McCrae & Costa, 1994, p. 173; Asendorpf & Van-Aken, 2003). Though to some extent adults can vary their behavior to fit the situations in which they find themselves, in general it seems that when it comes to personality traits, "You can't teach old dogs new tricks."

Check Your Understanding

1. Eysenck stated that personality could be reduced to three basic dimensions: _____, _____ and _____.

2. Peter is competent, self-disciplined, responsible, and well organized. In terms of the Big Five model of personality, he is high in

   a. Agreeableness   **c.** Emotional stability

   b. Conscientiousness   **d.** Intellect

3. Sherry is warm, assertive, energetic, and enthusiastic. According to the Big Five model of personality, she is high in

   a. Extraversion   **c.** Emotional stability

   b. Agreeableness   **d.** Openness to experience

The Psychodynamic Approach

Psychodynamic theories of personality assert that unconscious processes primarily determine personality and that personality is heavily influenced by experience. As discussed in Chapter 1: The Science of Psychology, Sigmund Freud originated the psychodynamic approach to understanding behavior.

■ SIGMUND FREUD

To this day, Sigmund Freud (1856–1939) is the best known and most influential of the psychodynamic theorists. Prior to Freud, the field of psychology had focused on consciousness—that is, on those thoughts and feelings of which we are aware. In a radical departure, Freud stressed the **unconscious**—the ideas, thoughts, and feelings of which we are *not* normally aware. Freud's ideas form the basis of **psychoanalysis**, a term that refers both to his theory of personality and to the form of therapy that he invented.

According to Freud, human behavior is based on unconscious instincts, or drives. Some instincts are aggressive and destructive; others, such as hunger, thirst, self-preservation, and sex, are necessary to the survival of the individual and the species. Freud used the term *sexual instincts* to refer not just to erotic sexuality, but also to the desire for virtually any form of pleasure. In this broad sense, Freud regarded the sexual instinct as the most critical factor in the development of personality.

How Personality Is Structured   Freud theorized that personality is formed around three structures: the id, the ego, and the superego. The **id** is the only structure present at birth and is completely unconscious (Figure 10–1). Consisting of all the unconscious urges and desires that continually seek expression, it operates according to the **pleasure principle**—that is, it tries to obtain immediate pleasure and to avoid pain. As soon as an instinct arises, the id seeks to gratify it. Because the id is not in contact with the real world, however, it has only two ways of obtaining gratification. One way is by reflex actions, such as coughing, which immediately relieve unpleasant sensations. The other is through fantasy, or *wish fulfillment*: A person forms a mental image of an object or a situation that partially satisfies the instinct and relieves the uncomfortable feeling. This kind of thought occurs most often in dreams and daydreams, but it may take other forms. For instance, if someone insults you and you spend the next half hour imagining clever retorts, you are engaging in wish fulfillment.

Mental images of this kind provide fleeting relief, but they cannot fully satisfy most needs. For example, just thinking about being with someone you love is a poor substitute for actually being with that person. Therefore, the id by itself is not very effective at gratifying instincts. It must eventually link to reality if it is to relieve its discomfort. The id's link to reality is the ego.

Freud conceived of the **ego** as the psychic mechanism that controls all thinking and reasoning activities. The ego operates partly consciously, partly *preconsciously*, and partly

---

Psychodynamic theories:

■ Emphasize _____ and

  _____

Sigmund Freud

■ Psychoanalysis: _____

■ Personality is composed of three

structures:

  ■ Id: _____

  ■ Ego: _____

  ■ Superego: _____

■ Libido: _____

■ Fixation: _____

■ Psychosexual stages of development:

_____ (   )

_____ (   )

_____ (   )

_____ (   )

_____ (   )

FIGURE 10–1

The structural relationship formed by the id, ego, and superego.
Often, Freud's conception of personality is depicted as an iceberg to illustrate how the vast workings of the mind occur beneath its surface. Notice that the ego is partly conscious, partly unconscious, and partly preconscious; it derives knowledge of the external world through the senses. The superego also works at all three levels. But the id is an entirely unconscious structure.

Source: Adapted from *New Introductory Lectures on Psychoanalysis*, by Sigmund Freud, 1933, New York: Carlton House.

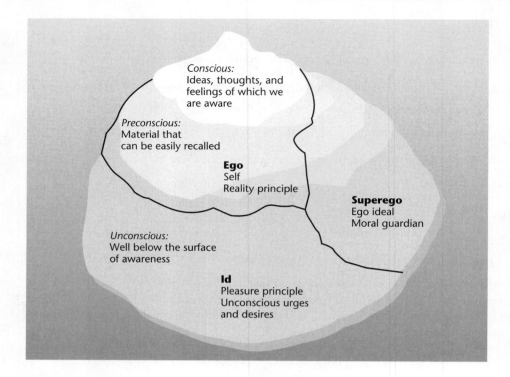

unconsciously. ("Preconscious" refers to material that is not currently in awareness but can be easily recalled.) The ego learns about the external world through the senses and sees to the satisfaction of the id's drives in the external world. But instead of acting according to the pleasure principle, the ego operates by the **reality principle:** By means of intelligent reasoning, the ego tries to delay satisfying the id's desires until it can do so safely and successfully. For example, if you are thirsty, your ego will attempt to determine how to quench your thirst effectively and safely (Figure 10–2).

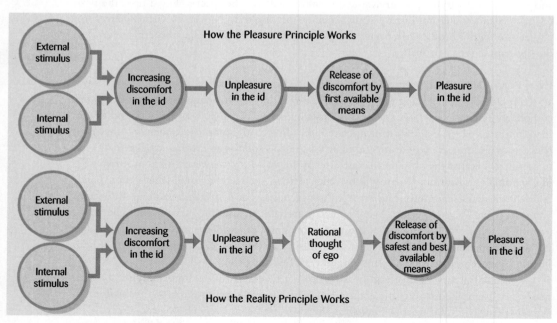

FIGURE 10–2

How Freud conceived the workings of the pleasure and reality principles.
Note that according to the reality principle, the ego uses rational thought to postpone the gratification of the id until its desires can be satisfied safely.

A personality consisting only of ego and id would be completely selfish. It would behave effectively, but unsociably. Fully adult behavior is governed not only by reality but also by the individual's conscience or by the moral standards developed through interaction with parents and society. Freud called this moral watchdog the **superego**. According to Freud, the superego also compares the ego's actions with an **ego ideal** of perfection and rewards or punishes the ego accordingly. Unfortunately, the superego is sometimes too harsh in its judgments. An artist dominated by such a punishing superego, for example, may realize the impossibility of ever equaling Rembrandt and so give up painting entirely.

Ideally, our id, ego, and superego work in harmony, with the ego satisfying the demands of the id in a reasonable, moral manner that is approved by the superego. We are then free to love and hate and to express our emotions sensibly and without guilt. When our id is dominant, our instincts are unbridled and we are likely to endanger ourselves and society. When our superego dominates, our behavior is checked too tightly and we are inclined to judge ourselves too harshly or too quickly, impairing our ability to act on our own behalf and enjoy ourselves.

How Personality Develops Freud's theory of personality development focuses on the way in which individuals satisfy the sexual instinct during the course of life. Freud thought of this instinct as a craving for sensual pleasure of all kinds, calling the energy generated by the sexual instinct **libido**. As infants mature, their libido focuses on various sensitive parts of the body during sequential stages of development. According to Freud, children's experiences at each of these stages stamp their personality with tendencies that endure into adulthood. If a child is deprived of pleasure (or allowed too much gratification) from the part of the body that dominates a certain stage, some sexual energy may remain permanently tied to that part of the body, instead of moving on in normal sequence to give the individual a fully integrated personality. This is called **fixation**, and Freud believed that it leads to immature forms of sexuality and to certain characteristic personality traits. Let's look more closely at the psychosexual stages that Freud identified and their presumed relationship to personality development.

In the **oral stage** (birth to 18 months), infants, who depend completely on other people to satisfy their needs, relieve sexual tension by sucking and swallowing; when their baby teeth come in, they obtain oral pleasure from chewing and biting. According to Freud, infants who receive too much oral gratification at this stage grow into overly optimistic and dependent adults; those who receive too little may turn into pessimistic and hostile people later in life. Fixation at this stage is linked to several personality characteristics, including lack of confidence, gullibility, sarcasm, and argumentativeness.

During the **anal stage** (roughly 18 months to 3.5 years), the primary source of sexual pleasure shifts from the mouth to the anus. Just about the time children begin to derive pleasure from holding in and excreting feces, toilet training takes place, and they must learn to regulate this new pleasure. In Freud's view, if parents are too strict in toilet training, some children throw temper tantrums and may live in self-destructive ways as adults. Others become obstinate, stingy, and excessively orderly. If parents are too lenient, their children may become messy, unorganized, and sloppy.

When children reach the **phallic stage** (after age 3), they discover their genitals and develop a marked attachment to the parent of the opposite sex while becoming jealous of the same-sex parent. In boys, Freud called this the **Oedipus complex**, after the character in Greek mythology who killed his father and married his mother. Girls go through a corresponding **Electra complex**, involving possessive love for their father and jealousy toward their mother. Most children eventually resolve these conflicts by identifying with the parent of the same sex. However, Freud contended that fixation at this stage leads to vanity and egotism in adult life, with men boasting of their sexual prowess and treating women with contempt, and with women becoming flirtatious and promiscuous. Phallic fixation may also prompt feelings of low self-esteem, shyness, and worthlessness.

At the end of the phallic period, Freud believed, children lose interest in sexual behavior and enter a **latency period**. During this period, which begins around the age of 5 or 6 and lasts until age 12 or 13, boys play with boys, girls play with girls, and neither sex takes much interest in the other.

At puberty, the individual enters the last psychosexual stage, the **genital stage**. At this time, sexual impulses reawaken and unfulfilled desires from infancy and childhood are satisfied. Ideally, the quest for immediate gratification of these desires yields to mature sexuality, in which postponed gratification, a sense of responsibility, and caring for others play a part.

Freud's theories have clearly expanded our understanding of personality, or they would not still be so vigorously debated today, more than 100 years after he proposed them. Freud's emphasis on the fact that we are not always—or even often—aware of the real causes of our behavior has fundamentally changed the way people view themselves and others. Freud's ideas have also had a lasting impact on history, literature, and the arts. Yet, Freud was a product of his time and place and he is certainly not without his critics (Dahl, 1996; C. Hall, 2005). His male-centered, phallic view of personality development in particular has come under criticism, especially because he also hypothesized that all little girls feel inferior because they do not have a penis. Critics have pointed out that he was apparently unable to imagine a connection between his female patients' sense of inferiority and their subordinate position in society.

■ OTHER PSYCHODYNAMIC THEORISTS

Freud's beliefs, particularly his emphasis on sexuality, were not completely endorsed even by his own colleagues. Carl Jung and Alfred Adler, two early associates of Freud, eventually broke with him and formulated their own psychodynamic theories of personality. Jung expanded the scope of the unconscious well beyond the selfish satisfactions of the id. Adler believed that human beings have positive—and conscious—goals that guide their behavior. Other psychodynamic theorists put greater emphasis on the ego and its attempts to gain mastery over the world. These neo-Freudians, principally Karen Horney and Erik Erikson, also focused more on the influence of social interaction on personality.

Carl Jung   Carl Jung (1875–1961) agreed with many of Freud's tenets, including his emphasis on the role of the unconscious in human behavior. But Jung contended that libido represents *all* life forces, not just the sexual ones. And where Freud viewed the id as a "cauldron of seething excitations" that the ego has to control, Jung saw the unconscious as the ego's source of strength and vitality. He also believed that the unconscious consists of the personal unconscious and the collective unconscious. The **personal unconscious** includes one's repressed thoughts, forgotten experiences, and undeveloped ideas, which may enter consciousness if an incident or a sensation triggers their recall. The **collective unconscious**, Jung's most original concept, comprises "thought forms," or collective memories, that are inherited from past generations and therefore are shared by all humans. He called these thought forms **archetypes**. Because all people have mothers, for example, the archetype of "mother" is universally associated with the image of one's own mother, with Mother Earth, and with a protective presence.

While Freud emphasized the primacy of the sexual instincts, Jung stressed the individual's rational and spiritual qualities. And while Freud considered development to be shaped in childhood, Jung thought that psychic development comes to fruition only during middle age. Jung brought a sense of historical continuity to his theories, tracing the roots of human personality back through our ancestral past; yet he also contended that a person moves constantly toward self-realization—toward blending all parts of the personality into a harmonious whole. Nonetheless, many psychologists have somewhat neglected Jung's ideas (Neher, 1996; Addison, 2005) for two reasons: (1) Jung broke with Freud, and (2) symbolism and mysticism characterize his theories. Recently, however, his concept of archetypes has been "rediscovered" by those interested in the power of myth (Ellens, 2002; Nuttall, 2002).

Alfred Adler   Alfred Adler (1870–1937), who served as president of the Vienna Psychoanalytic Society in 1910, nonetheless disagreed sharply with Freud's concept of the conflict between the selfish id and the morality-based superego. Adler's early thinking was focused on the individual's attempt to overcome physical weaknesses, an effort he called **compensation**. Later,

---

Other Psychodynamic Theorists

Carl Jung

- Libido represents _____

_____

- Personal unconscious: _____

_____

- Collective unconscious: _____

_____

Alfred Adler

- Compensation: _____

_____

- Fixation on feelings of personal inferiority that results in emotional and social paralysis is called an

_____

- Later theory: _____

Karen Horney

- Feelings of _____ and _____ are more important than sexuality.

- Neurotic lifestyles: _____ type, _____ type, _____ type

- Biology is not _____

- Gender differences derived from _____, not _____

Erik Erikson

- Emphasized the quality of _____

_____

- According to Erikson, only when children feel_____ and _____, in their own eyes and in society's, will they develop a secure sense of identity.

According to Carl Jung, we all inherit from our ancestors collective memories or "thought forms" that people have had in common since the dawn of human evolution. The image of a motherlike figure with protective, embracing arms is one such primordial thought form that stems from the important, nurturing role of women throughout human history. This thought form is depicted here in this Bulgarian clay figure of a goddess that dates back some six or seven thousand years.

A contemporary representation from American culture of the Jungian archetype of the Wise Old Man can be seen in Yoda (from the *Star Wars* films). Although this theatrical image is not universally associated with the archetype, it is one of culture's ways of capturing and expressing it.

"I'm only a _good_ dane."

he broadened his views to include efforts to overcome *feelings* of inferiority that may or may not have a basis in reality. He thought that such feelings often spark positive development and personal growth. Still some people become so fixated on their feelings of inferiority that they become paralyzed and develop what Adler called an **inferiority complex.** Even later in his life, Adler again shifted his theoretical emphasis in a more positive direction when he concluded that strivings for superiority and perfection are more important to personality development than overcoming feelings of inferiority. Because of his emphasis on positive, socially constructive goals and on striving for perfection, Adler is considered by many psychologists to be the father of humanistic psychology, a topic that will be explored in greater depth shortly.

Karen Horney   Karen Horney (1885–1952), another psychodynamic personality theorist greatly indebted to Freud, nevertheless took issue with some of his most prominent ideas, especially his analysis of women and his emphasis on sexual instincts. Based on her experience as a practicing therapist in Germany and the United States, Horney concluded that nonsexual factors—such as the need for a sense of basic security and the person's response to real or imagined threats—play an even larger role in development than does sexuality. For Horney, *anxiety*—an individual's reaction to real or imagined dangers—is a powerful motivating force. Even well-adjusted people experience anxiety and threats to their basic security, but because their childhood environment enabled them to satisfy their basic emotional needs, they have developed effective ways of dealing with emotional problems and threats to their safety. In contrast, other adults have difficulty dealing with basic feelings of insecurity and anxiety and, as a result, they become trapped in neurotic lifestyles. The overly *submissive* personality type has an overriding need to give in or to submit to others and feels safe only when receiving their protection and guidance. In contrast, the overly *aggressive* personality masks submissive feelings by relating to others in a hostile and domineering manner. Finally, the *detached* type copes with basic anxiety by withdrawing from other people. This person seems to be saying, "If I withdraw, nothing can hurt me."

Karen Horney, a psychotherapist during the first half of the twentieth century, disagreed with Freud's emphasis on sexual instincts. She considered environmental and social factors, especially the relationships we have as children, to be the most important influences on personality.

ENDURING ISSUES   STABILITY/CHANGE

Is Biology Destiny?

Horney believed that adults can continue to develop and change throughout life. Because biology is not destiny, adults can come to understand the source of their basic anxiety and try to eliminate neurotic anxiety. Horney's belief (and that of other psychodynamic thinkers) in the possibility of change through self-understanding also relates to the mind–body question. Psychodynamic therapies, which involve delving into past experiences and hidden motives, rely on the premise that destructive thought patterns and behaviors can change through mental effort only.

Horney also opened the way to a more constructive and optimistic understanding of male and female personality. She emphasized that culture, rather than anatomy, determines many of the characteristics that differentiate women from men, and she pointed out that those cultural forces can be changed. For example, when women feel dissatisfied with their gender or men are overly aggressive, the explanation is likely to be found in their social status and social roles, not in their anatomy; fortunately, social status and social roles can be changed. Indeed, she was a forerunner of contemporary thinkers who believe that individuals can change culture and society and, in the process, transform human relationships.

Erik Erikson, another psychodynamic theorist, also stressed the importance of parent-child relationships for shaping personality. His eight-stage theory of personality development is still influential today.

Evaluating the Psychodynamic Approach

■ Difficult to translate psychodynamic theories into _____ that can be tested _____

■ Five propositions, central to all psychodynamic theories, have withstood the tests of time:

_____

_____

_____

_____

_____

Erik Erikson   Erik Erikson and his eight psychosocial stages were introduced in Chapter 9: Life-Span Development. Erikson was a psychodynamic theorist who studied with Freud in Vienna and was psychoanalyzed by Freud's daughter, Anna. Erikson agreed with much of Freud's thinking on sexual development and the influence of libidinal needs on personality. He also agreed that development occurs in distinct stages, each of which has characteristic challenges or conflicts that must be addressed and resolved in order for the individual to develop optimally (see the Summary Table: Stages of Development: Erikson and Freud on p. 253). But like Karen Horney, Erikson took a socially oriented view of personality development. In particular, he emphasized the quality of parent-child relationships. Children can be disciplined in a way that leaves them with a feeling of being loved or of being hated. The difference is largely based on the atmosphere of a home. The important point is that children should feel that their own needs and desires are compatible with those of society. Only when children feel competent and valuable, in their own eyes and in society's, will they develop a secure sense of identity. In this way, Erikson's psychosocial theory of development shifted the focus of Freud's personality theory to ego development.

■ EVALUATING THE PSYCHODYNAMIC APPROACH

Some aspects of psychodynamic theory, especially Freud's views of female sexuality, are clearly out of date. The following five propositions, however, are central to all psychodynamic theories and have withstood the tests of time (Huprich & Keaschuk, 2006; Westen, 1998):

1. Much of *mental* life is unconscious; as a result, people may behave in ways that they themselves do not understand.
2. Mental processes (such as emotions, motivations, and thoughts) operate in parallel and thus may lead to conflicting feelings.
3. Not only do stable personality patterns begin to form in childhood, but early experiences also strongly affect personality development.
4. Our mental representations of ourselves, of others, and of our relationships tend to guide our interactions with other people.
5. Personality development involves learning to regulate sexual and aggressive feelings as well as becoming socially interdependent rather than dependent.

It is often difficult to translate psychodynamic personality theories into hypotheses that can be tested scientifically. But whatever their merit as science, psychodynamic theories attempt to explain the root causes of all human behavior. The sheer magnitude of this undertaking helps to account for their lasting attractiveness.

Check Your Understanding

1. An angry parent imagines hitting a child for misbehaving, but decides instead to discuss the misbehavior with the child and to point out why the behavior was wrong. After hearing the child's explanation for the behavior, the parent feels guilty for having been so angry. According to Freud, the parent's anger arises from the _____; the decision to discuss the problem is the result of the _____, and the guilt derives from the _____.

   a. Ego; superego; id   **c.** Ego; id; superego

   b. Id; ego; superego   **d.** Id; superego; ego

2. Match the following personality characteristics with fixation at the appropriate stage in Freud's theory of development.

   _____ Obstinate, stingy, excessively orderly   **a.** Oral stage

   _____ Gullible, sarcastic, argumentative   **b.** Anal stage

   _____ Low self-esteem, shyness, worthlessness   **c.** Phallic stage

The Humanistic Approach

Humanistic personality theory emphasizes that people are positively motivated and that they progress toward higher levels of functioning—in other words, that there is more to human existence than dealing with hidden conflicts. Humanistic psychologists believe that life is a process of opening oneself to the world around and experiencing joy in living. They stress people's potential for growth and change, as well as the ways they experience their lives right now—rather than dwelling on how they felt or acted in the past. This approach holds everyone personally responsible for their own lives. Finally, humanists also believe that given reasonable life conditions, people will develop in desirable directions. Adler's concept of striving for perfection laid the groundwork for later humanistic personality theorists such as Abraham Maslow and Carl Rogers. Maslow's theory of the hierarchy of needs leading to self-actualization was discussed in Chapter 8: Motivation and Emotion. We now turn to Rogers's theory of self-actualization.

■ CARL ROGERS

One of the most prominent humanistic theorists of the twentieth century, Carl Rogers (1902–1987), contended that men and women develop their personalities in the service of positive goals. According to Rogers, every organism is born with certain innate capacities, capabilities, or potentialities—"a sort of genetic blueprint, to which substance is added as life progresses" (Maddi, 1989, p. 102). The goal of life, Rogers believed, is to fulfill this genetic blueprint, to become the best of whatever each person is inherently capable of becoming. Rogers called this biological push toward fulfillment the **actualizing tendency**. Although Rogers maintained that the actualizing tendency characterizes all organisms—plants, animals, and humans—he noted that human beings also form images of themselves, or *self-concepts*. Just as people try to fulfill their inborn biological potential, so, too, they attempt to fulfill their own self-concept, their conscious sense of who they are and what they want to do with their lives. Rogers called this striving the **self-actualizing tendency**. If you think of yourself as "intelligent" and "athletic," for example, you will strive to live up to those images of yourself.

When self-concept is matched closely with inborn capacities, an individual is likely to become what Rogers called a **fully functioning person**. Such people are self-directed: They

---

Humanistic personality theory:

■ _____

Carl Rogers

■ Actualizing tendency: _____

_____

■ Self-actualizing tendency: _____

_____

■ Fully functioning person: _____

_____

■ Unconditional positive regard: _____

_____

■ Conditional positive regard: _____

_____

Evaluating the Humanistic Approach

■ Central tenet _____ is difficult, if not impossible, to test scientifically

■ Some support for specific _____ _____ from theories

■ Perhaps overly _____ view of human nature

■ Reflects Western values of _____

decide for themselves what it is they wish to do and to become, even though their choices may not always be sound ones. They are not unduly swayed by other people's expectations for them. Fully functioning people are also open to experience—to their own feelings as well as to the world and other people around them—and thus, they find themselves "increasingly willing to be, with greater accuracy and depth, that self which [they] most truly [are]" (Rogers, 1961, pp. 175–176).

According to Rogers, people tend to become more fully functioning when they are brought up with **unconditional positive regard**, or the experience of being treated with warmth, respect, acceptance, and love regardless of their own feelings, attitudes, and behaviors.

But often parents and other adults offer children what Rogers called **conditional positive regard**: They value and accept only certain aspects of the child. The acceptance, warmth, and love that the child receives from others then depend on the child's behaving in certain ways and fulfilling certain conditions. In the process, self-concept comes to resemble the inborn capacity less and less, and the child's life deviates from the genetic blueprint.

When people lose sight of their inborn potential, they become constricted, rigid, and defensive. They feel threatened and anxious, and they experience considerable discomfort and uneasiness. Because their lives are directed toward what other people want and value, they are unlikely to experience much real satisfaction in life. At some point, they may realize that they do not really know who they are or what they want.

■ EVALUATING THE HUMANISTIC APPROACH

The central tenet of most humanistic personality theories—that the overriding purpose of the human condition is to realize one's potential—is difficult, if not impossible, to verify scientifically. The resulting lack of scientific evidence and rigor is one of the major criticisms of these theories. In addition, some critics claim that humanistic theories present an overly optimistic view of human beings and fail to take into account the evil in human nature. Others contend that the humanistic view fosters self-centeredness and narcissism, reflecting Western values of individual achievement rather than universal human potential.

Nonetheless, Maslow and, especially, Rogers did attempt to test some aspects of their theories scientifically. For example, Rogers studied the discrepancy between the way people perceived themselves and the way they ideally wanted to be. He discovered that people whose real selves differed considerably from their *ideal* selves were more likely to be unhappy and dissatisfied.

Check Your Understanding

1. Barbara was brought up with unconditional positive regard. According to Rogers, she is likely to

a. Be vain and narcissistic

b. Feel that she is valued regardless of her attitudes and behavior

c. Have self-concepts that do not correspond very closely to her inborn capacities

d. Both (b) and (c) are true.

2. Your friend has always known that she wants to be a doctor. When you ask her how she knows that, she says, "That's just who I am. It's what I want to do with my life." Rogers calls the push toward fulfilling this sense of who she is

a. Being fully functioning

b. Engaging in a compensatory process

c. Expressing a high need for achievement

d. The self-actualizing tendency

The Cognitive–Social Learning Approach

Cognitive–social learning theories hold that people internally organize their expectancies and values to guide their own behavior. This set of personal standards is unique to the individual, growing out of his or her own life history. The person's behavior then is the product of the interaction of cognitions (how one thinks about a situation and how one views his or her behavior in that situation), learning and past experiences (including reinforcement, punishment, and modeling), and the immediate environment.

■ EXPECTANCIES, SELF-EFFICACY, AND LOCUS OF CONTROL

Albert Bandura (1977, 1986, 1997), arguably the most influential contemporary personality theorist, asserts that people evaluate a situation according to certain internal **expectancies**, such as personal preferences, and this evaluation affects their behavior. Environmental feedback that follows the actual behavior, in turn, influences future expectancies. These experience-based expectancies lead people to conduct themselves according to unique **performance standards**, individually determined measures of excellence by which they judge their own behavior. Those who succeed in meeting their own internal performance standards develop an attitude that Bandura calls **self-efficacy** (Bandura & Locke, 2003). For example, two young women trying a video game for the first time may experience the situation quite differently, even if their scores are similarly low. One with a high sense of self-efficacy may find the experience fun and may eagerly wish to gain the skills necessary to go on to the next level, whereas the one with a lower sense of self-efficacy may be disheartened by getting a low score, assume she will never be any good at video games, and never play again.

Julian Rotter identified one particularly prevalent expectancy, or cognitive strategy, by which people evaluate situations—and he called it **locus of control** (Rotter, 1954). People with an *internal locus* of control are convinced that they can control their own fate. They believe that through hard work, skill, and training, they can find reinforcements and avoid punishments. People with an *external locus* of control do not believe they control their fate. Instead, they are convinced that chance, luck, and the behavior of others determine their destiny and that they are helpless to change the course of their lives.

ENDURING ISSUES PERSON/SITUATION

How Consistent Are We?

We have seen that trait theorists tend to believe that behavior is relatively consistent across situations. "Agreeable" people tend to be agreeable in most situations most of the time. In contrast, cognitive–social learning theorists view personality as the relatively stable cognitive processes that underlie behavior, but behavior itself is the product of the person and the situation: At any time, our actions are influenced by the people around us and by the way we think we are supposed to behave in a given situation. According to this latter view, although underlying personality is relatively stable, behavior is likely to be more inconsistent than consistent from one situation to another.

If behavior is relatively inconsistent across situations, why does it *appear* to be more consistent than it actually is? Why is the trait view of personality so compelling? One explanation is that, because we see a person only in those situations that tend to elicit the same behavior, we tend to assume that they are consistent across a wide range of situations. Moreover, there is considerable evidence that people need to find consistency and stability even in the face of inconsistency and unpredictability. We, therefore, see consistency in the behavior of others even when there is none (Mischel, 2003; Mischel & Shoda, 1995).

Cognitive-social learning theories:

■ Hold that people internally organize their _____ and _____ to guide their own _____

Expectancies, Self-Efficacy, and Locus of Control

■ Performance standards: _____

■ Self-efficacy: _____

■ Locus of control: _____

Evaluating the Cognitive–Social Learning Approach

■ Key concepts can be _____ and _____

■ Accounts for inconsistencies in _____

■ Already has numerous _____

Both Bandura and Rotter have tried to combine personal variables (such as expectancies) with situational variables in an effort to understand the complexities of human behavior. Both theorists believe that expectancies become part of a person's *explanatory style*, which, in turn, greatly influences behavior. Explanatory style, for example, separates optimists from pessimists—it is, for example, what causes two beginners who get the same score on a video game to respond so differently.

■ EVALUATING THE COGNITIVE–SOCIAL LEARNING APPROACH

It is still too early to say how well cognitive–social learning theories will account for the complexity of human personality, but they seem to have great potential. They put mental processes back at the center of personality, and they focus on conscious behavior and experience. The key concepts of these theories, such as self-efficacy and locus of control, can be defined and studied scientifically, which is not true of the key concepts of psychodynamic and humanistic theories. Moreover, cognitive–social learning theories help explain why people behave inconsistently, an area in which trait approaches fall short. Cognitive-social learning theories of personality have also spawned useful therapies that help people recognize and change a negative sense of self-efficacy or explanatory style. In particular, as we will see in Chapter 13, these therapies have helped people overcome depression. Self-efficacy theory has also been embraced by management theorists because of its practical implications for work performance. Many studies conducted over more than 20 years have shown a positive correlation between self-efficacy and performance in workplaces, schools, and clinical settings.

Check Your Understanding

1. In Bandura's view, the belief that people can control their own fate is known as _____-_____.

2. Rey Ramos grew up in the South Bronx, an urban ghetto in which young males are more likely to go to jail than they are to graduate from high school. He said, "My father always said you cannot change anything; destiny has everything written for you. But, I rebelled against that, and I told him I was going to make my own destiny." According to cognitive–social learning theories of personality, which of the following is most descriptive of Rey?

   a. He has an internal locus of control.

   b. He has a low sense of self-efficacy.

   c. He is compensating for feelings of inferiority.

   d. He has an external locus of control.

The Personal Interview

■ Unstructured interview: _____

_____

■ Structured interview: _____

_____

Direct Observation

■ Observe behavior in _____

_____

■ Method tends to be _____

and _____

■ Behavior may be affected by _____

_____

Personality Assessment

In some ways, testing personality is very similar to testing intelligence. In both cases, something intangible and invisible is trying to be measured. And in both cases, a "good test" is one that is both *reliable* and *valid*: It gives dependable and consistent results, and it measures what it claims to measure (Chapter 7). But there are special difficulties in measuring personality.

Because personality reflects *characteristic* behavior, researchers are not interested in someone's *best* behavior. They are interested in *typical* behavior—how a person usually behaves in ordinary situations. Further complicating the measurement process, factors such as fatigue, a desire to impress the examiner, and fear of being tested can profoundly affect a person's behavior in a personality-assessment situation. For the intricate task of measuring personality, psychologists use four basic tools: the personal interview, direct observation of behavior, objective tests, and projective tests.

■ THE PERSONAL INTERVIEW

An interview is a conversation with a purpose: to obtain information from the person being interviewed. Some interviews are *unstructured*—the interviewer asks people questions and lets the interview unfold, asking follow-up questions whenever appropriate. When conducting systematic research on personality, investigators more often rely on the *structured* interview. In these interviews, the order and content of the questions are fixed and the interviewer adheres to the set format. Although less personal, this kind of interview allows the interviewer to obtain comparable information from everyone interviewed. Generally speaking, structured interviews are more likely to elicit information about sensitive topics that might not come up spontaneously in an unstructured interview.

■ DIRECT OBSERVATION

Another way to assess personality is to observe a person's actions in everyday situations over a long period. Social learning theorists prefer this method of assessing personality because it allows them to see how situation and environment interact to influence behavior. Ideally, the observers' unbiased accounts of the person's behavior paint an accurate picture of that behavior, but an observer runs the risk of misinterpreting the true meaning of an act. For example, the observer may think that children are being hostile when they are merely protecting themselves from the class bully. An expensive and time-consuming method of research, direct observation may also yield faulty results whenever the presence of the observer affects people's behavior.

■ OBJECTIVE TESTS

To avoid depending on the skills of an interviewer or the interpretive abilities of an observer in assessing personality, psychologists use **objective tests**, also called *personality inventories*. Generally, these *written* tests are administered and scored according to a standard procedure and usually are constructed so that the person merely chooses a "yes" or "no" response or selects one answer among many choices.

Objective tests are the most widely used tools for assessing personality, but they have two serious drawbacks. First, they rely entirely on self-reporting. If people do not know themselves well, cannot be entirely objective about themselves, or want to paint a particular picture of themselves, self-report questionnaire results have limited usefulness. Second, if people have taken personality questionnaires previously, their familiarity with the test format may affect their responses to it. This is a particular problem with college students, who are likely to participate in many research studies that rely on personality inventories.

Because of their interest in measuring personality traits accurately, trait theorists favor objective tests. Cattell, for example, developed a 374-question personality test called the **Sixteen Personality Factor Questionnaire**. As to be expected, the 16PF (as it is usually called) provides scores on each of the 16 traits originally identified by Cattell. More recently, objective tests such as the **NEO-PI-R** have been developed to assess the Big Five major personality traits (Costa & McCrae, 2006). The NEO-PI-R yields scores on each of the Big Five traits as well as each of the 30 facets.

The most widely used and thoroughly researched objective personality test is the **Minnesota Multiphasic Personality Inventory (MMPI-2)**. Respondents are asked to answer "true," "false," or "cannot say" to such questions as "Once in a while I put off until tomorrow what I ought to do today," "At times I feel like swearing," and "There are people who are trying to steal my thoughts and ideas." Some of the items repeat very similar thoughts in different words: For example, "I tire easily" and "I feel weak all over much of the time." This redundancy provides a check on the possibility of false or inconsistent answers.

Researchers have derived a number of clinical scales from this test, including ratings for depression, paranoia, hysteria, and hypochondriasis. These scales make the MMPI-2 a useful tool for differentiating among psychiatric populations. For the present, it is sufficient to note that to a lesser extent, the MMPI-2 has also been used to assess more normal personality dimensions, such as extraversion-introversion and assertiveness.

■ PROJECTIVE TESTS

Owing to their belief that people are often unaware of the determinants of their behavior, psychodynamic theorists tend to discount self-report objective personality tests. Instead, they prefer

---

Objective Tests

■ Objective tests (personality inventories): _____

_____

■ Rely on _____

■ Sixteen Personality Factor Questionnaire (16PF): Measures

_____

■ NEO-PI-R: Measures _____

_____

■ Minnesota Multiphasic Personality Inventory (MMPI-2): Provides _____

_____

as well as _____

Projective Tests

■ Projective tests: _____

_____

■ Rorschach Test: Test consisting of

_____

■ Thematic Apperception Test (TAT):

_____

■ Flexible, difficult to fake, may reflect _____, _____, or _____ of which the person is _____

■ Depend heavily on _____;
uncertain validity and reliability,
especially in _____

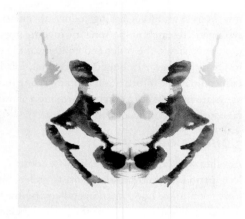
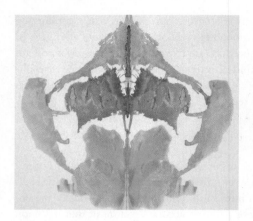

FIGURE 10–3
Inkblots used in the Rorschach projective test.

projective tests of personality. Most projective tests consist of simple, ambiguous stimuli that can elicit an unlimited number of responses. After looking at an essentially meaningless graphic image or at a vague picture, the test taker explains what the material means. Alternatively, the person may be asked to complete a sentence fragment, such as "When I see myself in the mirror, I . . . " The tests offer no clues regarding the "best way" to interpret the material or to complete the sentence.

The **Rorschach Test** is the best known and one of the most frequently used projective personality tests. It is named for Hermann Rorschach (1884–1922), a Swiss psychiatrist and psychoanalyst, who in 1921 published the results of his research on interpreting inkblots as a key to personality (Figure 10–3). Each inkblot design is printed on a separate card and is unique in form, color, shading, and white space. People are asked to specify what they see in each blot. Test instructions are minimal, so people's responses will be completely their own. After interpreting all the blots, the person goes over the cards again with the examiner and explains which part of each blot prompted each response. There are different methods of interpreting a person's responses to the blots on the Rorschach test, some of which produce more valid results than others.

Somewhat more demanding is the **Thematic Apperception Test (TAT)**. It consists of 20 cards that display one or more human figures in deliberately ambiguous situations (Figure 10–4). A person is shown the cards one by one and asked to create a complete story about each

FIGURE 10–4
A sample item from the Thematic Apperception Test (TAT).
In the photo, the person is making up a story to explain the scene in the painting. The examiner then interprets and evaluates the person's story for what it reveals about her personality.

Source: Reprinted by permission of the publishers from Henry A. Murray, *Thematic Apperception Test,* Plate 12F, Cambridge, Mass.: Harvard Univ. Press, © 1943 by the President and Fellows of Harvard College, © 1971 by Henry A. Murray.

picture, including what led up to the scene depicted, what the characters are doing at that moment, what their thoughts and feelings are, and what the outcome will be.

Although various scoring systems have been devised for the TAT, examiners usually interpret the stories in the light of their personal knowledge of the storyteller. One key in evaluating the TAT is determining who the test taker identifies with—the story's hero or heroine, or one of the minor characters. The examiner then determines what the attitudes and feelings of the character reveal about the storyteller. The examiner also assesses each story for content, language, originality, organization, consistency, and recurring themes such as the need for affection, repeated failure, or parental domination.

Projective tests have several advantages. Because they are flexible and can even be treated as games or puzzles, people can take them in a relaxed atmosphere, without the tension and self-consciousness that sometimes accompany objective tests. Often, the purpose of the test is not obvious—to make faking responses more difficult. Some psychologists believe that projective tests can uncover unconscious thoughts and fantasies, such as latent sexual or family problems. In any event, the accuracy and usefulness of projective tests depend largely on the skill of the examiner in eliciting and interpreting responses. Both the Rorschach and the TAT may open up a conversation between a clinician and a patient who is reluctant or unable to talk about personal problems. Both tests may also provide insight into motives, events, or feelings of which the person is unaware. But because of their inherent ambiguity and the fact that interpreting answers to the test relies heavily on the skill of the examiner, their validity and reliability, especially in cross-cultural settings, have been called into question (Hofer & Chasiotis, 2004). As a result, their use has declined somewhat since the 1970s.

Check Your Understanding

1. _____ tests require people to fill out questionnaires, which are then scored according to a standardized procedure.

2. In _____ tests of personality, people are shown ambiguous stimuli and asked to describe them or to make up a story about them.

3. You are consulting a psychologist who asks you to take a personality test. She shows you pictures of people and asks you to write a complete story about each picture. The test is most likely the

   a. Minnesota Multiphasic Personality Inventory

   b. Rorschach Test

   c. Thematic Apperception Test

   d. NEO-PI-R

Chapter Review

www.psychologythecore.com

Personality refers to an individual's unique pattern of thoughts, feelings, and behaviors that persists over time and across situations. Key to this definition is the concept of distinctive differences among individuals and the concept of personality's stability and endurance.

Personality Traits

Personality traits describe ways in which people can differ. Cattell, using **factor analysis**, concluded that no more than two dozen traits could capture the complexity of human personality. Eysenck reduced that number to just three dimensions. Contemporary researchers tend to agree that there may be just five overarching and universal personality traits: extraversion, agreeableness, conscientiousness, emotional stability, and openness to experience (also called culture or intellect). Each of these traits has facets or components that give rise to a total of 30 aspects of personality. The same **Big Five** traits appear in other cultures and in some other species. Research shows these traits are influenced strongly by heredity.

Trait theories are primarily descriptive—to provide a way of classifying personalities—but they do not explain why someone's personality develops as it does. Moreover, there is some question about whether the complexity of human personality can be reduced to just a few traits and whether the Big Five traits are the best way to describe the basic traits of personality.

The Psychodynamic Approach

Psychodynamic theories of personality emphasize **unconscious** factors and personal life experience as crucial to understanding human personality. Freud's theory of personality and his approach to therapy are called **psychoanalysis**.

According to Freud, personality is made of three structures. The **id**, the only personality structure present at birth, is completely unconscious and operates according to the **pleasure principle**. The **ego**, operating according to the **reality principle**, attempts to satisfy id impulses safely and effectively in the real world. The **superego**, which acts as the moral guardian or conscience, helps the person function in society by comparing the ego's actions with the **ego ideal** of perfection. Freud used the term *sexual instinct* to refer to the desire for virtually any form of pleasure. As infants mature, their **libido**, or energy generated by the sexual instinct, focuses on sensitive parts of the body. A **fixation** occurs when a child is deprived of or receives too much pleasure from the part of the body that dominates one of the five developmental stages—**oral**, **anal**, **phallic**, **latency**, and **genital**. During the phallic stage, strong attachment to the parent of the opposite sex and jealousy of the parent of the same sex is termed the **Oedipus complex** in boys and the **Electra complex** in girls. Next, the child enters the latency period, characterized by a lack of interest in sexual behavior. Finally, at puberty, the individual enters the genital stage of mature sexuality.

Freud's view of human nature has had a profound effect on our understanding of human behavior, but it has also been subject to heated criticism. Even members of his own psychoanalytic school differed with him, particularly with respect to his emphasis on sexuality. For example, while Freud saw the id as a "cauldron of seething excitations," Jung expanded the scope of the unconscious well beyond selfish satisfactions of the id. Jung believed that the unconscious consisted of the **personal unconscious**, encompassing an individual's repressed thoughts, forgotten experiences, and undeveloped ideas; and the **collective unconscious**, a subterranean river of memories and behavior patterns flowing to us from previous generations. Certain universal thought forms, called **archetypes**, give rise to mental images or mythological representations and play a special role in shaping personality.

Alfred Adler believed that people possess innate positive motives and strive toward personal and social perfection. He originally proposed that the principal determinant of personality was the individual's attempt to overcome physical weakness (**compensation**), but he later modified his theory to stress the importance of *feelings* of inferiority, whether or not those feelings are justified. When people become so fixated on their feelings of inferiority that they become paralyzed by them, they are said to have an **inferiority complex**. Still later, Adler proposed that strivings for superiority and perfection, both in one's own life and in the society in which one lives, are crucial to personality development.

Karen Horney proposed that *anxiety*—a person's reaction to real or imagined dangers or threats—is a stronger motivating force than the sexual drive. Anxious adults are likely to become trapped in neurotic lifestyles and become overly submissive, overly aggressive, or detached. By emphasizing that culture and not anatomy determines many of the personality traits that differentiate women from men and that culture can be changed, Horney became a forerunner of feminist psychology.

Erik Erikson argued that the quality of the parent-child relationship affects the development of personality because, out of this interaction, the child either feels competent and valuable and is able to form a secure sense of identity or feels incompetent and worthless and fails to build a secure identity. Erikson proposed that each person moves through eight stages of development, each involving a more successful versus a less successful adjustment.

Psychodynamic theories have had a profound impact on the way we view ourselves and others. Several key concepts that are shared by all psychodynamic theories have withstood the tests of time. But it is often difficult to translate psychodynamic personality theories into hypotheses that can be tested scientifically.

The Humanistic Approach

Freud and many of his followers believed that personality grows out of the resolution of unconscious conflicts and developmental crises from the past. In contrast, **humanistic personality theory** emphasizes that we are positively motivated and progress toward higher levels of functioning; and it stresses people's potential for growth and change in the present.

Carl Rogers contended that all people are born with certain innate potentials and the **actualizing tendency** to realize their biological potential as well as their conscious sense of who they are (the **self-actualizing tendency**). A **fully functioning person** is one whose self-concept closely matches his or her inborn capabilities. This is a likely outcome when a child is raised in an atmosphere characterized by **unconditional positive regard** as opposed to **conditional positive regard**.

There is a lack of scientifically derived evidence for humanistic theories of personality. In addition, these theories are criticized for taking too rosy a view of human nature, for fostering self-centeredness, and for reflecting Western values of individual achievement.

The Cognitive–Social Learning Approach

Cognitive–social learning theories of personality view behavior as the product of cognitions, learning and past experiences, and the immediate environment.

Albert Bandura maintains that certain internal **expectancies** determine how a person evaluates a situation and that this evaluation has an effect on the person's behavior. These expectancies prompt people to conduct themselves according to unique **performance standards**, individually determined measures of excellence by which they judge their behavior. Those who succeed in meeting their own internal performance standards develop an attitude that Bandura calls **self-efficacy**. According to Julian Rotter, one particularly prevalent expectancy is **locus of control**. People with an internal locus of control believe that they can control their own fate through their actions. Those with an external locus of control believe that chance, luck, and the behavior of others determine their destiny. Finally, because social learning theorists believe behavior is the product of the person and the situation, it is not surprising that they believe behavior is likely to be more inconsistent than consistent from one situation to another.

It is still too early to say how well cognitive–social learning theories will account for the complexity of human personality, but they seem to have great potential. Cognitive–social learning theories avoid the narrowness of trait theories. They also lend themselves to scientific study to a much greater degree than do psychodynamic and humanistic theories. They also explain why people behave inconsistently, an area in which the trait theories fall short. Cognitive–social learning theories have also spawned therapies that have been used effectively to treat depression.

Personality Assessment

Psychologists use four different methods to assess personality: the personal interview, direct observation of behavior, **objective tests**, and **projective tests**. During an unstructured interview, the interviewer asks questions and lets the interview unfold, posing follow-up questions where appropriate. In a structured interview, the order and the content of the questions are fixed and the interviewer does not deviate from the format. Structured interviews are more likely to be used for systematic research on personality because they elicit comparable information from all interviewees.

Direct observation of a person over a period of time enables researchers to assess how a person's personality is expressed in a variety of situations. This technique is expensive and time-consuming. The observer may misinterpret the meaning of a given behavior. And the mere presence of the observer may affect people's behavior.

Objective tests ask respondents to answer specific questions about their own behavior and thoughts. Cattell's **Sixteen Personality Factor Questionnaire (16PF)** provides scores on 16 basic personality traits, whereas the **NEO-PI-R** reports scores for each of the Big Five traits and their associated facets. The **Minnesota Multiphasic Personality Inventory (MMPI-2)**, originally developed as an aid to diagnose mental disorders, also provides scores on some nonpsychiatric dimensions of personality.

Psychodynamic theorists, who believe that much behavior is determined by unconscious processes, tend to discount tests that rely on self-reports. They are more likely to use projective tests consisting of ambiguous stimuli that can elicit an unlimited number of interpretations based on these unconscious processes. Two such tests are the **Rorschach Test** and the **Thematic Apperception Test (TAT)**. Because the stimuli in these tests are ambiguous and the responses are unstructured, their reliability and validity depends heavily on the skill of the examiner.

Chapter 11
Stress and Health Psychology

Go to *The Core Online* at **www.psychologythecore.com** to get the most up-to-date information for your introductory psychology course. The content online is an important part of what you are learning—the content there can help prepare you for your test! It includes up-to-date examples, simulations, video clips, and practice quizzes. Also be sure to check out the *Blog* to hear directly from the authors on what current events and latest research are most relevant to your course materials.

The first time you log in, you will need the access code packaged with your textbook. If you do not have a code, please go to **www.mypearsonstore.com** and enter the ISBN of your textbook (**0-13-603344-X**) to purchase the code.

Chapter 11 Stress and Health Psychology

Stress: The body's reaction to any environmental demand that creates a state of tension or threat and requires change or adaptation (**stressor**)

Adjustment: Any effort to cope with stress

11 1 Sources of Stress

Change
- Anything—good or bad—that requires change has the potential to be experienced as stressful.
- The more change that a situation requires, the more stressful the situation becomes.

Everyday Hassles
- Everyday hassles include life's petty annoyances, irritations, and frustrations.
- **Pressure:** Demand to speed up, intensify, or change the direction of one's behavior or live up to a higher standard of performance
- **Frustration:** Being prevented from reaching a goal because something or someone stands in the way
  —Delays
  —Lack of resources
  —Losses
  —Failure
  —Discrimination
- **Conflict:** Two or more incompatible demands, opportunities, needs, or goals
  —**Approach/approach conflict:** Being simultaneously attracted to two desirable possibilities
  —**Avoidance/avoidance conflict:** Being confronted with two undesirable or threatening possibilities
  —**Approach/avoidance conflict:** Being both attracted to and repelled by the same goal

Self-Imposed Stress
- Stress that arises from self-defeating or unrealistic thoughts

11 2 Coping With Stress

Direct Coping
- Intentional efforts to change a stressful situation include:
  —**Confrontation:** Acknowledging a stressful situation and addressing the problem head-on
  —**Compromise:** Deciding on a more realistic solution or goal when an ideal solution or goal is not practical
  —**Withdrawal:** Avoiding a stressful situation when other forms of coping are not practical

Defensive Coping
- **Defense mechanisms:** Techniques for deceiving oneself about the causes of a stressful situation to reduce pressure, frustration, conflict, and anxiety that might otherwise be unbearable
- Most often used when an individual either cannot identify or cannot deal directly with the source of severe stress
- Can be maladaptive when the defense mechanism interferes with the ability to deal directly with a problem or creates more problems than it solves
  —**Denial:** Refusal to acknowledge a painful or threatening reality
  —**Repression:** Blocking out all awareness of painful feelings, thoughts, and memories
  —**Projection:** Attributing one's own motives, ideas, or feelings to others
  —**Identification:** Taking on the characteristics of someone else
  —**Regression:** Reverting to childlike behavior
  —**Intellectualization:** Analyzing stressful problems intellectually and without emotion
  —**Reaction formation:** Expressing, with exaggerated intensity, ideas and emotions that are the opposite of one's own
  —**Displacement:** Redirection of motives and emotions from one's original objects to substitute objects
  —**Sublimation:** Transforming repressed motives or feelings into more socially acceptable forms

Socioeconomic and Gender Differences in Coping With Stress
- Stress often takes a greater toll on people in lower socioeconomic classes: poor neighborhoods are especially stressful, and people in lower socioeconomic classes often have fewer resources for coping with hardship and stress.
- When under stress, men are more likely to withdraw, get into arguments, or turn to alcohol. Women are more likely to ruminate about the problem, spend time with their family, or call on friends.

11 3 How Stress Affects Health

Health psychology: Explores how psychological factors influence wellness and illness

- **General Adaptation Syndrome (GAS)**: Stages in the reaction to stress proposed by Hans Selye
  - —Alarm reaction: Mobilization of the body's coping resources occurs
  - —Resistance: Physical symptoms and other signs of strain appear; intensification of coping efforts
  - —Exhaustion: Physical and emotional resources are depleted further; increased use of ineffective defense mechanisms
- Psychological stress can cause physical illness in at least two ways:
  - —The body is not designed for the biological changes that accompany prolonged stress.
  - —Stress has a powerful negative effect on the body's immune system, the focus of the field of **psychoneuroimmunology (PNI)**.

11 4 Staying Healthy

- Ways to reduce the negative impact of stress on health:
  - —Exercise
  - —Relaxation training
  - —Social support network
  - —Religion
  - —Altruism
  - —Proactive coping
  - —Positive reappraisal
  - —Humor
  - —Avoiding smoking

11 5 Extreme Stress

Sources of Extreme Stress
- Unemployment
- Divorce and separation
- Bereavement
- Catastrophes

Posttraumatic Stress Disorder
- Psychological disorder resulting from severely stressful events such as war, serious accidents, and violent crimes
- Characterized by nightmares, flashbacks, and withdrawal from job and family
- Individual characteristics predispose some people to PTSD more than others.
- Some people experience positive growth as a result of significant trauma.

11 6 The Well-Adjusted Person

- There is no consensus among psychologists regarding what constitutes good adjustment.
- Some alternative ways of viewing good adjustment include:
  - —Living according to social norms
  - —Enjoying the difficulties and ambiguities of life and treating them as challenges to be overcome and opportunities for psychological growth
  - —Specific criteria
    - Does the action realistically meet the demands of the situation or does it simply postpone resolving the problem?
    - Does the action meet the individual's needs?
    - Is the action compatible with the well-being of others?

Difficult situations are common in everyday life, and so, too, is stress. Everyone is familiar with the knotted stomach, pounding heart, or anxious feelings when the car breaks down in traffic, when the computer crashes before the data was backed up, when running late and caught in a traffic jam, or when under pressure to meet deadlines. Whenever people feel threatened physically or psychologically, when they wonder if they can cope with the demands of their environment, and when their heart pounds and their stomach feels queasy, they are experiencing **stress**—the body's reaction to a difficult situation that disrupts a person's normal functioning and state of well-being. But stress is not always "bad"; it can have positive as well as negative consequences. Indeed, most people would be bored with an existence that held no challenges or surprises. Moreover, stress can stimulate effort and spark creativity. Even when a situation is hopeless and a happy ending is impossible, people often report that they have grown, acquired new coping skills and resources, and perhaps experienced a spiritual or religious transformation as a result of stress.

But experiencing too much stress over too long a period can contribute to physical and psychological problems. **Health psychology** focuses on how the mind and body interact. Specifically, health psychologists seek to understand how psychological factors influence wellness and illness. Numerous studies have found that people suffering from acute or chronic stress may be more vulnerable to everything from the common cold to an increased risk for heart disease. New research is uncovering the biological mechanisms that link stress to lowered immunity and poor health. The challenge for health psychologists is to find ways to facilitate **adjustment** to stress, to prevent stress from becoming physically and emotionally debilitating, and to *promote* healthy behavior and well-being.

This chapter looks at common sources of stress, explores why some people are more vulnerable to stress than others, and examines strategies for coping with stress. Then, a discussion follows regarding how acute or chronic stress sometimes can make people more susceptible to physical illness by weakening their immune system. The challenge, discussed in the sections that follow, is to find ways to reduce stress and promote good health and a sense of well-being even among those who have suffered extreme stress.

ENDURING ISSUES   in Stress and Health Psychology

← → In this chapter, we again encounter several of the "Enduring Issues" that interest all psychologists regardless of their area of specialization. To what extent do the methods that people use in coping with stress depend on the environment in which they find themselves (person–situation)? Can psychological stress cause physical illness (mind–body)? To what extent do people respond differently to severe stress (diversity–universality)?

Sources of Stress

The term **stressor** refers to any environmental demand that creates a state of tension or threat and requires change or adaptation. Many situations prompt individuals to change their behavior in some way, but only some of these situations cause stress. Consider, for example, stopping at a traffic signal that turns red. Normally, this involves no stress. But now imagine that you are rushing to an important appointment or to catch a train and the red light will surely make you late. Here, stress is triggered because the situation not only requires adaptation, but it produces tension and distress as well.

Some events, such as wars and natural disasters, are inherently stressful. Danger is real, lives are threatened, and often, there is little or nothing people can do to save themselves. Stress is not limited, however, to dangerous or unpleasant situations. Even everyday events or good things can also cause stress, because they necessitate a change or adaptation. For example, a wedding is often a stressful, as well as an exciting, event. A promotion at work is gratifying, but it demands that the individual relate to new people in new ways, learn to carry more responsibility, and perhaps work longer hours.

Stress: The body's reaction to any _____ that creates a state of tension or threat and requires _____ or _____

Adjustment: Any effort to _____ with _____

Change

- Anything—good or bad—that requires _____ has the potential to be experienced as _____.

- The more _____ that a situation requires, the more _____ the situation becomes.

■ CHANGE

All stressful events involve change. But most people have a strong preference for order, continuity, and predictability in their lives. Therefore, anything—good or bad—that requires change has the potential to be experienced as stressful. The more change that a situation requires, the more stressful the situation becomes. In fact, the relationship between change and stress is so close that many questionnaires measure stress simply by asking about the amount of change people have experienced in their lives.

■ EVERYDAY HASSLES

Stress can also arise from everyday "hassles." Seemingly minor matters can take their toll, such as having a zipper break, waiting in a long line, misplacing car keys, or having a petty argument with a friend. Richard Lazarus (1922–2002) believed that big events matter so much because they trigger numerous little hassles that eventually overwhelm us with stress. "It is not the large dramatic events that make the difference," Lazarus noted, "but what happens day in and day out, whether provoked by major events or not" (Lazarus, 1981, p. 62). Research confirms that people who have recently suffered a major traumatic event are more likely to experience a sustained stress reaction when exposed to minor stressors or hassles they might usually be able to tolerate (Cross, 2003). In the end, major *and* minor events are stressful, because they lead to feelings of pressure, frustration, and conflict.

Pressure   **Pressure** is another common source of stress. Pressure occurs when one feels forced to speed up, intensify, or shift the direction of behavior or to meet a higher standard of performance. In part, pressure can arise from within, from very personal goals and ideals. Because of our concern about our intelligence, appearance, popularity, or talents, we may push ourselves to reach ever higher standards of excellence. This kind of pressure can be constructive. It may lead, for example, to a serious effort to learn to play a musical instrument, which can ultimately bring us great pleasure. On the other hand, internal pressure can be destructive whenever our aims are impossible to achieve.

A sense of pressure may also derive from outside influences. Among the most significant and consistent of these are seemingly relentless demands that we compete, that we adapt to the rapid rate of change in our society, and that we live up to what our family and close friends expect of us. The forces that push us to compete affect nearly all relationships in American life. We compete for grades, for popularity, for sexual and marital partners, and for jobs. We are taught to see failure as shameful. Hence, the pressure to win can be intense.

Frustration   **Frustration** occurs when a person is prevented from reaching a goal because something or someone stands in the way. Frustration can arise from a number of sources in addition to daily hassles. *Delays* are annoying because our culture puts great stock in the value of time. *Lack of resources* is frustrating to those who cannot afford the new cars or lavish vacations they desire. *Losses*, such as the end of a love affair or a cherished friendship, cause frustration because they often make those involved feel helpless, unimportant, or worthless. *Failure* generates intense frustration in our competitive society. *Discrimination*, too, can be extremely frustrating when individuals or groups are denied opportunities or recognition simply because of their sex, age, religion, or skin color.

Conflict   Of all life's troubles, conflict is probably the most common. A boy does not want to go to his aunt's for dinner, but neither does he want to listen to his parents complain if he stays home. A student finds that both of the required courses she wanted to take this semester are given at the same hours on the same days. **Conflict** arises when we face two or more incompatible demands, opportunities, needs, or goals. We can never completely resolve conflict. Either we must give up some of our goals, modify some of them, delay our pursuit of some of them, or resign ourselves to not attaining all our goals. Whatever we do, we are bound to experience some frustration, thereby adding to the stressfulness of conflicts.

All major life changes involve a certain amount of stress. This is partly because major life changes typically bring strong emotions, and even joy and elation can arouse the body and begin to take a toll on its resources. Major life events can also be stressful because any new experience requires some adjustment.

Everyday Hassles

■ Everyday hassles include life's petty

_____, _____,

and _____.

■ Pressure: _____

■ Frustration: Being prevented from

_____ because _____,

such as: _____

_____

■ Conflict: Two or more _____

demands, opportunities, needs, or

goals

Approach/approach conflict: _____

_____

Avoidance/avoidance conflict: _____

_____

Approach/avoidance conflict: _____

_____

Self-Imposed Stress

■ Stress that arises from _____

_____

Much of the stress we experience in our lives arises not from major traumas but from small everyday hassles such as traffic jams, petty arguments, and equipment that fails when we need it most.

In the 1930s, Kurt Lewin (1890–1947) described two opposite tendencies of conflict: approach and avoidance. When something attracts us, we want to approach it; when something frightens us, we try to avoid it. Lewin (1935) showed how different combinations of these tendencies create three basic types of conflict: approach/approach conflict, avoidance/avoidance conflict, and approach/avoidance conflict.

Approach/approach conflict occurs when a person is simultaneously attracted to two appealing goals. Being accepted for admission at two equally desirable colleges or universities is an example. The stress that occurs in approach/approach conflict is that in choosing one desirable option, we must give up the other.

The reverse is **avoidance/avoidance conflict**, in which we confront two undesirable or threatening possibilities, neither of which has any positive attributes. When faced with an avoidance/avoidance conflict, people usually try to escape the situation altogether. If escape is impossible, people often simply wait for events to resolve their conflict for them.

An **approach/avoidance conflict**, in which a person is both attracted to and repelled by the same goal, is the most common form of conflict. The closer we come to a goal with good and bad features, the stronger our desires grow both to approach and to avoid; but Lewin proposed that the tendency to avoid increases more rapidly than does the tendency to approach. Eventually, everyone reaches a point at which the tendency to approach equals the tendency to avoid the goal. Afraid to go any closer, they stop and vacillate, making no choice at all, until the situation changes.

■ SELF-IMPOSED STRESS

So far, we have considered external sources of stress. Sometimes, however, people create problems for themselves quite apart from stressful events in their environment. For example, some people believe that "it is essential to be loved or approved by almost everyone for everything I do." For such people, any sign of disapproval will be a source of considerable stress. Others believe that "I must be competent, adequate, and successful at everything I do." For them, the slightest sign of failure or inadequacy means that they are worthless human beings. Still other people believe that "it is disastrous if everything doesn't go the way I would like." These people feel upset, miserable, and unhappy when things do not go perfectly. As seen in Chapter 12: Psychological Disorders, self-defeating thoughts such as these can contribute to psychological disorders.

Check Your Understanding

1. Indicate whether each of the following statements is true (T) or false (F).

   a. _____ Change that results from "good" events, such as marriage or job promotion, does not produce stress.

   b. _____ Stressful events nearly always involve changes in our lives.

   c. _____ Big events in life are always much more stressful than everyday hassles.

2. Bob wants to go to graduate school for a degree in pharmacology, but he is very concerned about the intense studying that will be required to complete the curriculum. Bob is faced with a(n)

   a. Offensive/defensive coping dilemma

   b. Direct/defensive coping dilemma

   c. Avoidance/avoidance conflict

   d. Approach/avoidance conflict

Coping With Stress

Whatever its source, stress requires that individuals cope—that is, it requires people to make cognitive and behavioral efforts to manage psychological stress. There are many different ways to cope with stress, but two general types of adjustment stand out: direct coping and defensive coping.

▪ DIRECT COPING

Direct coping refers to intentional efforts to change an uncomfortable situation. Direct coping tends to be problem oriented and tends to focus on the immediate issue. For example, when we are threatened, frustrated, or in conflict, we have three basic choices for coping directly: confrontation, compromise, or withdrawal.

Acknowledging that there is a problem for which a solution must be found, attacking the problem head-on and pushing resolutely toward the goal is called **confrontation**. The hallmark of the "confrontational style" is making intense efforts to cope with stress and to accomplish one's aims. Doing so may involve learning skills, enlisting other people's help, or just trying harder. Or it may require steps to change either oneself or the situation. Confrontation may also include expressions of anger. Anger may be effective, especially if we really have been treated unfairly and if we express our anger with restraint instead of exploding in rage.

Compromise is one of the most common and effective ways of coping directly with conflict or frustration. People often recognize that they cannot have everything they want and that they cannot expect others to do just what they would like them to do. In such cases, they may decide to settle for less than what they originally sought.

In other circumstances, the most effective way of coping with stress is to withdraw from the situation. When people realize that their adversary is more powerful than they are, that there is no way they can effectively modify themselves or the situation, that there is no possible compromise, and that any form of aggression would be self-destructive, **withdrawal** is a positive and realistic response. Although withdrawal can be an effective method of coping, it has built-in dangers. The person who has given up on a situation is in a poor position to take advantage of a more effective solution if one should come along. And, in some cases, withdrawal can lead to maladaptive avoidance, such as when a person caught in a bad marriage makes the decision that divorce is the best course of action, then avoids all close relationships in the future.

▪ DEFENSIVE COPING

Thus far, we have discussed coping with stress that arises from recognizable sources. But there are times when people either cannot identify or cannot deal directly with the source of their stress. For example, you might return to a parking lot to discover that your car has been damaged. In other cases, a problem may be so emotionally threatening that it cannot be faced directly: Perhaps someone close to you is terminally ill, or, after 4 years of hard work, you have failed to gain admission to medical school and may have to abandon your plan to become a doctor.

In such situations, people may turn to **defense mechanisms** as a way of coping. Defense mechanisms are techniques for *deceiving* oneself about the causes of a stressful situation to reduce pressure, frustration, conflict, and anxiety. The self-deceptive nature of the defense mechanisms led Freud to conclude that they are entirely unconscious, but not all psychologists agree that they always spring from unconscious conflicts over which one has little or no control. Often, individuals realize that they are pushing something out of their memory or are otherwise deceiving themselves. For example, nearly everyone has blown up at another person even though they knew they were really angry at someone else. Whether defense mechanisms operate consciously or unconsciously, they provide a means of coping with stress that might otherwise be unbearable.

Denial and Repression **Denial** is the refusal to acknowledge a painful or threatening reality. Although denial is a positive response in some situations, it clearly is not in other situations. Frequent drug users who insist that they are merely "experimenting" with drugs are using

---

Direct Coping

▪ Intentional efforts to change a stressful situation include:
- Confrontation:_____
- Compromise:_____
- Withdrawal:_____

Defensive Coping

▪ Defense mechanisms:_____
_____
▪ Most often used when an individual either cannot _____ or cannot _____ with the source of severe stress
▪ Can be maladaptive when the defense mechanism interferes with _____
_____ or _____
- Denial:_____
- Repression:_____
- Projection:_____
- Identification:_____
- Regression:_____
- Intellectualization:_____
- Reaction formation:_____
- Displacement:_____
- Sublimation:_____

denial. As we saw in Chapter 9, Elisabeth Kübler-Ross proposed that many people who learn they are dying of cancer react initially with denial. The person may deny that he was ever told he was dying. Or he may insist that an error has been made.

In denial, people block out situations that they cannot otherwise handle. In **repression**, individuals block out painful feelings, thoughts, and memories. Many war veterans have no recollection at all of some of the horrors they witnessed. Some victims of childhood sexual abuse repress all memories of those events. Denial and repression are the most basic defense mechanisms. These psychic strategies form the basis for several other defensive ways of coping.

Projection If a problem cannot be denied or completely repressed, we may be able to distort its nature so that we can handle it more easily through **projection**, which refers to the attribution of one's own motives, ideas, or feelings onto others. For example, a corporate executive who feels guilty about the way he rose to power may project his own ruthless ambition onto his colleagues. He simply is doing his job, he believes, whereas his associates are all crassly ambitious and consumed with power.

Identification The reverse of projection is **identification**: taking on the characteristics of someone else, so that we can share vicariously in that person's triumphs and overcome any feelings of inadequacy. A parent with unfulfilled career ambitions may come to identify with one of her children. When the child is promoted, the parent may feel personally triumphant. Sometimes, identification is used to cope with situations in which a person feels utterly helpless. For example, in a hostage situation, victims sometimes seek to please their captors and may identify with them as a way of coping defensively with unbearable and inescapable stress. This is called the "Stockholm Syndrome," named after four Swedes who were held captive in a bank vault for nearly a week, and upon their release defended their captors.

Regression People under severe stress may revert to childlike behavior through a process called **regression**. Why do people regress? One explanation is that the person may be unable to tolerate feeling helpless. Children, on the other hand, feel helpless and dependent every day, so becoming more childlike can make total dependency or helplessness more bearable. But regression is not always the result of imposed dependency or helplessness. Adults who cry or throw temper tantrums when their arguments fail may expect those around them to react sympathetically, as their parents did when they were children. Inappropriate as it may seem, such immature and manipulative behavior sometimes works—at least for a while.

Intellectualization **Intellectualization** is a subtle form of denial in which we detach ourselves from our feelings about our problems by analyzing them intellectually and thinking of them almost as though they concerned other people. Imagine that someone who has been diagnosed with cancer shows little or no emotional reaction. Rather, he or she spends day after day gathering information about the disease. Such a person may be intellectualizing what would otherwise be an intolerable situation.

Reaction Formation The term **reaction formation** refers to a behavioral form of denial in which people express, with exaggerated intensity, ideas and emotions that are the opposite of their own. *Exaggeration* is the clue to this behavior. The woman who extravagantly praises a rival may be covering up jealousy over her opponent's success. Reaction formation may also be a way of convincing ourselves that our motives are pure. The man who feels ambivalent about being a father may devote a disproportionate amount of time to his children in an attempt to prove to *himself* that he is a good father.

Displacement **Displacement** involves the redirection of repressed motives and emotions from their original objects to substitute objects. The man who has always wanted to be a father, but who learns that he cannot have children, may become extremely attached to a pet or to a niece or nephew. The classic example of displacement is the person who, experiencing stress on the job, comes home and kicks the cat.

Sublimation   Sublimation refers to transforming repressed motives or feelings into more socially acceptable forms. Aggressiveness, for instance, might be channeled into competitiveness in business or sports. A strong and persistent desire for attention might be transformed into an interest in acting or politics. From the Freudian perspective, sublimation is not only necessary but also desirable. People who can transform their sexual and aggressive drives into more socially acceptable forms are clearly better off, for they are able at least partially to gratify instinctual drives with relatively little anxiety and guilt. Moreover, society benefits from the energy and effort that such people channel into the arts, literature, science, and other socially useful activities.

Does defensive coping mean that a person is immature, unstable, or on the edge of a "breakdown"? Is direct coping adaptive and is defensive coping maladaptive? The answer is "not necessarily." In some cases of prolonged and severe stress, lower-level defenses may not only contribute to one's overall ability to adjust but also may even become essential to survival. In the short run, especially when there are few other options, defenses may reduce anxiety and thus allow the person to work out more effective modes of adaptation. Over the long run, however, defenses can hinder successful adjustment. Defense mechanisms are maladaptive when they interfere with a person's ability to deal directly with a problem or when they create more problems than the person can solve.

ENDURING ISSUES   PERSON/SITUATION

Coping Strategies

Individuals use various coping strategies in different combinations and in different ways to deal with stressful events. It is tempting to conclude that styles of coping, like personality, reside within the individual. Yet, a good deal of research indicates that the amount of stress people encounter and how they cope with it depend to a significant degree on the environment in which they live (Almeida, 2005; Taylor & Repetti, 1997).

■ SOCIOECONOMIC AND GENDER DIFFERENCES IN COPING WITH STRESS

Consider the impact of socioeconomic status on stress and coping. In poor neighborhoods, addressing even the basic tasks of living is stressful. Housing is often substandard and crowded; there are fewer stores and these stores offer lower quality goods; crime and unemployment rates are likely to be high; and schools have lower teacher-student ratios, high staff turnover, and more part-time teachers. In short, people living in poor neighborhoods have to deal with more stress than people who live in better neighborhoods. Moreover, people in lower socioeconomic classes often have fewer means for coping with hardship and stress, fewer people to turn to, and fewer community resources to draw upon for support during stressful times. Taken together, the greater levels of stress and fewer resources for coping with stress help to explain why stress often takes a much greater toll on people in lower socioeconomic classes.

Are there also gender differences in experiencing and coping with stress? The answer seems to be "yes"—at least under some circumstances. In one study of 300 dual-income couples, women and men felt equally stressed by the state of their marriage, their jobs, and how well their children were doing. However, the women in this study experienced greater stress than men when problems developed in long-term relationships, largely because they were more committed to their personal and professional relationships than were the men (Barnett, Brennan, & Marshall, 1994). Women and men also appear to respond differently to the stress caused by an automobile accident, with women experiencing more stress both immediately after the accident and several months later (Bryant & Harvey, 2003). Other research indicates

Socioeconomic and Gender Differences in Coping With Stress

■ Stress often takes a greater toll on people in _____ socioeconomic classes: _____ neighborhoods are especially stressful, and people in _____ socioeconomic classes often have fewer _____ for coping with hardship and stress.

■ When under stress, men are more likely to _____, _____, or _____.

Women are more likely to _____, _____, or _____.

that men and women often use different ways of coping with stress. For example, when men are down or depressed, they are more likely than women to turn to alcohol; when women are blue, sad, or mad, they are more likely to ruminate about the problem, revisiting negative emotions and the events that led up to them in their minds (Husong, 2003; Nolen-Hoeksema & Harrell, 2002). Moreover, women often deal with stress by using a *tend-and-befriend response*, spending time with their family or calling friends. In contrast, men more often withdraw or get into arguments (Taylor et al., 2000; Volpe, 2004).

Check Your Understanding

1. Confronting problems, compromising, or withdrawing from the situation entirely are all forms of _____ coping.

2. _____ coping is a means of dealing with situations that people feel unable to resolve.

3. Bill is very frustrated because he did quite poorly on several midterm exams. After returning from an especially difficult exam, he yells at his roommate for leaving clothes strewn around the floor. Bill's reaction is most likely the result of which defense mechanism?

   a. Projection   **c.** Sublimation

   b. Reaction formation   **d.** Displacement

How Stress Affects Health

To understand how the body responds to stress, let's first examine how people react to danger. Suppose you are walking alone down an unfamiliar street late at night and you notice that a suspicious stranger is following you. Suddenly, your heart begins to pound, your respiration increases, and you develop a queasy feeling in your stomach. What is happening to you? The hypothalamus, a center deep in your brain, is reacting to your perception of danger by organizing a generalized response that affects several organs throughout your body (Figure 11–1).

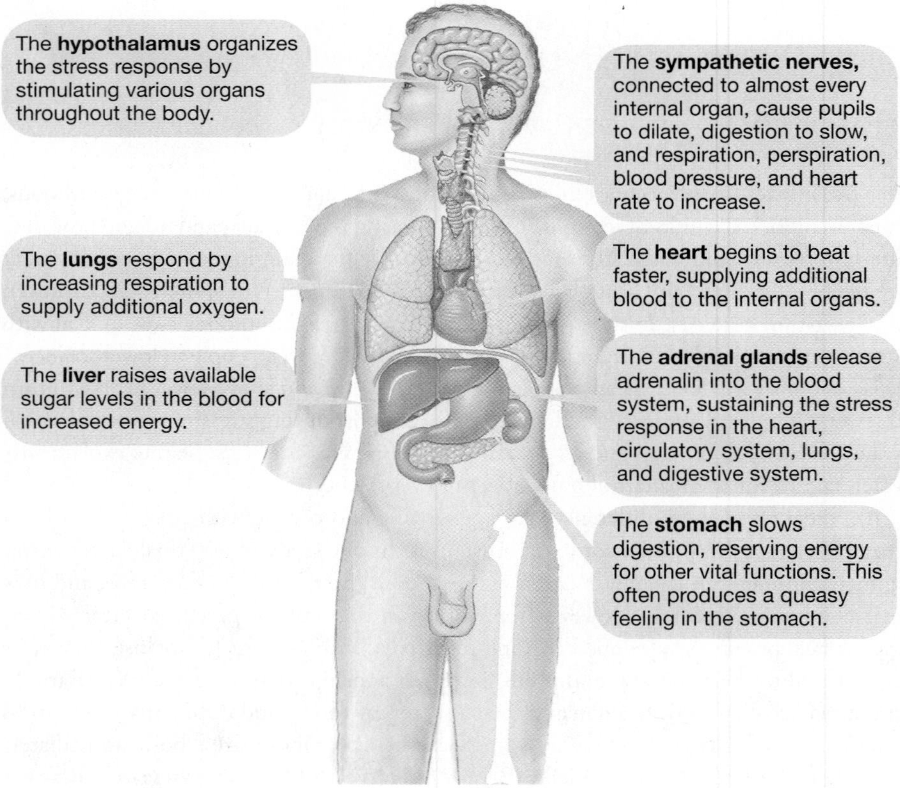

The **hypothalamus** organizes the stress response by stimulating various organs throughout the body.

The **sympathetic nerves,** connected to almost every internal organ, cause pupils to dilate, digestion to slow, and respiration, perspiration, blood pressure, and heart rate to increase.

The **lungs** respond by increasing respiration to supply additional oxygen.

The **heart** begins to beat faster, supplying additional blood to the internal organs.

The **liver** raises available sugar levels in the blood for increased energy.

The **adrenal glands** release adrenalin into the blood system, sustaining the stress response in the heart, circulatory system, lungs, and digestive system.

The **stomach** slows digestion, reserving energy for other vital functions. This often produces a queasy feeling in the stomach.

FIGURE 11–1
The physiological response to stress.
When the body is confronted with a stressful situation, the hypothalamus stimulates the sympathetic nervous system and the adrenal glands to release stress hormones. Other organs, including the stomach and liver, also respond.

Source: "Invisible wounds," June 2000, by R. F. Mollica. *Scientific American*, p. 54. Figure by Laurie Grace.

Almost immediately, the hypothalamus stimulates the sympathetic branch of the autonomic nervous system and the adrenal glands to release stress hormones such as adrenaline and norepinephrine into the blood. This process in turn leads to increases in heart rate, blood pressure, respiration, and perspiration. Other organs also respond; for example, the liver increases the available sugar in the blood for extra energy and the bone marrow increases the white blood cell count to combat infection. Conversely, the rate of some bodily functions decreases; for example, the rate of digestion slows down, thus accounting for the queasy feeling in the stomach.

The noted physiologist Walter Cannon (1871–1945) first described the basic elements of this sequence of events as a *fight-or-flight response*, because it appeared that its primary purpose was to prepare an animal to respond to external threats by either attacking or fleeing from them (Cannon, 1929). Cannon also observed that this physiological mobilization occurred uniformly regardless of the nature of the threat. For instance, the fight-or-flight response can be triggered by physical trauma, fear, emotional arousal, or simply having a really bad incident happen at work or school. The adaptive significance of the fight-or-flight response in people was obvious to Cannon, because it assured the survival of early humans when faced with danger.

Extending Cannon's theory of the fight-or-flight response, the Canadian physiologist Hans Selye (pronounced SAY-lee) (1907–1982) proposed that people react to physical and psychological stress in three stages, which he collectively called the **general adaptation syndrome**, or GAS (Selye, 1956, 1976). These three stages are alarm reaction, resistance, and exhaustion.

Stage 1—*alarm reaction*—is the first response to stress. It begins when the body recognizes that it must fend off some physical or psychological danger. Emotions run high. Activity of the sympathetic nervous system is increased, resulting in the release of hormones from the adrenal gland. Individuals become more sensitive and alert, respiration and heartbeat quicken, muscles tense, and other physiological changes are experienced as well. All these changes help the person to mobilize coping resources. At the alarm stage, one might use either direct or defensive coping strategies. If neither of these approaches reduces the stress, one eventually enters the second stage of adaptation.

During Stage 2—*resistance*—physical symptoms and other signs of strain appear as the person struggles against increasing psychological disorganization. The individual intensifies his or her use of direct and defensive coping techniques. If the person is successful in reducing the stress, he or she will return to a more normal state. But if the stress is extreme or prolonged, the person may turn in desperation to inappropriate coping techniques and cling to them rigidly, despite the evidence that the techniques are not working. When that happens, physical and emotional resources are depleted further, and signs of psychological and physical wear and tear become even more apparent.

In the third stage—*exhaustion*—individuals draw on increasingly ineffective defense mechanisms in a desperate attempt to bring the stress under control. Some people lose touch with reality and show signs of emotional disorder or mental illness at this stage. Others show signs of "burnout," including an inability to concentrate, irritability, procrastination, and a cynical belief that nothing is worthwhile. Physical symptoms such as skin or stomach problems may erupt, and some victims of burnout turn to alcohol or drugs to cope with the stress-induced exhaustion. If the stress continues, the person may suffer irreparable physical or psychological damage or even death.

Stress is a major contributing factor in the development of coronary heart disease (CHD), the leading cause of death and disability in the United States (Rosengren et al., 2004). Frequent or chronic stress as well as negative emotions such a fear, anger, and depression can damage the heart and blood vessels, increase blood pressure, trigger arrhythmias (erratic heartbeats that may lead to sudden death), and increase cholesterol levels (which causes a plaque buildup and, over time, "hardening" and eventually blockage of the arteries).

Scientists have long suspected that stress also affects the functioning of the immune system. Recall that the immune system is strongly affected by hormones and signals from the

---

Health psychology:

- General adaptation syndrome (GAS): Stages in _____ proposed by Hans Selye
  - Alarm reaction: _____
  - Resistance: _____
  - Exhaustion: _____
- Psychological stress can cause physical illness in at least two ways:

  _____

  _____

> **ENDURING ISSUES MIND/BODY**
>
> ### Psychological Stress and Physical Illness
>
> How exactly does psychological stress lead to or influence physical illness? First, when we experience stress, our heart, lungs, nervous system, and other physiological systems are forced to work harder. The human body is not designed to be exposed for long periods to the powerful biological changes that accompany alarm and mobilization; so, when stress is prolonged, we are more likely to experience some kind of physical disorder. Second, stress has a powerful negative effect on the body's immune system, and prolonged stress can destroy the body's ability to defend itself from disease. Indirectly, stress may also lead to unhealthy behaviors such as smoking, drinking, overeating, or skipping meals, not getting enough exercise, and avoiding regular medical checkups, which can, in turn, lead to illness and poor overall health.

brain. Researchers in the field of **psychoneuroimmunology (PNI)** study the interaction between stress on the one hand and immune, endocrine, and nervous system activity on the other. To the extent that stress disrupts the functioning of the immune system, it can impair health (S. Cohen & Herbert, 1996). Chronic stress—from caring for an elderly parent, living in poverty, depression (Kiecolt-Glaser & Glaser, R. 2002), or even living with a spouse with cancer (Mortimer et al., 2005)—has been linked to suppressed functioning of the immune system (Irwin, 2002).

Increased stress may make people more susceptible to influenza (Tseng, Padgett, Dhabhar, Engler, & Sheridan, 2005) and upper respiratory infections, such as the common cold (S. Cohen, 1996; S. Cohen et al., 2002). For example, volunteers who reported being under severe stress and who had experienced two or more major stressful events during the previous year were more likely to develop a cold when they were exposed to a cold virus (Cohen, Tyrrell, & Smith, 1991). A control group of volunteers who reported lower levels of stress was less likely to develop cold symptoms even though the individuals were exposed equally to the virus. There is also some evidence of a relationship between stress and cancer (Herberman, 2002), but there is considerable controversy over whether such a relationship exists in humans (Reiche, Morimoto, & Nunes, 2005).

Check Your Understanding

1. Which of the following describes the sequence of stages in the "general adaptation syndrome"?

   a. Resistance, alarm, exhaustion

   b. Excitement, resistance, death

   c. Alarm, resistance, exhaustion

   d. Arousal, resistance, exhaustion

   e. None of the above are correct.

2. Coronary heart disease is largely hereditary. However, the incidence of coronary heart disease varies among genetically identical twins depending on their attitudes toward work, existence of problems at home, and use of leisure time. This finding illustrates that

   a. Psychological factors may be important determinants of physical illness.

   b. Genetically identical twins are constitutionally weaker than fraternal twins.

   c. Coronary heart disease occurs regardless of psychological well-being.

   d. Sensitivity to stress is genetically programmed.

Staying Healthy

Stress may be part of life, but there are proven ways to reduce the negative impact of stress on your body and your health. *Exercise* is a good beginning. Running, walking, biking, swimming, or other aerobic exercise lowers your resting heart rate and blood pressure, so that your body not only does not react as strongly to stress but also recovers from it more quickly. *Relaxation training* is another stress buster. Numerous studies indicate that relaxation techniques lower stress and improve immune functioning. Relaxation involves more than flopping on the couch with the TV zapper, however. Healthful physical relaxation requires lying quietly and alternately tensing and relaxing every voluntary muscle in your body—from your head to your toes—to learn how to recognize muscle tension, as well as to learn how to relax your body. Breathing exercises can have the same effect: If you are tense, then deep, rhythmic breathing may be difficult, but learning to do so relieves bodily tension (see Chapter 4: States of Consciousness for a discussion of meditation and Chapter 5: Learning for a discussion of biofeedback, both of which can be useful in relaxing and reducing stress).

A strong network of friends and family who provide *social support* can help to reduce stress and contribute to good health. Exactly why the presence of a strong social support system is related to health is not fully understood. Whatever the underlying mechanism, most people can remember times when other people made a difference in their lives by giving them good advice, helping them to feel better about themselves, providing assistance with chores and responsibilities or financial help, or simply by "hanging out" with them.

Health psychologists are also investigating the role *religion* may play in reducing stress and bolstering health. For example, research has found that elderly people who pray or attend religious services regularly enjoy better health and markedly lower rates of depression than those who do not (Koenig, McCullough, & Larson, 2000). Other studies have shown that having a religious commitment may also help to moderate high blood pressure and hypertension (Levin & Vanderpool, 1989; Wilkins, 2005).

Altruism—reaching out and giving to others because doing so brings one pleasure—is another effective way to reduce stress. Caring for others tends to take our minds off our own problems, to make us realize that others may be worse off than we are, and to foster the feeling that we are involved in something larger than our own small slice of life. Altruism may also channel loss, grief, or anger into constructive action. An example is Mothers Against Drunk Driving (MADD), an organization founded by a mother whose child was killed by a drunk driver.

■ Ways to reduce the negative impact of stress on health:

_____

_____

_____

_____

_____

_____

_____

_____

_____

Doing yoga exercises regularly is a direct way of coping with stress that can enhance feelings of well-being while improving balance and flexibility.

How you appraise events in your environment—and how you appraise your ability to cope with potentially unsettling, unpredictable events—also affects stress and its impact on health. *Proactive coping* is the psychological term for anticipating stressful events and taking advance steps to avoid them or to minimize their impact. Proactive coping does not mean "expect the worst"; constant vigilance actually increases stress and may damage health. Rather, proactive coping means (as in the Boy Scout motto), "Be prepared." This may include accumulating resources (time, money, social support, and information), recognizing potential stress in advance, and making realistic plans.

In many cases, you cannot change or escape stressful circumstances, but you can change the way you think about things. *Positive reappraisal* helps people to make the best of a tense or painful situation. A low grade can be seen as a warning sign, not a catastrophe. A job you hate provides information on what you really want in your career. Rather than brood about a nasty remark from your sister, ask what does this tell you about *her*? Positive reappraisal does not require you to become a "Pollyanna" (the heroine of a novel who was optimistic to the point of being ridiculous). Rather, it requires finding new meaning in a situation or finding a perspective or insight that you had overlooked.

One of the most effective, stress-relieving forms of reappraisal is *humor*. As Shakespeare so aptly put it in *The Winter's Tale*: "A merry heart goes all the day/Your sad tires in a mile" (Act IV, Scene 3). Journalist Norman Cousins (1981) attributed his recovery from a life-threatening disease to regular "doses" of laughter. Watching classic comic films, he believed, reduced both his pain and the inflammation in his tissues. He wrote:

> What was significant about the laughter . . . was not just the fact that it provides internal exercise for a person flat on his or her back—a form of jogging for the innards—but that it creates a mood in which the other positive emotions can be put to work, too. In short, it helps make it possible for good things to happen. (Cousins, pp. 145–146)

Learning how to avoid and cope with stress is important, but the *positive psychology* movement (introduced in Chapter 1) has prompted many health psychologists to explore other ways to promote good health by adopting a healthier lifestyle. The importance of regular aerobic exercise (such as jogging, brisk walking, or swimming) for maintaining a healthy body is well established. In addition, health psychologists have shown that regular aerobic exercise can also help people cope better with stress and help them to feel less depressed, more vigorous, and more energetic. Avoiding cigarettes is another component of a healthy lifestyle. Fewer Americans smoke today than in the past, and more than half of those who did smoke have quit. However, cigarette smoking still poses a serious health threat to the millions of people who continue to smoke (Mody & Smith, 2006).

Check Your Understanding

1. Indicate whether each of the following three statements is true (T) or false (F).

   a. _____ Research has been unable to find a relationship between stress and the strength of the body's immune system.

   b. _____ Increased stress may make individuals more susceptible to the common cold.

   c. _____ People who attend religious services regularly enjoy better health than those who do not attend regularly.

2. You are going through a particularly stressful event. According to Selye's *general adaptation syndrome*, your first response to the stress is likely to be

   a. Increased activity in the sympathetic nervous system and heightened sensitivity and alertness

   b. Reliance on defense mechanisms in an effort to bring the stress quickly under control

   c. Inability to concentrate, irritability, and procrastination

   d. Increased activity in the immune system to ward off potential diseases

Extreme Stress

Extreme stress marks a radical departure from everyday life, such that a person cannot continue life as before and, in some cases, the individual never fully recovers. What are some major causes of extreme stress? What effect do they have on people? How do people cope?

■ SOURCES OF EXTREME STRESS

Unemployment   Unemployment is a source of extreme stress. In fact, when the jobless rate rises, there is an increase in first admissions to psychiatric hospitals, infant mortality, deaths from heart disease, alcohol-related diseases, and suicide (Almgren, Guest, Immerwahr, & Spittel, 2002; Brenner, 1973, 1979; Rayman & Bluestone, 1982; White & Waghorn, 2004). Many unemployed workers report high blood pressure, alcoholism, heavy smoking, and anxiety. Family strain often increases as well. "Things just fell apart," one worker said after he and his wife found themselves suddenly unemployed. Not surprisingly, being unemployed also decreases an individual's sense of well-being and happiness (Creed & Klisch, 2005).

Divorce and Separation   The deterioration or ending of an intimate relationship is another potent stressor. After a breakup, both partners often feel they have failed at one of life's most important endeavors, but strong emotional ties often continue to bind the pair. If only one spouse wants to end the marriage, the initiator may feel sadness and guilt at hurting the other partner; the rejected spouse may feel anger, humiliation, and guilt over his or her role in the failure. Even if the separation was a mutual decision, ambivalent feelings of love and hate can make life turbulent, often for many years. Of course, adults are not the only ones who are stressed by divorce. As seen in Chapter 9, divorce can have serious and far-reaching effects on children as well.

Bereavement   For decades, it was widely held that following the death of a loved one, people go through a necessary period of intense grief during which they work through their loss and, about a year later, pick up and go on with their lives. Psychologists and physicians, as well as the public at large, have endorsed this cultural wisdom. But research indicates that this view of loss may be a myth (Wortman & Silver, 1989). Not everyone is intensely distressed when a loved one dies. Often, people have prepared for the loss, said their goodbyes, and feel little remorse or regret when death eventually occurs. Indeed, they may be relieved that their loved one is no longer suffering. Thus, not everyone will feel or act distraught upon the death of a loved one and not everyone needs to work through their grief. Another myth is that people who find meaning in the death, who come to a spiritual or existential understanding of why it happened, cope better than those who do not. In reality, people who do not seek greater understanding are the best adjusted and least depressed. Finally, the notion that people should recover from a loss within a year or so is perhaps the most damaging. Parents trying to cope with the death of an infant and adults whose spouse or child died suddenly in a vehicle accident often continue to experience painful memories and wrestle with depression years later. But because they have not recovered "on schedule," members of their social network may become unsympathetic. Unfortunately, the people who need support most may hide their feelings because they do not want to make other people uncomfortable. Often, they fail to seek treatment because they, too, believe they should recover on their own.

Catastrophes   Catastrophes, natural and otherwise—including floods, earthquakes, violent storms, fires, and plane crashes—produce certain psychological reactions common to all stressful events. At first, in the *shock stage*, "the victim is stunned, dazed, and apathetic" and sometimes even "stuporous, disoriented, and amnesic for the traumatic event." Then, in the *suggestible stage*, victims are passive and quite ready to do whatever rescuers tell them to do. In the third phase, the *recovery stage*, emotional balance is

The death of a loved one is a source of extreme stress for many people. Recently, psychologists have questioned traditional notions about the grieving process.

Sources of Extreme Stress

- _____
- _____
- _____
- _____

Posttraumatic Stress Disorder

- Psychological disorder resulting from _____ such as _____, _____, and _____
- Characterized by _____, _____, and _____
- _____ predispose some people to PTSD more than others
- Some people experience positive _____ as a result of significant trauma.

regained but anxiety often persists, and victims may need to recount their experiences repeatedly. In later stages, survivors may feel irrationally guilty because they lived while others died (Straton, 2004).

■ POSTTRAUMATIC STRESS DISORDER

Wartime experiences often cause soldiers intense and disabling combat stress that persists long after they have left the battlefield. Similar reactions—including bursting into rage over harmless remarks, sleep disturbances, cringing at sudden loud noises, psychological confusion, uncontrollable crying, and silently staring into space for long periods—are also frequently seen in survivors of serious accidents, especially children, and of violent crimes such as rapes and muggings (Fairbrother & Rachman, 2006).

Severely stressful events can cause a psychological disorder known as **posttraumatic stress disorder (PTSD)**. Dramatic nightmares in which the victim re-experiences the terrifying event exactly as it happened are common—as are daytime flashbacks, in which the victim relives the trauma. Often, victims of PTSD withdraw from social life and from job and family responsibilities. PTSD can set in immediately after a traumatic event or within a short time afterward. But sometimes, months or years may go by in which the victim seems to have recovered from the experience, and, without warning, psychological symptoms reappear, then may disappear only to recur repeatedly.

The experiences of soldiers have heightened interest in PTSD. For example, more than one third of the soldiers who served in Vietnam experienced PTSD at some point afterward (Ozer, Best, Lipsey, & Weiss, 2003). Many veterans of World War II, who are now elderly, still have nightmares from which they awake sweating and shaking. The memories of combat continue to torment them after more than half a century (Port, Engdahl, & Frazier, 2001). Recently, therapists have begun to observe a new phenomenon: Veterans who seemed to be healthy and well adjusted throughout their postwar lives suddenly develop symptoms of PTSD when they retire and enter their "golden years" (Sleek, 1998; van Achterberg, Rohrbaugh, & Southwick, 2001).

Soldiers are not the only victims of war. Indeed, during the twentieth century, civilian deaths outnumbered military deaths in most wars. For many, the immediate response following a traumatic event is one of shock. After the initial shock passes, individual reactions to trauma vary considerably, but they commonly include: heightened emotionality, irritability, nervousness, difficulty with concentration, changes in sleep patterns, and physical symptoms (such as nausea, headaches, chest pain, and even depression). Some civilians also experience long-lasting and severe problems, such as exhaustion, hatred, mistrust, and the symptoms of PTSD. Figure 11–2 shows the devastating effects of war on civilians based on composite statistics obtained after recent civil wars.

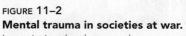
FIGURE 11–2
Mental trauma in societies at war.
In societies that have undergone the stress of war, nearly everyone suffers some psychological reaction, ranging from serious mental illness to feelings of demoralization. Rates of clinical depression are as high as 50%.

Source: "Invisible wounds," June 2000, by R. F. Mollica. *Scientific American*, p. 54. Figure by Laurie Grace.

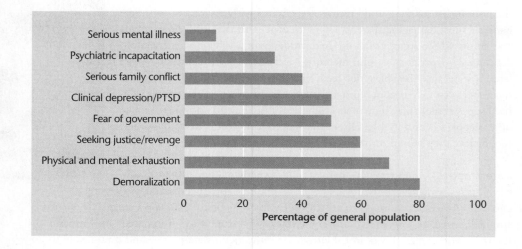

Reactions to Severe Stress

Not everyone who is exposed to severely stressful events (such as heavy combat or childhood sexual abuse) develops PTSD. Although more than half of the American population is exposed to a severely traumatic event at some time, less than 10% will develop symptoms of PTSD (Ozer et al., 2003). Individual characteristics—including gender, personality, a family history of mental disorders, prior exposure to trauma, substance abuse among relatives, and even preexisting neurological disorders—appear to predispose some people to PTSD more than others. Both men and women who have a history of emotional problems are more likely to experience severe trauma and to develop PTSD as a consequence of trauma. Not surprisingly, people who may already be under extreme stress (perhaps caused by a health problem or interpersonal difficulties) prior to experiencing a traumatic event are at greatest risk.

Some psychologists have found that following a significant trauma, a few particularly stable individuals experience a *positive* form of personal growth called *posttraumatic growth* (Calhoun & Tedeschi, 2001). In rare instances in which posttraumatic growth occurs, it appears to emerge largely from an individual's struggle to reconcile his or her loss through religious or existential understanding. When it does occur, posttraumatic growth is more likely to be seen in young adults than in older people (Powell, Rosner, Butollo, Tedeschi, & Calhoun, 2003).

Recovery from posttraumatic stress disorder is strongly related to the amount of emotional support survivors receive from family, friends, and community. Treatment consists of helping those who have experienced severe trauma to come to terms with their terrifying memories. Immediate treatment near the site of the trauma coupled with the expectation that the individual will return to everyday life is often effective. Reliving the traumatic event in a safe setting is also crucial to successful treatment. This helps desensitize people to the traumatic memories haunting them.

Check Your Understanding

1. Indicate whether each of the following statements is true (T) or false (F).

    a. _____ If people who are bereaved following the death of a spouse or child have not recovered after a year or so, this outcome indicates that they are coping abnormally.

    b. _____ Catastrophes (such as floods, earthquakes, violent storms, fires, and plane crashes) produce different psychological reactions than do other kinds of stressful events.

    c. _____ Most children whose parents divorce experience serious and long-term problems.

    d. _____ Posttraumatic stress disorder can appear months or even years after a traumatic event.

2. Your friend Patrick has just survived a traumatic event. Which of the following would you *least* expect to observe?

    a. Difficulty sleeping, frequent nightmares

    b. Physical symptoms, such as nausea and headaches

    c. Irritability, rapid mood changes, and nervousness

    d. A healthy appetite and increased interest in food and eating

- There is no consensus among psychologists regarding what constitutes _____.

- Some alternative ways of viewing good adjustment include:

  - _____
  _____
  - _____
  _____

- Specific criteria
  Does the action realistically meet _____?
  Does the action meet _____?
  Is the action compatible with _____?

The Well-Adjusted Person

Adjustment is any effort to cope with stress, but determining what constitutes *good* adjustment is difficult. Some psychologists believe it is the ability to live according to social norms. Others argue that, because society is not always right if people accept social standards blindly, they renounce the right to make individual judgments. Yet another view is that well-adjusted people enjoy the difficulties and ambiguities of life; these people treat difficulties as challenges to be overcome and opportunities for psychological growth. Specific criteria can be used when evaluating adjustment and judging an action, including:

1. Does the action realistically meet the demands of the situation or does it simply postpone resolving the problem?
2. Does the action meet the individual's needs?
3. Is the action compatible with the well-being of others?

As we have seen, there are many standards for judging whether an individual is well adjusted. A person deemed well adjusted by one standard might not be considered well adjusted by other standards. The same principle holds true when we try to specify what behaviors are "abnormal"—which is the topic of the next chapter.

Check Your Understanding

1. Your roommate is attempting to deal with a particularly stressful set of events in her life. You wonder whether she is coping well or whether there is cause for concern. Which of the following criteria would be *least* useful in making that judgment?

   a. Whether her behavior is realistically meeting the demands of the situation

   b. Whether she is doing what society says people should do in such a situation

   c. Whether her behavior is interfering with the well-being of others around her

   d. Whether her actions are effectively meeting her needs

Chapter Review

 www.psychologythecore.com

Sources of Stress

We experience **stress** when we are faced with a tense or threatening situation (**stressor**) that requires us to change or adapt our behavior. Life-and-death situations, such as war and natural disasters, are inherently stressful. Even events that usually are viewed as positive, such as a wedding or a job promotion, can be stressful because they require change, adaptation, and **adjustment**. How we adjust to the stress affects our health, since prolonged or severe stress can contribute to physical and psychological disorders. **Health psychologists** try to find ways to prevent stress from becoming debilitating and to promote healthy behaviors.

Because most people strongly desire order in their lives, any event involving change will be experienced as stressful. Stress can also arise from everyday "hassles" such as **pressure**, **frustration**, and **conflict** (including **approach/approach conflict**, **avoidance/avoidance conflict**, and **approach/avoidance conflict**). Sometimes, however, people create problems for themselves quite apart from stressful events in their environment.

Coping With Stress

People generally adjust to stress in one of two ways: *Direct coping* describes any action people take to change an uncomfortable situation, whereas *defensive coping* denotes the various ways people convince themselves—through a form of self-deception—that they are not really threatened or do not really want something they cannot get.

There are several ways of coping directly with stress. **Confrontation** involves admitting to ourselves that there is a problem that needs to be solved and attacking the problem head-on. In the process, we may learn new skills, enlist other people's aid, or try harder to reach our goal. **Compromise** usually requires adjusting expectations or desires; the conflict is resolved by settling for less than what originally was sought. **Withdrawal** involves distancing oneself from the source of stress. The danger of withdrawal is that it may become a maladaptive habit.

When a stressful situation arises and there is little that can be done to deal with it directly, people often turn to **defense mechanisms** as a way of coping. Defense mechanisms are ways of deceiving ourselves about the causes of stressful events, thus reducing conflict, frustration, pressure, and anxiety. **Denial** is the refusal to acknowledge a painful or threatening reality. **Repression** is the blocking out of unacceptable thoughts or impulses from consciousness. When we cannot deny or repress a particular problem, we might resort to **projection**—attributing our repressed motives or feelings to others, thereby locating the source of our conflict outside ourselves. **Identification** may occur when people feel completely powerless. People who adopt this technique take on others' characteristics to gain a sense of control or adequacy. People under severe stress sometimes revert to childlike behavior, called **regression**. Because adults cannot stand feeling helpless, becoming more childlike can make total dependency or helplessness more tolerable. A subtle form of denial is seen in **intellectualization**, when people emotionally distance themselves from a particularly disturbing situation. **Reaction formation** refers to a behavioral form of denial in which people express with exaggerated intensity ideas and emotions that are the opposite of their own. Through **displacement**, repressed motives and feelings are redirected from their original objects to substitute objects. **Sublimation** involves transforming repressed emotions into more socially accepted forms. Defensive coping can help us adjust to difficult circumstances, but it can also lead to maladaptive behavior whenever it interferes with our ability to deal constructively with a difficult situation.

People handle stress differently, in part because of the environment in which they live. People in low-income groups living in poor neighborhoods often experience more stress and have fewer personal and community resources to draw on for support as well as fewer coping strategies. Men and women also differ in their exposure to stress and often have different ways of coping with stress.

How Stress Affects Health

Physiologist Hans Selye contended that people react to physical and psychological stress in three stages. In Stage 1 (*alarm reaction*) of the **general adaptation syndrome (GAS)**, the body recognizes that it must fight off some physical or psychological danger, resulting in quickened respiration and heart rate, increased sensitivity and alertness, and a highly charged emotional state—a physical adaptation that augments our coping resources and helps us to regain self-control. If direct or defensive coping mechanisms fail to reduce the stress, we progress to Stage 2 (*resistance stage*), during which physical symptoms of strain appear as we intensify our efforts to cope both directly and defensively. If these attempts to regain psychological equilibrium fail, psychological disorganization rages out of control until we reach Stage 3 (*exhaustion*). During this phase, we use increasingly ineffective defense mechanisms to bring the stress under control. At this point, some people lose touch with reality, whereas others show signs of "burnout," such as shorter attention spans, irritability, procrastination, and general apathy.

The body's biological responses to stress are known to be important factors in the development of coronary heart disease (CHD). Stress can also suppress the functioning of the immune system, the focus of the relatively new field of **psychoneuroimmunology (PNI)**, leaving people more susceptible to a wide range of illnesses.

Staying Healthy

We can reduce the negative impact of stress on our health by trying to reduce stress and by maintaining a healthy lifestyle, which equips the body to cope with stress that is unavoidable.

Exercising regularly and relaxation training reduce the body's responses to stress. Having a strong network of social support is also related to healthier adjustment. Regular participation in religious services also appears to moderate stress as does altruistic behavior. Finally, people can take steps to minimize the impact of stressful events by anticipating stressful events and preparing for them (proactive coping), by making the best of difficult situations (positive reappraisal), and by maintaining a sense of humor.

Apart from studying ways to avoid and cope with stress, many health psychologists are concerned with promoting good health through healthier lifestyles. Eating a well-balanced diet, getting regular exercise, not smoking, and avoiding high-risk behaviors are all important contributors to a healthy life.

Extreme Stress

Extreme stress derives from a number of sources, including unemployment, divorce and separation, bereavement, combat, and natural catastrophes.

Posttraumatic stress disorder is a response to intense and disabling stressors such as war, serious accidents, and violent crimes. The symptoms, which affect less than 10% of those who are exposed to a severely traumatic event, include daytime flashbacks, social and occupational withdrawal, sleeplessness, and nightmares. These symptoms may persist for years. Personal characteristics make some people more likely than others to experience PTSD. A few particularly stable individuals may actually experience a *positive* form of personal growth following severe trauma.

The Well-Adjusted Person

Psychologists disagree on what constitutes good adjustment. Some believe that well-adjusted people live according to social norms. Others disagree, arguing that well-adjusted people enjoy overcoming challenging situations and that this ability leads to growth and self-fulfillment. Finally, some psychologists use specific criteria to evaluate a person's ability to adjust, such as how well the adjustment solves the problem and satisfies both personal needs and the needs of others.

Chapter 12
Psychological Disorders

Go to *The Core Online* at **www.psychologythecore.com** to get the most up-to-date information for your introductory psychology course. The content online is an important part of what you are learning—the content there can help prepare you for your test! It includes up-to-date examples, simulations, video clips, and practice quizzes. Also be sure to check out the *Blog* to hear directly from the authors on what current events and latest research are most relevant to your course materials.

The first time you log in, you will need the access code packaged with your textbook. If you do not have a code, please go to **www.mypearsonstore.com** and enter the ISBN of your textbook (0-13-603344-X) to purchase the code.

Chapter 12 Psychological Disorders

12 1 Perspectives on Psychological Disorders

Perspectives on Abnormal Behavior
- Society: Failure to fulfill expectations and meet prevailing standards
- Individual: Feelings of low self-esteem, rejection, unhappiness
- Mental health professional: Presence of diagnostic symptoms, maladaptive behavior, psychological discomfort, inability to function well in life

The Prevalence of Psychological Disorders
- Prevalence varies from 4% in Asia to 12% in the Americas and 15% in the United States.

Historical Views of Psychological Disorders
- Mentally ill were often believed to be witches or possessed by the devil.

Contemporary Views of Psychological Disorders
- **Biological model:** Result of physiological disorders
- **Psychoanalytic model:** Symbolic expression of unconscious conflicts
- **Cognitive-behavioral model:** Learned maladaptive ways of thinking and acting
- **Diathesis-stress model:** Biological predisposition (diathesis) triggered by stressful circumstances
- **Systems (biopsychosocial) approach:** "Lifestyle diseases" arising from biological risk factors, psychological stress, and societal pressures

Classifying Psychological Disorders
- Most widely used system for classifying psychological disorders is the fourth edition of the *Diagnostic and Statistical Manual of Mental Disorders (DSM-IV-TR)*.

12 2 Mood Disorders

Mood disorders: Disturbances in mood or prolonged emotional state
- **Depression:** Characterized by overwhelming feelings of sadness, lack of interest in activities, excessive guilt, feelings of worthlessness
- **Mania:** Characterized by euphoria, extreme physical activity, excessive talkativeness, distractedness, grandiosity
- **Bipolar disorder:** Alternating periods of mania and depression

12 3 Anxiety Disorders

Anxiety disorders: Characterized by inappropriate fear and anxiety
- **Specific phobia:** Intense, paralyzing, unreasonable fear of something
- **Social phobia:** Excessive, inappropriate fear connected with social situations
- **Agoraphobia:** Intense fear of being alone or of being in public places
- **Panic disorder:** Characterized by recurring sudden, unpredictable, and overwhelming experiences of intense fear or terror without any reasonable cause
- **Generalized anxiety disorder:** Characterized by prolonged vague, but intense fears
- **Obsessive-compulsive disorder:** Characterized by involuntary thoughts that recur or compulsive rituals

12 4 Psychosomatic and Somatoform Disorders

Psychosomatic disorders: Illnesses that have a valid physical basis, but are largely caused by psychological factors; all illnesses are, to some extent, psychosomatic

Somatoform disorders: Symptoms of illness without an identifiable physical cause
- **Conversion disorder:** Dramatic specific disability without organic cause
- **Hypochondriasis:** Insistence that minor symptoms mean serious illness

12 5 Dissociative Disorders

Dissociative disorders: Some part of a person's personality or memory is separated from the rest.
- **Dissociative amnesia:** Unusual loss of memory without an organic cause
- **Dissociative fugue:** Flight from home and the assumption of a new personality
- **Dissociative identity disorder:** Separation of the personality into two or more distinct personalities
- **Depersonalization disorder:** Sudden feelings of strange changes or differences
- Childhood abuse and/or biological factors are believed to be causes.

12 6 Sexual and Gender-Identity Disorders

- **Sexual dysfunction**: Loss or impairment of the ability to function effectively during sex
  —Erectile disorder (ED)
  —Female sexual arousal disorder
  —Sexual desire disorders
  —Orgasmic disorders
  —Premature ejaculation
  —Vaginismus

- **Paraphilias**: Use of unconventional sex objects or situations
  —Fetishism   —Transvestic fetishism
  —Voyeurism   —Sexual sadism
  —Exhibitionism   —Sexual masochism
  —Frotteurism   —Pedophilia

- **Gender-identity disorders**: Desire to become, or the insistence that one really is, a member of the other sex

12 7 Personality Disorders

Personality disorders: Inflexible and maladaptive ways of thinking and behaving

- **Schizoid personality disorder**: Withdrawal and lacking feeling for others
- **Paranoid personality disorder**: Inappropriate suspicion and mistrust of others
- **Dependent personality disorder**: Inability to make decisions independently; cannot tolerate being alone
- **Avoidant personality disorder**: Social isolation resulting from fear of rejection
- **Narcissistic personality disorder**: Exaggerated sense of self-importance; desire for constant admiration
- **Borderline personality disorder**: Instability in self-image, mood, and interpersonal relationships
- **Antisocial personality disorder**: Violent, criminal, or unethical behavior; inability to feel affection for others

12 9 Childhood Disorders

- **Attention-deficit hyperactivity disorder (ADHD)**: Characterized by inattention, impulsiveness, and hyperactivity
- **Psychostimulant**: Drugs that increase ability to focus attention in people with ADHD
- **Autistic disorder**: Characterized by lack of social instincts and strange motor behavior
- **Autistic spectrum disorder (ASD)**: A range of disorders involving varying degrees of impairment in communication skills and social interactions, with restricted, repetitive, and stereotyped patterns of behavior

12 8 Schizophrenic Disorders

Schizophrenic disorders: Marked by dramatic disruptions in thought and communication, inappropriate emotions, and bizarre behavior that lasts for years

Psychotic (psychosis): Characterized by a loss of touch with reality

Insanity: Legal term to describe mentally disturbed people who are not considered responsible for their criminal actions

Hallucinations: False sensory experiences

Delusions: False beliefs about reality

- Biological and environmental factors alike contribute to:
  —**Disorganized schizophrenia**: Bizarre, childlike behaviors
  —**Catatonic schizophrenia**: Disturbed motor behavior
  —**Paranoid schizophrenia**: Extreme suspiciousness, bizarre delusions
  —**Undifferentiated schizophrenia**: Clear symptoms that do not match other categories

12 10 Gender and Cultural Differences in Psychological Disorders

Gender Differences
- Nearly all psychological disorders affect men and women alike.
- Men are more likely to suffer from substance abuse and antisocial personality disorder.
- Women show higher rates of depression, agoraphobia, simple phobia, and obsessive-compulsive disorder.

Cultural Differences
- Gender and cultural differences are less likely to be seen in disorders that have a strong biological component.

Jack was a very successful chemical engineer known for the meticulous accuracy of his work. But Jack also had a "little quirk." He constantly felt compelled to double-, triple-, and even quadruple-check things to assure himself that they were done properly. For example, when leaving his apartment in the morning, he occasionally got as far as the garage—but invariably he would go back to make certain that the door was locked securely and the stove, lights, and other appliances were turned off. Going on a vacation was particularly difficult for him because his checking routine was so exhaustive and time consuming. Yet, Jack insisted that he would never want to give up this chronic checking. Doing so, he said, would make him "much too nervous."

Jonathan was a 22-year-old auto mechanic whom everyone described as a loner. He seldom engaged in conversation and seemed lost in his own private world. At work, the other mechanics took to whistling sharply whenever they wanted to get his attention. Jonathan also had a "strange look" on his face that could make customers feel uncomfortable. But his oddest behavior was his assertion that sometimes he had the distinct feeling his dead mother was standing next to him, watching what he did. Although Jonathan realized that his mother was not really there, he nevertheless felt reassured by the illusion of her presence. He took great care not to look or reach toward the spot where he felt his mother was, because doing so inevitably made the feeling go away.

Cases adapted from *Abnormal Psychology in a Changing World* (5th ed.) by J. S. Nevis, S. A. Rathus, & B. Green (2005). Upper Saddle River, NJ: Prentice Hall.

ENDURING ISSUES   in Psychological Disorders

As we explore psychological disorders in this chapter, we will again encounter some of the "Enduring Issues" that interest psychologists. A recurring topic is the relationship between genetics, neurotransmitters, and behavior disorders (mind–body). We will also see that many psychological disorders arise because a vulnerable person encounters a particularly stressful environment (person–situation). As you read the chapter, think about how you would answer the question "What is normal?" and how the answer to that question has changed over time and differs even today across cultures (diversity–universality). Consider also whether a young person with a psychological disorder is likely to suffer from it later in life and, conversely, whether a well-adjusted young person is immune to psychological disorders later in life (stability–change).

Perspectives on Psychological Disorders

■ PERSPECTIVES ON ABNORMAL BEHAVIOR

When is a person's behavior abnormal? This is not always easy to determine. There is no doubt about the abnormality of a man who dresses in flowing robes and accosts pedestrians on the street claiming to be Jesus Christ or a woman who dons an aluminum-foil helmet to prevent space aliens from "stealing" her thoughts. But not all instances of abnormal behavior are so clear. Let's consider the two people just described. Both of them exhibit unusual behavior, but does their behavior deserve to be labeled "abnormal"? Do these people have a genuine psychological disorder?

The answer depends in part on the perspective you take. As Table 12–1 summarizes, society, the individual, and the mental health professional adopt different perspectives when distinguishing abnormal behavior from normal behavior. The main standard of abnormality in society is whether the behavior fails to conform to prevailing ideas about what is socially expected of people. In contrast, when individuals assess the abnormality of their own behavior,

Perspectives on Abnormal Behavior

■ Society: Failure to _____

and _____

■ Individual: Feelings of _____,

_____, _____

■ Mental health professional: Presence

of diagnostic symptoms, _____

behavior, psychological _____,

inability to _____ in life

The Prevalence of Psychological Disorders

■ Prevalence varies from 4% in

_____ to 12% in _____

and 15% in _____.

Historical Views of Psychological Disorders

■ Mentally ill were often believed to

be _____ or _____.

TABLE 12–1   Perspectives on Psychological Disorders

	STANDARDS/VALUES	MEASURES
Society	Orderly world in which people assume responsibility for their assigned social roles (e.g., breadwinner, parent), conform to prevailing mores, and meet situational requirements	Observations of behavior, extent to which a person fulfills society's expectations and measures up to prevailing standards
Individual	Happiness, gratification of needs	Subjective perceptions of self-esteem, acceptance, and well-being
Mental Health Professional	Sound personality structure characterized by growth, development, autonomy, environmental mastery, ability to cope with stress, adaptation	Clinical judgment, aided by behavioral observations and psychological tests of such variables as self-concept; sense of identity; balance of psychic forces; unified outlook on life; resistance to stress; self-regulation; the ability to cope with reality; the absence of mental and behavioral symptoms; adequacy in interpersonal relationships

Source: H. H. Strupp and S. W. Hadley (1977). A tripartite model of mental health and therapeutic outcomes with special reference to negative effects on psychotherapy. *American Psychologist, 32,* 187–196. © 1977 by the American Psychological Association. Adapted by permission of the authors.

their main criterion is whether that behavior fosters a sense of unhappiness and lack of well-being. Mental health professionals take still another perspective. They assess abnormality chiefly by looking for maladaptive *personality traits, psychological discomfort* regarding a particular behavior, and evidence that the behavior is preventing the person from *functioning well in life.*

These three approaches to identifying abnormal behavior are not always in agreement. For example, Jack is not really bothered by his compulsive behavior (in fact, he sees it as a way of relieving anxiety); and Jonathan is not only content with being a loner, but he also experiences great comfort from the illusion of his dead mother's presence. Thus, from the *individual* perspective, neither of them would be likely to say he has a psychological disorder. From *society's* perspective, Jonathan's behavior would certainly qualify as abnormal; Jack's probably would not. *Mental health professionals* would diagnose both men as suffering from psychological disorders because the behaviors they exhibit impair their ability to function well in everyday settings or in social relationships. The point is that there is no hard and fast rule as to what constitutes abnormal behavior. Distinguishing between normal and abnormal behavior always depends on the perspective taken.

Identifying behavior as abnormal is also a matter of degree. To understand why, imagine that Jack is still prone to double-checking, but he does not check repeatedly. As for Jonathan, he only occasionally withdraws from social contact; and he has had the sense of his dead mother's presence just twice over the last three years. In these less severe situations, a mental health professional would not be so ready to diagnose a mental disorder. Clearly, great care must be taken when separating mental health and mental illness into two *qualitatively* different categories. It is often more accurate to think of mental illness as simply being *quantitatively* different from normal behavior—that is, different in degree. The line between one and the other is often somewhat arbitrary.

■ THE PREVALENCE OF PSYCHOLOGICAL DISORDERS

How common are psychological disorders in the United States? Are they increasing or decreasing over time? Are some population groups more prone to these disorders than others? These questions interest psychologists and public health experts who are concerned with both the prevalence and the incidence of mental health problems. *Prevalence* refers to the frequency with which a given disorder occurs at a given time. If there were 100 cases of depression in a population of 1,000, the prevalence of depression would be 10%. The *incidence* of a disorder

In the seventeenth century, French physicians tried various devices to cure their patients of "fantasy and folly."

refers to the number of new cases that arise in a given period. If there were 10 new cases of depression in a population of 1,000 in a single year, the incidence would be 1% per year.

The American Psychiatric Association funded an ambitious and wide-ranging study of the prevalence of psychological disorders, which involved interviewing more than 20,000 people around the country. The results were surprising: 15% of the population was found to be experiencing a clinically significant mental disorder, and 6% was experiencing a significant substance abuse disorder (Narrow, Rae, Robins, & Regier, 2001). The most common mental disorders were anxiety disorders, followed by phobias and mood disorders (all of which are described in detail later in this chapter). Schizophrenia, a severe mental disorder that often involves hospitalization, was found to afflict 1% of the population, or more than 2 million people. Substance abuse problems were found in 6% of the population, with abuse of alcohol being three times more prevalent than abuse of all other drugs combined.

More recently, diagnostic interviews with more than 60,000 people in 14 countries around the world showed that over a 1-year period, the prevalence of moderate or serious psychological disorders varied widely from 12% of the population in the Americas to 7% in Europe, 6% in the Middle East and Africa, and just 4% in Asia (World Health Organization [WHO] World Mental Health Survey Consortium, 2004).

■ HISTORICAL VIEWS OF PSYCHOLOGICAL DISORDERS

The place and times also contribute to how mental disorders are defined. As late as the eighteenth century, the emotionally disturbed person was believed to be a witch or one possessed by the devil. Gradually, there was a move away from viewing the mentally ill as witches and possessed by demons, and they were increasingly confined to public and private asylums. Even though these institutions were founded with good intentions, most were little more than prisons. In the worst cases, inmates were chained down and deprived of food, light, or air to "cure" them.

Little was done to ensure humane standards in mental institutions until 1793, when Philippe Pinel (1745–1826) became director of the Bicêtre Hospital in Paris. Under his direction, patients were released from their chains and allowed to move about the hospital grounds, rooms were made more comfortable and sanitary, and questionable and violent medical treatments were abandoned. Pinel's reforms were soon followed by similar efforts in England and, somewhat later, in the United States where Dorothea Dix (1802–1887), a schoolteacher from Boston, led a nationwide campaign for the humane treatment of people with mental illness. Under her influence, the few existing asylums in the United States gradually were turned into hospitals.

The basic reason for the failed—and sometimes abusive—treatment of mentally disturbed people throughout history has been the lack of understanding of the nature and causes of psychological disorders. Although our knowledge is still inadequate, important advances in understanding abnormal behavior have led to three influential but conflicting models of abnormal behavior: the biological model, the psychoanalytic model, and the cognitive-behavioral model.

■ CONTEMPORARY VIEWS OF PSYCHOLOGICAL DISORDERS

The Biological Model The **biological model** holds that psychological disorders are caused by physiological malfunctions of, for example, the nervous system or the endocrine glands—

Contemporary Views of Psychological Disorders

■ Biological model: Result of _____ disorders

■ Psychoanalytic model: Symbolic expression of _____

■ Cognitive-behavioral model: Learned maladaptive ways of _____

■ Diathesis-stress model: Biological predisposition (diathesis) triggered by _____

■ Systems (biopsychosocial) approach: "Lifestyle diseases" arising from _____ risk factors, _____ stress, and _____ pressures often stemming from hereditary factors. Evidence is growing in support of the biological model of mental illness. Moreover, advances in the new interdisciplinary field of *neuroscience* leaves little doubt that our understanding of the role of biological factors in mental illness will continue to expand.

The Psychoanalytic Model   According to the **psychoanalytic model**, behavior disorders are symbolic expressions of unconscious conflicts that usually can be traced to childhood. For example, a man who behaves violently toward women may be unconsciously expressing rage at his mother for being unaffectionate toward him during his childhood. The psychoanalytic model argues that in order to resolve their problems effectively, people must become aware that the source of their problems lies in their childhood and infancy.

The Cognitive-Behavioral Model   The **cognitive-behavioral model** suggests that psychological disorders, as with all behavior, result from learning. From this perspective, fear, anxiety, sexual deviations, and other maladaptive behaviors are learned—and they can be unlearned.

The cognitive-behavioral model stresses both internal and external learning processes in the development and treatment of psychological disorders. For example, a bright student who believes that he is academically inferior to his classmates and cannot perform well on a test may not put much effort into studying. Naturally, he performs poorly, and his poor test score both punishes his minimal efforts and confirms his belief that he is academically inferior. This student is caught up in a vicious cycle (Albano & Barlow, 1996). A cognitive-behavior therapist might try to modify both the young man's dysfunctional studying behavior and his inaccurate and maladaptive cognitive processes.

The cognitive-behavioral model has led to innovations in the treatment of psychological disorders, but the model has been criticized for its limited perspective, especially its emphasis on environmental causes and treatments.

The Diathesis-Stress Model and Systems Theory   The **diathesis-stress model** suggests that a biological predisposition called a **diathesis** must combine with a stressful circumstance before the predisposition to a mental disorder is manifested. According to this model, some people are biologically prone to developing a particular disorder under stress, whereas others are not.

The **systems approach**, also known as the *biopsychosocial model*, examines how biological risks, psychological stresses, and social pressures and expectations combine to produce psychological disorders. According to this model, emotional problems are "lifestyle diseases" that, much like heart disease and many other physical illnesses, result from a combination of risk factors and stresses. Because this model casts a broad net in search of the causes of psychological disorders, it is the model discussed in this chapter and the next.

■ CLASSIFYING PSYCHOLOGICAL DISORDERS

For nearly 40 years, the American Psychiatric Association (APA) has issued a manual describing and classifying the various kinds of psychological disorders. This publication, the *Diagnostic and Statistical Manual of Mental Disorders* (*DSM*), has been revised four times. The fourth edition, text revision *DSM-IV-TR* (American Psychiatric Association, 2000), was coordinated with the tenth edition of the World Health Organization's *International Classification of Diseases*.

The *DSM-IV-TR* provides a complete list of mental disorders, with each category painstakingly defined in terms of significant behavior patterns so that diagnoses based on it will be reliable (Table 12–2). Although the manual provides careful descriptions of symptoms of different disorders to improve consistent diagnosis, it is generally silent on cause and treatment. The DSM has gained increasing acceptance because its detailed criteria for diagnosing mental disorders have made diagnosis much more reliable. Today, it is the most widely used classification of psychological disorders. Some of the key categories are discussed in greater detail in the next section.

The cognitive-behavioral view of mental disorders suggests that people can learn—and unlearn—thinking patterns that affect their lives unfavorably. For example, an athlete who is convinced she will not win may not practice as hard as she should and end up "defeating herself."

Classifying Psychological Disorders

■ Most widely used system for classifying psychological disorders is

_____

_____

_____

TABLE 12–2 Diagnostic Categories of DSM-IV-TR

CATEGORY	EXAMPLE
Disorders Usually First Diagnosed in Infancy, Childhood, or Adolescence	Mental retardation, learning disorders, autistic disorder, attention-deficit/hyperactivity disorder
Delirium, Dementia, and Amnestic and Other Cognitive Disorders	Delirium, dementia of the Alzheimer's type, amnestic disorder
Mental Disorders Resulting From a General Medical Condition	Psychotic disorder resulting from epilepsy
Substance-Related Disorders	Alcohol dependence, cocaine dependence, nicotine dependence
Schizophrenia and Other Psychotic Disorders	Schizophrenia, schizoaffective disorder, delusional disorder
Mood Disorders	Major depressive disorder, dysthymic disorder, bipolar disorder
Anxiety Disorders	Panic disorder with agoraphobia, social phobia, obsessive-compulsive disorder, posttraumatic stress disorder, generalized anxiety disorder
Somatoform Disorders	Somatization disorder, conversion disorder, hypochondriasis
Factitious Disorders	Factitious disorder with predominantly physical signs and symptoms
Dissociative Disorders	Dissociative amnesia, dissociative fugue, dissociative identity disorder, depersonalization disorder
Sexual and Gender-Identity Disorders	Hypoactive sexual desire disorder, male erectile disorder, female orgasmic disorder, vaginismus
Eating Disorders	Anorexia nervosa, bulimia nervosa
Sleep Disorders	Primary insomnia, narcolepsy, sleep terror disorder
Impulse-Control Disorders	Kleptomania, pyromania, pathological gambling
Adjustment Disorders	Adjustment disorder with depressed mood, adjustment disorder with conduct disturbance
Personality Disorders	Antisocial personality disorder, borderline personality disorder, narcissistic personality disorder, dependent personality disorder

Check Your Understanding

1. Indicate whether the following statements are true (T) or false (F).

a. _____ The line separating normal from abnormal behavior is somewhat arbitrary.

b. _____ About two thirds of Americans are suffering from one or more serious mental disorders at any given time.

c. _____ The cognitive view of mental disorders suggests that they arise from unconscious conflicts, often rooted in childhood.

2. You are talking to a friend whose behavior has you concerned. She says, "Look, I'm happy. I feel good about myself, and I think things are going well." Which viewpoint on mental health is reflected in her statement?

a. Society's view

b. The individual's view

c. The mental health professional's view

d. Both (b) and (c) are true.

3. A friend asks you, "What causes people to have psychological disorders?" You respond, "Most often, it turns out that some people are biologically prone to developing a particular disorder. When they have some kind of stressful experience, the predisposition shows up in their behavior." What view of psychological disorders are you taking?

a. Psychoanalytic model

b. Cognitive model

c. Behavioral model

d. Diathesis-stress model

Mood Disorders

Most people have a wide emotional range; they can be happy or sad, animated or quiet, cheerful or discouraged, or overjoyed or miserable, depending on the circumstances. In some people with **mood disorders**, this range is greatly restricted. They seem stuck at one or the other end of the emotional spectrum—either consistently excited and euphoric or consistently sad—regardless of life circumstances. Others with mood disorders alternate between the extremes of euphoria and sadness.

DEPRESSION

The most common mood disorder is **depression**, a state in which a person feels overwhelmed with sadness. Depressed people lose interest in the things they normally enjoy. Intense feelings of worthlessness and guilt leave them unable to feel pleasure. They are tired and apathetic, sometimes to the point of being unable to make the simplest decisions. *Clinical depression* is different from the "normal" kind of depression that all people experience from time to time. Only when depression is long lasting and goes well beyond the typical reaction to stressful life events is it classified as a mood disorder (American Psychological Association, 2000). Many clinically depressed people feel as though they have failed utterly in life, and they tend to blame themselves for their problems. Seriously depressed people often have insomnia and a lack of interest in food and sex. They may have trouble thinking or concentrating—even to the extent of finding it difficult to read a newspaper. In fact, difficulty in concentrating and subtle changes in short-term memory are sometimes the first signs of the onset of depression. Depression is two to three times more prevalent in women than in men (Inaba et al., 2005).

One of the most severe hazards of depression, as well as some of the other disorders described in this chapter, is that people may become so miserable that they no longer wish to live. Abraham Lincoln wrote, in 1841:

> I am now the most miserable man living. If what I feel were equally distributed to the whole human family, there would not be one cheerful face on earth. Whether I shall ever be better I can not tell; I awfully forebode I shall not. To remain as I am is impossible; I must die or be better, it appears to me. (Shenk, 2005, p. 62)

People considering suicide are overwhelmed with hopelessness. They feel that things cannot get better, and they see no way out of their difficulties. Telling a suicidal person that things are not really so bad does no good; in fact, the person may only view this as further evidence that no one understands his or her suffering. But most suicidal people do want help, however much they may despair of obtaining it. If a friend or family member seems at all suicidal, getting professional help is urgent. A community mental health center is a good starting place, as are the national suicide hotlines.

MANIA AND BIPOLAR DISORDER

Another mood disorder, which is less common than depression, is **mania**, a state in which the person becomes euphoric or "high," extremely active, excessively talkative, and easily distracted. People suffering from mania may become grandiose—that is, their self-esteem is greatly inflated. They typically have unlimited hopes and schemes, but little interest in realistically carrying them out. People in a manic state sometimes become aggressive and hostile toward others as their self-confidence grows more and more exaggerated. At the extreme, people going through a manic episode may become wild, incomprehensible, or violent until they collapse from exhaustion.

The mood disorder in which both mania and depression are present is known as bipolar disorder. In people with **bipolar disorder**, periods of mania and depression alternate (each lasting from a few days to a few months), sometimes with periods of normal mood in between. Research suggests that bipolar disorder is much less common than depression and, unlike depression, occurs equally in men and women.

CAUSES OF MOOD DISORDERS

Researchers have identified many of the causes of mood disorders, but they do not know exactly how these elements combine to cause a mood disorder. Genetics play an important role in the development of depression, particularly in bipolar disorder. Mood disorders are also related to chemical imbalances in the brain, principally to high and low levels of certain neurotransmitters. It is possible that the chemical imbalances are a result of heredity. But it is equally

---

Mood disorders: Disturbances in _____ or prolonged _____

- Depression: Characterized by overwhelming feelings of _____, lack of _____, excessive _____, feelings of _____
- Mania: Characterized by _____, extreme _____, excessive _____, _____, _____
- Bipolar disorder: Alternating periods of _____

possible that they are caused by stressful life events: Just as biology affects psychological experience, psychological experience can alter a person's biological functioning. The answer is not yet fully known.

Several psychological factors are also believed to play a role in causing mood disorders. For example, Aaron Beck (1967, 1976, 1984) has proposed that during childhood and adolescence, some people undergo wrenching experiences such as the loss of a parent, severe difficulties in gaining parental or social approval, or humiliating criticism from teachers and other adults. One response to such experience is to develop a negative self-concept—a feeling of incompetence or unworthiness that has little to do with reality but that is maintained by a distorted and illogical interpretation of real events. When a new situation arises that resembles the situation under which the self-concept was learned, these same feelings of worthlessness and incompetence may be activated, resulting in depression. Considerable research supports Beck's view of depression. Moreover, as will be seen in Chapter 13, therapy based on Beck's theories has proven quite successful in treating depression.

Difficulties in interpersonal relationships are also linked to depression. Yet, not every person who experiences a troubled relationship becomes depressed. As the systems approach would predict, it appears that a genetic predisposition or cognitive distortion is necessary before a distressing close relationship or other significant life stressor will result in a mood disorder.

ENDURING ISSUES PERSON/SITUATION

The Chicken or the Egg?

It is sometimes difficult to tease apart the relative contribution of the person's biological or cognitive tendencies and the social situation. People with certain depression-prone genetic or cognitive tendencies may be more likely than others to encounter stressful life events by virtue of their personality and behavior. For example, studies show that depressed people tend to evoke anxiety and even hostility in others, partly because they require more emotional support than people feel comfortable giving. As a result, people tend to avoid those who are depressed, and this shunning can intensify the depression. In short, depression-prone and depressed people may become trapped in a vicious circle that is at least partly of their own making.

Check Your Understanding

1. Bob is "down in the dumps" most of the time. He is having a difficult time dealing with any criticism he receives at work or at home. On most days, he feels that he is a failure, despite the fact that he is successful in his job and his family is happy. Although he participates in various activities outside the home, he finds no joy in anything. He says he is constantly tired, but he has trouble sleeping. It is most likely that Bob is suffering from

   a. Clinical depression
   b. Generalized anxiety disorder
   c. Depersonalization disorder
   d. Somatoform disorder

2. Mary almost seems to be two different people. At times, she is a hyperactive, nonstop talker (sometimes talking so fast that nobody can understand her). At those times, her friends say she is "bouncing off the walls." But then, she changes and becomes terribly sad, loses interest in eating, spends much of her time in bed, and rarely says a word. It is most likely that Mary is suffering from

   a. Dissociative identity disorder
   b. Depression
   c. Bipolar disorder
   d. Schizophrenia

Anxiety Disorders

All of us are afraid from time to time, but we usually know why we are fearful. Our fear is caused by something appropriate and identifiable, and it passes with time. In the case of **anxiety disorders**, however, either the person does not know why he or she is afraid or the anxiety is inappropriate to the circumstances. In either case, the person's fear and anxiety just do not seem to make sense.

A **specific phobia** is an intense, paralyzing fear of something that perhaps should be feared, but the fear is excessive and unreasonable. In fact, the fear in a specific phobia is so great that it leads the person to avoid routine or adaptive activities and thus interferes with life functioning. Of course, many people have fears. It is appropriate, for example, to be a bit fearful as an airplane takes off or lands. But when people are so afraid of snakes that they cannot go to a zoo, walk through a field, or even look at pictures of snakes without trembling, they may be said to have a phobia.

Most people also feel some mild fear or uncertainty in social situations, but when these fears interfere significantly with life functioning, they are considered **social phobias**. Intense fear of public speaking is a common form of social phobia. In other cases, simply talking with people or eating in public causes such severe anxiety that the phobic person will go to great lengths to avoid these situations.

Agoraphobia is much more debilitating than social phobia. This term comes from Greek and Latin words that literally mean "fear of the marketplace," but the disorder typically involves multiple, intense fears such as the fear of being alone, of being in public places from which escape might be difficult, of being in crowds, of traveling in an automobile, or of going through tunnels or over bridges. Agoraphobia can greatly interfere with life functioning: Some sufferers are so fearful that they will venture only a few miles from home; others will not leave their home at all.

Another type of anxiety disorder is **panic disorder**, which is characterized by recurring episodes of a sudden, unpredictable, and overwhelming fear or terror. Panic attacks occur without any reasonable cause and are accompanied by feelings of impending doom, chest pain, dizziness or fainting, sweating, difficulty breathing, and fear of losing control or dying. Panic attacks usually last only a few minutes, but they can recur for no apparent reason. Panic attacks not only cause tremendous fear while they are happening, but also they leave a dread of having another panic attack that can persist for days or even weeks after the original episode. In some cases, this dread is so overwhelming that it can lead to the development of agoraphobia: To prevent a recurrence, people may avoid any circumstance that might cause anxiety, clinging to people or situations that help keep them calm.

In the various phobias and panic attacks, a specific source of anxiety exists, such as fear of heights, fear of social situations, or fear of being in crowds. In contrast, **generalized anxiety disorder** is defined by prolonged vague but intense fears that are not attached to any particular object or circumstance. Generalized anxiety disorder perhaps comes closest to the everyday meaning attached to the term *neurotic*. Its symptoms include the inability to relax, muscle tension, rapid heartbeat or pounding heart, apprehensiveness about the future, constant alertness to potential threats, and sleeping difficulties.

A very different form of anxiety disorder is **obsessive-compulsive disorder (OCD)**. *Obsessions* are involuntary thoughts or ideas that keep recurring despite the person's attempts to stop them, whereas *compulsions* are repetitive, ritualistic behaviors that a person feels compelled to perform. One common type of compulsion is checking: repeatedly performing some kind of behavior to make sure that something was or was not done. Recall Jack, the engineer described at the beginning of the chapter, who felt compelled to double- and triple-check whether his doors were locked or his lights were off. People who experience obsessions and compulsions often do not seem particularly anxious, so why is this disorder considered an anxiety disorder? The answer is that when such people try to stop their irrational behavior—or when someone else tries to stop them—they experience severe anxiety. In other words, the obsessive-compulsive behavior seems to have developed to keep anxiety under control.

Finally, two types of anxiety disorder are clearly caused by some specific highly stressful event. Some people who have lived through fires, floods, tornadoes, or disasters (such as an

---

Anxiety disorders: Characterized by inappropriate _____ and _____

- Specific phobia: Intense, paralyzing, _____ fear of something
- Social phobia: Excessive, inappropriate fear connected with

_____

- Agoraphobia: Intense fear of _____ or of being _____
- Panic disorder: Characterized by _____ sudden, unpredictable, and overwhelming experiences of intense fear or terror without any _____
- Generalized anxiety disorder: Characterized by prolonged _____, but _____ fears
- Obsessive-compulsive disorder: Characterized by _____ thoughts that recur or compulsive _____

airplane crash) experience repeated episodes of fear and terror after the event itself is over. If the anxious reaction occurs soon after the event, the diagnosis is *acute stress disorder*. If it takes place long after the event is over, particularly in cases of military combat or rape, the diagnosis is likely to be *posttraumatic stress disorder*, discussed in Chapter 11: Stress and Health Psychology.

What causes anxiety disorders? Some phobias are triggered by specific events: A young child who is bitten by a dog may develop a fear of all dogs. But in most cases, it appears that phobias are *prepared responses*; that is, through evolution the individual may have become biologically predisposed to associate certain stimuli with intense fears (see Chapter 5: Learning). For example, the vast majority of snakes and spiders are harmless but they are frequently the source of phobias. On the other hand, people are much more likely to be injured in an automobile accident than by a snake or spider bite; yet, car phobias are quite rare.

Psychologists working from the biological perspective point to evidence that there is an inherited predisposition to anxiety disorders. Researchers have even located some specific genetic sites that may predispose people toward anxiety disorders (Goddard et al., 2004; Hamilton et al., 2004), although the evidence linking specific kinds of anxiety disorders to genetic factors is less clear (Oltmanns & Emery, 2006).

Finally, the role that internal psychological distress may play in producing feelings of anxiety should be considered. Most psychoanalytic theorists believe that anxiety disorders arise when unacceptable impulses or thoughts (usually sexual or aggressive) threaten to overwhelm the ego and break through into consciousness. The person is unaware of the unconscious conflict but experiences the early warning signal of anxiety. Phobias convert vague, uncontrollable anxiety into a specific fear that, at least in theory, can be controlled.

Check Your Understanding

1. According to the psychoanalytic view, anxiety results from _____.

2. The fact that we are much more likely to develop phobias about spiders and snakes than about real threats suggests that phobias are _____.

3. Indicate whether the following two statements are true (T) or false (F).

    a. _____ The fear in a specific phobia often interferes with life functions.

    b. _____ People who experience obsessions and compulsions appear highly anxious.

4. Barbara becomes intensely fearful whenever she finds herself in crowds or in public places from which she might not be able to escape easily. It is most likely that Barbara is suffering from

    a. Generalized anxiety disorder   c. Agoraphobia

    b. Panic disorder   d. Acute stress disorder

Psychosomatic disorders: Illnesses that have a valid physical basis, but are largely caused by _____; all illnesses are, to some extent, _____

Somatoform disorders: Symptoms of illness without _____

■ Conversion disorder: Dramatic specific disability without _____

■ Hypochondriasis: Insistence that minor symptoms mean _____

Psychosomatic and Somatoform Disorders

ENDURING ISSUES MIND/BODY

Psychosomatic and Somatoform Disorders

The term *psychosomatic* perfectly captures the interplay of *psyche* (mind) and *soma* (body), which characterizes these disorders. A **psychosomatic disorder** is a real, physical disorder, but one that has, at least in part, a psychological cause. In contrast, **somatoform disorders** are characterized by physical symptoms that do not have any identifiable, underlying biological cause. In both cases, the close relationship between mind and body is immediately evident.

Modern medicine increasingly leans toward the idea that all physical ailments are, to some extent, "psychosomatic"—in the sense that stress, anxiety, and various states of emotional arousal alter body chemistry, the functioning of bodily organs, and the body's immune system (which is vital in fighting infections). Tension headaches, for example, are caused by muscle contractions brought on by stress. The headache is real, but it is called "psychosomatic" because psychological factors (such as stress and anxiety) appear to play an important role in causing the symptoms. In Chapter 11: Stress and Health Psychology, we discussed at some length the fact that frequent or chronic stress as well as negative emotions such as fear, anger, and depression can cause extensive damage to the heart and blood vessels and significantly impair the immune system.

Somatoform disorders are especially puzzling. People suffering from these disorders believe that they are physically ill and describe symptoms that match those of physical illnesses, but medical examinations reveal no organic problems. One of the more dramatic forms of somatoform disorder involves complaints of paralysis, blindness, deafness, seizures, loss of feeling, or pregnancy. In these **conversion disorders**, no physical causes can be found, yet the symptoms are real. Yet another somatoform disorder is **hypochondriasis**. Here, the person interprets some small symptom—perhaps a cough, a bruise, or perspiration—as a sign of a serious disease. Although the symptom may actually exist, there is no evidence that the serious illness does.

Somatoform disorders (especially conversion disorders) present a challenge for psychological theorists because they seem to involve some kind of unconscious processes. Freud concluded that the physical symptoms were often related to traumatic experiences buried in a patient's past. Cognitive-behavioral theorists look for ways in which the symptomatic behavior is being rewarded. From the biological perspective, research has shown that at least some diagnosed somatoform disorders actually were real physical illnesses that were overlooked or misdiagnosed. For example, some cases of "conversion disorder" have proved to be the result of neurological problems such as epilepsy or multiple sclerosis. Nevertheless, most cases of conversion disorder cannot be explained by current medical science. These cases pose as much of a theoretical challenge today as they did when conversion disorders captured Freud's attention more than a century ago.

Check Your Understanding

1. Bob is concerned about a few warts that have appeared on his arms. His doctor says that they are just warts and are not a concern, but Bob believes they are cancerous and that he will die from them. He consults another doctor and then another, both of whom tell him they are just normal warts, but he remains convinced they are cancerous and he is going to die. It appears that Bob is suffering from

   a. Hypochondriasis

   b. A psychosomatic disorder

   c. A somatoform disorder

   d. A phobia

2. John is a writer, but work on his latest novel has come to a halt because he has lost all feeling in his arm and his hand. His doctor can find no physical cause for his problem; however, there is no question that he no longer has feeling in his arm and that he can no longer hold a pencil or type on a keyboard. It seems likely that John is suffering from

   a. Bipolar disorder

   b. Hypochondriasis

   c. Conversion disorder

   d. Dissociative disorder

When she was found by a Florida park ranger, Jane Doe was suffering from amnesia. She could not recall her name, her past, or how to read and write. She never regained her memory of the past.

Dissociative disorders: Some part of a person's personality or memory is _____

- Dissociative amnesia: Unusual loss of _____ without _____

- Dissociative fugue: Flight from home and the _____

- Dissociative identity disorder: Separation of the personality into _____

- Depersonalization disorder: Sudden feelings of _____ or _____

- _____ and/or_____ factors are believed to be causes.

Dissociative Disorders

To the observer and to the sufferer, **dissociative disorders** are among the most puzzling forms of mental disorders. *Dissociation* means that part of an individual's personality appears to be separated from the rest, and, for some reason, the person cannot reassemble the pieces. The disorder usually takes the form of memory loss (**dissociative amnesia**). Less often, there may be amnesia along with a complete, though generally temporary, change in identity (**dissociative fugue**). In **dissociative identity disorder**, commonly known as *multiple personality disorder*, several distinct personalities emerge at different times. This dramatic disorder has been the subject of popular fiction and films, but most psychologists believe it to be rare. In true multiple personality, the various personalities are distinct people with their own names, identities, memories, mannerisms, speaking voices, and even IQs. Sometimes, the personalities are so separate they do not know they inhabit a body with other "people." At other times, the personalities do know of the existence of other "people" and even make disparaging remarks about them. Typically, the personalities contrast sharply with one another, as though each one represents different aspects of the same person—one being the more socially acceptable, "nice" side of the person and the other being the darker, more uninhibited or "evil" side.

A far less dramatic (and much more common) dissociative disorder is **depersonalization disorder**, in which the person suddenly feels changed or different in a strange way. Some people feel that they have left their bodies, whereas others find that their actions have suddenly become mechanical or dreamlike. This kind of feeling is especially common during adolescence and young adulthood, when our sense of ourselves and our interactions with others change rapidly. Only when the sense of depersonalization becomes a long-term or chronic problem or when the alienation impairs normal social functioning can this be classified as a dissociative disorder.

The origins of dissociative identity disorders are not fully understood. Dissociative disorders, as with conversion disorders, seem to involve some kind of unconscious processes. Trauma is one important psychological factor in the onset of these disorders. In many cases, childhood abuse in particular seems to play a role. The child learns to cope with abuse by a process of dissociation—by having the abuse, in effect, happen to "someone else," that is, to a personality who is not conscious most of the time. Biological factors may also play a role. Dissociation and amnesia are commonly associated with aging and disorders such as Alzheimer's disease; and dissociative experiences are a common consequence of the ingestion of drugs such as LSD. Nevertheless, all of these observations are only tantalizing clues to solving the mystery of what causes dissociative disorders.

Check Your Understanding

1. A person who was being interrogated by the police confessed on tape to having committed several murders. When the alleged killer was brought to trial, his lawyers agreed that the voice on the tape belonged to their client. But they asserted that the person who confessed was another personality that lived inside the body of their client. In other words, they claimed that their client was suffering from

   a. Depersonalization disorder   **c.** Conversion disorder

   b. Dissociative identity disorder   **d.** Bipolar disorder

2. You are reading the newspaper and come across a story of a young man who was found wandering the streets with no recollection of who he was, where he came from, or how he got there. You suspect that he is most likely suffering from

   a. Depersonalization disorder   **c.** Conversion disorder

   b. Dissociative amnesia   **d.** Bipolar disorder

Sexual and Gender-Identity Disorders

What's Normal?

Ideas about what is normal and abnormal in sexual behavior vary with the times, the individual, and, sometimes, the culture. Alfred Kinsey and his associates showed years ago (Kinsey, Pomeroy, & Martin, 1948; Kinsey, Pomeroy, Martin, & Gebhard, 1953) that many Americans enjoy a variety of sexual activities—some forbidden by law. We also know that there are a number of sexual universals such as great interest in sex, sexual attractiveness based on signs of health, avoidance of incest, and sexual relations carried out in private. Despite the wide variation in courtship, marriage customs, and other sexual practices among cultural groups, some things remain universally human—and others are universally shunned. Throughout the late twentieth century, as psychologists became more aware of the diversity of "normal" sexual behaviors, they began to narrow their definition of abnormal sexual behavior. Today, the *DSM-IV-TR* recognizes only three main types of sexual disorders: sexual dysfunction, paraphilias, and gender-identity disorders, all of which will be discussed next.

Sexual dysfunction is the loss or impairment of the ordinary physical responses of sexual function (Figure 12–1). In men, this usually takes the form of **erectile disorder** or **erectile dysfunction (ED)**, the inability to achieve or maintain an erection. In women, it often takes the form of **female sexual arousal disorder**, the inability to become sexually excited or to reach orgasm. (These conditions were once called "impotence" and "frigidity," respectively, but professionals in the field have rejected these terms as negative and judgmental.) Occasional problems with achieving or maintaining an erection in men or with lubrication or reaching orgasm in women are common. Only when the condition is frequent or constant and when enjoyment of sexual relationships becomes impaired should it be considered serious.

Although medications such as Viagra, Levitra, and Cialis appear to help most male patients overcome ED, they are of little value unless a man is first sexually aroused. Unfortunately, some men and women find it difficult or impossible to experience any desire for sexual activity to begin with. **Sexual desire disorders** involve a lack of interest in sex or perhaps an active distaste for it. Other people are able to experience sexual desire and maintain arousal but are unable to reach orgasm, the peaking of sexual pleasure and the release of sexual tension. These people are said to experience **orgasmic disorders**. Among the other problems that can occur during the sexual response cycle are **premature ejaculation,** a fairly common disorder, and **vaginismus**, involuntary muscle spasms in the outer part of a woman's vagina during sexual excitement that make intercourse impossible. Again, the occasional experience of such problems is common; the *DSM-IV-TR* considers them dysfunctions only when they are "persistent and recurrent."

A second group of sexual disorders, known as **paraphilias**, involves the use of unconventional sex objects or situations to obtain sexual arousal. Most people have unusual sexual fantasies at some time, which can be a healthy stimulant of normal sexual enjoyment. However, **fetishism**—the repeated use of a nonhuman object such as a shoe or underwear as the preferred or exclusive method of achieving sexual excitement—is considered a sexual disorder. Other unconventional patterns of sexual behavior are **voyeurism**, watching other people have sex or spying on people who are nude; achieving arousal by **exhibitionism**, the exposure of one's genitals in inappropriate situations, such as in front of strangers; **frotteurism**, achieving sexual arousal by touching or rubbing against a nonconsenting person in public situations

- Sexual dysfunction: Loss or impairment of the ability to _____
  - Erectile disorder (ED): _____
  - Female sexual arousal disorder: _____
  - Sexual desire disorders: _____
  - Orgasmic disorders: _____
  - Premature ejaculation: _____
  - Vaginismus: _____
- Paraphilias: Use of unconventional _____ or situations
  - Fetishism: _____
  - Voyeurism: _____
  - Exhibitionism: _____
  - Frotteurism: _____
  - Transvestic fetishism: _____
  - Sexual sadism: _____
  - Sexual masochism: _____
  - Pedophilia: _____
- Gender-identity disorders: Desire to become, or the insistence that one really is, _____

FIGURE 12–1
Sexual dysfunction in the United States.
This graph shows the prevalence of the most common types of sexual dysfunction in men and women, by age group.
Source: *USA Today*, May 18, 1999, p. 7D. Data from the National Health and Social Life Survey, published in the *Journal of the American Medical Association*, February 1999. © 1999, *USA Today*. Reprinted with permission.

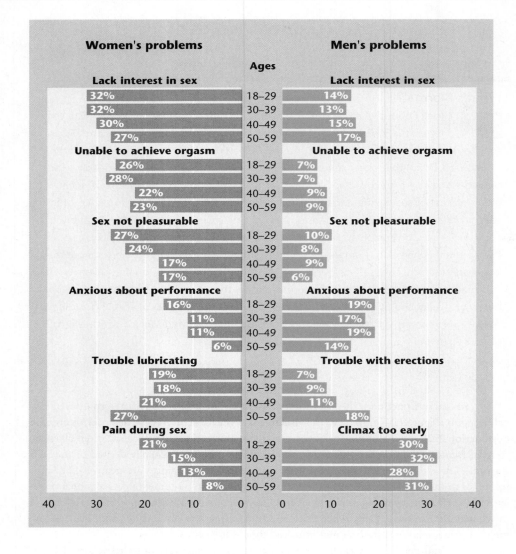

such as in a crowded subway car; and **transvestic fetishism**, wearing clothes of the opposite sex for sexual excitement and gratification. **Sexual sadism** ties sexual pleasure to aggression. To attain sexual gratification, sadists humiliate or physically harm sex partners. **Sexual masochism** is the inability to enjoy sex without accompanying emotional or physical pain. Sexual sadists and masochists sometimes engage in mutually consenting sex, but at times sadistic acts are inflicted on nonconsenting partners.

One of the most serious paraphilias is **pedophilia**, which according to *DSM-IV-TR* is defined as engaging in sexual activity with a child, generally under the age of 13. Child sexual abuse is shockingly common in the United States; and the abuser usually is someone close to the child, rather than a stranger. Although there is no single cause of pedophilia, some of the most common explanations are that pedophiles cannot adjust to the adult sexual role; that they turn to children as sexual objects in response to stress in adult relationships in which they feel inadequate; or that they have records of unstable social adjustment and generally commit sexual offenses against children in response to a temporary aggressive mood. Studies also indicate that the majority of pedophiles have histories of sexual frustration and failure; tend to perceive themselves as immature; and are rather dependent, unassertive, lonely, and insecure (L. J. Cohen & Galynker, 2002).

Gender-identity disorders involve the desire to become—or the insistence that one really is—a member of the other sex. Some little boys, for example, want to be girls instead. They may reject boys' clothing, feel a desire to wear their sisters' clothes, and play only with girls and with toys that are considered "girls' toys." Similarly, some girls wear boys' clothing and play only with boys and "boys' toys." When such children are uncomfortable being a male or a female and are unwilling to accept themselves as such, the diagnosis is **gender-identity disorder in children** (Zucker, 2005). The causes of gender-identity disorders are not known, but the research evidence suggests that biological factors, such as prenatal hormonal imbalances, are major contributors. Family dynamics and learning experiences, however, may also be contributing factors.

Check Your Understanding

Match each of the following terms with the appropriate description.

____ Pedophilia

____ Gender-identity disorder

____ Female sexual arousal disorder

____ Paraphilias

a. The inability for a woman to become sexually excited or to reach orgasm

b. Involve the use of unconventional sex objects or situations to obtain sexual arousal

c. Recurrent, intense sexually arousing fantasies, sexual urges, or behaviors involving sexual activity with a prepubescent child

d. The desire to become—or the insistence that one really is—a member of the other biological sex

Personality Disorders

In Chapter 10: Personality, we saw that despite having certain characteristic views of the world and ways of doing things, people normally can adjust their behavior to fit different situations. But some people, starting at some point early in life, develop inflexible and maladaptive ways of thinking and behaving that are so exaggerated and rigid that they cause serious distress to themselves or problems to others. People with such **personality disorders** range from harmless eccentrics to cold-blooded killers.

Schizoid personality disorder is characterized by odd or eccentric behavior. People with this disorder lack the ability or desire to form social relationships and have no warm or tender feelings for others. Such loners cannot express their feelings and appear cold, distant, and unfeeling. Moreover, they often seem vague, absentminded, indecisive, or "in a fog." Because their withdrawal is so complete, persons with schizoid personality disorder seldom marry and may have trouble holding jobs that require them to work with or relate to others.

People with **paranoid personality disorder** also appear to be odd. Although they often see themselves as rational and objective, they are guarded, secretive, devious, scheming, and argumentative. They are suspicious and mistrustful even when there is no reason to be; they are hypersensitive to any possible threat or trick; and they refuse to accept blame or criticism even when it is deserved.

A cluster of personality disorders characterized by anxious or fearful behavior includes dependent personality disorder and avoidant personality disorder. People with **dependent personality disorder** are unable to make decisions on their own or to do things independently. Rather, they rely on parents, spouses, friends, or others to make the major choices in their lives and usually are extremely unhappy being alone. Their underlying fear seems to be that they will be rejected or abandoned by important people in their lives. In **avoidant personality disorder**, the person is timid, anxious, and fearful of rejection. It is not surprising that this social anxiety leads to isolation, but unlike the schizoid type, the person with avoidant personality disorder *wants* to have close relationships with others.

Another cluster of personality disorders is characterized by dramatic, emotional, or erratic behavior. People with **narcissistic personality disorder**, for example, display a grandiose sense of self-importance and a preoccupation with fantasies of unlimited success. Such people believe that they are extraordinary, need constant attention and admiration, display a sense of

Personality disorders:

_____ and _____

ways of thinking and behaving

- Schizoid personality disorder: Withdrawal and lacking _____

- Paranoid personality disorder: Inappropriate _____ and _____ of others

- Dependent personality disorder: Inability to _____ independently; cannot tolerate _____

- Avoidant personality disorder: Social isolation resulting from _____

- Narcissistic personality disorder: Exaggerated sense of _____; desire for _____

- Borderline personality disorder: _____ in self-image, mood, and interpersonal relationships

- Antisocial personality disorder: _____, _____, or _____ behavior; inability to feel _____ for others

entitlement, and tend to exploit others. They are given to envy and arrogance, and they lack the ability to really care for anyone else.

Borderline personality disorder is characterized by marked instability in self-image, mood, and interpersonal relationships. People with this personality disorder tend to act impulsively and, often, self-destructively. They feel uncomfortable being alone and often manipulate self-destructive impulses in an effort to control or solidify their personal relationships. Borderline personality disorder is common and serious.

One of the most widely studied personality disorders is **antisocial personality disorder**. People who exhibit this disorder lie, steal, cheat, and show little or no sense of responsibility, although they often seem intelligent and charming at first. The "con man" exemplifies many of the features of the antisocial personality, as does the person who compulsively cheats business partners, because she or he knows their weak points. Antisocial personalities rarely show any anxiety or guilt about their behavior. Indeed, they are likely to blame society or their victims for the antisocial actions that they themselves commit. As you might suspect, people with antisocial personality disorder are responsible for a good deal of crime and violence.

As one might expect from systems theory, personality disorders seem to result from a combination of biological predisposition, difficult life experiences, and an unhealthy social environment. However, researchers are a long way from understanding the ways in which these factors combine to produce a particular kind of disorder.

Check Your Understanding

1. Match the following personality disorders with the appropriate description.

_____ Schizoid personality disorder	**a.** Shows instability in self-image, mood, and relationships
_____ Paranoid personality disorder	**b.** Is fearful and timid
_____ Dependent personality disorder	**c.** Is mistrustful even when there is no reason
_____ Avoidant personality disorder	**d.** Lacks the ability to form social relationships
_____ Borderline personality disorder	**e.** Is unable to make own decisions

2. John represents himself as a stockbroker who specializes in investing the life savings of elderly people, but he never invests the money. Instead, he puts it into his own bank account and flees the country. When he is caught and asked how he feels about financially destroying the lives of elderly people, he explains, "Hey, if they were stupid enough to give me their money, they deserved what they got." John is most likely suffering from _____ personality disorder.

a. Dependent   **c.** Antisocial

b. Avoidant   **d.** Borderline

3. Jennifer is a graduate student who believes that her thesis will completely change the way that scientists view the universe. She believes that she is the only person intelligent enough to have come up with the thesis, that she is not appreciated sufficiently by other students and faculty, and that nobody on her thesis committee is sufficiently knowledgeable to judge its merits. Assuming that her thesis is not, in fact, revolutionary, it would appear that Jennifer is suffering from _____ personality disorder.

a. Paranoid   **c.** Borderline

b. Narcissistic   **d.** Antisocial

Schizophrenic Disorders

A common misconception is that *schizophrenia* means "split personality." But, as seen earlier, split personality (or multiple personality) is actually a dissociative identity disorder. The misunderstanding comes from the fact that the root *schizo* derives from the Greek verb meaning "to split." What is split in schizophrenia is not so much personality as the connections among thoughts.

Schizophrenic disorders are severe conditions marked by disordered thoughts and communications, inappropriate emotions, and bizarre behavior that lasts for months or even years. People suffering from schizophrenia are out of touch with reality, which is to say that they are **psychotic**. Psychosis is sometimes confused with insanity, but the terms are not synonymous. **Insanity** is the legal term for people who are found not to be responsible for their criminal actions.

People with schizophrenia often suffer from **hallucinations**, false sensory perceptions that usually take the form of hearing voices that are not really there. They also frequently have **delusions**—false beliefs about reality with no factual basis—that distort their relationships with their surroundings and with other people. Often, they are unable to communicate with others because when they speak, their words are incoherent.

Disorganized schizophrenia includes some of the more bizarre symptoms of schizophrenia, such as giggling, grimacing, and frantic gesturing. People suffering from disorganized schizophrenia show a childish disregard for social conventions and may urinate or defecate at inappropriate times. They are active, but aimless, and they are often given to incoherent conversations.

In **catatonic schizophrenia**, motor activity is severely disturbed. People in this state may remain immobile, mute, and impassive. They may behave in a robotlike fashion when ordered to move, and they may even let doctors put their arms and legs into uncomfortable positions that they maintain for hours. At the opposite extreme, they may become excessively excited, talking and shouting continuously.

Paranoid schizophrenia is marked by extreme suspiciousness and complex delusions. People with paranoid schizophrenia may believe themselves to be Napoleon or the Virgin Mary, or they may insist that Russian spies with laser guns are constantly on their trail because they have learned some great secret. As they are less likely to be incoherent or to look or act "crazy," these people can appear more "normal" than people with other schizophrenic disorders when their delusions are compatible with everyday life. They may, however, become hostile or aggressive toward anyone who questions their thinking or delusions. Note that this disorder is far more severe than paranoid personality disorder, which does not involve bizarre delusions or loss of touch with reality.

Finally, **undifferentiated schizophrenia** is the classification developed for people who have several of the characteristic symptoms of schizophrenia—such as delusions, hallucinations, or incoherence—yet do not show the typical symptoms of any other subtype of the disorder.

Because schizophrenia is such a serious disorder, considerable research has been directed at discovering its causes. Many studies suggest that there is a biological predisposition to schizophrenia (see Figure 2–17). The thinking is that perhaps heredity causes faulty regulation of neurotransmitters, such as dopamine and glutamate, or pathology in structures of the brain (Flashman & Green, 2004; Javitt & Coyle, 2004). But so far, scientists have found only average differences in brain structure and chemistry between schizophrenic and healthy people.

But Figure 2–17 tells another story as well. Note that although identical twins are genetically identical, half of the identical twins of people with schizophrenia do not develop schizophrenia. Thus, genetics cannot be the whole story. Environmental factors—ranging from disturbed family relations to taking drugs to biological damage that may occur at any age, even before birth (Bresnahan, Schaefer, Brown, & Susser, 2005)—must also figure in determining whether a person will develop schizophrenia. As you would expect from systems theory, the various explanations for schizophrenic disorders are not mutually exclusive. Genetic factors are universally acknowledged, but many theorists believe that only a combination of biological, psychological, and social factors produces schizophrenia. According to systems theory, genetic factors predispose some people to schizophrenia; and family interaction and life stress activate the predisposition.

- Schizophrenic disorders: Marked by dramatic disruptions in _____ and _____, inappropriate _____, and bizarre _____ that lasts for years
- Psychotic (psychosis): Characterized by a _____
- Insanity: Legal term for mentally disturbed people who are not considered _____
- Hallucinations: False _____
- Delusions: False beliefs about

_____

- Biological and environmental factors alike contribute to:
  - Disorganized schizophrenia: _____, _____ behaviors
  - Catatonic schizophrenia: Disturbed _____ behavior
  - Paranoid schizophrenia: Extreme _____, bizarre _____
  - Undifferentiated schizophrenia: Clear symptoms that do not

_____

Check Your Understanding

1. Indicate whether the following two statements are true (T) or false (F).

   a. _____ Schizophrenia is almost the same thing as multiple personality disorder.

   b. _____ Studies indicate that a biological predisposition to schizophrenia may be inherited.

2. The book *A Beautiful Mind* is about John Nash, a mathematical genius. In young adulthood, he became convinced that people were spying on him and hunting him down. He searched for secret codes in numbers, sent bizarre postcards to friends, and made no sense when he spoke. On the basis of this description, it seems most likely that he was suffering from

   a. Disorganized schizophrenia   b. Catatonic schizophrenia

   c. Undifferentiated schizophrenia   d. Paranoid schizophrenia

3. Your roommate asks you what the difference is between "hallucinations" and "delusions." You tell her

   a. Hallucinations involve false beliefs, while delusions involve false sensory perceptions.

   b. Hallucinations occur primarily in schizophrenic disorders, while delusions occur primarily in dissociative disorders.

   c. Hallucinations involve false sensory perceptions, while delusions involve false beliefs.

   d. There is no difference; those are just two words for the same thing.

Childhood Disorders

■ Attention-deficit hyperactivity disorder (ADHD): Characterized by_____, _____, and _____

■ Psychostimulant: Drugs that increase _____ in people with ADHD

■ Autistic disorder: Characterized by lack of _____ and strange _____ behavior

■ Autistic spectrum disorder (ASD): A range of disorders involving varying degrees of impairment in _____ and _____, with _____, _____, and _____ patterns of behavior

Childhood Disorders

Children may suffer from conditions already discussed in this chapter—for example, depression and anxiety disorders. But other disorders are either characteristic of children or are first evident in childhood. The *DSM-IV-TR* contains a long list of disorders usually first diagnosed in infancy, childhood, or adolescence. Two of these disorders are attention-deficit hyperactivity disorder and autistic disorder.

Attention-deficit hyperactivity disorder (ADHD) was once known simply as *hyperactivity*. The new name reflects the fact that children with the disorder typically have trouble focusing their attention in the sustained way that other children do. Instead, they are easily distracted, often fidgety and impulsive, and almost constantly in motion. Many theorists believe that this disorder—which affects 3 to 5% of all school-age children and is much more common in boys than girls—is present at birth, but that it becomes a serious problem only after the child starts school. The class setting demands that children sit quietly, pay attention as instructed, follow directions, and inhibit urges to yell and run around. The child with ADHD simply cannot conform to these demands.

The cause of ADHD is not yet known, but considerable evidence indicates biological factors play an important role. Neuroimagining studies, for example, reveal individuals with ADHD display altered brain functioning when presented with tasks that require shifting attention. The deficiency appears to involve the frontal lobe (see Chapter 2: The Biological Basis of Behavior), which normally recruits appropriate regions of the brain to solve a problem. In people with ADHD, however, the frontal lobe sometimes activates brain centers unrelated to solving a problem.

Family interaction and other social experiences may be more important in preventing the disorder than in causing it; that is, some exceptionally competent parents and patient, tolerant teachers may be able to teach "difficult" children to conform to the demands of schooling. Although some psychologists train the parents of children with ADHD in these management skills, the most frequent treatment for these children is a type of drug known as a **psychostimulant**. Psychostimulants do not work by "slowing down" hyperactive children; rather, they appear to increase the children's ability to focus their attention so that they can attend to the task at hand, which decreases their hyperactivity and improves their academic performance. Unfortunately, psychostimulants often produce only short-term benefits; and their use and possible overuse in treating ADHD children is controversial (LeFever, Arcona, & Antonuccio, 2003).

A very different and profoundly serious disorder that usually becomes evident in the first few years of life is **autistic disorder**. Autistic children fail to form normal attachments to parents, remaining distant and withdrawn into their own separate worlds. As infants, they may even show distress at being picked up or held. As they grow older, they typically do not speak or they develop a peculiar speech pattern called *echolalia*, in which they repeat the words said to them. Autistic children typically show strange motor behavior, such as repeating body movements endlessly or walking constantly on tiptoe. They do not play as normal children do; they are not at all social and may use toys in odd ways, constantly spinning the wheels on a toy truck or tearing paper into strips. Autistic children often display the symptoms of retardation, but it is hard to test their mental ability because they generally do not talk. The disorder lasts into adulthood in the great majority of cases.

In recent years, autistic disorder has come to be viewed as just one dimension of a much broader range of developmental disorders known as **autistic spectrum disorder (ASD)** (Dawson & Toth, 2006; Simpson et al., 2005). Individuals with disorders in the autistic spectrum display symptoms that are similar to those seen in autistic disorder, but the severity of the symptoms is often quite reduced. For example, high-functioning children with a form of ASD known as *Asperger syndrome* may show difficulty interacting with other people, but may have little or no problem with speech or intellectual development.

One explanation for the inability of individuals within the autistic spectrum to develop normal patterns of social interaction holds they may not understand or correctly interpret others' thoughts and feelings. This *theory of mind* explanation argues that because they do not realize other people may have different thoughts, emotions, and attitudes than their own, they often have problems communicating with and relating socially to them (Attwood, 2005; Papp, 2006). For example, a child with Asperger syndrome may not understand why others do not know the answer to a question they know the answer to, or why they may take a point of view different from their own. This failure to comprehend another person's point of view or opinion is often a source of frustration leading to inappropriate social responses.

We do not know what causes autism, although most theorists believe that it results almost entirely from biological conditions. Some causes of mental retardation, such as fragile X syndrome (see Chapter 7: Cognition and Mental Abilities), also seem to increase the risk of autistic disorder. Recent evidence suggests that genetics also play a strong role in causing the disorder (Lamb, Moore, Bailey, & Monaco, 2000; Nurmi et al., 2003; Rodier, 2000; Rutter, 2005), though no specific gene or chromosome responsible for autistic disorder has yet been identified (Shastry, 2005).

Check Your Understanding

1. Indicate whether the following statements are true (T) or false (F).

    a. _____ ADHD is much more common in boys than in girls.

    b. _____ Psychostimulants work by "slowing down" hyperactive children.

    c. _____ Most theorists believe that autistic disorder results almost entirely from biological conditions.

2. Mary is a 7-year-old who is easily distracted and who has great difficulty concentrating. While reading or studying, her attention will often be drawn to events going on elsewhere. She is fidgety, impulsive, and never seems to stop moving. She finds it almost impossible to sit quietly, pay attention, and follow directions. Marie is most likely suffering from

    a. Attention-deficit hyperactivity disorder   **c.** Echolalia

    b. Autistic disorder   **d.** Disorganized personality disorder

Gender and Cultural Differences in Psychological Disorders

■ GENDER DIFFERENCES

For the most part, men and women are similar with respect to mental disorders, but differences do exist. Many studies have concluded that women have a higher rate of psychological disorders than do men, but this is an oversimplification. We do know that more women than men are *treated* for mental disorders. But this cannot be taken to mean that more women than men have mental disorders; in our society, it is much more acceptable for women to discuss their emotional difficulties and to seek professional help openly. It may be that mental disorders are equally common among men—or even more common—but that men do not so readily show up in therapists' offices and, therefore, are not counted in the studies.

Moreover, mental disorders for which there seems to be a strong biological component, such as bipolar disorder and schizophrenia, are distributed fairly equally between the sexes. Differences tend to be found for those disorders *without* a strong biological component—that is, disorders in which learning and experience play a more important role. For example, men are more likely than women to suffer from substance abuse and antisocial personality disorder. Women, on the other hand, are more likely to suffer from depression, agoraphobia, simple phobia, and obsessive-compulsive disorder. These tendencies, coupled with the fact that gender differences observed in the United States are not always seen in other cultures, suggest that socialization plays a part in developing a disorder: When men display abnormal behavior, it is more likely to take the forms of drinking too much and acting aggressively; when women display abnormal behavior, they are more likely to become fearful, passive, hopeless, and "sick."

One commonly reported difference between the sexes concerns marital status. Men who are separated or divorced or who have never married have a higher prevalence of mental disorders than married men and women who are separated or divorced or who have never married. Those data suggest that for men, marriage and family provide a haven. Conversely, the prevalence of psychological disorders among married women is the highest of all. The explanation appears to lie in the fact that marriage, family relationships, and child rearing are likely to be far more stressful for women than they are for men (see Chapter 9: Life-Span Development). In addition, women are more likely than men to be the victims of incest, rape, and marital battery. As one researcher has commented, "for women, the U.S. family is a violent institution" (Koss, 1990, p. 376).

Chapter 11 noted that the effects of stress are proportional to the extent to which a person feels alienated, powerless, and helpless. Alienation, powerlessness, and helplessness are more prevalent in women than in men. These factors are especially common among minority women, so it is not surprising that the prevalence of psychological disorders is greater among them than among other women (Laganà & Sosa, 2004). In addition, these factors play an especially important role in anxiety disorders and depression—precisely those disorders experienced most often by women. Not surprisingly, the rate of depression among women is twice that of men.

In summary, women do seem to have higher rates of anxiety disorders and depression than do men. The explanation appears to lie in the fact that women experience greater stress than men do—in part, as a result of feeling alienated and powerless, and in part, as a result of the added stress of family life for most women.

ENDURING ISSUES DIVERSITY/UNIVERSALITY

Are We All Alike?

The frequency and nature of some psychological disorders vary significantly among the world's different cultures (Halbreich & Karkun, 2006; López & Guarnaccia, 2000). This suggests that many disorders have a strong cultural component, or that diagnosis is somehow related to culture. On the other hand, disorders that are known to have a strong genetic component generally display a more uniform distribution across different cultures.

■ CULTURAL DIFFERENCES

As the U.S. population becomes more diverse, it is increasingly important for mental health professionals to be aware of cultural differences if they are to understand and diagnose disorders among people of various cultural groups. Many disorders occur only in particular cultural groups. For example, *ataque de nervios*—literally translated as "attack of nerves"—is a culturally specific phenomenon seen predominately among Latinos. The symptoms of *ataque de nervios* generally include the feeling of being out of control, which may be accompanied by fainting spells, trembling, uncontrollable screaming and crying, and, in some cases, verbal or physical aggressiveness. Afterward, many people do not recall the attack, and they quickly return to normal functioning. Another example, *taijin kyofusho* (roughly translated as "fear of people"), involves a morbid fear that one's body or actions may be offensive to others. *Taijin kyofusho* is rarely seen outside Japan. Other cross-cultural investigations have found differences in the course of schizophrenia and in the way childhood psychological disorders are manifest among different cultures.

For some psychological disorders, the prevalence among males and females also differs markedly among countries. For instance, in the United States and most developed nations, females generally display a markedly higher incidence of depression than males. But in many underdeveloped countries of the world, such as Iran, Uganda, or Nigeria, very little or no gender difference in the incidence of depression is found (Culbertson, 1997).

Check Your Understanding

1. Mental disorders for which there seems to be a strong _____ component are distributed fairly equally between the sexes.

2. More women than men are treated for mental disorders. Is this statement true (T) or false (F)?

3. There is greater cultural variation in those abnormal behaviors with strong genetic causes. Is this statement true (T) or false (F)?

Chapter Review

 www.psychologythecore.com

Perspectives on Psychological Disorders

Society, the individual, and the mental health professional use different criteria when distinguishing abnormal behavior from normal behavior. Mental health professionals look for maladaptive behavior, psychological discomfort, and evidence that the person's ability to function well in life is impaired. There is no clear-cut distinction between mental health and mental illness. The line between the two is often somewhat arbitrary, and the difference between them is often simply a difference in degree.

According to research, 15% of the population is suffering from one or more clinically significant mental disorders at any given point in time (the *prevalence* of psychological disorders). Cross-culturally, the prevalence varies from 4% in Asia to 12% in the Americas.

As late as the eighteenth century, the mentally ill were regarded as witches or as people possessed by the devil. Gradually, the mentally ill were confined to public and private asylums. But little was done to ensure humane standards in mental institutions until the late 1700s. In modern times, three approaches have helped to advance our understanding of abnormal behavior: the biological, the psychoanalytic, and the cognitive behavioral.

The **biological model** holds that abnormal behavior is caused by physiological disorders, especially of the brain. There is considerable evidence in support of this view, though it is only part of the picture. The **psychoanalytic model** holds that abnormal behavior is a symbolic expression of unconscious conflicts that generally can be traced to childhood. The **cognitive-behavioral model** states that psychological disorders arise when people learn maladaptive ways of thinking and acting.

The **diathesis-stress model** integrates the biological and environmental perspectives. According to this view, psychological disorders develop when a biological predisposition (**diathesis**) is triggered by stressful circumstances. Another attempt at integrating causes is the **systems** (biopsychosocial) **approach,** which contends psychological disorders are "lifestyle diseases" arising from a combination of biological risk factors, psychological stresses, and societal pressures.

The most widely used system for classifying psychological disorders is the fourth edition of the *Diagnostic and Statistical Manual of Mental Disorders* (*DSM-IV-TR*). This manual provides careful descriptions of the symptoms of different disorders, though it is silent on causes and treatment.

Mood Disorders

Most people have a wide emotional range, but in some people with **mood disorders**, this range is greatly restricted. They seem stuck at one or the other end of the emotional spectrum, or they may alternate back and forth between periods of euphoria and sadness.

The most common mood disorder is **depression**, in which a person feels overwhelmed with sadness, loses interest in activities, and displays such other symptoms as excessive guilt, feelings of worthlessness, insomnia, and loss of appetite. One of the most severe hazards of depression, as well as some of the other disorders described in this chapter, is that people may become so miserable that they no longer wish to live.

People suffering from **mania** become euphoric ("high"), extremely active, excessively talkative, and easily distracted. They typically have unlimited hopes and schemes, but little interest in realistically carrying them out. At the extreme, they may collapse from exhaustion. Manic episodes usually alternate with depression. Such a mood disorder, in which both mania and depression are alternately present and are sometimes interrupted by periods of normal mood, is known as **bipolar disorder**.

Mood disorders can result from a combination of biological, psychological, and social factors. Genetics and chemical imbalances in the brain seem to play an important role in the development of depression and, especially, bipolar disorder. Unrealistically negative views about the self also occur in many depressed people, although it is uncertain whether these cause the depression or are caused by it. Finally, social factors, such as troubled relationships, have also been linked with mood disorders.

Anxiety Disorders

Normal fear is caused by something identifiable and the fear subsides with time. With **anxiety disorders**, however, either the person does not know the source of the fear or the anxiety is inappropriate to the circumstances.

A **specific phobia** is an intense, paralyzing, unreasonable fear of something. A **social phobia** is excessive, inappropriate fear connected with social situations or performances in front of other people. **Agoraphobia,** a less common and much more debilitating type of anxiety disorder, involves multiple, intense fears such as the fear of being alone, of being in public places, or of other situations involving separation from a source of security. **Panic disorder** is characterized by recurring sudden, unpredictable, and overwhelming experiences of intense fear or terror without any reasonable cause. **Generalized anxiety disorder** is defined by prolonged vague, but intense fears that, unlike phobias, are not attached to any particular object or circumstance. In contrast, **obsessive-compulsive disorder** involves either involuntary thoughts that recur despite the person's attempt to stop them or compulsive rituals that a person feels compelled to perform. Two other types of anxiety disorder are caused by highly stressful events. If the anxious reaction occurs soon after the event, the diagnosis is *acute stress disorder*; if it occurs long after the event is over, the diagnosis is *posttraumatic stress disorder*.

Psychologists with a biological perspective propose that a predisposition to anxiety disorders may be inherited because these types of disorders tend to run in families. Moreover, it appears that many phobias are *prepared responses*; that is, through evolution we may have become biologically predisposed to associate certain stimuli with intense fears. Most psychoanalytic theorists believe that anxiety disorders arise when unacceptable impulses or thoughts (usually sexual or aggressive) threaten to overwhelm the ego and break through into consciousness.

Psychosomatic and Somatoform Disorders

Psychosomatic disorders are illnesses that have a valid physical basis, but are largely caused by psychological factors such as excessive stress and anxiety. In contrast, **somatoform disorders** are characterized by physical symptoms without any identifiable physical cause. Examples are **conversion disorder** (a dramatic specific disability without organic cause), and **hypochondriasis** (insistence that minor symptoms mean serious illness).

Modern medicine increasingly leans toward the idea that all physical ailments are to some extent "psychosomatic"—caused by stress, anxiety, and emotional arousal. But somatoform disorders pose as much of a theoretical challenge today as they did a century ago.

Dissociative Disorders

In **dissociative disorders**, some part of a person's personality or memory is separated from the rest. **Dissociative amnesia** involves the loss of at least some significant aspects of memory. When an amnesia victim leaves home and assumes an entirely new identity, the disorder is known as **dissociative fugue**. In **dissociative identity disorder** *(multiple personality disorder)*, several distinct personalities emerge at different times. In **depersonalization disorder**, the person suddenly feels changed or different in a strange way.

The causes of dissociative disorders are obscure. In many cases, childhood abuse in particular seems to play a role. And in at least some cases, biological factors seem to be involved as well.

Sexual and Gender-Identity Disorders

The *DSM-IV-TR* recognizes three main types of sexual disorders: sexual dysfunction, paraphilias, and gender-identity disorders.

Sexual dysfunction is the loss or impairment of the ability to function effectively during sex. In men, this may take the form of **erectile disorder (ED)**, the inability to achieve or keep an erection; in women, it often takes the form of **female sexual arousal disorder**, the inability to become sexually excited or to reach orgasm. **Sexual desire disorders** involve a lack of interest in or an active aversion to sex. People with **orgasmic disorders** experience both desire and arousal but are unable to reach orgasm. Other problems that can occur include **premature ejaculation**—the male's inability to inhibit orgasm as long as desired—and **vaginismus**—involuntary muscle spasms in the outer part of a woman's vagina during sexual excitement that make intercourse impossible.

Paraphilias involve the use of unconventional sex objects or situations. These disorders include **fetishism, voyeurism, exhibitionism, frotteurism, transvestic fetishism, sexual sadism,** and **sexual masochism.** One of the most serious paraphilias is **pedophilia**, engaging in sexual relations with children.

Gender-identity disorders involve the desire to become, or the insistence that one really is, a member of the other sex. **Gender-identity disorder in children** is characterized by rejection of one's biological gender as well as the clothing and behavior society considers appropriate to that gender during childhood.

Personality Disorders

Personality disorders are enduring, inflexible, and maladaptive ways of thinking and behaving that are so exaggerated and rigid that they cause serious inner distress or conflicts with others. One group of personality disorders is characterized by odd or eccentric behavior. People who exhibit **schizoid personality disorder** lack the ability or desire to form social relationships and have no warm feelings for other people; those with **paranoid personality disorder** are inappropriately suspicious, hypersensitive, and argumentative. Another cluster of personality disorders is characterized by anxious or fearful behavior. Examples are **dependent personality**

disorder (the inability to think or act independently) and **avoidant personality disorder** (social anxiety leading to isolation). A third group of personality disorders is characterized by dramatic, emotional, or erratic behavior. For instance, people with **narcissistic personality disorder** have an overblown sense of self-importance, whereas those with **borderline personality disorder** show much instability in self-image, mood, and interpersonal relationships. Finally, people with **antisocial personality disorder** chronically lie, steal, and cheat with little or no remorse. Because this disorder is responsible for a good deal of crime and violence, it creates the greatest problems for society.

Schizophrenic Disorders

In multiple-personality disorder, consciousness is split into two or more distinctive personalities, each of which is coherent and intact. This condition is different from **schizophrenic disorders**, which involve dramatic disruptions in thought and communication, inappropriate emotions, and bizarre behavior that lasts for years. People with schizophrenia are out of touch with reality, which is to say that they are **psychotic**. Usually they cannot live a normal life unless successfully treated with medication. They often suffer from **hallucinations** (false sensory perceptions) and **delusions** (false beliefs about reality). Subtypes of schizophrenic disorders include **disorganized schizophrenia** (childish disregard for social conventions), **catatonic schizophrenia** (mute immobility or excessive excitement), **paranoid schizophrenia** (extreme suspiciousness related to complex delusions), and **undifferentiated schizophrenia** (characterized by a diversity of symptoms).

Many studies suggest that there is a biological predisposition to schizophrenia. But twin studies show that environmental factors—ranging from disturbed family relations to taking drugs to biological damage that may occur at any age, even before birth—must also figure in determining whether a person will develop schizophrenia.

Childhood Disorders

DSM-IV-TR contains a long list of disorders usually first diagnosed in infancy, childhood, or adolescence. Children with **attention-deficit hyperactivity disorder (ADHD)** are highly distractible, often fidgety and impulsive, and almost constantly in motion. The **psychostimulants** frequently prescribed for ADHD appear to slow such children down because they increase the ability to focus attention on routine tasks. **Autistic disorder** is a profound developmental problem identified in the first few years of life. It is characterized by a failure to form normal social attachments, by severe speech impairment, and by strange motor behaviors. A much broader range of developmental disorders known as **autistic spectrum disorder (ASD)** is used to describe individuals with symptoms that are similar to those seen in autistic disorder, but may be less severe as is the case in *Asperger syndrome*. The *theory of mind* holds that individuals within the autistic spectrum have difficulty understanding other people's thoughts and emotions.

Gender and Cultural Differences in Psychological Disorders

Although nearly all psychological disorders affect both men and women, there are some gender differences in the degree to which some disorders are found. Men are more likely to suffer from substance abuse and antisocial personality disorder; women show higher rates of depression, agoraphobia, simple phobia, and obsessive-compulsive disorder. In general, gender differences are less likely to be seen in disorders that have a strong biological component. This tendency is also seen cross-culturally, where cultural differences are observed in disorders not heavily influenced by genetic and biological factors. These gender and cultural differences support the systems view that biological, psychological, and social forces interact as causes of abnormal behavior.

Chapter 13
Therapies

Go to *The Core Online* at **www.psychologythecore.com** to get the most up-to-date information for your introductory psychology course. The content online is an important part of what you are learning—the content there can help prepare you for your test! It includes up-to-date examples, simulations, video clips, and practice quizzes. Also be sure to check out the *Blog* to hear directly from the authors on what current events and latest research are most relevant to your course materials.

The first time you log in, you will need the access code packaged with your textbook. If you do not have a code, please go to **www.mypearsonstore.com** and enter the ISBN of your textbook (**0-13-603344-X**) to purchase the code.

Chapter 13 Therapies

Psychotherapy: A wide variety of psychological techniques used to treat psychological disorders

13 1 Insight Therapies

Insight therapies: Goal is to increase self-awareness and self-understanding to foster better adjustment

Psychoanalysis
- Designed to bring hidden feelings and motives to conscious awareness so that the person can deal with them more effectively
- **Free association:** Disclosing whatever thoughts or fantasies come to mind
- **Insight:** Becoming aware of what was formerly unconscious
- Neo-Freudian analysts focus more on coping with current problems; they favor face-to-face discussions and taking an active role.

Client-Centered Therapy
- **Client-centered (person-centered) therapy:** Treatment for psychological problems based on the client's view of the world
- Therapist provides unconditional positive regard
- Goal is to gain insight into current feelings and to help the person become fully functioning

Gestalt Therapy
- **Gestalt therapy:** Emphasizes the here and now, wholeness of the personality
- Goal is to become aware of conflicting inner feelings and to become more genuine in everyday interactions

13 3 Cognitive Therapies

Cognitive therapies: Focus on changing maladaptive ways of thinking

Stress-Inoculation Therapy
- **Stress-inoculation therapy:** Using self-talk to "coach" oneself through stressful situations by suppressing negative thoughts and replacing them with positive thoughts

Rational-Emotive Therapy
- **Rational-emotive therapy (RET):** Challenges irrational and self-defeating beliefs that people hold about themselves and the world

Beck's Cognitive Therapy
- **Beck's cognitive therapy:** Helps people to examine dysfunctional thoughts and to think more objectively and positively about themselves and their life situations

13 2 Behavior Therapies

Behavior therapies teach the person new, more satisfying ways of behaving using the basic principles of learning

Therapies Based on Classical Conditioning
- **Systematic desensitization:** Learning to remain in a deeply relaxed state while confronting feared situations
- **Flooding:** Exposing phobic people to feared situations at full intensity for a prolonged period
- **Aversive conditioning:** Eliminating undesirable behavior by associating it with pain and discomfort

Therapies Based on Operant Conditioning
- **Behavior contracting:** Client and therapist agree on certain behavioral goals and on the reinforcement that the client will receive on reaching them
- **Token economy:** Tokens that can be exchanged for rewards are used for positive reinforcement of adaptive behaviors.

Therapies Based on Observational Learning
- Observational learning can be used to treat problem behaviors such as phobias.

13 4 Group Therapies

- **Group therapy:** Clients meet regularly with others to help one another achieve insight into feelings and behaviors
- Offer a circle of support for clients, shared insights into problems, and the opportunity to obtain psychotherapy at a lower cost
- **Family therapy:** Goal is to improve communication, increase empathy, share responsibilities, and reduce conflict
- **Couple therapy:** Goal is to improve the patterns of communication and mutual expectations

13 5 Effectiveness of Psychotherapy

- Formal psychotherapy helps approximately two thirds of the people treated compared to at most one third of those who are not treated.
- There is no overall difference in the effectiveness of different therapies.
- Each kind of therapy works better for some problems than for others
  —Insight therapy: Best suited to people seeking self-understanding, relief of inner conflict and anxiety, or better relationships with others
  —Behavior therapy: Most appropriate for the treatment of specific anxieties or other well-defined behavioral problems
  —Family therapy: More effective than individual counseling for the treatment of drug abuse
  —Cognitive therapies: Most effective for the treatment of depression and anxiety disorders

13 6 Biological Treatments

Biological treatments: Used in conjunction with, or instead of, psychotherapy

Drug Therapies
- The most common and often effective form of biological therapy; costs less than psychotherapy
- The major types of psychoactive medications include: antipsychotic drugs, antidepressants, lithium carbonate to treat bipolar disorder, psychostimulants to treat attention deficit hyperactive disorder, and antianxiety medications to reduce tension and stress.
- Some medications produce undesirable side effects and are potentially addictive.

Electroconvulsive Therapy
- **Electroconvulsive therapy (ECT)** involves passing a mild electrical current through the brain for a short period.
- As a last resort, ECT is used to treat severe, prolonged depression.

Psychosurgery
- **Psychosurgery** is brain surgery directed at changing one's behavior or emotional state; it has unpredictable, potentially severe side effects.

13 7 Institutionalization and Its Alternatives

Institutionalization refers to confinement in a mental hospital.

- **Deinstitutionalization** refers to releasing people who have severe psychological disorders back into the community for treatment outside the hospital.
- In practice, deinstitutionalization has often failed because:
  —Follow-up care and housing often are unavailable or underfunded.
  —Persons often are incapable of meeting their own needs.
  —Without supervision, many stop taking their drugs.
  —The social stigma related to mental illness is a major obstacle to rehabilitation.
- Prevention
  —**Primary prevention** involves improving the social environment through assistance to parents, education, and family planning.
  —**Secondary prevention** involves identifying high-risk groups and intervening to direct service to them.
  —**Tertiary prevention** involves helping hospitalized patients return to the community and educating that community to prepare for their return.

13 8 Client Diversity and Treatment

- Gender differences
  —Generally, treatment given to women is the same as that given to men.
  —The American Psychological Association provides guidelines to ensure that women receive treatment that is not tied to traditional, stereotypical ideas about appropriate behavior for the sexes.
- Cultural differences
  —Having different cultural backgrounds or belonging to different racial or ethnic groups can lead to misunderstandings in therapy.
  —Treatment and prevention must be tailored to the beliefs and cultural practices of the person's ethnic group.

■ **Psychotherapy:** A wide variety of
_____ used to
treat psychological disorders

To many people, the term **psychotherapy** still evokes an image of a psychologist or psychiatrist sitting silently in a chair, while a client, reclining on a nearby couch, recounts traumatic events in his or her life. As the anxious client reveals dreams, fantasies, fears, and obsessions, the therapist nods, scribbles a few words in a notebook, and perhaps asks a question or two. The therapist rarely offers the client advice . . . and never reveals details of his or her own personal life.

This cliché of psychotherapy has some truth to it—scenes such as this one do occur. But psychotherapy takes many forms—literally hundreds of variations practiced by several different types of mental-health professionals. In contrast to the image of the clinical, detached analyst, most psychotherapists are warm, understanding, and willing to offer at least some direct information and advice. In some forms of psychotherapy, therapists are very directive, even confrontational, in exploring their clients' thoughts and feelings, some types of psychotherapy occur outside of the therapist's office, as clients confront their fears in real life. Other psychotherapies treat couples or entire families, and still others treat groups of people with similar problems or goals. Many people tend to be confused about the effectiveness of psychotherapy. Some people who have gone through therapy claim that it changed their lives; others complain that it made little difference. The public's perception of the effectiveness of psychotherapy is particularly important now that health care costs have escalated and treatments of psychological disorders are being monitored more closely in terms of their costs and outcomes.

The future of psychotherapy rests in demonstrating the effectiveness of different treatments for different problems. In this chapter, the major types of therapies used to treat psychological disorders are surveyed. Included among these treatments are individual psychotherapies employed by clinical psychologists and psychiatrists in private practice and in institutions, as well as group therapies. Research comparing the effectiveness of different forms of psychotherapies is examined, and the role of medication and other biological therapies is considered. Finally, the important issues of institutionalization, deinstitutionalization, and prevention are discussed.

This review of individual psychotherapies follows the sequence of their historical development. Insight therapies were developed early in the twentieth century, followed by behavior therapies in the 1960s and 1970s, and more recently by cognitive therapies and biological therapies.

ENDURING ISSUES   in Therapies

The underlying assumption behind providing therapy for psychological disorders is the belief that people are capable of changing (stability–change). Throughout this chapter, you will have many opportunities to think about whether people suffering from psychological disorders can change significantly and whether they can change even without therapeutic intervention. In the discussion of biological treatments for psychological disorders, we will again encounter the issue of mind–body. Finally, the enduring issue of diversity–universality will arise again when we discuss the challenges therapists face when treating people from cultures other than their own.

Insight Therapies

Many of the individual psychotherapies used in private practice and in institutions fall under the heading of **insight therapies**. Although the details of various insight therapies differ, their common goal is to give people a better awareness and understanding of their feelings, motivations, and actions in the hope that this will lead to better adjustment. Three major insight therapies are examined in this chapter: psychoanalysis, client-centered therapy, and Gestalt therapy.

■ PSYCHOANALYSIS

Psychoanalysis is designed to bring hidden feelings and motives to conscious awareness so that the person can deal with them more effectively.

In Freudian psychoanalysis, the client is instructed to talk about whatever comes to mind, with as little editing as possible and without inhibiting or controlling thoughts and fantasies. This process is called **free association**. Freud believed that the resulting "stream of consciousness" would provide insight into the person's unconscious mind. During the early stages of psychoanalysis, the analyst remains impassive, mostly silent, and out of the person's sight. In classical psychoanalysis, the client lies on a couch while the neutral analyst sits behind the client. The analyst's silence is a kind of "blank screen" onto which the person eventually projects unconscious thoughts and feelings.

Eventually, clients may test their analyst by talking about desires and fantasies that they have never revealed to anyone else. But the analyst maintains neutrality throughout, showing little of his or her own feelings and personality. When clients discover that their analyst is not shocked or disgusted by their revelations, they are reassured and can then transfer to their analyst feelings they have toward authority figures from their childhood. This process is known as **transference**. When the person feels good about the analyst, *positive transference* is the result.

As people continue to expose their innermost feelings, they begin to feel increasingly vulnerable. They want reassurance and affection, but their analyst remains silent. Their anxiety builds. Threatened by their analyst's silence and by their own thoughts, clients may feel cheated and perhaps may accuse their analyst of being a money grabber. Or they may suspect that their analyst is really disgusted by their disclosures or is laughing about them behind their backs. This *negative transference* is believed to be a crucial step in psychoanalysis, because it presumably reveals negative feelings toward authority figures and resistance to uncovering repressed emotions.

As therapy progresses, the analyst takes a more active role and begins to *interpret* or suggest alternative meanings for clients' feelings, memories, and actions. The goal of interpretation is to help people to gain **insight**—to become aware of what was formerly outside their awareness. As what was unconscious becomes conscious, clients may come to see how their childhood experiences have determined how they currently feel and act. Analysts encourage their clients to confront childhood events and to recall them fully. As these clients relive their childhood traumas, they become able to resolve conflicts they could not resolve in the past. *Working through* old conflicts is believed to provide people with the chance to review and revise the feelings and beliefs that underlie their problems.

The consulting room where Freud met his clients. Note the position of Freud's chair at the head of the couch. In order to encourage free association, the psychoanalyst has to function as a blank screen onto which the client can project his or her feelings. To accomplish this, Freud believed, the psychoanalyst has to stay out of sight of the client.

■ Insight therapies: Goal is to _____

_____

Psychoanalysis

■ Designed to bring hidden feelings and motives to_____ so that the person can _____

_____

■ Free association: _____

_____

■ Insight: _____

■ Neo-Freudian analysts focus more on _____ ; they favor _____ and _____ .

Client-Centered Therapy

■ Client-centered (person-centered) therapy: Treatment for psychological problems based on _____

■ Therapist provides _____

■ Goal is to _____ and to help person become _____

Gestalt Therapy

■ Gestalt therapy: Emphasizes _____, _____

■ Goal is to _____

Only a small percentage of people who seek therapy go into traditional psychoanalysis. As Freud himself recognized, analysis requires great motivation to change and an ability to deal rationally with whatever the analysis uncovers. Moreover, traditional analysis may take five years or longer, with three, sometimes five, sessions a week. Few people can afford this kind of treatment. Fewer still possess the verbal and analytical skills necessary to discuss thoughts and feelings in this detailed way. And many want more immediate help for their problems. Moreover, for those with severe disorders, psychoanalysis is not effective.

Finally, since Freud invented psychoanalysis around the turn of the twentieth century, psychodynamic personality theory has changed significantly, as seen in Chapter 10: Personality. Many of these changes have led to modified psychoanalytic techniques as well as to different therapeutic approaches. For example, although Freud felt that to understand the present, people must understand the past, most neo-Freudians encourage their clients to cope directly with current problems in addition to, or as a way of, addressing unresolved conflicts from the past. Neo-Freudians also favor face-to-face discussions; and most take an active role in analysis from the start by interpreting their client's statements freely and suggesting topics for discussion.

■ CLIENT-CENTERED THERAPY

Carl Rogers, the founder of **client-centered** (or **person-centered**) **therapy**, took pieces of the neo-Freudians' views and revised and rearranged them into a radically different approach to therapy. According to Rogers, the goal of therapy is to help people to become fully functioning, to open them up to all of their experiences and to all of themselves. Such inner awareness is a form of insight, but for Rogers, insight into current feelings was more important than insight into unconscious wishes with roots in the distant past. Rogers called his approach to therapy *client centered* because he placed the responsibility for change on the person with the problem.

Rogers believed that people's defensiveness, rigidity, anxiety, and other signs of discomfort stem from their experiences of *conditional positive regard*. They have learned that love and acceptance are contingent on conforming to what other people want them to be. By contrast, the cardinal rule in person-centered therapy is for the therapist to express *unconditional positive regard*—that is, to show true acceptance of clients no matter what they may say or do. Rogers felt that this was a crucial first step toward getting clients to accept themselves.

Rather than taking an objective approach, Rogerian therapists try to understand things from the clients' point of view. They are also emphatically *nondirective*. They do not suggest reasons why clients feel as they do or how they might better handle a difficult situation. Instead, they try to reflect clients' statements, sometimes asking questions and sometimes hinting at feelings that clients have not put into words.

■ GESTALT THERAPY

Gestalt therapy is largely an outgrowth of the work of Frederick (Fritz) Perls (1893–1970). Perls began his career as a psychoanalyst but later turned vehemently against Freud and psychoanalytic techniques. He felt that "Freud invented the couch because he could not look people in the eye" (Perls, 1969, p. 118). Gestalt therapy emphasizes the here and now and encourages face-to-face confrontations in an effort to help people become more genuine or "real" in their day-to-day interactions. It may be conducted with individuals or with "encounter groups." The therapist is active and directive, and the emphasis is on the *whole* person. (The term *Gestalt* means "whole.") The therapist's role is to "fill in the holes in the personality to make the person whole and complete again" (Perls, 1969, p. 2).

Gestalt therapists use various techniques to try to make people aware of their feelings. For example, they tell people to "own their feelings" by talking in an active, rather than a passive way: "I feel angry when he's around" instead of "He makes me feel angry when he's around." In this way, Gestalt therapists remind clients that they alone are responsible for their feelings and, ultimately, their lives. They may also ask people to speak to a part of themselves that they imagine to be sitting next to them in an empty chair. The objective is to get clients to become more aware of their conflicting inner feelings and, with this insight, to become more genuine.

Although Freud, Rogers, and Perls originated the three major forms of insight therapy, others have developed hundreds of variations on this theme. Most involve a therapist who is far more active and emotionally engaged with clients than traditional psychoanalysts thought fit. These therapists give clients direct guidance and feedback, commenting on what they are told rather than just listening to their clients in a neutral manner.

Another general trend in recent years is toward **short-term psychodynamic therapy**. For most people, this usually means meeting once a week for a fixed period. Insight remains the goal, but the course of treatment is usually limited—for example, to 25 sessions. With the trend toward a time-limited framework, insight therapies have become more problem—or symptom—oriented, with greater focus placed on the person's current life situation and relationships. Although contemporary insight therapists do not discount childhood experiences, they view people as being less at the mercy of early childhood events than did Freud.

Check Your Understanding

1. _____ therapies focus on giving people clearer understanding of their feelings, motives, and actions.

2. _____ _____ is a technique in psychoanalysis whereby the client lets thoughts flow without interruption or inhibition.

3. The process called _____ involves having clients project their feelings of authority figures onto their therapist.

4. Rogerian therapists show that they value and accept their clients by providing them with _____ _____ regard.

5. Indicate whether the following statements are true (T) or false (F):

   a. ___ Psychoanalysis is based on the belief that problems are symptoms of inner conflicts dating back to childhood.

   b. ___ Rogers's interest in the process of therapy was one avenue of exploration that did not prove very fruitful.

   c. ___ In Gestalt therapy, the therapist is active and directive.

   d. ___ Gestalt therapy emphasizes the client's problems in the present.

Behavior Therapies

Behavior therapies sharply contrast with insight-oriented approaches. They concentrate on changing people's *behavior*, rather than on discovering insights into their thoughts and feelings. Behavior therapies are based on the belief (described in Chapter 5: Learning) that all behavior, whether normal or abnormal, is learned. People suffering from hypochondriasis *learn* that they get attention when they are sick; people with paranoid personalities *learn* to be suspicious of others. Behavior therapists also assume that maladaptive behaviors *are* the problem, not symptoms of deeper underlying causes. Thus, the job of the therapist is simply to teach the person new, more satisfying ways of behaving using the basic principles of learning, such as classical conditioning, operant conditioning, and modeling.

■ THERAPIES BASED ON CLASSICAL CONDITIONING

As seen in Chapter 5, *classical conditioning* involves the repeated pairing of a neutral stimulus with one that evokes a certain reflex response. Eventually, the formerly neutral stimulus alone comes to elicit the same response. The approach is one of learned stimulus-response associations. Several variations on classical conditioning have been used to treat psychological problems.

- Behavior therapies teach the person new, _____ using the basic principles of learning

Therapies Based on Classical Conditioning

- Systematic desensitization: _____

_____

- Flooding: _____

_____

- Aversive conditioning: _____

_____

Therapies Based on Operant Conditioning

- Behavior contracting: _____

_____

- Token economy: _____

_____

Therapies Based on Observational Learning

- Observational learning can be used to treat _____ such as

_____

Desensitization and Flooding   **Systematic desensitization**, a method for gradually reducing fear and anxiety, is one of the oldest behavior therapy techniques (Wolpe, 1990). The method works by gradually associating a new response (relaxation) with stimuli that have been causing anxiety. First, the therapist develops a *hierarchy of fears*—a list of situations from the least to the most anxiety provoking. Then the therapist teaches the person how to relax, including mental and physical techniques of relaxation. Once the person has mastered deep relaxation, she or he begins work at the bottom of the hierarchy of fears. People who are deathly afraid of flying, for example, might first simply drive to an airport. When they are able to do this without anxiety, they may move on to walking near a plane on the ground. When they can do that calmly, they may go inside a stationary plane. Eventually, they may take a short flight. Numerous studies show that systematic desensitization helps many people overcome their fears and phobias (Hazel, 2005; McNeil & Zvolensky, 2000; Wang & Chen, 2000).

The technique of *flooding* is a less familiar and more frightening method of desensitization. It involves full-intensity exposure to a feared stimulus for a prolonged period (Pollard, 2000; Wolpe, 1990). For example, someone with a powerful fear of snakes might be forced to handle dozens of snakes, or someone with an overwhelming fear of spiders might be forced to stroke a tarantula and allow it to crawl up an arm. If you think that flooding is an unnecessarily harsh method, remember how debilitating many untreated anxiety disorders can be to a person (see Chapter 12: Psychological Disorders).

Aversive Conditioning   Another classical conditioning technique is **aversive conditioning**, in which pain and discomfort are associated with the behavior that the person wants to unlearn. Aversive conditioning has been used with limited success to treat alcoholism, obesity, smoking, and some psychosexual disorders. For example, the taste and smell of alcohol are sometimes paired with drug-induced nausea and vomiting. Before long, clients feel sick just seeing a bottle of liquor. The long-term effectiveness of this technique has been questioned. When pain and discomfort no longer follow, the undesired behavior may reemerge. In addition, aversive conditioning is a controversial technique because of its unpleasant nature.

■ THERAPIES BASED ON OPERANT CONDITIONING

In *operant conditioning*, a person learns to behave in a certain way because that behavior is reinforced, or rewarded. One therapy based on the principle of reinforcement is called **behavior**

The people in these photographs are overcoming a simple phobia: fear of snakes. After practicing a technique of deep relaxation, people in desensitization therapy work from the bottom of their hierarchy of fears up to the situation that provokes the greatest fear or anxiety. Here, people progress from handling rubber snakes (*top left*) to viewing live snakes through a window (*top center*) and finally to handling live snakes. This procedure can also be conducted vicariously in the therapist's office, where clients combine relaxation techniques with imagining anxiety-provoking scenes.

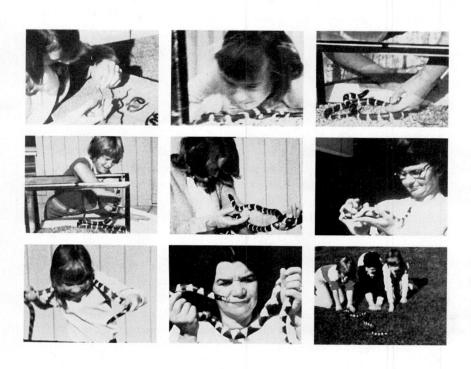

contracting. The therapist and the client agree on behavioral goals and on the reinforcement that the client will receive when he or she reaches those goals. These goals and reinforcements are often written in a contract that binds both the client and the therapist. For instance, a contract to help a person stop smoking might read: "For each day that I smoke fewer than 20 cigarettes, I will earn 30 minutes of time to go bowling. For each day that I exceed the goal, I will lose 30 minutes from the time that I have accumulated." Behavior contracting is often effective when the behavior is specific and goals can be identified.

Another therapy based on operant conditioning is called the **token economy**. Token economies generally are used in schools and hospitals, where controlled conditions are most feasible. People are rewarded with tokens or points for behaviors that are considered appropriate and adaptive. The tokens or points can be exchanged for desired items and privileges. On the ward of a mental hospital, for example, improved grooming habits might earn points that can be used to purchase special foods or weekend passes. Token economies have proved effective in modifying the behavior of people who are resistant to other forms of treatment, such as those with chronic schizophrenia. The positive changes in behavior, however, do not always generalize to everyday life outside the hospital or clinic, where adaptive behavior is not always reinforced and maladaptive behavior is not always punished.

■ THERAPIES BASED ON OBSERVATIONAL LEARNING

The behavior therapies discussed so far rely on classical and operant conditioning principles to change behavior. But, as seen in Chapter 5, human nature can be studied by watching other people. *Observational learning* can also be used to treat problem behavior. In a now classic demonstration, Albert Bandura and his colleagues helped people to overcome a snake phobia by showing them films in which models confronted snakes and gradually moved closer and closer to them (Bandura, Blanchard, & Ritter, 1969).

Check Your Understanding

1. Maria is in an alcoholism treatment program in which she must take a pill every morning. If she drinks alcohol during the day, she immediately feels nauseous. This treatment is an example of
   - **a.** Transference
   - **b.** Flooding
   - **c.** Aversive conditioning
   - **d.** Desensitization

2. Robert is about to start a new job in a tall building, but he is deathly afraid of riding in elevators. He sees a therapist who first teaches him how to relax. Once he has mastered that skill, the therapist asks him to relax while imagining that he is entering the office building. Once he can do that without feeling anxious, the therapist asks him to relax while imagining standing in front of the elevator doors, and so on until Robert can completely relax while imagining riding in elevators. This therapeutic technique is known as
   - **a.** Transference
   - **b.** Desensitization
   - **c.** Behavior contracting
   - **d.** Flooding

Cognitive Therapies

Cognitive therapies are based on the belief that when people can change their distorted ideas about themselves and the world, they also can change their problem behaviors and make their lives more enjoyable. The task facing cognitive therapists is to identify erroneous ways of thinking and to correct them. This focus on learning new ways of thinking shares many similarities with behavior therapies, which also focus on learning. In fact, many professionals consider themselves to be *cognitive-behavior therapists*—therapists who combine both cognitive and behavior therapies. Three popular forms of cognitive therapy are stress-inoculation therapy, rational-emotive therapy, and Aaron Beck's cognitive approach.

■ STRESS-INOCULATION THERAPY

As people go about their lives, they talk to themselves constantly—proposing courses of action, commenting on their performance, expressing wishes, and so on. **Stress-inoculation therapy** makes use of this self-talk to help people cope with stressful situations. The client is taught to suppress any negative thoughts and to replace them with positive, "coping" thoughts. Take a student with exam anxiety who faces every test telling herself, "Oh no, another test. I'm so nervous. I'm sure I won't think calmly enough to remember the answers. If only I'd studied more. If I don't get through this course, I'll never graduate!" This pattern of thought only makes anxiety worse. With the help of a cognitive therapist, the student learns a new pattern of self-talk: "I studied hard for this exam, and I know the material well. I looked at the textbook last night and reviewed my notes. I should be able to do well. If some questions are hard, they won't all be, and even if it's tough, my whole grade doesn't depend on just one test." Then, the person tries out the new strategy in a real situation, ideally one of only moderate stress (e.g., a short quiz). Finally, the person is ready to use the strategy in a more stressful situation, such as a final exam. Stress-inoculation therapy works by turning the client's thought patterns into a kind of vaccine against stress-induced anxiety.

■ RATIONAL-EMOTIVE THERAPY

Another type of cognitive therapy, **rational-emotive therapy (RET)**, developed by Albert Ellis (1913–2007), is based on the view that most people in need of therapy hold a set of irrational and self-defeating beliefs (A. Ellis, 1973, 2001). They believe that they should be competent at *everything*, liked by *everyone, always* treated fairly, quick to find solutions to *every* problem, and so forth. Such beliefs involve absolutes—"musts" and "shoulds"—that allow for no exceptions, making no room for mistakes. When people with such irrational beliefs come up against real-life struggles, they often experience excessive psychological distress. For example, when a college student who believes that he must be liked by everyone is not invited to join a certain fraternity, he may view the rejection as a catastrophe and become deeply depressed rather than just feeling disappointed.

Rational-emotive therapists confront such dysfunctional beliefs vigorously, using a variety of techniques, including persuasion, challenge, commands, and theoretical arguments. Studies have shown that RET often does enable people to reinterpret their negative beliefs and experiences in a more positive light, decreasing the likelihood of becoming depressed (Blatt, Zuroff, Quinlan, & Pilkonis, 1996; Bruder et al., 1997).

■ BECK'S COGNITIVE THERAPY

One of the most important and promising forms of cognitive therapy for treating depression is known simply as **cognitive therapy**. Sometimes, it is referred to as "Beck's cognitive therapy," after Aaron Beck who developed it (Beck, 1967), to avoid confusion with the broader category of cognitive therapies.

Beck believes that depression results from inappropriately self-critical patterns of thought about the self. Such people have unrealistic expectations of themselves, magnify their failures, make sweeping negative generalizations about themselves from little evidence, notice only negative feedback from the outside world, and interpret anything less than total success as failure. This negative chain of thinking may spiral downward from small setbacks, until the person concludes that he or she is worthless. According to Beck, the downward spiral of negative, distorted thoughts is at the heart of depression.

Beck's assumptions about the cause of depression are very similar to those underlying RET, but the style of treatment differs considerably. Cognitive therapists are much less challenging and confrontational than rational-emotive therapists. Instead, they try to help clients examine each dysfunctional thought in a supportive, but objectively scientific manner ("Are you *sure* your whole life will be totally ruined if you break up with Frank? What is your evidence for that? Didn't you once tell me how happy you were *before* you met him?"). As with RET, Beck's cognitive therapy tries to lead the person to more realistic and flexible ways of thinking.

Check Your Understanding

1. Larry has difficulty following his boss's directions. Whenever his boss asks him to do something, Larry panics. Larry enters a stress-inoculation program. Which is most likely to be the first step in this program?

   a. Have Larry volunteer to do a task for his boss.

   b. Show Larry a film in which employees are asked to do tasks and they perform well.

   c. Ask Larry what he says to himself when his boss asks him to perform a task.

   d. Ask Larry how he felt when he was a child and his mother asked him to do something.

2. Sarah rushes a sorority but is not invited to join. She has great difficulty accepting this fact and, consequently, becomes deeply depressed. She sees a therapist who vigorously challenges and confronts her in an effort to show her that her depression comes from an irrational, self-defeating belief that she must be liked and accepted by everyone. This therapist is most likely engaging in

   a. Rational-emotive therapy

   b. Stress-inoculation therapy

   c. Flooding

   d. Desensitization therapy

Group Therapies

Some therapists believe that treating several people simultaneously is preferable to treating each alone. Such **group therapy** allows the client and the therapist to see how the person acts around others. If a person is painfully anxious and tongue-tied, chronically self-critical, or hostile and aggressive, these tendencies will show up quickly in a group.

Group therapies have other advantages, too. A good group offers social support, a feeling that one is not the only person in the world with problems. Group members can also help one another learn useful new behaviors (such as how to express feelings and how to disagree without antagonizing others). Interactions in a group can lead people toward insights into their own behavior, such as why they are so defensive or why they feel compelled to complain constantly. Finally, because group therapy consists of several clients "sharing" a therapist, it is less expensive than individual therapy.

There are many kinds of group therapy. Some groups follow the general outlines of the therapies already mentioned. Others are oriented toward a very specific goal, such as stopping smoking, drinking, or overeating. Some have a single, but more open-ended goal—for example, a happier family or romantic relationship.

- Group therapy: Clients meet regularly with others to _____

- Offer a circle of _____, shared insights into _____, and the opportunity to obtain _____

- Family therapy: Goal is to _____, _____, _____ and _____

- Couple therapy: Goal is to improve the patterns of _____ and _____

Carl Rogers (*far right*) leading a group therapy session. Rogers is the founder of client-centered therapy.

Family therapy is one form of group therapy. Family therapists believe that if one person in the family is having problems, it is often a signal that the entire family needs assistance. Family therapists do not try to reshape the personalities of family members. Instead, the primary goals of family therapy are improving family communication, encouraging family members to become more empathetic, getting them to share responsibilities, and reducing conflict within the family. To achieve these goals, all family members must believe that they will benefit from changes in their behavior.

Couple therapy is another form of group therapy designed to assist partners who are having difficulties with their relationship. In the past, this therapy was generally called *marital therapy*, but the term "couple therapy" is considered more appropriate today because it captures the broad range of partners who may seek help. Most couple therapists concentrate on improving patterns of communication and mutual expectations. For example, each member of the couple might be taught to share inner feelings and to listen to and understand the partner's feelings before responding to them. In other cases, behavioral techniques might be used to help a couple to develop a schedule for exchanging specific caring actions, such as helping with chores around the house, making time to share a special meal together, or remembering special occasions with a gift or card.

Because an estimated 40 million Americans suffer some kind of psychological problem and because the cost of individual treatment can be so high, more and more people faced with life crises are turning to low-cost self-help groups. Most groups are small, local gatherings of people who share a common problem or predicament and who provide mutual assistance. Alcoholics Anonymous is perhaps the best-known self-help group, but self-help groups are available for virtually every life problem.

Do these self-help groups work? In many cases, they do (Galanter, Hayden, Castañeda, & Franco, 2005; Kurtz, 2004; McKellar, Stewart, & Humphreys, 2003; Ouimette et al., 2001). Such groups also help to prevent more serious psychological disorders by reaching out to people who are near the limits of their ability to cope with stress. The social support they offer is particularly important in an age when divorce, geographic mobility, and other factors have reduced the ability of the family to comfort people.

Check Your Understanding

1. Which of the following is an advantage of group therapy?

   a. The client has the experience of interacting with other people in a therapeutic setting.

   b. It often reveals a client's problems more quickly than individual therapy.

   c. It can be cheaper than individual therapy.

   d. All of the above.

2. You are talking to a clinical psychologist who explains that, in her view, it is a mistake to try to treat a client's problems in a vacuum. Quite often, well-adjusted members of a family can help the client cope more effectively. Other times, the client's progress is slowed because of other people in the family. She is most likely a

   a. Self-help therapist   **c.** Proximity therapist

   b. Family therapist   **d.** Social-attribution therapist

3. Imagine that you believe most problems between partners arise because the partners do not share their inner feelings and do not truly listen to and try to understand each other. You meet with them together and teach them to spend more time listening to the other person and trying to understand what the other person is really saying. Your beliefs are closest to which of the following kinds of therapists?

   a. Gestalt therapists   **c.** Family therapists

   b. Rational-emotive therapists   **d.** Couple therapists

Effectiveness of Psychotherapy

As noted, some psychotherapies are generally effective, but how much better are they than no treatment at all? Researchers have found that two thirds of the people who receive formal therapy improve, compared to one third who improve without receiving any formal treatment at all. Because many people who do not receive formal therapy nonetheless get therapeutic help from friends, clergy, physicians, and teachers, the recovery rate for people who receive *no* therapeutic support at all is probably even less than one third.

One very extensive study designed to evaluate the effectiveness of psychotherapy was reported by *Consumer Reports*. Largely under the direction of psychologist Martin E. P. Seligman (1995), this investigation surveyed 180,000 *Consumer Reports* subscribers on everything from automobiles to mental health. Approximately 7,000 people from the total sample responded to the mental health section of the questionnaire that assessed satisfaction and improvement in people who had received psychotherapy, with the following results:

First, the vast majority of respondents reported significant overall improvement after therapy. Second, there was no difference in the overall improvement score among people who had received therapy alone and those who had combined psychotherapy with medication. Third, no differences were found between the various forms of psychotherapy. Fourth, no differences in effectiveness were indicated among psychologists, psychiatrists, and social workers, although marriage counselors were seen as less effective. And fifth, people who had received long-term therapy reported more improvement than those who had received short-term therapy. This last result, one of the most striking findings of the study, is illustrated in Figure 13–1.

The *Consumer Reports* study lacked the scientific rigor of more traditional investigations designed to assess psychotherapeutic efficacy. For example, it did not use a control group to assess change in people who did not receive therapy. Moreover, it relied entirely on self-report by those who chose to share information on their mental health. Nevertheless, it provides broad support for the idea that psychotherapy does work.

- Formal psychotherapy helps approximately _____ of the people treated compared to at most _____ of those who are not treated.
- There is _____ overall difference in the effectiveness of different therapies.
- Each kind of therapy works better for some problems than for others
  - Insight therapy: Best suited to people seeking _____, _____ or _____
  - Behavior therapy: Most appropriate for the treatment of _____ or _____ behavioral problems
  - Family therapy: More effective than individual counseling for the treatment of _____
  - Cognitive therapies: Most effective for the treatment of _____ and _____

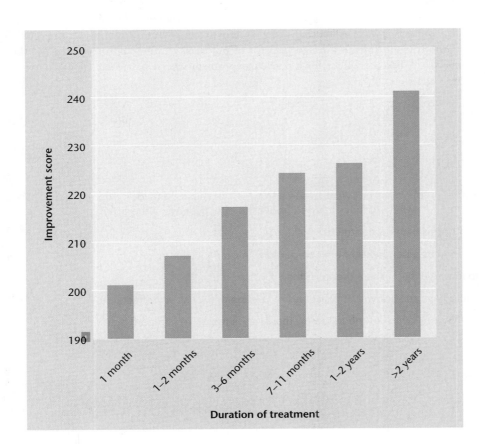

FIGURE 13–1
Duration of therapy and improvement.
One of the most dramatic results of the *Consumer Reports* (1995) study on the effectiveness of psychotherapy was the strong relationship between reported improvement and the duration of therapy.

Source: Adapted from "The effectiveness of psychotherapy: The *Consumer Reports* study," by M. E. P. Seligman, 1995. *American Psychologist, 50,* 965–974. © 1995 by the American Psychological Association. Adapted with permission.

As seen earlier, the various forms of psychotherapy are based on very different views about what causes mental disorders and, at least on the surface, these forms approach the treatment of mental disorders in different ways. Why, then, is there no difference in their effectiveness? To answer this question, some psychologists have focused their attention on what the various forms of psychotherapy have in common, rather than emphasizing their differences (Carter 2006; Roberts, Kewman, Mercer, & Hovell, 1993):

1. All forms of psychotherapy provide people with an *explanation for their problems*. Often, along with this explanation, a new perspective comes that provides clients with specific actions to help them cope more effectively.
2. Most forms of psychotherapy offer people *hope*. Because most people who seek therapy have low self-esteem and feel demoralized and depressed, hope and the expectation for improvement increase their feelings of self-worth.
3. All major types of psychotherapy engage the client in a *therapeutic alliance* with a therapist. Although their therapeutic approaches may differ, effective therapists are warm, empathetic, and caring people who understand the importance of establishing a strong emotional bond with their clients that is built on mutual respect and understanding (Norcross, 2002; Wampold, 2001).

Together, these nonspecific factors common to all forms of psychotherapy appear, at least in part, to explain why most people who receive some form of therapy show benefits, as compared with those who receive no therapeutic help at all.

Still, some kinds of psychotherapy seem to be particularly appropriate for certain people and problems. Insight therapy, for example, seems to be best suited to people seeking profound self-understanding, relief of inner conflict and anxiety, or better relationships with others. Behavior therapy is apparently most appropriate for treating specific anxieties or other well-defined behavioral problems, such as sexual dysfunctions. Family therapy is generally more effective than individual counseling for the treatment of drug abuse. Cognitive therapies have been shown to be effective treatments for depression and seem to be promising treatments for anxiety disorders as well. The trend among the majority of psychotherapists today is toward **eclecticism**—that is, moving away from commitment to a single form of therapy and toward a broad package of potential treatments from which the therapist selects the best treatment for a particular problem with a particular client (Carter, 2006; Slife & Reber, 2001).

Check Your Understanding

1. Your friend is experiencing anxiety attacks, but does not want to see a therapist because "they don't do any good." Which of the following replies most accurately reflects what you have learned about the effectiveness of therapy?

   a. "You're right. Psychotherapy is no better than no treatment at all."

   b. "Actually, even just initiating therapy has a beneficial effect compared with doing nothing."

   c. "You're at least twice as likely to improve if you see a therapist than if you don't."

   d. "Therapy could help you, but you'd have to stick with it for at least a year before it has any effect."

2. John is suffering from moderate depression. Which of the following therapies is most likely to help him?

   a. Insight therapy

   b. Cognitive therapy

   c. Behavioral contracting

   d. Group therapy

TABLE 13–1   Major Types of Psychoactive Medications

THERAPEUTIC USE	CHEMICAL STRUCTURE*	TRADE NAME*
Antipsychotics	Phenothiazines	Thorazine, Therazine, Olanzapine, Risperdal, Clozapine
Antidepressants	Tricyclics	Elavil
	MAO inhibitors	Nardil
	SSRIs	Paxil, Prozac, Zoloft
	SNRI	Effexor
Psychostimulants	Amphetamines	Dexedrine
	Other	Ritalin, Adderall
Antiseizure	Carbamazepine	Tegretol
Antianxiety	Benzodiazepines	Valium
Sedatives	Barbiturates	
Antipanic	Tricyclics	Tofranil
Antiobsessional	Tricyclics	Anafranil

*The chemical structures and especially the trade names listed in this table are representative examples, rather than an exhaustive list, of the many kinds of medications available for the specific therapeutic use.

Source: Kierman et al., 1994 (adapted and updated).

Biological Treatments

Biological treatments—a group of approaches including medication, electroconvulsive therapy, and psychosurgery—may be used to treat psychological disorders in addition to, or instead of, psychotherapy. Traditionally, the only mental health professionals licensed to offer biological treatments were psychiatrists, who are physicians, but some states now permit specially trained psychologists to prescribe drugs. Therapists without such training often work with physicians who prescribe medication for their clients. In many cases in which biological treatments are used, psychotherapy is also recommended.

■ DRUG THERAPIES

Medication is used frequently and effectively to treat a number of different psychological problems (Table 13–1). Two major reasons for the widespread use of drug therapies today are the development of several very effective psychoactive medications and the fact that drug therapies can cost much less than psychotherapy.

Antipsychotic Drugs   Before the mid-1950s, drugs were not widely used to treat psychological disorders because the only available sedatives induced sleep as well as calm. Then, the major tranquilizers *reserpine* and the *phenothiazines* were introduced. In addition to alleviating anxiety and aggression, both drugs reduce psychotic symptoms, such as hallucinations and delusions, and, for that reason, they are called **antipsychotic drugs**.

Antidepressant Drugs   Until the end of the 1980s, there were only two main types of antidepressant drugs (both named for their chemical properties): *monoamine oxidase inhibitors (MAO inhibitors)* and *tricyclics*. Both drugs work by increasing the concentration of the neurotransmitters serotonin and norepinephrine in the brain. Both are effective for most people with serious depression, but both produce a number of serious and troublesome side effects.

In 1988, Prozac (fluoxetine) came onto the market. This drug works by reducing the uptake of serotonin in the nervous system, thus increasing the amount of serotonin active in

■ Biological treatments: Used in conjunction with, or instead of, _____

Drug Therapies

■ The most common and often effective form of biological therapy; costs less than _____

■ The major types of psychoactive medications include:

  ■ _____

  ■ _____

  ■ _____

  ■ _____

  ■ _____

■ Some medications produce _____ and are _____.

ENDURING ISSUES   MIND/BODY

Antipsychotic Drugs

Antipsychotic medications sometimes have dramatic effects. People who take them can go from being perpetually frightened, angry, confused, and plagued by auditory and visual hallucinations to being totally free of such symptoms. However, these drugs only alleviate symptoms while the person is taking the drug. Therefore, most people must take antipsychotics for years—perhaps for the rest of their lives. In turn, this can lead to discomfort because antipsychotic drugs can also have numerous undesirable side effects, including blurred vision, weight gain, constipation, and temporary neurological impairments such as muscular rigidity or tremors. Another problem is that antipsychotics are of little value in treating the problems of social adjustment that people with schizophrenia face outside an institutional setting. Because many discharged people fail to take their medications, relapse is common. However, when drug therapy is effectively combined with psychotherapy, the relapse rate can be reduced. The fact that a combination of drugs and psychotherapy often works better than either approach used alone underscores the highly complex relationship between mind and body.

the brain at any given moment (Figure 13–2). For this reason, Prozac is part of a group of psychoactive drugs known as *selective serotonin reuptake inhibitors (SSRIs)*. (See Chapter 2: The Biological Basis of Behavior.) Today, several second-generation SSRIs are available for the treatment of depression, including Paxil (paroxetine), Zoloft (sertraline), and Effexor (venlafaxine HCl). For many patients, correcting the imbalance in these chemicals in the brain reduces their symptoms of depression and relieves the associated symptoms of anxiety. Moreover, because these drugs have fewer side effects than do MAO inhibitors or tricyclics, they have been heralded in the popular media as "wonder drugs" for the treatment of depression.

Today, antidepressant drugs are not only used to treat depression, but they also have shown promise in treating generalized anxiety disorder, panic disorder, obsessive-compulsive disorder, social phobia, and posttraumatic stress disorder. Antidepressant drugs such as the SSRIs do not work for everyone, however. At least one fourth of the patients with major depressive

FIGURE **13–2**
How do the SSRIs work?
Antidepressants such as Prozac, Paxil, and Zoloft belong to a class of drugs called SSRIs (selective serotonin reuptake inhibitors). These drugs reduce the symptoms of depression by blocking the reabsorption (or reuptake) of serotonin in the synaptic space between neurons. The increased availability of serotonin to bind to receptor sites on the receiving neuron is believed to be responsible for the ability of these drugs to relieve the symptoms of depression.

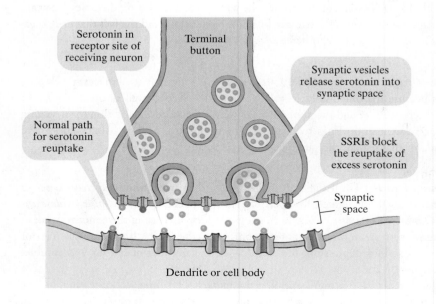

Serotonin in receptor site of receiving neuron

Terminal button

Synaptic vesicles release serotonin into synaptic space

Normal path for serotonin reuptake

SSRIs block the reuptake of excess serotonin

Synaptic space

Dendrite or cell body

disorders do not respond to antidepressant drugs. Moreover, for some patients, these drugs produce unpleasant side effects, including nausea, insomnia, headaches, anxiety, and impaired sexual functioning. They can also cause severe withdrawal symptoms in patients who abruptly stop taking them.

Lithium   Bipolar disorder, or manic depression, is frequently treated with lithium carbonate. Lithium is not a drug, but a naturally occurring salt that helps level out the wild and unpredictable mood swings of manic depression. It is effective in treating bipolar disorder in approximately 75% of cases. It is not known exactly how lithium works, but recent studies indicate that it may act to stabilize the levels of specific neurotransmitters or alter the receptivity of specific synapses (G. Chen & Manji, 2006). Unfortunately, some people with bipolar disorder stop taking lithium when their symptoms improve—against the advice of their physicians—leading to a relatively high relapse rate.

Other Medications   Several other medications can be used to alleviate the symptoms of various psychological problems (Table 13–1). *Psychostimulants*, for example, heighten alertness and arousal. Some psychostimulants, such as Ritalin, are commonly used to treat children with attention-deficit hyperactivity disorder. In these cases, the drugs have a calming, rather than a stimulating effect. As with the antidepressants, some professionals worry that psychostimulants are being overused, especially with young children. *Antianxiety medications*, such as Valium, are commonly prescribed as well. Quickly producing a sense of calm and mild euphoria, these medications are often used to reduce general tension and stress. Because they are potentially addictive, however, they must be used with caution. Another class of drugs, the *sedatives*, produce both calm and drowsiness, and they are used to treat agitation or to induce sleep. These drugs, too, can become addictive.

■ ELECTROCONVULSIVE THERAPY

Electroconvulsive therapy (ECT) is most often used for cases of prolonged and severe depression that do not respond to other forms of treatment. The technique involves briefly passing a mild electric current through one or both hemispheres of the brain. No one knows exactly why ECT works, but its effectiveness has been clearly demonstrated. In addition, the fatality rate for ECT is markedly lower than for people taking antidepressant drugs (Henry, Alexander, & Sener, 1995). Still, ECT has many critics and its use remains controversial. Side effects include brief confusion, disorientation, and memory impairment, though research suggests that unilateral ECT produces fewer side effects and is only slightly less effective than the traditional method. In view of the side effects, ECT is usually considered a "last-resort" treatment after all other methods have failed.

■ PSYCHOSURGERY

Psychosurgery refers to brain surgery performed to change a person's behavior and emotional state. This is a drastic step, especially because the effects of psychosurgery are difficult to predict. In a *prefrontal lobotomy*, the frontal lobes of the brain are severed from the deeper centers beneath them. The assumption is that in extremely disturbed people, the frontal lobes intensify emotional impulses from the lower brain centers (chiefly, the thalamus and hypothalamus). Unfortunately, lobotomies can work with one person and fail completely with another—possibly producing permanent, undesirable side effects, such as the inability to inhibit impulses or a near-total absence of feeling.

Prefrontal lobotomies are rarely performed today. In fact, very few psychosurgical procedures are done, except as desperate attempts to control such conditions as intractable psychoses, Parkinson's disease, epilepsy that does not respond to other treatments, severe obsessive-compulsive disorders, and pain in a terminal illness.

Electroconvulsive Therapy

■ Electroconvulsive therapy (ECT) involves _____

■ As a last resort, ECT is used to treat _____

Psychosurgery

■ Psychosurgery is _____ directed at changing one's _____ or _____; it has unpredictable, potentially severe _____

Check Your Understanding

1. Bipolar disorder (also called manic-depressive illness) is often treated with _____.

2. Which of the following is true of psychosurgery?

   a. It never produces undesirable side effects.

   b. It is useless in controlling pain.

   c. It is widely used today.

   d. Its effects are hard to predict.

3. Although it is considered effective in treating depression, electroconvulsive therapy (ECT) is considered a treatment of last resort because of its potential negative side effects. Is this statement true (T) or false (F)?

4. Brian is suffering from schizophrenia. Which of the following biological treatments is most likely to be effective in reducing or eliminating his symptoms?

   a. Any drug, such as a phenothiazine, that blocks the brain's receptors for dopamine

   b. Selective serotonin reuptake inhibitors (SSRIs), such as Paxil and Prozac

   c. Lithium carbonate

   d. Electroconvulsive therapy

Institutionalization and Its Alternatives

For persons with severe mental illness, hospitalization has been the treatment of choice in the United States for the past 150 years. Many different kinds of hospitals offer such care. When most people think of "mental hospitals," however, large, state-run institutions come to mind. These public hospitals, many with beds for thousands of patients, were often built in rural areas in the nineteenth century. The idea was that a country setting would calm patients and help restore their mental health. Despite the good intentions behind the establishment of these hospitals, they generally have not provided adequate care or therapy for their residents. Perpetually underfunded and understaffed, state hospitals often have been little more than warehouses for victims of serious mental illness who were unwanted by their families. Except for new arrivals who often were treated intensively in the hope of quickly discharging them, patients received little therapy besides drugs; and most spent their days watching television or staring into space. Under these conditions, many patients became completely apathetic and accepted a permanent "sick role."

The development of effective drug therapies starting in the 1950s led to a number of changes in state hospitals. First, people who were agitated could now be sedated with drugs. Although the drugs often produced lethargy, this was considered an improvement over the use of physical restraints. The second major, and more lasting, result of the new drug therapies was the widespread release of people who had severe psychological disorders back into the community—a policy called **deinstitutionalization**. The full effects of deinstitutionalization are unknown, but it is obvious that deinstitutionalization, though a worthy ideal, has had dire effects on patients and society. Many released patients are unable to obtain adequate follow-up care or housing and are incapable of meeting their own needs. Consequently, every major U.S. city now has a population of mentally ill men and women living in makeshift shelters or sleeping in doorways, bus stations, parks, and other public spaces. Surveys indicate that nearly 40% of homeless people are mentally ill (Burt et al., 1999). Discharged people often find poorly funded community mental health centers—or none at all. Without supervision, they often stop taking the drugs that made their release possible in the first place; consequently, their psychotic symptoms return. The patients are further burdened by the social stigma of mental illness, which may be the largest single obstacle to their rehabilitation.

Lacking adequate funding and staff, mental hospitals frequently were crowded and failing in their ability to provide adequate treatment to their residents.

Beginning in the 1950s and 1960s, the policy of deinstitutionalization led to the release of many individuals, who, without proper follow-up care, ended up living on the streets. Although not all homeless people are mentally ill, estimates suggest that nearly 40% of homeless persons suffer from some type of mental disorder.

Suicide hotlines and other crisis intervention programs are secondary prevention measures designed to serve individuals and groups at high risk for mental disorders.

This situation is tragic not only for the mentally ill homeless, who are easy prey for criminals, but for society as well. The public finds their constant presence unpleasant; and compassion for them is waning to the point that public officials feel pressured to "get them off the street." Most mental health professionals now agree that many chronically ill patients should not be released to live "in the community" without better planning, more funding, more community support, and readily available short-term rehospitalization for those who require it.

Are there any alternatives to deinstitutionalization other than rehospitalizing patients? For several decades, Charles Kiesler (1934–2002) argued vigorously for forms of treatment that avoid hospitalization altogether (Kiesler & Simpkins, 1993). Kiesler (1982b) examined 10 controlled studies in which seriously disturbed people were randomly assigned either to hospitals or to an alternative program. The alternative programs took many forms: training patients living at home to cope with daily activities; assigning patients to a small, homelike facility in which staff and residents share responsibility for residential life; placing patients in a hostel and offering therapy and crisis intervention; providing family-crisis therapy and day care treatment; providing visits from public-health nurses combined with medication; and offering intensive outpatient counseling combined with medication. All these alternatives involved daily professional contact and skillful preparation of the community to receive the patients. Even though the hospitals to which some people in these studies were assigned provided very good patient care—probably substantially above average for institutions in the United States—9 of the 10 studies found that the outcome was more positive for alternative treatments than for the more expensive hospitalization. Moreover, the people who received alternative care were less likely to undergo hospitalization later, thus suggesting that hospitalizing those with mental illness is a self-perpetuating process. Many such people "could be treated in alternative settings more effectively and less expensively," Kiesler concluded (1982a, p. 358).

Yet another approach to managing mental illness is trying to prevent it in the first place. This requires finding and eliminating the conditions that cause or contribute to mental disorders and substituting conditions that foster well-being. Prevention takes three forms: primary, secondary, and tertiary.

- Institutionalization refers to _____ _____

- Deinstitutionalization refers to _____ _____

- In practice, deinstitutionalization has failed because:

    - _____ and _____ often are unavailable or underfunded.

    - Persons are often incapable of _____

    - Without supervision, many _____

    - The _____ related to mental illness is a major obstacle to rehabilitation.

Prevention

- Primary prevention involves improving the social environment through _____, _____, and _____.

- Secondary prevention involves _____ and _____.

- Tertiary prevention involves helping hospitalized patients _____ and _____

Primary prevention refers to efforts to improve the overall environment so that new cases of mental disorders do not develop. Family planning and genetic counseling are two examples of primary prevention programs. Other primary prevention programs aim at increasing personal and social competencies in a wide variety of groups. For example, there are programs designed to help mothers encourage problem-solving skills in their children and programs to enhance competence and adjustment among elderly persons. Current campaigns to educate young people about drugs, alcohol abuse, violence, and date rape are other examples of primary prevention.

Secondary prevention involves identifying groups at high risk for mental disorders—for example, abused children, people who have recently divorced, those who have been laid off from their jobs, and victims of terrorist incidents. The main thrust of secondary prevention is *intervention* with such high-risk groups—that is, detecting maladaptive behavior early and treating it promptly. One form of intervention is *crisis intervention*, which includes such programs as suicide hotlines. Another is the establishment of short-term crisis facilities at which a therapist can provide face-to-face counseling and support, although so far there is no evidence that such "psychological first aid" is effective (McNally, Bryant, & Ehlers, 2003).

The main objective of **tertiary prevention** is to help people adjust to community life after release from a mental hospital. For example, hospitals often grant passes to encourage people to leave the institution for short periods before their release. Other tertiary prevention measures are halfway houses, where people find support and skills training during the period of transition between hospitalization and full integration into the community, as well as nighttime and outpatient programs that provide supportive therapy while people live at home and hold down full-time jobs. Tertiary prevention also includes efforts to educate the community that the person will reenter.

Preventing behavior disorders has been the ideal of the mental health community since at least 1970, when the final report of the Joint Commission on Mental Health of Children called for a new focus on prevention in mental health work. Ironically, because preventive programs usually are long range and indirect, they are often the first mental health programs to be eliminated in times of economic hardship. Such cuts, predicated on cost effectiveness, exemplify the old adage about being penny wise and pound foolish.

Check Your Understanding

1. Harold argues that institutionalizing people who suffer from serious mental illnesses is not only the most effective way to treat them, but also the least expensive. On the basis of what you have learned in this chapter, which of the following would be the most appropriate reply?

a. "Mental institutions are indeed the least expensive form of treatment, but they also are the least effective treatment option."

b. "You're right. Mental institutions are both the least expensive form of treatment and the most effective treatment option."

c. "Actually, mental institutions not only are the most expensive form of treatment, they are also the least effective treatment option."

d. "Actually, mental institutions are the most expensive form of treatment, but they are the most effective treatment option."

2. Your community is especially aware of the importance of preventing psychological disorders. So far, financial support has been provided for family planning, genetic counseling, increasing competence among the elderly, and educational programs aimed at reducing the use of drugs and acts of violence. From this description, it is clear that your community is putting its emphasis on

a. Primary prevention efforts

b. Secondary prevention efforts

c. Tertiary prevention efforts

Client Diversity and Treatment

A major topic of this book is human *diversity*, the wide range of differences that exist in human beings. Although everyone shares certain basic human characteristics as individuals and as groups, each of us has our own distinctive traits and ways of responding to the world. Do such human differences affect the treatment of psychological problems? Two areas that researchers have explored to answer this question are gender differences and cultural differences.

As shown in Chapter 12: Psychological Disorders, there are significant gender differences in the prevalence of many psychological disorders. If gender differences exist in the prevalence of psychological disorders, are there gender differences in their treatment as well? In most respects, the treatment given to women is the same as that given to men, a fact that has become somewhat controversial. However, because most therapists are male and most vocational and rehabilitation programs are male oriented, some critics of "equal treatment" have claimed that women in therapy are often encouraged to adopt traditional, male-oriented views of what is "normal" or "appropriate." For instance, some male therapists urge women to adapt or conform passively to their surroundings. Not all male therapists are sensitive to the fact that much of the stress that women experience comes from trying to cope with a world in which they are not treated equally (Brown & Ballou, 1992). For these reasons, there has been an increase recently in the number of "feminist therapists." These therapists help their female clients to become aware of the extent to which their problems derive from external controls and inappropriate sex roles; to become more conscious of and attentive to their own needs and goals; and to develop a sense of pride in their womanhood, rather than passively accepting or identifying with the status quo. In addition, the American Psychological Association (1978) has established a detailed set of guidelines regarding treatment of women in psychotherapy that are intended, in part, to ensure that women receive treatment that is not tied to traditional ideas about appropriate behavior for the sexes.

Misunderstanding can also arise in therapy when a client and a therapist come from different cultural backgrounds or belong to different racial or ethnic groups.

Because most traditional therapeutic programs are male oriented, many female clients seek out female therapists who are more sensitive to their situation.

ENDURING ISSUES   DIVERSITY/UNIVERSALITY

On Being Culture Bound

Imagine the following scenario: A Native American client being interviewed by a psychologist stares at the floor. He answers questions politely, but during the entire consultation, he looks away continually, never meeting the doctor's eye. This body language might lead the psychologist to suppose that the man is depressed or has low self-esteem—unless, that is, the psychologist knows that in the person's culture, avoiding eye contact is a sign of respect.

This example shows how culture-bound are our ideas of what constitutes normal behavior. When psychotherapist and client come from different cultures, misunderstandings of speech, body language, and customs are almost inevitable. Even when client and therapist are of the same nationality and speak the same language, but belong to different racial and ethnic groups, there can be striking differences. Some African American people, for example, are wary of confiding in a Caucasian therapist—so much so that their wariness is sometimes mistaken for paranoia. In addition, many African American patients perceive African American therapists as being more understanding and accepting of their problems than Caucasian therapists are (Thompson & Alexander, 2006). For this reason, many African American people will seek out African American therapists, a tendency that is becoming more common as larger numbers of African American middle-class people enter therapy (Diala et al., 2000; Snowden & Yamada, 2005).

- Gender differences
  - Generally, _____ given to women is the same as that given to men.
  - The American Psychological Association provides guidelines to ensure that _____

- Cultural differences
  - Having _____ or belonging to _____ can lead to misunderstandings in therapy.
  - Treatment and prevention must be tailored to the _____ and _____ of the person's _____

One of the challenges for U.S. therapists in recent years has been to treat immigrants, many of whom have fled such horrifying circumstances at home that they arrive in the United States exhibiting posttraumatic stress disorder. These refugees must overcome not only the effects of past trauma but also the new stresses of settling in a strange country, which often include separation from their families, ignorance of the English language, and inability to practice their traditional occupations. Therapists in such circumstances must learn something of their clients' culture. Often, therapists must conduct interviews through an interpreter—hardly an ideal circumstance for therapy.

Finally, therapists need to recognize that some disorders afflicting people from other cultures may not exist in Western culture at all. For example, as seen in Chapter 12, *taijin kyofusho* (roughly translated as "fear of people") involves a morbid fear that one's body or actions may be offensive to others. Because this disorder is rarely seen outside Japan, American therapists require specialized training to recognize it.

Ultimately, the best solution to the difficulties of serving a multicultural population is to train therapists of many different backgrounds so that members of ethnic, cultural, and racial groups can choose therapists of their own group when they wish to do so. Research has shown that psychotherapy is more likely to be effective when the client and the therapist share a similar cultural background (Gibson & Mitchell, 2003; Pedersen & Carey, 2003). Similarly, efforts aimed at preventing mental illness in society must be sensitive to cultural diversity. Many intervention programs have proved unsuccessful because they failed to take into account the appropriate cultural norms and values of the group being served. To be effective, treatment and prevention approaches must reflect the beliefs and cultural practices of the person's ethnic group.

Check Your Understanding

1. An immigrant from the Middle East who speaks very little English seeks assistance from an American psychotherapist who only speaks English. Which of the following problems may interfere with the therapeutic process?

    a. Misunderstanding each other's body language

    b. The therapist's lack of familiarity with the cultural norms and values of the immigrant's home country

    c. Need for an interpreter

    d. All of the above

2. Preventing and treating psychological disorders is especially challenging in a society such as ours, which has a culturally diverse population. Which of the following is *not* a constructive way of dealing with this challenge?

    a. Therapists need to recognize that some disorders afflicting people from other cultures may not exist in Western culture at all.

    b. Therapists from many different backgrounds need to receive training so that people who wish to do so can be treated by a therapist who shares their cultural background.

    c. Clients should be treated by therapists who represent the dominant culture so that they can best adapt to their new environment.

    d. Intervention programs need to take into account the cultural norms and values of the group being served.

Chapter Review  www.psychologythecore.com

Psychotherapy refers to the use of psychological techniques to treat psychological disorders. Psychotherapy takes many forms—literally hundreds of variations practiced by several different types of mental health professionals.

Insight Therapies

The various **insight therapies** share the common goal of providing people with better awareness and understanding of their feelings, motivations, and actions to foster better adjustment. Among these are psychoanalysis, client-centered therapy, and Gestalt therapy.

Many African American clients are more comfortable dealing with a therapist of the same racial background.

Psychoanalysis is based on the belief that psychological problems stem from feelings and conflicts repressed during childhood. These repressed feelings can be revealed through **free association**, a process in which the client discloses whatever thoughts or fantasies come to mind without inhibition. As therapy progresses, clients transfer to their analyst feelings they have toward authority figures from their childhood, a process known as **transference;** the analyst also takes a more active, interpretive role. The goal of interpretation is to help people to gain **insight**—to become aware of what was formerly outside their awareness. Only a small percentage of people who seek therapy go into traditional psychoanalysis. Most neo-Freudians encourage their clients to cope directly with current problems in addition to, or as a way of, addressing unresolved conflicts from the past. Neo-Freudians also favor face-to-face discussions, and most take an active role in analysis from the start by interpreting their client's statements freely and suggesting topics for discussion.

Carl Rogers believed treatment for psychological problems should be based on the client's view of the world rather than that of the therapist. The therapist's most important task in this approach, called **client-centered,** or **person-centered, therapy,** is to provide unconditional positive regard for clients so they will become fully functioning, open to all of their experiences and to all of themselves.

Gestalt therapy helps people to become more aware of their conflicting inner feelings and, with this insight, to become more genuine in their interactions. Unlike Freud, who sat quietly out of sight while his clients dredged up memories from the past, the Gestalt therapist confronts the person, emphasizes the present, and focuses on the *whole* person.

Contemporary insight therapists are more actively involved than traditional psychoanalysts, offering clients direct guidance and feedback. An especially significant development is the trend toward **short-term psychodynamic therapy**, in which the course of treatment is time limited and oriented toward current life situations and relationships, rather than childhood traumas.

Behavior Therapies

Behavior therapies are based on the belief that all behavior is learned and therefore people can be taught more satisfying ways of behaving. The job of the therapist is to teach the person new, more satisfying ways of behaving using the basic principles of learning.

One therapeutic application of classical conditioning is **systematic desensitization**, in which people learn to remain in a deeply relaxed state while confronting feared situations. *Flooding,* which exposes phobic people to feared situations at full intensity for a prolonged period, is a harsh but often effective method of desensitization. In **aversive conditioning**, the goal is to eliminate undesirable behavior by associating it with pain and discomfort.

Therapies based on operant conditioning encourage or discourage behaviors by reinforcing or punishing them. In **behavior contracting**, client and therapist agree on certain behavioral goals and on the reinforcement that the client will receive on reaching them. In the **token economy** technique, tokens that can be exchanged for rewards are used for positive reinforcement of adaptive behaviors.

Observational learning can also be used to treat problem behaviors such as phobias.

Cognitive Therapies

Cognitive therapies focus not so much on maladaptive behaviors as on maladaptive ways of thinking. By changing people's distorted, self-defeating ideas about themselves and the world, cognitive therapies help to encourage better coping skills and adjustment.

The things people say to themselves as they go about their daily lives can encourage either success or failure, a self-confident outlook, or acute anxiety. With **stress-inoculation therapy,** clients learn how to use self-talk to "coach" themselves through stressful situations.

Rational-emotive therapy (RET) is based on the idea that emotional problems derive from a set of irrational and self-defeating beliefs that people hold about themselves and the world. The therapist vigorously challenges these dysfunctional beliefs, enabling clients to reinterpret their experiences in a more positive light.

Beck's **cognitive therapy** has proved especially effective in treating depression. Aaron Beck believes that depression results from strongly and inappropriately self-critical thought patterns. In a similar way as RET but in a less confrontational manner, cognitive therapists try to help such people think more objectively and positively about themselves and their life situations.

Group Therapies

Group therapies are based on the idea that psychological problems are at least partly interpersonal and are therefore best approached in a group. Group therapies offer a circle of support for clients, shared insights into problems, and the opportunity to obtain psychotherapy at a lower cost. Among the many different kinds of group therapy are self-help groups, **family therapy**, and **couple therapy.**

Effectiveness of Psychotherapy

Formal psychotherapy helps about two thirds of the people treated. In addition, many people who do not receive formal therapy get therapeutic help from friends, clergy, physicians, and teachers. Thus, the recovery rate for people who receive *no* help at all is probably quite low.

All therapies provide an explanation of problems, hope, and an alliance with a caring, supportive person. But each kind of therapy works better for some problems than for others. Insight therapy, for example, seems to be best suited to people who seek profound self-understanding, relief of inner conflict and anxiety, or better relationships with others. Behavior therapy is most appropriate for treating specific anxieties or other well-defined behavioral problems. Family therapy is generally more effective than individual counseling for the treatment of drug abuse. Cognitive therapies have been shown to be effective treatments for depression and are promising treatments for anxiety disorders as well. The current trend in therapy is toward **eclecticism,** which recognizes the value of a broad treatment package rather than commitment to a single form of therapy.

Biological Treatments

Biological treatments—including medication, electroconvulsive therapy, and psychosurgery—are often used in conjunction with psychotherapy. Traditionally, psychiatrists (who are physicians) were the only mental health professionals licensed to offer biological treatments. However, some states now extend that privilege to specially trained clinical psychologists.

Drugs are the most common form of biological therapy. **Antipsychotic drugs** are valuable in treating schizophrenia. They do not cure the disorder, but they reduce its symptoms, although side effects can be severe. Antidepressant drugs alleviate depression, though some also have unpleasant side effects. Antidepressant drugs have also shown promise in treating generalized anxiety disorder, panic disorder, obsessive-compulsive disorder, social phobia, and posttraumatic stress disorder. Lithium carbonate is often used to treat bipolar disorder. Psychostimulants heighten alertness and arousal; they also alleviate some of the symptoms of attention-deficit hyperactivity disorder. Antianxiety medications are often used to reduce general tension and stress. Sedatives are often used to treat agitation or to induce sleep.

Electroconvulsive therapy (ECT), which involves briefly passing an electric current through the brain of the patient, is sometimes used as a last resort treatment for cases of severe depression that do not respond to other treatments. Newer forms of ECT are given to only one side of the brain.

Psychosurgery is brain surgery performed to change a person's behavior and emotional state. It is rarely used today, and then only as a last, desperate measure on people who have severe and intractable problems and do not respond to any other form of treatment.

Institutionalization and Its Alternatives

For most of the past 150 years, institutionalization in large mental hospitals was the most common treatment for people with severe mental illness. Patients with serious mental disorders were given shelter and some degree of treatment, but a great many never recovered enough to be released. With the advent of antipsychotic drugs in the 1950s, a trend began toward **deinstitutionalization,** in which people with serious mental disorders were integrated back into the community. However, poorly funded community mental health centers and other support services have proved inadequate to the task of caring for previously institutionalized patients with mental disorders. Many patients stop taking their medication, become psychotic, and end up homeless on the streets. Thus, although the concept of deinstitutionalization may have been a good idea in principle, in practice it has failed for many patients and for society.

Alternatives to hospitalization include living at home with adequate supports provided to all family members; living in small, homelike facilities in which residents and staff share responsibilities; living in hostels with therapy and crisis intervention provided; and receiving intensive outpatient counseling or frequent visits from public-health nurses. Most alternative treatments involve daily professional contact and skillful preparation of the family and community. Most studies have found more positive outcomes from alternative treatments than from hospitalization.

Prevention refers to efforts to reduce the incidence of mental illness before it arises. **Primary prevention** consists of improving the social environment through assistance to parents, education, and family planning. **Secondary prevention** involves identifying high-risk groups and providing direct service to them. **Tertiary prevention** involves helping hospitalized patients return to the community and educating that community to prepare for their return.

Client Diversity and Treatment

Given that human beings differ as much as they do, it is not surprising that a one-size-fits-all concept is not always appropriate in the treatment of psychological problems. In recent years, the special needs of women and of people from other cultures have particularly occupied the attention of mental health professionals.

In most respects, the treatment given to women is the same as that given to men. However, there is some concern that women in therapy may be encouraged by male therapists to adopt traditional, male-oriented views of what is "normal" or "appropriate." Thus, many women have turned to "feminist therapists." The American Psychological Association has issued guidelines to ensure that women receive treatment that is not tied to traditional ideas about appropriate behavior for the sexes.

When a client and therapist come from different cultural backgrounds or belong to different racial or ethnic groups, misunderstandings can arise in therapy. Therapists must recognize that cultural differences exist in the nature of the psychological disorders that affect people. Treatment and prevention must be tailored to the beliefs and cultural practices of the person's ethnic group.

Chapter 14
Social Psychology

Go to *The Core Online* at **www.psychologythecore.com** to get the most up-to-date information for your introductory psychology course. The content online is an important part of what you are learning—the content there can help prepare you for your test! It includes up-to-date examples, simulations, video clips, and practice quizzes. Also be sure to check out the *Blog* to hear directly from the authors on what current events and latest research are most relevant to your course materials.

The first time you log in, you will need the access code packaged with your textbook. If you do not have a code, please go to **www.mypearsonstore.com** and enter the ISBN of your textbook (**0-13-603344-X**) to purchase the code.

Chapter 14 Social Psychology

Social psychology: The scientific study of how people's thoughts, feelings, and behaviors are influenced by the behaviors and characteristics of other people

14 1 Social Cognition

Social cognition: The collecting and assessing of information about other people

Forming Impressions

- **Schema** (plural: **schemata**): An organized set of beliefs and expectations based on past experience that is presumed to apply to all people in a category
- **Primacy effect**: First impressions are more influential than later experience
- **Self-fulfilling prophecy**: When preconceptions about people bring about the behavior expected of them
- **Stereotype**: A set of characteristics presumed to be shared by all members of a social category

Attribution

- **Attribution theory**: How people make judgments about the causes of behavior
  - *Internal attribution*: Attributing the causes of behavior to characteristics of the person
  - *External attribution*: Attributing the causes of behavior to characteristics of the situation
- **Actor-observer bias**: Tendency to attribute the behavior of others to internal factors (the **fundamental attribution error**) and to attribute one's own behavior to situational factors
- **Defensive attribution**: Tendency to attribute one's successes to one's own efforts or qualities and to attribute one's failures to external factors
- **Just-world hypothesis**: Attribution error based on the assumption that bad things happen to bad people and good things happen to good people

Interpersonal Attraction

- Three key determinants of attraction:
  - **Proximity**: How close people live to one another
  - Similarity of attitudes, interests, values, backgrounds, and beliefs
  - Physical attractiveness

14 2 Attitudes

The Nature of Attitudes

- **Attitude**: A relatively stable organization of beliefs, feelings, and behavior tendencies toward something or someone
- Three components of attitudes that are often consistent with one another:
  - Beliefs: Facts, opinions, and general knowledge of the object
  - Feelings: Emotions associated with the object
  - Behavior tendencies: Inclinations to act in certain ways toward the object
- Factors that determine whether an attitude is likely to match behavior
  - Strength of the attitude
  - How easily it comes to mind
  - How noticeable a particular attitude is in a given situation
  - How relevant the attitude is to the particular behavior in question
  - Whether a person is low **self-monitoring** or high self-monitoring

Prejudice, Discrimination, and Racism

- **Prejudice**: An unfair, intolerant, or unfavorable view of a group of people
- **Discrimination**: An unfair act or a series of acts directed against an entire group of people or individual members of that group
- **Racism**: The belief that members of certain racial or ethnic groups are innately inferior to one or more other groups or individuals
- Sources of prejudice and discrimination:
  - **Frustration-aggression theory**: Frustration resulting in anger and hostility toward scapegoats
  - **Authoritarian personality**: Bigoted, rigidly conventional, suspicious, mistrusting, preoccupied with power and toughness
  - Social conformity

Changing Attitudes

- Persuasion
  - Seize and retain attention
  - Get comprehension and acceptance of the message
  - Four key elements in persuasion:
    - Source
    - Medium
    - Message
    - Audience
- **Cognitive dissonance**: Discomfort resulting from two contradictory cognitions, or beliefs, at the same time
- Self-persuasion

14 3 Social Influence

Social influence: The process by which people affect the perceptions, attitudes, and actions of others

Cultural Influences

- Culture, acquired through formal instruction, imitation, modeling, is a major source of social influence.
- **Cultural truisms:** Beliefs or values that most members of a society accept as self-evident
- **Norm:** Culturally shared idea or expectation about how to behave

Conformity

- **Conformity:** Response to pressure exerted by norms that are generally unstated
- In small groups, conformity increases to a maximum of four opponents and is higher when the task is difficult or ambiguous; just one "ally" greatly reduces conformity.
- Conformity is greater when a person is attracted to the group, expects to interact with its members in the future, holds a position of relatively low status, and does not feel completely accepted by the group.
- Conformity is greater in collectivist cultures as opposed to individualist cultures.

Compliance

- **Compliance:** Change of behavior in response to an explicitly stated request
  - *Foot-in-the-door effect:* Once people have granted a small request, they are more likely to comply with a larger one.
  - *Lowball procedure:* Once committed, people are more likely to remain committed despite increases in the price.
  - *Door-in-the-face effect:* When people refuse to comply with an unreasonable request, they will be more likely to comply with a second, more reasonable request.

Obedience

- **Obedience:** Compliance with a command or a direct order, generally from a person in authority
- Obedience is more likely when:
  - The person giving the orders has power.
  - The person receiving the orders remains under surveillance.
  - Responsibility for an act is shared by others.

14 4 Social Action

Deindividuation

- **Deindividuation:** Losing one's personal sense of responsibility in a group

Helping Behavior

- Helping behavior can be caused by self-interest.
- **Altruistic behavior:** Helpful actions not linked to personal gain
- Factors that affect the likelihood of helping behavior:
  - Less likely when other people are present (**bystander effect**), the situation is ambiguous, and the culture is individualistic
  - More likely when one person feels a sense of personal responsibility for another, is empathetic, in a good mood, is not shy or fearful, is greatly in need of approval, or the culture is collectivist

Groups and Decision Making

- In some cases, groups make decisions that are less sound than those made by individuals:
  - **Polarization:** The tendency for people to become more extreme in their attitudes as a result of group discussion
  - **Risky shift:** Special case of polarization in which groups take more risks than the members of the group would if working alone
- Groups are more effective than individuals only under certain circumstances.

Leadership

- **Great-person theory:** Leaders are extraordinary people who assume positions of influence and are able to shape events around them regardless of the circumstances.
- An alternative theory states that social and economic factors influence the emergence of a leader who happens to be *the right person in the right place at the right time.*
- **Contingency theory:**
  - When conditions are either very favorable or very unfavorable for the leader, the most effective leader is the one who is task oriented.
  - When conditions are moderately favorable, the most effective leader is relationship oriented.
- Gender differences: Women tend to have a more democratic, collaborative, and interpersonally oriented style of managing that is generally more effective than the directive and task-oriented leadership style common among men as far as winning acceptance for their ideas and instilling self-confidence.

Police never apologized for arresting Sher Singh as a terrorist after the September 11, 2001, attacks in the United States.

On September 12, 2001, the day after the terrorist attacks on the Pentagon and the World Trade Center, Sher Singh, a telecommunications consultant from Virginia, managed to catch a train home from Boston where he had been on a business trip. Singh was very much like any other shocked and sorrowful American on that day—except for one small difference: As a member of the Sikh religion, Singh, unlike most Americans, wore a full beard and a turban.

The train made a scheduled stop in Providence, Rhode Island, about an hour outside of Boston. But oddly, the stop dragged on for a very long time. Singh began to wonder what was wrong. Suddenly law-enforcement officers burst into his coach and pulled him off the train at gunpoint. They were searching for four Arab men who had evaded authorities in a Boston hotel. A Sikh, however, is not an Arab. A Sikh belongs to a Hindu sect that comes from India, not the Middle East.

On the station platform, Singh was abruptly handcuffed and asked about his citizenship. Assurances that he was a U.S. citizen did not satisfy the officers. They asked him whether or not he had a weapon. Singh informed them that, as a devout Sikh, he is required to carry a miniature ceremonial sword. They promptly arrested Singh and pushed him through a crowd of onlookers to a waiting police car. According to news reports, as Singh passed by, some teenagers shouted, "Let's kill him!" while a woman yelled, "Burn in Hell!" As a terrorist suspect, Singh was photographed, fingerprinted, and strip-searched. He was held in custody at police headquarters until 9:00 p.m. While he was jailed, news media nationwide had displayed a photo of him side by side with a photo of Osama bin Laden. Eventually, all charges against Sher Singh were dropped.

How could this blatant case of mistaken identity have happened? Why were police so convinced that Sher Singh could be a fugitive terrorist? Researchers who specialize in the field of social psychology help provide some answers. **Social psychology** is the scientific study of how people's thoughts, feelings, and behaviors are influenced by the behaviors and characteristics of other people, whether these behaviors and characteristics are real, imagined, or inferred. Sher Singh was clearly a victim of imagined and inferred characteristics formed on the basis of his ethnic appearance. As you read about the findings of social psychologists in this chapter, you will discover that Singh's experience is far from unique. Every day, people make judgments about others that often are based on very little "real" evidence. The process by which such impressions are formed, whether or not they are accurate, is part of a fascinating area of social psychology known as *social cognition*.

ENDURING ISSUES   in Social Psychology

A key issue throughout this chapter is the extent to which a particular behavior reflects personal characteristics—such as attitudes and values—versus situational characteristics—such as the behavior of others and social expectations (person–situation). A second key issue in this chapter concerns the extent to which there are differences in social behavior among people in different cultures (individuality–universality).

Social Cognition

Part of the process of being influenced by other people involves organizing and interpreting information about them to form first impressions, to try to understand their behavior, and to determine to what extent we are attracted to them. This collecting and assessing of information about other people is called **social cognition**. Social cognition is a major area of interest to social psychologists.

■ FORMING IMPRESSIONS

Forming first impressions of people is more complex than you may think. You must direct your attention to various aspects of the person's appearance and behavior and make a rapid

■ Social psychology: _____

_____

■ Social cognition: _____

_____

assessment of what those characteristics mean. How do you complete this process? What cues do you interpret? How accurate are your impressions?

When we meet someone for the first time, we notice a number of things about that person—clothes, gestures, manner of speaking, body build, and facial features. We then draw on these cues to fit the person into a category. Associated with each category is a **schema**—an organized set of beliefs and expectations based on past experience that is presumed to apply to all members of that category. Over time, as we continue to interact with people, we add new information about them to our mental files. But because **schemata** (singular: *schema*) influence the information we notice and remember, our later experiences usually do not influence us nearly so much as our earliest impressions. This phenomenon is called the **primacy effect**.

Why do schemata have such a powerful effect on our perceptions of other people? Humans have been called "cognitive misers" (Fiske & Taylor, 1991; Madon, 1999). Instead of exerting ourselves to interpret every detail that we learn about a person, we are stingy with our mental efforts. If we are warned specifically to beware of first impressions or if we are encouraged to interpret information about others slowly and carefully, the primacy effect can be weakened or even eliminated. Generally speaking, however, once we have formed an impression about someone, we do not exert the mental effort to change it. As a result, schemata can sometimes lead us astray, luring us into "seeing" things about a person that we do not actually observe. Schemata can even help us create the behavior we expect from other people. In a classic study, pairs of participants played a competitive game (Snyder & Swann, 1978). The researchers told one member of each pair that his or her partner was either hostile or friendly. The players who were led to believe that their partner was hostile behaved differently toward that partner than did the players led to believe that their partner was friendly. In turn, those treated as hostile actually began to display hostility. In fact, these people continued to show hostility later, when they were paired with new players who had no expectations about them at all. The expectation of hostility seemed to produce actual aggressiveness, and this behavior persisted. When we bring about expected behavior in another person in this way, our impression becomes a **self-fulfilling prophecy**.

Considerable scientific research has shown how teacher expectations can take the form of a self-fulfilling prophecy and can influence student performance in the classroom (Harris & Rosenthal, 1985; Rosenthal, 2002; Trouilloud, Sarrazin, Bressoux, Bressoux, & Bois, 2006). That finding has been named the *Pygmalion effect*, after the mythical sculptor who created the statue of a woman and brought it to life. Although the research does not suggest that high teacher expectations can turn an "F" student into an "A" student, it does show that high *and* low expectations can exert a powerful influence on student achievement. One study, for example, compared the performance of "at risk" ninth-grade students who had been assigned to regular classrooms with that of students assigned to experimental classrooms that received a year-long intervention aimed at increasing teachers' expectations. After 1 year, the students in the experimental classrooms had higher grades in English and history than the students who were not in the intervention classrooms. Two years later, the experimental students were less likely to drop out of high school (Weinstein et al., 1991).

A **stereotype**—a set of characteristics presumed to be shared by all members of a social category—is a special kind of schema. A stereotype can involve almost any distinguishing personal attribute, such as age, sex, race, occupation, place of residence, or membership in a certain group. When our first impression of a person is governed by a stereotype, we tend to infer things about that person solely on the basis of some key distinguishing feature and to ignore facts that are inconsistent with the stereotype, no matter how apparent they are. As a result, we may perceive things about the person selectively or inaccurately, thereby perpetuating our initial stereotype. As Sher Singh learned after the terrorist attacks of September 11, 2001, many Americans have a stereotype that bearded males wearing turbans are from the Middle East and are potential terrorists.

■ ATTRIBUTION

Social interaction is filled with occasions that invite people to make judgments about the causes of behavior. When something unexpected or unpleasant occurs, it is a common tendency to

Suppose you are a new teacher entering this classroom on the first day of school in September. Do you have any expectations about children of any ethnic or racial groups that might lead to a self-fulfilling prophecy?

wonder about it and try to understand it. The observations by social psychologists about how people go about attributing causes to behavior form the basis of **attribution theory**.

ENDURING ISSUES PERSON/SITUATION

Interpreting Behavior

The study of attribution, or how people explain their own and other people's behavior, focuses on when and why people interpret behavior as reflecting personal traits or social situations. An early attribution theorist, Fritz Heider (1896–1998), argued that people attribute behavior to either internal or external causes, but not both (Heider, 1958). Thus, one might conclude that a classmate's lateness was caused by his laziness (a personal factor, or an _internal_ attribution) or by traffic congestion (a situational factor, or an _external_ attribution). Suppose you run into a friend at the supermarket. You greet him warmly, but he barely acknowledges you, mumbles "Hi," and walks away. You feel snubbed and try to figure out why he acted like that. Did he behave that way because of something in the situation? Did you do something that offended him? Was he having no luck finding the groceries he wanted? Had someone had just blocked his way by leaving a cart in the middle of an aisle? Or did something within him, some personal trait such as moodiness or arrogance, prompt him to behave that way?

How do people decide whether to attribute a given behavior to internal or external causes? According to Harold Kelley (1921–2003), people rely on three kinds of information about the behavior: distinctiveness, consistency, and consensus (Kelley, 1967, 1973). For example, if your instructor asks you to stay briefly after class so she can talk with you, you will probably try to figure out what lies behind her request by asking yourself three questions.

First, how _distinctive_ is the instructor's request? Does she often ask students to stay and talk (low distinctiveness) or is such a request unusual (high distinctiveness)? If she often asks students to speak with her, you will probably conclude that she has personal reasons for talking with you. But if her request is highly distinctive, you will probably conclude that something about you, not her, underlies her request.

Second, how _consistent_ is the instructor's behavior? Does she regularly ask you to stay and talk (high consistency) or is this a first for you (low consistency)? If she has consistently made this request of you before, you will probably guess that this occasion is like those others. But if her request is inconsistent with past behavior, you will probably wonder whether some particular event—perhaps something you said in class—motivated her to request a private conference.

Finally, what degree of _consensus_ among teachers exists regarding this behavior? Do your other instructors ask you to stay and talk with them (high consensus) or is this instructor unique in making such a request (low consensus)? If it is common for your instructors to ask to speak with you, this instructor's request is probably because of something about you or because of something in the situation. But if she is the only instructor ever to ask to speak privately with you, it is probably something about her—an internal motive or a concern—that accounts for her behavior.

Unfortunately, the causal attributions people make are often vulnerable to _biases_. For example, imagine that you are at a party and you see Ted, an acquaintance, walk across the room carrying several plates of food and a drink. As he approaches his chair, Ted spills food on himself. You may attribute the spill to Ted's personal characteristics—he is clumsy. Ted, however, is likely to make a very different attribution. He likely will attribute the spill to an external factor—he was carrying too many other things or the carpet was uneven.

Did this accident happen because of poor driving or because the driver swerved to avoid a child in the street? The fundamental attribution error says that we are more likely to attribute behavior of others to internal causes, such as poor driving, rather than situational factors, such as a child who darted into the street.

This is an example of **actor-observer bias**—the tendency to explain the behavior of others as caused by *internal* factors, while attributing one's own behavior to *external* forces. For example, during World War II some Europeans risked their own safety to help Jewish refugees who were being persecuted in Nazi-occupied Europe. From the perspective of an observer, the tendency is to attribute this behavior to personal qualities. Indeed, Robert Goodkind, chairman of the foundation that honored the rescuers, called for parents to "inculcate in our children the values of altruism and moral courage as exemplified by the rescuers." Clearly, Goodkind was making an internal attribution for the heroic behavior. This is sometimes called the **fundamental attribution error**—the tendency to attribute others' behavior to causes within themselves. The rescuers themselves, however, attributed their actions to external factors. One said, "We didn't feel like rescuers at all. We were just ordinary students doing what we had to do" (Lipman, 1991).

A related class of biases is called **defensive attribution**. These types of attributions occur when people are motivated to present themselves well, either to impress others or to feel good about themselves (Aronson, Wilson, & Akert, 2005; Gyekye & Salminen, 2006). One example of a defensive attribution is the *self-serving bias*, which is a tendency to attribute one's successes to one's own personal attributes while chalking up one's failures to external forces beyond one's control (Sedikides, Gaertner, & Toguchi, 2003; R. A. Smith & Weber, 2005). Students do this all the time. They tend to regard exams on which they do well as good indicators of their abilities and exams on which they do poorly as bad indicators (R. A. Smith, 2005). Similarly, teachers are more likely to assume responsibility for students' successes than for their failures (R. A. Smith, 2005). In one survey of more than 800,000 high school seniors, less than 1% said they were below average in "ability to get along with others," while more than half said they were in the top 10%. In another survey, less than 80% of the respondents said that Mother Teresa was likely to go to heaven, though 87% said that they themselves were likely to do so (Shermer, 2004).

A second type of defensive attribution comes from thinking that people get what they deserve: Bad things happen to bad people, and good things happen to good people. This is called the **just-world hypothesis** (Aronson, Wilson, & Akert, 2005; Blader & Tyler, 2002; Lerner, 1980). When misfortune strikes someone, people often jump to the conclusion that the person deserved it, rather than giving full weight to situational factors that may have been responsible. Why do people behave this way? One reason is that doing so gives them the comforting illusion that such a thing could never happen to them. By reassigning the blame for a terrible misfortune from a chance event (something that could happen to anyone) to the victim's own negligence, people delude themselves into believing that they could never suffer such a fate (Dalbert, 2001).

■ INTERPERSONAL ATTRACTION

A third aspect of social cognition involves interpersonal attraction. When people meet, what determines whether they will like each other? This is the subject of much speculation and even mystification, with popular explanations running the gamut from fate to compatible astrological signs. Romantics believe that irresistible forces propel them toward an inevitable meeting with their beloved, but social psychologists take a more hardheaded view. They have found that attraction and the tendency to like someone else are closely linked to such factors as *proximity*, *similarity*, and *physical attractiveness*.

Proximity is a critical factor in determining attraction. The closer two people live to each other, the more likely they are to interact. Conversely, two people separated by considerable geographic distance are not likely to run into each other and thus have little chance to develop a mutual attraction.

Moreover, people who live near each other are more likely to share similar attitudes, interests, values, backgrounds, and beliefs. And *similarity* is a powerful determinant of interpersonal attraction. When we know that someone shares our attitudes and interests and makes us feel appreciated, we tend to have more positive feelings toward that person. It is nice to be around others who agree with our choices and beliefs. If similarity is a determinant of attraction, what about the notion that opposites attract? Are not people sometimes attracted to

Interpersonal Attraction

■ Three key determinants of attraction:

  ■ Proximity: _____

  ■ Similarity of _____,

  _____, _____, _____,

  and _____

  ■ _____ attractiveness

others who are completely different from them? Extensive research has failed to confirm this notion. In long-term relationships, where attraction plays an especially important role, people overwhelmingly prefer to associate with people who are similar to themselves (Buss, 1985; McPherson, Smith-Lovin, & Cook, 2001). In some cases in which people's attraction seems to be founded on their lack of similarity, their critical qualities are not so much opposites as they are complements. Complementary traits are needs or skills that complete or balance each other. For example, a person who likes to care for and fuss over others will be most compatible with a mate who enjoys receiving such attention. Complementarity nearly always occurs between people who share similar goals and values and are willing to adapt to each other. True opposites are unlikely even to meet each other, much less interact long enough to achieve such compatibility.

Physical attractiveness can powerfully influence the conclusions we reach about a person's character. Research shows that we tend to presume that attractive people are more intelligent, interesting, happy, kind, sensitive, moral, and successful than people who are not perceived as attractive. As a result, we tend to give good-looking people the benefit of the doubt: If they do not live up to our expectations during the first encounter, we give them a second chance, ask for or accept a second date, or seek further opportunities for interaction. These reactions can give attractive people substantial advantages in life and can lead to self-fulfilling prophecies. Physically attractive people may come to think of themselves as interesting and sensitive because they have been treated as though they are. Conversely, unattractive people may come to see themselves as uninteresting or insensitive because they have always been regarded that way.

Check Your Understanding

1. When the first information a person receives about another person weighs more heavily in forming an impression than later information does, the _____ effect is being experienced.

2. The tendency to attribute the behavior of others to internal causes and one's own behavior to external causes is called the _____-_____ _____.

3. The tendency to attribute the behavior of others to personal characteristics is the _____ _____ error.

4. You meet someone at a party who is outgoing, is entertaining, and is someone with a great sense of humor. A week later, your paths cross again but, this time, the person seems very shy, withdrawn, and humorless. Most likely, your impression of this person after the second meeting is that he or she

   a. Is actually shy, withdrawn, and humorless, despite your initial impression

   b. Is actually outgoing and entertaining but was just having a bad day

   c. Is low in self-monitoring

   d. Both (b) and (c) are correct

Attitudes

The phrase "I don't like his attitude" is a telling one. People are often told to "change your attitude" or make an "attitude adjustment." An **attitude** is a relatively stable organization of beliefs, feelings, and behavior tendencies toward something or someone—called an *attitude object*. Attitudes are important mainly because they often influence our behavior. Discrimination, for example, is often caused by prejudiced attitudes. Psychologists wonder how attitudes are formed and how they can be changed.

■ THE NATURE OF ATTITUDES

An attitude has three major components: *evaluative beliefs* about the object, *feelings* about the object, and *behavior tendencies* toward the object. Beliefs include facts, opinions, and general knowledge about the object. Feelings encompass love, hate, like, dislike, and similar sentiments. Behavior tendencies refer to our inclinations to act in certain ways toward the object—to approach it, avoid it, and so on. For example, our attitude toward a political candidate includes our beliefs about the candidate's qualifications and positions on crucial issues and our expectations about how the candidate will vote on those issues. We also have feelings about the candidate—like or dislike, trust or mistrust. And because of these beliefs and feelings, we are inclined to behave in certain ways toward the candidate—to vote for or against the candidate, to contribute time or money to the candidate's campaign, to make a point of attending or staying away from rallies for the candidate, and so forth.

These three aspects of an attitude are often consistent with one another. For example, when we have positive feelings toward something, we tend to have positive beliefs about it and to behave positively toward it. This tendency does not mean, however, that our every action will accurately reflect our attitudes. For example, our feelings about going to dentists are often negative, yet most of us make an annual visit anyway. Let's look more closely at the relationship between attitudes and behavior.

ENDURING ISSUES   PERSON/SITUATION

Attitudes and Behavior

The relationship between attitudes and behavior is not always straightforward. Variables such as the strength of the attitude, how easily it comes to mind, how noticeable a particular attitude is in a given situation, and how relevant the attitude is to the particular behavior in question help to determine whether a person will act in accordance with an attitude. Moreover, some people consistently match their actions to their attitudes while others have a tendency to override their own attitudes in order to behave properly in a given situation. As a result, attitudes predict behavior better for some people than for others. People who rate highly on **self-monitoring** are especially likely to override their attitudes to behave in accordance with others' expectations. Before speaking or acting, those who score high in self-monitoring observe the situation for clues about how they should react. Then they try to meet those "demands," rather than behave according to their own beliefs or sentiments. In contrast, those who score low in self-monitoring express and act on their attitudes with great consistency, showing little regard for situational clues or constraints.

Attitude Development   How do people acquire their attitudes? Many of the most basic attitudes derive from early, direct personal experience. Children are rewarded with smiles and encouragement when they please their parents, and they are punished through disapproval when they displease them. These early experiences give children enduring attitudes. Attitudes are also formed by imitation. Children mimic the behavior of their parents and peers, acquiring attitudes even when no one is deliberately trying to shape them.

But parents are not the only source of attitudes. Teachers, friends, and even famous people are also important in shaping our attitudes. New fraternity or sorority members, for example, may model their behavior and attitudes on upper-class members. A student who idolizes a teacher may adopt many of the teacher's attitudes toward controversial subjects, even if they run counter to attitudes of parents or friends.

The mass media, particularly television, also have a great impact on attitude formation. Television bombards us with messages—not merely through its news and entertainment, but also through commercials. Without experience of their own against which to measure the merit of these messages, children are particularly susceptible to the influence of television on their attitudes.

▪ PREJUDICE, DISCRIMINATION, AND RACISM

Although the terms *prejudice* and *discrimination* are often used interchangeably, they actually refer to different concepts. **Prejudice**—an attitude—is an unfair, intolerant, or unfavorable

---

The Nature of Attitudes

- Attitude: A relatively stable organization of _____, _____, and _____ toward _____

- Three components of attitudes that are often consistent with one another:
  - Beliefs: _____, _____, and _____ of the object
  - Feelings: _____ associated with the object
  - Behavior tendencies: Inclinations to _____ toward the object

- Factors that determine whether an attitude is likely to match behavior
  - _____ of the attitude
  - How easily it _____
  - How _____ a particular attitude is in a given situation
  - How relevant the attitude is to _____
  - Whether a person is _____ self-monitoring or _____ self-monitoring

Prejudice, Discrimination, and Racism

- Prejudice: An _____,

_____, or _____

view of a group of people

- Discrimination: An _____ or

_____ directed against

_____ or

_____

- Racism: The belief that members of

certain racial or ethnic groups are

_____ to one or more

other groups or individuals

- Sources of prejudice and

discrimination:

- Frustration-aggression theory:

Frustration resulting in

_____ and

_____ toward _____

- Authoritarian personality:

Bigoted, rigidly conventional,

suspicious, mistrusting,

preoccupied with _____

and _____

- Social _____

Signs such as this were common in the South before the Civil Rights movement.

view of a group of people. **Discrimination**—a behavior—is an unfair act or a series of acts directed against an entire group of people or individual members of that group. As you would expect from our discussion of attitudes and behavior, prejudice and discrimination do not always occur together. It is possible to be prejudiced against a particular group without openly behaving in a hostile or discriminatory manner toward its members. It is also possible to discriminate against people without being prejudiced against them. A prejudiced storeowner may smile at an African American customer, for example, to disguise opinions that could hurt his business. Likewise, many institutional practices can be discriminatory even though they are not based on prejudice.

As with all attitudes, prejudice has three components: beliefs, feelings, and behavioral tendencies. Prejudicial beliefs are virtually always negative stereotypes. Along with stereotyped beliefs, prejudiced attitudes usually are marked by strong emotions, such as dislike, fear, hatred, or loathing. And prejudice typically is accompanied by strong behavioral tendencies such as avoidance, hostility, and discrimination.

Many theories have attempted to identify the sources of prejudice. According to the **frustration-aggression theory,** prejudice is the result of people's frustrations (Allport, 1954; E. R. Smith & Mackie, 2005). As seen in Chapter 8: Motivation and Emotion, under some circumstances, frustration can spill over into anger and hostility. People who feel exploited and oppressed often cannot vent their anger against an identifiable or proper target, so they displace their hostility onto those even "lower" on the social scale than themselves. The result is prejudice and discrimination. The people who are the victims of this displaced aggression, or *scapegoats,* are blamed for the problems of the times.

Another theory locates the source of prejudice in a bigoted or an **authoritarian personality** (Adorno, Frenkel-Brunswick, Levinson, & Sanford, 1950; Altemeyer, 2004). Authoritarian people tend to be rigidly conventional. They favor following the rules and abiding by tradition and are hostile to those who defy social norms. They respect and submit to authority and are preoccupied with power and toughness. Looking at the world through a lens of rigid categories, they are cynical about human nature, fearing, suspecting, and rejecting all groups other than those to which they belong. Prejudice is only one expression of their suspicious, mistrusting views.

In addition, prejudice and discrimination may originate in people's attempts to conform. If we associate with people who are prejudiced, we are more likely to go along with their ideas than to resist them. The pressures of social conformity help to explain why children quickly absorb the prejudices of their parents and playmates long before they have formed their own beliefs and opinions on the basis of experience. Peer pressure often makes it "cool" or acceptable to express certain biases rather than to behave tolerantly toward members of other social groups.

Racism is the belief that members of certain racial or ethnic groups are *innately* inferior to members of one or more other groups. Racists believe that intelligence, industry, morality, and other valued traits are biologically determined and therefore cannot be changed. Racism leads to *either-or* thinking: Either you are one of "us," or you are one of "them." An *in-group* is any group of people that feels a sense of solidarity and exclusivity in relation to nonmembers. An *out-group*, in contrast, is a group of people outside this boundary and thus is viewed as competitors, enemies, or different and unworthy of respect. These terms can be applied to opposing sports teams, rival gangs, and political parties, or to entire nations, regions, religions, and ethnic or racial groups. According to the *in-group bias*, members see themselves not just as different, but also as superior to members of out-groups. In extreme cases, members of an in-group may see members of an out-group as less than human and feel hatred that may lead to violence, civil war, and even genocide.

■ CHANGING ATTITUDES

A man watching television on Sunday afternoon ignores scores of beer commercials, but he listens to a friend who recommends a particular brand. A political speech convinces one woman to vote for the candidate but the same speech leaves her next-door neighbor determined to vote against him. Why would a personal recommendation have greater persuasive power than an expensively produced television commercial? How can two people with similar initial views derive completely different messages from the same speech? What makes one attempt to change attitudes fail and another succeed? Are some people more resistant to attitude change than others are?

The Process of Persuasion   The first step in persuasion is to seize and retain the audience's attention. As competition has stiffened, advertisers have become increasingly creative in catching your attention. For example, ads that arouse emotions, especially feelings that make you want to act, can be memorable and thus persuasive. Humor, too, is an effective way to keep you watching or reading an ad that you would otherwise ignore. Other ads "hook" the audience by involving them in a narrative. A commercial might open with a dramatic scene or situation—for example, two people seemingly "meant" for each other but not yet making eye contact—and the viewer stays tuned to find out what happens. Some commercials even feature recurring characters and story lines so that each new commercial in the series is really the latest installment in a soap opera. Even annoying ads can still be effective in capturing attention, because people tend to notice them when they appear.

Capturing attention is only the first step in persuasion. The audience must also comprehend and accept the message. The *communication model* of persuasion spotlights four key elements to achieve these goals: the source, the message itself, the medium of communication, and the characteristics of the audience. Persuaders manipulate each of these factors in the hopes of changing your attitudes.

The effectiveness of a persuasive message depends first on its *source*, the author or communicator who appeals to the audience to accept the message. Source credibility is especially important when we are not otherwise inclined to pay attention to the message. For example, we are less likely to change our attitude about the oil industry's antipollution efforts if the president of a major refining company tells us about them than if we hear the same information from an impartial commission appointed to study the situation. However, over time, even a message from an unreliable source may become influential. Apparently, we are inclined to forget the source, while remembering the content. Not surprisingly, this is known as the *sleeper effect* (Kumkale & Albarracín, 2004).

In cases where we have some interest in the message, the content of the message itself plays a greater role than source credibility in determining whether we change our attitudes. For example, people tend to tune out messages that contradict their own point of view. Thus, messages are generally more successful when they present both sides of an issue. A two-sided presentation also is likely to make the speaker seem less biased and thus more credible: We are likely to have greater respect and trust for a communicator who acknowledges that there is another side to a controversial issue. Messages that create fear sometimes work well, too, but when a message generates too much fear, it has the potential to turn off the audience and be ignored.

When it comes to choosing an effective *medium* of persuasion, written documentation is best suited to making people understand complex arguments, whereas videotapes or live presentations are more effective with an audience that already grasps the gist of an argument (Chaiken & Eagly, 1976). Most effective, however, are face-to-face appeals or the lessons of our own experience.

Some of the most critical factors in changing attitudes—and the most difficult to control—have to do with the *audience*. Attitudes are most resistant to change whenever (1) the audience has a strong commitment to its present attitudes, (2) those attitudes are shared by others, and (3) the attitudes were instilled during early childhood by a pivotal group such as the family. The *discrepancy* between the content of the message and the present

Changing Attitudes

- Persuasion
  - Seize and retain _____
  - Get _____ and
    _____ of the message
  - Four key elements in persuasion:

    _____

    _____

    _____

- Cognitive dissonance: Discomfort resulting from two contradictory _____ or _____, at the same time
- Self-persuasion

LAST CALL.
When closing time comes around, don't get behind the wheel. Get in front of a phone. Call a friend, or call a cab. **MADD**
Mothers Against Drunk Driving

For an ad to affect our behavior, it must first attract our attention. This one also generates fear, which can sometimes be effective.

Source: © MADD. Used by permission.

attitudes of the audience also affects how well the message will be received. Up to a point, the greater the difference between the two, the greater the likelihood of attitude change, as long as the person delivering the message is considered an expert on the topic. If the discrepancy is too great, however, the *audience* may reject the new information altogether, even though it comes from an expert.

Finally, certain personal characteristics make some people more susceptible to attitude change than others. People with low self-esteem are influenced more easily, especially when the message is complex and hard to understand. Highly intelligent people tend to resist persuasion because they can think of counterarguments more easily.

With so many clever strategies focused on seizing and holding your attention, how can you shield yourself from unwanted influences and resist persuasive appeals? Start by reminding yourself that these are deliberate attempts to influence you and to change your behavior. Research shows that to a great extent, "forewarned is forearmed." Another strategy for resisting persuasion is to analyze ads to identify which attention-getting strategies are at work. Make a game of deciphering the advertisers' "code" instead of falling for the appeal of the advertisement. In addition, raise your standards for the kinds of messages that are worthy of your attention and commitment.

Cognitive Dissonance One of the more fascinating approaches to understanding the process of attitude change is the theory of cognitive dissonance, developed by Leon Festinger (1919–1989). **Cognitive dissonance** exists whenever a person has two contradictory cognitions, or beliefs, at the same time (Festinger, 1957). "I am a considerate and loyal friend" is one cognition; "Yesterday I repeated some juicy gossip I heard about my friend Chris" is another cognition. These two cognitions are dissonant—each one implies the opposite of the other. According to Festinger, cognitive dissonance creates unpleasant psychological tension, which motivates us to try to resolve the dissonance in some way.

Sometimes changing one's attitude is the easiest way to reduce the discomfort of dissonance. I cannot easily change the fact that I have repeated gossip about a friend; therefore, it is easier to change my attitude toward my friend. If I conclude that Chris is not really a friend but simply an acquaintance, then my new attitude now fits my behavior—spreading gossip about someone who is *not* a friend does not contradict the fact that I am loyal and considerate to those who *are* my friends.

Discrepant behavior that contradicts an attitude does not necessarily bring about attitude change, however, because there are other ways a person can reduce cognitive dissonance. One alternative is to *increase the number of consonant elements*—that is, the thoughts that are consistent with one another. For example, I might recall the many times I defended Chris when others were critical of him. Now my repeating a little bit of gossip seems less at odds with my attitude toward Chris as a friend. Another option is to reduce the importance of one or both dissonant cognitions. For instance, I could tell myself, "The person I repeated the gossip to was Terry, who doesn't really know Chris very well. Terry doesn't care and won't repeat it. It was no big deal, and Chris shouldn't be upset about it." By reducing the significance of my disloyal action, I reduce the dissonance that I experience and so make it less necessary to change my attitude toward Chris.

But why would someone engage in behavior that goes against an attitude in the first place? One answer is that cognitive dissonance is a natural part of everyday life. Simply choosing between two or more desirable alternatives leads inevitably to dissonance. Suppose you are in the market for a computer but cannot decide between a Dell (Windows) and a Macintosh. If you choose one, all of its bad features and all the good aspects of the other contribute to dissonance. After you have bought one of the computers, you can reduce the dissonance by changing your attitude: You might decide that the other keyboard was not "quite right" and that some of the "bad" features of the computer you bought are not so bad after all.

You may also engage in behavior at odds with an attitude because you are enticed to do so. Perhaps someone offers you a small bribe or reward: "I will pay you 25 cents just to try my product." Curiously, the larger the reward, the smaller the change in attitude that is likely to result. When rewards are large, dissonance is at a minimum and attitude change is small, if it happens at all. Apparently, when people are convinced that there is a good reason to do something that goes against their beliefs ("I'll try almost anything in exchange for a large cash incentive"), they experience little dissonance, and their attitudes are not likely to shift, even though their behavior may change for a time. If the reward is small, however—just barely enough to induce behavior that conflicts with one's attitude—dissonance will be great, maximizing the chances of attitude change: "I only got 25 cents to try this product, so it couldn't have been the money that attracted me. I must really like this product after all." The trick is to induce the behavior that goes against an attitude, while leaving people feeling personally responsible for the dissonant act. In that way, they are more likely to change their attitudes than if they feel they were blatantly induced to act in a way that contradicted their beliefs.

One of the best antidotes to prejudice is contact among people of different racial groups. Working on class projects together, for example, can help children to overcome negative stereotypes about others.

In the final analysis, the most effective means of changing attitudes—especially important attitudes, behaviors, or lifestyle choices—may be self-persuasion (Aronson, 2003; Gordijn, Postmes, & de Vries, 2001). In contrast to traditional, direct techniques of persuasion, people are put in situations in which they are motivated to persuade themselves to change their attitudes or behavior. For example, many educators hoped that school integration would reduce racial prejudices. But often the reverse proved true: Although they attended the same schools and classes, African American and Caucasian children tended to "self-segregate." However, when children were assigned to small, culturally diverse study groups, in which they were forced to cooperate, attitudes changed—albeit slowly. Insults and put-downs, often ethnically based, decreased. Having learned both to teach and to listen to "others," students emerged from the experience with fewer group stereotypes and greater appreciation of individual differences. This outcome, in turn, made them less likely to stereotype others. In a nutshell, maintaining one's prejudice is difficult when working with diverse individuals who do not fit preconceived notions (cognitive dissonance).

Check Your Understanding

1. A(n) _____ is a fairly stable organization of beliefs, feelings, and behavioral tendencies directed toward some object, such as a person or group.

2. Indicate whether the following statements are true (T) or false (F).

   a. ___ The best way to predict behavior is to measure attitudes.

   b. ___ Prejudice is the act of treating someone unfairly.

   c. ___ Messages are more persuasive when they present both sides of an argument.

   d. ___ A person who has two contradictory beliefs at the same time is likely to experience cognitive dissonance.

3. Two people listen to a discussion on why their government should increase defense spending. John has never really thought much about the issue, while Jane has participated in marches and demonstrations against increased defense spending. Which person is *less* likely to change their attitude about defense spending?

   a. Jane   **b.** John   **c.** Both are equally likely to change their attitude.

Social Influence

Social influence refers to the process by which people—individually or collectively—affect the perceptions, attitudes, and actions of others. One form of social influence—attitude change—was discussed in the previous section. The next section focuses on how the presence or actions of some can control the behavior of others without regard to underlying attitudes.

■ Social influence: The process by which people affect the _____, _____, and _____ of others

Cultural Influences

■ _____, acquired through _____, _____, _____, is a major source of social influence.

■ Cultural truisms: _____ or _____ that most members of a society accept as self-evident

■ Norm: Culturally shared idea or expectation about how to _____

■ CULTURAL INFLUENCES

Culture is a major source of social influence. To some extent, culture influences people through formal instruction. For example, your parents might have reminded you from time to time that certain actions are considered "normal" or the "right way" to behave. But more often, people learn cultural lessons through modeling and imitation. One result of such learning is the unquestioning acceptance of **cultural truisms**—beliefs or values that most members of a society accept as self-evident (Aronson, Wilson, & Akert, 2005; Maio & Olson, 1998). People are rewarded (reinforced) for doing as their companions and fellow citizens do in most situations—for going along with the crowd. This social learning process is one of the chief mechanisms by which a culture transmits its central lessons and values.

In the course of comparing and adapting one's own behavior to that of others, people learn the norms of their culture. A **norm** is a culturally shared idea or expectation about how to behave. As in the preceding examples, norms are often steeped in tradition and strengthened by habit. Other cultures often seem strange to those whose norms are very different. It is tempting to conclude that *different* means "wrong," simply because unfamiliar patterns of behavior can make people feel uncomfortable. To transcend their differences and get along better with those from other cultures, people must find ways to overcome such discomfort.

One technique for understanding other cultures is the *cultural assimilator*, a strategy for perceiving the norms and values of another group (Kempt, 2000). This technique teaches by example, asking students to explain why a member of another culture has behaved in a particular way. For example, why do the members of a Japanese grade school class silently follow their teacher single file through a park on a lovely spring day? Are they afraid of being punished for disorderly conduct if they do otherwise? Are they naturally placid and compliant? Once you understand that Japanese children are raised to value the needs and feelings of others over their own selfish concerns, their orderly, obedient behavior seems much less perplexing. Cultural assimilators encourage people to remain open-minded about others' norms and values by challenging such cultural truisms as "Our way is the right way."

■ CONFORMITY

Accepting cultural norms should not be confused with conformity. For instance, millions of Americans drink coffee in the morning but not because they are conforming. They drink coffee because they like and desire it. **Conformity,** in contrast, implies a conflict between an individual and a group that is resolved when individual preferences or beliefs yield to the norms or expectations of the larger group.

Since the early 1950s, when Solomon Asch (1907–1996) conducted the first systematic study of the subject, conformity has been a major topic of research in social psychology. Asch (1956) demonstrated in a series of experiments that people, under some circumstances, will conform to group pressures even when this action forces them to deny obvious physical evidence. He asked people in a small group to view cards with several lines of differing lengths; then, he asked each of them to choose the card with the line most similar to the line on a comparison card. As you can see from Figure 14–1, the correct choice was clear. However, all but one of the people in the group were confederates of the experimenter who deliberately gave the wrong answer on some of the trials. This procedure put the dissenter on the spot: Should he conform to what he knew to be a wrong answer and agree with the group, thereby denying the evidence of his own eyes, or should he disagree with the group, thereby risking the social consequences of nonconformity?

Overall, participants conformed and gave the wrong answer on about 35% of the trials. There were large individual differences, however; and in subsequent research, experimenters discovered that two sets of factors influence the likelihood that a person will conform: characteristics of the situation and characteristics of the person.

Why do Japanese schoolchildren behave in such an orderly way? How does your answer compare with the discussion of cultural influences?

ENDURING ISSUES PERSON/SITUATION

Conformity

Asch found that the *size* of the group affects conformity. The likelihood of conformity increased with group size until four confederates were present. Adding more confederates did not increase the likelihood of the person conforming to the erroneous group judgment.

Another important situational factor is the degree of *unanimity* in the group. If just one confederate broke the perfect agreement of the majority by giving the correct answer, conformity among participants in the Asch experiments dropped. Apparently, having just one "ally" eases the pressure to conform. The ally does not even have to share the person's viewpoint—just breaking the unanimity of the majority is enough to reduce conformity.

The *nature of the task* is still another situational variable that affects conformity. For instance, conformity has been shown to vary with the difficulty and ambiguity of a task. When the task is difficult or poorly defined, conformity tends to be higher (Blake, Helson, & Mouton, 1956). In an ambiguous situation, people are less sure of their own opinion and more willing to conform to the majority view.

Personal characteristics also influence conforming behavior. The more a person is attracted to the group, expects to interact with its members in the future, holds a position of relatively low status, and does not feel completely accepted by the group, the greater the likelihood that person will conform.

Conformity Across Cultures   A Chinese proverb states that "if one finger is sore, the whole hand will hurt." In a *collectivist culture* such as China, community and harmonious relationships are very important. Although members of all societies show a tendency to conform, you might suspect that people in such cultures would be more likely to conform to the will of the group than would members of *individualist cultures* (which value independence and personal achievement). That is indeed the case. Levels of conformity in collectivist cultures as diverse as Fiji, Zaire, Hong Kong, Lebanon, Zimbabwe, Kuwait, Japan, and Brazil are considerably higher than that found by Asch in the United States.

■ COMPLIANCE

Conformity is a response to pressure exerted by norms that are generally unstated. In contrast, **compliance** is a change of behavior in response to an explicitly stated request. One technique for inducing compliance is the so-called *foot-in-the-door effect*. Every salesperson knows that the moment a prospect allows the sales pitch to begin, the chances of making a sale improve greatly. The same effect operates in other areas of life: Once people have granted a small request (such as signing a petition), they are more likely to comply with a larger one (a request for money).

Another strategy commonly used by salespeople is the *lowball procedure*. The first step is to induce a person to agree to do something. The second step is to raise the cost of compliance. Among dealers of new cars, lowballing works like this: The dealer persuades the customer to buy a new car by reducing the price well below that offered by competitors. Once the customer has agreed to buy the car, however, the terms of the sale shift (for example, the trade-in value promised by the manager of used cars is cut); in the end, the car may be more costly than it would be at other dealerships. Despite the added costs, many customers follow through on their commitment to buy. Although the original inducement was the low price (the "lowball" that the salesperson originally pitched), once committed, the buyer remains committed to the now pricier car.

Under certain circumstances, a person who has refused to comply with an unreasonable request will be more likely to comply with a second, more reasonable request. This phenomenon

Conformity

- Conformity: Response to pressure exerted by _____ that are generally _____

- In small groups, conformity increases to a maximum of _____ and is higher when the task is _____ or _____; just one "ally" greatly _____ conformity.

- Conformity is greater when a person is _____ to the group, expects to _____ _____ in the future, holds a position of _____ _____, and does not feel _____ by the group.

- Conformity is greater in _____ cultures as opposed to _____ cultures.

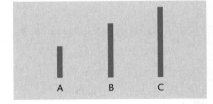

FIGURE 14–1
Asch's experiment on conformity.
In Asch's experiment on conformity, participants were shown a comparison card like the top one and asked to indicate which of the three lines on the bottom card was the most similar. Participants frequently chose the wrong line in order to conform to the group choice.

Compliance

- Compliance: Change of behavior in response to _____

  - *Foot-in-the-door effect*: Once people have granted a _____ request, they are more likely to comply with _____.

  - *Lowball procedure*: Once committed, people are more likely to _____ despite increases in the price.

  - *Door-in-the-face effect*: When people refuse to comply with an unreasonable request, they will be more likely to comply with _____ _____.

Obedience

- Obedience: Compliance with _____, generally from _____

- Obedience is more likely when:

  - The person giving the orders has _____

  - The person receiving the orders _____

  - Responsibility for an act is _____ by others.

Nazi concentration camps are a shocking example of the extremes to which people will go to obey orders. How do you explain the behaviors of the people who ran these camps?

has been dubbed the *door-in-the-face effect*. For example, in one study researchers approached students and asked them to make an unreasonably large commitment: Would they counsel delinquent youths at a detention center for two years? Nearly everyone declined, thus effectively "slamming the door" in the researcher's face. But when later asked to make a much smaller commitment—supervising children during a trip to the zoo—many of the same students quickly agreed.

■ OBEDIENCE

Compliance is agreement to change behavior in response to a request. **Obedience** is compliance with a command or a direct order, generally from a person in authority, such as a police officer, principal, or parent, who can back up the command with some sort of force if necessary. Obedience embodies social influence in its most direct and powerful form.

The powerful effect of obedience was demonstrated in a famous series of experiments conducted by Stanley Milgram (1933–1984). Milgram hired people to help him with a learning experiment and told them that they were to teach other people, the "learners," by giving them electric shocks when they gave the wrong answers. The shocks could be given in various intensities from "slight shock" to "severe shock." The participants were told to increase the intensity of the shock each time the learner made a mistake. As the shocks increased in intensity, the learners began to protest that they were being hurt. They cried out in pain and became increasingly upset as the shocking continued. Finally, they stopped responding altogether. The participants giving the shocks often became concerned and frightened and asked if they could stop. The experimenter politely but firmly pointed out that they were expected to continue. This was the crux of the experiment. Milgram was not doing a learning experiment at all—he was investigating obedience. Unbeknownst to the participants, the shock machine was fake and the "learners" were actually Milgram's accomplices who had been trained to act as though they were being hurt. Milgram actually wanted to find out how much shock people would deliver simply out of obedience to the experimenter. Incredibly, 65% of the participants went on to administer the highest level of shock even though many of them worried that the shocks were causing serious damage (Milgram, 1963). Milgram's research has been replicated in different cultures using male and female participants (P. B. Smith & Bond, 1999).

What factors influence the degree to which people will do what they are told? Studies in which people were asked to put a dime in a parking meter by people wearing uniforms show that one important factor is the amount of power vested in the person giving the orders. People obeyed a guard whose uniform looked like that of a police officer more often than they obeyed a man dressed either as a milkman or as a civilian. Another factor is surveillance. If we are ordered to do something then are left alone, we are less likely to obey than when we are being watched, especially when the act seems unethical to us. Milgram, for instance, found that his "teachers" were less willing to give severe shocks when the experimenter was out of the room. Milgram's experiments revealed other factors that influence a person's willingness to follow orders. When the victim was in the same room as the "teacher," obedience dropped sharply. When another "teacher" was present, someone who refused to give shocks, obedience also dropped. But when responsibility for an act was shared, so that the person was only one of many doing it, the degree of obedience was much greater.

Why do people willingly obey an authority figure, even when doing so means violating their own principles? Milgram (1974) suggested that people come to see themselves as the agents of *another* person's wishes and therefore as not responsible for the obedient actions or their consequences. Once this shift in self-perception has occurred, obedience follows, because in their own minds, they have relinquished control of their actions. For example, you may recall that in the aftermath of the Abu Ghraib prison scandal, the enlisted personnel who were photographed abusing prisoners insisted that they did so only on orders from higher authorities. An alternative explanation is that perhaps obedient participants do not succumb to situational forces, but rather fail to *perceive* the situation correctly (Nissani, 1990). Thus, in Milgram's study, the participants began with the belief that the experiment would be safe and that the experimenter would be trustworthy. The real emotional struggle for the obedient participants, then, may not have been in deciding whether to obey malevolent orders, but in recognizing that a trusted authority figure proved to be treacherous.

Check Your Understanding

1. The fact that people are more likely to comply with a smaller request after they have refused a larger one is called the _____ effect.

2. Indicate whether the following statements are true (T) or false (F).

    a. ___ Research shows that compliance is often higher in collectivist cultures than in noncollectivist ones.

    b. ___ Solomon Asch found that people were much more likely to conform in groups of four or more people.

    c. ___ A person is more likely to conform to the group when the group's task is ambiguous or difficult than when it is easy and clear.

3. You answer the telephone and hear the caller say, "Good morning. My name is _____ and I'm calling on behalf of XYZ. How are you today?" Right away, you know this caller is using which of the following social influence techniques?

    a. The lowball technique

    b. The assimilator technique

    c. The foot-in-the-door technique

    d. The door-in-the-face technique

Social Action

The various kinds of social influence just discussed may take place even when no one else is physically present. Let's now turn to processes that *do* depend on the presence of others. Specifically, let's examine processes that occur when people interact one-on-one and in groups, beginning with the phenomenon of deindividuation.

Deindividuation

■ Deindividuation: Losing one's

_____ in a group

Helping Behavior

■ Helping behavior can be caused by

_____

■ Altruistic behavior: Helpful actions

not linked to _____

■ Factors that affect the likelihood of

helping behavior:

  ■ Less likely when other people are

  _____ (bystander effect), the

  situation is _____, and the

  culture is _____

  ■ More likely when one person

  feels a sense of _____

  for another, is _____,

  in a good mood, is not shy or

  _____, is greatly in

  need of approval, or the culture is

  _____

■ DEINDIVIDUATION

We have seen several cases of social influence in which people act differently in the presence of others from the way they would if they were alone. The most striking and frightening instance of this phenomenon is *mob behavior*. Some well-known violent examples of mob behavior include the beatings and lynchings of African Americans in the 1950s and 1960s, the looting that sometimes accompanies urban rioting, and the wanton destruction of property that mars otherwise peaceful protests and demonstrations. One reason for mob behavior is that people can lose their personal sense of responsibility in a group, especially in a group subjected to intense pressures and anxiety. This process is called **deindividuation** because people respond not as individuals, but as anonymous parts of a larger group. In general, the more anonymous one feels in a group, the less responsible he or she begins to feel (Aronson, Wilson, & Akert, 2005).

But deindividuation only partly explains mob behavior. Another contributing factor is the *snowball effect*: If just one dominant and persuasive person convinces just a few people, those few will convince others, who will convince still others, and the group soon becomes an unthinking mob. Moreover, large groups provide *protection*. Anonymity makes it difficult to press charges. If two, or even 10, people start smashing windows, they will probably be arrested. However, if a thousand people smash windows, very few of them will be caught or punished.

■ HELPING BEHAVIOR

Mob behavior seems to support the unfortunate—and inaccurate—notion that when people get together, they will become more destructive and irresponsible than they would be individually. In fact, instances of cooperation and mutual assistance are at least as abundant as examples of human conflict and hostility. We need only to recall the behavior of people all over the United States in the aftermath of the September 11, 2001, terrorist attacks on the World Trade Center and the Pentagon or the rush of assistance to victims of Hurricane Katrina to find thousands of people working together and helping one another.

What are some of the social forces that can promote helping behavior? One force is perceived self-interest. For example, an employee offers the boss a ride home from the office because the employee knows that a promotion depends on how much he or she is liked by the boss. A person volunteers to feed a neighbor's cat while the neighbor is away because the person wants the neighbor to return the favor. But when helpful actions are not linked to such personal gain, they are considered altruistic. **Altruistic behavior** refers to helpful actions performed with no expectation of recognition or reward in return, except perhaps the good feeling that comes from helping someone in need. For example, many altruistic acts are directed toward strangers in the form of anonymous charitable donations, as is often demonstrated in the aftermath of a natural disaster.

Under what conditions is helpful behavior most likely to occur? People often assume that there is a "helping personality" or a set of traits that determines who is helpful and who is not. This is unlikely. Several conditions, both individual and situational, combine to determine when help will be offered.

The most important situational variable affecting the likelihood of helping behavior is the *presence of other people*. In a phenomenon called the **bystander effect**, the probability that a person will help someone else in trouble decreases as the number of bystanders present increases. In one experiment, people filling out a questionnaire heard a taped "emergency" in the next room, complete with a crash and screams. Of those who were alone, 70% offered help to the unseen victim, but of those who waited with a companion—a stranger who did nothing to help—only 7% offered help (Latané & Rodin, 1969). Another situational factor that affects helping behavior is *ambiguity*. Any factors that make it harder for others to recognize a genuine emergency reduce the probability of altruistic actions.

The personal characteristics of bystanders also affect helping behavior. Not all bystanders are equally likely to help a stranger. Increasing the amount of *personal responsibility* that one person feels for another boosts the likelihood that help will be extended. The amount of *empathy* that we feel toward another person affects our willingness to help, too. *Mood* also makes a difference: A person in a good mood is more likely to help another in need than is someone who is in a neutral or bad mood (Aronson, Wilson, & Akert, 2005; Salovey, Mayer, & Rosenhan, 1991). In addition, helping behavior is more likely to come from people who are *not shy* or *do not fear negative evaluation* for helping (Karakashian, Walter, Christopher, & Lucas, 2006). Finally, when others are watching, people who score high on the *need for approval* are more likely to help than are low scorers (Jonas, Schimel, Greenberg, & Pyszczynski, 2002; Satow, 1975).

ENDURING ISSUES DIVERSITY/UNIVERSALITY

Helping Behavior Across Cultures

Just as it is unlikely that there is such a thing as a "helping personality," it is doubtful that there is such a thing as a "helping culture"—that is, a society, nation, or group whose members are invariably "more helpful" than those of other groups. Psychologists have instead focused on the cultural factors that make helping more or less likely to take place.

Individualism-collectivism is an important dimension in this area: It seems plausible that members of individualist cultures feel less obligated to help other people than do members of collectivist cultures. A study using Indian and American participants investigated this possibility (Miller, Bersoff, & Harwood, 1990). Participants were presented with helping scenarios involving either a stranger, a friend, or a close relative whose need was either minor, moderate, or extreme. There were no cultural differences in cases of extreme need; members of both cultures reported being equally willing to help. But the two groups differed in cases of minor needs. Almost three times as many Indians (from a collectivist culture) as Americans (from an individualist culture) felt obligated to help in a scenario involving a close friend or a stranger asking for minor assistance. Even within collectivist cultures, however, the prediction of when help will be offered can be problematic (Triandis, 1994, 2001). Some members of collectivist societies are reluctant to offer help to anyone outside their in-group. They are therefore less likely to help strangers. Other cultures treat strangers as members of their group until the strangers' exact status can be determined.

■ GROUPS AND DECISION MAKING

There is a tendency in American society to turn over important decisions to groups. In the business world, key decisions are often made around a conference table rather than behind one person's desk. In politics, major policy decisions are seldom vested in just one person. Groups of advisers, cabinet officers, committee members, or aides meet to deliberate and forge a course of action. In the courts, a defendant may request a trial by jury, and for some serious crimes, jury trial is required by law. The nine members of the U.S. Supreme Court render group decisions on legal issues affecting the entire nation.

Many people trust these group decisions more than decisions made by individuals. Yet, the dynamics of social interaction within groups sometimes conspire to make group decisions *less* sound than those made by someone acting alone. Social psychologists are intrigued by how this outcome happens.

Polarization in Group Decision Making People often assume that an individual acting alone is more likely to take risks than a group considering the same issue. This assumption remained unchallenged until the early 1960s when research showed that groups often take more risks than the members of the group would if working alone. This phenomenon is known as the **risky shift**.

The risky shift is simply one aspect of a more general group phenomenon called **polarization**—the tendency for people to become more extreme in their attitudes as a result of

Groups and Decision Making

■ In some cases, groups make decisions that are _____ sound than those made by individuals:

　■ Polarization: The tendency for people to become _____ in their attitudes as a result of

　_____

　■ Risky shift: Special case of polarization in which groups _____ than the members of the group would if working alone

■ Groups are more effective than individuals only under certain circumstances.

group discussion. Polarization begins when group members discover during discussion that they share views to a greater degree than they realized. Then, in an effort to be seen in a positive light by the others, at least some group members become strong advocates for what is potentially the dominant sentiment in the group. Arguments leaning toward one extreme or the other not only reassure people that their initial attitudes are correct, but they also intensify those attitudes so that the group as a whole becomes more extreme in its position (Liu & Latané, 1998). So, if you want a group decision to be made in a cautious, conservative direction, you should be certain that the members of the group hold cautious and conservative views in the first place. Otherwise, the group decision may polarize in the opposite direction.

The Effectiveness of Groups   Another common assumption about groups is that "Two heads are better than one." In fact, groups are more effective than individuals only under certain circumstances. For one thing, their success depends on the *task* they face. Whenever the requirements of the task match the skills of the group members, the group is likely to be more effective than any single individual. But even when task and personnel are perfectly matched, the ways in which group members *interact* can reduce the group's effectiveness. For example, high-status individuals tend to exert more influence in groups, so if they do not possess the best problem-solving skills, group decisions may suffer. Another factor affecting group interaction and effectiveness is *group size*. The larger the group, the more likely it is to include someone who has the skills needed to solve a difficult problem. On the other hand, it is much harder to coordinate the activities of a large group. In addition, large groups may be more likely to encourage *social loafing*, the tendency of group members to exert less individual effort on the assumption that others in the group will do the work. Finally, the quality of group decision making also depends on the *cohesiveness* of a group. When the people in a group like one another and feel committed to the goals of the group, cohesiveness is high. Under these conditions, members may work hard for the group, spurred by high morale. But cohesiveness can also undermine the quality of group decision making. If the group succumbs to *groupthink*, strong pressure to conform may prevent its members from criticizing the emerging group consensus (Janis, 1982, 1989). The result may be disastrous decisions—such as the Bay of Pigs invasion, the Watergate burglary and cover-up, or the ill-fated *Columbia* and *Challenger* space flights.

■ LEADERSHIP

Every group has a leader, but how do group leaders come to the fore? For many years, the predominant answer was the **great-person theory,** which states that leaders are extraordinary people who assume positions of influence and are able to shape events around them. In this view, people such as George Washington, Winston Churchill, and Nelson Mandela were "born leaders" who would have led their nations in extraordinary ways at any time in history.

Most historians and psychologists now regard this theory as naive because it ignores social and economic factors. An alternative theory holds that leadership emerges when the right person is in the right place at the right time. For instance, in the late 1950s and early 1960s, Dr. Martin Luther King Jr. rose to lead the Civil Rights movement in the United States. Dr. King was clearly a "great person"—intelligent, dynamic, eloquent, and highly motivated. Yet, had the times not been right (had he lived 30 years earlier, for example), it is doubtful that he would have been as successful as he was.

Recently, social scientists have argued that there is more to leadership than either the great-person theory or the right-place-at-the-right-time theory implies. Rather, the leader's traits, certain aspects of the situation in which the group finds itself and the response of the group and the leader to each other are all important considerations. Fred Fiedler's *contingency theory* of leader effectiveness is based on such a transactional view of leadership (Fiedler, 1993, 2002).

According to Fiedler's theory, personal characteristics are important to the success of a leader. One kind of leader is *task oriented*, concerned with doing the task well—even at the expense of worsening relationships among group members. Other leaders are *relationship oriented,*

Leadership

■ Great-person theory: Leaders are extraordinary people who assume positions of _____ and are able to _____ regardless of the circumstances.

■ An alternative theory states that social and economic factors influence the emergence of a leader who happens to be the right _____ in the right _____ at the right _____.

■ Contingency theory:

■ When conditions are either very favorable or very unfavorable for the leader, the most effective leader is the one who is _____ oriented.

■ When conditions are moderately favorable, the most effective leader is _____ oriented.

■ Gender differences: Women tend to have a more _____, _____, and _____ oriented style of managing that is generally _____ effective than the directive and task-oriented leadership style common among men as far as winning acceptance for their ideas and instilling self-confidence.

concerned with maintaining group cohesiveness and harmony. Which style is most effective depends on situational factors. Fiedler has shown that when conditions are either very favorable (good leader-member relations, structured tasks, high leader power) or very unfavorable (poor leader-member relations, unstructured task, low leader power) for the leader, the most effective leader is the one who is task oriented. However, when conditions within the group are only moderately favorable for the leader, the most effective leader is one who is concerned about maintaining good interpersonal relations. The contingency view of leadership, which has received a great deal of support from research conducted in the laboratory as well as in real-life settings, clearly indicates that there is no such thing as an ideal leader for all situations. "Except perhaps for the unusual case," Fiedler states, "it is simply not meaningful to speak of an effective or of an ineffective leader; we can only speak of a leader who tends to be effective in one situation and ineffective in another" (Fiedler, 1967, p. 261).

One theory of leadership holds that the particularly effective leader is the right person in the right place at the right time. For the American Civil Rights movement, Martin Luther King Jr. was such a leader.

ENDURING ISSUES DIVERSITY/UNIVERSALITY

Women as Leaders

Research has shown that the leadership styles of men and women vary considerably. In one five-year study of 2,482 managers in more than 400 organizations, female and male coworkers said that women make better managers than men (Kass, 1999). The reason seems to be that many female managers have added such traditionally "masculine" task-oriented traits as decisiveness, planning, and setting standards to such "feminine" relationship-oriented assets as communication, feedback, and empowering other employees, whereas many male managers still rely on an autocratic style that emphasizes individual competition and achievement (Eagly, 2003). For example, one review concluded that, in contrast to the directive and task-oriented leadership style common among men, women tend to have a more democratic, collaborative, and interpersonally oriented style of managing employees (O'Leary & Flanagan, 2001). Moreover, a woman's more collaborate style of leadership is often able to overcome any preconceived resistance to her leadership (Lips, 2002).

Another large-scale review of 45 studies of gender and leadership found women's leadership styles are generally more effective than traditional male leadership styles (Eagly, Johannesen-Schmidt, & van-Engen, 2003). This review found that female leaders are generally more effective than male leaders at winning acceptance for their ideas and instilling self-confidence in their employees (Lips, 2002). Results similar to these have prompted some experts to call for specialized women-only leadership training programs to assist women in developing their full feminine leadership potential independent of male influence (Vinnicombe & Singh, 2003).

Check Your Understanding

1. Match each of the following terms with the appropriate description.

_____ Deindividuation

_____ Bystander effect

_____ Polarization

_____ Groupthink

a. The tendency for people to become more extreme in their attitudes as a result of group discussion

b. Reduced willingness to criticize an emerging group consensus as a result of strong pressure to conform

c. Loss of personal sense of responsibility in a group

d. The probability that a person will help someone else in trouble decreases as the number of other people present increases

2. In a situation in which leader-member relations are poor, the group's task is unstructured, and the leader has little power, according to Fiedler's contingency model of leadership which of the following is true?

a. The most effective leader is likely to be task oriented.

b. The most effective leader is likely to be relationship oriented.

c. Neither task-oriented leaders nor relationship-oriented leaders are likely to be effective.

d. Both task-oriented leaders and relationship-oriented leaders are likely to be effective.

Chapter Review    www.psychologythecore.com

Social psychology is the scientific study of how people's thoughts, feelings, and behaviors are influenced by the behaviors and characteristics of other people.

Social Cognition

Forming impressions, explaining others' behavior, and experiencing interpersonal attraction are examples of **social cognition**, the process of taking in and assessing information about other people. It is one way that people are influenced by others' thoughts, feelings, and behaviors.

When forming impressions of others, we often rely on **schemata**, or sets of expectations and beliefs about categories of people. A **stereotype**, a set of characteristics presumed to be shared by all members of a social category, is a particular kind of schema. Impressions are also affected by the order in which information is acquired. First impressions are especially strong (the **primacy effect**), in part because people are "cognitive misers": Once they have formed an impression about someone, they do not exert the mental effort to change it. First impressions can also bring about the very behavior expected from other people, a process known as **self-fulfilling prophecy**. One example of a self-fulfilling prophecy is the *Pygmalion effect* in which both high and low teacher expectations have been shown to exert a powerful influence on student achievement.

Attribution theory holds that people seek to understand human behavior by attributing it either to internal causes (such as personality) or external causes (such as situational factors). In making such judgments, there is reliance on three aspects of the behavior: distinctiveness, consistency, and consensus. However, causal attributions are often vulnerable to biases. For example, people tend to explain the behavior of others as caused by *internal* factors, while attributing their own behavior to *external* forces (the **actor-observer bias**). The **fundamental attribution error** refers specifically to this tendency to overemphasize others' personal traits in attributing causes to their behavior. **Defensive attribution** motivates people to explain their own actions in ways that protect their self-esteem. *Self-serving bias* refers to the tendency to attribute personal successes to internal factors and personal failures to external ones. The **just-world hypothesis** may lead individuals to blame the victim when bad things happen to other people.

Proximity is important in determining attraction. People who do not live or work near each other are unlikely to have a chance to develop a mutual attraction. People who are similar in attitudes, interests, backgrounds, and values tend to like one another. Finally, people also tend to like physically attractive people, as well as attributing to them, correctly or not, many positive personal characteristics, such as being intelligent and interesting.

Attitudes

An **attitude** is a relatively stable organization of beliefs, feelings, and tendencies to act in certain ways toward something or someone. The three major components of attitudes are (1) evaluative beliefs about the attitude object, (2) feelings about that object, and (3) behavioral tendencies toward it. These three components are very often (but not always) consistent with one another. Attitudes are important because they often influence behavior. However, behavior does not always accurately reflect attitudes. Variables such as the strength of the attitude, how easily it comes to mind, how noticeable a particular attitude is in a given situation, and how relevant the attitude is to the particular behavior in question help to determine whether a person will act in accordance with an attitude. Also, people who are high on **self-monitoring** are more likely to override their attitudes to meet the demands of the situation.

Many of our most basic attitudes derive from early, direct personal experience with parents and peers. Teachers, friends, the mass media and even famous people are also important in shaping attitudes.

Prejudice is an unfair negative attitude directed toward a group and its members, whereas **discrimination** is unfair behavior directed against an entire group of people or individual members of that group. Prejudice and discrimination do not always occur together. As do all attitudes, prejudice has three components: beliefs, feelings, and behavioral tendencies. Prejudicial beliefs are virtually always negative stereotypes. Prejudice is usually marked by strong emotions, such as dislike, fear, hatred, or loathing as well as behavioral tendencies such as avoidance, hostility, and discrimination. **Racism** is the belief that members of certain racial or ethnic groups are *innately* inferior to one or more other groups.

One explanation for prejudiced attitudes is the **frustration-aggression theory,** which states that people who feel exploited and oppressed displace their hostility toward the powerful onto *scapegoats*—people who are "lower" on the social scale than they are. Another theory links prejudice to the **authoritarian personality,** a rigidly conventional and bigoted type marked by exaggerated respect for authority and hostility toward those who defy society's norms. Finally, conformity to the prejudices of one's social group can also explain prejudice.

Attitudes can change in response to persuasion. The first step in persuasion is to get the audience's attention. Then the task is to get the audience to comprehend and accept the message. According to the *communication model*, persuasion is a function of the source, the message itself, the medium of communication, and the characteristics of the audience.

Attitudes may also change when new actions, beliefs, or perceptions contradict preexisting attitudes and create **cognitive dissonance.** In particular, behaving in a way that does not correspond to one's attitudes can lead to attitude change that, in turn, reduces cognitive dissonance. The most effective means of changing attitudes—especially important attitudes, behaviors, or lifestyle choices—may be *self-persuasion*.

Social Influence

Social influence refers to the process by which the presence of other people affects perceptions, attitudes, and actions. The power of social influence is especially apparent in the study of cultural influences and of conformity, compliance, and obedience.

The culture in which you are immersed has an enormous influence on your thoughts and actions. Culture dictates differences in diet, dress, and personal space. One result of this is the unquestioning acceptance of **cultural truisms**—beliefs or values that most members of a society accept as self-evident. Eating pizza, shunning rattlesnake meat, dressing in jeans rather than a loincloth, and feeling uncomfortable when others stand very close to you when they speak are all results of living in American culture. As we adapt our behavior to that of others, we learn the behavioral **norms** of our culture, as well as its beliefs and values.

Voluntarily yielding one's preferences, beliefs, or judgments to those of a larger group is called **conformity.** Research by Solomon Asch and others has shown that characteristics of both the situation and the person influence the likelihood of conforming. Cultural influences on the tendency to conform also exist, with people in collectivist cultures often being more prone to conformity than those in noncollectivist ones.

Compliance is a change in behavior in response to an explicit request. One technique to encourage compliance is the *foot-in-the-door effect,* or getting people to go along with a small request to make them more likely to comply with a larger one. Another technique is the *lowball procedure*, which involves initially offering a low price to win commitment, then gradually escalating the cost. Also effective is the *door-in-the-face effect,* or initially making an unreasonable request that is bound to be turned down but will perhaps generate enough guilt to foster compliance with another less extreme request.

Obedience is compliance with a command or direct order. Classic research by Stanley Milgram showed that many people were willing to obey orders to administer harmful shocks to other people. Obedience to an authority figure was more likely when the authority figure issuing the order was nearby. They were also more likely to obey the command when the person being given the shock was some distance from them. According to Milgram, obedience is brought on by the constraints of the situation.

Social Action

Immersion in a large, anonymous group may lead to **deindividuation,** the loss of a sense of personal responsibility for one's actions. Deindividuation can sometimes lead to violence or other forms of irresponsible behavior. The greater the sense of anonymity, the more this effect occurs.

Helping someone in need without expectation of a reward is called **altruistic behavior.** Altruism is influenced by situational factors, such as the presence of other people. According to the **bystander effect,** a person is less apt to offer assistance when other potential helpers are present, especially when the others do nothing. Factors within the individual that encourage helping behavior include a sense of personal responsibility, empathy, being in a good mood, and not being shy or fearful. When others are watching, people high in need for approval are more likely to help. Helping behavior is more likely to occur in collectivist cultures than in individualist cultures when the need is not extreme.

Contrary to the belief that groups are less likely than individuals to make extreme, unsound, or risky decisions, research shows that groups often take more risks than the members of the group would if working alone (a phenomenon known as the **risky shift**). More generally, people become more extreme rather than less extreme in their attitudes as a result of group discussion (a phenomenon known as **polarization**).

Contrary to the belief that "two heads are better than one," research shows that groups are more effective than individuals only under certain circumstances: when the requirements of the task match the skills of the group members, whenever high-status individuals who lack the best problem-solving skills do not exert undue influence and when the size of the group is large enough to include people with the requisite skills but not so large that it becomes unwieldy or when people engage in *social loafing*. Finally, a cohesive group may or may not be more effective than a less cohesive group. In very cohesive groups, there may be a tendency toward *groupthink*, an unwillingness to criticize the emerging group consensus even when it seems misguided.

According to the **great-person theory,** leadership is a function of personal traits that qualify one to lead others. An alternative theory attributes leadership to being in the right place at the right time. According to the transactional view, traits of the leader and traits of the group interact with certain aspects of the situation to determine what kind of leader will come to the fore. Fred Fiedler's *contingency theory* focused on two contrasting leadership styles: task oriented and relationship oriented. The effectiveness of each style depends on the nature of the task, the relationship of the leader with group members, and the leader's power over the group.

Recent research indicates that women in leadership positions tend to have a more democratic, collaborative, and interpersonally oriented style of managing employees than do men in similar positions. As a result, female leaders are generally more effective than male leaders at winning acceptance for their ideas and instilling self-confidence in their employees.

Most of the experiments described in this book involve measuring one or more variables and analyzing the data statistically. The design and scoring of all the tests are also based on statistical methods. **Statistics** is a branch of mathematics that provides techniques for sorting out quantitative facts and ways of drawing conclusions from them. Statistics let people organize and describe data quickly, guide the conclusions they draw, and help them make inferences.

Statistical analysis is essential to conducting an experiment or designing a test, but statistics can only handle numbers—groups of them. To use statistics, the psychologist first must measure things—count and express them in quantities.

Scales of Measurement

No matter what is being measured—height, noise, intelligence, attitudes—a scale has to be used. The data to be collected determines the scale to use and, in turn, the scale used helps determine the conclusions drawn from the data.

Nominal Scales   A nominal scale is a set of arbitrarily named or numbered categories. If we decide to classify a group of people by the color of their eyes, we are using a nominal scale. We can count how many people have blue, green, or brown eyes, and so on, but we cannot say that one group has more or less eye color than the other. The colors are simply different. Because a nominal scale is better for classifying than for measuring, it is the least informative kind of scale. If we want to compare our data more precisely, we will have to use a scale that tells us more.

Ordinal Scales   If we list horses in the order in which they finish a race, we are using an ordinal scale. On an **ordinal scale**, data are ranked from first to last according to some criterion. An ordinal scale tells the order, but it says nothing about the distances between what is ranked first and second or ninth and tenth. It does not tell us how much faster the winning horse ran than the horses that placed or showed. If a person ranks her preferences for various kinds of soup—pea soup first, then tomato, then onion, and so on—we know what soup she likes most and what soup she likes least, but we have no idea how much better she likes tomato than onion, or whether pea soup is far more favored than either one of them.

Because we do not know the distances between the items ranked on an ordinal scale, we cannot add or subtract ordinal data. If mathematical operations are necessary, we need a still more informative scale.

Interval Scales   An interval scale is often compared to a ruler that has been broken off at the bottom—it only goes from, say, 5.5 to 12. The intervals between 6 and 7, 7 and 8, 8 and 9, and so forth are equal, but there is no zero. A Fahrenheit or Celsius thermometer is an interval scale—even though a certain degree registered on such thermometer specifies a certain state of cold or heat, there is no such thing as the absence of temperature. One day is never twice as hot as another; it is only so many equal degrees hotter.

An interval scale tells us how many equal-size units one thing lies above or below another thing of the same kind, but it does not tell us how many times bigger, smaller, taller, or fatter one thing is than another. An intelligence test cannot tell us that one person is three times as intelligent as another, only that he or she scored so many points above or below someone else.

Ratio Scales　We can only say that a measurement is two times as long as another or three times as high when we use a **ratio scale**, one that has a true zero. For instance, if we measure the snowfall in a certain area over several winters, we can say that six times as much snow fell during the winter in which we measured a total of 12 feet as during a winter in which only 2 feet fell. This scale has a zero—there can be no snow.

Measurements of Central Tendency

Usually, when we measure a number of instances of anything—from the popularity of TV shows to the weights of 8-year-old boys to the number of times a person's optic nerve fires in response to electrical stimulation—we get a distribution of measurements that range from smallest to largest or lowest to highest. The measurements will usually cluster around some value near the middle. This value is the **central tendency** of the distribution of the measurements.

Suppose, for example, you want to keep 10 children busy tossing rings around a bottle. You give them three rings to toss each turn, the game has six rounds, and each player scores one point every time he or she gets the ring around the neck of the bottle. The highest possible score is 18. The distribution of scores might end up like this: 11, 8, 13, 6, 12, 10, 16, 9, 12, 3.

What could you quickly say about the ring-tossing talent of the group? First, you could arrange the scores from lowest to highest: 3, 6, 8, 9, 10, 11, 12, 12, 13, and 16. In this order, the central tendency of the distribution of scores becomes clear. Many of the scores cluster around the values between 8 and 12. There are three ways to describe the central tendency of a distribution. We usually refer to all three as the *average*.

The arithmetical average is called the **mean**—the sum of all the scores in the group divided by the number of scores. If you add up all the scores and divide by 10, the total number of scores in this group of ring tossers, you find that the mean for the group is 10.

The **median** is the point that divides a distribution in half—50% of the scores fall above the median and 50% fall below. In the ring-tossing scores, five scores fall at 10 or below, five at 11 or above. The median is thus halfway between 10 and 11, which is 10.5.

The point at which the largest number of scores occurs is called the **mode**. In our example, the mode is 12. More people scored 12 than any other.

■ DIFFERENCES AMONG THE MEAN, MEDIAN, AND MODE

If we take many measurements of anything, we are likely to get a distribution of scores in which the mean, median, and mode are all about the same—the score that occurs most often (mode) will also be the point that half the scores are below and half above (median). And the same point will be the arithmetical average (mean). This is not always true, of course, and small samples rarely come out so symmetrically. In these cases, we often have to decide which of the three measures of central tendency—mean, median, or mode—will tell us what we want to know.

For example, a shopkeeper wants to know the general incomes of passersby so he can stock the right merchandise. He might conduct a rough survey by standing outside his store for a few days from 12:00 p.m. to 2:00 p.m. and asking every tenth person who walks by to check a card showing the general range of his or her income. Suppose most of the people checked the ranges between $25,000 and $60,000 a year. However, a couple of the people made a lot of money—one checked $100,000 to $150,000 and the other checked the $250,000-or-above box. The mean for the set of income figures would be pushed higher by those two large figures and would not really tell the shopkeeper what he wants to know about his potential customers. In this case, he would be wiser to use the median or the mode.

Suppose instead of meeting two people whose incomes were so great, he noticed that people from two distinct income groups walked by his store—several people checked the box for $25,000–$35,000, and several others checked $50,000–$60,000. The shopkeeper would find that his distribution was bimodal. It has two modes—$30,000 and $55,000. This might be more useful to him than the mean, which could lead him to think his customers were a unit with an average income of about $40,000.

Another way of approaching a set of scores is to arrange them into a **frequency distribution**—that is, to select a set of intervals and count how many scores fall into each interval. A frequency distribution is useful for large groups of numbers; it puts the number of individual scores into more manageable groups.

Suppose a psychologist tests memory. She asks 50 college students to learn 18 nonsense syllables, then records how many syllables each student can recall two hours later. She arranges her raw scores from lowest to highest in a rank distribution:

2	6	8	10	11	14
3	7	9	10	12	14
4	7	9	10	12	15
4	7	9	10	12	16
5	7	9	10	13	17
5	7	9	11	13	
6	8	9	11	13	
6	8	9	11	13	
6	8	10	11	13	

The scores range from 2 to 17, but 50 individual scores are too cumbersome to work with. So, she chooses a set of 2-point intervals and tallies the number of scores in each interval:

Interval	Tally	Frequency
1–2		1
3–4		3
5–6		6
7–8		9
9–10		13
11–12		8
13–14		7
15–16		2
17–18		1

Now she can tell at a glance what the results of her experiment were. Most of the students had scores near the middle of the range, and very few had scores in the high or low intervals. She can see these results even better when she uses the frequency distribution to construct a bar graph—a **frequency histogram**. Marking the intervals along the horizontal axis and the frequencies along the vertical axis would give her the graph shown in Figure A–1. Another way is to construct a **frequency polygon**, a line graph. A frequency polygon drawn from the same set of data is shown in Figure A–2. Note that the figure is not a smooth curve, since the points are connected by straight lines. With many scores, however, and with small intervals, the angles would smooth out, and the figure would resemble a rounded curve.

The Normal Curve

Ordinarily, if we take enough measurements of almost anything, we get a *normal distribution*. Tossing coins is a favorite example of statisticians. If you tossed 10 coins into the air 1,000 times and recorded the heads and tails on each toss, your tabulations would reveal a normal

FIGURE A–1
A frequency histogram for a memory experiment.
The bars indicate the frequency of scores within each interval.

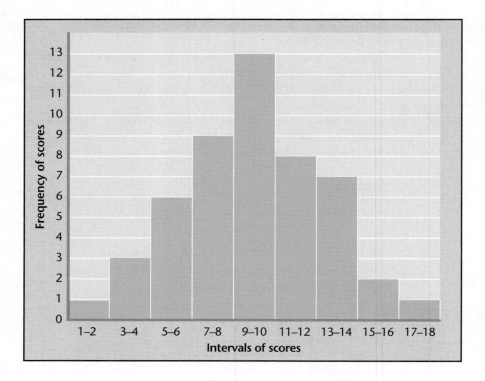

distribution. Five heads and five tails would be the most frequent, followed by four heads/six tails and six heads/six tails, and so on down to the rare all heads or all tails.

Plotting a normal distribution on a graph yields a particular kind of frequency polygon, called a **normal curve**. Figure A–3 shows data on the heights of 1,000 men. Superimposed over the bars that reflect the actual data is an "ideal" normal curve for the same data. Note that the curve is absolutely symmetrical—the left slope parallels the right slope exactly. Moreover, the mean, median, and mode all fall on the highest point on the curve.

The normal curve is a hypothetical entity. No set of real measurements shows such a smooth gradation from one interval to the next, or so purely symmetrical a shape. But because so many things do approximate the normal curve so closely, the curve is a useful model for much that we measure.

FIGURE A–2
A frequency polygon drawn from data used in Figure A–1.
The dots, representing the frequency of scores in each interval, are connected by straight lines.

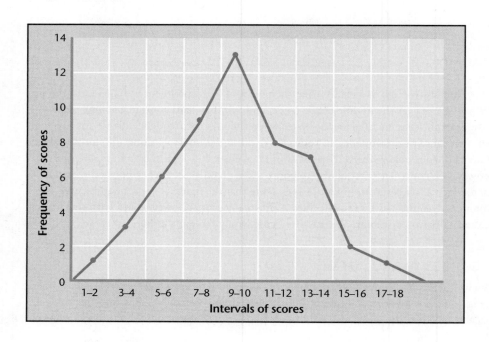

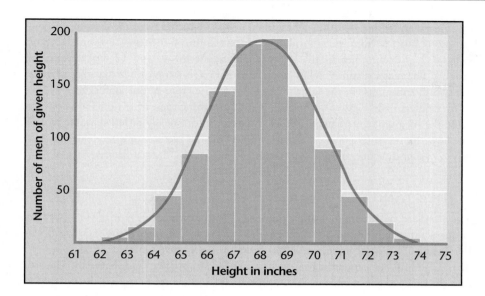

FIGURE A–3
A normal curve.
This curve is based on measurements of the heights of 1,000 adult males.

Source: From Hill, 1966.

SKEWED DISTRIBUTIONS

If a frequency distribution is asymmetrical—when most of the scores are gathered at either the high end or the low end—the frequency polygon will be skewed. The hump will sit to one side or the other, and one of the curve's tails will be disproportionately long.

 If a high school mathematics instructor, for example, gives her students a sixth-grade arithmetic test, we would expect nearly all the scores to be quite high. The frequency polygon would probably look like the one in Figure A–4. But if a sixth-grade class were asked to do advanced algebra, the scores would probably be quite low. The frequency polygon would be very similar to the one shown in Figure A–5.

 Note, too, that the mean, median, and mode fall at different points in a skewed distribution, unlike in the normal curve, where they coincide. Usually, when you know that the mean is greater than the median of a distribution, you can predict that the frequency polygon will be skewed to the right. When the median is greater than the mean, the curve will be skewed to the left.

BIMODAL DISTRIBUTIONS

We have already mentioned a bimodal distribution in our description of the shopkeeper's survey of his customers' incomes. The frequency polygon for a bimodal distribution has two humps—one for each mode. The mean and the median may be the same (Figure A–6) or different (Figure A–7).

MEASURES OF VARIATION

Sometimes, it is not enough to know the distribution of a set of data and their mean, median, and mode. Suppose an automotive safety expert feels that too much damage occurs in tail-end accidents because automobile bumpers are not all the same height. It is not enough to know what the average height of an automobile bumper is. The safety expert also wants to know about the variation in bumper heights: How much higher is the highest bumper than the mean? How do bumpers of all cars vary from the mean? Are the latest bumpers closer to the same height?

RANGE

The simplest measure of variation is the **range**—the difference between the largest and smallest measurements. Perhaps the safety expert measured the bumpers of 1,000 cars

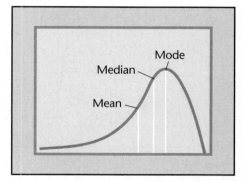

FIGURE A–4
Distribution skewed left.
Most of the scores are gathered at the high end of the distribution, causing the hump to shift to the right. Because the tail on the left is longer, we say that the curve is skewed to the left. Note that the *mean, median,* and *mode* are different.

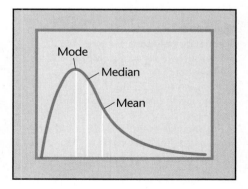

FIGURE A–5
Distribution skewed right.
In this distribution, most of the scores are gathered at the low end, so the curve is skewed to the right. The *mean, median,* and *mode* do not coincide.

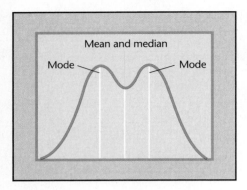

FIGURE A–6
Bimodal distribution: Example 1.
A bimodal distribution in which the *mean* and the *median* are the same.

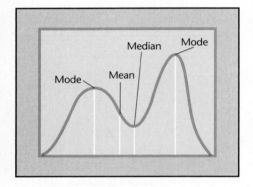

FIGURE A–7
Bimodal distribution: Example 2.
In this bimodal distribution, the *mean* and the *median* are different.

FIGURE A–8
Frequency polygons for two sets of measurements of automobile bumper heights.
Both are normal curves, and in each distribution the *mean, median,* and *mode* are 15. But the variation from the mean is different, causing one curve to be flattened and the other to be much more sharply peaked.

2 years ago and found that the highest bumper was 18 inches from the ground, the lowest only 12 inches from the ground. The range was thus 6 inches—18 minus 12. This year the highest bumper is still 18 inches high, the lowest still 12 inches from the ground. The range is still 6 inches. Moreover, our safety expert finds that the means of the two distributions are the same—15 inches off the ground. But look at the two frequency polygons in Figure A–8—there is still something the expert needs to know, because the measurements cluster around the mean in drastically different ways. To find out how the measurements are distributed around the mean, our safety expert has to turn to a slightly more complicated measure of variation—the standard deviation.

■ THE STANDARD DEVIATION

The **standard deviation**, in a single number, tells us much about how the scores in any frequency distribution are dispersed around the mean. Calculating the standard deviation is one of the most useful and widely employed statistical tools.

To find the standard deviation of a set of scores, we first find the mean. Then we take the first score in the distribution, subtract it from the mean, square the difference, and jot it down in a column to be added up later. We do the same for all the scores in the distribution. Then we add up the column of squared differences, divide the total by the number of scores in the distribution, and find the square root of that number. Figure A–9 shows the calculation of the standard deviation for a small distribution of scores.

In a normal distribution, however peaked or flattened the curve, about 68% of the scores fall between one standard deviation above the mean and one standard deviation below the mean (see Figure A–10). Another 27% fall between one standard deviation and two standard deviations on either side of the mean, and 4% more between the second and third standard deviations on either side. Overall, then, more than 99% of the scores fall between three standard deviations above and three standard deviations below the mean. This makes the standard deviation useful for comparing two different normal distributions.

Now let us see what the standard deviation can tell our automotive safety expert about the variations from the mean in the two sets of data. The standard deviation for the cars measured 2 years ago is about 1.4. A car with a bumper height of 16.4 is one standard deviation above the mean of 15; one with a bumper height of 13.6 is one standard deviation below the mean. Because the engineer knows that the data fall into a normal distribution, he can figure that about 68% of the 1,000 cars he measured will fall somewhere between these two heights: 680 cars will have bumpers between 13.6 and 16.4 inches high. For the more recent set of data, the standard deviation is just slightly less than 1. A car with a

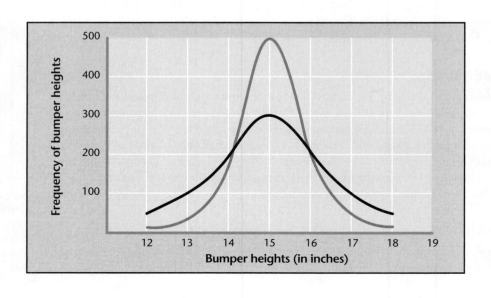

Number of scores = 10		Mean = 7
Scores	Difference from mean	Difference squared
4	7 – 4 = 3	$3^2 = 9$
5	7 – 5 = 2	$2^2 = 4$
6	7 – 6 = 1	$1^2 = 1$
6	7 – 6 = 1	$1^2 = 1$
7	7 – 7 = 0	$0^2 = 0$
7	7 – 7 = 0	$0^2 = 0$
8	7 – 8 = – 1	$– 1^2 = 1$
8	7 – 8 = – 1	$– 1^2 = 1$
9	7 – 9 = – 2	$– 2^2 = 4$
10	7 – 10 = – 3	$– 3^2 = 9$

Sum of squares = 30

÷

Number of scores = 10

Variance = 3

Standard deviation = $\sqrt{3}$ = 1.73

FIGURE A–9
Standard deviation.
Step-by-step calculation of the *standard deviation* for a group of 10 scores with a mean of 7.

bumper height of about 14 inches is one standard deviation below the mean; a car with a bumper height of about 16 is one standard deviation above the mean. Thus, in this distribution, 680 cars have bumpers between 14 and 16 inches high. This tells the safety expert that car bumpers are becoming more similar, although the range of heights is still the same (6 inches), and the mean height of bumpers is still 15.

Measures of Correlation

Measures of central tendency and measures of variation can be used to describe a single set of measurements—such as the children's ring-tossing scores—or to compare two or more sets of measurements—such as the two sets of bumper heights. Sometimes, however, we need to know whether two sets of measurements are in any way associated with each other—whether or not they are correlated. Is parental IQ related to children's IQ? Does the need for achievement relate to the need for power? Is watching violence on TV related to aggressive behavior?

One fast way to determine whether two variables are correlated is to draw a **scatter plot.** We assign one variable (X) to the horizontal axis of a graph, the other variable (Y) to the vertical axis. Then we plot a person's score on one characteristic along the horizontal axis and his or her score on the second characteristic along the vertical axis. Where the two scores intersect,

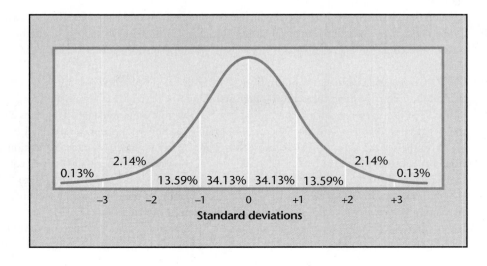

FIGURE A–10
Normal curve.
A normal curve, divided to show the percentage of scores that fall within each *standard deviation* from the *mean.*

FIGURE A–11
Correlations.
Scatter plots provide a picture of the strength and direction of a correlation.

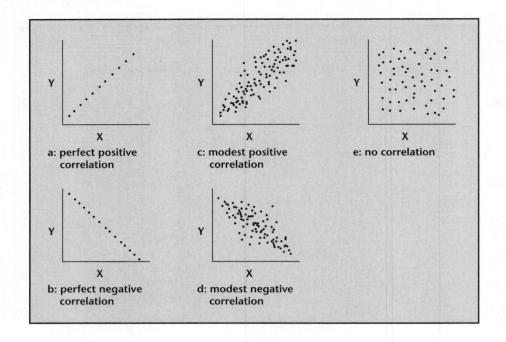

a: perfect positive correlation

c: modest positive correlation

e: no correlation

b: perfect negative correlation

d: modest negative correlation

we draw a dot. When several scores have been plotted in this way, the pattern of dots tells whether the two characteristics are in any way correlated with each other.

If the dots on a scatter plot form a straight line running between the lower left-hand corner and the upper right-hand corner, as they do in Figure A–11a, we have a perfect positive correlation—a high score on one of the characteristics is always associated with a high score on the other one. A straight line running between the upper left-hand corner and the lower right-hand corner, as in Figure A–11b, is the sign of a perfect negative correlation—a high score on one of the characteristics is always associated with a low score on the other one. If the pattern formed by the dots is cigar shaped in either of these directions, as in Figures A–11c and d, we have a modest correlation—the two characteristics are related but not highly correlated. If the dots spread out over the whole graph, forming a circle or a random pattern, as they do in Figure A–11e, there is no correlation between the two characteristics.

A scatter plot can give us a general idea of whether a correlation exists and how strong it is. To describe the relation between two variables more precisely, we need a **correlation coefficient**—a statistical measure of the degree to which two variables are associated. The correlation coefficient tells us the degree of association between two sets of matched scores—that is, to what extent high or low scores on one variable tend to be associated with high or low scores on another variable. It also provides an estimate of how well we can predict from a person's score on one characteristic how high he or she will score on another characteristic. If we know, for example, that a test of mechanical ability is highly correlated with success in engineering courses, we could predict that success on the test would also mean success as an engineering major.

Correlation coefficients can run from +1.0 to −1.0. The highest possible value (+1.0) indicates a perfect positive correlation—high scores on one variable are always and systematically related to high scores on a second variable. The lowest possible value (−1.0) means a perfect negative correlation—high scores on one variable are always and regularly related to low scores on the second variable. In life, most things are far from perfect, so most correlation coefficients fall somewhere between +1.0 and −1.0. A correlation smaller than ±.20 is considered very low, from ±.20 to ±.40 is low, from ±.40 to ±.60 is moderate, from ±.60 to ±.80 is high, and from ±.80 to ±1.0 is very high. A correlation of zero indicates that there is no correlation between two sets of scores—no regular relation between them at all.

Correlation tells us nothing about causality. If we found a high positive correlation between participation in elections and income levels, for example, we still could not say that being wealthy made people vote or that voting made people wealthy. We would still not know which came first, or whether some third variable explained both income levels and voting behavior. Correlation only tells us that we have found some association between scores on two specified characteristics.

Using Statistics to Make Predictions

Behind the use of statistics is the hope that we can generalize from our results and use them to predict behavior. We hope, for example, that we can use the record of how well a group of rats run through a maze today to predict how another group of rats will do tomorrow, that we can use a person's scores on a sales aptitude test to predict how well he or she will sell life insurance, that we can measure the attitudes of a relatively small group of people about pollution control to indicate what the attitudes of the whole country are.

First, we have to determine whether our measurements are representative and whether we can have confidence in them. In Chapter 1, "The Science of Psychology", we discussed this problem when we considered the problem of proper sampling.

■ PROBABILITY

Errors based on inadequate sampling procedures are somebody's fault. Other kinds of errors occur randomly. In the simplest kind of experiment, a psychologist will gather a representative sample, split it randomly into two groups, and then apply some experimental manipulation to one of the groups. Afterward, the psychologist will measure both groups and determine whether the experimental group's score is now different from the score of the control group. But even if there is a large difference between the scores of the two groups, it may still be wrong to attribute the difference to the manipulation. Random effects might influence the results and introduce error.

Statistics give the psychologist many ways to determine precisely whether the difference between the two groups is really significant, whether something other than chance produced the results, and whether the same results would be obtained with different subjects. These probabilities are expressed as measures of **significance.** If the psychologist computes the significance level for the results as .05, he or she knows that there are 19 chances out of 20 that the results are not due to chance. But there is still 1 chance in 20—or a .05 likelihood—that the results are due to chance. A .01 significance level would mean that there is only 1 chance in 100 that the results are due to chance.

Using Meta-Analysis in Psychological Research

In several places in this text, we have presented findings from reviews of psychological research in which a research team has summarized a wide selection of literature on a topic in order to reach some conclusions on that topic. There are several crucial decisions to be made in such a process: Which research reports should be included? How should the information be summarized? What questions might be answered after all the available information is gathered?

Traditionally, psychologists reviewing the literature in a particular area relied on the *box-score method* to reach conclusions. That is, after collecting all the relevant research reports, the researcher simply counted the number supporting one conclusion or the other, much like keeping track of the scoring in nine innings of a baseball game (hence, the term *box score*). For example, if there were 200 studies of gender differences in aggressive behavior, researchers might find that 120 of them showed that males were more aggressive than females, 40 showed the opposite pattern, and 40 showed no evidence of gender differences. On the basis of these box scores, the reviewer might conclude that males are more likely than females to act aggressively.

Today, researchers tend to rely on a more sophisticated strategy known as **meta-analysis.** Meta-analysis provides a way of statistically combining the results of individual

FIGURE A–12
Meta-Analysis.
Meta-analysis enables researchers to combine the results of individual studies to reach an overall conclusion.

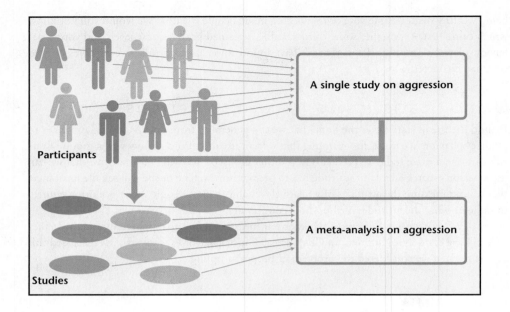

research studies to reach an overall conclusion. In a single experiment, each participant contributes data to help the researcher reach a conclusion. In a meta-analysis, each published study contributes data to help the reviewer reach a conclusion, as Figure A–12 illustrates. Rather than relying on the raw data of individual participants, meta-analysis treats the results of entire studies as its raw data. Meta-analysts begin by collecting all available research reports that are relevant to the question at hand. Next, they statistically transform these results into a common scale for comparison. That way differences in sample size (one study might have used 50 participants, another 500), in the magnitude of an effect (one study might have found a small difference, another a more substantial one), and in experimental procedures (which might vary from study to study) can be examined using the same methods.

The key element in this process is its statistical basis. Rather than keeping a tally of "yeas" and "nays," meta-analysis allows the reviewer to determine both the strength and the consistency of a research conclusion. For example, instead of simply concluding that there were more studies that found a particular gender difference, the reviewer might determine that the genders differ by .06 of a percentage point or that across all the studies, the findings are highly variable.

Meta-analysis has proved to be a valuable tool for psychologists interested in reaching conclusions about a particular research topic. By systematically examining patterns of evidence across individual studies whose conclusions vary, psychologists are able to gain a clearer understanding of the findings and their implications.

Chapter 1

The Rise of Scientific Psychology
Answers: **1.** 1800s (or ninteenth century); **2.** a; **3.** d

Contemporary Approaches to Psychology
Answers: **1.** c; **2.** a; **3.** b

Enduring Issues in Psychology
Answers: **1.** person–situation—d, nature–nurture—e, stability–change—a, diversity–universality—b, mind–body—c; **2.** c

Psychology as Science
Answers: **1.** a (T), b (T), c (T), d (F), e (T), f (F)

Research Methods in Psychology
Answers: **1.** naturalistic observation; **2.** correlational; **3.** experimental; **4.** independent, dependent; **5.** random, representative

Ethics and Psychology
Answers: **1.** c; **2.** a

Chapter 2

Neurons: The Messengers
Answers: **1.** d; **2.** f; **3.** a; **4.** h; **5.** k; **6.** b; **7.** j; **8.** e; **9.** g; **10.** c; **11.** i

The Central Nervous System
Answers: **1.** c; **2.** d; **3.** a; **4.** b; **5.** c

The Peripheral Nervous System
Answers: **1.** (S); **2.** (P); **3.** (S); **4.** (P); **5.** a

The Endocrine System
Answers: **1.** c; **2.** d; **3.** b; **4.** a; **5.** c

Genes, Evolution, and Behavior
Answers: **1.** (T); **2.** (F); **3.** c

Chapter 3

The Nature of Sensation
Answers: **1.** receptor cell; **2.** d; **3.** c

Vision
Answers: **1.** d; **2.** c; **3.** a; **4.** f; **5.** b; **6.** e; **7.** b

Hearing
Answers: **1.** c, b, d, e, a; **2.** a

The Other Senses
Answers: **1.** sweet, sour, salty, bitter, and umami; **2.** kinesthetic; **3.** a

Perception
Answers: **1.** c; **2.** b; **3.** d; **4.** a; **5.** b

Chapter 4

Sleep
Answers: **1.** selective attention; **2.** circadian; **3.** paradoxical; **4.** a

Dreams
Answers: **1.** REM; **2.** two; **3.** manifest, latent; **4.** d

Drug-Altered Consciousness
Answers: **1.** a. (F); b. (T); c. (T); d. (T); **2.** d

Meditation and Hypnosis
Answers: **1.** c; b; a; **2.** c

Chapter 5

Classical Conditioning
Answers: **1.** classical conditioning; **2.** unconditioned stimulus—b; unconditioned response—d; conditioned stimulus—a; conditioned response—c; **3.** d.

Operant Conditioning
Answers: **1.** negative, positive; **2.** avoidance training; **3.** punishment; **4.** d

Factors Shared by Classical and Operant Conditioning
Answers: **1.** spontaneous recovery; **2.** stimulus generalization; **3.** d; **4.** a

Cognitive Learning
Answers: **1.** c; a; b; **2.** a (T); b (F)

Chapter 6

The Sensory Registers
Answers: **1.** a. (T), b. (F), c. (F), d. (F); **2.** b

Short-Term Memory
Answers: **1.** short-term; **2.** b; **3.** a

Long-Term Memory
Answers: **1.** beginning, end; **2.** c; **3.** d

The Biology of Memory
Answers: **1.** b; **2.** a

Forgetting
Answers: **1.** c; a; b; **2.** d

Special Topics in Memory
Answers: **1.** (F); **2.** a; **3.** c

Chapter 7

Building Blocks of Thought
Answers: **1.** language, images, concepts; **2.** a. (T); b. (T); c. (T); **3.** a

Language, Thought, and Culture
Answers: **1.** b; **2.** a. (T); b. (T); c. (F)

Nonhuman Thought and Language
Answers: **1.** a; **2.** c

Problem Solving
Answers: **1.** algorithm—c, heuristic—a, hill climbing—b, means-end analysis—e, working backward—d, subgoal creation—f; **2.** d

Decision Making
Answers: **1.** representativeness heuristic—c, availability heuristic—a, confirmation bias—b; **2.** c; **3.** d

Intelligence and Mental Abilities
Answers: **1.** a. (F), b. (F), c. (T), d. (T); **2.** intelligence quotient, I.Q., 100

Heredity, Environment, and Intelligence
Answers: **1.** a. (F), b. (F); **2.** a; **3.** b

Creativity
Answer: **1.** c

Answers to Problems in Chapter 7

Problem 1 Fill each of the smaller spoons with salt from the larger spoon. That step will require four teaspoons of salt, leaving exactly four teaspoons of salt in the larger spoon.

Problem 2 As shown in the figure below, fill spoon C with the salt from spoon A (now A has 5 teaspoons of salt and C has 3). Pour the salt from spoon C into spoon B (now A has 5 teaspoons of salt and B has 3). Again, fill spoon

C with the salt from spoon A. (This leaves A with only two teaspoons of salt, while B and C each have three.) Fill spoon B with the salt from spoon C. (This step leaves one teaspoon of salt in spoon C, while B has five teaspoons and A has only two.) Pour all the salt from spoon B into spoon A. (Now A has seven teaspoons of salt and C has one.) Pour all the salt from spoon C into spoon B and fill spoon C from spoon A. (This step leaves four teaspoons of salt in A, one teaspoon in C, and three teaspoons in C.) Finally, pour all the salt from spoon C into spoon B. (This step leaves four teaspoons of salt in spoons A and B, which is the solution.)

Problem 3 Take one of the short pieces of chain shown in the figure below and open all three links. (This step costs 6 cents.) Use those three links to connect the remaining three pieces of chain. (Hence, closing the three links costs 9 cents.)

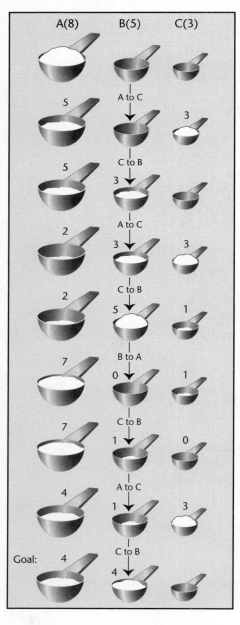

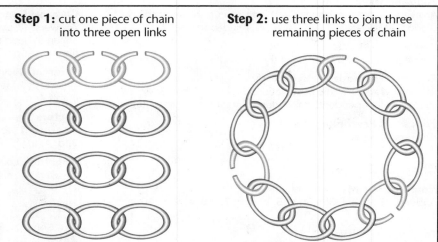

Step 1: cut one piece of chain into three open links

Step 2: use three links to join three remaining pieces of chain

Problem 4 One way to solve this problem is to draw a diagram of the ascent and the descent, as in the figure below. From this drawing, you can see that, indeed, there is a point that the monk passes at exactly the same time on both days. Another way to

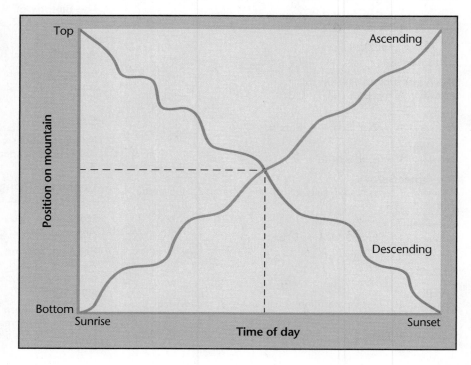

approach this problem is to imagine that there are two monks on the mountain; one starts ascending at 7 a.m., while the other starts descending at 7 a.m. on the same day. Clearly, sometime during the day the monks must meet somewhere along the route.

Problem 5 This problem has four possible solutions, one of which is shown in the figure to the right.

Problem 6 There are 15 possible solutions to this problem, of which this is one: First, one hobbit and one orc cross the river in the boat; the orc remains on the opposite side while the hobbit rows back. Next, three orcs cross the river; two of those orcs remain on the other side (making a total of three orcs on the opposite bank) while one orc rows back. Now three hobbits and one orc row the boat back. Again, three hobbits row across the river, at which point all five hobbits are on the opposite bank with only two orcs. Then, one of the orcs rows back and forth across the river twice to transport the remaining orcs to the opposite side.

Answers to Intelligence Test Questions in Chapter 7

1. Idleness refers to the state of being inactive, not busy, unoccupied; laziness means an unwillingness or a reluctance to work. Laziness is one possible cause of idleness, but not the only cause.
2. If you face west, your right ear will face north.
3. Obliterate means to erase or destroy something completely.
4. An hour *and* a week are measures of time.
5. Alternative F is the correct pattern.
6. Seventy-five cents will buy nine pencils.
7. Alternative D is correct. A crutch is used to help someone who has difficulty with locomotion; spectacles are used to help someone who has difficulty with vision.
8. Alternative D is correct. The second figure is the same shape and size but with diagonal cross-hatching from upper left to lower right.
9. Figures 3, 4, and 5 can be covered completely by using some or all of the given pieces.

Chapter 8

Perspectives on Motivation
Answers: **1.** e; **2.** c; **3.** b; **4.** a; **5.** f; **6.** d

Hunger and Thirst
Answers: **1.** c; **2.** a

Sex
Answers: **1.** c; **2.** b; **3.** a; **4.** b

Other Important Motives
Answers: **1.** achievement; **2.** a

Emotions
Answers: **1.** a; **2.** c

Communicating Emotion
Answers: **1.** facial expressions; **2.** display rules; **3.** b

Chapter 9

Research Methods in Developmental Psychology
Answers: **1.** c; **2.** c

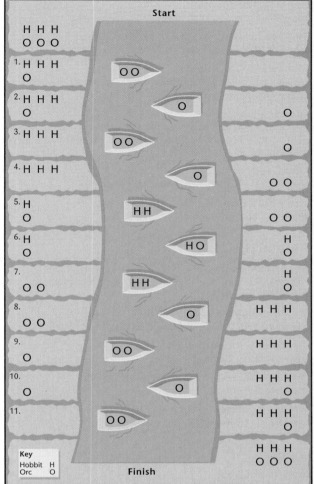

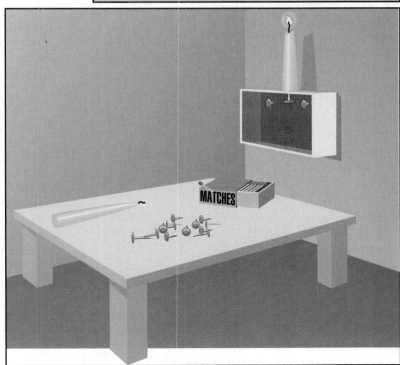

Answer to problem shown in Figure 7–5 on page 185

Prenatal Development
Answers: **1.** b; c; a; d; **2.** c

The Newborn
Answers: **1.** easy, difficult, slow to warm up, shy; **2.** b

Infancy and Childhood
Answers: **1.** infancy—b, toddlerhood—c, preschool years—d, elementary school years—a; **2.** c

Adolescence
Answers: **1.** growth spurt, puberty; **2.** identity, role confusion; **3.** identity achievement, identity foreclosure, moratorium, identity diffusion; **4.** (F)

Adulthood
Answers: **1.** intimacy—isolation, generativity—stagnation; **2.** c

Late Adulthood
Answers: **1.** a (F), b (F), c (F), d (T); **2.** d

Chapter 10

Personality Traits
Answers: **1.** emotional stability, introversion-extraversion, psychoticism; **2.** b; **3.** a

The Psychodynamic Approach
Answers: **1.** b; **2.** a. anal, b. oral, c. phallic

The Humanistic Approach
Answers: **1.** b; **2.** d

The Cognitive–Social Learning Approach
Answers: **1.** self-efficacy; **2.** a

Personality Assessment
Answers: **1.** objective; **2.** projective; **3.** c

Chapter 11

Sources of Stress
Answers: **1.** a. (F); b. (T); c. (F); **2.** d

Coping With Stress
Answers: **1.** direct; **2.** defensive; **3.** d

How Stress Affects Health
Answers: **1.** c; **2.** a

Staying Healthy
Answers: **1.** a. (F); b. (T); c. (T); **2.** a

Extreme Stress
Answers: **1.** a. (F); b. (F); c. (F); d. (T); **2.** d

The Well-Adjusted Person
Answers: **1.** b

Chapter 12

Perspectives on Psychological Disorders
Answers: **1.** a. (T); b. (F); c. (F); **2.** b; **3.** d

Mood Disorders
Answers: **1.** a; **2.** c

Anxiety Disorders
Answers: **1.** unconscious conflicts; **2.** prepared responses; **3.** (T); **4.** (F); **5.** c

Psychosomatic and Somatoform Disorders
Answers: **1.** a; **2.** c

Dissociative Disorders
Answers: **1.** b; **2.** b

Sexual and Gender-Identity Disorders
Answers: **1.** c; **2.** d; **3.** a; **4.** b

Personality Disorders
Answers: **1.** d; c; e; b; a; **2.** c; **3.** b

Schizophrenic Disorders
Answers: **1.** a. (F); b. (T); **2.** d; **3.** c

Childhood Disorders
Answers: **1.** a. (T); b. (F); c. (T); **2.** a.

Gender and Cultural Differences in Psychological Disorders
Answers: **1.** biological; **2.** (T); **3.** (F)

Chapter 13

Insight Therapies
Answers: **1.** insight; **2.** free association; **3.** transference; **4.** unconditional positive; **5.** a. (T), b. (F), c. (T), d. (T)

Behavior Therapies
Answers: **1.** c; **2.** b

Cognitive Therapies
Answers: **1.** c; **2.** a

Group Therapies
Answers: **1.** d; **2.** b; **3.** d

Effectiveness of Psychotherapy
Answers: **1.** c; **2.** b

Biological Treatments
Answers: **1.** lithium; **2.** d; **3.** (T); **4.** a

Institutionalization and Its Alternatives
Answers: **1.** c; **2.** a

Client Diversity and Treatment
Answers: **1.** d; **2.** c

Chapter 14

Social Cognition
Answers: **1.** primacy; **2.** actor-observer bias; **3.** fundamental attribution; **4.** b

Attitudes
Answers: **1.** attitude; **2.** a. (F), b. (F), c. (T), d. (T); **3.** a

Social Influence
Answers: **1.** door-in-the-face; **2.** a. (T), b. (F), d. (T); **3.** c

Social Action
Answers: **1.** c; d; a; b; **2.** a

absolute threshold The least amount of energy that can be detected as a stimulation 50% of the time.

achievement motive The need to excel or to overcome obstacles.

actor-observer bias The tendency to explain the behavior of others as caused by internal factors, while attributing one's own behavior to external forces.

actualizing tendency According to Rogers, the drive of every organism to fulfill its biological potential and become what it is inherently capable of becoming.

adaptation An adjustment of the senses to the level of stimulation they are receiving.

adjustment Any effort to cope with stress.

adoption studies Research carried out on children who were adopted at birth by parents not related to them for the purpose of determining the relative influence of heredity and environment on human behavior.

adrenal glands Two endocrine glands located just above the kidneys.

aerial perspective Monocular cue to distance and depth based on the fact that more distant objects are likely to appear hazy and blurred.

affiliation motive The need to be with others.

afterimage Sense experience that occurs after a visual stimulus has been removed.

aggression Behavior aimed at doing harm to others; also, the motive to behave aggressively.

agoraphobia An anxiety disorder that involves multiple, intense fears of crowds, public places, and other situations that require separation from a source of security such as the home.

alcohol Depressant that is the intoxicating ingredient in whiskey, beer, wine, and other fermented or distilled liquors.

algorithm A step-by-step method of problem solving that guarantees a correct solution.

all-or-none law Principle that the action potential in a neuron does not vary in strength; either the neuron fires at full strength or it does not fire at all.

altered states of consciousness Mental states that differ noticeably from normal waking consciousness.

altruistic behavior Helping behavior that is not linked to personal gain.

Alzheimer's disease A neurological disorder, most commonly found in late adulthood, characterized by progressive losses in memory and cognition and by changes in personality.

amphetamines Stimulant drugs that initially produce "rushes" of euphoria often followed by sudden "crashes" and, sometimes, severe depression.

amplitude The magnitude of a wave; in sound, the primary determinant of loudness.

anal stage Second stage in Freud's theory of personality development, in which a child's erotic feelings center on the anus and on elimination.

anorexia nervosa A serious eating disorder that is associated with a distorted body image and an intense fear of weight gain.

antipsychotic drugs Drugs used to treat very severe psychological disorders, particularly schizophrenia.

antisocial personality disorder Personality disorder that involves a pattern of violent, criminal, or unethical, exploitative behavior and an inability to feel affection for others.

anxiety disorders Disorders in which anxiety is a characteristic feature or the avoidance of anxiety seems to motivate abnormal behavior.

apnea Sleep disorder characterized by breathing difficulty in falling asleep or remaining asleep throughout the night.

approach/approach conflict According to Lewin, the result of simultaneous attraction to two appealing possibilities, neither of which has any negative qualities.

approach/avoidance conflict According to Lewin, the result of being simultaneously attracted to and repelled by the same goal.

archetypes In Jung's theory of personality, thought forms common to all human beings, stored in the collective unconscious.

arousal theory Theory of motivation that proposes that organisms seek an optimal level of arousal.

association areas Areas of the cerebral cortex in which incoming messages from the separate senses are combined into meaningful impressions and outgoing messages from the motor areas are integrated.

attachment Emotional bond that develops in the first year of life that makes human babies cling to their caregivers for safety and comfort.

attention The selection of some incoming information for further processing.

attention-deficit hyperactivity disorder (ADHD) A childhood disorder characterized by inattention, impulsiveness, and hyperactivity.

attribution theory The theory that addresses the question of how people make judgments about the causes of behavior.

attitude Relatively stable organization of beliefs, feelings, and behavior tendencies directed toward something or someone—the attitude object.

auditory nerve The bundle of axons that carries signals from each ear to the brain

authoritarian personality A personality pattern characterized by rigid conventionality, exaggerated respect for authority, and hostility toward those who defy society's norms.

autistic disorder A childhood disorder characterized by lack of social instincts and strange motor behavior.

autistic spectrum disorder (ASD) A range of disorders involving varying degrees of impairment in communication skills, social interactions, and restricted, repetitive, and stereotyped patterns of behavior.

autonomic nervous system Part of the peripheral nervous system that carries messages between the central nervous system and the internal organs.

autonomy Sense of independence; a desire not to be controlled by others.

availability A heuristic by which a judgment or decision is based on information that is most easily retrieved from memory.

aversive conditioning Behavioral therapy techniques aimed at eliminating undesirable behavior patterns by teaching the person to associate them with pain and discomfort.

avoidance/avoidance conflict According to Lewin, the result of facing a choice between two undesirable possibilities, neither of which has any positive qualities.

avoidance training Learning a desirable behavior to prevent the occurrence of something unpleasant, such as punishment.

avoidant personality disorder Personality disorder in which the person's fears of rejection by others lead to social isolation.

axon Single, long fiber extending from the cell body; carries outgoing messages.

babbling A baby's vocalizations, consisting of repetition of consonant-vowel combinations.

barbiturates Potentially deadly depressants, first used for their sedative and anticonvulsant properties, now used only to treat such conditions as epilepsy and arthritis.

basilar membrane Vibrating membrane in the cochlea of the inner ear; it contains sense receptors for sound.

behavior contracting Form of operant conditioning therapy in which the client and therapist set behavioral goals and agree on reinforcements that the client will receive on reaching those goals.

behavior genetics Study of the relationship between heredity and behavior.

behavior therapies Therapeutic approaches that are based on the belief that all behavior—normal and abnormal—is learned and that the objective of therapy is to teach people new, more satisfying ways of behaving.

behavioral approach Viewpoint that the only legitimate object of scientific study is observable, measurable behavior.

behaviorism School of psychology, based on the behavioral approach, that was especially influential in the mid-twentieth century.

Big Five Five traits or basic dimensions currently considered to be of central importance in describing personality.

binocular cues Cues to distance and depth that require the use of both eyes.

biofeedback A technique that uses monitoring devices to provide precise information about internal physiological processes, such as heart rate or blood pressure, to teach people to gain voluntary control over these functions.

biographical (or retrospective) study A method of studying developmental changes by reconstructing a person's past through interviews and inferring the effects of past events on current behaviors.

biological approach Perspective that focuses on the relationship between behavior, thoughts, and emotions on the one hand and biological processes on the other.

biological model View that psychological disorders have a biochemical or physiological basis.

biological treatments A group of approaches, including medication, electroconvulsive therapy, and psychosurgery, that are sometimes used to treat psychological disorders in conjunction with, or instead of, psychotherapy.

bipolar cells Neurons that have only one axon and one dendrite; in the eye, these neurons connect the receptors on the retina to the ganglion cells.

bipolar disorder A mood disorder in which periods of mania and depression alternate, sometimes with periods of normal mood intervening.

blind spot The place on the retina where the axons of all the ganglion cells leave the eye and where there are no receptors.

body mass index (BMI) A numerical index calculated from a person's height and weight that is used to indicate health status and predict disease risk.

borderline personality disorder Personality disorder characterized by marked instability in self-image, mood, and interpersonal relationships.

brainstorming A problem-solving strategy in which an individual or group produces numerous ideas and evaluates them only after all ideas have been collected.

brightness The nearness of a color to white as opposed to black.

brightness constancy Perceiving the brightness of an object as the same, even though the amount of light reaching the retina changes.

bulimia nervosa An eating disorder characterized by binges of eating followed by self-induced vomiting.

bystander effect The tendency for an individual's helpfulness in an emergency to decrease as the number of passive bystanders increases.

Cannon-Bard theory Theory that states that the experience of emotion occurs simultaneously with biological changes.

case study A detailed, in-depth description and analysis of one person or a few individuals.

catatonic schizophrenia Schizophrenic disorder in which disturbed motor behavior is prominent.

central nervous system (CNS) Division of the nervous system that consists of the brain and spinal cord.

central tendency Tendency of scores to congregate around some middle value.

cerebellum Structure in the hindbrain that controls certain reflexes and coordinates the body's movements.

cerebral cortex Outer surface of the two cerebral hemispheres.

cerebrum Largest portion of the brain, composed of the two cerebral hemispheres.

childhood (infantile) amnesia Difficulty adults have remembering experiences from their first two years of life.

chromosomes Pairs of threadlike bodies within the cell nucleus that contains the genes.

chunking The grouping of information into meaningful units for easier handling by short-term memory.

circadian rhythm A regular biological rhythm with a period of approximately 24 hours.

classical (or Pavlovian) conditioning Type of learning in which a response naturally elicited by one stimulus comes to be elicited by a different, formerly neutral, stimulus.

client-centered (or person-centered) therapy Nondirectional form of therapy developed by Carl Rogers that calls for unconditional positive regard of the client by the therapist with the goal of helping the client become fully functioning.

cliques Groups of adolescents with similar interests and strong mutual attachment.

cocaine Drug derived from the coca plant that, although producing a sense of euphoria by stimulating the sympathetic nervous system, also leads to anxiety, depression, and addictive cravings.

cochlea Part of the inner ear containing fluid that vibrates, which in turn causes the basilar membrane to vibrate.

cohort A group of people born during the same period in historical time.

cognition The processes whereby people acquire and use knowledge.

cognitive approach Viewpoint that mental processes such as thoughts and memories, though not directly observable, can nonetheless be studied scientifically.

cognitive-behavioral model View that psychological disorders result from learning maladaptive ways of thinking and behaving.

cognitive dissonance Perceived inconsistency between two cognitions.

cognitive learning Learning that depends on mental processes that are not directly observable.

cognitive map A learned mental image of a spatial environment that may be called on to solve problems when stimuli in the environment change.

cognitive-social learning theories Personality theories that view behavior as the product of the interaction of cognitions, learning and past experiences, and the immediate environment.

cognitive theory States that emotional experience depends on one's perception or judgment of a situation.

cognitive therapies Psychotherapies that emphasize changing clients' perceptions of their life situation as a way of modifying their behavior; therapies that depend on identifying and changing inappropriately negative and self-critical patterns of thought.

collective unconscious In Jung's theory of personality, the level of the unconscious that is inherited and common to all members of a species.

color constancy An inclination to perceive familiar objects as retaining their color despite changes in sensory information.

compensation According to Adler, the person's effort to overcome imagined or real personal weaknesses.

compensatory model A rational decision-making model in which choices are systematically evaluated on various criteria.

compliance Change of behavior in response to an explicit request from another person or group.

compromise Deciding on a more realistic solution or goal when an ideal solution or goal is not practical.

concepts Mental categories for classifying objects, people, or experiences.

concrete-operational stage In Piaget's theory, the stage of cognitive development between 7 and 11 years of age in which the individual can attend to more than one thing at a time and understand someone else's point of view, though thinking is limited to concrete matters.

conditional positive regard In Rogers's theory, acceptance and love that depend on another's behaving in certain ways and on fulfilling certain conditions.

conditioned response (CR) After conditioning, the response an organism produces when a conditioned stimulus is presented.

conditioned stimulus (CS) An originally neutral stimulus that is paired with an unconditioned stimulus and eventually produces the desired response in an organism when presented alone.

conditioned taste aversion Conditioned avoidance of certain foods even when there is only one pairing of conditioned and unconditioned stimuli.

cones Receptor cells in the retina responsible for color vision.

confirmation bias The tendency to look for evidence in support of a belief and to ignore evidence that would disprove a belief.

conflict Simultaneous existence of incompatible demands, opportunities, needs, or goals.

conformity Voluntarily yielding to social norms, even at the expense of one's preferences.

confrontation Acknowledging a stressful situation directly and attempting to find a solution to the problem or to attain the difficult goal.

consciousness Awareness of various cognitive processes, such as sleeping, dreaming, concentrating, and making decisions.

content validity Refers to a test's having an adequate sample of questions measuring the skills or knowledge it is supposed to measure.

contingency A reliable "if-then" relationship between two events, such as a CS and a US.

control group In a controlled experiment, the group not subjected to a change in the independent variable; used for comparison with the experimental group.

convergence A visual depth cue that comes from muscles controlling eye movement as the eyes turn inward to view a nearby stimulus.

convergent thinking Thinking that is directed toward one correct solution to a problem.

conversion disorders Somatoform disorders in which a dramatic specific disability has no physical cause but instead seems related to psychological problems.

cornea The transparent protective coating over the front part of the eye.

corpus callosum Thick band of nerve fibers connecting the left and right cerebral hemispheres.

correlation coefficients Statistical measures of the degree of association between two variables.

correlational research Research technique based on the naturally occurring relationship between two or more variables.

counterfactual thinking Thinking about alternative realities and things that never happened.

couple therapy A form of group therapy intended to help troubled partners improve their problems of communication and interaction.

creativity The ability to produce novel and socially valued ideas or objects.

criterion-related validity Validity of a test as measured by a comparison of the test score and independent measures of what the test is designed to measure.

critical period A time when certain internal and external influences have a major effect on development; at other periods, the same influences will have little or no effect.

cross-sectional study A method of studying developmental changes by comparing people of different ages at about the same time.

cultural truisms Beliefs that most members of a society accept as self-evidently true.

culture-fair tests Intelligence tests designed to eliminate cultural bias by minimizing skills and values that vary from one culture to another.

dark adaptation Increased sensitivity of rods and cones in darkness.

daydreams Apparently effortless shifts in attention away from the here and now into a private world of make-believe.

decay theory A theory that argues that the passage of time causes forgetting.

decibel Unit of measurement for the loudness of sounds.

defense mechanisms Self-deceptive techniques for reducing stress, including denial, repression, projection, identification, regression, intellectualization, reaction formation, displacement, and sublimation.

defensive attribution The tendency to attribute one's successes to one's own efforts or qualities and one's failures to external factors.

deindividuation A loss of personal sense of responsibility in a group.

deinstitutionalization Policy of treating people with severe psychological disorders in the larger community or in small residential centers such as halfway houses, rather than in large public hospitals.

delusions False beliefs about reality that have no basis in fact.

denial Refusal to acknowledge a painful or threatening reality.

deoxyribonucleic acid (DNA) Complex molecule in a double-helix configuration that is the main ingredient of chromosomes and genes that forms the code for all genetic information.

dendrites Short fibers that branch out from the cell body and pick up incoming messages.

dependent personality disorder Personality disorder in which the person is unable to make choices and decisions independently and cannot tolerate being alone.

dependent variable Variable in an experiment that is measured to see how it is altered by manipulations in the independent variable.

depersonalization disorder Dissociative disorder chiefly characterized by the person suddenly feeling changed or different in a strange way.

depressants Chemicals that slow down behavior or cognitive processes.

depression A mood disorder characterized by overwhelming feelings of sadness, lack of interest in activities, and perhaps excessive guilt or feelings of worthlessness.

developmental psychology The study of the changes that occur in people from birth through old age.

diathesis Biological predisposition.

diathesis-stress model View that people biologically predisposed to a mental disorder (those with a certain diathesis) will tend to exhibit that disorder when particularly affected by stress.

difference threshold The smallest change in stimulation that can be detected 50% of the time; also called the *just-noticeable difference (jnd)*.

discrimination   An unfair act or series of acts taken toward an entire group of people or individual members of that group.

disorganized schizophrenia   Schizophrenic disorder in which bizarre and childlike behaviors are common.

displacement   Shifting repressed motives and emotions from an original object to a substitute object.

display rules   Culture-specific rules that govern how, when, and why expressions of emotion are appropriate.

dissociative amnesia   Disorder characterized by loss of memory for past events without organic cause.

dissociative disorders   Disorders in which some aspect of the personality seems separated from the rest.

dissociative fugue   Disorder that involves flight from home and the assumption of a new identity with amnesia for past identity and events.

dissociative identity disorder (also multiple personality disorder)   Disorder characterized by the separation of the personality into two or more distinct personalities.

divergent thinking   Thinking that meets the criteria of originality, inventiveness, and flexibility.

double-blind procedure   Experimental design useful in studies of the effects of drugs, in which neither the subject nor the researcher knows at the time of administration that subjects are receiving an active drug and are receiving an inactive substance.

dreams   Vivid visual and auditory experiences created by the mind during sleep and occurring primarily during REM periods of sleep.

drive   State of tension or arousal that motivates behavior.

drive-reduction theory   Theory stating that motivated behavior is aimed at reducing a state of bodily tension or arousal and returning the organism to homeostasis.

dualism   A view that holds that thoughts and feelings (the mind) are distinct from the world of real objects and our bodies.

eclecticism   Psychotherapeutic approach that recognizes the value of a broad treatment package over a rigid commitment to one particular form of therapy.

ego   Freud's term for the part of the personality that mediates between environmental demands (reality), conscience (superego), and instinctual needs (id); now often used as a synonym for "self."

ego ideal   The part of the superego that consists of standards of what one would like to be.

egocentric   Unable to see things from another's point of view.

eidetic imagery   The ability to reproduce unusually sharp and detailed images of something one has seen.

elaborative rehearsal   The linking of new information in short-term memory to familiar material stored in long-term memory.

Electra complex/Oedipus complex   According to Freud, a child's sexual attachment to the parent of the opposite sex and jealousy toward the parent of the same sex; generally occurs in the phallic stage.

electroconvulsive therapy (ECT)   Biological therapy in which a mild electrical current is passed through the brain for a short period, often producing convulsions and temporary coma; used to treat severe, prolonged depression.

elevation   Monocular cue to distance and depth based on the fact that the higher on the horizontal plane an object is, the farther away it appears.

embryo   A developing human between 2 weeks and 3 months after conception.

emotion   A feeling, such as fear, joy, or surprise, that underlies behavior.

emotional intelligence   (IQ) According to Goleman, a form of intelligence that refers to how effectively people perceive and understand their own emotions and the emotions of others and can regulate and manage their emotional behavior.

emotional memories   Learned emotional responses to various stimuli.

endocrine glands   Glands that release hormones into the bloodstream.

episodic memories   The portion of long-term memory that stores personally experienced events.

erectile disorder (ED)   Inability of a male to achieve or maintain an erection; also *erectile dysfunction.*

evolutionary/sociological approach   An approach to psychology that is concerned with the evolutionary origins of behaviors and mental processes, their adaptive value, and the purposes they continue to serve.

exhibitionism   Compulsion to expose one's genitals in public to achieve sexual arousal.

expectancies   In Bandura's view, what a person anticipates in a situation or as a result of behaving in certain ways.

experimental group   In a controlled experiment, the group subjected to a change in the independent variable.

experimental method   Research technique in which an investigator deliberately manipulates selected events or circumstances and measures the effects of those manipulations on subsequent behavior.

experimenter bias   Expectations by the experimenter that might influence the results of an experiment or its interpretation.

explicit memory   Memory for information that people can readily express in words and are aware of having; these memories can be intentionally retrieved from memory.

extinction   A decrease in the strength or frequency, or stopping, of a learned response because of failure to continue pairing the US and CS (classical conditioning) or withholding of reinforcement (operant conditioning).

extrinsic motivation   Desire to perform a behavior to obtain an external reward or avoid punishment.

factor analysis   A statistical technique that identifies groups of related objects; used by Cattell to identify clusters of traits.

family studies   Studies of heritability in humans based on the assumption that when genes influence a certain trait, close relatives should be more similar on that trait than distant relatives.

family therapy   A form of group therapy that sees the family as at least partly responsible for the individual's problems and that seeks to change all family members' behaviors to the benefit of the family unit as well as the troubled individual.

feature detectors   Specialized brain cells that only respond to particular elements in the visual field such as movement or lines of specific orientation.

female sexual arousal disorder   Inability of a woman to become sexually aroused or to reach orgasm.

fetal alcohol syndrome (FAS)   Disorder that occurs in children of women who drink alcohol during pregnancy; characterized by facial deformities, heart defects, stunted growth, and cognitive impairments.

fetishism   A paraphilia in which a nonhuman object is the preferred or exclusive method of achieving sexual excitement.

fetus   A developing human between 3 months after conception and birth.

fixation   According to Freud, a partial or complete halt at some point in the individual's psychosexual development.

fixed-interval schedule   A reinforcement schedule in which the correct response is reinforced after a fixed length of time since the last reinforcement.

fixed-ratio schedule   A reinforcement schedule in which the correct response is reinforced after a fixed number of correct responses.

flashbulb memory   A vivid memory of a certain event and the incidents surrounding it even after a long time has passed.

forebrain   Top part of the brain; includes the thalamus, hypothalamus, limbic system, and cerebral cortex.

formal-operational stage In Piaget's theory, the stage of cognitive development beginning about 11 years of age in which the individual becomes capable of abstract thought.

fovea Area of the retina that is the center of the visual field.

framing The perspective from which people interpret information before making a decision.

fraternal twins Twins developed from two separate fertilized ova and, therefore, different in genetic makeup.

free association A psychoanalytic technique that encourages the person to talk without inhibition about whatever thoughts or fantasies come to mind.

frequency The number of cycles per second in a wave; in sound, the primary determinant of pitch.

frequency distribution A count of the number of scores that falls within each of a series of intervals.

frequency histogram Type of bar graph that shows frequency distributions.

frequency polygon Type of line graph that shows frequency distributions.

frequency theory Theory that pitch is determined by the frequency with which hair cells in the cochlea fire.

frontal lobe Part of the cerebral cortex responsible for voluntary movement; important for attention, goal-directed behavior, and appropriate emotional experiences.

frotteurism Compulsion to achieve sexual arousal by touching or rubbing against a nonconsenting person in public situations.

frustration The feeling that occurs when a person is prevented from reaching a goal.

frustration-aggression theory Theory asserting that, under certain circumstances, people who are frustrated in their goals turn their anger away from the proper, powerful target and toward another, less powerful target that is safer to attack.

fully functioning person According to Rogers, an individual whose self-concept closely resembles his or her inborn capacities or potentials.

functional fixedness Tendency to perceive only a limited number of uses for an object, thus interfering with the process of problem solving.

functionalism School of psychology that is concerned with how an organism uses its perceptual abilities to function in its environment.

fundamental attribution error The tendency of people to overemphasize personal causes for other people's behavior.

ganglion cells Neurons that connect the bipolar neurons in the eyes to the brain.

gate control theory The theory that a "neurological gate" in the spinal cord controls the transmission of pain messages to the brain.

gender constancy The realization that gender does not change with age.

gender identity A little girl's knowledge that she is a girl and a little boy's knowledge that he is a boy.

gender-identity disorder in children Rejection of one's biological gender in childhood, along with the clothing and behavior that society considers appropriate to that gender.

gender-identity disorders Disorders that involve the desire to become, or the insistence that one really is, a member of the other biological sex.

gender-role awareness Knowledge of what behavior is appropriate for each gender.

gender stereotypes General beliefs about characteristics that men and women are presumed to have.

general adaptation syndrome (GAS) According to Selye, the three stages the body passes through as it adapts to stress: alarm reaction, resistance, and exhaustion.

generalized anxiety disorder An anxiety disorder characterized by prolonged vague but intense fears that are not attached to any particular object or circumstance.

genes Elements that control the transmission of traits; found on the chromosomes.

genetics Field of study focused on the traits that are transmitted from one generation to the next.

genital stage In Freud's theory of personality development, the final stage of normal adult sexual development, which is usually marked by mature sexuality.

genotype Entire unique genetic makeup of an organism.

Gestalt psychology School of psychology that studies how people perceive and experience objects as whole patterns.

Gestalt therapy An insight therapy that emphasizes the wholeness of the personality and attempts to reawaken people to their emotions and sensations in the present.

ghrelin A hormone produced in the stomach and small intestines that increases appetite.

giftedness Refers to superior IQ combined with demonstrated or potential ability in such areas as academic aptitude, creativity, and leadership.

glucose A simple sugar used by the body for energy.

gonads Reproductive glands—testes in males and ovaries in females.

grammar The language rules that determine how sounds and words can be combined and used to communicate meaning within a language.

great-person theory Theory that states that leadership results from personal qualities and traits that qualify one to lead others.

group tests Written intelligence tests administered by one examiner to many people at one time.

group therapy Type of psychotherapy in which clients meet regularly to interact and help one another achieve insight into their feelings and behavior.

growth spurt A rapid increase in height and weight that occurs during adolescence.

hallucinations Sensory experiences in the absence of external stimulation.

hallucinogens Any of a number of drugs, such as LSD and mescaline, that distort visual and auditory perception.

health psychology A subfield of psychology concerned with the relationship between psychological factors and physical health and illness.

hertz (Hz) Cycles per second; unit of measurement for the frequency of sound waves.

heuristics Rules of thumb that help in simplifying and solving problems, although they do not guarantee a correct solution.

hierarchy of needs Theory of motivation advanced by Maslow that holds that higher order motives involving social and personal growth only emerge after lower level motives related to survival have been satisfied.

higher-order conditioning Conditioning based on previous learning; the conditioned stimulus serves as an unconditioned stimulus for further training.

hill climbing A heuristic, problem-solving strategy in which each step moves you progressively closer to the final goal.

hindbrain Area containing the medulla, pons, and cerebellum.

hindsight bias Tendency to see outcomes as inevitable and predictable after the outcome is known.

holophrases One-word sentences commonly used by children under 2 years of age.

homeostasis State of balance and stability in which the organism functions effectively.

hormones   Chemical substances released by the endocrine glands that help regulate bodily activities.

hues   The aspects of color that correspond to names such as red, green, and blue.

humanistic approach   Perspective that emphasizes the importance of realizing one's full human potential.

humanistic personality theory   Any personality theory that asserts the fundamental goodness of people and their striving toward higher levels of functioning.

hypnosis   Trancelike state in which a person responds readily to suggestions

hypochondriasis   A somatoform disorder in which a person interprets insignificant symptoms as signs of serious illness in the absence of any organic evidence of such illness.

hypotheses   Specific, testable predictions derived from a theory.

id   In Freud's theory of personality, the collection of unconscious urges and desires that continually seek expression.

identical twins   Twins developed from a single fertilized ovum and, therefore, are identical in genetic makeup at the time of conception.

identification   Taking on the characteristics of someone else to avoid feeling incompetent.

identity crisis   A period of intense self-examination and decision making; part of the process of identity formation.

identity formation   Erickson's term for the development of a stable sense of self necessary to make the transition from dependence on others to dependence on oneself.

image   A mental representation of a sensory experience.

implicit memory   Memory for information that people cannot readily express in words and may not be aware of having; these memories cannot be intentionally retrieved from memory.

imprinting   The tendency in certain species to follow the first moving thing (usually its mother) it sees after it is born or hatched.

incentive   External stimulus that prompts goal-directed behavior.

independent variable   Variable in an experiment that is manipulated to test its effects on other, dependent variables.

inferiority complex   In Adler's theory, the fixation on feelings of personal inferiority that results in emotional and social paralysis.

information-processing model   View of memory as a computer-like process of encoding, storing, and retrieving information.

insanity   Legal term for mentally disturbed people who are considered not responsible for their criminal actions.

insight   Awareness of previously unconscious feelings and memories and how they influence present feelings and behavior; learning that occurs rapidly as a result of understanding all the elements of a problem.

insight therapies   A variety of individual psychotherapies designed to give people a better awareness and understanding of their feelings, motivations, and actions in the hope that this will help them to adjust.

insomnia   Sleep disorder characterized by difficulty in falling asleep or remaining asleep throughout the night.

instincts   Inborn, inflexible, goal-directed behaviors that are characteristic of an entire species.

insulin   Hormone secreted by the pancreas that regulates carbohydrate metabolism.

intellectualization   Thinking abstractly about stressful problems as a way of detaching oneself from them.

intelligence   A general term referring to the ability or abilities involved in learning and adaptive behavior.

intelligence quotient (IQ)   A numerical value given to intelligence that is determined from the scores on an intelligence test on the basis of a score of 100 for average intelligence.

intermittent pairing   Pairing the conditioned stimulus and the unconditioned stimulus on only a portion of the learning trials.

interneurons (or association neurons)   Neurons that carry messages from one neuron to another.

interposition   Monocular distance cue in which one object, by partly blocking a second object, is perceived as being closer.

interval scale   Scale with equal distances between the points or values, but without a true zero.

intrinsic motivation   A desire to perform a behavior that stems from the enjoyment derived from the behavior itself.

ions   Electrically charged particles found inside and outside the neuron.

iris   The colored part of the eye that regulates the size of the pupil.

James-Lange theory   Theory that states that stimuli cause physiological changes in human bodies and that emotions result from those physiological changes.

just-noticeable difference (jnd)   The smallest change in stimulation that can be detected 50% of the time; also called *difference threshold*.

just-world hypothesis   Attribution error based on the assumption that bad things happen to bad people and good things happen to good people.

kinesthetic senses   Senses of muscle movement, posture, and strain on muscles and joints.

language   A flexible system of communication that uses sounds, rules, gestures, or symbols to convey information.

language acquisition device   A hypothetical neural mechanism for acquiring language that is presumed to be "wired into" all humans.

latency period   In Freud's theory of personality, a period in which the child appears to have no interest in the other sex; occurs after the phallic stage.

latent learning   Learning that is not immediately reflected in a behavior change.

law of effect (or principle of reinforcement)   Thorndike's theory that behavior consistently rewarded will be "stamped in" as learned behavior and behavior that brings about discomfort will be "stamped out."

learned helplessness   Failure to take steps to avoid or escape from an unpleasant or aversive stimulus that occurs as a result of previous exposure to unavoidable painful stimuli.

learning   The process by which experience or practice results in a relatively permanent change in behavior or potential behavior.

learning set   The ability to become increasingly more effective in solving problems as more problems are solved.

lens   The transparent part of the eye behind the pupil that focuses light onto the retina.

leptin   A hormone released by fat cells that reduces appetite.

libido   According to Freud, the energy generated by the sexual instinct.

light adaptation   Decreased sensitivity of rods and cones in bright light.

limbic system   Ring of structures that plays a key role in learning, motivation, and emotion.

linear perspective   Monocular cue to distance and depth based on the fact that two parallel lines seem to come together at the horizon.

linguistic determinism   Belief that thought and experience are determined by language.

linguistic relativity hypothesis   Whorf's idea that patterns of thinking are determined by the specific language one speaks.

locus of control   According to Rotter, an expectancy about whether reinforcement is under internal or external control.

long-term memory (LTM)   The portion of memory that is more or less permanent, corresponding to everything we "know."

long-term potentiation (LTP)   A long-lasting change in the structure or function of a synapse that increases the efficiency of neural transmission and is believed to be related to how information is stored by neurons.

longitudinal studies A method of studying developmental changes by evaluating the same people at different points in their lives.

lysergic acid diethylamide (LSD) Hallucinogenic or "psychedelic" drug that produces hallucinations and delusions similar to those occurring in a psychotic state.

mania A mood disorder characterized by euphoric states, extreme physical activity, excessive talkativeness, distractedness, and, sometimes, grandiosity.

marijuana A mild hallucinogen that produces a "high" often characterized by feelings of euphoria, a sense of well-being, and swings in mood from gaiety to relaxation; may also cause feelings of anxiety and paranoia.

maturation An automatic biological unfolding of development in an organism as a function of the passage of time.

mean Arithmetical average calculated by dividing a sum of values by the total number of cases.

means-end analysis A heuristic strategy that aims to reduce the discrepancy between the current situation and the desired goal at a number of intermediate points.

median Point that divides a set of scores in half.

meditation Any of the various methods of concentration, reflection, or focusing of thoughts undertaken to suppress the activity of the sympathetic nervous system.

medulla Structure in the hindbrain that controls essential life support functions including breathing, heart rate, and blood pressure.

memory Ability to remember things that have been experienced, imagined, and learned.

menarche First menstrual period.

menopause The time in a woman's life when menstruation ceases.

mental representations Mental images or symbols (such as words) used to think about or remember an object, a person, or an event.

mental retardation Condition of significantly subaverage intelligence combined with deficiencies in adaptive behavior.

mental set The tendency to perceive and to approach problems in certain ways.

meta-analysis A statistical procedure for combining the results of several studies so the strength, consistency, and direction of the effect can be estimated.

midbrain Region between the hindbrain and the forebrain; important for hearing and sight and is one of several places in the brain where pain is registered.

midlife crisis A time when adults discover they no longer feel fulfilled in their jobs or personal lives and attempt to make a decisive shift in career or lifestyle.

midlife transition According to Levinson, a process whereby adults assess the past and formulate new goals for the future.

Minnesota Multiphasic Personality Inventory (MMPI-2) The most widely used objective personality test, originally intended for psychiatric diagnosis.

mnemonics Techniques that make material easier to remember.

mnemonists People with highly developed memory skills.

mode Point at which the largest number of scores occurs.

monocular cues Cues to distance and depth that require only one eye.

mood disorders Disturbances in mood or prolonged emotional state.

morphemes The smallest meaningful units of speech, such as simple words, prefixes, and suffixes.

motion parallax Monocular distance cue in which objects closer than the point of visual focus seem to move in the direction opposite to the viewer's moving head and objects beyond the focus point appear to move in the same direction as the viewer's head.

motive Specific need or desire, such as hunger, thirst, or achievement, that prompts goal-directed behavior.

motor (or efferent) neurons Neurons that carry messages from the spinal cord or brain to the muscles and glands.

myelin sheath White fatty covering found on some axons.

narcissistic personality disorder Personality disorder in which the person has an exaggerated sense of self-importance and is in need of constant admiration.

narcolepsy Hereditary sleep disorder characterized by sudden nodding off during the day and sudden loss of muscle tone following moments of emotional excitement.

natural selection Mechanism, proposed by Charles Darwin in his theory of evolution, that states that organisms best adapted to their environment tend to survive and transmit their genetic characteristics to succeeding generations; whereas, organisms with less adaptive characteristics tend to vanish from the earth.

naturalistic observation Research method involving the systematic study of animal or human behavior in natural settings rather than in the laboratory.

negative reinforcers Events whose reduction or termination increases the likelihood that ongoing behavior will recur.

neonates Newborn babies.

NEO-PI-R An objective personality test designed to assess the Big Five personality traits.

nerve (or tract) Group of axons bundled together.

neural impulse (or action potential) The firing of a nerve cell.

neural plasticity Ability of the brain to change in response to experience.

neurofeedback A biofeedback technique that monitors brain waves with the use of an EEG to teach people to gain voluntary control over their brain wave activity.

neurogenesis Growth of new neurons.

neurons Individual cells that are the smallest unit of the nervous system.

neuroscience The study of the brain and the nervous system.

neurotransmitters Chemicals released by the synaptic vesicles that travel across the synaptic space and affect adjacent neurons.

night terrors Often terrifying dreams that occur during NREM sleep from which a person is difficult to awaken.

nightmares Frightening dreams that occur during REM sleep.

nominal scale A set of categories for classifying objects.

non-REM (NREM) sleep Non-rapid-eye-movement stages of sleep that alternate with REM stages during the sleep cycle.

nonshared environment Unique aspects of the environment that are experienced differently by siblings, even though they are reared in the same family.

norm A shared idea or expectation about how to behave.

normal curve Hypothetical, bell-shaped, distribution curve that occurs when a normal distribution is plotted as a frequency polygon.

obedience Change of behavior in response to a command from another person, typically an authority figure.

object permanence The concept that things continue to exist even when they are out of sight.

objective tests Personality tests that are administered and scored in a standard way.

observational (or vicarious) learning Learning by observing other people's behavior.

observer bias Expectations or biases of the observer that might distort or influence his or her interpretation of what was actually observed.

obsessive-compulsive disorder (OCD) Anxiety disorder in which a person feels driven to think disturbing thoughts or to perform senseless rituals.

occipital lobe Part of the cerebral cortex that receives and interprets visual information.

Oedipus complex/Electra complex According to Freud, a child's sexual attachment to the parent of the opposite sex and jealousy toward the parent of the same sex; generally occurs in the phallic stage.

olfactory bulb The smell center in the brain.

operant behaviors Behaviors designed to operate on the environment in a way that will gain something desired or avoid something unpleasant.

operant (or instrumental) conditioning Type of learning in which behaviors are emitted (in the presence of specific stimuli) to earn rewards or avoid punishments.

opiates Drugs derived from the opium poppy, such as opium and heroin, that dull the senses and induce feelings of euphoria, well-being, and relaxation; synthetic drugs resembling opium derivatives are also classified as opiates.

opponent-process theory Theory of color vision that holds that three pairs of color receptors (yellow-blue, red-green, black-white) respond to determine the color one experiences.

optic nerve The bundle of axons of ganglion cells that carries neural messages from each eye to the brain.

oral stage First stage in Freud's theory of personality development, in which the infant's erotic feelings center on the mouth, lips, and tongue.

ordinal scale Scale indicating order or relative position of items according to some criterion

organ of Corti Structure on the surface of the basilar membrane that contains the receptor cells for hearing.

orgasmic disorders Inability to reach orgasm in a person able to experience sexual desire and maintain arousal.

oval window Membrane across the opening between the middle ear and inner ear that conducts vibrations to the cochlea.

panic disorder Anxiety disorder characterized by recurrent panic attacks in which the person suddenly experiences intense fear or terror without any reasonable cause.

paranoid personality disorder Personality disorder in which the person is inappropriately suspicious and mistrustful of others.

paranoid schizophrenia Schizophrenic disorder marked by extreme suspiciousness and complex, bizarre delusions.

paraphilias Sexual disorders in which unconventional objects or situations cause sexual arousal.

parasympathetic division Branch of the autonomic nervous system that calms and relaxes the body.

parietal lobe Part of the cerebral cortex that receives sensory information from all over the body.

participants Individuals whose reactions or responses are observed in an experiment.

Pavlovian (or classical) conditioning Type of learning in which a response naturally elicited by one stimulus comes to be elicited by a different, formerly neutral, stimulus.

pedophilia Desire to have sexual relations with children as the preferred or exclusive method of achieving sexual excitement.

peer group A network of same-aged friends and acquaintances who give one another emotional and social support.

perception The brain's process of organizing and interpreting sensory information to give it meaning.

perceptual constancy The tendency to perceive objects as stable and unchanging despite changes in sensory stimulation.

performance standards In Bandura's theory, standards that people develop to rate the adequacy of their own behavior in a variety of situations.

performance tests Intelligence tests that minimize the use of language.

peripheral nervous system (PNS) Division of the nervous system that connects the central nervous system to the rest of the body.

personal unconscious In Jung's theory of personality, one of the two levels of the unconscious; contains the individual's repressed thoughts, forgotten experiences, and undeveloped ideas.

personality An individual's unique pattern of thoughts, feelings, and behaviors that persists over time and across situations.

personality disorders Disorders in which inflexible and maladaptive ways of thinking and behaving learned early in life cause distress to the person or conflicts with others.

personality traits Dimensions or characteristics on which people differ in distinctive ways.

phallic stage Third stage in Freud's theory of personality development, in which erotic feelings center on the genitals.

phenotype Characteristics of an organism; determined by both genetics and experience.

pheromones Chemicals that communicate information to other organisms through smell.

phonemes The basic sounds that make up any language.

pitch Auditory experience corresponding primarily to frequency of sound vibrations, resulting in a higher or lower tone.

pituitary gland Located on the underside of the brain, it produces the largest number of the body's hormones.

place theory Theory that pitch is determined by the location of greatest vibration on the basilar membrane.

placebo Chemically inactive substance used for comparison with active drugs in experiments on the effects of drugs.

pleasure principle According to Freud, the way in which the id seeks immediate gratification of an instinct.

polarization Condition of a neuron when the inside is negatively charged relative to the outside; for example, when the neuron is at rest; also, a shift in attitudes by members of a group toward more extreme positions than the ones held before group discussion.

polygenic inheritance Process by which several genes interact to produce a certain trait; responsible for a person's most important traits.

pons Structure in the midbrain that regulates sleep and wake cycles.

positive psychology An emerging field of psychology that focuses on positive experiences, including subjective well-being, self-determination, the relationship between positive emotions and physical health, and the factors that allow individuals, communities, and societies to flourish.

positive reinforcers Events whose presence increases the likelihood that ongoing behavior will recur.

posttraumatic stress disorder (PTSD) Psychological disorder characterized by episodes of anxiety, sleeplessness, and nightmares resulting from some disturbing past event.

prejudice An unfair, intolerant, or unfavorable attitude toward a group of people.

premature ejaculation Inability of a male to inhibit orgasm as long as desired.

prenatal development Development from conception to birth.

preoperational stage In Piaget's theory, the stage of cognitive development between 2 and 7 years of age in which the individual becomes able to use mental representations and language to describe, remember, and reason about the world, though only in an egocentric fashion.

preparedness A biological readiness to learn certain associations because of their survival advantages.

pressure Any demand to speed up, intensify, or change the direction of one's behavior or live up to a higher standard of performance.

primacy effect The fact that early information about someone weighs more heavily than later information in influencing one's impression of that person.

primary drives Unlearned drive, such as hunger, that are based on a physiological state.

primary motor cortex Section of the frontal lobe responsible for voluntary movement.

primary prevention Techniques and programs to improve the social environment so that new cases of mental disorders do not develop.

primary reinforcers Reinforcers that are rewarding in themselves, such as food, water, or sex.

primary somatosensory cortex Area of the parietal lobe in which messages from the sense receptors are registered.

principles of conservation The concept that the quantity of a substance is not altered by reversible changes in its appearance.

proactive interference The process by which information already in memory interferes with new information.

problem representation The first step in solving a problem; involves interpreting or defining the problem.

procedural memories The portion of long-term memory that stores information relating to skills, habits, and other perceptual-motor tasks.

projection Attributing one's repressed motives, feelings, or wishes to others.

projective tests Personality tests, such as the Rorschach inkblot test, consisting of ambiguous or unstructured material.

prototype (or model) According to Rosch, a mental model containing the most typical features of a concept.

proximity How close two people live to each other.

psychoanalysis Theory of personality Freud developed, as well as the form of therapy he invented.

psychoanalytic model View that psychological disorders result from unconscious internal conflicts.

psychoactive drugs Chemical substances that change moods and perceptions.

psychobiology Area of psychology that focuses on the biological foundations of behavior and mental processes.

psychodynamic approach Belief that behavior results from psychological factors that interact within the individual, often outside conscious awareness.

psychodynamic theories Personality theories contending that behavior results from psychological forces that interact within the individual, often outside conscious awareness.

psychology The scientific study of behavior and mental processes.

psychoneuroimmunology (PNI) A new field that studies the interaction between stress on the one hand and immune, endocrine, and nervous system activity on the other.

psychosomatic disorder Disorder in which real physical illness is largely caused by psychological factors, such as stress and anxiety.

psychostimulant Drugs that increase ability to focus attention in people with ADHD.

psychosurgery Brain surgery performed to change a person's behavior and emotional state; a biological therapy rarely used today.

psychotherapy The use of psychological techniques to treat personality and behavior disorders.

psychotic (psychosis) Behavior characterized by a loss of touch with reality.

puberty The onset of sexual maturation, with accompanying physical development.

pupil A small opening in the iris through which light enters the eye.

punishers Stimuli that follows a behavior and decreases the likelihood that the behavior will be repeated.

punishment Any event whose presence decreases the likelihood that ongoing behavior will recur.

racism Prejudice and discrimination directed at a particular racial group.

rapid-eye movement (REM) or paradoxical sleep Sleep stage characterized by rapid eye movements and increased dreaming.

random sample Sample in which each potential participant has an equal chance of being selected.

range Difference between the largest and smallest measurements in a distribution.

ratio scale Scale with equal distances between the points or values and with a true zero.

rational-emotive therapy (RET) A directive cognitive therapy based on the idea that clients' psychological distress is caused by irrational and self-defeating beliefs and that the therapist's job is to challenge such dysfunctional beliefs.

reaction formation Expression of exaggerated ideas and emotions that are the opposite of one's repressed beliefs or feelings.

reality principle According to Freud, the way in which the ego seeks to satisfy instinctual demands safely and effectively in the real world.

receptor cell A specialized cell that responds to a particular type of energy.

receptor sites Locations on a receptor neuron into which a specific neurotransmitter fits.

regression Reverting to childlike behavior and defenses.

reinforcers A stimuli that follows a behavior and increases the likelihood that the behavior will be repeated.

reliability Ability of a test to produce consistent and stable scores.

representative sample Sample carefully chosen so that the characteristics of the participants correspond closely to the characteristics of the larger population.

representativeness A heuristic by which a new situation is judged on the basis of its resemblance to a stereotypical model.

repression Excluding uncomfortable thoughts, feelings, and desires from consciousness.

response generalization Giving a response that is somewhat different from the response originally learned to that stimulus.

resting potential Electrical charge across a neuron membrane resulting from more positive ions concentrated on the outside and more negative ions on the inside.

reticular formation (RF) Network of neurons in the hindbrain, the midbrain, and part of the forebrain, whose primary function is to alert and arouse the higher parts of the brain.

retina The lining of the eye containing receptor cells that are sensitive to light.

retinal disparity Binocular distance cue based on the difference between the images cast on the two retinas when both eyes are focused on the same object.

retroactive interference Process by which new information interferes with information already in memory.

retrograde amnesia Inability to recall events preceding an accident or injury, but without loss of earlier memory.

risky shift Greater willingness of a group than an individual to take substantial risks.

rods Receptor cells in the retina responsible for night vision and perception of brightness.

Rorschach test A projective test composed of ambiguous inkblots; the way people interpret the blots is believed to reveal aspects of their personality.

rote rehearsal Retaining information in memory simply by repeating it again and again.

sample A subset of a population.

saturation The purity of a color.

scatter plot Diagram showing the association between scores on two variables.

schedule of reinforcement In operant conditioning, the rule for determining when and how often reinforcers will be delivered.

schema (*skee-mah*) A set of beliefs or expectations about something or someone based on past experience; plural *schemata*.

schizoid personality disorder Personality disorder in which a person is withdrawn and lacks feelings for others.

schizophrenic disorders Severe disorders in which there are disturbances of thoughts, communications, and emotions, including delusions and hallucinations.

scientific method An approach to knowledge that relies on collecting data, generating a theory to explain the data, producing testable hypotheses based on the theory, and testing those hypotheses empirically.

secondary drives Learned drives, such as ambition, that are not based on a physiological state.

secondary prevention Programs to identify groups that are at high risk for mental disorders and to detect maladaptive behavior in these groups and treat it promptly.

secondary reinforcers Reinforcers whose value is acquired through association with other primary or secondary reinforcers.

selection studies Studies that estimate the heritability of a trait by breeding animals with other animals that have the same trait.

self-actualizing tendency According to Rogers, the drive of human beings to fulfill their self-concepts, or the images they have of themselves.

self-efficacy According to Bandura, the expectancy that one's efforts will be successful.

self-fulfilling prophecy The process in which a person's expectation about another elicits behavior from the second person that confirms the expectation.

self-monitoring The tendency for an individual to observe the situation for cues about how to react.

semantic memories The portion of long-term memory that stores general facts and information.

sensation The experience of sensory stimulation.

sensory (or afferent) neurons Neurons that carry messages from sense organs to the spinal cord or brain.

sensory-motor stage In Piaget's theory, the stage of cognitive development between birth and 2 years of age in which the individual develops object permanence and acquires the ability to form mental representations.

sensory registers Entry points for raw information from the senses.

serial position effect The finding that when asked to recall a list of unrelated items, performance is better for the items at the beginning and end of the list.

set point theory Theory that states that a person's body is genetically predisposed to maintaining a certain weight by changing its metabolic rate and activity level in response to caloric intake.

sex-typed behavior Socially prescribed ways of behaving that differ for boys and girls.

sexual desire disorders Disorders in which the person lacks sexual interest or has an active distaste for sex.

sexual dysfunction Loss or impairment of the ordinary physical responses of sexual function.

sexual masochism Inability to enjoy sex without accompanying emotional or physical pain.

sexual orientation Refers to the direction of one's sexual interest toward members of the same sex, the other sex, or both sexes.

sexual response cycle The typical sequence of events, including excitement, plateau, orgasm, and resolution, characterizing sexual response in males and females.

sexual sadism Obtaining sexual gratification from humiliating or physically harming a sex partner.

shape constancy A tendency to see an object as the same shape no matter the angle from which it is viewed.

shaping Reinforcing successive approximations to a desired behavior.

short-term memory (STM) Working memory; briefly stores and processes selected information from the sensory registers.

short-term psychodynamic therapy Insight therapy that is time limited and focused on trying to help clients correct the immediate problems in their lives.

significance Probability that results obtained were because of chance.

signs Stereotyped communications about an animal's current state.

Sixteen Personality Factor Questionnaire Objective personality test created by Cattell that provides scores on the 16 traits he identified.

size constancy Perceiving an object as the same size regardless of the image it casts on the retina.

Skinner box A box often used in operant conditioning of animals; it limits the available responses and thus increases the likelihood that the desired response will occur.

social cognition Knowledge and understanding concerning the social world and the people in it (including oneself).

social influence The process by which others individually or collectively affect one's perceptions, attitudes, and actions.

social learning theorists Psychologists whose view of learning emphasizes the ability to learn by observing a model or receiving instructions, without firsthand experience by the learner.

social phobias Anxiety disorders characterized by excessive, inappropriate fears connected with social situations or performances in front of other people.

social psychology The scientific study of the ways in which the thoughts, feelings, and behaviors of one individual are influenced by the real, imagined, or inferred behavior or characteristics of other people.

socialization Process by which children learn the behaviors and attitudes appropriate to their family and culture.

sociocultural approach Contemporary approach to psychology that emphasizes the ways in which culture, gender, race, and ethnicity can affect virtually all aspects of human behavior.

somatic nervous system Part of the peripheral nervous system that carries messages from the senses to the central nervous system and between the central nervous system and the skeletal muscles.

somatoform disorders Disorders in which there is an apparent physical illness for which there is no organic basis.

sound A psychological experience created by the brain in response to changes in air pressure received by the auditory system.

sound waves Changes in air pressure caused when molecules of air or fluid collide with one another and then move apart again.

specific phobia Anxiety disorder characterized by an intense, paralyzing fear of something.

spinal cord Complex cable of neurons that runs down the spine, connecting the brain to most of the rest of the body.

split-half reliability A method of determining test reliability by dividing the test into two parts and checking the agreement of scores on both parts.

spontaneous recovery The reappearance of an extinguished response after the passage of time, without training.

standard deviation Statistical measure of variability in a group of scores or other values.

statistics A branch of mathematics that psychologists use to organize and analyze data.

stereotype A set of characteristics presumed to be shared by all members of a social category.

stimulants Drugs, including amphetamines and cocaine, that stimulate the sympathetic nervous system and produce feelings of optimism and boundless energy.

stimulus discrimination Learning to respond to only one stimulus and to inhibit the response to all other stimuli.

stimulus generalization The transfer of a learned response to different but similar stimuli.

strain studies Studies of the heritability of behavioral traits using animals that have been inbred to produce strains that are genetically similar to one another.

stranger anxiety Fear of unfamiliar people which usually emerges around 7 months, reaching its peak at 12 months and declining during the second year.

stress A state of psychological tension or strain.

stress-inoculation therapy Type of cognitive therapy that trains clients to cope with stressful situations by learning a more useful pattern of self-talk.

stressor Any environmental demand that creates a state of tension or threat and requires change or adaptation.

structuralism School of psychology that stresses the basic units of experience and the combinations in which they occur.

subgoals Intermediate, more manageable goals used in one heuristic strategy to make it easier to reach the final goal.

sublimation Redirecting repressed motives and feelings into more socially acceptable channels.

substance abuse A pattern of drug use that diminishes the ability to fulfill responsibilities at home, work, or school and that results in repeated use of a drug in dangerous situations or that leads to legal difficulties related to drug use.

substance dependence A pattern of compulsive drug taking that results in tolerance, withdrawal symptoms, or other specific symptoms for at least a year.

superego According to Freud, the social and parental standards the individual has internalized; the conscience and the ego ideal.

suprachiasmatic nucleus (SCN) A cluster of neurons in the hypothalamus that receives input from the retina regarding light and dark cycles and is involved in regulating the biological clock.

survey research Research technique in which questionnaires or interviews are administered to a selected group of people.

sympathetic division Branch of the autonomic nervous system that prepares the body for quick action in an emergency.

synapse Area composed of the axon terminal of one neuron, the synaptic space, and the dendrite or cell body of the next neuron.

synaptic space (or synaptic cleft) Tiny gap between the axon terminal of one neuron and the dendrites or cell body of the next neuron.

synaptic vesicles Tiny sacs in a terminal button that release chemicals into the synapse.

systems approach View that biological, psychological, and social risk factors combine to produce psychological disorders; also known as the *biopsychosocial* model of psychological disorders.

systematic desensitization Behavioral technique for reducing a person's fear and anxiety by gradually associating a new response (relaxation) with stimuli that have been causing the fear and anxiety.

taste buds Structures on the tongue that contain the receptor cells for taste.

temperament Characteristic patterns of emotional reactions and emotional self-regulation.

temporal lobe Part of the cerebral hemisphere that helps regulate hearing, balance, and equilibrium, and certain emotions and motivations.

teratogens Toxic substances such as alcohol or nicotine that cross the placenta and may result in birth defects.

terminal button (or synaptic knob) Structure at the end of an axon terminal branch.

tertiary prevention Programs to help people adjust to community life after release from a mental hospital.

testosterone The primary male sex hormone.

texture gradient Monocular cue to distance and depth based on the fact that objects seen at greater distances appear to be smoother and less textured.

thalamus Forebrain region that relays and translates incoming messages from the sense receptors, except those for smell.

Thematic Apperception Test (TAT) A projective test composed of ambiguous pictures about which a person is asked to write a complete story.

theory Systematic explanation of a phenomenon; it organizes known facts, allows people to predict new facts, and permits them to exercise a degree of control over the phenomenon.

theory of multiple intelligences Howard Gardner's theory that there is not one intelligence, but rather many intelligences, each of which is relatively independent of the others.

threshold of excitation Level an impulse must exceed to cause a neuron to fire.

thyroid gland Endocrine gland located below the voice box that produces the hormone thyroxin.

tip-of-the-tongue phenomenon (or TOT) Knowing a word, but not being able to immediately recall it.

token economy Operant conditioning therapy in which people earn tokens (reinforcers) for desired behaviors and exchange them for desired items or privileges.

transduction The conversion of physical energy into coded neural signals.

transference The client's carrying over to the analyst feelings held toward childhood authority figures.

transvestic fetishism Wearing the clothes of the opposite sex to achieve sexual gratification.

triarchic theory of intelligence Sternberg's theory that intelligence involves mental skills (analytical intelligence), insight and creative adaptability (creative intelligence), and environmental responsiveness (practical intelligence).

trichromatic (three-color) theory Theory of color vision that holds that all color perception derives from three different color receptors in the retina (usually red, green, and blue receptors).

twin studies Studies of identical and fraternal twins to determine the relative influence of heredity and environment on human behavior.

unconditional positive regard In Rogers's theory, the full acceptance and love of another person regardless of his or her behavior.

unconditioned response (UR) A response that takes place in an organism whenever an unconditioned stimulus occurs.

unconditioned stimulus (US) A stimulus that invariably causes an organism to respond in a specific way.

unconscious In Freud's theory, all the ideas, thoughts, and feelings of which we are not and normally cannot become aware.

undifferentiated schizophrenia Schizophrenic disorder in which there are clear schizophrenic symptoms that do not meet the criteria for another subtype of the disorder.

vaginismus Involuntary muscle spasms in the outer part of the vagina that make intercourse impossible.

validity Ability of a test to measure what it has been designed to measure.

variable-interval schedule A reinforcement schedule in which the correct response is reinforced after varying lengths of time following the last reinforcement.

variable-ratio schedule A reinforcement schedule in which a varying number of correct responses must occur before reinforcement is presented.

vestibular senses The senses of body position and movement in space.

vicarious reinforcement (or punishment) Reinforcement or punishment experienced by models that affects the willingness of others to perform the behaviors they learned by observing those models.

visual acuity The ability to distinguish fine details visually.

voyeurism Desire to watch others having sexual relations or to spy on nude people.

waking consciousness Mental state that encompasses the thoughts, feelings, and perceptions that occur when people are awake and reasonably alert.

Weber's law The principle that the jnd for any given sense is a constant fraction or proportion of the stimulation being judged.

Wechsler Adult Intelligence Scale—Third Edition (WAIS-III) An individual intelligence test developed especially for adults; measures both verbal and performance abilities.

Wechsler Intelligence Scale for Children—Third Edition (WISC-III) An individual intelligence test developed especially for school-aged children; measures verbal and performance abilities and also yields an overall IQ score.

withdrawal Avoiding a situation when other forms of coping are not practical.

working backward A heuristic strategy in which one works backward from the desired goal to the given conditions.

Abramson, C. I., & Aquino, I. S. (2002). Behavioral studies of learning in the Africanized honey bee (*Apis mellifera L.*). *Brain, Behavior, and Evolution, 59,* 68–86.

Ackerman, D. (1995). *A natural history of the senses.* New York: Vintage.

Addison, A. (2005). The first formal reaction to C. G. Jung's departure from psychoanalysis: Sandor Ferenczi's review of *Symbols of Transformation. Journal of Analytical Psychology, 50,* 551–552.

Adorno, T. W., Frenkel-Brunswick, E., Levinson, D. J., & Sanford, R. N. (1950). *The authoritarian personality.* New York: Harper & Row.

Aiken, L. R., & Groth-Marnat, G. (2005). *Psychological testing and assessment* (12th ed.). Boston: Allyn & Bacon.

Ainsworth, M. D. (1977). Attachment theory and its utility in cross-cultural research. In P. H. Leiderman, S. R. Tulkin, & A. Rosenfields (Eds.), *Culture and infancy: Variation in the human experience* (pp. 49–67). New York: Academic Press.

Ainsworth, M. D. (1989). Attachments beyond infancy. *American Psychologist, 44,* 709–716.

Albano, A. M., & Barlow, D. H. (1996). Breaking the vicious cycle: Cognitive-behavioral group treatment for socially anxious youth. In E. D. Hibbs & P. S. Jensen (Eds.), *Psychosocial treatments for child and adolescent disorders: Empirically based strategies for clinical practice* (pp. 43–62). Washington, DC: American Psychological Association.

Albeck, S., & Kaydar, D. (2002). Divorced mothers: Their network of friends, pre- and post-divorce. *Journal of Divorce and Remarriage, 36,* 111–138.

Allgood-Merten, B., Lewinsohn, P. M., & Hops, H. (1990). Sex differences and adolescent depression. *Journal of Abnormal Psychology, 99,* 55–63.

Allport, G. W. (1954). *The nature of prejudice.* New York: Anchor.

Allport, G. W., & Odbert, H. S. (1936). Trait-names: A psycholexical study. *Psychological Monographs, 47*(1, Whole No. 211).

Almeida, D. M. (2005). Resilience and vulnerability to daily stressors assessed via diary methods. *Current Directions in Psychological Science, 14,* 64–68.

Almgren, G., Guest, A., Immerwahr, G., & Spittel, M. (2002). Joblessness, family disruption, and violent death in Chicago, 1970–90. *Social Forces, 76,* 1465–1493.

Altabe, M. N., & Thompson, J. K. (1994). Body image. In *Encyclopedia of human behavior* (Vol. 1, pp. 407–414). San Diego, CA: Academic Press.

Altemeyer, B. (2004). Highly dominating, highly authoritarian personalities. *Journal of Social Psychology, 144,* 421–447.

Alzheimer's Association. (2006). *Alzheimer's facts and figures.* Retrieved May 11, 2006, from http://www.alz.org/AboutAD/statistics.asp.

Amedi, A., Merabet, L. B., Bermpohl, F., & Pascual-Leone, A. (2005). The occipital cortex in the blind: Lessons about plasticity and vision. *Current Directions in Psychological Science, 14,* 306–311.

Amen, D. G., Stubblefield, M., Carmichael, B., & Thisted, R. (1996). Brain SPECT findings and aggressiveness. *Annals of Clinical Psychiatry, 8,* 129–137.

American Psychological Association. (1978). Guidelines for therapy with women. *American Psychologist, 33,* 1122–1123.

American Psychological Association. (1992). *Ethical principles of psychologists and code of conduct.* Washington, DC: Author.

American Psychiatric Association (APA). (1994). *Diagnostic and statistical manual of mental disorders* (4th ed.). Washington, DC: Author.

American Psychological Association. (2000, November). Facts & figures. *Monitor on Psychology, 31,* 10.

American Psychological Association. (2003). *Ethical principles of psychologists and code of conduct.* Retrieved October 1, 2007, from http://www.apa.org/ethics/code2002.html#intro

Anastasi, A., & Urbina, S. (1997). *Psychological testing* (7th ed.). Upper Saddle River, NJ: Prentice Hall.

Andrews, J. A., & Lewinsohn, P. M. (1992). Suicidal attempts among older adolescents: Prevalence and co-occurrence with psychiatric disorders. *Journal of the American Academy of Child and Adolescent Psychiatry, 31,* 655–662.

Archer, J. (1996). Sex differences in social behavior: Are the social role and evolutionary explanations compatible? *American Psychologist, 51,* 909–917.

Aronson, E. (2003). *The social animal* (9th ed.). New York: Worth.

Aronson, E., Wilson, T. D., & Akert, R. M. (2005). *Social Psychology* (5th ed.). Upper Saddle River, NJ: Prentice Hall.

Arrigo, J. M., & Pezdek, K. (1997). Lessons from the study of psychogenic amnesia. *Current Directions in Psychological Science, 6,* 148–152.

Asch, S. E. (1956). Studies of independence and conformity: I. A minority of one against a unanimous majority. *Psychological Monographs, 70*(9, Whole No. 416).

Asendorpf, J. B., & Van-Aken, M. A. G. (2003). Validity of Big Five personality judgments in childhood: A 9-year longitudinal study. *European Journal of Personality, 17,* 1–17.

Astur, R. S., Taylor, L. B., Marnelak, A. N., Philpott, L., & Sutherland, R. J. (2002). Humans with hippocampus damage display severe spatial memory impairments in a virtual Morris water task. *Behavioural Brain Research, 132,* 77–84.

Attwood, T. (2005). Theory of mind and Asperger's syndrome. In L. J. Baker & L. A. Welkowitz (Eds.), *Asperger's syndrome: Intervening in schools, clinics, and communities* (pp. 11–41). Mahwah, NJ: Erlbaum.

Baddeley, A. D. (1986). *Working memory.* New York: Clarendon Press/Oxford University Press.

Baddeley, A. D. (2002). Is working memory still working? *European Psychologist, 7,* 85–97.

Bagemihl, B. (2000). *Biological exuberance: Animal homosexuality and natural diversity.* New York: St. Martin's Press.

Bahrick, H. P. (1984). Semantic memory in permastore: Fifty years of memory for Spanish learned in school. *Journal of Experimental Psychology: General, 113,* 1–31.

Bahrick, H. P., Bahrick, P. O., & Wittlinger, R. P. (1974, December). Those unforgettable high school days. *Psychology Today,* 50–56.

Baillargeon, R. (1994). How do infants learn about the physical world? *Current Directions in Psychological Science, 3,* 133–140.

Bandura, A. (1965). Influence of models' reinforcement contingencies on the acquisition of imitative responses. *Journal of Personality and Social Psychology, 1*, 589–595.

Bandura, A. (1977). *Social learning theory*. Englewood Cliffs, NJ: Prentice Hall.

Bandura, A. (1986). *Social foundations of thought and action: A social cognitive theory*. Englewood Cliffs, NJ: Prentice Hall.

Bandura, A. (1997). *Self-efficacy: The exercise of control*. New York: Freeman.

Bandura, A. (2004). Model of causality in social learning theory. In A. Freeman, M. J. Mahoney, P. DeVito, & D. Martin (Eds.), *Cognition and psychotherapy* (2nd ed., pp. 25–44). New York, NY: Springer.

Bandura, A., & Locke, E. A. (2003). Negative self-efficacy and goal effects revisited. *Journal of Applied Psychology, 8*, 87–99.

Barnett, R. C., Brennan, R. T., & Marshall, N. L. (1994). Gender and the relationship between parent role quality and psychological distress: A study of men and women in dual-earner couples. *Journal of Family Issues, 15*, 229–252.

Barron, F. (1963). *Creativity and psychological health*. Princeton, NJ: Van Nostrand.

Bartlett, F. C. (1932). *Remembering: A study in experimental and social psychology*. New York: Macmillan.

Bauer, P. J. (1996). What do infants recall of their lives? Memory for specific events by one- to two-year-olds. *American Psychologist, 51*(1), 29–41.

Baumeister, A. A., & Baumeister, A. A. (2000). Mental retardation: Causes and effects. In M. Hersen & R. T. Ammerman (Eds.), *Advanced abnormal child psychology* (2nd. ed., pp. 327–355). Mahwah, NJ: Erlbaum.

Baumeister, R. F., & Leary, M. R. (2000). The need to belong: Desire for interpersonal attachments as a fundamental human motivation. In E. T. Higgins & A. W. Kruglanski (Eds.), *Motivational science: Social and personality perspectives* (pp. 24–49). New York: Psychology Press.

Baumrind, D. (1972). Socialization and instrumental competence in young children. In W. W. Hartup (Ed.), *The young child: Reviews of research* (Vol. 2, pp. 202–224). Washington, DC: National Association for the Education of Young Children.

Baumrind, D. (1991). Parenting styles and adolescent development. In J. Brooks-Gunn, R. Lerner, & A. C. Petersen (Eds.), *The encyclopedia of adolescence* (Vol. 2, pp. 746–758). New York: Garland.

Baumrind, D. (1996). The discipline controversy revisited. *Family Relations: Journal of Applied Family and Child Studies, 45*, 405–414.

Beck, A. T. (1967). *Depression: Clinical, experimental and theoretical aspects*. New York: Harper (Hoeber).

Beck, A. T. (1976). *Cognitive therapy and emotional disorders*. New York: International Universities Press.

Beck, A. T. (1984). Cognition and therapy. *Archives of General Psychiatry, 41*, 1112–1114.

Benokraitis, N. V. (2004). *Marriages and families: Changes, choices, and constraints* (5th ed.). Upper Saddle River, NJ: Prentice Hall.

Benton, D., & Roberts, G. (1988). Effect of vitamin and mineral supplementation on intelligence of a sample of schoolchildren. *Lancet, 1*, 140–144.

Berkowitz, L., & Harmon-Jones, E. (2004). Toward an understanding of the determinants of anger. *Emotion, 4*, 107–130.

Berr, C. (2002). Oxidative stress and cognitive impairment in the elderly. *Journal of Nutrition, Health and Aging, 6*, 261–266.

Bertenthal, B. I., Campos, J. J., & Kermoian, R. (1994). An epigenetic perspective on the development of self-produced locomotion and its consequences. *Current Directions in Psychological Science, 3*, 140–145.

Bettencourt, B. A., & Miller, N. (1996). Gender differences in aggression as a function of provocation: A meta-analysis. *Psychological Bulletin, 119*, 422–427.

Bilkey, D. K., & Clearwater, J. M. (2005). The dynamic nature of spatial encoding in the hippocampus. *Behavioral Neuroscience, 119*, 1533–1545.

Blader, S. L., & Tyler, T. R. (2002). Justice and empathy: What motivates people to help others? In M. Ross & M. D. T. Miller (Eds.), *The justice motive in everyday life* (pp. 226–250). New York: Cambridge Univ. Press.

Blake, R. R., Helson, H., & Mouton, J. (1956). The generality of conformity behavior as a function of factual anchorage, difficulty of task and amount of social pressure. *Journal of Personality, 25*, 294–305.

Blatt, S. J., Zuroff, D. C., Quinlan, D. M., & Pilkonis, P. (1996). Interpersonal factors in brief treatment of depression: Further analysis of the NIMH Treatment of Depression Collaborative Research Program. *Journal of Consulting and Clinical Psychology, 64*, 162–171.

Block, J. (1971). *Lives through time*. Berkeley, CA: Bancroft.

Bonanno, G. A., Wortman, C. B., & Nesse R. M. (2004). Prospective patterns of resilience and maladjustment during widowhood. *Psychology and Aging, 19*, 260–271.

Bosma, H., van Boxtel, M. P. J., Ponds, R. W. H. M., Houx, P. J. H., & Jolles, J. (2003). Education and age-related cognitive decline: The contribution of mental workload. *Educational Gerontology, 29*, 165–173.

Bosworth, R. G., & Dobkins, K. R. (1999). Left-hemisphere dominance for motion processing in deaf signers. *Psychological Science, 10*, 256–262.

Bouchard, T. J. Jr. (1984). Twins reared together and apart: What they tell us about human diversity. In S. W. Fox (Ed.), *Individuality and determinism* (pp. 147–178). New York: Plenum.

Bouchard, T. J. Jr. (1996). IQ similarity in twins reared apart: Findings and responses to critics. In R. J. Sternberg & E. Grigorenko (Eds.), *Intelligence: Heredity and environment* (pp. 126–160). New York: Cambridge Univ. Press.

Bovbjerg, D. H. (2003). Conditioning, cancer, and immune regulation. *Brain, Behavior and Immunity, 17* [Special issue: *Biological mechanisms of psychosocial effects on disease: Implications for cancer control*], S58–S61.

Bowden, E. M., & Jung-Beeman, M. (2003). Aha! Insight experience correlates with solution activation in the right hemisphere. *Psychonomic Bulletin and Review, 10*, 730–737.

Bower, B. (2006, February 11). Self-serve brains: Personal identity veers to the right hemisphere. *Science News, 169*, 90–92.

Brannon, E. M., & Terrace, H. S. (1998, October 23). Ordering of the numerosities 1–9 by monkeys. *Science, 282*, 746–749.

Brenner, M. H. (1973). *Mental illness and the economy*. Cambridge, MA: Harvard Univ. Press.

Brenner, M. H. (1979). Influence of the social environment on psychopathology: The historic perspective. In J. E. Barrett (Ed.), *Stress and mental disorder*. New York: Raven.

Bresnahan, M., Schaefer, C. A., Brown, A. S., & Susser, E. S. (2005). Prenatal determinants of schizophrenia: What we have learned thus far? *Epidemiologiae Psichiatria Sociale, 14*, 194–197.

Brim, O. (1999). *The McArthur Foundation study of midlife development.* Vero Beach, FL: The McArthur Foundation.

Broadbent, D. E. (1958). *Perception and communication.* New York: Pergamon.

Brobert, A. G., Wessels, H., Lamb, M. E., & Hwang, C. P. (1997). Effects of day care on the development of cognitive abilities in 8-year-olds: A longitudinal study. *Developmental Psychology, 33*, 62–69.

Brody, J. E. (2004, February 24). Age-fighting hormones put men at risk, too. *New York Times*, p. D7.

Brody, L., & Hall, J. (2000). Gender, emotion, and expression. In M. Lewis & J. Haviland-Jones (Eds.), *Handbook of emotions* (2nd ed., pp. 338–349). New York: Guilford.

Brown, L. S., & Ballou, M. (1992). *Personality and psychopathology: Feminists reappraisals.* New York: Guilford.

Brown, R., & McNeill, D. (1966). The "tip of the tongue phenomenon." *Journal of Verbal Learning and Verbal Behavior, 8*, 325–337.

Bruder, G. E., Stewart, M. W., Mercier, M. A., Agosti, V., Leite, P., Donovan, S., et al. (1997). Outcome of cognitive-behavioral therapy for depression: Relation to hemispheric dominance for verbal processing. *Journal of Abnormal Psychology, 106*, 138–144.

Bryant, R. A., & Harvey, A. G. (2003). Gender differences in the relationship between acute stress disorder and posttraumatic stress disorder following motor vehicle accidents. *Australian and New Zealand Journal of Psychiatry, 37*, 226–229.

Buist, C. M. (2002). Reducing essential hypertension in the elderly using biofeedback assisted self-regulatory training. *Dissertation Abstracts International: Section B: The Sciences and Engineering, 63*, 516.

Buklina, S. B. (2005). The corpus callosum, interhemisphere interactions, and the function of the right hemisphere of the brain. *Neuroscience and Behavioral Physiology, 35, 473*–480.

Burt, M. R., Aron, L. Y., Douglas, T., Valente, J., Lee, E., & Iwen, B. (1999). Homelessness: Programs and the people they serve. Retrieved October 25, 2007, from http://www.urban.org/UploadedPDF/homelessness.pdf

Bushman, B. J. (2002). Does venting anger feed or extinguish the flame? Catharsis rumination, distraction, anger, and aggressive responding. *Personality and Social Psychology Bulletin, 28, 724*–731.

Bushman, B. J., & Baumeister, R. F. (1998). Threatened egotism, narcissism, self-esteem, and direct and displaced aggression: Does self-love or self-hate lead to violence? *Journal of Personality & Social Psychology, 75*, 219–229.

Buss, D. M. (1985). Human mate selection. *American Scientist, 73*, 47–51.

Buss, D. M. (1990). The evolution of anxiety and social exclusion. *Journal of Social and Clinical Psychology, 9*, 196–210.

Buss, D. M. (1991). Evolutionary personality psychology. *Annual Review of Psychology, 42*, 459–491.

Buss, D. M. (2000). *The dangerous passion: Why jealousy is as necessary as love and sex.* New York: Free Press.

Buss, D. M. (2004). *Evolutionary psychology: The new science of the mind* (2nd ed.). Boston: Pearson Education.

Buss, D. M. (2005). *The handbook of evolutionary psychology.* Hoboken, NJ: John Wiley & Sons.

Byne, W. (1994). The biological evidence challenged. *Scientific American, 270*, 50–55.

Cahill, L., & McGaugh, J. L. (1998). Mechanisms of emotional arousal and lasting declarative memory. *Trends in Neurosciences, 21*, 294–299.

Calhoun, L. G., & Tedeschi, R. G. (2001). Posttraumatic growth: The positive lessons of loss. In R. A. Neimeyer (Ed.), *Meaning reconstruction & the experience of loss* (pp. 157–172). Washington, DC: American Psychological Assoc.

Callahan, R. (2000, January 13). Tall Polish men have tall kids, study says. *Charlotte Observer*, p. 12A.

Camperio-Ciani A., Corna, F., & Capiluppi C. (2004). Evidence for maternally inherited factors favouring male homosexuality and promoting female fecundity. *Proceedings of the Royal Society of London B., 271*, 2217–2221.

Camras, L., Meng, Z., Ujiie, T., Dharamsi, S., Myake, K., Oster, H., et al. (2002). Observing emotion in infants: Facial expression, body behavior, and rater judgments of responses to an expectancy-violating event. *Emotion, 2*, 179–193.

Cannon, W. B. (1929). *Bodily changes in pain, hunger, fear, and rage*, (Rev. ed.) New York: D. Appleton and Co.

Carr, D., & Friedman, M. A. (2005). Is obesity stigmatizing? Body weight, perceived discrimination, and psychological well-being in the United States. *Journal of Health and Social Behavior, 46*, 244–259.

Carr, M., Borkowski, J. G., & Maxwell, S. E. (1991). Motivational components of underachievement. *Developmental Psychology, 27*, 108–118.

Carrère, S., Mittmann, A., Woodin, E., Tabares, A., & Yoshimoto, D. (2005). Anger dysregulation, depressive symptoms, and health in married women and men. *Nursing Research, 54*, 184–192.

Carroll, M. E., & Overmier, B. J. (2001) *Animal research and human health: Advancing human welfare through behavioral science.* Washington, DC: American Psychological Association.

Carter, J. A. (2006). Theoretical pluralism and technical eclecticism. In C. D. Goodheart, A. E. Kazdin, & R. J. Sternberg (Eds.), *Evidence-based psychotherapy: Where practice and research meet* (pp. 63–79). Washington, DC: American Psychological Association.

Carter, R. (1998). *Mapping the mind.* Berkeley, CA: Univ. of California Press.

Cattell, J. M. (1906). *American men of science: A biographical directory.* New York: Science Press.

Cattell, R. B. (1965). *The scientific analysis of personality.* Baltimore: Penguin.

Cattell, R. B., & Kline, P. (1977). *The specific analysis of personality and motivation.* New York: Academic Press.

Cerri, M. M. (2005). Recovered memory: Historical and theoretical foundations of the debate. *Dissertation Abstracts International: Section B: The Sciences and Engineering, 65, 4820.*

Chaiken, S., & Eagly, A. H. (1976). Communication modality as a determinant of message persuasiveness and message comprehensibility. *Journal of Personality and Social Psychology, 34*, 605–614.

Chance, P. (1992). The rewards of learning. *Phi Delta Kappan, 73*, 200–207.

Chapman, R. A. (2006). *The clinical use of hypnosis in cognitive behavior therapy.* New York: Springer Publishing.

Chen, G., & Manji, H. K. (2006). The extracellular signal-regulated kinase pathway: An emerging promising target for mood stabilizers. *Current Opinion in Psychiatry, 19*, 313–323.

Chen, J-Q., & Gardner, H. (2005). Assessment based on multiple-intelligences theory. In D. P. Flanagan & P. L. Harrison (Eds.), *Contemporary intellectual assessment: Theories, tests, and issues* (pp. 77–102). New York: Guilford.

Cherry, C. (1966). *On human communication: A review, a survey, and a criticism* (2nd ed.). Cambridge, MA: MIT Press.

Chervin, R. D., Killion, J. E., Archbold, K. H., & Ruzicka, D. L. (2003). Conduct problems and symptoms of sleep disorders in children. *Journal of the American Academy of Child and Adolescent Psychiatry, 42*, 201–208.

Chomsky, N. (1957). *Syntactic structures*. The Hague: Mouton.

Chomsky, N. (1986). *Knowledge of language: Its nature, origins and use.* New York: Praeger.

Chomsky, N. (1998). *On language.* New York: The New Press.

Chomsky, N., Place, U., & Schoneberger, T. (2000). The Chomsky-Place correspondence 1993–1994. *Analysis of Verbal Behavior, 17*, 7–38.

Chuang, Y. C. (2002). Sex differences in mate selection preference and sexual strategy: Tests for evolutionary hypotheses. *Chinese Journal of Psychology, 44*, 75–93.

Chwalisz, K., Diener, E., & Gallagher, D. (1988). Autonomic arousal feedback and emotional experience: Evidence from the spinal cord injured. *Journal of Personality and Social Psychology, 54*, 820–828.

Clapham, M. M. (2004). The convergent validity of the Torrance Tests of Creative Thinking and Creativity Interest Inventories. *Educational and Psychological Measurement, 64*, 828–841.

Clarke-Stewart, K. A., Christian, P. G., & Fitzgerald, L. M. (1994). *Children at home and in day care.* Hillsdale, NJ: Erlbaum.

Clements, M. (1996, March 17). Sex after 65. *Parade Magazine*, 4–5, 7.

Cohen, L. J., & Galynker, I. I. (2002). Clinical features of pedophilia and implications for treatment. *Journal of Psychiatric Practice, 8*, 276–289.

Cohen, S. (1996). Psychological stress, immunity, and upper respiratory infections. *Current Directions in Psychological Science, 5*, 86–88.

Cohen, S., & Herbert, T. B. (1996). Health psychology: Psychological factors and physical disease from the perspective of human psychoneuroimmunology. *Annual Review of Psychology, 47*, 113–142.

Cohen, S., Hamrick, N., Rodriguez, M. S., Feldman, P. J., Rabin, B. S., & Manuck, S. B. (2002). Reactivity and vulnerability to stress-associated risk for upper respiratory illness. *Psychosomatic Medicine, 64*, 302–310.

Cohen, S., Tyrrell, D. A., & Smith, A. P. (1991). Psychological stress and susceptibility to the common cold. *New England Journal of Medicine, 325*, 606–612.

Cohn, L. D. (1991). Sex differences in the course of personality development: A meta-analysis. *Psychological Bulletin, 109*, 252–266.

Colcombe, S., & Kramer, A. F. (2003). Fitness effects on the cognitive function of older adults: A meta-analytic study. *Psychological Science, 14*, 125–130.

Coley, R. L., & Chase-Lansdale, L. (1998). Adolescent pregnancy and parenthood: Recent evidence and future directions. *American Psychologist, 53*, 152–166.

Collaer, M. L., & Hines, M. (1995). Human behavioral sex differences: A role for gonadal hormones during early development? *Psychological Bulletin, 118*, 55–107.

Collins, W. A., Maccoby, E. E., Steinberg, L., Hetherington, E. M., & Bornstein, M. H. (2000). Contemporary research on parenting: The case for nature and nurture. *American Psychologist, 55*, 218–232.

Conger, J. J., & Petersen, A. C. (1991). *Adolescence and youth* (4th ed.). New York: HarperCollins.

Conway, M. A. (1996). Failures of autobiographical remembering. In D. Hermann, C. McEvoy, C. Hertzog, P. Hertel, & M. K. Johnson (Eds.), *Basic and applied memory research: Theory in context.* Mahwah, NJ: Erlbaum.

Cooke, C. A. (2004). Young people's attitudes towards guns in America, Great Britain and Western Australia. *Aggressive Behavior, 30*, 93–104.

Costa, P. T., Jr., & McCrae, R. R. (1992). *Revised NEO Personality Inventory (NEO-PI-R) and NEO Five-Factor Inventory (NEO-FFI) professional manual.* Odessa, FL: Psychological Assessment Resources.

Cousins, N. (1981). *Anatomy of an illness as perceived by the patient.* New York: Bantam.

Creed, P. A., & Klisch, J. (2005). Future outlook and financial strain: Testing the personal agency and latent deprivation models of unemployment and well-being. *Journal of Occupational Health Psychology, 10*, 251–260.

Crooks, R., & Bauer, K. (2002). *Our sexuality* (8th ed.). Belmont CA: Wadsworth.

Cross, M. R. (2003). The relationship between trauma history, daily hassles, and physical symptoms. *Dissertation Abstracts International: Section B: The Sciences and Engineering, 63*, 43–64.

Culbertson, F. M. (1997). Depression and gender: An international review. *American Psychologist, 52*, 25–31.

Dahl, E. K. (1996). The concept of penis envy revisited: A child analyst listens to adult women. *Psychoanalytic Study of the Child, 51*, 303–325.

Dalbert, C. (2001). *The justice motive as a personal resource: Dealing with challenges and critical life events.* New York: Kluwer Academic/Plenum.

Dalton, P., Doolittle, N., & Breslin, P. A. S. (2002). Gender-specific induction of enhanced sensitivity to odors. *Nature Neuroscience, 5*, 199–200.

Darwin, C. R. (1859). *On the origin of species.* London: John Murray.

Darwin, C. R. (1872). *The origin of species by means of natural selection, or the preservation of favoured races in the struggle for life.* London: John Murray.

Davidson, R. J., Kabat-Zinn, J., Schumacher, J., Rosenkranz, M., Muller, D., Santorelli, S. F., et al. (2003). Alterations in brain and immune function produced by mindfulness meditation. *Psychosomatic Medicine, 65*, 564–570.

Dawson, G., & Toth, K. (2006). Autism spectrum disorders. In D. Cicchetti & D. J. Cohen (Eds.), *Developmental psychopathology, Vol 3: Risk, disorder, and adaptation* (2nd ed., pp. 317–357). Hoboken, NJ: John Wiley & Sons.

De la Fuente, M. (2002). Effects of antioxidants on the immune system aging. *European Journal of Clinical Nutrition, 56*(Suppl. 3), S5–8.

Deci, E. L., Koestner, R. & Ryan, R. M. (2001). Extrinsic rewards and intrinsic motivation in education: Reconsidered once again. *Review of Educational Research, 71*, 1–27.

Deci, E. L., Koestner, R., & Ryan, R. M. (1999). A meta-analytic review of experiments examining the effects of extrinsic rewards on intrinsic motivation. *Psychological Bulletin, 125*, 627–668.

Dennerstein, L., Dudley, E., & Guthrie, J. (2002). Empty nest or revolving door? A prospective study of women's quality of life in midlife during the phase of children leaving and re-entering the home. *Psychological Medicine, 32*, 545–550.

DePaulo, B. M., Lindsay, J. J., Malone, B. E., Muhlenbruck, L., Charlton, K., & Cooper, H. (2003). Cues to deception. *Psychological Bulletin, 129*, 74–118.

Dess, N. K., & Foltin, R.W. (2005). The ethics cascade. In C. K. Akins, S. Panicker, & C. L. Cunningham (Eds.), *Laboratory animals in research and teaching: Ethics, care, and methods* (pp. 31–39). Washington, DC: American Psychological Association.

Diala, C., Muntaner, C., Walrath, C., Nickerson, K., LaVeist, T. A., & Leaf, P. J. (2000). Racial differences in attitudes toward professional mental health care and in the use of services. *American Journal of Orthopsychiatry, 70*, 455–464.

Doty, R. L. (1989). Influence of age and age-related diseases on olfactory function. *Annals of the New York Academy of Sciences, 561*, 76–86.

Durex Global Sex Survey (2005). Retrieved April 13, 2006, from http://www.durex.com/cm/gss2005result.pdf

Eacott, M. J. (1999). Memory for the events of early childhood. *Current Directions in Psychological Science, 8*, 46–48.

Eagly, A. H. (2003). The rise of female leaders. *Zeitschrift-fur-Sozialpsychologie, 34*, 123–132.

Eagly, A. H., & Steffen, V. J. (1986). Gender and aggressive behavior: A meta-analytic review of the social psychological literature. *Psychological Bulletin, 100*, 309–330.

Eagly, A. H., Johannesen-Schmidt, M. C., & van-Engen, M. L. (2003). Transformational, transactional, and laissez-faire leadership styles: A meta-analysis comparing women and men. *Psychological Bulletin, 129*, 569–591.

Eccles, J., Midgley, C., Wigfield, A., Buchanan, C. M., Reuman, D., Flanagan, C., et al. (1993). Development during adolescence: The impact of stage-environment fit on young adolescents' experiences in school and families. *American Psychologist: Special Issue: Adolescence, 48*, 90–101.

Eichenbaum, H., & Fortin, N. (2003). Episodic memory and the hippocampus: It's about time. *Current Directions in Psychological Science, 12*, 53–57.

Ekman, P. (2003). *Emotions revealed: Recognizing faces and feelings to improve communication and emotional life.* New York: Henry Holt.

Ekman, P., & Davidson, R. J. (1993). Voluntary smiling changes regional brain activity. *Psychological Science, 4*, 342–345.

Ekman, P., & Friesen, W. V. (1971). Constants across cultures in the face and emotion. *Journal of Personality and Social Psychology, 17*, 124–129.

Ekman, P., & Friesen, W. V. (1975). *Unmasking the face.* Englewood Cliffs, NJ: Prentice Hall.

Ekman, P., & O'Sullivan, M. (1991).Who can catch a liar? *American Psychologist, 46*, 913–920.

Ekman, P., Friesen, W. V., O'Sullivan, M., Chan, A., Diacoyanni-Tarlatzis, I., Heider, K., et al. (1987). Universals and cultural differences in the judgments of facial expressions of emotion. *Journal of Personality and Social Psychology, 53*, 712–717.

Ekman, P., Sorenson, E. R., & Friesen, W. V. (1969). Pancultural elements in facial displays of emotion. *Science, 164*, 86–88.

El-Ad, B., & Lavie, P. (2005). Effect of sleep apnea on cognition and mood. *International Review of Psychiatry, 17*, 277–282.

Elfenbein, H. A., & Ambady, N. (2002). On the universality and cultural specificity of emotion recognition: A meta-analysis. *Psychological Bulletin, 128*, 203–235.

Elfenbein, H. A., & Ambady, N. (2003). Universals and cultural differences in recognizing emotions. *Current Directions in Psychological Science, 12*, 159–164.

Elkins, G. R., & Rajab, M. H. (2004). Clinical hypnosis for smoking cessation: Preliminary results of a three-session intervention. *International Journal of Clinical and Experimental Hypnosis, 52*, 73–81.

Ellens, J. H. (2002). Psychological legitimization of violence by religious archetypes. In C. E. Stout (Ed.), *The psychology of terrorism: Theoretical understandings and perspectives, Vol. III. Psychological dimensions to war and peace* (pp. 149–162). Westport, CT: Praeger/Greenwood.

Elliott, M. E. (1996). Impact of work, family, and welfare receipt on women's self-esteem in young adulthood. *Social Psychology Quarterly, 59*, 80–95.

Ellis, A. (1973). *Humanistic psychotherapy: The rational emotive approach.* New York: Julian.

Ellis, A. (2001). *Overcoming destructive beliefs, feelings, and behaviors: New directions for Rational Emotive Behavior Therapy.* Amherst, NY: Prometheus.

Ellis, L., & Coontz, P. D. (1990). Androgens, brain functioning, and criminality: The neurohormonal foundations of antisociality. In L. Ellis & H. Hoffman (Eds.), *Crime in biological, social, and moral contexts* (pp. 36–49). New York: Praeger.

Ellis, L., Robb, B., & Burke, D. (2005). Sexual orientation in United States and Canadian college students. *Archives of Sexual Behavior, 34*, 569–581.

Elloy, D. F., & Mackie, B. (2002). Overload and work-family conflict among Australian dual-career families: Moderating effects of support. *Psychological Reports, 91*, 907–913.

Ellsworth, P. C. (2002). Appraisal processes in emotion. In R. R. Davidson, K. R. Scherer, & H. H. Goldsmith (Eds.), *Handbook of affective science* (pp. 233–248). New York: Oxford Univ. Press.

Enard, W., Przeworski, M., Fisher, S. E., Lai, C. S., Wiebe, V., Kitano, T., et al. (2002). Molecular evolution of FOXP2, a gene involved in speech and language. *Nature, 418*, 869–872.

Epel, E. S., Lin, J., Wilhelm, F. H., Wolkowitz, O. M., Cawthon, R., Adler, N. E., et al. (2006). Cell aging in relation to stress arousal and cardiovascular disease risk factors. *Psychoneuroendocrinology, 31*, 277–287.

Esterson, A. (2002). The myth of Freud's ostracism by the medical community in 1896–1905: Jeffrey Masson's assault on truth. *History of Psychology, 5*, 115–134.

Eysenck, H. J. (1976). *The measurement of personality.* Baltimore, MD: Univ. Park.

Fagot, B. I. (1994). Parenting. In *Encyclopedia of human behavior* (Vol. 3, pp. 411–419). San Diego, CA: Academic Press.

Fairbrother, N., & Rachman, S. (2006). PTSD in victims of sexual assault: Test of a major component of the Ehlers-Clark theory. *Journal of Behavior Therapy and Experimental Psychiatry, 37*, 74–93.

Farroni, T., Massaccesi, S., Pividori, D., & Johnson, M. (2004). Gaze following in newborns. *Infancy, 5*, 39–60.

Federal Bureau of Investigation. (2005). *Crime in the United States: 2004. Uniform Crime Reports.* Washington, DC: Government Printing Office.

Feinberg, T. D., & Keenan, J. P. (2005). Where in the brain is the self? *Consciousness and Cognition, 14*, 647–790.

Feldhusen, J. F., & Goh, B. E. (1995). Assessing and accessing creativity: An integrative review of theory, research, and development. *Creativity Research Journal, 8,* 231–247.

Festinger, L. (1957). *A theory of cognitive dissonance.* Evanston, IL: Row, Peterson.

Fiedler, F. E. (1967). *A theory of leadership effectiveness.* New York: McGraw-Hill.

Fiedler, F. E. (1993). The leadership situation and the black box contingency theories. In M. Chemers & R. Ayman (Eds.), *Leadership theory and research: Perspective and directions* (pp. 1–28). San Diego, CA: Academic Press.

Fiedler, F. E. (2002). The curious role of cognitive resources in leadership. In R. E. Riggio & S. E. Murphy (Eds.), *Multiple intelligences and leadership. LEA's organization and management series* (pp. 91–104). Mahwah, NJ: Erlbaum.

Field, T. M. (1986). Interventions for premature infants. *Journal of Pediatrics, 109,* 183–191.

Fischer, A. H., Rodriguez-Mosquera, P. M., van-Vianen, A. E. M., & Manstead, A. S. R. (2004). Gender and culture differences in emotion. *Emotion, 4,* 87–94.

Fischhoff, B., & Downs, J. (1997). Accentuate the relevant. *Psychological Science, 8,* 154–158.

Fiske, S. T., & Taylor, S. E. (1991). *Social cognition* (2nd ed.). New York: McGraw-Hill.

Flashman, L. A., & Green, M. F. (2004). Review of cognition and brain structure in schizophrenia: Profiles, longitudinal course, and effects of treatment. *Psychiatric Clinics of North America, 27,* 1–18.

Flavell, J. H. (1999). Cognitive development: Children's knowledge about the mind. *Annual Review of Psychology, 50,* 21–45.

Flier, J. S., & Maratos-Flier, E. (1998). Obesity and the hypothalamus: Novel peptides for new pathways. *Cell, 92,* 437–440.

Ford, W. C. L., North, K., Taylor, H., Farrow, A., Hull, M. G. R., & Golding, J. (2000). Increasing paternal age is associated with delayed conception in a large population of fertile couples: Evidence for declining fecundity in older men. *Human Reproduction, 15,* 1703–1708.

Frank, M. G. (2006). Research methods in detecting deception research. In J. A. Harrigan, R. Rosenthal, & K. R. Scherer (Eds.), *The new handbook of methods in nonverbal behavior research* (pp. 341–368). New York: Oxford Univ. Press.

Freud, S. (1900). The interpretation of dreams. In J. Strachey (Ed.), *The standard edition of the complete psychological works of Sigmund Freud* (Vol. 5). London: Hogarth.

Freud, S. (1933). *New introductory lectures on psychoanalysis.* New York: Carlton.

Friedland, R. P., Fritsch, T., Smyth, K. A., Koss, E., Lerner, A. J., Chen, C. H., et al. (2001). Patients with Alzheimer's disease have reduced activities in midlife compared with healthy control-group members. *Proceedings of the National Academy of Sciences, USA, 98,* 3440–3445.

Frijda, N. H., Markam, S., & Sato, K. (1995). Emotions and emotion words. In J. A. Russell, J-M. Fernàndez-Dols, A. S. R. Manstead, & J. C. Wellenkamp (Eds.), *Everyday conceptions of emotion: An introduction to the psychology, anthropology and linguistics of emotion* (pp. 121–143). New York: Kluwer Academic/Plenum.

Furstenberg, F. F., Jr., Brooks-Gunn, J., & Chase-Lansdale, L. (1989). Teenaged pregnancy and childbearing. *American Psychologist, 44,* 313–320.

Gable, S. L., & Haidt, J. (2005). What (and why) is positive psychology? *Review of General Psychology, 9 (Special issue: Positive Psychology),* 103–110.

Gabrieli, J. D. E. (1998). Cognitive neuroscience of human memory. *Annual Review of Psychology, 49,* 87–115.

Gage, F. H. (2003). Brain, repair yourself. *Scientific American, 289*(3), 46–53.

Galanter, M., Hayden, F., Castañeda, R., & Franco, H. (2005). Group therapy, self-help groups, and network therapy. In R. J. Frances, S. I. Miller, & A. H. Mack (Eds.), *Clinical textbook of addictive disorders* (3rd ed., pp. 502–527). New York: Guilford.

Gallahue, D. L., & Ozmun, J. C. (2006). Motor development in young children. In B. Spodek & O. N. Saracho (Eds.), *Handbook of research on the education of young children* (2nd ed., pp. 105–120). Mahwah, NJ: Erlbaum.

Gallup, G. G., Jr. (1985). Do minds exist in species other than our own? *Neuroscience and Biobehavioral Reviews, 9,* 631–641.

Gallup, G. G., Jr. (1998). Self-awareness and the evolution of social intelligence. *Behavioural Processes, 42,* 239–247.

Garbarino, J. (1999). *Lost boys: Why our sons turn violent and how we can save them.* New York: Free Press.

Gardner, H. (1983). *Frames of mind: The theory of multiple intelligences.* New York: Basic Books.

Gardner, H. (2004). *Frames of mind: The theory of multiple intelligences.* New York: Basic Books.

Garnets, L. K. (2002). Sexual orientation in perspective. *Cultural Diversity and Ethnic Minority Psychology, 8,* 115–129.

Garry, M., & Polaschek, D. L. L. (2000). Imagination and memory. *Current Directions in Psychological Science, 9,* 6–10.

Geen, R. G. (1998). Aggression and antisocial behavior. In D. Gilbert, S. T. Fiske, & G. Lindzey (Eds.), *Handbook of social psychology* (4th ed., Vol. 2, pp. 317–356). Boston: McGraw-Hill.

Gehring, J. (2001, April 4). U.S. seen losing edge on education measures. *Education Week.* Retrieved October 16, 2007, from http://www.ecs.org/clearinghouse/25/19/2519.htm

George, L. K. (2001). The social psychology of health. In R. H. Binstock & L. K. George (Eds.), *Handbook of the psychology of aging* (5th ed., pp. 217–237). San Diego: Academic Press.

Gerkens, D. (2005). Are recovered memories accurate? *Dissertation Abstracts International: Section B: The Sciences and Engineering, 66,* 2321.

Getzels, J. W., & Jackson, P. (1962). *Creativity and intelligence.* New York: Wiley.

Gibson, R. L., & Mitchell, M. (2003). *Introduction to counseling and guidance* (6th ed.). Upper Saddle River, NJ: Prentice Hall.

Gilligan, C. (1982). *In a different voice: Psychological theory and women's development.* Cambridge, MA: Harvard Univ. Press.

Gilligan, C. (1992, August). *Joining the resistance: Girls' development in adolescence.* Paper presented at the meeting of the American Psychological Association, Montreal, Canada.

Goddard, A. W., Mason, G. F., Rothman, D. L., Behar, K. L., Petroff, O. A. C., & Krystal, J. H. (2004). Family psychopathology and magnitude of reductions in occipital cortex GABA levels in panic disorder. *Neuropsychopharmacology, 29,* 639–640.

Goerge, R. M., & Lee, B. J. (1997). Abuse and neglect of the children. In R. A. Maynard (Ed.), *Kids having kids: Economic costs and social consequences of teen pregnancy* (pp. 205–230). Washington, DC: Urban Institute Press.

Goleman, D. (1997). *Emotional intelligence.* New York: Bantam.

Goleman, D., Boyatzis, R., & McKee, A. (2002). *Primal leadership: Realizing the power of emotional intelligence.* Boston: Harvard Business School Press.

Gonsalkorale, W. M., Miller, V., Afzal, A., & Whorwell, P. J. (2003). Long-term benefits of hypnotherapy for irritable bowel syndrome. *Gut, 52,* 1623–1629.

Goodall, J. (1971). *In the shadow of man.* New York: Dell.

Goode, E. (2000, August 8). How culture molds habits of thought. *New York Times,* pp. D1–D4.

Gopnik, A. (1996). The post-Piaget era. *Psychological Science, 7,* 221–225.

Gordijn, E. H., Postmes, T., & de Vries, N. K. (2001). Devil's advocate or advocate of oneself: Effects of numerical support on pro- and counter-attitudinal self-persuasion. *Personality and Social Psychology Bulletin, 27,* 395–407.

Gosling, S. D., & John, O. P. (1999). Personality dimensions in nonhuman animals: A cross-species review. *Current Directions in Psychological Science, 8,* 69–75.

Green, J. P., & Lynn, S. J. (2000). Hypnosis and suggestion-based approaches to smoking cessation: An examination of the evidence. *International Journal of Clinical and Experimental Hypnosis* [Special Issue: *The status of hypnosis as an empirically validated clinical intervention*], *48,* 195–224.

Greene, S. M., Anderson, E. R., Doyle, E. A., & Riedelbach, H. (2006). Divorce. In G. G. Bear & K. M. Minke (Eds.), *Children's needs III: Development, prevention, and intervention* (pp. 745–757). Washington, DC: National Association of School Psychologists.

Guérin, D. (1994, August). *Fussy infants at risk.* Paper presented at the meeting of the American Psychological Association, Los Angeles.

Guthrie, R. (1976). *Even the rat was white.* New York: Harper & Row.

Gyekye, S. A., & Salminen, S. (2006). The self-defensive attribution hypothesis in the work environment: Co-workers' perspectives. *Safety Science, 44,* 157–168.

Halbreich, U., & Karkun, S. (2006). Cross-cultural and social diversity of prevalence of postpartum depression and depressive symptoms. *Journal of Affective Disorders, 91,* 97–111.

Hall, C. (2005). A 21st-century view of female genital anxiety. *Psychoanalytic Social Work, 12,* 37–49.

Hall, G. S. (1904). *Adolescence: Its psychology and its relations to physiology, anthropology, sex, crime, religion and education* (Vol. 1). New York: Appleton-Century-Crofts.

Hallschmid, M., Benedict, C., Born, J., Fehm, H.-L., & Kern, W. (2004). Manipulating central nervous mechanisms of food intake and body weight regulation by intranasal administration of neuropeptides in man. *Physiology & Behavior, 83,* 55–64.

Hamilton, S. P., Slager, S. L., de Leon, A. B., Heiman, G. A., Klein, D. F., Hodge, S. E., et al. (2004). Evidence for genetic linkage between a polymorphism in the Adenosine 2A receptor and panic disorder. *Neuropsychopharmacology, 29,* 558–565.

Hammack, P. L. (2005). The life course development of human sexual orientation: An integrative paradigm. *Human Development, 48,* 267–290.

Hammen, C. L., Gitlin, M., & Altshuler, L. (2000). Predictors of work adjustment in bipolar I patients. A naturalistic longitudinal follow-up. *Journal of Consulting & Clinical Psychology, 68,* 220–225.

Haney, M., Hart, C. L., Vosburg, S. K., Nasser, J., Bennett, A., Zubaran, C., et al. (2004). Marijuana withdrawal in humans: Effects of oral THC or divalproex. *Neuropsychopharmacology, 29,* 158–170.

Harley, H. E., Roitblat, H. L., & Nachtigall, P. E. (1996). Object representation in the bottlenose dolphin (*Tursiops truncatus*): Integration of visual and echoic information. *Journal of Experimental Psychology: Animal Behavior Processes, 22,* 164–174.

Harlow, H. F. (1949). The formation of learning sets. *Psychological Review, 56,* 51–65.

Harlow, H. F. (1958). The nature of love. *American Psychologist, 13,* 673–685.

Harlow, H. F., & Zimmerman, R. R. (1959). Affectional responses in the infant monkey. *Science, 130,* 421–432.

Harrell, R. F., Woodyard, E., & Gates, A. I. (1955). *The effect of mother's diet on the intelligence of the offspring.* New York: Teacher's College, Columbia Bureau of Publications.

Harris, J. R. (1998). *The nurture assumption: Why children turn out the way they do.* New York: Free Press.

Harris, M., & Rosenthal, R. (1985). Mediation of the interpersonal expectancy effect: A taxonomy of expectancy situations. In P. Blanck (Ed.), *Interpersonal expectations: Theory, research, and application* (pp. 350–378). New York: Cambridge Univ. Press.

Harvey, E. (1999). Short-term and long-term effects of early parental employment on children of the National Longitudinal Survey of Youth. *Developmental Psychology, 35,* 445–459.

Hayne, H. (2004). Infant memory development: Implications for childhood amnesia. *Developmental Review, 24,* 33–73.

Hazel, M. T. (2005). Visualization and systematic desensitization: Interventions for habituating and sensitizing patterns of public speaking anxiety. *Dissertation Abstracts International Section A: Humanities and Social Sciences, 66,* 30.

Hedges, L. V., & Nowell, A. (1995, July 7). Sex differences in mental test scores, variability, and numbers of high-scoring individuals. *Science, 269,* 41–45.

Heider, F. (1958). *The psychology of interpersonal relations.* New York: Wiley.

Helgesen, S. (1998). *Everyday revolutionaries: Working women and the transformation of American life.* New York: Doubleday.

Hendrick, C. & Hendrick, S. S. (2003). Romantic love: Measuring Cupid's arrow. In S. J. Lopez & C. R. Snyder (Eds.), *Positive psychological assessment: A handbook of models and measures* (pp. 235–249). Washington, DC: American Psychological Association.

Henkel, L. A., Franklin, N., & Johnson, M. K. (2000). Cross-modal source monitoring confusions between perceived and imagined events. *Journal of Experimental Psychology: Learning, Memory, & Cognition, 26,* 321–335.

Henry, J. A., Alexander, C. A., & Sener, E. K. (1995). Relative mortality from overdose of antidepressants. *British Medical Journal, 310,* 221–224.

Herberman, R. B. (2002). Stress, natural killer cells, and cancer. In H. G. Koenig & H. J. Cohen (Eds.), *The link between religion and health: Psychoneuroimmunology and faith factor* (pp. 69–83). London: Oxford Univ. Press.

Herman, C. P., Roth, D. A., & Polivy, J. (2003). Effects of the presence of others on food intake: A normative interpretation. *Psychological Bulletin, 129,* 873–886.

Hermann, B. P., Seidenberg, M., Sears, L., Hansen, R., Bayless, K., Rutecki, P., et al. (2004). Cerebellar atrophy in temporal lobe epilepsy affects procedural memory. *Neurology, 63,* 2129–2131.

Hermann, C., & Blanchard, E. B. (2002). Biofeedback in the treatment of headache and other childhood pain. *Applied Psychophysiology and Biofeedback, 27*, 143–162.

Hetherington, E. M., Bridges, M., & Insabella, G. M. (1998). What matters? What does not? Five perspectives on the association between marital transitions and children's adjustment. *American Psychologist, 53*, 167–184.

Hidehiro, W., & Makoto, M. (2006). Classical conditioning of activities of salivary neurones in the cockroach. *Journal of Experimental Biology 209*, 766–779.

Hilgard, E. R., Hilgard, J. R., & Kaufmann, W. (1983). *Hypnosis in the relief of pain* (2nd ed.). Los Altos, CA: Kaufmann.

Hinton, E. C., Parkinson, J. A., Holland, A. J., Arana, F. S., Roberts, A. C., & Owen, A. M. (2004). Neural contributions to the motivational control of appetite in humans. *European Journal of Neuroscience, 20*, 1411–1418.

Hofer, J., & Chasiotis, A. (2004). Methodological considerations of applying a TAT-type picture-story test in cross-cultural research. *Journal of Cross Cultural Psychology, 35*, 224–241.

Hoffrage, U., Hertwig, R., & Gigerenzer, G. (2000). Hindsight bias: A by-product of knowledge updating? *Journal of Experimental Psychology: Learning, Memory & Cognition, 26*, 566–581.

Hollis, K. L. (1997). Contemporary research on Pavlovian conditioning: A "new" functional analysis. *American Psychologist, 52*, 956–965.

Hopkins, B., & Westra, T. (1990). Motor development, maternal expectation, and the role of handling. *Infant Behavior and Development, 13*, 117–122.

Howe, M. L., & Courage, M. (1993). On resolving the enigma of infantile amnesia. *Psychological Bulletin, 113*, 305–326.

Hsu, L. K. (1996). Epidemiology of the eating disorder. *Psychiatric Clinics of North America, 19*, 681–700. http://profiles.nlm.nih.gov/NN/Views/Exhibit/narrative/smoking.html

Hudson, J. A., & Sheffield, E. G. (1998). Deja vu all over again: Effects of reenactment on toddlers' event memory. *Child Development, 69*, 51–67.

Huebner, A. M., Garrod, A., & Snarey, J. (1990). *Moral development in Tibetan Buddhist monks: A cross-cultural study of adolescents and young adults in Nepal*. Paper presented at the meeting of the Society for Research in Adolescence, Atlanta, GA.

Hunt, M. (1994). *The story of psychology*. New York: Anchor/Random House.

Huprich, S. K., & Keaschuk, R. A. (2006). Psychodynamic psychotherapy. In F. Andrasik, (Ed.), *Comprehensive handbook of personality and psychopathology: Adult psychopathology* (Vol. 2, pp. 469–486). Hoboken, NJ: John Wiley & Sons.

Husong, A. M. (2003). Further refining the stress-coping model of alcohol involvement. *Addictive Behaviors, 28*, 1515–1522.

Hyde, J. S. (1986). Gender differences in aggression. In J. S. Hyde & M. C. Linn (Eds.), *The psychology of gender differences: Advances through meta-analysis* (pp. 51–66). Baltimore: Johns Hopkins Univ. Press.

Hyde, J. S. (2005). The gender similarities hypothesis. *American Psychologist, 60*, 581–592.

Hyde, J. S., & Linn, M. C. (1988). Gender differences in verbal ability: A meta-analysis. *Psychological Bulletin, 104*, 53–69.

Hyde, J. S., Fennema, E., & Lamon, S. J. (1990). Gender differences in mathematics performance: A meta-analysis. *Psychological Bulletin, 107*, 139–155.

Hyman, I. E., Husband, T. H., & Billings, F. J. (1995). False memories of childhood experiences. *Applied Cognitive Psychology, 9*, 181–197.

Inaba, A., Thoits, P. A., Ueno, K., Gove, W. R., Evenson, R. J., & Sloan, M. (2005). Depression in the United States and Japan: Gender, marital status, and SES patterns. *Social Science & Medicine, 61*, 2280–2292.

Irwin, M. (2002). Psychoneuroimmunology of depression: Clinical implications. *Brain, Behavior and Immunity, 16*, 1–16.

Izard, C. E. (1971). *The face of emotion*. New York: Appleton-Century-Crofts.

Izard, C. E. (1980). Cross-cultural perspectives on emotion and emotion communication. In H. C. Triandis & W. J. Lonner (Eds.), *Handbook of cross-cultural psychology* (Vol. 3). Boston: Allyn & Bacon.

Izard, C. E. (1994). Innate and universal facial expressions: Evidence from developmental and cross-cultural research. *Psychological Bulletin, 115*, 288–299.

Jaakkola, K., Fellner, W., Erb, L., Rodriguez, M., & Guarino, E. (2005). Understanding of the concept of numerically "less" by bottlenose dolphins (*Tursiops truncatus*). *Journal of Comparative Psychology, 119*, 296–303.

Jackson, O. (2004). Episodic memory in the brain: Association, recognition, and prediction. *Dissertation Abstracts International: Section B: The Sciences and Engineering, 64*, 4647.

Jacobi, C., Hayward, C., de Zwaan, M., Kraemer, H. C., & Agras, W. S. (2004). Coming to terms with risk factors for eating disorders: Application of risk terminology and suggestions for a general taxonomy. *Psychological Bulletin, 130*, 19–65.

Jacobs, W. J., & Nadel, L. (1998). Neurobiology of reconstructed memory. *Psychology, Public Policy, & Law, 4*, 1110–1134.

James, W. (1890). *The principles of psychology*. New York: Holt.

Jang, K. L., Livesley, W. J., McCrae, R. R., Angleitner, A., & Riemann, R. (1998). Heritability of facet-level traits in a cross-cultural twin sample: Support for a hierarchical model of personality. *Journal of Personality and Social Psychology, 74*, 1556–1565.

Janis, I. L. (1982). *Groupthink: Psychological studies of policy decisions and fiascoes* (2nd ed.). Boston: Houghton Mifflin.

Janis, I. L. (1989). *Crucial decisions: Leadership in policymaking and crisis management*. New York: Free Press.

Janos, P. M., & Robinson, N. M. (1985). Psychosocial development in intellectually gifted children. In F. D. Horowitz & M. O'Brien (Eds.), *Gifted and talented: Developmental perspectives* (pp. 149–195). Washington, DC: American Psychological Association.

Javitt, D. C., & Coyle, J. T. (2004). Decoding schizophrenia. *Scientific American, 290*(1), 48–55.

Johnson, C. (2002). Obesity, weight management, and self-esteem. In T. A. Wadden & A. J. Stunkard, *Handbook of obesity treatment* (pp. 480–493). New York: Guilford.

Johnson, W., & Krueger, R. F. (2004). Genetic and environmental structure of adjectives describing the domains of the Big Five model of personality: A nationwide US twin study. *Journal of Research in Personality, 38*, 448–472.

Johnson, W., Bouchard, T. J. Jr., Segal, N. L., & Samuel, J. (2005). General intelligence and reading performance in adults: Is the genetic factor structure the same as for children? *Personality and Individual Differences, 38,* 1413–1428.

Johnston, L. D., O'Malley, P. M., Bachman, J. G., & Schulenbert, J. E. (2004). Monitoring the future national results on adolescent drug use: Overview of key findings. *NIH Publication No. 05-5726,* Bethesda, MD: National Institute on Drug Abuse.

Jonas, E., Schimel, J., Greenberg, J., & Pyszczynski, T. (2002). The Scrooge Effect: Evidence that mortality salience increases prosocial attitudes and behavior. *Personality and Social Psychology Bulletin, 28,* 1342–1353.

Julius, M., Harburg, E., Cottington, E. M., & Johnson, E. H. (1986). Anger-coping types, blood pressure, and all-cause mortality: A follow-up in Tecumseh, Michigan (1971–1983). *American Journal of Epidemiology, 124,* 220–233.

Kadotani, H., Kadotani, T., Young, T., Peppard, P. E., Finn, L., Colrain, I. M., et al. (2001). Association between apolipoprotein E C 4 and sleep-disordered breathing in adults. *Journal of the American Medical Association, 285,* 2888–2890.

Kagan, J. (1994, October 5). The realistic view of biology and behavior. *Chronicle of Higher Education,* p. A64.

Kagan, J., & Snidman, N. (1991). Infant predictors of inhibited and uninhibited profiles. *Psychological Science, 2,* 40–44.

Kagan, J., & Snidman, N. (2004). *The long shadow of temperament.* Cambridge, MA: Belknap/Harvard Univ. Press.

Kagan, J., Reznick, J. S., Snidman, N., Gibbons, J., & Johnson, M. O. (1988). Childhood derivatives of inhibition and lack of inhibition to the unfamiliar. *Child Development, 59,* 1580–1589.

Kahneman, D., & Tversky, A. (1996). On the reality of cognitive illusions. *Psychological Review, 103,* 582–591.

Kandel, E. R. (2001). The molecular biology of memory storage: A dialogue between genes and synapses. *Science, 294,* 1030–1038.

Karakashian, L. M., Walter, M. I., Christopher, A. N., & Lucas, T. (2006). Fear of negative evaluation affects helping behavior: The bystander effect revisited. *North American Journal of Psychology, 8,* 13–32.

Kass, S. (1999, September). Employees perceive women as better managers than men, finds five-year study. *APA Monitor,* p. 6.

Kawai, N., & Matsuzawa, T. (2000). Cognition: Numerical memory span in a chimpanzee. *Nature, 403,* 39–40.

Keel, P. K., & Klump, K. L. (2003). Are eating disorders culture-bound syndromes? Implications for conceptualizing their etiology. *Psychological Bulletin, 129,* 747–769.

Kelley, H. H. (1967). Attribution theory in social psychology. In D. Levine (Ed.), *Nebraska Symposium on Motivation* (Vol. 15, pp. 192–238). Lincoln: Univ. of Nebraska Press.

Kelley, H. H. (1973). The process of causal attribution. *American Psychologist, 28,* 107–128.

Kempt, H. (2000). Culture assimilator training for students with limited English proficiency at the University of Mississippi intensive English program. *Dissertation Abstracts International Section A: Humanities and Social Sciences, 60,* 2773.

Kendall-Tackett, K. A. (2001). *The hidden feelings of motherhood: Coping with stress, depression, and burnout.* Oakland, CA: New Harbinger.

Kiecolt-Glaser, J. K., & Glaser, R. (2002). Depression and immune function: Central pathways to morbidity and mortality. *Journal of Psychosomatic Research, 53,* 873–876.

Kiesler, C. A. (1982a). Mental hospitals and alternative care: Noninstitutionalization as a potential public policy for mental patients. *American Psychologist, 37,* 349–360.

Kiesler, C. A. (1982b). Public and professional myths about mental hospitalization: An empirical reassessment of policy-related beliefs. *American Psychologist, 37,* 1323–1339.

Kiesler, C. A., & Simpkins, C. G. (1993). *The unnoticed majority in psychiatric inpatient care.* New York: Plenum.

King, J. E., Weiss, A., & Farmer, K. H. (2005). A chimpanzee (*Pan troglodytes*) analogue of cross-national generalization of personality structure: Zoological parks and an African sanctuary. *Journal of Personality, 73,* 389–410.

Kingstone, A., Enns, J. T., Mangun, G. R., & Gazzaniga, M. S. (1995). Right hemisphere memory superiority: Studies of a split-brain patient. *Psychological Science, 6,* 118–121.

Kinsey, A. C., Pomeroy, W. B., & Martin, C. E. (1948). *Sexual behavior in the human male.* Philadelphia: Saunders.

Kinsey, A. C., Pomeroy, W. B., Martin, C. E., & Gebhard, P. H. (1953). *Sexual behavior in the human female.* Philadelphia: Saunders.

Kirsch, I., Montgomery, G., & Saperstein, G. (1995). Hypnosis as an adjunct to cognitive behavioral psychotherapy: A meta-analysis. *Journal of Consulting and Clinical Psychology, 63,* 214–220.

Kisilevsky, B., Hains, S., Lee, K., Xie, X., Huang, H., Ye, H., et al. (2003). Effects of experience on fetal voice recognition. *Psychological Science, 14,* 220–224.

Kleim, J. A., Vij, K., Ballard, D. H., & Greenough, W. T. (1997). Learning-dependent synaptic modifications in the cerebellar cortex of the adult rat persist for at least four weeks. *Journal of Neuroscience, 17,* 717–721.

Klein, G. S. (1951). The personal world through perception. In R. R. Blake & G. V. Ramsey (Eds.), *Perception: An approach to personality* (pp. 328–355). New York: Ronald Press.

Kling, K. C., Hyde, J. S., Showers, C. J., & Buswell, B. N. (1999). Gender differences in self-esteem: A meta-analysis. *Psychological Bulletin, 125,* 470–500.

Knight, G. P., Fabes, R. A., & Higgins, D. A. (1996). Concerns about drawing causal inferences from meta-analyses: An example in the study of gender differences in aggression. *Psychological Bulletin, 119,* 410–421.

Knight, J. A. (2000). The biochemistry of aging. *Advances in Clinical Chemistry, 35,* 1–62.

Koenig, H. G., McCullough, M. E., & Larson, D. B. (2000). *Handbook of religion and health.* New York: Oxford Univ. Press.

Kohlberg, L. (1969). Stage and sequence: The cognitive-developmental approach to socialization. In D. A. Goslin (Ed.), *Handbook of socialization theory and research* (pp. 347-380). Chicago: Rand McNally.

Kohlberg, L. (1979). *The meaning and measurement of moral development* (Clark Lectures). Worcester, MA: Clark Univ.

Kohlberg, L. (1981). *The philosophy of moral development* (Vol. 1). San Francisco: Harper & Row.

Komiya, N., Good, G. E., & Sherrod, N. B. (2000). Emotional openness as a predictor of college students' attitudes toward seeking psychological help. *Journal of Counseling Psychology, 47,* 138–143.

Koss, M. P. (1990). Violence against women. *American Psychologist, 45,* 374–380.

Kosslyn, S. M. (2002). Einstein's mental images: The role visual, spatial, and motoric representations. In A. M. Galaburda, S. M. Kosslyn, & C. Yves (Eds.), *The languages of the brain* (pp. 271–287). Cambridge, MA: Harvard Univ. Press.

Kramer, A. F., & Willis, S. L. (2002). Enhancing the cognitive vitality of older adults. *Current Directions in Psychological Science, 11*, 173–176.

Krasne, F. B., & Glanzman, D. L. (1995). What we can learn from invertebrate learning. *Annual Review of Psychology, 46*, 585–624.

Kübler-Ross, E. (1969). *On death and dying.* New York: Macmillan.

Kübler-Ross, E. (1975). *Death: The final stage of growth.* Englewood Cliffs, NJ: Prentice Hall.

Kulik, J., & Brown, R. (1979). Frustration, attribution of blame, and aggression. *Journal of Experimental Social Psychology, 15*, 183–194.

Kumkale, G. T., & Albarracín, D. (2004). The sleeper effect: A meta-analytic review. *Psychological Bulletin, 130*, 143–172.

Kurdek, L. A. (2005). What do we know about gay and lesbian couples? *Current Directions in Psychological Science, 14*, 251–254

Kurdek, L. A., Fine, M. A., & Sinclair, R. J. (1995). School adjustment in sixth graders: Parenting transitions, family climate, and peer norm effects. *Child Development, 66*, 430–445.

Kurtz, L. D. (2004). Support and self-help groups. In C. D. Garvin, L. M. Gutiérrez, & M. J. Galinsky (Eds.), *Handbook of social work with groups* (pp. 139–159). New York: Guilford.

Lachman, M. E. (2004). Development in midlife. *Annual Review of Psychology, 55*, 305–331.

Laganà, L., & Sosa, G. (2004). Depression among ethnically diverse older women: The role of demographic and cognitive factors. *Educational Gerontology, 30*, 801–820.

Laird, J. (2003). Lesbian and gay families. In F. Walsh (Ed.), *Normal family processes: Growing diversity and complexity* (3rd ed., pp. 176–209). New York: Guilford.

Lamb, J. A., Moore, J., Bailey, A., & Monaco, A. P. (2000). Autism: Recent molecular genetic advances. *Human Molecular Genetics, 9*, 861–868.

Lambert, W. W., Solomon, R. L., & Watson, P. D. (1949). Reinforcement and extinction as factors in size estimation. *Journal of Experimental Psychology, 39*, 637–641.

Latané, B., & Rodin, J. (1969). A lady in distress: Inhibiting effects of friends and strangers on bystander intervention. *Journal of Experimental Social Psychology, 5*, 189–202.

Lazarus, R. S. (1981, July). Little hassles can be hazardous to health. *Psychology Today*, 58–62.

Lazarus, R. S. (1991a). Cognition and motivation in emotion. *American Psychologist, 46*, 352–367.

Lazarus, R. S. (1991b). *Emotion and adaptation.* New York: Oxford Univ. Press.

Lazarus, R. S. (1991c). Progress on a cognitive-motivational-relational theory of emotion. *American Psychologist, 46*, 819–834.

Leary, M. R., Kowalski, R. M., Smith, L., & Phillips, S. (2003). Teasing, rejection, and violence: Case studies of the school shootings. *Aggressive Behavior, 29*, 202–214.

Leborgne, L., Maziere, J. C., & Andrejak, M. (2002). Oxidative stress, atherogenesis, and cardiovascular risk factors. *Archives des Maladies du Coeur et des Vaisseaux, 95*, 805–814.

Lee, S., Chan, Y. Y. L., & Hsu, L. K. G. (2003). The intermediate term outcome of Chinese patients with anorexia nervosa in Hong Kong. *American Journal of Psychiatry, 160*, 967–972.

LeFever, G. B., Arcona, A. P., & Antonuccio, D. O. (2003). ADHD among American schoolchildren: Evidence of overdiagnosis and overuse of medication. *Scientific Review of Mental Health Practice, 2*, 49–60.

Lerner, M. J. (1980). *The belief in a just world: A fundamental delusion.* New York: Plenum.

Leschied, A. W., & Cummings, A. L. (2002). Youth violence: An overview of predictors, counseling interventions, and future directions. *Canadian Journal of Counseling, 36*, 256–264.

LeVay, S., & Hamer, D. H. (1994). Evidence for a biological influence in male homosexuality. *Scientific American, 270*, 44–49.

Levin, F. R., McDowell, D., Evans, S. M., Nunes, E., Akerele, E., Donovan, S., et al. (2004). Pharmacotherapy for marijuana dependence: A double-blind, placebo-controlled pilot study of divalproex sodium. *American Journal on Addictions, 13*, 21–32.

Levin, J. S., & Vanderpool, H. Y. (1989). Is religion therapeutically significant for hypertension? *Social Science and Medicine, 29*, 69–78.

Levinson, D. J. (1978). *The seasons of a man's life.* New York: Knopf.

Levinson, D. J. (1986). A conception of adult development. *American Psychologist, 41*, 3–13.

Levinson, D. J. (1987). *The seasons of a woman's life.* New York: Knopf.

Lewin, K. A. (1935). *A dynamic theory of personality* (K. E. Zener & D. K. Adams, trans.). New York: McGraw-Hill.

Lipman, S. (1991). *Laughter in Hell: The use of humor during the Holocaust.* Northvale, NJ: J. Aronson.

Lippa, R. R. (2005). *Gender, nature, and nurture* (2nd ed.). Mahwah, NJ: Erlbaum.

Lips, H. M. (2002). *A new psychology of women: Gender, culture*, and *ethnicity* (2nd ed.). New York: McGraw-Hill.

Liu, J. H., & Latané, B. (1998). Extremitization of attitudes: Does thought-and-discussion-induced polarization cumulate? *Basic and Applied Social Psychology, 20*, 103–110.

Livesley, W. J., Jang, K. L., & Vernon P. A. (2003). Genetic basis of personality structure. In T. Millon & M. J. Lerner, (Eds.), *Handbook of psychology: Personality and social psychology* (Vol. 5, pp. 59–83). New York: John Wiley & Sons.

Loehlin, J. C., Horn, J. M., & Willerman, L. (1997). Heredity, environment, and IQ in the Texas adoption study. In R. J. Sternberg & E. Grigorenko (Eds.), *Intelligence: Heredity and environment* (pp. 105-125). New York: Cambridge Univ. Press.

Loehlin, J. C., McCrae, R. R., Costa, P. T., & John, O. P. (1998). Heritability of common and measure-specific components of the Big Five personality traits. *Journal of Research in Personality, 32*, 431–453.

Loftus, E. F. (1993). Psychologists in the eyewitness world. *American Psychologist, 48*, 550–552.

Loftus, E. F. (1997). Repressed memory accusations: Devastated families and devastated patients. *Applied Cognitive Psychology, 11*(1), 25–30.

Loftus, E. F., & Hoffman, H. G. (1989). Misinformation and memory: The creation of new memories. *Journal of Experimental Psychology: General, 118*, 100–114.

Loftus, E. F., & Palmer, J. C. (1974). Reconstruction of automobile destruction: An example of the interaction between language and memory. *Journal of Verbal Learning and Verbal Behavior, 13*, 585–589.

Loftus, E. F., & Pickrell, J. E. (1995). The formation of false memories. *Psychiatric Annals, 25*, 720–725.

Loftus, E. F., Coan, J. A., & Pickrell, J. E. (1996). Manufacturing false memories using bits of reality. In L. Reder (Ed.), *Implicit memory and metacognition* (pp. 195–220). Mahwah, NJ: Erlbaum.

López, S. R., & Guarnaccia, P. J. J. (2000). Cultural psychopathology: Uncovering the social world of mental illness. *Annual Review of Psychology, 51,* 571–598.

Luria, A. R. (1968). *The mind of a mnemonist* (L. Solotaroff, Trans.). New York: Basic Books.

Lynn, S. J., & Kirsch, I. (2006a). Anxiety disorders. In S. J. Lynn & I. Kirsch (Eds.), *Essentials of clinical hypnosis: An evidence-based approach* (pp. 135–157). Washington, DC: American Psychological Association.

Lynn, S. J., & Kirsch, I. (2006b). Posttraumatic Stress Disorder. In S. J. Lynn & I. Kirsch (Eds.), *Essentials of clinical hypnosis: An evidence-based approach* (pp. 159–173). Washington, DC: American Psychological Association.

Lynn, S. J., & Kirsch, I. (2006c). Smoking cessation. In S. J. Lynn & I. Kirsch (Eds.), *Essentials of clinical hypnosis: An evidence-based approach* (pp.79–98). Washington, DC: American Psychological Association.

Lynn, S. J., Kirsch, I., & Koby, D. G. (2006). Pain management, behavioral medicine, and dentistry with Danielle G. Koby. In S. J. Lynn & I. Kirsch (Eds.), *Essentials of clinical hypnosis: An evidence-based approach* (pp. 175–196). Washington, DC: American Psychological Association.

Maccoby, E. E. (1998). *The two sexes: Growing up apart, coming together.* Cambridge, MA: Belknap.

Maccoby, E. E., & Jacklin, C. N. (1974). *The psychology of sex differences.* Stanford, CA: Stanford University Press.

Maddi, S. R. (1989). *Personality theories: A comparative approach* (5th ed.). Homewood, IL: Dorsey.

Madon, S. J. (1999). The best guess model of stereotyping: Information seekers versus cognitive misers. *Dissertation Abstracts International: Section B: The Sciences and Engineering, 59,* 6517.

Maio, G. R., & Olson, J. M. (1998). Values as truisms: Evidence and implications. *Journal of Personality and Social Psychology, 74,* 294–311.

Maloney, M. P., & Ward, M. P. (1976). *Psychological assessment: A conceptual approach.* New York: Academic Press.

Mann, T., Sherman, D., & Updegraff, J. (2004). Dispositional motivations and message framing: A test of the congruency hypothesis in college students. *Health Psychology, 23,* 330–334.

Manns, J. R., Hopkins, R. O., & Squire, L. R. (2003). Semantic memory and the human hippocampus. *Neuron, 38,* 127–133.

Maquet, P., Laureys, S., Peigneus, P., Fuchs, S., Petiau, C., Phips, C., et al. (2000). Experience-dependent changes in cerebral activation during human REM sleep. *Nature: Neuroscience, 3,* 831–836.

Maranto, C. L., & Stenoien, A. F. (2000). Weight discrimination: A multidisciplinary analysis. *Employee Responsibilities and Rights Journal, 12,* 9–24.

Marcia, J. E. (1980). Identity in adolescence. In J. Adelson (Ed.), *Handbook of adolescent psychology.* New York: Wiley.

Markovic, B. M., Dimitrijevic, M., & Jankovic, B. D. (1993). Immunomodulation by conditioning: Recent developments. *International Journal of Neuroscience, 71,* 231–249.

Maslow, A. H. (1954). *Motivation and personality.* New York: Harper & Row.

Masters, W. H., & Johnson, V. E. (1966). *Human sexual response.* Boston: Little, Brown.

Matsumoto, D. (2000). *Culture and psychology: People around the world* (2nd ed.). Belmont, CA: Wadsworth/Thomson Learning.

Mazzoni, G. A. L. & Memon, A. (2003). Imagination can create false autobiographical memories. *Psychological Science, 14,* 186–188.

McClelland, D. C., & Atkinson, J. W. (1948). The projective expression of needs: I. The effect of different intensities of the hunger drive on perception. *Journal of Psychology, 25,* 205–222.

McCrae, R. R., & Costa, P. T., Jr. (1994). The stability of personality: Observations and evaluations. *Current Directions in Psychological Science, 3,* 173–175.

McCrae, R. R., & Costa, P. T., Jr. (1997). Personality trait structure as a human universal. *American Psychologist, 52,* 509–516.

McGeer, E. G., Klegeris, A., & McGeer, P. L. (2005). Inflammation, the complement system and the diseases of aging. *Neurobiology of Aging, 26,* S94–S97.

McIntyre, C. K., Marriott, L. K., & Gold, P. E. (2003). Cooperation between memory systems: Acetylcholine release in the amygdala correlates positively with performance on a hippocampus-dependent task. *Behavioral Neuroscience, 117,* 320–326.

McKellar, J., Stewart, E., & Humphreys, K. (2003). Alcoholics Anonymous involvement and positive alcohol-related outcomes: Cause, consequence, or just a correlate? A prospective 2-year study of 2,319 alcohol-dependent men. *Journal of Consulting and Clinical Psychology 71,* 302–308.

McNally, R. J. (2003a). Experimental approaches to the recovered memory controversy. In M. F. Lenzenweger & J. M. Hooley (Eds.), *Principles of experimental psychopathology: Essays in honor of Brendan A. Maher* (pp. 269–277). Washington, DC: American Psychological Association.

McNally, R. J. (2003b). Recovering memories of trauma: A view from the laboratory. *Current Directions in Psychological Science, 12,* 32–35.

McNally, R. J., Bryant, R. A., & Ehlers, A. (2003). Does early psychological intervention promote recovery from posttraumatic stress? *Psychological Science in the Public Interest, 4,* 45–79.

McNeil, B. J., Pauker, S. G., Sox, H. C., Jr., & Tversky, A. (1982). On the elicitation of preferences for alternative therapies. *New England Journal of Medicine, 306,* 1259–1262.

McNeil, D. W., & Zvolensky, M. J. (2000). Systematic desensitization. In A. E. Kazdin (Ed.), *Encyclopedia of psychology* (Vol. 7, pp. 533–535). Washington, DC: American Psychological Association.

McPherson, J. M., Smith-Lovin, L., & Cook, J. M. (2001). Birds of a feather: Homophily in social networks. *Annual Review of Sociology, 27,* 415–444.

Mednick, S. A. (1962). The associative basis of creativity. *Psychological Review, 69,* 220–232.

Melzack, R. (1980). Psychological aspects of pain. In J. J. Bonica (Ed.), *Pain.* New York: Raven.

Melzack, R., & Katz, J. (2004). The gate control theory: Reaching for the brain. In T. Hadjistavropoulos & K. Craig (Eds.), *Pain: Psychological perspectives* (pp. 13–34). Mahwah, NJ: Erlbaum.

Michael, R. T., Gagnon, J. H., Laumann, E. O., & Kolata, G. (1994). *Sex in America.* Boston: Little, Brown.

Milgram, S. (1963). Behavioral study of obedience. *Journal of Abnormal and Social Psychology, 67,* 371–378.

Milgram, S. (1974). *Obedience to authority: An experimental view.* New York: Harper & Row.

Miller, G. E., & Cohen, S. (2001). Psychological interventions and the immune system: A meta-analytic review and critique. *Health Psychology, 20,* 47–63.

Miller, J. G., Bersoff, D. M., & Harwood, R. L. (1990). Perceptions of social responsibilities in India and the United States: Moral imperatives or personal decisions? *Journal of Personality and Social Psychology, 58,* 33–47.

Milner, B. (1959). The memory defect in bilateral hippocampal lesions. *Psychiatric Research Reports, 11,* 43–52.

Milner, B., Corkin, S., & Teuber, H. H. (1968). Further analysis of the hippocampal amnesic syndrome: 14-year follow-up study of H. M. *Neuropsychologia, 6,* 215–234.

Mischel, W. (2003). Challenging the traditional personality psychology paradigm. In R. J. Sternberg (Ed.), *Psychologists defying the crowd: Stories of those who battled the establishment and won* (pp. 139–156). Washington, DC: American Psychological Association.

Mischel, W., & Shoda, Y. (1995). A cognitive-affective system theory of personality: Reconceptualizing situations, dispositions, dynamics, and invariance in personality structure. *Psychological Review, 102,* 246–268.

Mody, R. R., & Smith, M. J. (2006). Smoking status and health-related quality of life: Findings from the 2001 Behavioral Risk Factor Surveillance System data. *American Journal of Health Promotion, 20,* 251–258.

Mohapel, P., Leanza, G., Kokaia, M., & Lindvall, O. (2005). Forebrain acetylcholine regulates adult hippocampal neurogenesis and learning. *Neurobiology of Aging, 26,* 939–946.

Monastra, V. J., Monastra, D. M., & George, S. (2002). The effects of stimulant therapy, EEG biofeedback, and parenting style on the primary symptoms of attention-deficit hyperactivity disorder. *Applied Psychophysiology and Biofeedback, 27,* 231–249.

Moore, K. A., Morrison, D. R., & Greene, A. D. (1997). Effects on the children born to adolescent mothers. In R. A. Maynard (Ed.), *Kids having kids: Economic costs and social consequences of teen pregnancy* (pp. 145–180). Washington, DC: Urban Institute Press.

Morgan, G. (2005). The resilience of language: What gesture creation in deaf children can tell us about how all children learn language. *Journal of Child Language, 32,* 925–928.

Mortimer, J. S. B., Sephton, S. E., Kimerling, R., Butler, L., Bernstein, A. S., & Spiegel, D. (2005). Chronic stress, depression and immunity in spouses of metastatic breast cancer patients. *Clinical Psychologist, 9,* 59–63.

Mroczek, D. K., & Kolarz, C. M. (1998). The effect of age on positive and negative affect: A developmental perspective on happiness. *Journal of Personality & Social Psychology, 75,* 1333–1349.

Mucci, A., Galderisi, S., Bucci, P., Tresca, E., Forte, A., Koenig, T., et al. (2005). Hemispheric lateralization patterns and psychotic experiences in healthy subjects. *Psychiatry Research: Neuroimaging, 139,* 141–154.

Murray, H. A. (1938). *Explorations in personality.* New York: Oxford Univ. Press.

Murray, J. L., Feuerstein, A. N., & Adams, D. C. (2006). Gender differences in moral reasoning and university student views on juvenile justice. *Journal of College and Character.* Retrieved October 20, 2007, from http://www.collegevalues.org/articles.cfm?a_1&id_617

Nakao, M., Kashiwagi, M., & Yano, E. (2005). Alexithymia and grief reactions in bereaved Japanese women. *Death Studies, 29,* 423–433.

Narrow, W. E., Rae, D. S., Robins, L. N., & Regier, D. A. (2001). Revised prevalence estimates of mental disorders in the United States: Using a clinical significance criterion to reconcile 2 survey estimates. *Archives of General Psychiatry, 59,* 115–123.

National Adolescent Health Information Center. (2004). *Fact Sheet on Suicide: Adolescents & Young Adults.* San Francisco, CA: Author, Univ. of California, San Francisco.

National Institute on Aging. (2006). The impact of Alzheimer's disease. Retrieved October 20, 2007, from http://www.nia.nih.gov/Alzheimers/Publications/UnravelingTheMystery/ImpactOfAlzheimerIll.htm

National Institute on Alcohol Abuse and Alcoholism. (2003). Does alcohol affect women differently? Retrieved October 5, 2007, from http://www.niaaa.nih.gov/FAQs/General-English/default.htm#women

National Institute on Drug Abuse. (2005). *NIDA InfoFacts: Methamphetamine.* Retrieved March 16, 2006, from http://www.nida.nih.gov/Infofacts/methamphetamine.html

National Mental Health Association. (2007). Young people and suicide. Alexandria, VA: National Mental Health Association. Retrieved October 20, 2007, from http://www1.nmha.org/suicide/youngPeople.cfm

Neher, A. (1991). Maslow's theory of motivation: A critique. *Journal of Humanistic Psychology, 31,* 89–112.

Neher, A. (1996). Jung's theory of archetypes: A critique. *Journal of Humanistic Psychology, 36,* 61–91.

Neisser, U. (1982). *Memory observed: Remembering in natural contexts.* San Francisco: Freeman.

Nevis, J. S., Rathus, A., & Green, B. (2005). *Abnormal psychology in a changing world* (5th ed.) Upper Saddle River, NJ: Prentice Hall.

Newcombe, N. S., Drummey, A. B., Fox, N. A., Lie, E., & Ottinger-Alberts, W. O. (2000). Remembering early childhood: How much, how, and why (or why not). *Current Directions in Psychological Science, 9,* 55–58.

Newland, M. C., & Rasmussen, E. B. (2003). Behavior in adulthood and during aging is affected by contaminant exposure in utero. *Current Directions in Psychological Science, 12,* 212–217.

Nickerson, R. S., & Adams, M. J. (1979). Long-term memory for a common object. *Cognitive Psychology, 11,* 287–307.

Niehoff, D. (1999). *The biology of violence (how understanding the brain, behavior, and environment can break the vicious circle of aggression).* New York: Free Press.

Nisbett, R. E., & Norenzayan, A. (2002). Culture and cognition. In H. Pashler & D. Medin (Eds.), *Steven's handbook of experimental psychology* (3rd ed.): *Vol. 2. Memory and cognitive processes* (pp. 561–597). New York: John Wiley & Sons.

Nisbett, R. E., Peng, K., Choi, I., & Norenzayan, A. (2001). Culture and systems of thought: Holistic versus analytic cognition. *Psychological Review, 108,* 291–310.

Nissani, M. (1990). A cognitive reinterpretation of Stanley Milgram's observations on obedience to authority. *American Psychologist, 45,* 1384–1385.

Nixon-Cave, K. A. (2001). Influence of cultural/ethnic beliefs and behaviors and family environment on the motor development of infants 12–18 months of age in three ethnic groups: African-American, Hispanic/Latino and Anglo-European. *Dissertation Abstracts International: Section B: The Sciences and Engineering, 6,* 2519.

Nolen-Hoeksema, S., & Harrell, Z. A. (2002). Rumination, depression, and alcohol use: Tests of gender differences. *Journal of Cognitive Psychotherapy,* 16, 391–403.

Norcross, J. C. (2002). *Psychotherapeutic relationships that work.* New York: Oxford Univ. Press.

Nurmi, E. L., Amin, T., Olson, L. M., Jacobs, M. M., McCauley, J. L., Lam, A. Y., et al. (2003). Dense linkage disequilibrium mapping in the 15q11-q13 maternal expression domain yields evidence for association in autism. *Molecular Psychiatry,* 8, 624–634.

Nuttall, J. (2002). Archetypes and architecture: The coniunctio of Canary Wharf. *Psychodynamic Practice: Individuals, Groups and Organizations,* 8, 33–53.

Nyberg, L., Marklund, P., Persson, J., Cabeza, R., Forkstarn, C., Petersson, K. M., et al. (2003). Common prefrontal activations during working memory, episodic memory, and semantic memory. *Neuropsychologia,* 41, 371–377.

O'Leary, V. E., & Flanagan, E. H. (2001). Leadership. In J. Worell (Ed.), *Encyclopedia of gender* (Vol. 2, pp. 245–257). San Diego, CA: Academic Press.

Offer, D., Ostrov, E., Howard, K. I., & Atkinson, R. (1988). *The teenage world: Adolescents' self-image in ten countries.* New York: Plenum.

Oltmanns, T. F., & Emery, R. E. (2006). *Abnormal psychology* (5th ed.). Upper Saddle River, NJ: Prentice Hall.

Ortiz, S. O., & Dynda, A. M. (2005). Use of intelligence tests with culturally and linguistically diverse populations. In D. P. Flanagan & P. L. Harrison (Eds.), *Contemporary intellectual assessment: Theories, tests, and issues* (pp. 545–556). New York: Guilford.

Ostrov, J. M., & Keating, C. F. (2004). Gender differences in preschool aggression during free play and structured interactions: An observational study. *Social Development,* 13, 255–277.

Ouimette, P., Humphreys, K., Moos, R. H., Finney, J. W., Cronkite, R., & Federman, B. (2001). Self-help group participation among substance use disorder patients with posttraumatic stress disorder. *Journal of Substance Abuse Treatment,* 20, 25–32.

Owen, C. J. (2005). The empty nest transition: The relationship between attachment style and women's use of this period as a time for growth and change. *Dissertation Abstracts International: Section B: The Sciences and Engineering,* 65, 3747.

Ozer, E. J., Best, S. R., Lipsey, T. L., & Weiss, D. S. (2003). Predictors of posttraumatic stress disorder and symptoms in adults: A meta-analysis. *Psychological Bulletin,* 129, 52–73.

Paikoff, R. L., & Brooks-Gunn, J. (1991). Do parent-child relationships change during puberty? *Psychological Bulletin,* 110, 47–66.

Paivio, A. (1986). *Mental representations: A dual coding approach.* New York: Oxford Univ. Press.

Papp, S. (2006). A relevance-theoretic account of the development and deficits of theory of mind in normally developing children and individuals with autism. *Theory and Psychology,* 16, 141–161.

Pare, D., Collins, D. R., & Guillaume, P. J. (2002). Amygdala oscillations and the consolidation of emotional memories. *Trends in Cognitive Sciences,* 6, 306–314.

Parr, L.A. (2003). Case study 10A. Emotional recognition by chimpanzees. In F. B. M. de Waal & P. L. Tyack (Eds.), *Animal social complexity: Intelligence, culture, and individualized societies* (pp. 288–292). Cambridge, MA: Harvard Univ. Press.

Patterson, C. J. (2000). Family relationships of lesbians and gay men. *Journal of Marriage and the Family,* 62, 1052–1069.

Patterson, D. R., & Jensen, M. P. (2003). Hypnosis and clinical pain. *Psychological Bulletin,* 129, 495–521.

Patterson, D. R., & Ptacek, J. T. (1997). Baseline pain as a moderator of hypnotic analgesia for burn injury treatment. *Journal of Consulting & Clinical Psychology,* 65, 60–67.

Paunonen, S. V., & Ashton, M. C. (2001). Big Five factors and facets and the prediction of behavior. *Journal of Personality and Social Psychology,* 81, 524–539.

Pavlov, I. P. (1927). *Conditional reflexes* (G. V. Anrep, trans.). London: Oxford Univ. Press.

Pawlowski, B., Dunbar, R. I. M., & Lipowicz, A. (2000) Evolutionary fitness: Tall men have more reproductive success. *Nature, 403,* p. 156.

Pedersen, P. B., & Carey, J. C. (2003). *Multicultural counseling in schools* (2nd ed.). Boston: Allyn & Bacon.

Pedlow, R., Sanson, A., Prior, M., & Oberklaid, F. (1993). Stability of maternally reported temperament from infancy to 8 years. *Developmental Psychology,* 29, 998–1007.

Peng, K., & Nisbett, R. E. (1999). Culture, dialectics, and reasoning about contradiction. *American Psychologist, 54,* 741–754.

Peplau, L. A. (2003). Human sexuality: How do men and women differ? *Current Directions in Psychological Science, 12,* 37–40.

Peplau, L. A., & Beals, K. P. (2004). The family lives of lesbians and gay men. In A. L. Vangelisti (Ed.), *Handbook of family communication* (pp. 233–248). Mahwah, NJ: Erlbaum.

Perry, B. D., & Pollard, R. (1998). Homeostasis, stress, trauma, and adaptation: A neurodevelopmental view of childhood trauma. *Child Adolescent Psychiatric Clinics of North America, 7,* 33–51.

Persky, H. (1983). Psychosexual effects of hormones. *Medical Aspects of Human Sexuality, 17,* 74–101.

Persson-Blennow, I., & McNeil, T. F. (1988). Frequencies and stability of temperament types in childhood. *Journal of the American Academy of Child and Adolescent Psychiatry, 27,* 619–622.

Peters, R. (2005). Aging and the brain. *Postgraduate Medical Journal, 82,* 84–88.

Peterson, L. R., & Peterson, M. J. (1959). Short-term retention of individual verbal items. *Journal of Experimental Psychology, 58,* 193–198.

Pew Research Center. (2007). Fewer mothers prefer full-time work. Retrieved October 20, 2007, from http://pewresearch.org/pubs/536/working-women

Pew Research Center for the People and the Press. (2002, September 5). *One year later: New Yorkers more troubled, Washingtonians more on edge.* Retrieved July 13, 2004, from http://peoplepress.org/reports/display.php3?PageID_632

Phares, J. (1984). *Clinical psychology: Concepts, methods and profession.* Ontario: The Dorsey Press.

Piaget, J. (1969). The intellectual development of the adolescent. In G. Caplan & S. Lebovici (Eds.), *Adolescence: Psychosocial perspectives.* New York: Basic Books.

Pinker, S. (1994). *The language instinct: How the mind creates language.* New York: Harper Collins.

Pinker, S. (1999). *Words and rules: The ingredients of language.* New York: Basic Books.

Pinker, S. (2002). *The blank slate: The modern denial of human nature.* New York: Viking.

Plomin, R. (1997). Identifying genes for cognitive abilities and disabilities. In R. J. Sternberg & E. Grigorenko (Eds.), *Intelligence: Heredity and environment* (pp. 89-104). New York: Cambridge Univ. Press.

Plomin, R. (1999). Parents and personality. *Contemporary Psychology, 44,* 269–271.

Plomin, R., & Rende, R. (1991). Human behavioral genetics. *Annual Review of Psychology, 42,* 161–190.

Plutchik, R. (1980). *Emotion: A psychoevolutionary synthesis.* New York: Harper & Row.

Pollard, C. A. (2000). Flooding. In A. E. Kazdin (Ed.), *Encyclopedia of psychology* (Vol. 3, pp. 377–379). Washington, DC: American Psychological Association.

Port, C. L., Engdahl, B., & Frazier, P. (2001). A longitudinal and retrospective study of PTSD among older prisoners of war. *American Journal of Psychiatry, 158,* 1474–1479.

Powell, S., Rosner, R., Butollo, W., Tedeschi, R. G., & Calhoun, L. G. (2003). Postraumatic growth after a war: A study with former refugees and displaced people in Sarajevo. *Journal of Clinical Psychology, 59,* 71–83.

Premack, D. (1971, May 21). Language in chimpanzee? *Science, 172,* 808–822.

Premack, D. (1976). *Intelligence in ape and man.* Hillsdale, NJ: Erlbaum.

Prickaerts, J., Koopmans, G., Blokland, A., & Scheepens, A. (2004). Learning and adult neurogenesis: Survival with or without proliferation? *Neurobiology of Learning and Memory, 81,* 1–11.

Puca, A. A., Daly, M. J., Brewster, S. J., Matise, T. C., Barrett, J., Shea-Drinkwater, M., et al. (2001). A genome-wide scan for linkages to human exceptional longevity identifies a locus on chromosome 4. *Proceedings of the National Academy of Sciences, USA, 98,* 10505–10508.

Querido, J., Warner, T., & Eyberg, S. (2002). Parenting styles and child behavior in African American families of preschool children. *Journal of Clinical Child and Adolescent Psychology, 31,* 272–277.

Rainer, G., & Miller, E. K. (2002). Timecourse of object-related neural activity in the primate prefrontal cortex during a short-term memory task. *European Journal of Neuroscience, 15,* 1244–1254.

Rayman, P., & Bluestone, B. (1982). *The private and social response to job loss: A metropolitan study.* Final report of research sponsored by the Center for Work and Mental Health, National Institute of Mental Health.

Read, J., Perry, B. D., Moskowitz, A., & Connolly, J. (2001). The contribution of early traumatic events to schizophrenia in some patients: A traumagenic neurodevelopmental model. *Psychiatry: Interpersonal and Biological Processes, 64,* 319–345.

Redelmeier, D. A., & Tversky, A. (2004). On the belief that arthritis pain is related to the weather. In E. Shafir (Ed.), *Preference, belief, and similarity: Selected writings by Amos Tversky* (pp. 377–381). Cambridge, MA: MIT Press.

Reiche, E. M. V., Morimoto, H. K., & Nunes, S. O. V. (2005). Stress and depression-induced immune dysfunction: Implications for the development and progression of cancer. *International Review of Psychiatry, 17,* 515–527.

Reinisch, J. M., Ziemba-Davis, M., & Sanders, S. A. (1991). Hormonal contributions to sexually dimorphic behavioral development in humans. *Psychoneuroendocrinology, 16,* 213–278.

Reiss, S. (2005). Extrinsic and intrinsic motivation at 30: Unresolved scientific issues. *Behavior Analyst, 28,* 1–14.

Renzulli, J. S. (1978). What makes giftedness? Reexamining a definition. *Phi Delta Kappan, 60,* 180–184, 216.

Reuter-Lorenz, P. A., & Miller, A. C. (1998). The cognitive neuroscience of human laterality: Lessons from the bisected brain. *Current Directions in Psychological Science, 7*(1), 15–20.

Richards, J., Encel, J., & Shute, R. (2003). The emotional and behavioural adjustment of intellectually gifted adolescents: A multidimensional, multiinformant approach. *High Ability Studies, 14,* 153–164.

Rini, C. K., Dunkel-Schetter, C., Wadhwa, P. D., & Sandman, C. A. (1999). Psychological adaptation and birth outcomes: The role of personal resources, stress, and sociocultural context in pregnancy. *Health Psychology, 18,* 333–345.

Roberts, A. H., Kewman, D. G., Mercer, L., & Hovell, M. (1993). The power of nonspecific effects in healing: Implications for psychosocial and biological treatments. *Clinical Psychology Review, 13,* 375–391.

Robinson, A., & Clinkenbeard, P. R. (1998). Giftedness: An exceptionality examined. *Annual Review of Psychology, 49,* 117–139.

Rodier, P. M. (2000). The early origins of autism. *Scientific American, 282*(2), 56–63.

Roese, N. J. (1997). Counterfactual thinking. *Psychological Bulletin, 121,* 133–148.

Rofe, Y., Hoffman, M., & Lewin, I. (1985). Patient affiliation in major illness. *Psychological Medicine, 15,* 895–896.

Rogers, C. R. (1961). *On becoming a person: A therapist's view of psychotherapy.* Boston: Houghton Mifflin.

Roitblat, H. L., Penner, R. H., & Nachtigall, P. E. (1990). Matching-to-sample by an echolocating dolphin (*Tursiops truncatus*). *Journal of Experimental Psychology: Animal Behavior Processes, 16,* 85–95.

Rolls, E. T. (2000). Memory systems in the brain. *Annual Review of Psychology, 51,* 599–630.

Rolls, E. T., Tovee, M. J., & Panzeri, S. (1999). The neurophysiology of backward visual masking: Information analysis. *Journal of Cognitive Neuroscience, 11,* 335–346.

Roper, R., & Shewan, D. (2002). Compliance and eyewitness testimony: Do eyewitnesses comply with misleading "expert pressure" during investigative interviewing. *Legal and Criminological Psychology, 7,* 155–163.

Rosch, E. H. (1973). Natural categories. *Cognitive Psychology, 4,* 328–350.

Rosch, E. H. (1978). Principles of categorization. In E. H. Rosch & B. B. Lloyd (Eds.), *Cognition and categorization* (pp. 27–48). Hillsdale, NJ: Erlbaum.

Rosch, E. H. (1998). Principles of categorization. In A. M. Collens & E. E. Smith (Eds.), *Readings in cognitive science: A perspective from psychology and artificial intelligence* (pp. 312–322). San Mateo, CA: Morgan Kaufman.

Rosch, E. H. (2002). Principles of categorization. In D. J. Levitin (Ed.), *Foundations of Cognitive Psychology: Core Readings* (pp. 251–270). Cambridge, MA: MIT Press.

Rose, R. J., Viken, R. J., Dick, D. M., Bates, J. E., Pulkkinen, L., & Kaprio, J. (2003). It *does* take a village: Nonfamilial environments and children's behavior. *Psychological Science, 14,* 273–277.

Rosengren, A., Hawken, S., Ôunpuu, S., Sliwa, K., Zubaid, M., Almahmeed, W. A., et al. (2004). Association of psychosocial risk factors with risk of acute myocardial infarction in 11,119 cases and 13,648 controls from 52 countries (the INTERHEART study): Case-control study. *Lancet, 364,* 953–962.

Rosenthal, R. (2002). The Pygmalion effect and its mediating mechanisms. In J. Aronson (Ed.), *Improving academic achievement: Impact of psychological factors on education* (pp. 25–36). San Diego, CA: Academic Press.

Rosenzweig, M. R. (1984). Experience, memory, and the brain. *American Psychologist, 39*, 365–376.

Rosenzweig, M. R. (1996). Aspects of the search for neural mechanisms of memory. *Annual Review of Psychology, 47*, 1–32.

Rosenzweig, M. R., & Leiman, A. L. (1982). *Physiological psychology.* Lexington, MA: Heath.

Rothblum, E. D., Brand, P. A., Miller, C. T., & Oetjen, H. A. (1990). The relationship between obesity, employment discrimination, and employment related victimization. *Journal of Vocational Behavior, 37*, 251–266.

Rottenstreich, Y., & Tversky, A. (1997). Unpacking, repacking, and anchoring: Advances in support theory. *Psychological Review, 104*, 406–415.

Rotter, J. B. (1954). *Social learning and clinical psychology.* Englewood Cliffs, NJ: Prentice Hall.

Ruifang, G., & Danling, P. (2005). A review of studies on the brain plasticity. *Psychological Science, 28*, 409–411.

Russell, J. A. (1991). Culture and the categorization of emotions. *Psychological Bulletin, 110*, 426–450.

Rutter, M. (1997). Nature-nurture integration: An example of antisocial behavior. *American Psychologist, 52*, 390–398.

Rutter, M. (2005). Genetic influences and autism. In F. R. Volkmar, R. Paul, A. Klin, & D. Cohen (Eds.), *Handbook of autism and pervasive developmental disorders, Vol. 1: Diagnosis, development, neurobiology, and behavior* (3rd ed., pp. 425–452). Hoboken, NJ: John Wiley & Sons.

Sabini, J., & Silver, M. (2005). Ekman's basic emotions: Why not love and jealousy? *Cognition & Emotion, 19*, 693–712.

Salgado, J. F., Moscoso, S., & Lado, M. (2003). Evidence of cross-cultural invariance of the Big Five personality dimensions in work settings. *European Journal of Personality, 1* (Suppl. 1), S67–S76.

Salovey, P., Mayer, J. D., & Rosenhan, D. L. (1991). Mood behavior. In M. S. Clark (Ed.), *Review of personality and social psychology: Prosocial behavior* (Vol. 12, pp. 215–237). Newbury Park, CA: Sage.

Sanford, R. N. (1937). The effects of abstinence from food upon imaginal processes: A further experiment. *Journal of Psychology, 3*, 145–159.

Saporta, I., & Halpern, J. J. (2002). Being different can hurt: Effects of deviation from physical norms on lawyers' salaries. *Industrial Relations: A Journal of Economy and Society, 41*, 442–466.

Saretzki, G., & Zglinicki, T. (2002). Replicative aging, telomeres, and oxidative stress. In D. Harman (Ed.), *Increasing healthy life span: Conventional measures and slowing the innate aging process. Annals of the New York Academy of Science* (Vol. 959, pp. 24–29). New York: New York Academy of Sciences.

Satow, K. K. (1975). Social approval and helping. *Journal of Experimental Social Psychology, 11*, 501–509.

Sattler, J. M. (2005). *Assessment of children: Behavioral and clinical applications* (5th ed.). La Mesa, CA: Jerome M. Sattler.

Savage-Rumbaugh, E. S., & Fields, W. M. (2000). Linguistic, cultural, and cognitive capacities of bonobos (*Pan paniscus*). *Culture and Psychology, 6*, 131–153.

Scarr, S. (1999). Freedom of choice for poor families. *American Psychologist, 54*, 144–145.

Schachter, S., & Singer, J. (1962). Cognitive, social, and physiological determinants of emotional state. *Psychological Review, 69*, 379–399.

Schachter, S., & Singer, J. E. (2001). Cognitive, social, and psychological determinants of emotional state. In G. W. Parrott (Ed.), *Emotions in social psychology: Essential readings* (pp. 76–93). Philadelphia: Psychology Press.

Schaie, K. W., & Willis, S. L. (2001). *Adult development and aging* (5th ed.). Upper Saddle River, NJ: Prentice Hall.

Scheibel, R. S., & Levin, H. S. (2004). Working memory and the functional anatomy of the frontal lobes. *Cortex, 40*, 218–219.

Scherer, K. R., Schorr, A., & Johnstone, T. (Eds.) (2001). *Appraisal processes in emotion: Theory, methods, research.* New York: Oxford Univ. Press.

Schiffman, S. S. (1997). Taste and smell losses in normal aging and disease. *Journal of the American Medical Association, 278*, 1357–1362

Schmahl, C. G., Vermetten, E., Elzinga, B. M., & Bremmer, J. D. (2004). A positron emission tomography study of memories of childhood abuse in borderline personality disorder. *Biological Psychiatry, 55*, 759–765.

Schoenthaler, S. J., Amos, S. P., Eysenck, H. J., Peritz, E., & Yudkin, J. (1991). Controlled trial of vitamin-mineral supplementation: Effects on intelligence and performance. *Personality and Individual Differences, 12*, 251–362.

Schwartz, P. (1994, November 17). Some people with multiple roles are blessedly stressed. *New York Times.*

Sedikides, C., Gaertner, L., & Toguchi, Y. (2003). Pancultural self-enhancement. *Journal of Personality and Social Psychology, 84*, 60–79.

Seligman, M. E. P. (1995). The effectiveness of psychotherapy: The *Consumer Reports* study. *American Psychologist, 50*, 965–974.

Seligman, M. E. P., & Csikzentmihalyi, M. (2000). Positive psychology. *American Psychologist, 55*, 5–14.

Seligman, M. E. P., & Maier, S. F. (1967). Failure to escape traumatic shock. *Journal of Experimental Psychology, 74*, 1–9.

Seligman, M. E. P., Steen, T. A., & Park, N. (2005). Positive psychology progress: Empirical validation of interventions. *American Psychologist, 60*, 410–421.

Selye, H. (1956). *The stress of life.* New York: McGraw-Hill.

Selye, H. (1976). *The stress of life* (Rev. ed.). New York: McGraw-Hill.

Shastry, B. S. (2005). Recent advances in the genetics of autism spectrum disorders: A mini-review. *British Journal of Developmental Disabilities, 51*, 129–142.

Shenk, J. W. (2005). *Lincoln's melancholy: How depression challenged a president and fueled his greatness.* NY: Houghton Mifflin.

Shermer, M. (2004). The enchanted glass. *Scientific American, 290*(5), 46.

Siegel, S. (2005). Drug tolerance, drug addiction, and drug anticipation. *Current Directions in Psychological Science, 14*, 296–300.

Simcock, G., & Hayne, H. (2002). Breaking the barrier? Children fail to translate their preverbal memories into language. *Psychological Science, 13*, 225–231.

Simpson, R. L., de Boer-Ott, S. R., Griswold, D. E., Myles, B. S., Byrd, S. E., Ganz, J. B., et al. (2005). *Autism spectrum disorders: Interventions and treatments for children and youth.* London: Corwin.

Singer, J. L. (1975). *The inner world of daydreaming.* New York: Harper Colophon.

Singh, D. (1993) Adaptive significance of female physical attractiveness: Role of waist-to-hip ratio. *Journal of Personality and Social Psychology, 65,* 293–307.

Skeels, H. M. (1938). Mental development of children in foster homes. *Journal of Consulting Psychology, 2,* 33–43.

Skeels, H. M. (1942). The study of the effects of differential stimulation on mentally retarded children: A follow-up report. *American Journal of Mental Deficiencies, 46,* 340–350.

Skeels, H. M. (1966). Adult status of children with contrasting early life experiences. *Monographs of the Society for Research in Child Development, 31*(3), 1–65.

Skinner, B. F. (1948). *Science and human behavior.* New York: Macmillan.

Skinner, B. F. (1957). *Verbal behavior.* Englewood Cliffs, NJ: Prentice Hall.

Sleek, S. (1998, May). Older vets just now feeling pain of war. *APA Monitor,* pp. 1, 28.

Slife, B. D., & Reber, J. S. (2001). Eclecticism in psychotherapy: Is it really the best substitute for traditional theories? In B. D. Slife & R. N. Williams (Eds.), *Critical issues in psychotherapy: Translating new ideas into practice* (pp. 213–233). Thousand Oaks, CA: Sage.

Smith, C. T., Nixon, M. R., & Nader, R. S. (2004). Posttraining increases in REM sleep intensity implicate REM sleep in memory processing and provide a biological marker of learning potential. *Learning & Memory, 11,* 714–719.

Smith, D. E., Roberts, J., Gage, F. H., & Tuszynski, M. H. (1999). Age-associated neuronal atrophy occurs in the primate brain and is reversible by growth factor gene therapy. *Proceedings of the National Academy of Sciences, 96,* 10893–10898.

Smith, E. R., & Mackie, D. M. (2005). Aggression, hatred, and other emotions. In J. F. Dovidio, P. Glick, & L. A. Rudman (Eds.), *On the nature of prejudice: Fifty years after Allport* (pp. 361–376). Malden, MA: Blackwell.

Smith, P. B., & Bond, M. H. (1999). *Social psychology across cultures: Analysis and perspectives* (2nd ed.). Boston: Allyn & Bacon.

Smith, R. A. (2005). The classroom as a social psychology laboratory. *Journal of Social & Clinical Psychology, 24* [Special issue: *Dispelling the fable of "Those who can, do, and those who can't, teach:" The (social and clinical) psychology of instruction*], 62–71.

Smith, R. A., & Weber, A. L. (2005). Applying social psychology in everyday life. In F. W. Schneider, J. A. Gruman, & L. M. Coutts (Eds.), *Applied social psychology: Understanding and addressing social and practical problems,* (pp. 75–99). Thousand Oaks, CA: Sage.

Snowden, L. R., & Yamada, A.-M. (2005). Cultural differences in access to care. *Annual Review of Clinical Psychology, 1,* 143–166.

Snyder, M., & Swann, W. B., Jr. (1978). Behavioral confirmation in social interaction: From social perception to social reality. *Journal of Experimental Social Psychology, 14,* 148–162.

Soussignan, R. (2002). Duchenne smile, emotional experience, and autonomic reactivity: A test of the facial feedback hypothesis. *Emotion, 2,* 52–74.

Spanos, N. P. (1996). *Multiple identities and false memories.* Washington, DC: American Psychological Association.

Spanos, N. P., Burgess, C. A., Burgess, M. F., Samuels, C., & Blois, W. O. (1997). *Creating false memories of infancy with hypnotic and nonhypnotic procedures.* Unpublished manuscript, Carlton Univ., Ottawa, Canada.

Spelke, E. S. (2005). Sex differences in intrinsic aptitude for mathematics and science? A critical review. *American Psychologist, 60,* 950–958.

Sperling, G. (1960). The information available in brief visual presentations. *Psychological Monographs, 74,* 1–29.

Sperry, R. W. (1964). The great cerebral commissure. *Scientific American, 210*(1), 42–52.

Sperry, R. W. (1968). Hemisphere disconnection and unity in conscious awareness. *American Psychologist, 23,* 723–733.

Sperry, R. W. (1970). *Perception in the absence of neocortical commissures.* In *Perception and its disorders* (Res. Publ. A.R.N.M.D., Vol. 48). New York: The Association for Research in Nervous and Mental Disease.

Squire, L. R., & Kandel, E. R. (1999). *Memory: From mind to molecules.* New York: Scientific American Library.

Steinke, W. R. (2003). Perception and recognition of music and song following right hemisphere stroke: A case study. *Dissertation Abstracts International: Section B: The Sciences and Engineering, 63,* 4948.

Sternberg, R. J. (1982, April). Who's intelligent? *Psychology Today,* pp. 30–39.

Sternberg, R. J. (1986). *Intelligence applied.* Orlando, FL: Harcourt Brace Jovanovich.

Sternberg, R. J. (2003). Intelligence. In D. K. Freedheim (Ed.), *Handbook of psychology: History of psychology* (Vol. 1, pp. 135–156). New York: John Wiley & Sons.

Sternberg, R. J., & Grigorenko, E. L. (2001). *Environmental effects on cognitive abilities.* Mahwah, NJ: Erlbaum.

Sternberg, R. J., Conway, B. E., Ketron, J. L., & Bernstein, M. (1981). People's conceptions of intelligence. *Journal of Personal and Social Psychology, 41,* 37–55.

Stevenson, H. W. (1992). Learning from Asian schools. *Scientific American, 265*(6), 70–76.

Stevenson, H. W. (1993). Why Asian students still outdistance Americans. *Educational Leadership,* 63–65.

Stevenson, H. W., Chen, C., & Lee, S.-Y. (1993, January 1). Mathematics achievement of Chinese, Japanese, and American children: Ten years later. *Science, 259,* 53–58.

Stevenson, H. W., Lee, S., & Mu, X. (2000). Successful achievement in mathematics: China and the United States. In F. M. van Lieshout & P. G. Heymans (Eds.), *Developing talent across the life-span* (pp. 167–183). Philadelphia: Psychology Press.

Stevenson, H. W., Lee, S.-Y., & Stigler, J. W. (1986, February 14). Mathematics achievement of Chinese, Japanese, and American children. *Science, 231,* 693–697.

Stock, M. B., & Smythe, P. M. (1963). Does undernutrition during infancy inhibit brain growth and subsequent intellectual development? *Archives of Disorders in Childhood, 38,* 546–552.

Storksen, I., Roysamb, E., & Holmen, T. L. (2006). Adolescent adjustment and well-being: Effects of parental divorce and distress. *Scandinavian Journal of Psychology, 47,* 75–84.

Straton, D. (2004). Guilt and PTSD. *Australian and New Zealand Journal of Psychiatry, 38,* 269–270.

Streeter, S. A., & McBurney, D. H. (2003). Waist-hip ratio and attractiveness. New evidence and a critique of a "critical test." *Evolution and Human Behaviour, 24,* 88–98.

Strickland, B. R. (2000). Misassumptions, misadventures, and the misuse of psychology. *American Psychologist, 55,* 331–338.

Strollo, P. J. Jr., & Davé, N. B. (2005). Sleep apnea. In D. J. Buysse (Ed.), *Sleep disorders and psychiatry* (pp. 77–105). Washington, DC: American Psychiatric Publishing.

Studer, J. R. (2000). Adolescent suicide: Aggression turned inward. In D. S. Sandhu & C. B. Aspy (Eds.), *Violence in American schools: A practical guide for counselors* (pp. 269–284). Alexandria, VA: American Counseling Association.

Surgeon General Report (1964). *Smoking and Health.* Retrieved October 8, 2007.

Szatkowska, I., Grabowska, A., & Szymanska, O. (2001). Evidence for involvement of ventro-medial prefrontal cortex in a short-term storage of visual images. *Neuroreport: for Rapid Communication of Neuroscience Research, 12,* 1187–1190.

Tamminga, C. A., & Vogel, M. (2005). Images in neuroscience: The cerebellum. *American Journal of Psychiatry, 162,* 1253.

Tappan, M. B. (2006). Mediated moralities: Sociocultural approaches to moral development. In M. Killen & J. G. Smetana (Eds.), *Handbook of moral development* (pp. 351–374). Mahwah, NJ: Erlbaum.

Taylor, S. E., & Repetti, R. L. (1997). Health psychology: What is an unhealthy environment and how does it get under the skin? *Annual Review of Psychology, 48,* 411–447.

Taylor, S. E., Klein, L. C., Lewis, B. P., Gruenewald, T. L., Gurung, R. A. R., & Updegraff, J. A. (2000). Biobehavioral responses to stress in females: Tend-and-befriend, not fight-or-flight. *Psychological Review, 107,* 411–429.

Terman, L. M. (1925). *Mental and physical traits of a thousand gifted children: Genetic studies of genius* (Vol. 1). Stanford, CA: Stanford Univ. Press.

Terrace, H. S., Son, L. K., & Brannon, E. M. (2003). Serial expertise of rhesus macaques. *Psychological Science, 14,* 66–73.

Thomas, A., & Chess, S. (1977). *Temperament and development.* New York: Brunner/Mazel.

Thompson, C. P., Cowan, T. M., & Frieman, J. (1993). *Memory search by a memorist.* Hillsdale, NJ: Erlbaum.

Thompson, V. L. S., & Alexander, H. (2006). Therapists' race and African American clients' reactions to therapy. *Educational Publishing Foundation, 43,* 99–110.

Thorndike, E. L. (1898). Animal intelligence. *Psychological Review Monograph, 2* (4, Whole No. 8).

Thurber, J. (1942). The secret life of Walter Mitty. In J. Thurber (Ed.), *My world and welcome to it* (pp. 72–81). New York: Harcourt, Brace and Co.

Thurstone, L. L. (1938). Primary mental abilities. *Psychometric Monographs, 1.*

Tolman, E. C., & Honzik, C. H. (1930). Introduction and removal of reward, and maze performance in rats. *University of California Publications in Psychology, 4,* 257–275.

Tomer, A. (Ed.) (2000). *Death attitudes and the older adult: Theories, concepts, and applications.* Philadelphia: Brunner-Routledge.

Treisman, A. (2004). Psychological issues in selective attention. In M. S. Gazzaniga (Ed.), *The cognitive neurosciences* (3rd ed., pp. 529–544). Cambridge, MA: MIT Press.

Treisman, A. M. (1960). Contextual cues in selective listening. *Quarterly Journal of Experimental Psychology, 12,* 242–248.

Treisman, A. M. (1964). Verbal cues, language and meaning in selective attention. *American Journal of Psychology, 77,* 206–219.

Tremblay, R. E., Hartup, W. W., & Archer, J. (Eds.). (2005). *Developmental origins of aggression.* New York: Guilford.

Triandis, H. C. (1994). *Culture and social behavior.* New York: McGraw-Hill.

Triandis, H. C. (2001). Individualism-collectivism and personality. *Journal of Personality, 69,* 907–924.

Trouilloud, D., Sarrazin, P., Bressoux, P., & Bois, J. (2006). Relation between teachers' early expectations and students' later perceived competence in physical education classes: Autonomy-supportive climate as a moderator. *Journal of Educational Psychology, 98,* 75–86.

Tseng, R. J., Padgett, D. A., Dhabhar, F. S., Engler, H., & Sheridan, J. F. (2005). Stress-induced modulation of NK activity during influenza viral infection: Role of glucocorticoids and opioids. *Brain, Behavior and Immunity, 19,* 153–164.

Turati, C. (2004). Why faces are not special to newborns: An alternative account of the face preference. *Current Directions in Psychological Science, 13,* 5–8.

Turkheimer, E. (1991). Individual and group differences in adoption studies of IQ. *Psychological Bulletin, 110,* 392–405.

Turkheimer, E., & Waldron, M. (2000). Nonshared environment: A theoretical, methodological, and quantitative review. *Psychological Bulletin, 126,* 78–108.

Turkheimer, E., Haley, A., Waldron, M., D'Onofrio, B., & Gottesman, I. I. (2003). Socioeconomic status modifies heritability of IQ in young children. *Psychological Science, 14,* 623–628.

U.S. Bureau of the Census. (2001). *The 65 years and over population: 2000.* Retrieved May 11, 2006 from http://www.census.gov/prod/2001pubs/c2kbr01-10.pdf.

U.S. Bureau of the Census. (2007a). Civilian population—Employment status by sex, race, and ethnicity: 1960 to 2005. Retrieved October 20, 2007, from http://www.census.gov/compendia/statab/tables/07s0575.xls.

U.S. Bureau of the Census. (2007b). Labor force participation rates by marital status, sex, and age: 1960 to 2005. Retrieved October 20, 2007, from http://www.census.gov/compendia/statab/tables/07s0582.xls.

Uddin, L. Q., Kaplan, J. T., Molnar-Szakacs, I., Zaidel, E., & Iacoboni, M. (2005). Self-face recognition activates a frontoparietal "mirror" network in the right hemisphere: An event-related fMRI study. *Neuroimage, 25,* 926–935.

Underwood, M. K. (2003). *Social aggression among girls.* New York: Guilford.

UNICEF. (2001). A league table of teenage births in rich nations. *Innocenti Report Card, 3.*

Vaillant, G. E. (1977). *Adaptation to life.* Boston: Little, Brown.

Vaillant, G. E. (2003). *Aging well: Surprising guideposts to a happier life from the landmark Harvard Study of Adult Development.* New York: Little, Brown.

Vallee, B. I. (1998). Alcohol in the Western world. *Scientific American, 278*(6), 80–85.

van Achterberg, M. E., Rohrbaugh, R. M., & Southwick, S. M. (2001). Emergence of PTSD in trauma survivors with dementia. *Journal of Clinical Psychiatry, 62,* 206–207.

Vermetten, E., & Bremner, J. D. (2002). Circuits and systems in stress: II. Applications to neurobiology and treatment in posttraumatic stress disorder. *Depression and Anxiety, 16,* 14–38.

Vinnicombe, S., & Singh, V. (2003). Women-only management training: An essential part of women's leadership development. *Journal of Change Management, 3,* 294–306.

Volpe, K. (2004, January). Taylor takes on "fight-or-flight." *APS Observer,* p. 21.

Votruba-Drzal, E., Coley, R. L., & Chase-Lansdale, P. L. (2004). Child care and low-income children's development: Direct and moderated effects. *Child Development, 75,* 296–312.

Wade, G. W. (2004). Regulation of body fat content? *American Journal of Physiology Regulatory, Integrative and Comparative Physiology, 286,* R14–R15.

Wampold, B. E. (2001). *The great psychotherapy debate: Models, methods, and findings.* Mahwah, NJ: Erlbaum.

Wang, C., & Chen, W. (2000). The efficacy of behavior therapy in 9 patients with phobia. *Chinese Mental Health Journal, 14,* 351–352.

Watanabe, H., Kobayashi, Y., Sakura, M., Matsumoto, Y., & Mizunami, M. (2003). Classical olfactory conditioning in the cockroach *Periplaneta americana. Zoological Science, 20,* 1447–1454.

Watson, J. B. (1913). Psychology as the behaviorist views it. *Psychological Review, 20,* 158–177.

Watson, J. B. (1924). *Behaviorism.* Chicago: University of Chicago Press.

Watson, J. B., & Rayner, R. (1920). Conditioned emotional reactions. *Journal of Experimental Psychology, 3,* 1–14.

Weinstein, R. S., Soule, C. R., Collins, F., Cone, J., Melhorn, M., & Simantocci, K. (1991). Expectations and high school change: Teacher-researcher collaboration to prevent school failure. *American Journal of Community Psychology, 9,* 333–363.

Weiss, S. J., Wilson, P., & Morrison, D. (2004). Maternal tactile stimulation and the neurodevelopment of low birth weight infants. *Infancy, 5,* 85–107.

Werker, J. F. (1989). Becoming a native listener. *American Scientist, 77,* 54–59.

Werker, J. F., & Desjardins, R. N. (1995). Listening to speech in the 1st year of life: Experiential influences on phoneme perception. *Current Directions in Psychological Science, 4,* 76–81.

Westen, D. (1998). Unconscious thought, feeling and motivation: The end of a century-long debate. In R. F. Bornstein & J. M. Masling (Eds.), *Empirical perspectives on the psychoanalytic unconscious* (pp. 1–43). Washington, DC: American Psychological Association.

Wetzel, W., Wagner, T., & Balschun, D. (2003). REM sleep enhancement induced by different procedures improves memory retention in rats. *European Journal of Neuroscience, 18,* 2611–2617.

Wheeler, M. A., Stuss, D. T., & Tulving. E. (1997). Toward a theory of episodic memory: The frontal lobes and autonoetic consciousness. *Psychological Bulletin, 121,* 331–354.

White, P., & Waghorn, G. (2004). Mental illness and employment status. *Australian and New Zealand Journal of Psychiatry, 38,* 174–175.

Whorf, B. L. (1956). *Language, thought, and reality.* New York: MIT Press–Wiley.

Wiggins, J. S. (Ed.). (1996). *The five-factor model of personality: Theoretical perspectives.* New York: Guilford.

Wilkins, V. M. (2005). Religion, spirituality, and psychological distress in cardiovascular disease. *Dissertation Abstracts International: Section B: The Sciences and Engineering, 66,* 3430.

Williams, J. E., Satterwhite, R. C., & Saiz, J. L. (1998). *The importance of psychological traits: A cross-cultural study.* New York: Plenum.

Willis, S. L., & Schaie, K.W. (1999). Intellectual functioning in midlife. In S. L. Willis & J. D. Reid (Eds.), *Life in the middle: Psychological and social development in middle age* (pp. 233–247). San Diego, CA: Academic Press.

Wilson, R. S., & Bennett, D. A. (2003). Cognitive activity and risk of Alzheimer's disease. *Current Directions in Psychological Science, 12,* 87–91.

Wilson, R. S., Bennett, D. A., Bienias, J. L., de Leon, C. F. M., Morris, M. C., & Evans, D. A. (2003). Cognitive activity and cognitive decline in a biracial community population. *Neurology, 61,* 812–816.

Wing, H. (1969). *Conceptual learning and generalization.* Baltimore, MD: Johns Hopkins Univ.

Wolfson, C., Wolfson, D. B., Asgharian, M., M'Lan, C. E., Ostbye, T., Rockwood, K., et al. (2001). Reevaluation of the duration of survival after the onset of dementia. *New England Journal of Medicine, 344,* 1111–1116.

Wood, W., Wong., F. Y., & Chachere, J. G. (1991). Effects of media violence on viewers' aggression in unconstrained social interaction. *Psychological Bulletin, 109,* 371–383.

Woods, S. C., Schwartz, M. W., Baskin, D. G., & Seeley, R. J. (2000). Food intake and the regulation of body weight. *Annual Review of Psychology, 51,* 255–277.

Woods, S. C., Seeley, R. J., Porte, D. Jr., & Schwartz, M. W. (1998, May 29). Signals that regulate food intake and energy homeostasis. *Science, 280,* 1378–1383.

Woodward, K. L., & Springen, K. (1992, August 22). Better than a gold watch. *Newsweek,* p. 71.

World Health Organization World Mental Health Survey Consortium. (2004). Prevalence, severity, and unmet need for treatment of mental disorders in the World Health Organization World Mental Health Surveys. *Journal of the American Medical Association, 291,* 2581–2590.

Wortman, C. B., & Silver, R. C. (1989). The myths of coping with loss. *Journal of Consulting & Clinical Psychology, 57,* 349–357.

Wright, R. (1994). *The moral animal: The new science of evolutionary psychology.* New York: Pantheon.

Wubbolding, R. E. (2005). The power of belonging. *International Journal of Reality Therapy, 24,* 43–44.

Wynn, K. (1995). Infants possess a system of numerical knowledge. *Current Directions in Psychological Science, 4,* 172–177.

Yaggi, H. K., Concato, J., Kernan,W. N., Lichtman, J. H., Brass, L. M., & Mohsenin, V. (2005). Obstructive sleep apnea as a risk factor for stroke and death. *New England Journal of Medicine, 353,* 2034–2041.

Yamamoto, K., & Chimbidis, M. E. (1966). Achievement, intelligence, and creative thinking in fifth-grade children: A correlational study. *Merrill-Palmer Quarterly, 12,* 233–241.

Yang, Q., & Chen, F. (2001). Behavior problems in children with simple obesity. *Chinese Journal of Clinical Psychology, 9,* 273–274.

Yoo, S-S., Hu, P. T., Gujar, N., Jolesz, F. A., & Walker, M. P. (2007). A deficit in the ability to form new human memories without sleep. *Nature Neuroscience, 10,* 385–392.

Zaragoza, M. S., & Mitchell, K. J. (1996). Repeated exposure to suggestion and the creation of false memories. *Psychological Science, 7,* 294–300.

Zimmer-Gembeck, M. J., Geiger, T. C., & Crick, N. R. (2005). Relational and physical aggression, prosocial behavior, and peer relations: Gender moderation and bidirectional associations. *Journal of Early Adolescence, 25,* 421–452.

Zucker, K. J. (2005). Gender identity disorder in children and adolescents. *Annual Review of Clinical Psychology, 1,* 467–492.

Zuckerman, M. (1979). *Sensation seeking: Beyond the optimal level of arousal*. Hillsdale, NJ: Erlbaum.

Zuckerman, M. (1994). *Behavioral expressions and biosocial bases of sensation seeking*. New York: Cambridge Univ. Press.

Zuckerman, M. (2000). Sensation seeking. In A. Kazdin (Ed.), *Encyclopedia of psychology*. Washington, DC: American Psychological Association.

Zuckerman, M. (2005). The neurobiology of impulsive sensation seeking: Genetics, brain physiology, biochemistry, and neurology. In C. Stough (Ed.), *Neurobiology of exceptionality* (pp. 31–52). New York: Kluwer/Plenum.

Photo Credits

Chapter 1
Opener: Chuck Savage Productions Inc.; 6 left ZUMA Press, right Courtesy of the Library of Congress; 8 Scott Camazine/Photo Researchers, Inc.; 12 from left to right: Arvind Garg/Getty Images, Inc – Liaison, Guido Vrola/Shutterstock, Picture Contact BV/Alamy, Steve Vidler/SuperStock; 14 B. Daemmrich/The Image Works; 16 Getty Images, Inc.; 17 Bill Anderson/Photo Researchers, Inc.

Chapter 2
Opener: Scott Camazine/Photo Researchers, Inc.; 34 Edwin R. Lewis, Professor Emeritus; 35 (c) Dan McCoy; 43 right Howard Sochurek/Woodfin Camp & Associates, left Scott Camazine/Alamy; 44 Brad Markel/Getty Images, Inc – Liaison; 50 CNRI/Science Photo Library/Science Source/Photo Researchers, Inc.; 51 animate4.com ltd./Photo Researchers, Inc. .

Chapter 3
Opener: Joaquin Palting/CORBIS- NY; 64 Bob Daemmrich/The Image Works; 76 Corbis/Bettmann; 77 Fujifotos/The Image Works; 82 Pawan Sinha and Tomaso Poggio. Photo (c)Dirck Halstead/Gamma Liaison; 83 (B) Vatikaki/Shutterstock.

Chapter 4
Opener: Piko/Photo Researchers, Inc.; 97 Will & Deni McIntyre/Photo Researchers, Inc.; 111 The Granger Collection; 115 Tibor Hirsch/Photo Researchers, Inc.

Chapter 5
Opener: Azzara Steve/Corbis/Sygma; 125 Gregory K. Scott/Photo Researchers, Inc.; 128 Walter Dawn/Photo Researchers, Inc.; 135 Carroll Seghers/Photo Researchers, Inc.; 140 (T)Library of Congress; (B) Lisa F. Young/Fotolia; 141 Albert Bandura.

Chapter 6
Opener: LWA-Sharie Kennedy/CORBIS- NY; 153 A.Brucelle/Corbis/Sygma, 154 (c) The New Yorker Collection 1997 Arnie Levin from cartoonbank.com. All Rights Reserved.; 158 Michele Burgess; 162 (c)The New Yorker Collection 1998 Mick Stevens from cartoonbank.com. All Rights Reserved.; 166 (c) Renee Lynn/CORBIS All Rights Reserved; 168 AP Wide World Photos.

Chapter 7
Opener: Rich LaSalle/Getty Images Inc. – Stone Allstock; 193 Bob Daemmrich/The Image Works; 199 Jeff Greenberg/Photo Researchers, Inc.; 200 Charles Gupton/Corbis/Bettmann; 202 James Schnepf/Getty Images, Inc – Liaison.

Chapter 8
Opener: Germanskydiver/Shutterstock; 217 left Camermann/The Image Works, right EDHAR/Shutterstock; 221 Michele Burgess; 222 Prill Mediendesign & Fotografie/istockphoto; 224 Harlow Primate Laboratory/University of Wisconsin; 225 Dave Sandford/Getty Images, Inc.; 228 Photos by Peter DaSilva for The New York Times.; 232 Chris Cameron/Alamy.

Chapter 9
Opener: Ryan McVay/PhotoDisc/Getty Images; 240 (c) Keith/CORBIS All Rights Reserved; 243 Andy Levin/Photo Researchers, Inc. ; 246 top left Spencer Grant/Getty Images, Inc – Liaison; 246 left middle Pearson Education/PH College; 246 left bottom Myrleen Ferguson Cate/PhotoEdit Inc.; 246 top middle Lew Merrim/Photo Researchers, Inc.; 246 top right John Eastcott/The Image Works; 246 bottom right Petro Feketa/Shutterstock; 248 Lew Merrim/Photo Researchers, Inc.; 252 Nina Leen/Getty Images/Time Life Pictures; 253 Laurence Dutton/Getty Images, Inc.; 255 Altrendo Images/Getty Images, Inc.; 267 Bob Daemmrich/The Image Works; 268 (c) Freda Leinwand.

Chapter 10
Opener: George Shelley/Masterfile Corporation; 285 top right Erich Lessing/Art Resource, NY; 285 top right LUCASFILM/20TH CENTURY FOX/Picture Desk, Inc./Kobal Collection; 285 bottom right Corbis/Bettmann; 286 Library of Congress; 292 top left Spencer Grant/Photo Researchers, Inc.; 292 top right Stanley Goldblatt/Photo Researchers, Inc.; 292 bottom right Ken Karp/Pearson Education/PH College.

Chapter 11
Opener: Spencer Grant/PhotoEdit Inc; 301 Grant LeDuc; 302 David W. Hamilton/Getty Images Inc. – Image Bank; 309 Philip North-Coombes/Getty Images Inc. – Stone Allstock; 311 Lawrence Migdale/Getty Images Inc. – Stone Allstock.

Chapter 12
Opener: Kent Larsson/Getty Images, Inc.; 322 Stock Montage, Inc./Historical Pictures Collection; 232 Jim Cummins/Getty Images, Inc.; 330 Susan Greenwood/Getty Images, Inc – Liaison.

Chapter 13
Opener: Zigy Kaluzny/Getty Images, Inc.; 347 Engelman Tom Photographer; 350 Albert Bandura; 353 Michael Rougier/Getty Images/Time Life Pictures; 360 Eric Roth/Photolibrary.com; 361 left Laima E. Druskis/Pearson Education/PH College; right M. Antman/The Image Works; 363 Zigy Kaluzny/Getty Images, Inc. – Stone Allstock; 365 Spencer Grant/PhotoEdit Inc.

Chapter 14
Opener: Stewart Cohen/Getty Images, Inc.; 372 AP Wide World Photos; 373 David Buffington/Getty Images, Inc.- Photodisc.; 374 PHILLIP HAYSON/Photolibrary.com; 378 CORBIS- NY; 379 (c)MADD. Used by permission.; 381 Richard Hutchings/PhotoEdit Inc.; 382 Alain Oddie/PhotoEdit Inc.; 384 Getty Images Inc. – Hulton Archive Photos; 389 William Langley/Getty Images, Inc. – Taxi.